The Development of European Competition Policy

This book considers a central issue of our time: the relationship between the macroeconomic objectives of political parties in democratic countries and the legal framework of market economies. The impressive panel of contributors examines social-democratic policies on cartels, market concentration and competition in different European countries, spanning a hundred-year period (specifically the interwar period, the initial postwar period, the 1960s and 1970s, the 1980s and 1990s, and the 2000s).

This thought-provoking volume challenges the dominant belief that the EU's economic system and competition policy were mainly influenced by neoliberal economic thinking, instead showing that Keynesian and social-democratic positions played a major role in the emergence of this system.

It will be valuable reading for advanced students, researchers and policymakers interested in modern economic history, industrial organization, political economy, European legal history and political science.

Brian Shaev is University Lecturer at the Institute for History at Leiden University, the Netherlands.

Sigfrido M. Ramírez Pérez is Researcher at the Max Planck Institute for European Legal History, Germany.

Routledge Explorations in Economic History

Edited by Lars Magnusson
Uppsala University, Sweden

France and the International Economy
From Vichy to the Treaty of Rome
Frances M. B. Lynch

Monetary Standards and Exchange Rates
M.C. Marcuzzo, L. Officer, A. Rosselli

Production Efficiency in Domesday England, 1086
John McDonald

Free Trade and its Reception 1815–1960
Freedom and trade: Volume I
Edited by Andrew Marrison

Conceiving Companies
Joint-stock politics in Victorian England
Timothy L. Alborn

The British Industrial Decline Reconsidered
Edited by Jean-Pierre Dormois and Michael Dintenfass

The Conservatives and Industrial Efficiency, 1951–1964
Thirteen wasted years?
Nick Tiratsoo and Jim Tomlinson

The Development of European Competition Policy
Social Democracy and Regulation
Edited by Brian Shaev and Sigfrido M. Ramírez Pérez

For more information about this series, please visit: www.routledge.com/Routledge-Explorations-in-Economic-History/book-series/SE0347

The Development of European Competition Policy

Social Democracy and Regulation

Edited by Brian Shaev and Sigfrido M. Ramírez Pérez

Routledge
Taylor & Francis Group
LONDON AND NEW YORK

First published 2024
by Routledge
4 Park Square, Milton Park, Abingdon, Oxon OX14 4RN

and by Routledge
605 Third Avenue, New York, NY 10158

Routledge is an imprint of the Taylor & Francis Group, an informa business

British Library Cataloguing-in-Publication Data
A catalogue record for this book is available from the British Library

ISBN: 978-1-138-54159-7 (hbk)
ISBN: 978-1-032-76998-1 (pbk)
ISBN: 978-1-351-01057-3 (ebk)

DOI: 10.4324/9781351010573

Typeset in Times New Roman
by Apex CoVantage, LLC

Contents

List of Contributors *vii*

1 **Introduction** 1
BRIAN SHAEV

2 **Social democracy and the cartel question: the case of the German SPD** 29
HARM G. SCHRÖTER

3 **Swedish social democracy and cartels, 1911–1953** 52
BIRGIT KARLSSON

4 **The German Trade Union Confederation and the cartel policy of the early European communities** 70
SEVERIN CRAMM

5 **"The economy is our destiny": socialists and the birth of European competition law, 1950–1962** 96
BRIAN SHAEV

6 **Ordering through competition? Pieter VerLoren van Themaat and social-democratic thinking about competition in the early postwar Netherlands, 1940s–1960s** 124
KARIN VAN LEEUWEN

7 **Social democracy and the foundations of European competition policy and law, 1950–1973** 146
SIGFRIDO M. RAMÍREZ PÉREZ

8 **Finnish social democrats and competition policy: from the first "cartel law" to the application for EU membership** 178
SUSANNA FELLMAN

9 **European Social Democracy, Community Competition Law and Industrial Policy during the crisis of the 1970s and 1980s** 204
DIMITRI ZURSTRASSEN

10 **The impossible social-democratic European competition policy, 1985–2000** 231
LAURENT WARLOUZET

11 **Rules and exceptions in the recent history of competition law, 2003–2017: technocracy or scope for a social-democratic perspective?** 252
WOLF SAUTER

12 **A social-democratic dilemma: Swedish competition policy in the 21st century** 279
JOHN LAPIDUS

Conclusion 299
VERA ŠĆEPANOVIĆ AND BRIAN SHAEV

Index *325*

Contributors

Severin Cramm is a docent at Hildesheim University, where he received a Ph.D. for a dissertation on the role of the German Trade Union Confederation in the early years of European integration. He has published in the *Journal of European Integration History* and in *Arbeit – Bewegung – Geschichte. Zeitschrift für historische Studien*. Furthermore, a book based on his dissertation will soon be published.

Susanna Fellman is a professor of business history at the School of Business, Economics and Law at the University of Gothenburg, Sweden. She holds the Torsten Söderberg and Ragnar Söderberg Chair in business history. Her main research interests are competition policy and international cartels from a historical perspective and the professionalization and modernization of management. She is currently an associate editor of the journal *Business History*.

Birgit Karlsson is a professor emerita of economic history at the University of Gothenburg. Her research covers many areas of twentieth-century history, including trade and foreign policy related to Sweden, Nazi Germany, and the Soviet Union. She has also studied the relationship between digitalization and work, with a focus on the steel industry. Lately, her interest has been directed toward questions related to cartels and competition.

John Lapidus is a research fellow in the Department of Economy and Society at the University of Gothenburg. His research interests include comparative welfare state and ongoing privatization processes of the provision and funding of central welfare services. He is the author of *The Quest for a Divided Welfare State: Sweden in the Era of Privatization* (Palgrave Macmillan, 2019).

Karin van Leeuwen is an assistant professor of European political history at the Faculty of Arts and Social Sciences, Maastricht University, where she co-leads the Law and History research network. Her research mostly focuses on the crossroads of legal and political history, combining expertise in Dutch history, international politics, and the history of European integration.

Sigfrido M. Ramírez Pérez is an associated researcher at the Max Planck Institute for Legal History and Legal Theory, Frankfurt-am-Main, and the scientific collaborator of Mondes Modernes et Contemporaines (MMC), ULB-Free

University Brussels. He has written, among others, about the history of European Union law, European trade unionism, and business networks in European integration. He has recently published about the history of European policies and regulations in the automotive sector.

Wolf Sauter is professor of law, markets and behaviour at the Vrije Universiteit (VU) Amsterdam, and an expert at the Authority for Consumers and Markets (ACM) in The Hague. He was previously professor of economic law in Groningen and Tilburg, and has worked as a national expert on secondment to DG Competition at the European Commission. He obtained his PhD from the European University Institute in Florence in 1996 for a thesis on competition law and industrial policy.

Vera Šćepanović is a university lecturer at the Institute for History at Leiden University, where she teaches in the international relations and European Union studies program. She was previously a post-doctoral Max Weber Fellow at the European University Institute in Florence and a visiting lecturer at the Central European University in Budapest. She works on international trade, foreign direct investment, and industrial policy in the European Union.

Harm G. Schröter has worked as a professor in the Departments of Economics, History, and Business Schools at universities in Germany, USA, Norway, and especially the University of Bergen. He published on European economic and business history (cartelization, cultural conditions of economic development, FDI, cooperatives, labor movement, Americanization, and business groups). He served as President of the European Business History Association and organized the First World Congress on Business History.

Brian Shaev is a university lecturer in the Institute for History at Leiden University, where he teaches in the international relations and European Union studies program. Previously, he was a postdoctoral researcher at the Centre for European Research at the University of Gothenburg (CERGU). Currently, he is writing a book titled *Transnational Socialism and European Integration: The Socialist Group in the Early European Parliament (1952–1973)*.

Laurent Warlouzet is a professor of history at the Paris Sorbonne University. A former postdoctoral fellow at the London School of Economics (LSE) and at the European University Institute (EUI), he has published *Governing Europe in a Globalizing World. Neoliberalism and Its Alternatives* (Routledge 2018) as well as *Towards a Fourth Paradigm in European Competition Policy? A Historical Perspective (1957–2022)* (available on SSRN).

Dimitri Zurstrassen is currently a researcher in the history of European integration at Sorbonne University, France, and UCLouvain, Belgium, where he is finishing his Ph.D. thesis on the evolution of EU industrial policy from 1974 to 2002. He has taken part in several research projects on the history of European integration, such as the oral history project of the European Commission (1986–2000) coordinated by UCLouvain and the oral history of the Court of Justice of the European Union, a research project coordinated by the Max Planck Institute for the History and Theory of Law based in Frankfurt am Main (Germany). He is also the author of several publications on EU industrial policy and national industrial policies.

1 Introduction

Brian Shaev

In 1961, West Berlin mayor Willy Brandt accepted the nomination to be a chancellor candidate for Germany's storied Social Democratic Party (SPD). In his speech laying out a governing program for that year's federal election, Brandt celebrated the Bonn Republic's prosperity as the "result of the common efforts of our entire people." He went on to lament that "the fruits of our common work are unjustly distributed" and singled out big businesses as the "real beneficiaries of economic policy up to now." Their prosperity, he argued, too often came at the cost of higher prices for consumers and the self-employed, and their growth far outstripped rising wages for workers, white-collar workers, government employees and professionals. "A new Federal government will therefore propose to improve the Cartel Law and expand the powers of the German Cartel Office," he announced.[1]

Though Brandt's SPD lost the 1961 elections, strengthening Germany's 1957 cartel law and adding new merger control regulatory powers became constant demands of the SPD in opposition, in the Grand Coalition with Christian Democrats (1966–69) and in the Social-Liberal Coalition led by Willy Brandt (1969–74).[2] Brandt's 1961 speech declared that the SPD would promote an independent Monopoly Commission to subject market-dominating businesses to "effective control." Though he left it unstated, the Monopoly Commission was not intended to be entirely independent. A year before the SPD had submitted a merger control proposal to the Bundestag that carved out a key role for political intervention. The Economic Minister would be empowered to grant exemptions to businesses holding market-dominating positions to continue operations if the minister considered their activities to be in the interests of the "general economy or of the general good."[3] After more than a decade of effort, the Social Democrats succeeded in 1973 in passing the first merger control law in continental Europe, which required mergers above a certain size to register and receive permission. If the Monopoly Commission found that a merger would create a market-dominating position, the merger would be banned but the economic minister had the discretional authority to grant permission. The Merger Control Law represented social-democratic preferences on regulating competition.

This history – the origins of the first Merger Control Law in continental Europe – has received almost no attention in scholarship on European competition policy. Social Democrats make fragmentary appearances in existing histories of

DOI: 10.4324/9781351010573-1

cartel and competition policy to support or oppose proposals from other political families.[4] Rarely has it been considered that Social Democrats made important and at times decisive contributions themselves to the form and development of competition policy in Europe. As cartel and competition policy has re-emerged as a topic of heavy interest in our contemporary context of rising oligopoly and inequality in what some have called a "New Gilded Age," it is time to re-examine its political and ideological origins.[5] This book has a mission of placing Social Democrats center stage in a political and legal history of economic policy and regulation that examines the evolution of European competition policy not as a brand new policy invented in the postwar period, but as a policy seriously rooted in the experiences of its member states, including in key political traditions in Finland, France, Germany, the Netherlands, Spain, and Sweden.

Furthermore, this introductory chapter contains new empirical materials on transnational socialist discussions on cartels in the Labour and Socialist International in 1927–31 and the role of competition policy in socialist planning ideas in the 1930s, as well as a summary of the cartel and competition policies of one of the pioneers in this political debate, the British Labour Party. Its concluding section discusses the collective findings of our first set of chapters dealing with the period from the turn-of-the-twentieth-century to the foundation of competition policy for a European common market in 1962. The book's conclusion picks up this history in the 1960s and takes it up to today. We argue that the influences for Europe's evolution from "a cartel paradise" in the first half of the twentieth century to the world's leading regulator of competition by the end of the twentieth century were far more diverse than has to date been suggested. The often essential role of socialists and social democrats in the formation of a regulatory culture of competition in twentieth-century Europe has been overlooked.

The implications of writing a heterodox political history of European cartel and competition policy extend beyond this specific legal and policy field. Legal scholar David Gerber, who has had a large impact on this field, famously argued that a right-wing group of German ordoliberals implanted a postwar culture and legal framework of competition into the politics and law of the early Federal Republic of Germany.[6] Ordoliberals believed that free competition was necessary for a free society and democracy, but broke with laissez-faire liberals in arguing that the state had to create and enforce a strong legal framework to guarantee competition and eliminate oligarchic and monopolistic practices. Gerber's focus is on the 1957 German competition law, the strongest anti-cartel law in Europe to that date and a foundation for Germany's postwar "economic constitution," an ordoliberal term. The German Act against Restraints on Competition was passed in 1957 partly in preparation for the opening of the European Economic Community (EEC) in 1958, which had its own cartel and competition framework in the Treaties of Rome. The importance of competition policy for European integration has been stressed especially by political scientists Michelle Cini, Lee McGowan and Stephen Wilks who label it "the strongest supranational policy of the early European Communities" and "the foundation stone of the entire European Union."[7] Scholars from diverse disciplines have long held that German ordoliberal competition policies were uploaded to the EEC through Commission Regulation 17/62, which launched the Common Market's competition policy in 1962.[8] However, if ordoliberal influences were hegemonic, it makes little sense that enforcing European competition policy was left, first to the High Authority and then to the European Commission, both political bodies, rather than to an independent competition agency as ordoliberals preferred.[9]

As discussed throughout our book, the origin story of ordoliberal hegemony in early European competition policy is no longer tenable. Ordoliberalism was but one of several influences on early European competition policy. A new political history of social-democratic thought and policies on regulating competition is a novel approach to the history of competition policy in Europe. Early scholarship in the 1980s by Volker Berghahn stressed transatlantic influences culminating in Germany's 1957 Competition Law, as German economic culture "Americanized" in the 1950s. Brigitte Leucht and Mel Marquis later claimed to find important US influences in the cartel provisions of the 1951 Treaty of Paris to create the European Coal and Steel Community (ECSC).[10] Gerber contested the "Americanization" thesis by asserting that German competition policy had indigenous roots, hence his emphasis on the German ordoliberal school of intellectuals, economists and key politicians.[11] An excellent recent dissertation by Anselm Küsters argues that early European competition policy had heterodox ideological and national origins in the 1950s–early 60s but that an "ordoliberalization" occurred in the 1960s–80s. He argues that considering socioeconomic conditions and outcomes was an essential element for ordoliberal ideas of competition in contrast to neoliberal concepts. In this respect, there was some ground for overlap between social-democratic and ordoliberal ideas because social democrats also saw competition policy as part of a larger macroeconomic policy vision.[12]

Beyond the important German case, there have been a variety of approaches to analyzing the history of cartels and regulation in twentieth-century Europe. Scholars have conducted a plethora of sectoral studies, many of which included forms of international cartelization, such as the aluminum, automobile and paper industries.[13] Another approach has been national case studies.[14] Recently, there have been important advances in business history, in which "cartel biographies" of single companies are used as windows into the oblique world of shadow collusion between businesses after certain forms of cooperation became illegal with the introduction of new competition regulations in the 1950s–60s.[15] Important histories have been written about international business actors like the International Chamber of Commerce and the Union des confédérations de l'industrie et des employeurs en Europe (UNICE), the business peak organization of the European communities, now called BusinessEurope.[16] Scholars have also taken institutional approaches, examining competition policy in the development of the ECSC High Authority and the early European Commission.[17] The approach in our book is closest in spirit to recent economic histories on national competition regulation and cartel registers by Susanna Fellman and Martin Shanahan, an edited legal history exploring links between law, politics, economics and European institutions by Kiran Klaus Patel and Heike Schweitzer, and international histories of interstate negotiations and compromise between national cultures of competition in European competition policy by Laurent Warlouzet.[18] Our book takes a comparative and transnational approach to uncover the contributions made by the social-democratic "political family" to cartel and competition policies at national and European levels.

In addition to the legal history of public policy and economic history more broadly, our book contributes to new historiography on European social democracy. "An economic history of politics" of the French Socialist Party by Matthieu Fulla shows the fruitfulness of analyzing socialist economic policies over several decades.[19] Talbot Imlay has urged scholars to take international socialism and its networks seriously, to focus on "practice" rather than ideology, while also emphasizing socialists' support for European integration.[20] His approach is also validated in our book. Furthermore, Fulla and Marc Lazar recently published a book on European socialists and the state that shows that social-democratic parties became increasingly statist over the course of the twentieth century.[21] Their broad findings are confirmed here in the case of cartel and competition policy, as we identify (see further) a clear tendency of social-democratic parties to favor greater state regulation of competition in the postwar period. Existing studies of social-democratic policies on competition are limited to a study of the early SPD by Hartmut Bechtold, a study of German social-democratic trade unionists and the monopoly question under Weimar, a long-durée account of SPD policy by Helen Callaghan and Martin Höpner, work on the Labour Party discussed further, and a history of the interwar Swedish Social Democratic Party (*Sveriges socialdemokratiska arbetareparti*, SAP) by John Lapidus, who has a chapter in our book.[22] Bechthold and Lapidus analyze the classical period of social-democratic cartel policy, before the introduction of major cartel legislation in the post–Second World War period, while Callaghan and Höpner present SPD cartel policy as (neo)liberal, without identifying the many ways in which it was not.

Setting the record straight concerning the diverse political origins of competition policy in Europe casts new light on the evolving relationship between businesses, democratic actors, and the state in the twentieth century. The history of state regulation of the economy is incomplete without a recognition that social-democratic parties often introduced the first cartel and competition law in their countries, or, in the case of the SPD, expanded national competition policy to include merger control. Highlighting social-democratic thought and contributions upsets long-held presumptions about (ordo)liberal hegemony over European cartel and competition policy in postwar Europe and (ordo)liberal dominance over the early European communities that later became the European Union. Social-democratic cartel and competition policy was designed to restrain the economic power of private business, to protect consumers and at times small and medium enterprises, and to insulate democratic politics from special interests. It was conceived as an instrument in the service of government's broader social and economic goals to "order" the economy, a concept ordoliberals also used. Political discretion – loathed by neo- and ordoliberals alike – was built into social-democratic policies, platforms and the laws they passed in parliaments in the 1950s–70s. Socialists therefore supported entrusting the High Authority and European Commission with the power to enforce competition policy rather than an independent agency. Hubert Buch-Hansen and Angela Wigger have perceptively argued, in contrast to much-established thinking, that European competition policy was a part of a system of "embedded liberalism" before the 1980s, in which markets were liberalized but at the same time restrained by Fordist production models, welfare states, and Keynesianism.[23] Social-democratic influences that subordinated competition to wider economic, political and social goals were pivotal in constructing this postwar competition paradigm. Our book argues that there was a social-democratic alternative to liberal conceptions of cartel and competition policy that contributed in concrete ways to the legal framework for regulating competition in postwar Europe and in the early European communities.

From the league of nations to economic planning: transnational socialism and the interwar cartel debate

The "golden age" of the Weimar Republic in 1925–29 took place in the context of a French-German rapprochement *and* the "apogee"[24] of the interwar cartel movement in Europe. International cartelization – in particular between French and German businesses – gained allure as a means of cementing peace among two of the fiercest antagonists of the First World War. That it ran parallel with international efforts to reach economic agreements to lower tariffs and free trade, which culminated in the moribund plan of French Prime Minister and Foreign Minister Aristide Briand for a European customs union in 1929–30, has long attracted the attention of historians of cartels and European integration alike.[25] Cartel historian Dominique Barjot argues that "the idea of European integration was in embryo" in proposals in the early 1930s to embed a customs union within a protective cartel framework.[26] French politician Louis Loucheur is at the center of these histories. His major contribution was to interlace reformist impulses in international relations with the drive to cartelization. Since 1921, Loucheur had envisioned industrial cartels to be the best means of reaching an economic – and by extension political – entente with Germany. Minister in eight French governments in 1925–31, Barjot describes him as a "fervent advocate of the European project," and, with Briand, "the most impor tant actor in the policy of "appeasement" with [Weimar] Germany." Loucheur was the primary initiator of the 1927 World Economic Conference where he promoted a "Europe of producers."[27] A leader in the *Gauche républicaine* party, a center-left party close to Radical Party, he became the primary "partisan of international ententes without state control"[28] and the main figure in the international campaign to promote cartelization as "an optimal solution for the problem of international economic governance" at the League of Nations.[29]

Loucheur's influential vision catalyzed socialists in the transnational Labour and Socialist International (LSI) into preparing their own policies on international cartelization. Already in 1923, the Industry Committee of the League of Nations was split between a pro-cartel faction close to industry and a pro-regulatory alliance of trade unions, consumer organizations, and representatives of the International Labour Organization.[30] Transnational efforts to craft an international socialist response in the late 1920s reveal two developments of particular importance for our book. First, socialists carved out their own position at transnational levels in favor of international regulation of cartels and presented it as an alternative to the leading international vision of a united, cartelized Europe. Second, while all socialist parties favored regulation, continental socialists proposed forms of supranational regulation while the UK Labour Party only supported national regulation.

In the interwar context, their proposals differed both from contemporary US ideas of antitrust (because they wanted to have public supervision of cartels rather than dissolve them) and from leading center-left pro-cartel European politicians like Loucheur. What they were most concerned about was the private and secretive nature of international cartelization and the lead role taken by business interests in the International Chamber of Commerce (ICC) in international economic debates. The ICC launched study commissions on cartels under the League of Nations with the purpose of gaining public support for private cartels as a means of promoting peace and prosperity. Marco Bertilorenzi argues that these commissions became "the principal vehicle for the legitimisation of the international cartel movement." Business interests were especially opposed to the publication of an international cartel register. Such proposals were considered unacceptable in transnational socialist circles. In early 1926, representatives of the Belgian Workers Party (*Parti ouvrier belge*, POB), the French Socialist Party (*Section française de l'Internationale ouvrière*, SFIO) and the German Social Democratic Party (*Sozialdemokratische Partei Deutschlands*, SPD) met to discuss their international economic visions as the French and German governments prepared a new trade treaty. A French participant, Ernest Poisson, called for public intervention to supervise international and national trusts.[31] The meeting's resolution stated:

> The Conference notes the general tendency of industry to conclude cartels and international consortia. Cartels, which could constitute a more rational organization of production and exchange, will lead to grave dangers for workers and consumers if they are abandoned solely to private initiative. The Conference therefore demands forcefully that they not be established without the supervision and approval of governments and parliaments.[32]

This transnational resolution by three of Europe's most important social-democratic parties was an opening shot in an international socialist counteroffensive on cartels. Over the next years, the transnational LSI emerged as the major political opponent of the interwar campaign for a "Europe of cartels" organized under the auspices of the League of Nations.

The 1927 World Economic Conference, formally proposed by the French government on Loucheur's initiative, was the first time an international conference including government representatives held prolonged discussions on international cartels. Divisions broke down by national preferences, with the UK and Scandinavian delegates tending toward anti-cartel positions, and continental Europeans toward pro-cartel positions, but also along ideological lines, with trade unionists insisting on a form of co-management with industry and cooperatives, full publicity of cartel registers and formal regulatory powers for the League of Nations.

The trade unions' position was vigorously opposed by private industrial interests.[33] Although small in number at the conference, trade unionists helped shift the discussion from the merits of cartels to the need for legal controls against their abuse.[34] Assessments made by socialists of the nature and development of the interwar international economy – and the place of cartels within it – bring out the ambivalence in interwar social-democratic competition policy. They also, though, pointed the way to a transnational socialist consensus that cartels must be actively supervised and controlled at the international level.

Disagreements at the World Economic Conference resulted in stalemate: the conference refused to take a position concerning the merits of cartelization. Instead, it listed advantages as well as disadvantages, and declared that policy should differentiate between "good" and "bad" cartels.[35] The League of Nations was entrusted to collect information and monitor cartel conduct. Though apparently defeated, international cartelization emerged from the conference with greater public legitimacy. Loucheur and pro-cartel business interests looked to the creation of an Economic Committee by the League of Nations in 1928, and the joint study committee, as the next stages of their cartelization campaign. National governments, in their view, should free cartels from state scrutiny, legally protect them and promote them internationally, while international institutions should limit themselves to facilitating cartelization by serving as information centers for businesses and propagandizers for the cartel cause to international civil society.[36] A cartel register was set up – but it was to remain private and could not be used to prosecute businesses for restrictive practices. Meanwhile, in expert meetings to prepare a new report on cartels, League economic officials, business representatives and trade unionists generally agreed on the benefits of cartelization in 1928–29, but trade unionists again demanded co-management that would include trade unions and formal supervisory powers for the League of Nations.[37]

The basic contour of the response from the LSI was already set out in its reaction to the 1927 World Economic Conference. Policy documents in preparation for the LSI's 1928 conference make clear that transnational socialists considered private cartels to be economic and political menaces – for some potential, for oth ers active menaces – that required control. At the same time, they considered them natural products of the latest stage of world capitalism that could not be simply discarded without risking economic destabilization. German economic expert and trade unionist Fritz Napthali's draft resolution states:

> A demand must be put forward for super-state control over international combinations of monopolist tendency. . . . The first task of this controlling organ would be to ensure publicity of all conventions concluded, its second task would be to intervene against any price policy exploiting the consumer and against unequal treatment of different markets.[38]

His views aligned with representatives of both British Labour parties (Labour and the leftwing Independent Labour Party), which also demanded that the new International Economic Office being discussed at the League of Nations be invested with powers to collect information, that international cartels guarantee nations equal treatment in sales and prices, and that this be enforced by an international court.[39] They diverged though in that the Labour Party representative proposed that the Economic Office be granted the power to make formal recommendations for international conventions on cartels, while Napthali, as highlighted earlier, sought solutions in "super-state," that is, supranational regulations.

As study commissions proliferated in 1928–31, international cartelization continued apace. Cartels became a main point of discussion in the LSI, which clearly intended to counter the pro-cartel campaign of Loucheur and private businesses. Napthali's policy submission to the LSI in 1928 on behalf of the SPD built on his work within Germany. The German Trade Union Confederation (ADGB) tasked leading social democrats, including Napthali, Rudolf Hilferding and Fritz Baade, to flesh out a concept of "economic democracy." Among its 12 demands were state supervision over cartels and monopolies as well as nationalizations.[40] His memorandum for the LSI, titled "On the economic situation of the postwar period and the economic policy of the working class," stated that the postwar economy was marked by three general tendencies: (1) a reproduction of world economic links destroyed during the First World War, (2) an accelerating industrialization taking place outside of Europe, particularly in the United States, and (3) the "encroachment of forms of organized capitalism vis-à-vis the free competitive economy in national spheres and through international combinations [*Verflechtungen*]." In Germany alone, the number of cartels, he estimated, had risen from 500–600 cartels before 1914 to well over 2,000, representing around two-thirds of the nominal capital of total stock ownership. He highlighted that *Verflechtungen* – a word that directly translates as interpenetration, interweaving or interdependence – took a diversity of forms, including taking capital shares in other businesses, exchanging patents and cooperative founding of subsidiaries, that is, the most developed form of international combinations along with mergers – and was present in many industries, among which he mentions synthetic chemicals, an allusion to the powerful potash syndicate Harm G. Schröter has researched,[41] as well as steel, coal, electricity, vinyl disks and linoleum. Compared to the prewar period, "<u>international cartelization, company- and trust-building</u>" (emphasis in original) have advanced at such strength that they have gained a whole new meaning. In today's economy, Napthali wrote, "A newly founded, self-standing business would have no chance of succeeding; it must immediately seek to join existing organizations," often as a subsidiary or company branch.[42]

Already in 1928, documents prepared for the LSI congress highlight the internationalization of cartels and the resulting incapacity of national governments to gain a grip on them. A Labour Party memorandum states,

> When economic units fell for the most part within the frontiers of single states, the State was able to exercise a certain degree of supervision . . . . But many economic bodies have become cosmopolitan, owe allegiance to no single State, and are outside effective supervision or regulation by a Single

> State; while others though coming within the jurisdiction of a single State, exert a powerful influence far beyond the frontiers of that throughout the world.[43]

Socialists contested the heavily propounded view that a "Europe of cartels" represented a path for peaceful economic development and French-German reconciliation. The LSI's joint resolution with the International Federation of Trade Unions (IFTU) in 1931 asserted, "The organisation of the world economic system by international trusts of finance and industry does not do away with national antagonisms." Rather, "within international cartels the national struggle for market rates is going on."[44]

Transnational socialist support for international cartel regulation at the League of Nations comes out as well in the 1930 debates of the Interparliamentary Union (IPU) on the "control of international trusts and cartels." The previous IPU conference in 1927 had selected Hungarian Trade Minister Joseph Szterényi and French Socialist Marius Moutet to prepare a draft resolution on international cartels. Moutet had to resign from this function after he lost his French assembly seat in 1928, though he then won a by-election in 1929. Szterényi's text began by declaring cartels "natural phenomena of economic life."[45] States should set up cartel registers and establish an independent body including worker representatives and consumers to monitor for abuses. The League of Nations should be charged with supervising cartel agreements and making proposals for international regulation but, for the time being, legal regulation should be developed within national spheres. As head of the French parliamentary delegation to the IPU, Moutet responded at the conference, "It is probable that if I had been one of the rapporteurs, the conclusions, at least in spirit, would have been much less favorable to trusts and cartels."[46] Cartels were not natural outgrowths of economic development, in his view, nor were private international cartels conducive to peace and Franco-German reconciliation. He posited that international ententes were only beneficial when collective interests predominated over private interests. Instead, he offered an international version of the French socialist concept of national "offices" for commodity management that would conciliate between consumer, producing and national interests. Moutet joined the US and Romanian delegations in abstaining on the IPU pro-cartel resolution, which was otherwise adopted unanimously.[47]

International trade unionism participated in the LSI's move to a more active stance on the cartel issue. The 1931 IFTU-LSI resolution, at the lowest point of the Great Depression in Europe, stated, "During recent years the elimination of free competition . . . has proceeded at an accelerated rate" and "represents a tendency common to all industrial nations." On the one hand,

> Complete or partial monopolies . . . reinforce the economic power of the capitalist groups [and] constitute a grave menace to workers and consumers generally. In addition, the price policy of monopolistic concerns often accentuates economic crises, and thus leads to increased unemployment.

Its most direct economic consequence was in "subjecting the consumers to price-control by capitalist monopolies" but equally important was its political impact of "forcing governments into an oppressive dependence upon capitalist plutocracy." On the other hand,

> It must be recognised that the growth of industrial consolidation means an advance towards an economically higher form of capitalism, and may provide a starting-point for the development of conscious planning of the economic system, such as the workers strive to secure in socialism.

For this reason, "Labour cannot join in a general condemnation of economic developments which tend to eliminate competition, but must rather aim at the public supervision and regulation of monopolistic organisations."

The 1931 IFTU-LSI resolution split the difference between supranational and advisory powers, settling on the phrase "supervision and regulation." Hence the resolution proposed (1) "Monopolistic concerns of all kinds should be placed under public supervision and regulation" with the involvement of trade unions and cooperative movements; (2) "The supervision of prices should be one of the functions of such public institutions"; (3) "There should be, similarly, international supervision of international trusts and cartels" under the League of Nations with the collaboration of the IFTU and the international cooperative movement; and (4) "nationally and internationally, there should be the fullest publicity regarding the financial and other operations of monopolistic concerns, and both national legislations and international convention[s]."[48]

That same year, socialist economic policymaking began to retreat from international solutions as international economic cooperation and trade collapsed. Pressure for a proactive policy to counter the depression was especially intense in Germany, where a disastrous deflationary policy fueled the rise of the National Socialist and Communist parties. Wladimir Woytinsky, former Menshevik and head of the ADGB's statistical office, took the initiative to propose an international plan to address the crisis, in line with socialist internationalist traditions. In his article "Active World Economic Policy," he called for an international "cartel control," and linked cartels with "price gouging in which the entire economy is plundered for the benefit of a few strong business groups."[49] Soon, though, "having become convinced of the futility of an international approach,"[50] he offered instead a plan specific to Germany in collaboration with trade unionist Fritz Tarnow and economist Fritz Baade known as the WTB-Plan. It was forcefully rejected by Napthali and Hilferding, still the leading SPD lights on economist policy. Nonetheless, the ADGB and the Allgemeiner freier Angestelltenbund (AfA), the white-collar union, adopted the WTB employment plan in the spring of 1932. Its guidelines called for an activist state cartel and monopoly office that would work closely with a banking office, a state trade monopoly office, and public enterprises in service of central planning. The paragraph devoted to competition reads:

> All cartels and similar concentrations of businesses as well as monopoly-like corporations und single enterprises are to be supervised by a state cartel

> and monopolies office. The Cartel and Monopoly Office will investigate on a permanent basis their construction, production and marketing practices as well as the setting of prices and influence them in the interests of the general welfare.[51]

The ADGB's affiliated unions launched a propaganda campaign in favor of the WTB-Plan, leading to a public split with the SPD, before the ADGB planning push petered out by the end of the year. National Socialists moved to fill the void, advocating an active employment plan based on public works and deficit spending akin to the policy the ADGB had crafted.

The Nazi takeover in 1933 and the interdiction of the SPD and ADGB in Germany came as profound shocks to international social democracy. Using the SPD's fatalism as a countermodel, Belgian socialist Henri De Man crafted a Labor Plan with clear similarities to the moribund WTB-Plan though with stronger patriotic and corporatist accents. Like Woytinsky, De Man preferred international solutions in the early 1930s but turned to national initiatives during a period now understood as one of deglobalization.[52] He also thought that cartels had helped cause and exacerbate the Great Depression because they increased price inflexibility. De Man's competition policy bears striking resemblance to the competition goals of the reformist SPD of the late 1950s, which sought to create a cross-class alliance, including the middle-class and small businesses, against economic oligarchy. The Plan's emphasis was on a mixed economy in which "the state would act as regulator as well as competitor of private enterprise."[53] Competition would be promoted and monopolies, in particular the credit, energy and raw materials sectors, would be nationalized. The function of nationalization was no longer justified on the basis of removing private ownership, but on enhancing public utility and management in service of national planning.[54] The plan envisioned a mixed economy of state-run enterprises and small and medium-businesses within a competitive but nationally coordinated economy.

As the LSI fell into abeyance in the early 1930s, transnational socialism became decentered from official party hierarchies. Networks of younger socialists and especially trade unionists learned from one another, and shared and promoted planning ideas of a "directed economy," including in International Planning conferences first hosted by De Man in 1934. A recent history by Tommaso Milani shines light on transnational influences of De Man's plan in the 1930s. He writes that "between the summer of 1933 and the early months of 1935, the most salient cleavage within Western social democracy [was] between planists and anti-planists."[55] This was nowhere more so than in France, where the planning campaign led to quite a row. Planism found fertile soil in eclectic corners of French socialism: among "neosocialists" steadily moving to the right (and some to fascism), among economic modernizers (*Révolution constructive*) and leftists (*Bataille socialiste*) and, most importantly, among burgeoning teams of economic experts in the Confédération générale du travial (CGT) trade union federation. For the CGT, planist competition policy resembled its 1920 policy in that "the degree of concentration will determine nationalization," but now the federation came out explicitly for a mixed economy of nationalized large businesses with small and medium private businesses (framed as a means of defending not only the working but also the middle class). Though French Socialist parliamentary leader Léon Blum shot down much of the planning agenda at the 1934 SFIO congress, including the idea of a mixed economy, he incorporated planist proposals for the socialization of credit and large monopolized industries, in particular railroads, mines and electricity, into the 1934 party congress resolution.[56] Only fully embraced by French Resistance movements during the Second World War, planist ideas in the later 1930s became watered down into a defense of the "small people" against the oligarchy of "two hundred families" in Popular Front discourses.[57]

French planism in the 1930s served as a "laboratory and training ground" for prominent postwar French socialist economic experts.[58] Among these were future ministers Robert Lacoste and Jules Moch, future EEC Commissioner Robert Marjolin, future Foreign Minister Christian Pineau, who oversaw the negotiations for the Treaties of Rome, and, perhaps most importantly, future Economics Minister André Philip, whose postwar influence on socialist competition policy is stressed in Sigfrido M. Ramírez Pérez's and Brian Shaev's chapters. Already impressed by De Man's attempts to construct a non-Marxist form of social democracy in the 1920s, Philip elaborated a comprehensive plan with clear affinities to De Man's in his 1935 *La Crise et l'Economie dirigée* [The Crisis and the Directed Economy]. He located part of interwar Germany's economic woes in its "concentrated economy . . . that added new disequilibria to pre-existing disequilibria and aggravated the situation."[59] On an international plane, competitive capitalism had converted to monopolistic capitalism and high tariffs served the "monopoly policy of large cartels" at collective expense.[60] Like De Man, his solution to monopolization was nationalization, for example, of mining, metalmaking, electricity, capital goods, transport and credit. National directing councils would operate beneficially, whereas cartels did not because national bodies would represent collective rather than private interests.[61] On the international level, Philip advocated international planning through cooperation between nationally directed economies. This position chimed with broader French Socialists proposals for national commodity offices as Moutet had advocated. A Wheat Office and a Coal Office, for instance, would provide kernels for international planning offices on the lines of the First World War–era Anglo-French commodity boards.[62] In 1933, future French President and socialist Vincent Auriol presented such ideas of an "international organization of credit, exchange and production" as the main goal of a future European federation.[63]

***

In considering the legacies of the interwar period for postwar transnational socialist discussions on cartels and competition, there emerges a relative discontinuity in the shift from (inter)national supervision and regulation of abuses to stricter anti-cartel positions more favorable to prohibition. At the same time, though, there was a relative continuity in the international socialist position that international institutions needed formal regulatory powers over international cartels. This policy would develop into a direct socialist contribution to the early development of European competition policy in the 1950s–60s. Furthermore, we can see the contours of future divisions between the Labour Party and continental socialist parties on supranational regulation. While both moved toward more restrictive positions on cartels in the interwar and postwar periods, continental socialists looked to grant formal powers to international institutions in both eras while Labour was resistant. As policymaking shifted back to national borders with the decline of internationalism in the 1930s, socialist competition policies became subsumed within larger debates about economic planning. Though planning strengthened ideas of a "mixed economy" in European social democracy, the socialist solution for monopolies was nationalization. Monopolies would obstruct planning in the collective interest were they to remain private. Nationalization was justified therefore in order to mobilize these sectors in service of economic planning.

The British Labour Party and cartel and competition policy, 1900–67

One party that does not have a chapter of its own in this book is the UK Labour Party. Its experience is important as it had one of the longest tenures in the government of socialist and labor parties in Europe. Here we take the opportunity to introduce a number of themes and approaches shared throughout our book by examining the Labour Party's positions and influence on cartel and competition policy from the party's foundation in 1900 until Labour Prime Minister Harold Wilson's application to join the EEC in 1967.

The pre–First World War Labour Party, in its infancy, and the Labour-aligned Fabian Society initially viewed cartels as beneficial for increasing economic efficiency – a view shared by Swedish and German Social Democrats – but they also argued that monopoly rent extraction impoverished the masses.[64] The first Labour Party conference in 1904 called for the regulation of trusts. The party emerged from the First World War with a new nationalization policy critical of private enterprise, though it still considered cartelization an advance on previous forms of industrial (dis)organization. Public anger at "war profiteers" coupled with labor unrest led to the creation of a Committee on Trusts in 1918 to investigate cartels. The Committee included prominent Fabians, most notably Sidney Webb. Turn-of-the-century Fabians, like their German SPD counterparts (see Harm G. Schröter's chapter), initially welcomed cartelization as an affirmation of cooperation over competition, a principle inherent in socialism, and considered it a progressive force to achieve economies of scale and economic efficiency. They warned simultaneously, though, of the dangers they posed to British society and politics. The Committee's non-Labour majority, by contrast, saw its work largely as a public relations exercise to diffuse public tensions concerning cartels without making meaningful reforms. Disillusioned, Webb and his colleagues resigned. Then began a period of government support for cartels and rationalization marked by a massive wave of business mergers in the 1920s, followed by a more proactive period of state support for domestic and international cartelization during the Great Depression in the 1930s. The Coal Mines Act of 1930 vigorously promoted by the Labour Party included a cartelization of the coal industry. Conservative governments that replaced former Labour leader Ramsay MacDonald's National Government in the 1930s were even more assiduous in encouraging industrial cartelization.[65] A rising generation of Labour economic experts, including Hugh Dalton and Hugh Gaitskell, elaborated new reformist economic policies in the 1930s in response to the Great Depression. Under the influence of economist James Meade, they made the extent of monopoly control over prices in a given economic sector the primary criterion in determining whether a sector should be nationalized.[66] The reformist faction's position resembles that adopted by the SAP in Birgit Karlsson's chapter, in which she argues that economic efficiency in regard to prices was the primary means for social democrats to assess the desirability of a cartel arrangement.

Like many continental neighbors, the UK developed a heavily cartelized economy from the 1920s until the passage of the 1956 Restrictive Trade Practices Act, which was reinforced by further legislation in the 1960s. After surviving a spurt of anti-cartel publications and initiatives during and immediately following the Second World War, British industrial cartelization revived to new heights in the 1950s, such that historian Neil Rollings estimates that 50–60% of British manufacturing output in 1958 fell under one or another form of cartelization.[67] Helen Mercer argues, "For most of this century the most coherent critique of private monopoly by a wider 'public' has been articulated by the labour movement – the Labour Party, the trade unions, and the Co-Ops." Her assertion introduces several themes that are developed through this book. First, labor and socialist parties, not conservative or liberal parties, generally expounded the most anti-cartel positions in their countries; even in cases when their parties were broadly "pro-cartel," they tended to support state or international regulation to supervise restrictive business practices. During the Second World War, anti-cartel attitudes in the Labour Party came to a particularly fervent pitch, under the influence of US wartime propaganda that tied cartelization to Nazi ideology, raucous anti-cartel pressures from the Labour backbench and the general anti-cartel climate in public opinion. This position came to fruition in the stridently anti-monopoly paper "The Control of Monopoly" coauthored by Gaitskell in 1943 for the Board of Trade. For Mercer, "The paper represented the high point of the evolution of antitrust proposals in Britain for many years to come, indeed ever since."[68] Gaitskell and Dalton defended the "prohibition" principle, by which cartels would be a priori banned (with the possibility of exemptions) and detailed controls would be placed on monopoly prices and trade associations, while a cartel register was to be established and a sweeping nationalization program would wash away private monopolies. They could not gain agreement within the Conservative-Labour wartime cabinet, however. Labour policy was further weakened by internal disunity because, as we shall see in other labor and socialist parties, significant figures came out for the "abuse" principle rather than prohibition, meaning that only the abuse of cartel positions rather than their existence was illegal. In 1945, the Labour Party triumphed in national elections and took power for the first time as sole party of government. Its campaign manifesto came to an intermediary position that revived language from interwar policy documents discussed earlier. It demanded: "Public supervision of monopolies and cartels with the aim of advancing industrial efficiency in the service of the nation. Anti-social restrictive practices will be prohibited."[69] The result was the 1948 Monopolies and

Mergers Act but "this Act was very much a damp squib," Jim Tomlinson argues, due to opposition from the Board of Trade and industry, as well as "ambiguity in Labour's thinking about competition," in which anti-monopoly perspectives competed with the party's more fervent nationalization agenda, similar in many ways to uncertainties at the time on cartel policy within the German SPD (see Schröter's and Shaev's chapters).[70]

Secondly, Labour Party policies must be analyzed in the broader universe of labor's socio-political milieu, the "labour movement," which included trade unions and cooperatives. For the most part, these non-party organizations pushed anti-cartel policies in line with the Labour Party. At other times, their interests pulled in different directions, for instance, between employment-focused trade unions and consumer-based cooperative movements. Such differences came to a head concerning resale price maintenance (also known as retail price maintenance), an anti-competitive practice that amounted to price-fixing between large distributors and retail shops, including groceries, though its defenders highlighted that it often led to lower prices in rural and more remote areas where competition generally did not exist. Cooperatives hankered for a ban on this practice, arguing that it drove up food and basic good prices for consumers, while trade unions were more circumspect, worrying about the impact a ban might have on employment in small retail stores. Thus, it was only in 1951, in the waning days of Clement Attlee's postwar Labour government, that Harold Wilson oversaw the publication of a White Paper calling for a total ban on resale price maintenance.[71] The Trade Union Congress (TUC) came out for public supervision and for a monopoly court and generally supported anti-cartel measures, but its goal was expressly not to ensure competitive markets and its anti-cartel position was at times undermined by the interests of individual unions, especially the textiles union, which considered cartelization necessary to maintain employment in this fragile sector.[72] The TUC's competition policy resembled in this way that of the postwar German trade union confederation as shown in Severin Cramm's chapter.

Overall, despite such ambiguities, the labor movement had the most anti-cartel position in postwar British politics and society – a feature it shared with the French Socialist, Dutch Labor, Finnish Social Democratic, and Swedish Social Democratic parties (even when several of these parties straddled pro- and anti-cartel positions) – and, from mid-1950s, the German SPD. The UK Conservative Party, meanwhile, is described as "a mouthpiece for business in parliament" in its opposition to anti-cartel laws, though it was eager to apply competition law to economic actors favored by Labour, that is to say, to nationalized businesses, trade unions and cooperatives.[73] Chapters in this book explore not only continuities and changes in the rationale of socialist cartel policies over time but also their concrete influence (or absence of influence) on the formation and development of national and European competition law. Mercer shares Tomlinson's general view, arguing that Labour's policy in government, which culminated in the 1948 Act, represented the defeat of Labour's wartime vision. Business pressure, civil servants' behind-the-scenes influence and increasing suspicion of the US government's international anti-cartel agenda led Labour to acquiesce in a weakening of its own vision, such that what emerged bore more in common with Conservative war-time designs. The act set up the Monopolies and Restrictive Practices Commission, but it was loaded with loopholes and the Commission had no power to impose sanctions or penalties on businesses. Nonetheless, businesses loathed the authority, which produced a steady stream of damning reports on restrictive activities during its existence from 1949 to 1956. Partly as a response to business pressure, a Conservative government dissolved the authority and replaced it with the 1956 Restrictive Trade Practices Act. This act appeared in ways more restrictive than the 1948 Act in that it placed the burden of proof that restrictive practices were in the public interest onto businesses themselves and instituted compulsory registration of cartels at the newly created Restrictive Practices Court. However, the act was lenient in regard to large business concentrations, in a number of ways reinforced resale price maintenance despite instituting a formal ban, and certain clauses specifically targeted trade unions and cooperatives. Nick Tiratsoo and Tomlinson write that "[t]he 1956 Act was criticised by the Labour Party as a 'Charter for Big Business,'" because it was mostly used against smaller firms.[74] In line with contemporaneous events in Germany, where the SPD evolved toward a stronger anti-cartel position than the governing Christian democrats and opposed the 1957 German competition law as too lenient, Labour MPs called the new act "bogus" and voted in opposition from an anti-cartel position in 1956.

Though the Conservative Party was moderately trending toward a pro-competition position through the postwar era, it was only in the context of its shift to favoring accession to the European Communities that it moved to a more anti-cartel position in the lead-up to its loss in the 1964 UK elections.[75] Thereafter, the new Labour government under Harold Wilson passed the Monopolies and Mergers Act in 1965, which established a stronger competition policy in this field than in EEC countries where laws to control mergers did not yet exist (until an SPD-Liberal government passed the Merger Law in 1973 discussed at this introduction's opening) and outlawed resale price maintenance. However, the next year Wilson's government founded the Industrial Reorganisation Corporation with the purpose of building "national champions" by spurring industrial mergers. This was in line with the contemporary *Zeitgeist* of the late 1960s in which European countries feared their industries did not have economies of scale to compete in new technological sectors with the United States and USSR.[76] The Conservatives split their votes on the 1965 Bill, with those voting in favor following Edward Heath's position that stronger competition laws would facilitate the UK's accession to the EEC. This was decidedly not, however, Labour's position, as the party still opposed UK accession at the time, though soon after Wilson pivoted to the 1967 British application to join the EEC. The crucial point in this regard – and in contrast to socialist parties in EEC countries – is that Labour generally opposed international laws to regulate cartels and competition. Back in the interwar period, let us recall, the Labour Party had presented weaker positions than the SFIO and SPD on questions of international powers to regulate business practices. The Attlee government adopted an even starker position during the negotiations in 1945–48 for the Havana Charter for an International Trade Organization, in which the Labour-led

British government looked to weaken US proposed rules as well as the international enforcement capacity of international institutions to regulate cartels.[77] As we shall see, however, continental socialists in the 1950s were moving in the opposite direction, evolving within a few years into the strongest supporters of a supranational European competition policy to ban cross-border cartels and regulate restrictive business practices in the EEC.

The evolution of social-democratic competition policy in Europe, 1900–62

Our book's timeframe spans the classical period of social democracy around the turn of the twentieth century to the early twenty-first century. In this introduction, we focus on social-democratic competition policy from its formative stage in the pre–First World War era up to the postwar period in which new national competition laws were introduced in a number of countries and competition policy became an essential part of European integration. As we shall see, even when political parties under examination took more "cartel-friendly" or restrictive positions, there was always some ambivalence in their views of competition. Furthermore, taking a long-term perspective, there was a clear tendency for social-democratic parties to move toward more restrictive positions on cartels and anticompetitive practices from the early twentieth century. Though their specific preferences in regard to competition often varied, social democrats in the 1950s–early 60s were far more hostile toward cartels and anticompetitive practices than they had been in the decades before. Most importantly, they were determined to do something about it and indeed, as our book will show, in many cases they did.

Social-democratic policies on competition can be conceptualized as a blend of socialist ideology, contemporary affinities with or critical engagement with nonsocialist ideas and fashions, and constituency pressures. All three elements could lead socialists to more favorable or critical positions on cartels and competition but the balance underwent considerable change over time. Schröter introduces us to the Marxist legacy in early German social democracy, in which monopolies represented the final stage of capitalism. The state would be compelled, in Karl Marx's view, to intervene to redress the consequences of the elimination of competition in a capitalist system that could only function on the basis of competition. Classical German social democracy in the 1890s–1910s picked up on Marx's ambivalence, including the reformist faction around Eduard Bernstein. Social democrats viewed cartels and monopolies negatively because they represented the culmination of the exploitative tendencies engrained in capitalism but also positively in that they signaled the looming collapse of capitalism and its replacement with a new system. That cartels and monopolies represented economies of scale that swept away less productive economic actors and were based on the cooperative principle encouraged socialists to view cartelization as a maturing process in the evolution of economic life preparing these sectors for socialization. This view was prominent not only in Germany but also in Sweden, as John Lapidus has shown for the 1920s[78] and Birgit Karlsson confirms in her chapter.

Socialist ambivalence on cartels and monopolies came from a recognition that, though they appeared to herald a possible socialist future, monopoly prices were materially damaging working-class constituencies in the here and now. Social-democratic parties in particular faced a constant struggle to balance producer and consumer interests. As self-proclaimed representatives of the industrial working classes, socialists were drawn to support business sectors that were often experiencing the highest levels of concentration, for example, shipbuilding, metal industries and coal mining. At times, the producer-consumer conflict could be attenuated by favoring cartelization in industrial sectors while opposing it in food and consumer goods sectors, as was the case in Sweden in the 1920s. At other times, social democrats were pulled in different directions by conflicts between their key constituencies and affiliated interest groups: trade unions, consumer organizations and cooperatives. The latter two usually pressured for stronger regulation of cartels and monopolies – though cooperatives at times found themselves having to defend their own status from competition legislation – while trade unions usually supported cartelization with the purpose of defending industrial sectors where trade-union membership was often highest.

Trade unionists and social democrats were heavily influenced by expert and scientific opinion in the 1890s–1920s that considered cartels modern advances in production that could end economic price wars through rational coordination between businesses and thereby prevent unemployment. Karlsson emphasizes how, in the 1920s, cartelization appeared in political and economic discussions as the best means of achieving economic rationalization at a time that Taylorist techniques were being implemented in haste in Europe. Trade-union support for cartelization, though, was not unanimous. Leftwing trade unionists like Toni Sender, for instance, claimed that artificially high cartel prices eliminated incentives to modernize, a direct attack on the prevalent opinion on cartels.[79] She held this opinion even though the German Metal Workers Union she was associated with developed a pro-cartel position, as Schröter shows. Sender's argument also finds reflection in Karlsson's analysis of Swedish social democracy, which evolved toward a moderately restrictive position in the 1930s due to rising concerns that cartels were economically inefficient and creating more rather than less unemployment during the Great Depression.

When socialists began joining governments, especially during the First World War, they favored state direction of cartel activities. They were particularly impressed by wartime commodity boards and other organizations that combined state and business interests to coordinate production and distribution in the interests of war economies. French Socialists wished to see wartime-era Allied Control Boards extended after the First World War.[80] Schröter discusses how Carl Legien, German trade-union leader and head of the IFTU, wanted to do so as well for production boards in which trade unions were officially represented, which led him to support Walther Rathenau's ideas of state economic management. State economic boards removed a key objection socialists had to cartels and monopolies: cartels' secretive nature and service to private rather than public interests, though socialists also often denounced cartels for war profiteering. Postwar governments quickly dismantled interventionist bodies by the early 1920s, however, and many socialist parties adopted socialization or nationalization policies instead as their preferred means of addressing private concentrations of economic power. In Germany, co-determination – the inclusion of elected trade-union representatives in company management – was considered a means of attenuating the dangers of private economic power by fostering "economic democracy" in addition to providing opportunities to improve workers' pay and working conditions.

As discussed earlier, an effort to build an international system of European cooperation based on Loucheur's proposal of a "Europe of cartels" prompted international socialism to formulate their own proposals. The LSI in 1928 – and again in 1931 in alliance with the IFTU – demanded public regulation of cartels and public registers, though socialists split over whether regulation should be internationally enforced under the League of Nations or under national law. We can observe a precedent for postwar socialist policies in these transnational discussions: the SPD supported international regulation in the interwar period and again from 1955 while the UK Labour Party preferred national regulation in both instances. The political move toward supporting planning in the 1930s – controversial as it was at first for many parties – can be seen as outgrowths of previous thinking in regard to cartels and competition. The collapse of the international economic system and the decline of international institutions like the League of Nations pushed socialist regulatory ambitions back into national spheres, even when ideological support remained for international solutions. Planning ideas drew on socialists' previous support for wartime economic boards. In many ways, it allowed a synthesis of socialists' otherwise ambivalent views on cartels: the productive functions of economic concentration and cooperation would remain while planning agencies would direct their activities toward the collective good rather than private interests at the public's expense. Furthermore, planning ideas opened up possibilities for direct representation of trade unions, cooperatives and consumer organizations in tripartite arrangements with the state and businesses.

Planning ideas *en vogue* in the 1930s were influential again in the postwar period. One of the reasons that the postwar Dutch Labor Party (*Partij van de Arbeid*, PvdA) was less concerned about cartels than some other social-democratic parties was that a PvdA-led government had instituted an extensive tripartite management body for economic affairs, the Publiekrechtelijke Bedrijfsorganisatie (PBO). This meant, as Karin van Leeuwen argues, that cartel activities could be steered in the national interest as tools of state economic policy in what cartel historians have labeled a postwar "cartel paradise."[81] Nonetheless, one faction of the PvdA represented by Gerard Nederhorst propounded the most hostile position toward cartels in the Dutch parliament in the 1940s–50s. As one of the most important PvdA representatives in European parliamentary bodies in the 1950s–60s, Nederhorst pushed for strong supranational regulation of cartels and competition as well, as I show in my chapter.

Social-democratic parties emerged from the Second World War with policies on cartels and competition that ran the range from nationalizations, to tripartite economic management, and to national and international regulation. Most often they were a blend, with the UK Labour Party enacting widespread nationalizations and a new law to regulate competition while opposing international regulation. The French Socialist Party, as Ramírez Pérez and Shaev discuss, initially focused on a nationalization agenda. After concerns grew that further nationalizations would strengthen the Communist Party, the party moved to support national and international regulation while also working closely to defend the interests of new state-owned companies like the French national coal company (*Charbonnages de France*). In our chapters, we see that postwar social-democratic parties had moved toward more restrictive positions favoring regulation than they had had before the war. Out of a network of French Socialists, state planning administrators and directors of state-owned companies came the inspiration for the legal form of the competition provisions proposed by Jean Monnet for the ECSC that inaugurated European competition law, Ramírez Pérez argues. Though still relatively lenient, the SAP passed Sweden's first major piece of competition legislation in 1953. The party had decided that increased state supervision was necessary to tackle "abuse." Its government set up a cartel register and state investigation capacities that targeted distribution chains, while leaving production cartels seen as favoring rationalization untouched, Karlsson argues. A social-democratic-led government in Finland passed a similar law in 1954. As Susanna Fellman discusses, it was also based on the "abuse" principle, set up a public register and banned resale price maintenance in distribution as well as bid ridding. She credits steady pressure from the cooperative movement and the anti-cartel far-left/communist party as well as international influences and the policy entrepreneurship of individual social democrats for the enactment of this competition law.

A partial exception was the German Social Democratic Party, but as Schröter discusses, the SPD position was not as pro-cartel as previously thought. Rather, it represented an ambivalent blend of views in the late 1940s. As the SPD's postwar nationalization policy appeared increasingly unrealistic in the early 1950s, the party moved decisively in a regulatory direction as the best means for controlling accumulations of economic power. As Severin Cramm analyzes, German trade union policy on cartels and competition largely ran parallel to and reinforced the move toward regulating cartels and anticompetitive practices in the SPD. Especially in Germany, the contention that cartels and private economic power reflected threats to political democracy was a primary impetus first for the social democrats' nationalization policy and then, from 1955, for its competition policy. The SPD evolved into the strongest advocates of competition policy in Germany by the second half of the 1950s, joining its postwar counterparts in Finland, France, the Netherlands, Sweden and the UK as the political party most favorable to regulating competition in their country (with the exception of far-left parties). The myopic scholarly focus on German ordoliberals, a minority faction on competition within the Christian Democratic Union (CDU), has led scholars to largely ignore that it was the SPD that was the most pro-competition party in Germany from the mid-1950s to the 70s. Business interests were largely opposed to the new competition laws, as were most right-wing and liberal parties. Even the famous 1957 German competition law was a weak shadow of Economic Minister Ludwig Erhard's original proposal due to opposition from business lobbies and Christian Democrats in the Bundestag.

The SPD voted against the 1957 German competition law because it was too lenient. Shaev shows how it joined the other socialist parties in the early European parliament to support Regulation 17/62, the foundation of European competition policy, though it would have preferred that supranational competition powers be stronger. If one were to follow the view that the 1957 German law and the first European competition regulation were (ordo)liberal in inspiration, that would mean that the SPD was the most (ordo)liberal party in Germany and the Socialist Group the most (ordo)liberal group in the European parliament. This view would, of course, be mistaken. It is increasingly untenable to claim that the 1957 German law was a great ordoliberal victory considering the wide range of exemptions that covered most of economic activity. The historiography of Regulation 17/62 is now much more complex than an older view that it entailed a direct transfer of ordoliberal ideas from Germany to the European stage. The regulation is now viewed more as a compromise between national preferences,[82] including the largely unexplored Dutch influence van Leeuwen emphasizes.

The idea that strong competition policy is intrinsically and incontrovertibly an ordoliberal idea is also untenable. First, social-democratic parties generally developed the most anti-cartel positions and were the most favorable to state regulation of cartels and anti-restrictive practices within the postwar politics of the European countries under study – but their ideas on competition cannot be described as "ordoliberal" even when they shared overlapping features. With the partial exception of the postwar PvdA (see van Leeuwen's chapter), socialists did not view competition as a value to be pursued in and of itself. Rather, socialist competition policy generally considered national competition policy an active political arm to be wielded in the service of the state's economic goals – as an agent of democratic control. In some countries like the Netherlands, it was (with tripartism) a replacement in a sense for nationalization policies, but elsewhere it could coexist with nationalization goals as socialists generally wanted publicly owned enterprises to be excluded from most aspects of competition law. Competition policy was not intended to be a neutral, technocratic or even a primarily legal field: in the UK but also in Germany, social democrats put much of competition policy in the hands of the economic minister. Van Leeuwen observes this social-democratic concept of competition policy on display in the figure of Pieter VerLoren van Themaat, director general of competition in the European Commission in the 1960s. For him, competition policy served a broader Keynesian macroeconomic policy that included investment policy, taxation and more.

Not only did Liberal parties generally oppose strong competition laws because they usually represented business interests, but also it is hard to point to any unambiguous victories of ordoliberal ideas in Germany or in the European Communities in the 1950s–early 60s that did not also have support from social democrats. Social-democratic parties generally represented the hardest anti-cartel position in postwar national and European politics. They passed national competition laws in numerous countries that restricted cartels and anticompetitive activity. It is time to restore their formative contribution to the history of competition policy in Europe. Our book demonstrates that there were alternative ideas to ordoliberalism that favored strong competition policy – and that the building of a new legal and political framework for competition in Europe only makes sense once we have a fuller appreciation of the efforts and influences of European social-democratic parties on the origins of European competition policy.

Notes

1 Das Regierungsprogramm der SPD. Ausserordentlicher Kongress der SPD, Bonn, 28 April 1961, *Neuer Vorwärts-Verlag*, 1961.
2 Brian Shaev, "International Cartels in the Political Origins of German Competition Policy, 1949–1953," in Susanna Fellman and Martin Shanahan (eds.), *A History of Business Cartels: International Politics, National Policies, and Anti-Competitive Behaviour* (New York: Routledge, 2022), 83–102.
3 Bundestag, Antrag der SPD, Drucksache III/2293, December 1960.
4 Lorenzo Federico Pace and Katja Seidel briefly mention trade union but not socialist support in their legal history of Regulation 17/62, Lorenzo Federico Pace and Katja Seidel, "The Drafting and the Role of Regulation 17: A Hard-Fought Compromise," in Kiran Klaus Patel and Heike Schweitzer (eds.), *The Historical Foundations of EU Competition Law* (Oxford: Oxford University Press, 2014), 54–88, here 71; there are mentions of SPD cartel policy in the lead-up to Germany's 1957 Cartel Law in James C. van Hook, *Rebuilding Germany: The Creation of the Social Market Economy, 1945–1957* (Cambridge: Cambridge University Press, 2007), Chapter 6 "The Social Market Economy and Competition," 233–289.
5 David B. Gruskey and Tamar Kricheli-Katz (eds.), *The New Gilded Age: The Critical Inequality Debates of Our Time* (Stanford: Stanford University Press, 2012).
6 David J. Gerber, "Constitutionalizing the Economy: German Neoliberalism, Competition Law and the 'New' Europe," *The American Journal of Comparative Law* 42, 25 (1994): 25–84.
7 Michelle Cini and Lee McGowan, *Competition Policy in the European Union* (London: Routledge, 2009); Lee McGowan and Stephen Wilks, "The First Supranational Policy in the European Union: Competition Policy," *European Journal of Political Research* 28 (1995): 141–169.
8 Sigrid Quack and Marie-Laure Djelic, "Adaption, Recombination and Reinforcement: The Story of Antitrust and Competition Law in Germany and Europe," in Wolfgang Streeck and Kathleen Thelen (eds.), *Beyond Continuity: Institutional Change in Advanced Political Economies* (Oxford: Oxford University Press, 2005), 255–281.
9 Yannis Karagiannis, "The Origins of European Competition Policy: Redistributive versus Ideational Explanations," *Journal of European Public Policy* 20, 5 (2013): 777–792, 779–780.
10 Volker Berghahn, *The Americanization of West German Industry, 1945–1973* (Leamington Spa: Berg, 1986); Brigitte Leucht and Mel Marquis, "American Influences on EEC Competition Law: Two Paths, How Much Dependence?" in Kiran Klaus Patel and Heike Schweitzer (eds.), *The Historical Foundations of EU Competition Law* (Oxford: Oxford University Press), 125–161.
11 Gerber, "Constitutionalizing the Economy."
12 Anselm Küsters, "The Making and Unmaking of Ordoliberal Language: A Digital Conceptual History of European Competition Law," PhD dissertation, Johann Wolfgang Goethe University, 2022.
13 Marco Bertilorenzi, *The International Aluminum Cartel, 1886–1978: The Business and Politics of a Cooperative Industrial Institution* (London: Routledge, 2016); Sigfrido M. Ramírez Pérez, "La politique de la concurrence de la Communauté Économique Européenne et l´industrie: l'exemple des accords sur la distribution automobile

(1972–1985)," *Histoire, économie et société* 27, 1 (2008): 63–77; Niklas Jensen-Eriksen, "Industrial Diplomacy and Economic Integration: The Origins of All-European Paper Cartels, 1959–72," *Journal of Contemporary History* 46, 1 (2011): 179–202.

14 Bram Bouwens and Joost Dankers, "The Invisible Handshake: Cartelization in the Netherlands, 1930–2000," *The Business History Review* 84, 4 (2010): 751–771; Bram Bouwens and Joost Dankers, "Competition and Coordination: Reconsidering Economic Cooperation in Dutch Business, 1900–2000," *Revue économique* 64, 6 (2013): 1105–1124.

15 Neil Rollings and Laurent Warlouzet, "Business History and European Integration: How EEC Competition Policy affected Companies' Strategies," *Business History* 62, 5 (2020): 717–742.

16 Marco Bertilorenzi, "Legitimising Cartels: The Joint Roles of the League of Nations and of the International Chamber of Commerce," in Susanna Fellman and Martin Shanahan (eds.), *Regulating Competition: Cartel Registers in the Twentieth-Century World* (London: Routledge, 2016), 30–47; Werner Bührer and Laurent Warlouzet, "Regulating Markets: Peak Business Associations and the Origins of European Competition Policy," in Wolfram Kaiser and Jan-Henrik Meyer (eds.), *Societal Actors in European Integration: Polity-Building and Policy-Making 1958–1992* (Basingstoke: Palgrave Macmillan, 2013), 59–83.

17 Tobias Witschke, *Gefahr für den Wettbewerb? Die Fusionskontrolle der Europäischen Gemeinschaft für Kohle und Stahl und die "Rekonstruktion" der Ruhrstahlindustrie 1950–1963* (Berlin: Akademie, 2014); Sibylle Hambloch, *Europäische Integration und Wettbewerbspolitik: Die Frühphase der EWG* (Baden-Baden: Nomos, 2009).

18 Fellman and Shanahan, *Regulating Competition*; Patel and Schweitzer, *The Historical Foundations of EU Competition Law*; Laurent Warlouzet, "The EEC/EU as an Evolving Compromise between French Dirigism and German Ordoliberalism (1957–1995)," *Journal of Common Market Studies* 57, 1 (2019): 77–93.

19 Matthieu Fulla, *Les Socialistes français et l'économie (1944–1981): Une Histoire économique du politique* (Paris: Presses de Sciences Po, 2016), 25; See also the approach in Brian Shaev, "Liberalising Regional Trade: Socialists and European Economic Integration," *Contemporary European History* 27, 2 (2018): 258–279.

20 Talbot Imlay, *The Practice of Socialist Internationalism: European Socialists and International Politics, 1914–1960* (Oxford: Oxford University Press, 2018); Talbot Imlay, "The Policy of Social Democracy is Self-Consciously Internationalist: The SPD's Internationalism after 1945," *Journal of Modern History* 86, 1 (2014): 81–123.

21 Mathieu Fulla and Marc Lazar (eds.), *European Socialists and the State in the Twentieth and Twenty-First Centuries* (Basingstoke: Palgrave Macmillan, 2020).

22 Hartmut Bechtold, *Die Kartellierung der deutschen Volkswirtschaft und die sozialdemokratische Theorie-Diskussion vor 1933* (Frankfurt am Main: Haag+Herchen Verlag, 1986); John Lapidus, "Why such a Permissive Attitude towards Monopolistic Associations? Social Democracy up to the First Swedish Law on Cartels in 1925," *Scandinavian Journal of History* 38, 1 (2013): 65–88; Dietmar Petzina, "Gewerkschaften und Monopolfrage vor und während der Weimarer Republik," in Dietmar Petzina, Werner Abelshauser and Ludwig Budrass (eds.), *Die Verantwortung des Staates für die Wirtschaft: ausgewählte Aufsätze* (Essen: Klartext, 2001), 46–69; Helen Callaghan and Martin Höpner write that from 1959 'Liberal competition policy was now endorsed as an end in itself' by the SPD. Helen Callaghan and Martin Höpner, "Changing Ideas: Organised Capitalism and the German Left," *West European Politics* 35, 3 (2012): 551–573, here 562.

23 Hubert Buch-Hansen and Angela Wigger, "Revisiting 50 Years of Market-Making: The Neoliberal Transformation of European Competition Policy," *Review of International Political Economy* 17, 1 (2010): 20–44. Pinar Akman and Hussein Kassim offer a similar argument. Pinar Akman and Hussein Kassim, "Myths and Myth-Making in the European Union: The Institutionalization and Interpretation of EU Competition Policy," *Journal of Common Market Studies* 48, 1 (2010): 111–132.

24 Bertilorenzi, "Legitimising Cartels," in Fellman and Shanahan, *Regulating Competition*, 34.

25 Eric Bussière and François Berger, "La France, la Belgique, l'Allemagne et les cartels de l'Entre-deux-guerres, Une méthode pour l'organisation économique de l'Europe," in Jürgen Elvert and Sylvain Schirmann, *Ces chers voisins: L'Allemagne, la Belgique et la France en Europe du XIe au XXI siècles* (Stuttgart: Franz Steiner, 2012), 221–242; Clemens August Wurm, "Internationale Kartelle und die deutsch-französischen Beziehungen 1924–1930: Politik, Wirtschaft, Sicherheit," in Stephen A. Schuker (ed.) *Deutschland und Frankreich: Vom Konflikt zur Aussöhnung. Die Gestaltung der westeuropäischen Sicherheit 1914–1963* (Oldenbourg: Oldenbourg Wissenschaftsverlag, 2000), 97–116.

26 Dominique Barjot, "Les cartels, une voie vers l'intégration européenne: Le rôle de Louis Loucheur (1872–1931)," *Revue économique* 64, 6 (2013): 1043–1066, here 1062.

27 Eric Bussière, "Premiers schémas européens et économie internationale durant l'entre-deux-guerres," *Relations internationales* 123, 3 (2005): 51–68, here 60.

28 Barjot, "Les cartels, une voie vers l'intégration européenne," 1061.

29 Bertilorenzi, "Legitimising Cartels," 31.

30 Wolfram Kaiser and Johan Schot, *Writing the Rules for Europe: Experts, Cartels and International Organizations* (Basingstoke: Palgrave Macmillan, 2014).

31 Ernest Poisson, "La Conférence de Bruxelles," *La Vie Socialiste*, 18 March 1926.

32 "La Conférence économique de Bruxelles," *La Vie Socialiste*, 18 March 1926.

33 See remarks at the conference by CGT leader Léon Jouhaux in Robert Liefmann, *International Cartels, Combines and Trusts* (London: Europa Publishing, 1927), 110.

34 David J. Gerber, *Global Competition: Law, Markets, and Globalization* (Oxford: Oxford University Press, 2010), 28–29.

35 Terushi Hara, "La conférence économique internationale de 1927 et ses effets sur la formation des cartels internationaux," in Dominique Barjot (ed.), *International Cartels Revisited: relating to the history of business development and international economic order* (Cormelles: Editions-Diffusions du Lys, 1994), 265–272.

36 Bertilorenzi, "Legitimising Cartels," 37.

37 Eric Bussière, "La SDN, les cartels, et l'organisation économique de l'Europe durant l'entre-deux-guerres," in Dominique Barjot (ed.), *International Cartels Revisited* (Cormelles: Editions-Diffusions du Lys, 1994), 273–283, here 278.

38 International Institute for Social History (IISH), Amsterdam, Labour and Socialist International (LSI), ARCHO1368.58, Third Congress of the L.S.I. Brussels. Draft Statement for item 4 of the agenda. Draft Resolution to the Economic Report for the Brussels Congress submitted by F. Napthali (Berlin).

39 IISH, LSI, ARCH01368.58, Third Congress of L.S.I. Brussels 1928. Draft Resolution of the I.L.P. (Great Britain) for Item 4. The Post-war Economic Situation and the Economic Policy of the Working Class; IISH, LSI, ARCH01368.58, Third Congress of L.S.I. Brussels, 1928. Draft statement for item 4) The Post-war Economic Situation and the Economic Policy of the Working-Class by C.T. Cramp.

40 Stefan Berger, "Between Challenging the Authoritarian State and Democratizing It: German Social Democracy, 1914–1945," in Mathieu Fulla and Marc Lazar (eds.), *European Socialists and the State* (Basingstoke: Palgrave Macmillan, 2020), 35–55, here 46.

41 Harm G. Schröter, "The International Potash Syndicate," in Dominique Barjot (ed.), *International Cartels Revisited* (Cormelles: Editions-Diffusions du Lys, 1994), 75–92.

42 IISH, LSI, ARCH01368.58, Über die wirtschaftliche Situation der Nachkriegszeit und die ökonomische Politik der Arbeiterklasse. Richtlinien zum Vortrag von Fritz Napthali. Berlin, den 11. Juli 1928.

43 The Post-war Economic Situation and the Economic Policy of the Working-Class by C.T. Cramp.

44 IISH, LSI, ARCH01368.784, Fighting World Economic Crisis and Unemployment. Pamphlet embodying the Findings of the Joint Unemployment Committee of the International Federation of Trade Unions and the Labour and Socialist International. Amsterdam, 1931.

45 *Union interparlementaire, Compte rendu de la XXVIe conférence tenue à Londres du 16 au 22 Juillet 1930* (Lausanne: Librarie Payot, 1931), 33–34.

46 *Ibid.*, 360–365.
47 *Ibid.*, 374–75.
48 Fighting World Economic Crisis and Unemployment.
49 Wladimir Woytinksy, "Aktive Weltwirtschaftspolitik," *Die Arbeit* 6 (1931).
50 George Garvy, "Keynes and the Economic Activists of Pre-Hitler Germany," *Journal of Political Economy* 83, 2 (1975), 391–405, here 399.
51 "Richtlinien des ADGB und des AfA-Bundes zum Umbau der Wirtschaft vom 21. Juni 1932," *Gewerkschafts-Zeitung* 27 (2 July 1932): 418–420.
52 Tommaso Milani, *Hendrik de Man and Social Democracy: The Idea of Planning in Western Europe, 1914–1940* (Basingstoke: Palgrave Macmillan, 2021), 120.
53 *Ibid.*, 63.
54 *Ibid.*, 131–137, 202.
55 *Ibid.*, 6.
56 Georges Lefranc, "Le courant planiste dans le mouvement ouvrier français de 1933 à 1936," *Le Mouvement social* 54 (1966): 69–89, here 78–79.
57 Jacques Amoyal, "Les origines socialistes et syndicalistes de la planification en France," *Le Mouvement social* 87 (1974), 137–169, here 149–150.
58 Milani, *Hendrik de Man*, 253.
59 André Philip, *Le Crise et l'économie dirigée* (Paris: Cluny, 1935), 56, 62–63.
60 *Ibid.*, 184–185.
61 *Ibid.*, 200–204.
62 Adéodat Compère-Morel, "Est-on décidé à faire quelque chose de hardi et de neuf?" *Bataille socialiste*, May 1934.
63 Vincent Auriol, "La dernière débâcle," *Combat Social*, 26 March 1933.
64 Jim Tomlinson, *Democratic Socialism and Economic Policy in the Attlee Years* (Cambridge: Cambridge University Press, 2004), 4–5; Jim Tomlinson, "Labour and the Economy," in Duncan Tanner, Pat Thane and Nick Tiratsoo (eds.), *Labour's First Century* (Cambridge: Cambridge University Press, 2007), 48–49.
65 Nick Tiratsoo and Jim Tomlinson, *The Conservatives and Industrial Efficiency, 1951–1964: Thirteen Wasted Years?* (London: Routledge, 2016), 15.
66 Elizabeth Durbin, *New Jerusalems: The Labour Party and the Economics of Democratic Socialism* (London: Routledge & Evan, 1985), 228.
67 Neil Rollings, *British Business in the Formative Years of European Integration* (Cambridge: Cambridge University Press, 2008), 195.
68 Helen Mercer, *Constructing a Competitive Order: The Hidden History of British Antitrust Policies* (Cambridge: Cambridge University Press, 2009), 56.
69 *Ibid.*, 87.
70 Tomlinson, *Democratic Socialism and Economic Policy*, 72.
71 Mercer, *Constructing a Competitive Order*, 151–52.
72 *Ibid.*, 92, 135.
73 *Ibid.*, 99.
74 Tiratsoo and Tomlinson, *The Conservatives and Industrial Efficiency*, 118.
75 *Ibid.*, 100–122.
76 Tomlinson, *Democratic Socialism and Economic Policy*, 153.
77 Gerber, *Global Competition Law*, 49.
78 Lapidus, "Why such a Permissive Attitude towards Monopolistic Associations?"
79 Brian Shaev, "From Cradle to Grave: The German Trade Union Federation's Wage, Welfare, and Competitiveness Program for the Weimar Republic," in Lucia Coppolaro and Lorenzo Mechi (eds.), *Free Trade and Social Welfare: Explorations in the Long Twentieth Century* (London: Routledge, 2020), 30–51.
80 Shaev, "Liberalising Regional Trade."
81 Bram Bouwens and Joost Dankers, "From Paradise to Hell. Post-War Cartel Policy and Practice in the Netherlands," *Entreprises et histoire* 76, 3 (2014): 58–71.
82 Warlouzet, "The EEC/EU as an Evolving Compromise."

Bibliography

Akman, Pinar and Hussein Kassim. "Myths and Myth-Making in the European Union: The Institutionalization and Interpretation of EU Competition Policy." *Journal of Common Market Studies* 48, 1 (2010): 111–132.

Amoyal, Jacques. "Les origines socialistes et syndicalistes de la planification en France." *Le Mouvement social* 87 (1974): 137–169.

Bechtold, Hartmut. *Die Kartellierung der deutschen Volkswirtschaft und die sozialdemokratische Theorie-Diskussion vor 1933*. Frankfurt a.M.: Haag+Herchen Verlag, 1986.

Berger, Stefan. "Between Challenging the Authoritarian State and Democratizing It: German Social Democracy, 1914–1945." In *European Socialists and the State in the Twentieth and Twenty-First Centuries* edited by Mathieu Fulla and Marc Lazar. Basingstoke: Palgrave Macmillan, 2020, 35–55.

Berghahn, Volker. *The Americanization of West German Industry, 1945–1973*. Leamington Spa: Berg, 1986.

Bertilorenzi, Marco. *The International Aluminum Cartel, 1886–1978: The Business and Politics of a Cooperative Industrial Institution*. London: Routledge, 2016.

Bertilorenzi, Marco. "Legitimising Cartels: The Joint Roles of the League of Nations and of the International Chamber of Commerce." In *Regulating Competition: Cartel Registers in the Twentieth-Century World* edited by Susanna Fellman and Martin Shanahan. London: Routledge, 2016, 30–47.

Bouwens, Bram and Joost Dankers. "Competition and Coordination: Reconsidering Economic Cooperation in Dutch Business, 1900–2000." *Revue économique* 64, 6 (2013): 1105–1124.

Bouwens, Bram and Joost Dankers. "The Invisible Handshake: Cartelization in the Netherlands, 1930–2000." *The Business History Review* 84, 4 (2010): 751–771.

Bouwens, Bram and Joost Dankers. "From Paradise to Hell. Post-War Cartel Policy and Practice in the Netherlands." *Entreprises et histoire* 76, 3 (2014): 58–71

Buch-Hansen, Hubert and Angela Wigger. "Revisiting 50 Years of Market-Making: The Neoliberal Transformation of European Competition Policy." *Review of International Political Economy* 17, 1 (2010): 20–44.

Bührer, Werner and Laurent Warlouzet. "Regulating Markets: Peak Business Associations and the Origins of European Competition Policy." In *Societal Actors in European Integration: Polity-Building and Policy-Making 1958–1992* edited by Wolfram Kaiser and Jan-Henrik Meyer. Basingstoke: Palgrave Macmillan, 2013, 59–83.

Bussière, Eric. "La SDN, les cartels, et l'organisation économique de l'Europe durant l'entre-deux-guerres." In *International Cartels Revisited: Relating to the History of Business Development and International Economic Order* edited by Dominique Barjot. Cormelles: Editions-Diffusions du Lys, 1994, 273–283.

Bussière, Eric. "Premiers schémas européens et économie internationale durant l'entre-deux-guerres." *Relations internationales* 123, 3 (2005): 51–68.

Bussière, Eric and François Berger. "La France, la Belgique, l'Allemagne et les cartels de l'Entre-deux-guerres, Une méthode pour l'organisation économique de l'Europe." In *Ces chers voisins: L'Allemagne, la Belgique et la France en Europe du XIe au XXI siècles* edited by Jürgen Elvert and Sylvain Schirmann. Stuttgart: Franz Steiner, 2012, 221–242.

Callaghan, Helen and Martin Höpner. "Changing Ideas: Organised Capitalism and the German Left." *West European Politics* 35, 3 (2012): 551–573.

Cini, Michelle and Lee McGowan, *Competition Policy in the European Union*. Basingstoke: Palgrave Macmillan, 2009.

Durbin, Elizabeth. *New Jerusalems: The Labour Party and the Economics of Democratic Socialism*. London: Routledge & Evan, 1985.

Fulla, Matthieu. *Les Socialistes français et l'économie (1944–1981): Une Histoire économique du politique*. Paris: Presses de Sciences Po, 2016.

Garvy, George. "Keynes and the Economic Activists of Pre-Hitler Germany." *Journal of Political Economy* 83, 2 (1975): 391–405.

Gerber, David J. "Constitutionalizing the Economy: German Neoliberalism, Competition Law and the 'New' Europe." *American Journal of Comparative Law* 42, 25 (1994): 25–84.

Gerber, David J. *Global Competition: Law, Markets, and Globalization*. Oxford: Oxford University Press, 2010.

Gruskey, David B. and Tamar Kricheli-Katz (eds.). *The New Gilded Age: The Critical Inequality Debates of Our Time*. Stanford: Stanford University Press, 2012.

Hambloch, Sibylle. *Europäische Integration und Wettbewerbspolitik: Die Frühphase der EWG*. Baden-Baden: Nomos, 2009.

Hara, Terushi. "La conférence économique internationale de 1927 et ses effets sur la formation des cartels internationaux." In *International Cartels Revisited: Relating to the History of Business Development and International Economic Order* edited by Dominique Barjot. Cormelles: Editions-Diffusions du Lys, 1994, 265–272.

Hook, James C. van Hook. *Rebuilding Germany: The Creation of the Social Market Economy, 1945–1957*. Cambridge: Cambridge University Press, 2007.

Jensen-Eriksen, Niklas. "Industrial Diplomacy and Economic Integration: The Origins of All-European Paper Cartels, 1959–72." *Journal of Contemporary History* 46, 1 (2011): 179–202.

Kaiser, Wolfram and Johan Schot. *Writing the Rules for Europe: Experts, Cartels and International Organizations*. Basingstoke: Palgrave Macmillan, 2014.

Karagiannis, Yannis. "The Origins of European Competition Policy: Redistributive versus Ideational Explanations." *Journal of European Public Policy* 20, 5 (2013): 777–792.

Küsters, Anselm. "The Making and Unmaking of Ordoliberal Language: A Digital Conceptual History of European Competition Law." PhD dissertation, Johann Wolfgang Goethe University, 2022.

Lapidus, John. "Why such a Permissive Attitude towards Monopolistic Associations? Social Democracy up to the First Swedish Law on Cartels in 1925." *Scandinavian Journal of History* 38, 1 (2013): 65–88.

Lefranc, Georges. "Le courant planiste dans le mouvement ouvrier français de 1933 à 1936." *Le Mouvement social* 54 (1966): 69–89.

Leucht, Brigitte and Mel Marquis. "American Influences on EEC Competition Law: Two Paths, How Much Dependence?" In *The Historical Foundations of EU Competition Law* edited by Kiran Klaus Patel and Heike Schweitzer. Oxford: Oxford University Press, 2014, 125–161.

Liefmann, Robert. *International Cartels, Combines and Trusts*. London: Europa Publishing, 1927.

McGowan, Lee and Stephen Wilks. "The First Supranational Policy in the European Union: Competition Policy." *European Journal of Political Research* 28 (1995): 141–169.

Mercer, Helen. *Constructing a Competitive Order: The Hidden History of British Antitrust Policies*. Cambridge: Cambridge University Press, 2009.

Milani, Tommaso. *Hendrik de Man and Social Democracy: The Idea of Planning in Western Europe, 1914–1940*. Basingstoke: Palgrave Macmillan, 2021.

Pace, Lorenzo Federico and Katja Seidel. "The Drafting and the Role of Regulation 17: A Hard-Fought Compromise." In *The Historical Foundations of EU Competition Law* edited by Kiran Klaus Patel and Heike Schweitzer. Oxford: Oxford University Press, 2014, 54–88.

Pérez, Sigfrido Ramírez M. "La politique de la concurrence de la Communauté Économique Européenne et l'industrie: l'exemple des accords sur la distribution automobile (1972–1985)." *Histoire, économie et société* 27, 1 (2008): 63–77.

Petzina, Dietmar. "Gewerkschaften und Monopolfrage vor und während der Weimarer Republik," in *Die Verantwortung des Staates für die Wirtschaft: ausgewählte Aufsätze* edited by Dietmar Petzina, Werner Abelshauser and Ludwig Budrass. Essen: Klartext, 2001, 46–69.

Philip, André. *Le Crise et l'économie dirigée*. Paris: Cluny, 1935.

Quack, Sigfrid and Marie-Laure Djelic. "Adaption, Recombination and Reinforcement: The Story of Antitrust and Competition Law in Germany and Europe." In *Beyond Continuity: Institutional Change in Advanced Political Economies* edited by Wolfgang Streeck and Kathleen Thelen. Oxford: Oxford University Press, 2005, 255–281.

Rollings, Neil. *British Business in the Formative Years of European Integration*. Cambridge: Cambridge University Press, 2008.

Schröter, Harm G. "The International Potash Syndicate." In *International Cartels Revisited: Relating to the History of Business Development and International Economic Order* edited by Dominique Barjot. Cormelles: Editions-Diffusions du Lys, 1994, 75–92.

Shaev, Brian. "From Cradle to Grave: The German Trade Union Federation's Wage, Welfare, and Competitiveness Programme for the Weimar Republic." In *Free Trade and Social Welfare: Explorations in the Long Twentieth Century* edited by Lucia Coppolaro and Lorenzo Mechi. London: Routledge, 2020, 30–51.

Shaev, Brian. "International Cartels in the Political Origins of German Competition Policy, 1949–1953." In *A History of Business Cartels: International Politics, National Policies, and Anti-Competitive Behaviour* edited by Susanna Fellman and Marti Shanahan. New York: Routledge, 2022, 83–102.

Shaev, Brian. "Liberalising Regional Trade: Socialists and European Economic Integration." *Contemporary European History* 27, 2 (2018): 258–279.

Tiratsoo, Nick and Jim Tomlinson. *The Conservatives and Industrial Efficiency, 1951–1964: Thirteen Wasted Years?* London: Routledge, 2016.

Tomlinson, Jim. *Democratic Socialism and Economic Policy in the Attlee Years*. Cambridge: Cambridge University Press, 2004.

Tomlinson, Jim. "Labour and the Economy." In *Labour's First Century* edited by Duncan Tanner, Pat Thane and Nick Tiratsoo. Cambridge: Cambridge University Press, 2007.

Union interparlementaire, Comte rendu de la XXVIe conférence tenue à Londres du 16 au 22 Juillet 1930. Lausanne: Librarie Payot, 1931.

Warlouzet, Laurent. "The EEC/EU as an Evolving Compromise between French Dirigism and German Ordoliberalism (1957–1995)." *Journal of Common Market Studies* 57, 1 (2019): 77–93.

Witschke, Tobias. *Gefahr für den Wettbewerb? Die Fusionskontrolle der Europäischen Gemeinschaft für Kohle und Stahl und die "Rekonstruktion" der Ruhrstahlindustrie 1950–1963*. Berlin: Akademie, 2014.

Woytinksy, Wladimir. "Aktive Weltwirtschaftspolitik." *Die Arbeit* 6 (1931).

Wurm, Clemens August. "Internationale Kartelle und die deutsch-französischen Beziehungen 1924–1930: Politik, Wirtschaft, Sicherheit." In *Deutschland und Frankreich: Vom Konflikt zur Aussöhnung. Die Gestaltung der westeuropäischen Sicherheit 1914–1963* edited by Stephen A. Schucker. Oldenbourg: Oldenbourg Wissenschaftsverlag, 2000, 97–116.

2 Social democracy and the cartel question

The case of the German SPD[1]

Harm G. Schröter

Introduction

A hundred years ago European decision-makers usually supported cartelization. Only after the Second World War did support for cartels change, evolving first to a neutral and then to a negative evaluation. This process took several decades. Historical scholarship has described decartelization in a general way, with some historians interpreting it as part of a broader Americanization process.[2] While to date scholars have explained the movement in general and its result, this contribution here takes up the question of actors. While *bourgeois* parties of the right and the center were said to support cartels "naturally" (see next), left-wing parties were thought to have been "naturally" against any collusion. However, this straight-forward perception from today's vantage point did not exist. For decades, the Social Democratic Party of Germany (*Sozialdemokratische Partei Deutschlands*, SPD) supported cartels. How can that be? This contribution tries to explain the change in the SPD's development from a passive supporter toward an active fighter against cartelization.

Why single out the SPD of all the different actors? Did not *bourgeois* parties change as well? Indeed, industrialists and their lobby organizations supported cartelization. For the non-left-wing parties, the central considerations were the prevailing economic paradigms and the influence of lobbying by pro-cartelization groups. But the non-workers parties' engagement in favor of cartels faded together with the change of the respective prevailing economic paradigm – perhaps a bit later but it did. Consequently for non-left-wing parties, the question was one of the economic paradigm, and not related to core political questions. The change of the paradigm has been taken up in the literature in a general way.[3] For the SPD, the question was much more complicated, and thus interesting: For this party, the question did involve not only a change in the prevailing economic paradigm but also others of long-term strategy concerning socialism and capitalism. For the SPD, short-term steps of immediate improvement of living-conditions stood against long-term considerations in favor of socialism. It is this contradiction that makes the SPD much more interesting than other actors in the decades-long debate around the cartelization question.

DOI: 10.4324/9781351010573-2

Another factor singles out the SPD as a worthy subject for a scholarly contribution: its high reputation on the international stage. Since long before the First World War, the British Labour Party and the SPD were the largest socialist parties in Europe in terms of membership. While Labour was known for its pragmatist approach to politics and economics, the strategic policy of the SPD was, to a large extent, governed by theoretical considerations. This traditional strength on theoretical questions made the SPD attractive to socialist parties of other countries, which often looked to their German sister organization as a *Leitbild*, in particular on issues such as cartels.[4] Consequently, when analyzing the *SPD and cartelization*, we to a large extent focus on core theoretical considerations within the international movement of socialist parties concerning that issue.

Our contribution is organized in the following way: We start with a short survey of the existing literature. Given that our perception today of cartelization is entirely different, not to say opposite, of most contemporaries' views between 1890 and 1950, we first need to present an introduction into their worldview. It is likewise necessary to provide a brief introduction into Marxist theory because, on the one hand, Marxism was the prevailing theory within the SPD, while on the other, again our general thinking today is quite different. Therefore, a brief introduction into Marxist theory is necessary for our understanding of the behavior of the socialist actors under investigation. The rest of the chapter is organized in a chronological way, first examining the discourse within the SPD and its policy toward cartelization up to 1914, then during the First World War and the interwar period up to the Nazis' seizure of power in 1933, and finally during the 1950s, up to the approval of a German law on cartelization in 1957.

The existing literature and our main thesis

Existing literature either focused on massive, strategic contradictions within the party, like Dieter Groh's work,[5] or judged these debates to be relatively minor compared to a single deep break stimulated by the Nazi-period and the Second World War, such as the view put forth by Helen Callaghan and Martin Höpner. The latter authors argue that there was a deep change of views after the war, which "represents a radical reversal of policy preferences held prior to the World War II."[6] In contrast, we will try to verify the following thesis:

> Concerning the issue of cartelization an abrupt change never occurred within the SPD. There was a gradual change from majority support prior to WWI to decline after WWII, and even after 1945, an important minority maintained an opposite conviction (supporting cartelization) into the 1950s.

The existing literature suffers from two important drawbacks: it is extremely limited in number, and the development of our problem only corresponds to a minor degree with reflections in the literature on the general development of the theoretical party-line. Callaghan and Höpner and their thesis of a deep rupture during the Nazi period (1933–1945) and immediately after the Second World War are right on their main issue: *Organized Capitalism*. They are also correct concerning the decline of cooperation with the Communist Party and maybe other issues, but not on the question of cartelization. Other important authors in our question are Eduard Reuffurth and Hartmut Bechtold.[7] While the former's work, dated 1930, reflects interesting contemporary views in a critical way, the latter seems to be quite near to the party and how it wanted to be perceived. Though also more than 30 years old, it does not seem outdated, but it is accessible, as most other literature used here, only for readers of German.

What are cartels and how to understand them?

We define a cartel as a written or unwritten contract of suppliers or buyers of the same good or service with the intention to change market-conditions to their advantage. Cartel contracts can be hierarchical in power but need to be horizontal, not vertical agreements. Syndicates are an advanced form of cartels, in which its members have externalized normal functions of an enterprise into an organization independent of the single firm. In most cases, syndicates centralize distribution.

Like mergers and acquisitions, cartels are one form of economic concentration. Though the phenomenon is much older, the issue of cartelization was first debated on a scholarly level by Friedrich Kleinwächter, an Austrian economist, in 1883.[8] He was reflecting on a wave of cartelization, which was triggered by the start of a world economic crisis in 1874. His publication gained limited attention. Karl Marx commented on cartelization in *Das Kapital*. He understood the phenomenon not as separate but as part and parcel of general concentration: "It is the termination of the capitalistic mode of production within the capitalistic mode of production itself. . . . It constructs in certain quarters the monopoly and thus demands state intervention."[9] Like Adam Smith, Karl Marx thought of a capitalism characterized by many, rather small, competing enterprises; consequently, any monopoly would represent a rather strange case and surely entail state-intervention to deal with it. Marx understood competition as a core issue of capitalism, and thus any monopoly would contradict the very principles of capitalism.

Cartelization thrived in Germany up to the Second World War. However, it was not more widespread in that country compared to others until a ruling of its highest court in 1897. That specific case was about two economic principles: freedom of trade against freedom of contract.[10] In an existing cartel, one cartel-member had violated the contract. Taken to court, it argued that the agreement was invalid from the beginning because it acted against freedom of trade. But the ruling was that private contract is valid also in courts. That entailed security for cartel-contracts and led to an upswing in cartelization in Germany. In its ruling, the court did not raise any other question, for instance, about arbitrage prices or other issues.

A major problem of that time were the swings in the economy. Nothing was known about that phenomenon; all theories were developed later. Economic up- and down-swings came suddenly and were feared by capitalists, workers, and the state alike: Capitalists could lose their investment; workers were dismissed from one hour to the next; and the state lost tax revenue. In that situation, cartels, especially those with a central direction of sales by a separate cartel-body (syndicates), were thought to be a remedy to this basic problem of capitalism. The German cartel expert Siegfried Tschierschky suggested the following:

> Imagine a picture in all detail of an organization working like clockwork. One will come to the conclusion that a dangerous disruption of the national economy, what we call crises, could be nearly completely eliminated, so long as a disruption is not caused externally by the world economy.[11]

A second reason brought forward to support cartelization was rationalization and the exclusion of overproduction. Capitalistic production is chaotic and not organized. Its defenders claim up to today that this is its greatest virtue, while its critics point to overproduction and waste. Cartels were thought to organize the processes of production and distribution in a much more rational and superior way without creating a waste of labor, goods, or finances.

Up to the Second World War, the European discourse on the cartel issue was predominantly occupied with economic stability, not with super-profits. The American perspective was always the other way round. For instance, in 1925, US-Minister of Trade Herbert Hoover wrote to the Secretary of State to claim that the international potash-syndicate was organized "to milk the rest of the world."[12] Hoover was entirely right, but generally Europeans looked for economic security and much less to consumer prices. Most European decision-makers of all political stripes supported cartelization of their own national industry.[13] Also at the world level, applause was louder than critique: The League of Nations and the International Chamber of Commerce "were the creators of a positive discourse about international cartelization, which legitimised cartels both economically and politically."[14] Still a minority of non-Marxist economists and politicians kept asking critical questions. Already in 1905 the renowned German economist Gustav von Schmoller proposed state-supervision of cartels. The organization of German industrialists RDI (*Reichsverband der Deutschen Industrie*) set up its own cartel registry in 1920 (*Kartellstelle*), and in doing so pre-empted the state from answering that demand.[15] In contrast to the SPD, cartel representatives had clear-cut ideas about cartelization. Jakob Herle (*Hauptgeschäftsführer des RDI* – director of the RDI) and Max Metzner (*stellvertretender Hauptgeschäftsführer des RDI* and director of its *Kartellstelle*) claimed a contradiction between the interests of industry and workers concerning whether cartels were "absolutely necessary."[16] In Europe, the cartel-supporting attitude changed only slowly during the *Golden Age Period* 1949–1973, the period of exceptional growth-rates. The SPD was a major political actor in the development of the initial support for and later discrimination on cartelization. That policy was directly related to her theoretical basis: Marxism.

Historical materialism as the foundation of strategic decision-making of the SPD

Historical Materialism (*Histomat*) is the philosophical explanation of Marxists of the course of history. According to Histomat, all history is characterized by economically defined social classes, which exploit other classes. In capitalism, the main and *antagonistic classes* are workers on the one hand and the bourgeois class (*bourgeoisie*) on the other. The latter exploits the former on the basis of the private property of the *means of production*, such as machines. Exploitation of mankind can end by means of the socialization of private property, which would entail a substantial improvement of living conditions. Socialism is the morally superior *mode of production*, because it excludes private property of the means of production and thus ends the exploitation of human beings. At the same time, it represents an economically superior order, because there are no antagonistic contradictions, which hamper improvements in productivity. Within capitalism, certain improvements of workers' living conditions are not impossible, but cannot change the principal antagonistic contradiction between workers and capitalists. Therefore, a socialist party needs to strive to achieve socialism. It is the party's principal aim; any party that renounces that aim cannot call itself a socialist party.

The transition from capitalism to socialism is called *revolution* (whether bloody or not and even its span of time are secondary questions), because it profoundly changes the mode of production. According to Histomat, a revolution will not happen before the specific mode of production has exhausted all its own possibilities of development, and consequently has no more room for maneuver. *Antagonistic class-struggle* will lead to adjustments within the specific mode of production but in the end inevitably leads to a revolution. During its last stages of development, traces of the next move will develop within the old core of production, for instance, the growth of capitalist elements within the feudal mode of production. The same is due to happen in capitalism; traces of the socialist mode of production will emerge in one way or another (for instance cartels, see further in the text). A revolution is not easy to achieve because the respective state protects the ruling class and its interests within all modes of production; in capitalism, for instance, capitalist private property is protected. Consequently, from the viewpoint of a socialist party, the state needs to experience a revolution (and again nothing is predicted as to whether this would happen in a bloody, short way or not).

That is, briefly, what Marxists within the SPD had in mind when making strategic decisions, also when dealing with questions of cartelization. The role of cartelization was to be evaluated in light of Histomat: what is the role of cartels in the development of capitalism? No party leader doubted that cartels exploit the working class, but the strategic question was: What is the comprehensive and theoretically correct evaluation of cartelization as a phenomenon? One line of analysis was: Cartelization is a sign of a high – or even the highest – development of capitalism. If this were so, then the emergence of cartels is an indicator that the capitalist mode of production has reached the end of its life-span. Connected to such a view, another idea might emerge: Can cartels be understood as traces of a future socialist mode of production? If one agrees with one or both of these arguments, the strategic value of cartelization for achieving socialism is positive. But Marxists could also evaluate cartels in a different way: No Marxist denied the exploitative function cartels performed at the expense of the working class. Consequently, cartelization could be understood as just one of the many adjustments, which prolong the life span of the capitalistic mode of production. From that perspective, cartels need to be understood as instruments of the capitalist class to slow down history's speed and delay its path toward socialism. This perception leads to a strict anti-cartel policy. Thus, also Marxists need not agree on the consequences of cartelization; they can and did entertain different and even contrasting views on it.

A third view that emerged within the SPD over time was a non-Marxist one: Since nobody knows when socialism would occur, it is more important to improve living conditions today than striving for the great and final aim. From that perspective, only the exploitative function of cartelization comes to the fore. Consequently, this exploitation is reason enough to abandon and interdict cartels. Many Marxists in the SPD concentrated on the great aim of socialism; in contrast, non-Marxist social democrats and trade unionists preferred to improve living conditions. An exaggerated reduction of both positions would be: While Marxists looked to the aim – "the aim is all," social democrats (without denying the aim) concentrated on the path – "the path is all."

SPD discourses on cartelization – general traces

When, in 1890, the previously interdicted Socialist Workers Party (*Sozialistische Arbeiterpartei*) was re-founded in Germany, it took the name SPD (Social Democratic Party of Germany – *Sozialdemokratische Partei Deutschlands*). This variation in name was not connected to any ideological change. In 1890, the majority of leadership and members were clearly Marxist. But two important developments started before the First World War: (1) a less orthodox group of Marxists, the *Revisionists* emerged and gained access to the highest circle of party leaders. These *Revisionists* developed into an ever more important wing of the party. (2) The SPD became a mass-party, which since 1912 attracted the largest share of all German votes until the elections of July 1932, when the World Economic Crisis reached its deepest point. It still remained a predominantly blue-collar worker's party, but the trend to attract more and more white-collar workers, members of the petty-bourgeoisie and so on, had begun. That process developed parallel to our question, the change in the socialist evaluation of cartels. From its 1959 party-convention in Bad Godesberg onward, the SPD claimed a renewal by transforming itself from a traditional worker's party (*Arbeiterpartei*) to a people's party (*Volkspartei*). During the same decade, it finally supported the interdiction of cartels, an evaluation that continues up to today. How could this change have happened?

Traditionally, the SPD was proud of its party members' high standard of ideological education and training – at least compared to other European socialist parties. The theoretical discourse was conducted not within the whole party but predominantly among a group of party leaders. It took place mainly between the majority-group of orthodox Marxists such as Karl Kautsky and Rosa Luxemburg on one side and the *Revisionists* on the other, the latter of whom called for verifying whether Marx's predictions for the future were still valid or needed to be overhauled. The leader of that minority-group was Eduard Bernstein. The fora of this strategic discourse were meetings, party conventions, and special print media such as *Sozialistische Monatshefte* (only the Revisionists) or books and booklets often edited by the publishing house *Dietz*.[17] Generally, the discussants were not very precise when using the term "cartel"; often they referred to any form of concentration as a cartel and combined together "trusts, cartels and concerns" in their analyses.

The party gazette *Vorwärts* was crucial in communicating the political party line to members and followers. How salient was the cartel issue in *Vorwärts*? Figure 2.1 provides a quantification of the term during the 40 years before the Nazis interdicted the paper in March 1933. It seems that within this period, party members were well-informed about cartelization; the term was used in an annual frequency that ranged from 22 to 211 times. Other key issues for the SPD figured less frequently: "class-struggle" (*Klassenkampf*) was mentioned between 24 and 122 times, and "mass-strike" (*Massenstreik*) between 1 and 160.[18] The quantitative evaluation tells us that cartelization was among the most important topics in Vorwärts, and consequently within the SPD, up to the party's interdiction by the Nazis. However, a qualitative check based on a couple of samples tells us that in most cases, party members were informed about the formation of cartels or their effects on prices, but only on a very few occasions on the strategic political discourse. For example, on September 6, 1901, Vorwärts informed its readers that sugar consumers have to pay a "three times increased" price, because of (a) customs and (b) the sugar cartel.[19] Furthermore, like party leaders, Vorwärts applied the term "cartel" not always in a precise way but rather as an expression for any type of association. In such a use of the term, political parties, workers, when forming trade unions, or single persons, when pursuing the same hobby, also formed a "cartel." Over the course of time, there was a greater precision in the use of the term.

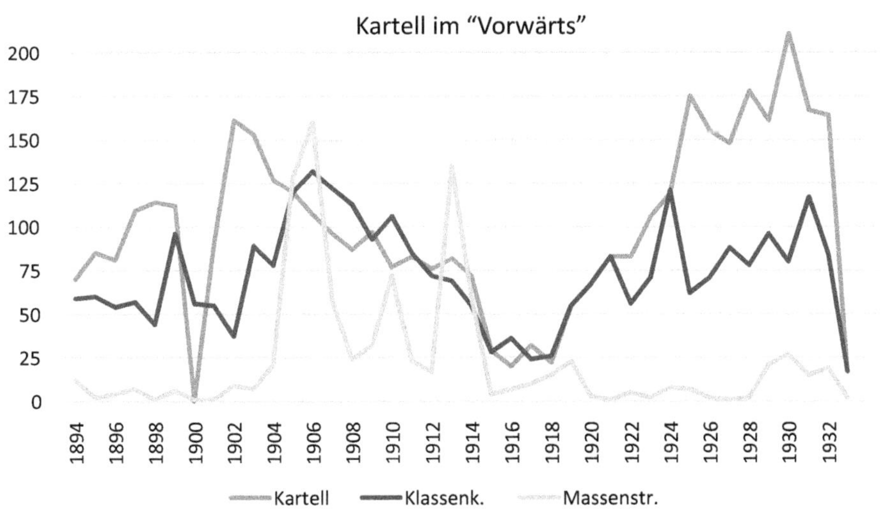

Figure 2.1 Annual frequency of three key terms *cartel*, *class-struggle*, and *mass-strike* in the SPD party-tabloid *Vorwärts*

The discourse of the SPD on cartelization up to and during the First World War

Usually, literature on the history of the SPD places the dispute between Marxists and revisionists at the fore.[20] However, in the question of cartelization, this division is useless because Friedrich Engels, Karl Kautsky, and Rosa Luxemburg as Marxists were supporting cartelization as well as the arch-revisionist Eduard Bernstein. Therefore, we first present the supporters of cartelization and their reasoning and afterward their opponents.

The first theoretical evaluation from a socialist's point of view was published by Bruno Schönlank. He argued that workers are the born enemies of cartels, because it would be they who in the end had to pay higher prices. On the other hand, he was convinced that cartels lift normal capitalist competition to a higher level, which in the end would be nearer to socialism (see further), and on that basis, he suggested supporting cartelization. This line became generally accepted by the aforementioned Marxists within the SPD, including party leader August Bebel. Also Bernstein supported this view, though from a different point of view. In his famous revisionist book published in 1899, he suggested that cartels, especially when internationally combined, would stabilize the business cycle, and thought it therefore foolish to "deny the superiority of organization over anarchic competition."[21] He imagined at that stage of development, capitalism could be transformed into socialism by means of democracy. Though this still was more or less a Marxist thought, Bernstein indeed wanted the SPD to break with Marxism and materialism and exchange them with the idealism of Immanuel Kant. Concerning our question, Marxists and revisionists both agreed to support cartelization on the basis of strategic, though different, reasons. Hartmut Bechtold has shown that the debate on cartelization at the party convention in 1894 demonstrated support for cartelization because it promoted economic concentration. The official speaker on the issue, Max Schippel, even suggested, "in general the consumer has nothing to fear from cartelization."[22] In spite of this, Wilhelm Schröder, another prominent SPD speaker, cast a negative light on cartels and trusts, calling them a "scourge" against workers.[23]

During the following years, as the factions fought over the party's policy line, arguments on cartels began to vary: Rosa Luxemburg maintained on the one hand that cartelization and concentration would by no means change the character of capitalism (a view which would support cartelization as a means to hasten capitalism toward its end).[24] On the other hand, she wrote: by cartelization "thousands of means and ways are thought up to cheat the masses of consumers"[25] (which was the main argument for a worker's party to act against cartelization). Also other party-leaders were not entirely strict in their argument for or against cartels. Before the First World War, Kautsky, Luxemburg, and also Rudolf Hilferding, Austrian and the rising star of socialist theory in the German language, questioned Bernstein's claim that socialism might be stepwise established without major crises via cartelization.[26] Still the vast majority supported cartelization, though for different reasons. In contrast, distinguished non-German leaders of the Second International, an international association of socialist parties, for instance, Vladimir Lenin or Eugen Varga, were outspoken in their condemnation of cartelization.[27]

In the decade leading up to the First World War, prominent SPD politician Karl Liebknecht and theoretical leaders Kautsky and Hilferding transferred the idea of economic competition, including its potential solution, that is cartelization, to the international political sphere. They suggested that international competition on colonies and other issues soon would enter (Kautsky, Liebknecht) or was already entering (Hilferding) a stage of international agreement (in their terms cartelization) between large powers such as the UK, France, Russia, and Germany. Unfortunately, they used the term "cartels and trusts" without any differentiation between these two different forms of organization or between political and economic issues in order to catch all forms of concentration.[28]

The First World War caused a deep rupture in the traditional European world, which is why a historian's concept of phases extends the "long 19th century" up to 1914. It also caused deep changes inside the SPD. Like most socialists of other states, SPD members of parliament supported their national government in fighting the war (except Liebknecht). Scarcity of material supply caused the German government to set up a monopoly organization for the allocation of all material goods except petrol and food. This *Kriegsrohstoffamt* was organized by Walter Rathenau, a distinguished German industrialist. Within the SPD, it was perceived as a major step toward a social economy from which it would be only a minor step toward socialism. Also food was allocated and distributed not according to money but by a state-organized bread-card system, which caused greater egalitarianism in the consumption patterns of middle-class and working-class families. This experience was well-received within the SPD, which wanted to keep these cartel-organizations up and running after the war. In 1915, Rudolf Hilferding suggested that this represented a new stage in the development of capitalism: "Organized Capitalism." Wilhelm Jansson, a Swedish subject who since the 1890s engaged himself in German worker's policy, was among the first to promote such ideas; among others, he edited the book *Monopolfrage und Arbeiterklasse* (The question of monopoly and the working class (Vorwärts, 1917)). One year earlier, he wrote in *Sozialistische Monatshefte* a lengthy article on the organization of industry after the war.[29] He advocated that cartels comprise whole branches of industry to enhance rationalization and export-strength work under state-supervision. Opting out of the respective monopoly would be granted only for self-supply to (a) very large enterprise and (b) worker's organizations, in other words, cooperatives. This last issue is interesting because for the first time cooperatives came on the agenda of the cartel-discourse. Many others took part in the discourse. Julius Karliski, one of the editors of *Sozialistische Monatshefte*, suggested that the surplus benefit, which these super-cartels unavoidably would generate, should be balanced by a special tax.[30]

Already in 1915 the top-leader of the trade-unions, Carl Legien, who in 1913 had become the first president of the International Federation of Trade Unions, wanted to keep these war organizations also in peace time. Both during the war and later, German trade unions made several suggestions concerning these monopoly organizations. They did not question them as such but suggested including worker's representatives at all levels of supervision after the war. During the First World War, German trade unions discussed questions of monopoly and cartelization much more vividly than the party SPD. Up to 1914, cartelization was not a major issue in the discourse of German trade unions. The change is the more remarkable, as within the UK, the trade unions had a large influence on the Labour Party, while in Germany, the relationship was the other way round. Finally, also the SPD party congress of 1917 perceived the war-monopoly organizations as a step forward toward socialism.[31] A general socialization of private property of means of production was no longer suggested, but private monopolies should be expropriated. But "cartel-like organizations" should come under the monitoring of a state agency (*Kartellamt*) with substantial power and workers' representation on its board.[32] In other words, private property, Marx's main issue, seemed to no longer be the decisive issue.

In 1917, radical Marxists separated from the SPD and founded a new party, which two years later became the Communist Party of Germany (KPD). The large majority of membership stayed with the SPD: As many Marxists had left, the split supported the revisionists' wing. The start of the German revolution in November 1918 gave the franchise to all women and caused representatives of labor (Carl Legien) and capital (Hugo Stinnes) to sign the Stinnes-Legien Contract on the eight-hour working day and official recognition of trade unions. While according to Marx the state is an organization of the bourgeoisie the purpose of which was to keep workers down, after the organizational changes for supplies during the war, the idea that the state represents a neutral authority became widespread (though not uncontested) within the SPD. In any case, there was no comprehensive discourse on cartelization inside the SPD during the war – as Figure 2.1 also indicates. Concerning our question, two important changes occurred during the First World War: (a) the trade unions entered the discourse on cartels, sometimes even initiating their own discussions (thus questioning the party's traditional political supremacy); and (b) the state was increasingly perceived as a neutral body and no longer simply an instrument in the hands of the bourgeoisie.

Window of opportunity? The SPD in government

The German revolution in November 1918 swept the SPD to power, and in theory, the party could have socialized all industry. In that case, the question of cartelization would have evaporated. But the SPD government acted slowly in that respect, looking for allies with bourgeois parties rather than with communists.[33] Experts of cartel research argued the SPD had not seized her chance of introducing socialism;[34] and also experts on the history of the party were critical.[35] In February 1919, the SPD leader Friedrich Ebert was elected president of the Reich (*Reichsspräsident*). The party was at the height of its political power. Until the summer of 1920, the SPD was by far the largest partner of three coalition governments. Unfortunately, three governments within only 17 months were more or less the average period; the 14 years of the Weimar Republic consumed no less than 21 governments. Based on the quickly changing preferences of the electorate, deep underlying social conflicts, and a series of economic and geopolitical crises, the political situation was extremely unstable during the whole period. This instability surely affected the discourse on cartels as well, the trends of which shifted several times. The revolution created a Commission of Socialization, tasked with first examining a potential socialization of the mines. Germany had many coal mines and the miners were highly organized. Supervisor of that Commission was the SPD Minister of Economics Rudolf Wissell and his State-Secretary Wichart von Moellendorff. The latter official was no party-member, but he had served as top-manager in war-monopoly organizations. He was against socialization, but in favor of the upkeep of monopolies in a social economy primarily aimed not at profits but at managing provisioning (*Gemeinwirtschaft*). This approach of preparing for but not executing a widespread socialization program was widely shared within the SPD. Also Kautsky, the old top theorist of the party and member of the socialization committee for the USPD, the independent social-democratic party, engaged himself against socialization in that moment.[36] The Marxist hard-liners had left the party anyway and had organized themselves in the KPD.

In February 1919, the Socialization Commission suggested socializing all coal mines, but neither Wissell nor von Moellendorf intended to do so. Their idea was to have comprehensive self-organized constructions like during the war, based on branches of industry with owners and workers on the supervisory boards. In fact, that would have resulted in state-monitored cartels. In the end, this solution was the result in the cases of coal and potash mining; the laws of February 23, and April 24, 1919, founded coal-syndicates and the potash-syndicate.[37] These syndicates represented extremely powerful cartels, because they by law organized the production and sales of all German mines. Wissell suggested a similar organization for electricity. When the respective law failed in Parliament in July 1919, he resigned because he saw no chance any more for his plans of a self-organized but state-controlled German economy. The reason for the SPD government to follow that line was twofold: On a tactical level, any socialization would have deepened the already-deep trenches between the political quarters and on a strategic level, cartels under state-supervision were thought to be a preparation for socialism, in which the economy would run according to planning.

The first major change in law was taken not by an SPD government but by a "bourgeois" coalition led by Gustav Stresemann. Though the SPD took part in this government, unaffiliated officials were responsible for the Decree on the Abuse of Economic Power (*Verordnung gegen Missbrauch wirtschaftlicher Machtstellungen*) dated November 2, 1923.[38] At that time, the SPD and the labor unions were concentrating more on daily problems than broader strategic considerations.

The lost war had undermined the German currency, which tended toward inflation. During the first years, this was beneficial for the government because it could repay its huge internal war-debt. While during the war German population had bought war-bonds, now it was easy to repay with inflated, worthless money. But from 1922 onward, inflation accelerated into hyperinflation, which nobody could stop or reverse with traditional means. In October 1922, postage for a letter was 6 Marks and one year later 10 million Marks. Everyday life became unbearable, and finally, in November, a totally new currency was introduced. It was this unbearable daily situation that caused the SPD, more precisely its faction in parliament, to act against cartels. In the debate, socialists connected cartels to extortion and racketeering. This view was underlined by the fact that many cartels boycotted consumer's cooperatives, which were part of the worker's milieu and movement. In the parliament's economic committee, the SPD asked for state supervision of cartels in June 1921. At the same time, SPD Chairman Hermann Müller (Franken) and later Chancellor (*Reichskanzler*) demanded that workers who were laid off due to boycotts of their businesses – mainly cooperatives – by cartels be compensated financially. Both initiatives were stopped by the SPD minister of economics Robert Schmidt, who mediated the lifting of the boycotts, and told the parliament that the time of a supervisory body for cartels had not yet come.[39] In spite of that, the same committee asked the government on May 16, 1922, and again on January 16, 1923, to act against extortion by cartels. These initiatives were important in bringing about the aforementioned cartel decree in 1923. The SPD faction was not content with the decree. Three years later, it again demanded state-supervision of cartels and a state-run cartel-register in the parliament. It renewed its demand in 1930, and finally, in 1932, the faction introduced in parliament its own proposal for a cartel law. However, during the SPD-led (second) cabinet of Müller (1928–1930), no initiatives against cartels, neither from parliament nor from government, are known. These (non-)activities raise several questions: Had the SPD turned into an anti-cartel party after the First World War? Or did its representatives in parliament not follow the party-line? If yes, for what reasons? Or – even worse – was parliamentary activity at the background of government abstinence just a show for the electorate, while the party-leaders followed their own, different agenda? Again we need to look into the party's internal discourse.

The Party's discourse during the 1920s and 1930s

In 1921, a new party program was agreed. It was designed by Eduard Bernstein and oriented toward a social economy (*Gemeinwirtschaft*). Though private property of the means of production remained untouched, all decision-making should be carried out by separate organizations jointly controlled by the state, owners, and workers' organizations. It was very much in line with the policy the SPD government pursued up to 1920. The party suggested that it now represented not only the working class but also all people who worked for their living. The idea of the SPD as a people's party was born, though short-lived. Also consumer's cooperatives claimed to be acting on behalf of not only their members but also all consumers. Quickly the cooperatives found themselves in a conflict with cartels that played an important role in the creation of the cartel decree of 1923.[40] During the following years of political and economic turmoil (right- and left-wings coups, inflation, French military occupation of the Ruhr-district), the SPD lost much of its power and consequently became more radical again, also because the USPD merged with the SPD. The renewed party program adopted in Heidelberg in 1925, written by Karl Kautsky and Rudolf Hilferding, was Marxist again.

Hilferding's promotion of the idea of *Organized Capitalism* became very important during these years. Austrian-born, he became German subject, worked several times as finance minister for the German Reich, and represented one of the SPD's brightest theorists. His interpretation of the contemporary sociopolitical order as Organized Capitalism was able to integrate left- and right-wing theory within the party. Karl Kautsky as a traditional Marxist maintained that capitalism would inevitably collapse in the end, undermined as it was by structural contradictions between workers and bourgeoisie. Consequently, a deepening of these contradictions would promote the end of capitalism. In contrast, Eduard Bernstein had shown that many of Marx's predictions were simply wrong and a new theoretical basis was needed. Organized Capitalism represented the highest form of economic concentration, of which cartels are one variation, and therefore Hilferding thought Organized Capitalism was very near to socialism.[41] Consequently, traditional Marxists expected socialist revolution to be imminent. Revisionists contended, by contrast, that it would be possible to take over the political and economic "commanding heights" (Lenin) by means of democracy. All forms of concentration reduced the number of these commanding heights and would facilitate the takeover. Thus, it was not just by chance that Rudolf Hilferding's influence became more and more decisive within the SPD during the Weimar Republic.

At the 1925 party congress, it was Hilferding who held the programmatic speech. He maintained that Marxist theory of economic concentration held true and that cartelization was not bad, because (a) it was a special form of concentration and (b) often a preparatory stage to form a more comprehensive enterprise.[42] Consequently, class struggle was lifted from the traditional level of workers against the bourgeoisie to the level of a privileged few against the rest of the population. The main struggle was now about power within the state and control of administration. At the congress, Hilferding said that the question was about "authority on the entirety."[43] Hilferding's position remained official party doctrine until the 1940s because there was no new party program before the Nazis interdicted the party in 1933.

Important support came from the labor unions. In 1926, the German Metal-Worker's Union (*Deutscher Metallarbeiter-Verband*) officially proclaimed that the

> concentration of industry towards trusts and the expansion of cartels and similar organizations, which on a national or international basis strive to monopolize markets, is recognized by workers as an expression of a development towards high-capitalism in which appear the first preparations for overcoming the chaos of production through an organized economy.[44]

Most important was the views of course of the umbrella trade union confederation, the ADGB. It represented by far the largest number of employees and, though independent, was officially aligned with the SPD.[45] The ADGB had founded its own center of economic research (*Forschungsstelle für Wirtschaftspolitik*), headed by Fritz (later Peretz) Naphtali. In 1928, Naphtali wrote the official theoretical memorandum of the ADGB, which was based on Hilferding's Organized Capitalism.[46]

The memorandum welcomed cartelization in general. Still the ADGB asked for state-supervision of all cartels, a demand that was also supported from the third column of the traditional workers milieu, the cooperatives.[47]

Hartmut Bechtold, a leading researcher on this phase, writes in his conclusion:

> After the attempt to exchange market economy by corporative social economy had failed, the party made no other attempt to economically operationalize a social utopia . . . . The party was not ready to say farewell to outlived ideologies.[48]

We disagree. Organized Capitalism was the theoretical vehicle to include both stepwise improvement of working and living conditions and a long-term perspective toward socialism. In any case, 12 years of Nazi-dictatorship, which entailed many losses,[49] caused a deep rupture in the party's perception of cartels.

SPD and cartelization after the Second World War

In spite of many losses of important members and an inevitable general questioning of the party's theoretical foundation, there were also links bridging the Nazi-period. The cartel question was virulent. The Nazis had cartelized the entirety of the German economy. In 1947, the Western Allies interdicted all agreements limiting competition, though they allowed exemptions on demand.[50] In spite of this, 10,000 cartels were thought to be still working in November 1948.[51] Already during the 1920s, a few SPD economists had criticized the party's fixation on socialism. The editor of the SPD theoretical journal *Die Neue Zeit* and professor of economics Emil Lederer was outspokenly against all monopolies, including cartels. Another professor, Eduard Heimann, who in 1919 acted as secretary general in the government's socialization committee, looked for a "Third Way" between capitalism and socialism. He was supported by a third one, Adolf (later Adolph) Löwe, another prominent researcher and SPD-member, who already favored a market economy without monopolies in the early 1930s.[52] After 1945, other intellectuals, such as Karl Schiller,[53] could build on this tradition. He, together with others, strongly advocated anti-cartel and anti-monopoly policy at the 1952 Dortmund party congress. The SPD agreed on a new platform at this congress that confirmed competition instead of concentration as the new economic paradigm. But still those SPD professors and intellectuals leading the anti-cartel charge represented only a small group.

The SPD was the only major party in West Germany that survived the Nazi period and thus could rebuild based on a prior tradition. However, the SPD also had to make major adjustments in the postwar context. There was little talk about Organized Capitalism after 1945; parts of it were more or less taken over while others were abandoned: economic democracy was welcomed but concentration was met with mistrust, as it was thought to be connected to the Nazis. Both analyses still had their supporters within the party. During the first decade after 1945, a comprehensive discussion took place. In 1945, the party launched again its traditional structures and ideas, partly as a worker's and a Marxist organization. Victor Agartz, supported by Marxists such as Wolfgang Abendroth,[54] still fought for Organized Capitalism and its monopoly phase and consequently for concentration. On the other hand, Helga Grebing could point to the fact that within the SPD, "socialism" had not been identical with "Marxism" since the 1920s.[55] The discourse changed the party, and in 1959, the famous *Godesberger Programm* redefined the SPD no longer as a predominantly worker's party striving for socialism, but as a people's party, open to all who were looking for better living conditions.

In 1945, the party's chairman Kurt Schumacher, "himself without his own . . . competence in economic theory,"[56] advocated a Third Way between capitalism and socialism: economic democracy while at the same time attacking economic concentration. That a planned economy did not automatically mean socialism was accepted, but many party members could not imagine a reconstruction of the country without comprehensive and deep-going planning. Everything could be bought only on bread-cards (or similar administrative entitlements) and even the Allies installed planning and distribution administrations for coal and other goods.[57] Important differences between this new coal authority and the old one based on a cartel were hard to find. At the same time, the Allies had interdicted all cartels and had started to dismantle large enterprises, such as IG Farben, Vereinigte Stahlwerke (United Steelworks), and Deutsche Bank. Distinguished SPD officials, Rolf Wagenführ, for example, could not imagine that competition could be beneficial: "In large parts of the economy free competition is irrational."[58] In short, during the first decade after 1945, the SPD had lost large parts of its theoretical basis, was occupied in a process of intense internal debate, and was no longer able to exert a large influence on the general political agenda on the question of cartelization. Besides the fact that the SPD was not in government, other issues such as co-determination within large enterprises introduced in 1951 and broadened in 1952, were more pressing at that moment. The 1951 law gave 50% of the vote in the supervisory board of large enterprises in the coal and steel industries to workers; the 1952 law allocated a third of these seats in all large enterprises to worker's representatives. With these two laws, advocates of Organized Capitalism could point to a great step forward. Under these conditions, it is interesting how the SPD delegates acted on cartel initiatives in the *Bundestag*, the new parliament.[59]

When Ludwig Erhard, minister of economics for the conservative CDU-led coalition, promoted an (ordo)liberal policy aiming at cartel-interdiction in 1949, he was opposed by both the SPD and the umbrella organization of the German Unions, the German Trade Union Confederation (*Deutscher Gewerkschaftsbund*, DGB). Each of them thought that interdiction of cartels would hamper a modern organization of the economy, which in their minds still meant a centrally planned economy.[60] In 1950, when Erhard and his staff worked on a first draft, the SPD parliamentary faction asked to talk about it officially in the federal parliament. Little came out of the discourse; on the one hand, the proposal was not yet ripe for a law, and on the other, the various factions and their lobby-groups could not agree on whether a cartel-law should be based on the principle of interdiction or only on that of abuse. Proposal No. 8 was discussed in the economic committee of the Bundestag, in which SPD deputies were heavily involved.[61] As Brian Shaev discusses, in the end, the committee decided to postpone everything to the following period of legislation.[62] The next important step took place in 1954; Erhard was again minister of economics. The proposed bill focused on concentrations, not exclusively on cartels, and as before the lines of discourse were not clear-cut along lines of party-membership. Large parts of Erhard's own CDU wanted a less strict anti-cartel law, while the main opposition party SPD now supported Erhard on this question. But also the SPD's larger milieu did not represent a single entity or view. For instance, the cooperatives, at that time important players, did not support comprehensive interdiction, because they feared that in the end, coops could also be considered special forms of cartels and prohibited.[63] In 1954, the second chamber (*Bundesrat*) voted down Erhard's suggestion; he was supported only by SPD representatives. Meanwhile, the cartel bill was now clearly based on the principle of interdiction, but the tug of wars went on concerning the amount and extension of exemptions. Dr. Joachim Schöne, an SPD deputy, pleaded several times for the principle of interdiction.[64] In 1957, the time was finally ripe for an anti-cartel law. The SPD succeeded in fighting back a number of exemptions of interdiction but remained disappointed that so many remained. On July 4, 1957, the law was approved, but the SPD voted against it. Erhard wanted only four exemptions but parliament voted for 11, including a broad exemption that seemed destined for extensive use: if it were determined that a cartel was "urgently necessary in the national interest and for the common welfare."[65] According to experts,[66] the law represented more or less what the industrial lobby had wanted in 1950, and consequently, the shape of the law was a reversal not only for the SPD but also for Erhard's liberal approach.

The opposition SPD faction was not content and made several interventions in the following years (1959, 1961, and 1962) and even launched its own law proposal in 1960. Georg Kurlbaum, who in 1957 gave the SPD's official line explaining why the party would vote against it, stated two years later that the law was "entirely ineffective"[67] and therefore was in urgent need of revision.

Conclusion

The cartel-discourse of the SPD was not only important for the party and Germany but also beyond, because the SPD was perceived by other social-democratic and socialist parties as a *Leitbild*. All agreed that cartels are detrimental to the working classes, because it is workers who, as consumers, have to pay higher prices compared to those that would be available through open competition. However, the SPD was not only a workers' but also, at the same time, a socialist party. The final aim was to overcome capitalism and install socialism. According to Marx, this would happen when capitalism has reached its highest form of development. Large economic concentration was seen as an indicator of progress toward this end; cartelization is one important form of concentration. Based on these Marxist premises, logic suggested not to hamper but to promote economic concentration in order to get nearer to the point of change, the revolution. Consequently, in the case of policy on cartelization, tactical aims of improving workers' living standards stood against the strategic aims of promoting socialist revolution. The SPD was well aware of this contradiction; the discourse sought a balance between these two principles. The stronger Marxists were in the party, the more it supported cartelization.

Previous literature suggested a clear and unique break: before the Second World War the SPD supported cartels and afterward it fought against them.[68] That presentation is too simple. Based on the combination of research on cartels on the one hand and on research on the party on the other, we could show that from the beginning in the 1890s up to the 1960s, both positions co-existed within circles of the highest party leaders. The thesis of a clear break cannot be upheld. Neither can be detected as a straightforward, linear development from a pro- toward an anti-cartel policy. Though the trend went in that direction the development was by no means easy and palpable. Up to the First World War, the SPD was unquestionably a Marxist party. But the party congregation in Kiel 1921, prepared under the influence of the revisionist Bernstein, showed a very flexible approach to socialism, while the more leftist Marxists remained in the USPD or KPD. When the USPD rejoined the SPD, a new platform was necessary and was prepared under the leadership of Hilferding. It therefore underlined a Marxist point of view and thus cartelization. This strategic attitude was contradicted by a tactical one. Party representatives (and labor unionists) at the same time increasingly complained about cartels and demanded a less friendly government policy or, at least, state-supervision of cartels. Parallel to this, a few intellectual party members already promoted a market economy that would ban cartels during the 1920s. This unclear situation was reflected by SPD (in)action in the government, when the party did little against cartels. SPD ministers even stopped some of the SPD's own parliamentary initiatives. When in opposition, however, its representatives asked for state control and presented an own draft on new, tougher legislation. This contradictory attitude does not show a straightforward approach. After 1945, the SPD was generally against cartelization; however, also then a minority still defended it. In 1957, when a relatively liberal law interdicting cartelization was passed in parliament, social democrats voted against it – because it considered the anti-cartel law to be too weak.

The stepwise and slow change concerning the cartel question was a reflection of a more fundamental change of the party. As long as Marxists thought socialism to be imminent, they supported economic concentration and cartelization as a preparatory step for socialism. When belief in Marxism faded, the party became more critical of cartelization. Thus, the SPD appeared neither before nor after the Second World War as a compact unit on the question of cartelization.

Notes

1 I thank the editors of this volume and the participants of the Gothenburg conference for critical and constructive comments – all errors are mine, of course. Special thanks to Brian Shaev, who put my contribution into readable English.

2 Harm G. Schröter, "Cartelization and Decartelization in Europe, 1870–1995: Rise and Decline of an Economic Institution," *Journal of European Economic History* 25, 1 (1996): 129–153; Jonathan Zeitlin and Gary Herrigel (eds.), *Americanization and its*

Limits. Reworking US Technology and Management in Post-War Europe and Japan (Oxford, OUP, 2000); Harm G. Schröter, *Americanization of the European Economy. A Compact Survey of American Economic Influence in Europe Since the 1880s* (Dordrecht: Springer, 2005).

3 See Lisa Murach-Brand, *Antitrust auf Deutsch. Der Einfluss der amerikanischen Alliierten auf das Gesetz gegen Wettbewerbsbeschränkungen (GWB) nach 1945* (Tübingen: Mohr-Siebeck, 2004); Schröter, *Americanization*, 67–71.

4 See, for instance, John Lapidus, *Social Democracy and the Swedish Welfare Model, Ideational Analyses of Attitudes Towards Competition, Individualization, Privatization*, vol. 13 (Gothenburg: Gothenburg Studies in Economic History, 2015).

5 Dieter Groh, *Negative Integration und revolutionärer Attentismus: die deutsche Sozialdemokratie am Vorabend des ersten Weltkrieges* (Frankfurt am Main: Verlag Ullstein, 1973).

6 Helen Callaghan and Martin Höpner, "Changing Ideas: Organized Capitalism and the German Left," *West European Politics* 35 (2012): 551–573, 552.

7 Eduard Reuffurth, *Die Stellung der deutschen Sozialdemokratie zum Problem der staatlichen Kartellpolitik* (Jena: Without Publisher, 1930); Hartmut Bechtold, *Die Kartellierung der deutschen Volkswirtschaft und die sozialdemokratische Theorie-Diskussion vor 1933* (Frankfurt am Main: Haag + Herchen, 1986). Between 1988 and1992 Bechtold was Head of the Economics Department of Hans Böckler Foundation, an institution of the labor unions.

8 Friedrich Kleinwächter, *Die Kartelle. Eine Frage der Organisation der Volkswirtschaft* (Innsbruck: Verlag der Wagner'schen Universitaets-Buchhandlung, 1883).

9 Translated by the author like all other translations in this contribution (Karl Marx and Friedrich Engels (eds.), *Das Kapital. Kritik der politischen Ökonomie, Book 3 Der Gesamtprozess der kapitalistischen Produktion*, 3 vols. (Berlin: Dietz, 1970), 454. Marx died in 1883, Engels edited the third volume of *Das Kapital* in 1894.

10 See: Klaus W. Richter, *Die Wirkungsgeschichte des deutschen Kartellrechts vor 1914. Eine rechts-historisch analytische Untersuchung* (Tübingen: Mohr Siebeck, 2007).

11 Siegfried Tschierschky, *Kartellpolitik, Eine analytische Untersuchung* (Berlin: C. Hymann 1930), 70.

12 Cited in Harm G. Schröter, "The International Potash Syndicate," in Dominique Barjot (ed.), *International Cartels Revisited* (Caen: Editions-Diffusion du Lys, 1994), 75–92.

13 Schröter, "Cartelization and Decartelization."

14 Marco Bertilorenzi, "Legitimising Cartels. The Joint Role of the League of Nations and of the International Chamber of Commerce," in Susanna Fellman and Martin Shanahan (eds.), *Regulating Competition: Cartel Registers in the Twentieth Century World* (New York; London: Routledge, 2016), 17–48, 45.

15 Eva-Maria Roelevink and Jan-Otmar Hesse, "Cartel Law and Cartel Register in German Twentieth-Century History," in Susanna Fellman and Martin Shanahan (eds.), *Regulating Competition* (New York: Routledge, 2022), 191–207.

16 Jakob Herle and Max Metzner, *Neue Beiträge zum Kartellproblem* (Berlin: Reimar Hobbing, 1929), 10.

17 For instance: Karl Kautsky, *Bernstein und das Sozialdemokratische Programm, Eine Antikritik* (Stuttgart: J. H. W. Dietz, 1899); Eduard Bernstein, *Zur Frage: Socialliberalismus oder Collectivismus?* (Berlin: Verlag der Sozialistischen Monatshefte, 1900).

18 The party debate on mass-strike was one of the most prominent discourses during our period. It evaluated the possibility to achieve major changes or even Socialism my means of comprehensive strikes.

19 *Vorwärts*, 6 September 1901.

20 See: Helga Grebing, *Geschichte der deutschen Arbeiterbewegung: ein Überblick* (Munich: DTV, 1972); Detlev Lehnert, *Reform und Revolution in der Strategiediskussion der klassischen Sozialdemokratie* (Bonn: Verlag Neue Gesellschaft, 1977).

21 Eduard Bernstein, *Die Voraussetzungen des Sozialismus und die Aufgaben der Sozialdemokratie* (Berlin: Dietz, 1992) (orig. 1899), 94.
22 Cited in: Bechtold, *Die Kartellierung der deutschen Volkswirtschaft*, 64.
23 Wilhelm Schröder, *Handbuch der Sozialdemokratischen Parteitage von 1863 bis 1910* (Munich: Birk, 1910).
24 Rosa Luxemburg, *Sozialreform oder Revolution* (Berlin: Dietz, 1974) (orig.: Verlag Leipziger Volkzeitung, 1899), 404ff, 450ff.
25 Idem, "Zweierlei Maß," in *Gesammelte Werke* (Berlin: Dietz, 1973), 431.
26 Martin Höpner, "Sozialdemokratie, Gewerkschaften und organisierter Kapitalismus, 1880–2002," in *MPIfG Discussion Paper 04/10* (Cologne, 2004), 14.
27 For Lenin cartels were just an instrument of the bourgeoisie to exploit the working class (see. Vladimir Lenin, "Über die national-kulturelle Autonomie," in *Werke*, vol. 19 (Berlin: Dietz, 1973), 498–502, 499), and idem, Rezension <on> Karl Kautsky, "Bernstein und das sozialdemokratische Programm. Eine Antikritik," in *Werke*, vol. 4 (Berlin: Dietz, 1972), 187–198, 197). On Varga see Mária Hidvégi, *Anschluss an den Weltmarkt. Ungarns elektrotechnische Leitunternehmen 1867–1949* (Göttingen: Vandenhoek & Ruprecht, 2016), 82, 216.
28 Karl Liebknecht, "Militarismus und Antimilitarismus," in Idem, *Schriften*, vol. 1 (Berlin: Dietz, 1958), 247–456, 269f; Rudolf Hilferding, *Das Finanzkapital* (Frankfurt am Main: Europäische Verlagsanstalt, 1973), 453; Karl Kautsky, "Ultra-Imperialism," *Die Neue Zeit*, 11 September 1914 (reprinted *New Left Review* 1/59, January–February 1970, 41–46).
29 Wilhelm Jansson, "Wirtschaft und Gewerkschaft nach dem Kriege," *Sozialistische Monatshefte* 18, 19 (1916): 953ff. For the general discourse was his book *Arbeiterinteressen und Kriegsergebnis. Ein gewerkschaftliches Kriegsbuch* (Berlin: Baumeister, 1915). In 1919, Jansson, who acted as a correspondent of the Swedish party daily *Social-Demokraten*, became Attaché for Social Issues at the Swedish Embassy in Berlin.
30 Julius Karliski, "Preisbildung," *Sozialistische Monatshefte* 2 (1916): 111; Idem, "Steuerprobleme," *Ibid* 4 (1916): 209ff, 214ff.
31 Bechtold, *Die Kartellierung der deutschen Volkswirtschaft*, 120ff.
32 Reuffurth, *Die Stellung der deutschen Sozialdemokratie*, 104.
33 Detlef Lehnert, *Sozialdemokratie zwischen Protestbewegung und Regierungspartei 1848–1983* (Frankfurt am Main: Suhrkamp, 1983), 119–143.
34 For instance Eva-Maria Roelevink, *Organnisierte Intransparenz. Das Kohlensyndikat und der Niederländische Markt 1915–1932* (München: C.H.Beck, 2015), 126.
35 "In 1918/19 the chance of a new economic policy was spoilt." ("1918/19 hatte man die Chance vertan, wirtschaftspolitisch neu zu beginnen.") Bechtold, *Die Kartellierung der deutschen Volkswirtschaft*, 170.
36 *Ibid.*, 131.
37 Roelevink, *Organnisierte Intransparenz*; Harm G. Schröter, *Die internationale Kaliwirtschaft 1918–1939. Zum Verhältnis von industrieller Kartellpolitik und Staatsinterventionismus* (Kassel: Kali & Salz AG, 1985). In contrast, the foundation of the nitrogen syndicate (Stickstoffsyndikat) in May 1919 was based on private initiative.
38 The decree did not change much. Abusive cartels could be interdicted and a special court on cartels was introduced. See: Roelevink and Hesse, "Cartel Law and Cartel Register," 196–197.
39 Reuffurth, *Die Stellung der deutschen Sozialdemokratie*, 128.
40 Fritz Voigt, "German Experience with Cartels and Their Control during the Pre-War and Post-War Periods," in John Perry Miller (ed.), *Competition, Cartels and Their Regulation* (Amsterdam: North Holland, 1962), 169–212, 180.
41 In 1927 at the party congregation in Kiel he said: "Organized capitalism means in reality the exchange of the capitalistic principle of free competition by the socialist principle of planned economy." Cited in: Günter Könke, *Organisierter Kapitalismus,*

Sozialdemokratie und Staat, Eine Studie zur Ideologie der sozialdemokratischen Arbeiterbewegung in der Weimarer Republik (1924–1932) (Stuttgart: Franz Steiner Verlag, 1987), 60.

42 See Bechtold, *Die Kartellierung der deutschen Volkswirtschaft*, 172.

43 Minutes of the Heidelberg party congregation 1925, 278, quoted after Bechtold, *Die Kartellierung der deutschen Volkswirtschaft*, 172.

44 Cited by Höpner, "Sozialdemokratie, Gewerkschaften und organisierter Kapitalismus," 15.

45 The ADGB had at its peak 1922 7.8 million members, while the next large one DGB counted 1.5 million.

46 Fritz Naphtali, *Wirtschaftsdemokratie: Ihr Wesen, Weg u. Ziel. Hrsg. im Auftrag des Allg. Dt. Gewerkschaftsbundes* (Berlin: Verlagsgesellschaft des Allg. Dt. Gewerkschaftsbundes, 1928).

47 Hans-Heinrich Barnikel, "Kartelle in Deutschland. Entwicklung, theoretische Ansätze und rechtliche Regelung," in Hans-Heinrich Barnikel (ed.), *Theorie und Praxis der Kartelle* (Darmstadt: Wissenschaftliche Buchgesellschaft, 1972), 1–64, 41.

48 Bechtold, *Die Kartellierung der deutschen Volkswirtschaft*, 181.

49 Only of the persons mentioned here: in February 1941 Hilferding died after being tortured. In June 1933, Naphtali escaped to Palestine and became several times a minister in government.

50 US-Zone: law nr. 56; UK-Zone: ordinance nr. 78; French Zone: decree 96.

51 "Insgesamt rechnet man in den Westzonen mit etwa 10.000 Kartellen, wovon 2.000 gemeldet sind." (*Wirtschafts- und Finanzzeitung*, Frankfurt am Main, Nr. 45, November 11, 1948).

52 Barnikel, "Kartelle in Deutschland," 60.

53 Later in government (1966–72) Schiller became a kind of super-minister, combining the ministries of economics and finances in one hand.

54 Agartz headed the Verwaltungsamt für Wirtschaft, the highest economic administration on the German side in the Bi-Zone (US- + UK Zones of Occupation).

55 Helga Grebing, "Der Sozialismus," in Axel Schildt and Arnold Sywottek (eds.), *Modernisierung im Wiederaufbau, Die westdeutsche Gesellschaft der 50er Jahre* (Bonn: Dietz, 1993), 646–658, 646.

56 *Ibid.*, 649.

57 1947–1952 the German-wide cartel Deutscher Kohlenverkauf, 1952–1956 replaced by the syndicate Gemeinschaftsorganisation Ruhrkohle. The European Coal- and Steel Community tolerated these syndicates not only in Germany but also in France and Belgium (Voigt, "German Experience with Cartels," 189).

58 Cited by Höpner, "Sozialdemokratie, Gewerkschaften und organisierter Kapitalismus," 25). Wagenführ later became director general at the Statistical Dept. of the EC.

59 See in detail the contribution of Brian Shaev in this volume on the ambiguous positions SPD politicians put forward on anti-cartel proposals in the Bundestag in 1950–1952.

60 Peter Hüttenberger, "Wirtschaftsordnung und Interessenpolitik in der Kartellgesetzgebung der Bundesrepublik 1949–1957," *Vierteljahrshefte für Zeitgeschichte* 24 (1976): 287–307, 294ff.

61 The SPD had six of 13 seats in that committee (Kurlbaum, Lange, Nölting, Pleiss, Schröder, and Weber), Hüttenberger, "Wirtschaftsordnung und Interessenpolitik," 299.

62 Brian Shaev in this volume.

63 Harry Westermann, "Genossenschaften und deutsche staatliche Kartellpolitik der Gegenwart in rechtlicher Sicht," *Zeitschrift für das gesamte Genossenschaftswesen* 4 (1954): 297–306, 302.

64 Vereinigte Wirtschaftsdienste, *Wirtschaftsspiegel* of March 31st, 1955; *Die Welt* Nr. 77, 1 April 1955; *Industriekurier* February 2nd, 1955; *Handelsblatt* Nr. 39, 4 April 1955.

65 *The Times* Nr. 53884, 4 July 1957.

66 Hüttenberger has presented the most deep-going research on the issue especially in parliament.
67 Georg Kurlbaum, "Antikartell- und Antimonopolpolitik," *Gewerkschaftliche Monatshefte* 15, 1 (1964): 22–27, 23. Central Board of DGB (eds.).
68 See footnote 6 of this chapter.

Bibliography

Barinkel, Hans-Heinrich Barnikel. "Kartelle in Deutschland. Entwicklung, theoretische Ansätze und rechtliche Regelung." In *Theorie und Praxis der Kartelle* edited by Hans-Heinrich Barnikel. Darmstadt: Wissenschaftliche Buchgesellschaft, 1972, 1–64.

Bechtold, Hartmut. *Die Kartellierung der deutschen Volkswirtschaft und die sozialdemokratische Theorie-Diskussion vor 1933*. Frankfurt am Main: Haag + Herchen, 1986.

Bernstein, Eduard. *Die Voraussetzungen des Sozialismus und die Aufgaben der Sozialdemokratie*. Berlin: Dietz, 1992 (orig. 1899).

Bernstein, Eduard. *Zur Frage: Socialliberalismus oder Collectivismus?* Berlin: Verlag der Sozialistischen Monatshefte, 1900.

Bertilorenzi, Marco. "Legitimising Cartels. The Joint Role of the League of Nations and of the International Chamber of Commerce." In *Regulating Competition: Cartel Registers in the Twentieth Century World* edited by Susanna Fellman and Martin Shanahan. New York & London: Routledge, 2016, 17–48.

Callaghan, Helen and Martin Höpner. "Changing ideas: Organized Capitalism and the German left." *West European Politics* 35 (2012): 551–573.

Grebing, Helga. "Der Sozialismus." In *Modernisierung im Wiederaufbau, Die westdeutsche Gesellschaft der 50er Jahre* edited by Axel Schildt and Arnold Sywottek. Bonn: Verlag J.H.W. Dietz Nachf., 1993, 646–658.

Grebing, Helga. *Geschichte der deutschen Arbeiterbewegung: ein Überblick*. Munich: DTV, 1972.

Groh, Dieter. *Negative Integration und revolutionärer Attentismus: die deutsche Sozialdemokratie am Vorabend des ersten Weltkrieges*. Frankfurt/Main: Verlag Ullstein, 1973.

Herle, Jakob and Max Metzner. *Neue Beiträge zum Kartellproblem*. Berlin: Reimar Hobbing, 1929.

Hidvégi, Mária. *Anschluss an den Weltmarkt. Ungarns elektrotechnische Leitunternehmen 1867–1949*. Göttingen: Vandenhoek & Ruprecht, 2016.

Hilferding, Rudolf. *Das Finanzkapital*. Frankfurt/Main: Europäische Verlagsanstalt, 1973 (Wien 1910).

Höpner, Martin. "Sozialdemokratie, Gewerkschaften und organisierter Kapitalismus, 1880–2002." *MPIfG Discussion Paper* 04/10, Cologne, 2004.

Hüttenberger, Peter. "Wirtschaftsordnung und Interessenpolitik in der Kartellgesetzgebung der Bundesrepublik 1949–1957." *Vierteljahrshefte für Zeitgeschichte* 24 (1976): 287–307.

Jansson, Wilhelm. *Arbeiterinteressen und Kriegsergebnis. Ein gewerkschaftliches Kriegsbuch*. Berlin: Baumeister, 1915.

Jansson, Wilhelm. "Wirtschaft und Gewerkschaft nach dem Kriege." *Sozialistische Monatshefte* 18, 19 (1916): 953.

Karliski, Julius. "Preisbildung." *Sozialistische Monatshefte* 2 (1916): 111.

Karliski, Julius. "Steuerprobleme." *Sozialistische Monatshefte* 4 (1916).

Kautsky, Karl. *Bernstein und das Sozialdemokratische Programm, Eine Antikritik*. Stuttgart: J. H. W. Dietz, 1899.

Kautsky, Karl. "Ultra-imperialism." *Die Neue Zeit*, 11 September 1914 (reprinted *New Left Review* 1/59, January-February 1970, 41–46).

Kleinwächter, Friedrich. *Die Kartelle. Eine Frage der Organisation der Volkswirtschaft*. Innsbruck: Verlag der Wagner'schen Universitaets-Buchhandlung, 1883.

Könke, Günter. *Organisierter Kapitalismus, Sozialdemokratie und Staat, Eine Studie zur Ideologie der sozialdemokratischen Arbeiterbewegung in der Weimarer Republik (1924–1932)*. Stuttgart: Franz Steiner Verlag, 1987.

Kurlbaum, Georg. "Antikartell- und Antimonopolpolitik." *Gewerkschaftliche Monatshefte* 15, 1 (1964): 22–27.

Lapidus, John. *Social Democracy and the Swedish Welfare Model, Ideational Analyses of Attitudes Towards Competition, Individualization, Privatization*, vol. 13. Gothenburg: Gothenburg Studies in Economic History, 2015.

Lehnert, Detlef. *Sozialdemokratie zwischen Protestbewegung und Regierungspartei 1848–1983*. Frankfurt/M: Suhrkamp, 1983.

Lehnert, Detlev. *Reform und Revolution in der Strategiediskussion der klassischen Sozialdemokratie*. Bonn: Verlag Neue Gesellschaft, 1977.

Lenin, Vladimir. "Rezension <on> Karl Kautsky, Bernstein und das sozialdemokratische Programm. Eine Antikritik." In *Werke*, vol. 4. Berlin: Dietz, 1972, 187–198.

Lenin, Vladimir. "Über die national-kulturelle Autonomie." In *Werke*, vol. 19. Berlin: Dietz, 1973, 498–502.

Liebknecht, Karl. "Militarismus und Antimilitarismus." In *Schriften*, vol. 1. Berlin: Dietz, 1958, 247–456.

Luxemburg, Rosa. *Sozialreform oder Revolution*. Berlin: Dietz, 1974 (orig. Verlag Leipziger Volkzeitung, 1899).

Marx, Karl and Friedrich Engels (eds.). *Das Kapital. Kritik der politischen Ökonomie, Book 3, Der Gesamtprozess der kapitalistischen Produktion*, vol. 3. Berlin: Dietz, 1970.

Murach-Brand, Lisa. *Antitrust auf Deutsch. Der Einfluss der amerikanischen Alliierten auf das Gesetz gegen Wettbewerbsbeschränkungen (GWB) nach 1945*. Tübingen: Mohr-Siebeck, 2004.

Naphtali, Fritz. *Wirtschaftsdemokratie: Ihr Wesen, Weg u. Ziel. Hrsg. im Auftrag des Allg. Dt. Gewerkschaftsbundes*. Berlin: Verlagsgesellschaft des Allg. Dt. Gewerkschaftsbundes, 1928.

Reuffurth, Eduard. *Die Stellung der deutschen Sozialdemokratie zum Problem der staatlichen Kartellpolitik*. Jena: (without publisher), 1930.

Roelevink, Eva-Maria. *Organnisierte Intransparenz. Das Kohlensyndikat und der Niederländische Markt 1915–1932*. Munich: C.H. Beck, 2015.

Roelevink, Eva-Maria and Jan-Otmar Hesse, "Cartel Law and Cartel Register in German Twentieth-Century History." In *A History of Business Cartels: International Politics, National Policies, and Anti-Competitive Behaviour* edited by Susanna Fellman and Marti Shanahan. New York: Routledge, 2022, 191–207.

Richter, Klaus W. *Die Wirkungsgeschichte des deutschen Kartellrechts vor 1914. Eine rechts-historisch analytische Untersuchung*. Tübingen: Mohr Siebeck, 2007.

Schröder, Wilhelm. *Handbuch der Sozialdemokratischen Parteitage von 1863 bis 1910*. Munich: Birk, 1910.

Schröter, Harm G. *Americanization of the European Economy. A Compact Survey of American Economic Influence in Europe Since the 1880s*. Dordrecht: Springer, 2005.

Schröter, Harm G. "Cartelization and Decartelization in Europe, 1870–1995: Rise and Decline of an Economic Institution." *Journal of European Economic History* 25, 1 (1996): 129–153.

Schröter, Harm G. *Die internationale Kaliwirtschaft 1918–1939. Zum Verhältnis von industrieller Kartellpolitik und Staatsinterventionismus*. Kassel: Kali & Salz AG, 1985.
Schröter, Harm G. "The International Potash Syndicate." In *International Cartels Revisited: Relating to the History of Business Development and International Economic Order* edited by Dominique Barjot. Cormelles: Editions-Diffusions du Lys, 1994, 75–92.
Tschierschky, Siegfried. *Kartellpolitik, Eine analytische Untersuchung*. Berlin: C. Hymann, 1930.
Voigt, Fritz. "German Experience with Cartels and Their Control During the Pre-War and Post-War Periods." In *Competition, Cartels and Their Regulation* edited by John Perry Miller. Amsterdam: North Holland, 1962, 169–212.
Westermann, Harry. "Genossenschaften und deutsche staatliche Kartellpolitik der Gegenwart in rechtlicher Sicht." *Zeitschrift für das gesamte Genossenschaftswesen* 4 (1954): 297–306.
Zeitlin, Jonathan and Gary Herrigel (eds.). *Americanization and Its Limits. Reworking US Technology and Management in Post-War Europe and Japan*. Oxford, Oxford University Press, 2000.

3 Swedish social democracy and cartels, 1911–1953

Birgit Karlsson

Introduction

This chapter illustrates the Swedish Social Democrats' attempts to deal with the problem of efficiency and justice when economies of scale had become dominating in most industries. Cartels had the potential to make production much more efficient and thereby lower prices. On the other hand, there was an inherent danger that the profits would not be used for making investments. The Social Democrats' problem was how to make sure that the increase of utilities achieved by production was used for investments (efficiency) and for achieving fair distribution (justice). Public investigations made after World War II indicated that cartels in many cases contributed to increased production. The Swedish Social democrats therefore came to adapt to the continental way of looking at cartels in opposition to the Anglo-American antitrust tradition. This meant that cartels were accepted as long as they contributed to the benefits of society. Social Democrats introduced stronger competition laws and regulations in the postwar era but only abuse was forbidden.

The Swedish Social Democratic Party was founded in 1889. It had a Marxist heritage expressed in the condemnation of the capitalist mode of production, which concentrated economic power in the hands of a few capitalists, while the large mass of workers remained poor and powerless. Cartels, trusts and monopolies were part of this process toward concentration of wealth. When social democrats came to power during the interwar period, they could have been expected to have forbidden cartels and monopolies, but this did not happen. Some legislation was approved but cartels remained perfectly legal in Sweden until 1993. This text aims to explain why cartels were, to a large extent, accepted by Swedish Social Democrats during the period 1911–1951.

Earlier research has depicted social democracy as hostile to trusts and cartels.[1] John Lapidus has questioned this view, arguing that social democrats were quite positive to cartels during the interwar period. He finds three main reasons for this; first, it was an advantage for future socialization if the nationalized companies were already organized in cartels. Second, the cartel organization meant a more rational organization, thereby creating more efficient production. And third, social democrats feared that the legislation against cartels could be used against trade

DOI: 10.4324/9781351010573-3

unions. He argues that the first motive was the most essential as long as the idea of socialization dominated political debate in that period.[2]

In this chapter, we would like to go further than these arguments by arguing that the relatively positive view on cartels mirrored the evolution of the social-democratic ideological development. We know from earlier research that the Social Democratic Party went through a period of ideological transformation during the first half of the 20th century. Initially, social democrats considered the private ownership of means of production a general problem of justice. It was not fair that this ownership would lead to such vast differences in income. Gradually, the problem of private ownership came to be conceptualized as a problem of efficiency. Private companies were not always efficient as demonstrated by their slow expansion and high prices for consumers.[3] Therefore, the regulation of cartels and competition were part of this political evolution from solving problems of justice and redistribution to deal with more general problems of economic development.

This chapter begins with an overview of legislation affecting cartels during the period 1911–1953. It is followed by a presentation of social-democratic ideological development during this period. Thereafter, it tackles the social-democratic debate on cartels and competition by analyzing the records of public debates in the Swedish Parliament (*Riksdag*), public investigations and political debates published in the social-democratic journal *Tiden*.

Two views on cartels: the theory of abuse

Cartels and other forms of cooperation grew in importance and number from the end of the 19th century all over the Western World. At the same time, the dominating economic doctrine was liberalism, according to which free competition was indispensable for the correct functioning of the economy. However, it was clear that the rosy picture of capitalism as a system with small companies, producing homogenous products without economies of scale, was increasingly outdated. When the state did not interfere in business matters, companies were on their way to abolishing free competition, especially where there existed advantages due to economies of scale. This development was confronted in different manners in the Western World. In the United States, legislation regulating competition by targeting cartels and trusts was developed quite early with the approval of the Sherman and Clayton Acts. Developments were very different in Germany where cartels were legally accepted if it could not be proven that their activities were against societal utility.[4] Sweden, during this period, saw cartels and the regulation of competition in the same way as Germany. It can be legally expressed as a tension between the principle of freedom of trade (or freedom to start businesses) and the principle of concluding agreements. In the German/Swedish tradition, the right to conclude agreements (*pacta sunt servanda*) was above the principle of freedom of trade.[5] Thus, it was not possible to forbid cartel agreements as such but only to make sure that the activities were not improperly used against the public interest: this is the so-called abuse doctrine.

The evolution of Swedish legislation on competition

Even if cartels were not forbidden, voices were raised in Sweden by the beginning of the 20th century that questioned their activities. There was a common view that there was a lack of knowledge about the phenomenon and public investigations were undertaken during the interwar period. The first law on cartels was the result of the work of *Trustlagstiftningskommittén*, which started its work in 1920, chaired by professor K. G. Westman, who was a professor in legal history and represented the agricultural party in Parliament. The law – *Lagen om undersökning angående monopolistiska företag och sammanslutningar* – was decided upon by the Parliament in 1925.[6] It was considered to be a mild law. A permanent commission was to be set up with the right to launch investigations when it suspected a cartel abuse. The principle of abuse was hereby vindicated. Cartels were legal, but cartel-abuse was forbidden and punished.

In 1936, a new public investigation started, led by Bertil Ohlin, leader of the liberal party. The committee finished its report in 1940, but by then, it was considered futile to undertake adequate measures.[7] After the war, the question came up again, and in 1946, a new law – *Lagen om övervakning av konkurrensbegräsning inom näringslivet* – was established according to which all cartels had to be registered. This was a way to enable public authorities to exercise control over cartels. This law was specifically targeted at cartels, but cartels were only a part of the larger question of the regulation of competition.[8]

A public investigation on competition and regulation was published in 1951.[9] It resulted in the first real law regulating competition – Konkurrensbegränsningslagen – in 1953.[10] Bidding cartels were forbidden. Other cartels were still legal, even if abuse was to be monitored, through registration and the possibility to make public the result of these investigations. In this law, cartels were not conceptualized as the only way of limiting competition. There were other forms of regulation, like the Resale Price Maintenance system. This system consisted in a concerted form of keeping retail prices high and protecting the least efficient producer. The new legislation prohibited this generalized practice.

Social democracy and fatalism: the origins of an ideological debate

The first decades of the 20th century were dramatic for the social-democratic movement in Sweden. The social-democratic leadership disavowed the path to socialism through a violent revolution, like in Russia, leading to a split in the party. The left wing formed the Swedish Social-Democratic Left Party, which from 1921 became the Communist Party of Sweden. After this split, a new party program was formulated in 1920, in which it was made clear that the transition to socialism would be the result of a gradual process. Private ownership was acceptable in enterprises that had not reached the stage of monopoly and thereby were not yet ripe for socialization. This illustrates one important dilemma in the social-democratic movement. The capitalist system's own logic would mean a development toward monopoly and one possibility was to allow this development to take place and then proceed to socialization. The other possibility discussed in the party program was to take action to stop the development toward monopoly, for example, by forming public enterprises operating in the same economic sector.

The question of "fatalism" within social democracy has been the focus of a scientific debate led by Herbert Tingsten, who studied the social-democratic ideological development. The problem was the Marxist view of capitalism, which included, on the one hand, a recognition of the dynamics of the capitalist system. Capitalism had a historical task to fulfill in developing the means of production toward higher and higher levels of efficiency. At the same time as this economically positive development took place, the capitalist system would create strong social tensions related to enormous differences in income. These tensions would lead to a collapse of the system and, as a result, workers would take over the means of production. In the case, however, that social democrats gained political support, it was not enough to wait for the collapse to happen. A social-democratic government had to do something to improve the conditions of workers.[11]

A precondition for adopting the fatalist standpoint was that capitalism generally improved efficiency in production, but this did not seem to happen during the interwar period. This brought a double-sided criticism toward the capitalist system: it was not only unfair but also inefficient. Production resources had not been used adequately, creating high unemployment, which meant that human capital was not used for increasing production. Crises occurred repeatedly – periods of overproduction and deflation obstructed the economy. There were banking crises and bankruptcies and the possibilities to plan for the future, which was necessary for making good investments, were limited. This created a situation for social democrats in which they actually reflected on the possibilities to help capitalism to fulfill its historical task. The paradox for social-democratic ideology relating to cartels can thus be found in that they wanted, on the one hand, to help capitalism fulfill its historical role but, on the other hand, they wanted to reap the fruits of increased efficiency quickly, in order to improve the conditions for workers. Gustav Möller, a social democrat, was one of the main proponents for increased efficiency in production as an argument in favor of socialization. In an article from 1918, he maintained that the common interest was achieving an increase in overall wealth. Poverty could not be abolished only through fairer distribution. Instead, society must become the owner of the means of production and through the organization of a planned economy make sure that production would take place in the most rational way possible.[12]

The question of socialization

The ideological development of social democracy during the 1930s and 1940s has been a topic for many researchers. Herbert Tingsten's argument was that the ideology of Swedish social democrats died when they abandoned Marxist fatalism. This view was challenged by Leif Lewin, who argued that there was still a clear social-democratic ideology formulated in the idea of the planned economy.

Planning society to make production more efficient was the main goal, since this would increase freedom for the majority.[13]

One way of describing the evolution of the aims of social-democratic policy is that it evolved from pursuing the socialization of production to the socialization of consumption. The question of socialization had been related to the social democrats' fight for power over the means of production. In 1920, a public investigation had the task to analyze how socialization could be realized. It concluded its work after 17 years and, when it published the results, it became clear that it did not propose the complete removal of market mechanisms or any sudden socializations (SOU 1936:7). During this period, leaders like Nils Karleby and Ernst Wigforss were important for the ideological development of social democracy. Nils Karleby was a journalist and a politician who sharply criticized the October revolution in Russia. He considered it to be non-socialist, since the preconditions for a socialist revolution in Russia were non-existent. Ernst Wigforss was an academic and finance minister several times between 1925 and 1949. He was one of the main architects behind the welfare state and also for the development of state-subsidized policies for diminishing unemployment during the 1929–1933 crisis. These persons were important for social democracy's development toward reformism.

During the interwar period, social democracy moved toward the conception that property was not an indivisible unit to be socialized, but rather consisted of a bundle of rights that could be progressively transferred to society. Formal ownership of production was less important than actual power to control economic development. It was a good thing if production was efficient and increased. This could be achieved within the framework of private ownership but the produced commodities should be distributed in a fairer way than had so far been the case.[14] This meant that the initial priority of controlling production came to be followed by a priority of questions of distribution and consumption. But there was still concern about how production was undertaken. Production had to be as effective as possible to enhance possibilities for consumption.

If the main critique against the capitalist system during the 1920s had been related to power relations and exploitation, this came to change during the economic crisis of 1929–1933. The main critique, instead, became related to the system's inability to make full use of society's resources, that is, production was not effective enough, as manifested by mass unemployment.[15]

The social-democratic government in 1933 managed to make the Parliament accept a substantial increase of public expenditure during the economic crisis. These measures were inspired by the theories of economists from the Stockholm School of Economics, which developed their theses parallel to Keynes. Gunnar Myrdal, a social democrat, and Bertil Ohlin, who led the Liberal party, were both professors in national economy and members of the Stockholm school. According to this line of thinking, the economy did not work efficiently. One sign of this was that it was unable to use resources in the form of labor. The state had to undertake measures to make use of these resources and finance public works, even if it would mean budget deficits. An intense political debate arose concerning whether or not it was responsible to finance employment by taking loans. As the measures were undertaken, they seemed to be effective. Unemployment diminished, which indicated that productive resources were more efficiently used. Later, it has been questioned whether this development can actually be explained by "Keynesian" policy, since in fact no budget deficit actually occurred. Nevertheless, it seemed at the time to be the right medicine.[16] Myrdal came to have influence over the continued social-democratic development of economic ideas.

From socialization to efficiency after 1945

The Social Democratic Party's view on intervention in the economy had shifted from the power aspect to the efficiency aspect. Inefficiency was considered to have its root in two phenomena – monopolistic practices and a lack of coordination and planning within branches and industries.[17] The deflation and unemployment after World War I could be avoided after World War II if there was enough planning and coordination. To make this possible, the government had to be much more economically active and undertake measures to increase demand. Myrdal was the main proponent of this policy as the fear of a new postwar economic crisis was taken seriously.[18] The commission for postwar planning undertook serious investigations into how all societal resources could be used in order to achieve increased efficiency and economic growth. This was also in full accordance with the social-democratic postwar program from 1944. The main goals for social democracy were formulated in terms of full employment, fair distribution and economic growth.[19] When it came to the problem of making production efficient, fragmentation in small units was seen as a problem, since it made rational planning problematic. Monopolies were another problem, because a monopolist could limit production as well as employment against the interests of consumers. The problem of monopolies could be solved either by socialization of monopolies or by encouraging competition. When it came to the fragmentation problem, no direct measures were identified, but planning in a rational way was seen as necessary.[20]

Social-democratic postwar planning became an important part of the large debate on planned economy that took place during the first years after the war. Some of the investigations dealt with industries that might become more efficient if they were socialized. The reasons for inefficiency were sometimes to be found in small-scale production, sometimes in a monopoly situation. The Myrdal commission suggested state regulations to deal with cartels and monopoly. These proposals met strong resistance from the bourgeois parties. At this time, the Social Democratic Party had come to the conclusion that if industries could achieve rationalizations without state interference, this was good enough for the party.[21] The central concern for them was that production be efficient and this could be evaluated by analyzing prices and competitiveness.

One dilemma for social democracy was to go beyond fatalism toward interventionism. Another dilemma, once planning had been chosen as the way to go, was the relation between economies of scale and competition. In those production sectors where economies of scale were important, there was an inherent development toward bigger units, which in turn implied more concentrated ownership.

This could increase efficiency by reducing costs per unit. On the other hand, there was a constant temptation for the owners to increase prices, since there was no or only a small degree of competition. How could efficiency in production be combined with low prices?

Summing up, Swedish Social Democrats were fully aware of the advantages of large-scale production. They were modernists and saw large problems in the traditional society, characterized by agricultural tradition and small-scale industry. They supported the development of industry and saw great possibilities in economies of scale, standardization and better organization. In the interwar situation, cartels could be seen as rational organizations, making use of the possibilities for economies of scale.

Debate and legislation on cartels

Questioning cartels in the Riksdag

Discussion on the potential need for legislation against cartels started in 1911 in the Swedish Parliament. The initiative came from a social democrat, Erik Palmstierna. He was a baron with radical views and deeply engaged in social questions. As a Member of Parliament, he represented the liberal party in 1909–1911 until he left the party. From 1911, he represented the social democrats and had minister posts in 1917–1920. Palmstierna was also a member of the committee that worked with trusts and cartels and was very active in the Parliament on these questions. He maintained that economic freedom during the 19th century had led to an enormously increased production but that this development was no longer sustainable: "The belief in the good effects of untamed competition was no longer possible to uphold."[22] Free competition was about to die as a result of the logic of mass production. According to Palmstierna, cartels and trusts had some advantages – private as well as social. The most important advantage of a trust/cartel was that it could adapt production to demand when there was knowledge of demand for commodities. If this adaptation was done properly, overproduction could be avoided. It could also be possible to avoid "some of these trade profits, advertisements and agents which are necessary for acquiring a place on the unorganized market but burdened production to a large extent."[23] If a market was well-organized, production could be divided between different factories. It would be possible to achieve standardization of commodities and prices and freight costs could be reduced. In the end, this would lead to more homogenous products for lower prices. The rational organization of business would serve a social purpose – downturns as well as upswings in the business cycles would be milder. Cartelized lines of businesses could, according to Palmstierna, play a positive role in society but had to accept social control. This argument would be repeated in many debates during the interwar period – if cartel representatives argued that the organizations brought social utility, this meant that cartels were not a private issue. If cartels served a social purpose, public control was justified.

In 1917, Palmstierna raised a new motion for measures to be undertaken in cases in which social interests had to be looked after against monopolies. The cases referred to were the sugar and milk trusts. During World War I, the public had experienced that trusts in sugar and milk production had not always contributed to social utility. The economic development in a country as a whole could no doubt be helped by trusts and cartels but the opposite could also be the case. Cartels and trusts could be obstacles to the development. Thus, investigations were needed.[24]

During the parliamentary debate, Palmstierna could note that there was no resistance in principle to control over trusts. He saw this as a natural result of development. Concentration of ownership in Sweden had increased in Sweden during the 20th century and this could mean possibilities to economize on both capital and labor. It could also lead to technical progress and possibilities to withstand foreign competition. It was repeated that production in the end served society, and a logical implication was that society must ensure that production serve the interests of society. The inherent danger in the concentration of production was that consumers might be plundered. Monopoly profits should not fall in the hands of private persons. Instead, they ought to be captured by society.[25]

In 1920, a motion in Parliament proposed setting up a controlling authority, which would have the right to examine accounts and elucidate net profit. It was, according to the motion, clear that unduly large profits existed and if this information was made public, it would create a strong moral pressure, which would force actors to undertake correction.[26] A committee was appointed to develop and propose legislation on control of trusts and other forms of company cooperation. The committee could confirm that there was a need for further investigations, and for state, measures to be undertaken. It was clear that some trusts and cartels in Sweden had tried to annihilate competition or place economically weaker competitors in unacceptable dependency.[27] But cartels and trusts were still considered to have the potential to be positive forces in economic development. Not even the social democrats wanted to create obstacles for their development "as long as [they were] loyal and did not violate the interests of others."[28]

The investigations led to legislation in 1925. One important problem to be considered was the difficulties for smaller companies to enter and establish themselves on the market where big companies already dominated and had organized cartels. When many firms cooperated, it was difficult to be an outsider. Retailers often found it impossible to refrain from agreements. Situations occurred in which the economically stronger part – company or cartel – was able to exercise increased power over the smaller company. The head of the department argued that legislation was necessary when amalgamations used unacceptable methods to annihilate competitors or make the economically weaker part dependent on the stronger.[29]

It can be noted that the question of power was central in these discussions, in at least two different dimensions. One was the difference in power between small and large companies, a situation in which small actors felt that their freedom to act was becoming more and more limited. Another dimension was the difference in power between producers and consumers. Monopolies meant that the producers had the power to increase prices in a way that was contrary to consumers' interests. Social democrats were critical of the imbalance in power in both dimensions. However, when cartels and trusts provided large economic advantages in terms of increased efficiency, it was not possible to stop an economic development. It was the abuse of power that was to be rejected in the social interest.

Good and bad cartels

The journal *Tiden* was founded in 1908 by the leader of the Social Democratic Party, Hjalmar Branting. The journal aimed to be a platform for socialist critique and politics. Its articles dealt with all kinds of subjects, cultural as well as political and ideological. During the interwar period, economic aspects came more into focus. For example, several articles commented on the development of monopolies and cartels.

There were cartels that were commented on in *Tiden* in a positive way. For example, an article written in 1926 noted that there were plans for a fusion of ironworks in Sweden. The iron producers had suffered for a long time, especially producers of ordinary steel. Production was considered to be split into too many plants. Another weakness was the lack of coordination between different producers when it came to sales operations. The author was, however, skeptical of proposals for state subsidies that had been brought up. Subsidizing one type of industry could never take place without the effect that other legitimate interests were put aside. The main incentive for the ironworks to coordinate was that their production costs were higher than the costs of the big producers on the continent. The conclusion was that horizontal cooperation was necessary.[30]

Similar views were apparent when discussing the crisis in the British coal industry. The commentator in *Tiden* could see many similarities with the Swedish iron industry as well as with the badly organized exploitation of the peasant forests in Sweden. The problem was described as economic individualism on a giant scale and conservative resistance against standardization of tools and machinery and an irrational use of transport capacity, related to diversified ownership.[31]

Other cartels were seen as much more problematic. One example was the so-called milk trust. During World War I, the price of milk increased rapidly in Stockholm. To provide the city's inhabitants with milk, an organization was created to transport milk in great quantities. The organization became similar to a cartel and prices rose. Even if there were other reasons for high milk prices in terms of draught and the export of cattle, the milk trust was considered to be responsible for part of the price increase.[32]

The problems of milk distribution were related to the war-time crisis and shortages of food. During the interwar period, social democrats were worried about protectionism, which also could create shortages. The international development toward protectionism was also seen as a problem. Social democrats were on the whole positive to free trade, since it in many cases led to increased competition and lower prices for consumers. In a 1922 *Tiden* article, it was pointed out that monopolies in practically all cases were to be found in areas that were protected by tariffs. This was true for sugar, mills, rolled oats and galoshes and earlier also cement. The simplest anti-monopoly policy was considered to be a rational free trade policy.[33]

For the sugar trust, protectionism in the form of tariffs had been crucial for the possibilities to regulate competition. By the end of the 19th century, interest in growing sugar beets increased and overproduction threatened. The refineries started to cooperate. Their organization thereby could seize power over the quantity of refining as well as the price of beets. When refineries cooperated, growers felt compelled to do the same, and in 1903, they became organized. In 1907, *Svenska sockerbruksaktiebolaget* was founded, including practically all sugar production in the country. The political issue connected to this was not the cooperation in itself, but the fact that there was overcapitalization. Capital increased, but no concentration of industry took place. According to social democrats, there were unnecessary boards as well as unnecessary directors. These anomalies led to the discussion of the sugar question in the Parliament in 1908. The chief of department argued that protection of domestic sugar production should not be higher than what was necessary for the sugar industry to survive and develop stably. The aim with protection was won when sugar could be sold at a price corresponding to production costs plus a reasonable profit. The problem was that the profit was considerably higher than reasonable. Negotiations led to lower tariffs and higher taxes. During the coming years, the state gained insight into the sugar trust and it was possible to compare it with production costs in Denmark and Germany. Costs were higher in Sweden. One main factor was the inefficient concentration of operations. There were too many factories. After a lot of problems during the 1920s when the state had to provide subsidies, a new way was tried in 1932. The trust gained a monopoly on imports and legislation on minimum prices on sugar as well as on beets. The burden of supporting the beet growers was thus placed on the consumers. Risk-taking in the sugar industry was minimized.[34]

The common view among social democrats was that concentration could be a good thing but that state subsidies should be avoided as much as possible. This is confirmed by comments on planned fusions within iron industry. The iron producers wanted tariffs or other types of state support. An article in *Tiden* commented that

> an association which aims to reduce production costs and improve sales is in all respects needed and worth support. A state subsidy was on the other hand not to be contemplated, if it did not contribute to the preservation of an economically profitable industry and the subsidies should in that case be provisional.[35]

It seems clear that social democrats, judging by the discussions in *Tiden*, all discussed the cartel – trust – monopoly problem in terms of efficiency. Efficiency was threatened if the business was dominated by small units, which did not rationalize and coordinate and did not have capital to invest in techniques that allowed large-scale production. But efficiency was also threatened if the producers in a monopolized area did not use their capital resources to organize production in an effective way. The main argument against the sugar trust was not that it was powerful but that the production was not organized efficiently. Both smallness and largeness could be problematic for efficiency.

The consumers' organization

Though the social democrats' attitude toward cartels, trusts and organized competition was ambivalent, this was not the case for the consumer cooperative movement. This movement had its root in local consumption associations, which joined together in Kooperativa förbundet (KF) in 1899. This consumer movement was not political, but many of the KF members and leading persons were social democrats. KF was the one actor that actually did something concrete to break the power of monopolies.[36] Criticisms of cartels was an important feature in KF advocacy. Its main claim was that the state should establish a mandatory register over cartels, which should be made public. The hope was that this kind of register would lead consumers to repudiate commodities produced in cartels, which would hopefully benefit KF products.[37]

KF wanted to break monopolies, which they considered to be harmful to the consumers, but in the beginning, their financial capacity was not very strong. However, it was to become strengthened as the association started wholesale business to provide the local associations with commodities. In 1921, a factory for producing margarine was started. The market for margarine was dominated by a private margarine cartel, which immediately started a price war against the KF margarine production. The price of margarine was halved in a few months, partly due to falling raw material costs. In the cooperative stores, the margarine cartel's products were almost totally replaced by KF margarine. The efforts by private producers to shut out KF production through price cuts failed. The KF plant was bigger and more modern and its distribution to cooperative stores was cost effective. The KF plant came during the following decades to generate cash flow to KF.[38]

Apart from the food industry, KF also became engaged in the rubber industry and the production of light bulbs. The price of light bulbs was 50% higher than in most other European countries and KF started production in 1931. KF was sued by the international cartel for light bulbs, but decided to make a deal with the cartel, including market sharing, price cooperation and use of patents.[39] During the interwar period, KF came to start production and buy companies in a number of areas. In 1950, KF was one of the biggest owner groups in Sweden, with a turnover corresponding to 5% of the total Swedish manufacturing industry.[40]

It should be noted that within the cooperative movement, the critique of cartels was harder than of monopolies. Monopolies were seen to have the capacity to organize production in a rational way, while cartels were seen more as protecting their weakest partners, which led to higher prices. This kind of thinking also showed up in *Tiden* when comments were made on the public investigation into trusts. Incentives for rationalization were regarded as high within the trusts, but if this only benefited the owners and not the consumers, the public had very little use for rationalization. Yet, harsher legislation was not seen as an option – it had not led to good results in the United States. Instead, publicity was seen as a possible tool. Consumers were expected to turn away from cartel products.[41]

There is no doubt that KF tried to break the power of the cartels in the areas where it started production. The main motive – to cut prices – was to some extent achieved. However, KF prices were only slightly lower than the private producers' prices. This was motivated by the cooperative ideologists by the implementation of the so-called Rochdale principles, which originated from the early cooperative movement in England. One of its principles was "prevalent prices," which meant that price cuts were not actively pushed for. Early attempts in that direction had led to defaults, and it was considered necessary to create surpluses for financing investments. There was also a strong skepticism against banks, which implied a reliance on self-financing. During the 1920s, the principle of prevalent prices came to be discussed and on certain occasions, a more active price policy was undertaken in order to cut prices. However, such efforts did not lead to any general policy change, even if voices were heard that argued that too much weight was placed on building equity and too little on price cuts.[42]

Public investigations on company cooperation

As previously mentioned, a public commission for investigating the extent of cooperation started its work in 1936. The committee was led by Ohlin. The other members represented different industrial and consumer interests. The work was finished in 1940, but by then, World War II made it impossible to undertake the suggested measures. During the late 1930s, tendencies toward cooperation had also increased as preparations for war became realized. The government was eager to have institutions to cooperate with in case of war and therefore encouraged industry associations. Their competence was considered necessary during trade negotiations and it was important for the government to have industrial partners that could represent different lines of business.

The directive to the commission was not to blow up the trusts. The Minister of Trade in the social-democratic government was outspoken when it came to cooperation. His view was that cooperation could without doubt have positive effects on industry. New markets could become available, distribution could be simplified and production rationalized and specialized. The comments in *Tiden* on the committee's proposals confirmed this view. The power of associations could be limited through real as well as potential competition but also through public opinion. The cooperative movement was considered successful in pressing down monopoly prices through competition or threats of competition. It was considered problematic to make general verdicts on the utility of associations. For example, there were associations whose only aim was to keep prices high to protect the least efficient producer. This must be considered harmful to society. On the other hand, there were organizations that cooperated to achieve better organization, technical development and research. These organizations had to be considered positive for social utility.[43]

Nevertheless, the conclusion of the commission was that concentration tendencies had become stronger. It was considered to be a societal interest that the state should undertake measures to increase competition to keep prices down.

As the war came to its close, the question was revived. Cartels were to be registered. A public authority should be created, which would have the right to undertake investigations if bad effects were suspected. The bourgeois members of the commission supported the main proposals even if they seem to have had some doubts regarding state interventions in the companies' competition situation.[44]

The alternative to socialization

Parallel to the investigation on competition, other public investigations took place related to socialization. The motive was expressed in terms of how the state could help industries to become more efficient. However, many of the investigations did not lead to results, for example the proposals on monopolies for coffee and oil. Socialization was only in certain cases seen as a solution. Often, like in the investigation on building material, it was claimed that rationalization was taking place, but that it was too slow, since all companies worked on their own and that knowledge was not spread with enough speed. Instead of socialization, it was suggested that a rationalization committee ought to be established.[45]

The party program from 1944 foresaw state measures to achieve structural rationalization. The proposals built on the view that the capitalist system was inefficient and wasteful and unable to make use of available resources. This situation changed after the war. Committee after committee all came to the conclusion that state measures were unnecessary to achieve efficiency. Private companies managed to solve their societal task without need for help from the state as full employment was achieved. Therefore, social democracy had proclaimed the principle that only if private entrepreneurship failed, would state have to interfere.[46]

When working with the new political program of 1944, the minister of finance, Ernst Wigforss, tried to explain the social-democratic principles for economic development. When regulations in the economy through state measures were proposed, it was because there was a lack of efficiency. Socialization was not a goal in itself; the goal was that economic life would have the organization form and performance ability to give the citizens a richer life – materially as well as spiritually. Increased degrees of freedom must be realized for everyone. If, for example, it was the case that there were cartels and trusts that held prices high, social democrats were prepared to discuss practical ways to deal with this. Socialization might be so problematic to achieve that it could be better to demand free competition. To achieve this, one might have to rely on cooperatives or the creation of state companies that were established in order to achieve a state of "free competition." The problems were practical and had to be solved in a practical way.[47] It seems that Wigforss actually meant that a certain degree of competition was necessary for efficiency reasons, and whether or not, this can be called "free competition" was an open question. If the room for consumption increased for the majority through access to more commodities at lower prices, this would mean increased feelings of freedom.

Legislative developments after World War II

The Law on Surveillance over Competition Regulations in 1946 was established when Myrdal was the responsible Minister. It is clear that his economic conceptions on competition were important for the formulation of the law. He was the main proponent of expansionism, and in the proposition, it was argued that incomplete competition could mean that the productive resources of society were not fully used. This would, in turn, lead to production results below maximum levels. Monopoly could mean rationalization, which was positive, but the experience was that monopoly over a longer time period meant that technical development lagged behind and that ineffective production methods were used.[48] The law implied that a public authority – *Monopolutredningsbyrån* (Bureau of Monopoly) – was to be created, which could undertake investigations if abuse was suspected. Firms or trade associations that had agreements affecting prices, production, turnovers or distribution should register these agreements in a cartel register. Special investigations should be undertaken when misuse or damaging effects of incomplete competition were feared.

In 1951, the previously mentioned public committee Nyetableringssakkunniga (experts on new establishment)[49] proposed that the legislative framework on competition should be strengthened. The principle was still that cartels and trusts were accepted but that abuse must be combated. Limitations of competition would be judged as negative when any of three criteria was fulfilled: firstly, if limitation of competition affected prices in a way that was negative for consumers; secondly, if efficiency in business was impaired; and last, but not least, if an individual's right to run a business was threatened. Each of these was considered harmful to society and against the public interest. They constituted the basis of the 1953 Law on Restrictive Trade Practices, the *Konkurrensbegränsningslagen*.[50]

This legislation reflected, to a large extent, the social-democratic view on competition. The party had by this time been in government for many years and was to stay there until 1976. Social-democratic ideology had in the beginning of the 1950s definitely moved in the direction of the socialization of consumption instead of production. Consumer interests in terms of low prices were the focus. When it came to legislation on competition, this became visible in the fact that the law forbade the gross price system (resale price maintenance). This system meant, according to its critics, that the price was decided by the actor with the highest costs. It counteracted rationalizations and thereby diminished space for reducing prices.[51] The abandonment of the gross price system was defended by Richard Sterner who was secretary in the Trade department and one of Myrdal's closest collaborators. He argued that rationalization within distribution lagged far behind rationalization in production and that forbidding the gross price system could contribute to this rationalization. Sterner was also the author of a publication in which the main arguments from the Nyetableringssakkunniga were summarized and promoted.[52]

There was thus an emphasis on increasing competition in the distribution area. When it came to production cartels, however, they were often seen as legitimate. The steel industry was an area in which cartels were common – 34 steel cartels were registered in the cartel register in 1950.[53] Their cooperation could often be legitimated in terms of rationality and efficiency and was on the whole accepted. An indication of the acceptance of production cartels is that cartels within steel and paper still existed and were seen as contributing to the exploitation of economies of scale in public investigations in 1968.[54]

Conclusion

The 1953 competition legislation implied that social democrats had come to the conclusion that cartels should not be forbidden. Cartels and similar associations were accepted, but abuse was not. Cartels had to be registered and had to accept public investigations if abuse was suspected. Their activities were to be evaluated by three criteria, all related to the concept of social utility: the first was that the associations contributed to rationalization; the second criteria related to the benefits for consumers in the form of lower prices; and the last criteria demanded that other producers be able to enter the market. When these three criteria were met, cooperation between companies was regarded as positive.

The argument of this article is that the social-democratic discussion on cartels exposed the double aims of social democracy. One aim was to increase production, and the other to make sure that products were distributed in a fair way. The historical task of capitalism was the development of productive forces. When it did not fulfill this task and became inefficient, social democrats found it to be their job to help capitalism to develop the way it should. Increasing efficiency could be achieved through better planning and, if needed, by socialization. When production had become efficient and made big profits possible, the surplus had to be distributed in a more equal way.

Cartels, trusts and monopolies had the potential to realize economies of scale and make investments to rationalize production. If they realized their potential, this would lead to decreasing costs, thereby making possible lower prices for consumers. If they did not fulfill this task, socialization was an option for social democrats. When public investigations came to the conclusion that it was not possible in most cases to argue that private industry was inefficient, it was difficult to advocate for socialization. It was also difficult to fight cartels for reasons of efficiency. The classical liberal model of free competition was supposed to lead to low prices for consumers and low profits for producers. Economies of scale were not foreseen in such pre-mass production analysis, and it can be argued that this chapter illustrates the Swedish Social Democrats' attempts to deal with the problem of how to achieve the same goals in an economy characterized by economies of scale.

Notes

1 Bo Rothstein, *Den korporativa staten* (Stockholm: Norstedts juridik, 1992), 218 and Torbjörn Lundqvist, *Konkurrensvisionens framväxt* (Stockholm: Nordstedts, 2003), 14.
2 John Lapidus, "Social Democracy and the Swedish Welfare Model," PhD dissertation, University of Gothenburg, 2015, 75–76.

3 Diane Sainsbury, *Swedish Social Democratic Ideology and Electoral Politics 1944–1948* (Stockholm: Almqvist & Wiksell International, 1980), 101.
4 Dudley Dillard, *Västeuropas och Förenta staternas ekonomiska historia* (Lund: Liber läromedel, 1980), 357–359.
5 Ulf Bernitz, *Svensk och europeisk marknadsrätt* (Stockholm: Nordstedts, 2005), 66.
6 SFS 1925:223.
7 SOU 1940:35.
8 SFS 1946:448.
9 SOU 1951:27.
10 SFS 1953:603.
11 Herbert Tingsten, *Den svenska socialdemokratins idéutveckling* (Stockholm: Aldus/Bonnier, 1941).
12 *Tiden*, 1918, 241–256.
13 Leif Lewin, "Planhushållningsdebatten," PhD dissertation, University of Uppsala, 1967.
14 Timothy Tilton, "The Swedish Road to Socialism: Ernst Wigforss and the Ideological Foundations of Swedish Social Democracy," *American Political Science Review* 73, 2 (June 1979): 505–520, here 515.
15 Tingsten, *Den svenska socialdemokratins idéutveckling*, 304 and Lewin, *Planhushållningsdebatten*, 121.
16 Karl Gustav Landgren, *Den "nya ekonomien" i Sverige* (Stockholm: Almqvist & Wicksell, 1960), Nils Unga, *Socialdemokratin och arbetslöshetsfrågan 1912–34* (Stockholm: Arkiv för studier i arbetarrörelsens historia, 1976).
17 Sainsbury, *Swedish Social Democratic Ideology and Electoral Politics*, 101.
18 Gunnar Myrdal, *Varning för fredsoptimism* (Stockholm: Bonnier, 1944).
19 *Arbetarrörelsens efterkrigsprogram. De 27 punkterna med motivering* (Stockholm, 1944).
20 Sainsbury, *Swedish Social Democratic Ideology and Electoral Politics*, 154.
21 Lewin, *Planhushållningsdebatten*, 255.
22 Riksdag, Motion AK 1911 56:2.
23 Riksdag, Motion AK 1911 56:11.
24 Riksdag, Protocol AK 1917 nr 34: 23–26.
25 Riksdag, Protocol AK 1913, 34:33–36.
26 Riksdag, Motion FK 1920, 60.
27 *Sociala meddelanden*, 1922, nr 4, 331–332.
28 Riksdag, Protocol FK 1920, 41:92–94.
29 Riksdag, Proposition 1925, 110:30–31.
30 *Tiden*, 1926, 184–186.
31 *Tiden*, 1926, 188–189.
32 *Tiden*, 1915, 340–347.
33 *Tiden*, 1922, 57.
34 *Tiden*, 1935, 93–101.
35 *Tiden*, 1926, 186.
36 Eli F. Heckscher, *Svenskt Arbete och Liv* (Stockholm: Aldus/Bonnier, 1967), 292–294.
37 Birgit Karlsson (ed.), *Organiserad samverkan* (Möklinta: Gidlund, 2014), 33.
38 *Ibid.*, 35.
39 *Ibid.*
40 Industridepartementet Ds 1981:12; Carl Fredriksson and Sten Ljunggren, *Kooperationens industrisektor i 1980-talets industri-Sverige* (Stockholm: Åberg, 1981), 30.
41 *Tiden*, 1929, 375–376.
42 E. Lindahl, "Det kooperativa programmet," in *Ekonomisk Tidskrift* (Uppsala: Almqvist & Wiksell, 1926).
43 *Tiden*, 1941, 1–4.

44 Lewin, *Planhushållningsdebatten*, 249–251
45 *Ibid.*, 157–158.
46 *Ibid.*, 333.
47 *Ibid.*, 233–234.
48 Riksdag, Proposition 1946, 264:11.
49 SOU 1951:27.
50 SFS 1953:603.
51 Riksdag, Protocol AK 1953, 21:134.
52 *Nationalekonomiska föreningens förhandlingar*, 1 November 1951, 84–85.
53 Kommerskollegium (ed.), *Kartellregistret, Monopolutredningsbyrån* (Stockholm, 1951).
54 SOU 1968:5.

Books and journals

Arbetarrörelsens efterkrigsprogram. De 27 punkterna med motivering. Stockholm, 1944.

Bernitz, Ulf. *Svensk och europeisk marknadsrätt.* Stockholm: Nordstedts, 2005.

Dillard, Dudley. *Västeuropas och Förenta staternas ekonomiska historia.* Lund: Liber läromedel, 1980.

Fredriksson, Carl and Sten Ljunggren. *Kooperationens industrisektor i 1980-talets industri-Sverige.* Stockholm: Åberg, 1981.

Heckscher, Eli F. *Svenskt Arbete och Liv.* Stockholm: Aldus/Bonnier, 1967.

Industrins struktur och konkurrensförhållanden. Stockholm: Statens offentliga utredningar, 1968, 5.

Karlsson, Birgit (ed.), *Organiserad samverkan.* Möklinta: Gidlund, 2014.

Kartellregistret, Monopolutredningsbyrån, Kommerskollegium. Monopolutredningsbyrån. Stockholm, 1951.

Konkurrensbegränsning. Stockholm: Statens offentliga utredningar, 1951, 27.

Landgren, Karl Gustav. *Den "nya ekonomien" i Sverige.* Stockholm: Almqvist & Wicksell, 1960.

Lapidus, John. "Social Democracy and the Swedish Welfare Model." PhD dissertation, University of Gothenburg, 2015.

Lewin, Leif. "Planhushållningsdebatten." PhD dissertation, University of Uppsala, 1967.

Lindahl, Erik. "Det kooperativa programmet." In *Ekonomisk Tidskrift.* Uppsala: Almqvist & Wiksell, 1926.

Lundqvist, Torbjörn. *Konkurrensvisionens framväxt.* Stockholm: Institutet för framtidsstudier, 2003.

Myrdal, Gunnar. *Varning för fredsoptimism.* Stockholm: Bonnier, 1944.

Nationalekonomiska föreningens förhandlingar. Stockholm, 1951.

Organiserad samverkan inom svenskt näringsliv. Stockholm: Statens offentliga utredningar, 1940, 35.

Rothstein, Bo. *Den korporativa staten.* Stockholm: Norstedts juridik, 1992.

Sainsbury, Diane. *Swedish Social Democratic Ideology and Electoral Politics 1944–1948.* Stockholm: Almqvist & Wiksell International, 1980.

Sociala meddelanden. Stockholm: Norstedts, 1922.

Tiden, månadsskrift för socialistisk kritik och politik. Stockholm: Sveriges socialdemokratiska arbetareparti, 1918–1935.

Tilton, Timothy. "The Swedish Road to Socialism: Ernst Wigforss and the Ideological Foundations of Swedish Social Democracy." *American Political Science Review* 73, 2 (June 1979).

Tingsten, Herbert. *Den svenska socialdemokratins idéutveckling*. Stockholm: Aldus/ Bonnier, 1941.
Unga, Nils. *Socialdemokratin och arbetslöshetsfrågan 1912–34*. Stockholm: Arkiv för studier i arbetarrörelsens historia, 1976.

Public print

Riksdagstryck Motioner och protokoll 1911–1953
Svensk Författningssamling 1925–1953.

4 The German Trade Union Confederation and the cartel policy of the early European communities

Severin Cramm

Introduction

While in the 1950s Germany was focused on rebuilding its economy, it was also preoccupied with the redefinition of its foreign policy in the international system. The fact that the two areas were closely intertwined is natural, especially with regard to the question of European competition regulations. Competition and antitrust policy was one of the most powerful and controversial parts of economic policy at the European level. From its foundation in 1949, the German Trade Union Confederation (*Deutscher Gewerkschaftsbund*, DGB) advocated for a large number of specific economic policy concepts that had a concrete impact on socialist theoretical discourses. For example, especially in the beginning of the 1950s, it called for the cartelization and nationalization of so-called key industries and the participation of trade unions in cartelized branches of the economy, while at the same time, it condemned cartelization for profit and economic power reasons and criticized initial approaches to cartel laws in West Germany. Only in the course of the 1950s did this change after internal debates and in the context of international contacts, which the DGB established primarily within the International Confederation of Free Trade Unions (ICFTU), in which the Western-oriented trade unions were organized after the Cold War division of the World Federation of Trade Unions (WFTU).

For these reasons, the aim of this chapter is to examine the competition policy of the German and international trade union movement against the background of European integration. The thesis is that the DGB strongly linked its European and international policy with the reorganization of German economic policy, in which the (de)cartelization of the economy became the central theme. In order to do justice to the practice-oriented perspective of the DGB, the focus will be on clearly documented and outlined legal projects, like the European Coal and Steel Community (ECSC) Treaty of 1951, the DGB's internal debates on the long-discussed German antitrust law, the antitrust provisions in the Treaties of Rome of 1957, and the reinterpretation and implementation of these provisions via Council Regulation 17/62. Following the argumentation of Wolfram Kaiser and Johan Schot, the chapter considers competition policy and law in the early days of European integration not as a break with European tradition, but as a continuation and advancement of

DOI: 10.4324/9781351010573-4

genuine European traditions.[1] The aim is to integrate the social, political and economic dimensions of DGB and ICFTU policy into a multi-perspective analysis.

A trade union perspective on competition policy and law in the mirror of European integration is an under-researched topic in both the historiography of European integration and overall historical trade union research. The trade union role in transnational politics is often neglected or underestimated in general. While older literature portrays trade unions as active social and economic forces at the European level, later research has argued that trade unions were "not an important factor in the EEC and the EC"[2] and that their political efforts "did not unfold."[3] This chapter is a part of a recent trend in research that is emphasizing that trade unions had a stronger influence than scholarship has to date recognized. Pioneering projects, for example, explore the possibilities and limits of trade unions' European policy[4] or investigate individual trade union fields of action[5] and actors in the integration process.[6] This chapter builds on this approach by examining the German and European antitrust policy of the trade unions between the founding of the DGB in 1949 and Regulation 17/62. Here it argues that the DGB evolved from being critically opposed to competition to an actor in favor of strict antitrust and competition rules. This took place through concrete economic policy debates, far-reaching theoretical discourses and, above all, international exchanges. Although this development, according to this thesis, was also the result of exchanges with the German government and contacts with various stakeholders, it was first and foremost based on long-standing traditions in which it was intrinsically anchored.

The founding of the German confederation of trade unions and the beginnings of German antitrust policy

During the late 1930s and 1940s, many European countries pursued an economic policy that tended toward planning. Generally, this included nationalization, direct interventions in the economy and a public policy supportive of cartels. After 1945, these concepts were fundamentally questioned and state competition policy shifted to promoting competition and antitrust policy. The particularly strong economic concentrations in Germany were partly blamed for the rise of National Socialism, which triggered a broad debate. After the Second World War, Germany was particularly affected in economic and infrastructural terms, which hindered the supply of the population and reconstruction. The occupying powers in the beginning consequently relied on a rebuilding of old structures. Therefore, in the particularly important coal and steel industries, joint management and organizational bodies were set. The trade unions were closely involved, as they were regarded as a democratically minded and above all economically well-informed group. The poor living conditions and high working hours in the reconstruction, especially in the Ruhr region, led to great dissatisfaction and wildcat Strikes. As Brian Shaev points out, these must be seen in close context with European integration. These strikes led to fears of a strengthening of communist forces in the region and, he argues, these fears are partly responsible for the later hesitant and ultimately hostile behavior of the German SPD and the biggest German metal workers union

(IG Metall) toward the coming Schuman Plan.[7] After at least halfway regulated economic conditions had been established and supply routes restored, the cartels and concentrations of power that had initially been rebuilt were targeted by the Allied powers. Based on the conviction that they had played a major role in the success and spread of National Socialism, the Allied forces enacted anti-cartel laws, which led to bans in the late 1940s. The basis for this approach was the Potsdam Agreement, which called for the decentralization of the German economy. The confusion between active economic coordination for reconstruction and politically desired deconcentration was gradually replaced by systematic decartelization laws in the occupied zones. How profound and successful the effects of these unbundling measures were on the West German economy is historiographically controversial.[8] In the end, the different policies of the occupation zones prevented strict action against the cartelized economy. The Bizone finally adopted the pragmatic British perspective in support of reconstruction in 1948. As David Gerber notes, allied laws had little exemplary character for later German and European antitrust legislation. They were perceived by German lawmakers and attorneys as imposed and foreign.[9]

In the immediate postwar period, the German trade unions were primarily concerned initially with reconstruction and self-organization. Only gradually did the occupying powers allow the formation of zone-wide trade unions; the most influential of these was the union in the British occupation zone, already known as the *Deutscher Gewerkschaftsbund* (German Trade Union Confederation, DGB). Shortly after its foundation, this forerunner of the national DGB spoke of a 'disastrous role' played by private monopolies and demanded an elimination of monopolistic structures through 'state planning' based on the Potsdam Agreement.[10]

In contrast to complete bans, however, the DGB demanded a state takeover of the companies and co-determination of the trade unions in accordance with their plans for reorganization. The aim was to 'democratize' the cartelized economy by involving trade unions in top management, and to fully nationalize the most important 'key industries.'[11] At its founding congress in Munich in 1949, the DGB was constituted as an association of individual trade unions. Three basic goals were adopted here: build a unified trade union federation, achieve co-determination for representatives of German workers in company boards, and maintain formal independence from political parties despite the DGB's close historic ties to the SPD. The DGB was a decisive factor in the economic policy of the postwar period in large part due to the declaration of party-political neutrality, since the DGB was thus able to develop its own theoretical concepts and campaign for support from the conservative German government. With a comparatively high degree of membership of over 40% of the workforce in the beginning of the 1950s, the DGB was a decisive representative body. On the question of antitrust legislation, the DGB maintained the basic attitude that the decartelization of the economy was desirable, but that co-determination and democratization of the economy should not be impaired. At first, the DGB remained very close to the official SPD rhetoric that tied cartels to the rise of Nazi rule. For instance, DGB chairman, Hans Böckler, told the DGB's founding congress that 'it must not happen again that economic agglomerations, translated into political power, destroy a democratic state structure, as happened to the German Republic and its Weimar Constitution.'[12]

In the late 1940s, the economic model of the Freiburg School was developed under the term *ordoliberalism*, which became particularly popular in the Christian Democratic Party (CDU). It represented a different approach to cartels and competition policy. While the DGB assessed economic concentrations as positive (at least in key industries or if under democratic control), the central thesis of ordoliberalism was the creation of as free competition as possible by unbundling and breaking up economic concentrations. Consumers and individual businesses needed federal law to withstand concentrations of power but beyond that, the state should not intervene. For ordoliberals, this economic vision should become the central objective of German competition policy. The debate between the social-democratic view and that of the CDU-led government of West Germany on economic policy issues was thus theoretically preordained.[13]

The first large-scale debate in postwar Germany was on the International Ruhr Authority (IAR). This body had been established by the allied powers in April 1949 to internationally supervise and control the coal and steel production in the Ruhr area – in the beginning without German participation. The SPD immediately and loudly protested against this breach of sovereignty of the West German people. Demonstrations against foreign rule also came from the mining and steelworkers' unions, which were directly affected by it. Shortly after Konrad Adenauer became Federal Chancellor of Germany, he announced in the Petersberg Declaration that he wished to join the International Ruhr Authority (IAR). Through this concession, Konrad Adenauer achieved far-reaching concessions of the Allies to German sovereignty. From the point of view of the SPD, however, German accession to the IAR legitimized foreign rule over the Ruhr industry. After this severe criticism from the social-democratic forces, an inner German agreement toward the IAR seemed remote. Adenauer needed support for his position to ensure political stability. The German trade unions had initially rejected the IAR in early 1949, also criticizing, in particular, the foreign control of German industry. While the DGB had still described the IAR as 'a one-sided supremacy' in accordance with the SPD at the beginning of 1949, the chairman of the DGB, Hans Böckler, declared in November 1949 after consultation with Adenauer that the DGB would support Adenauer's move. Within the DGB and SPD, Böckler defended this step against harsh criticism, arguing that further dismantling in the Ruhr region could be halted. The trade unions also achieved participation with a seat in the IAR.[14]

Germany's first antitrust legislation, which surfaced in 1949, was clearly based on Christian-democratic-backed ordoliberal ideas.[15] This bill, known as the 'Josten draft,' had been designed by experts since 1946 on the initiative of the Council of States of the American Occupation Zone, headed by Paul Josten, pre-NS head of the cartel department at the Reich Ministry of Economics.[16] As the first serious proposal for a German antitrust and competition law, it was intensively discussed and continuously developed further by the federal government and various interest groups. The Josten draft was based on an almost complete ban on cartels and harmful economic concentrations. It provided for the creation of an independent

Monopoly Office, which would define norms to combat harmful economic power concentrations. The office would be enabled to impose regulations, including fines and prohibit mergers.[17] At the beginning of 1950, it became apparent that a concrete draft law was possible. The question of Allied, and in particular, American influence on this early draft is quite controversial in research. Frank Pitzer points out that although no direct cooperation with the allied powers can be proven in the late proposal, indirect pressure from allied supervision was noticeable. Nevertheless, he points to the genuinely German ordoliberal basis of the draft law.[18] Brigitte Leucht refers to the role of US representatives as mediators and pressure exerters.[19] Lisa Murrach-Brandt, however, describes these early influences as an impulse for an internal advancement based on European traditions.[20]

However, the proposal was ultimately rejected by Economic Minister Ludwig Erhard because it was too radical politically. Still, it became the cornerstone for later proposals.[21] Criticism of the draft came, for example, from the largest German employers' association, the Federation of German Industries (BDI), which rejected the far-reaching prohibition clause and preferred an abuse clause, which was to come into effect only if a dominant market position was demonstrably exploited. It argued that this principle had been proven in Germany and that an abuse principle would weaken Germany's competitiveness within Europe.[22] A similar argumentation was adopted by the German trade unions in this early phase. In particular, the trade union-oriented Wirtschaftswissenschaftliches Institut (WWI) repeatedly commented on cartel issues. Rolf Wagenführ, who became the head of statistical offices after the West German merger of the statistical trade union offices, argued in the tradition of some socialist theoretical considerations from the interwar period (like the Swedish Social Democrats in Birgit Karlsson's chapter) that a cartelized capitalist economy would be a natural step on the way to socialism as free competition was irrational and public control was required to organize the market economy (see also Harm G. Schröter's chapter in this publication.) With this, the WWI employee, who went on to work in the European institutions as first director general of its Statistical Office, argued that unions would have to stand up for ordering in the market, which in many cases would mean maintaining inter-company ties.[23]

The DGB expressed its concerns later in much more detail. In a 52-page brochure, 'The Illusion of Free Competition' ('Die Illusion des freien Wettbewerbs') published in 1950, the DGB's view is placed in the context of the DGB's co-determination and democratization policies. The brochure addressed the Josten draft very explicitly. Although it rejected cartels and monopolies that lead to increased prices and exploitation, it also condemned a fundamental ban. As the introduction stated:

> We are against monopolistic practices as far as they affect production. We are in favor of regulatory measures (which have nothing to do with the capitalist cartel) as far as they enable organized research standardization . . . of production and higher performance. We are also opposed to ruinous competition; on the contrary, long-term redeployment and lack of mobility of productive forces require protection and control and specific healing.[24]

In addition, individual exceptions were discussed. For example, the trade unions demanded that no separate regulations be introduced for branded goods. Non-profit organizations (such as trade unions) should also be explicitly excluded from the law. The DGB also demanded that condition cartels receive automatic approval unless revoked, simply because of their frequency. 'Exclusively large industrial branches of organization' were to be converted into common property because of their inevitable monopoly position. The federation argued that the entire basic concept of a free economy based on the broadest possible competition could never be achieved, because the entrepreneurial ownership of the means of production ran counter to it. Furthermore, it would not be desirable anyway because it would hinder research, exacerbate structural crises and restrict rationalization. The bill for restrictive competitive practices was therefore fundamentally rejected on the basis of what was still a clear criticism of capitalism from an economic planning perspective.[25] A later publication then delineated nine central requirements, among which were 'special legal measures for companies with a dominant market position,' 'the creation of a central monopoly commission as a department of the Federal Ministry of Economics and Technology,' publicity of restrictive agreements among businesses, and the creation of an independent monopoly court, the decisions of which would be made public. The DGB's Federal Executive Committee sent these demands in a letter to the German parliament demanding that they be taken into account in any German cartel legislation under consideration.[26]

The Schuman plan negotiations and the first European antitrust legislation

In May 1950, French Foreign Minister Robert Schuman proposed that French and German coal and steel production should be subject to a joint supranational authority open to other European countries. This was intended to improve production and quality and ensure the supply of coal on equal terms. The plan seemed ambitious, as the coal and steel industries were of great importance for the reconstruction of Europe and for overall economic development. Especially after the Monnet Plan, which initially provided for an external restriction and control of the German coal and steel industry, the proposal for equal cooperation at the international level was rather surprising. These industries were also essential to the arms industry, and Schuman's proposal was couched in a pacifist language that it would make another war impossible between France and Germany.

Adenauer's government, building on its policy of 'Westpolitik,' quickly declared its support for the plan. The SPD, on the other hand, found it difficult to support the project. It took also a surprisingly long time for the DGB to openly position itself on the Schuman plan, considering that the plan would have massive implications for the Ruhr area, one of the core areas of German trade union membership. At an ICFTU conference in Düsseldorf in May 1950, Franz Grosse and Hans vom Hoff of the DGB stated that the plan was 'not a cartel in the old sense' and that the 'idea of the Schuman Plan was generally accepted.'[27] After a phone call from the high-ranking diplomat in the Foreign Office, Herbert Blankenhorn, Hans vom Hoff finally wrote a letter to Konrad Adenauer on June 7, 1950, in which he expressed cautious trade-union support for the plan under the condition that the trade unions be included in the negotiations.[28] Adenauer again needed support for such a politically controversial plan with far-reaching effects on Germany. He accepted the offer, thus inviting Hans vom Hoff, Rolf Wagenführ and Franz Grosse to join the German delegation at the intergovernmental negotiations. The trade unions were pleased that Robert Schuman had included the goal of 'the equalization and improvement of the living conditions of workers in these industries'[29] and hoped that on this basis, they would be able to achieve better trade union participation in the German political process.

In June 1950, the negotiations began on a positive and optimistic note. Then, in the autumn of 1950, Monnet surprised the German side in the negotiations by supporting US demands that very far-reaching unbundling measures and antitrust legislation be included in the community under the supervision of the supranational High Authority. This would ultimately have resulted in the unbundling of the Ruhr region. Exceptions should only be permitted with the approval of the High Authority. After heated arguments, both the French and German sides drew up proposals for a cartel article in the treaties. The French proposals went relatively far in this respect, prohibiting all practices that could affect competition, production quotas, products, customers or resources. The German side did not initially envisage such far-reaching antitrust and competition provisions. The German trade unions in particular played a role in the debates on these drafts and spoke out against far-reaching unbundling. The pressure becomes clear, for example, with the unbundling of the Coal Sales Syndicate (DKV) and the German coal and mining management (DKBL) that were initially set up to ensure sufficient provisions for the population and the reconstruction in postwar Germany. The trade unions were heavily involved in the management and administration of these organizations. Accordingly, the DGB had a particular interest in maintaining the organization and, above all, trade union participation within the framework of what would become the ECSC. However, when it became clear in the course of the negotiations that the unbundling of the organizations was not to be prevented, the DGB increased the pressure on Adenauer by threatening to withdraw from the negotiations should the decartelization articles find their way into the Treaties. There followed several rounds of crisis talks – the DGB consulted the French and German negotiators, and then Jean Monnet, Konrad Adenauer and the American High Commissioner – as a result of which the dismantling of these organizations became only part of the transitional provisions.[30] Even though the German side finally acquiesced to a far-reaching ban on cartels in negotiations with the French and American representatives in 1951, the trade unions became particularly active in efforts to prevent or mitigate the smashing of the Ruhr cartels.

In contrast to the cautious support of the Schuman Plan by the DGB, the mechanical industry workers' union (IG Metall) and the coal miners' union (IG Bergbau) took an increasingly public stance against it. Initially, these unions adopted an ambivalent stance, particularly in view of the cautious approval of the DGB and ICFTU. However, this changed at the latest by the time the first draft treaty was presented in May 1951. On the one hand, their industries were directly affected by the unbundling; on the other hand, they feared a resurgence of communist tendencies in their companies that might result from any negative effects of the Schuman Plan much more than the trade union confederation executive.[31] At a meeting of the Advisory Board, IG Metall came to the conclusion that it could not approve the treaty in this form 'under any circumstance.'[32] In particular, the then chairman of IG Metall, Walter Freitag, argued inside the DGB executive, that 'in his opinion, France alone has an interest in the realization of this plan, since all the advantages are on its side'[33] and complained that the interests of IG Metall were being ignored since it was not directly represented in the DGB delegation to the negotiations.

Regardless, the result of the international negotiations was a strict competition and antitrust law, which prohibited cartels in principle with the possibility of exemptions, and provided for merger control with a monopoly ban, to be overseen by the independent High Authority. This made the anti-cartel provisions of the ECSC Treaty (Articles 65 and 66) more comprehensive than all the cartel laws in the member states, which were either currently in progress or based on outdated laws. The text of the ECSC Treaty severely restricted the contractual freedom of the coal and steel companies.[34] The resulting Treaty of Paris was signed in April 1951. It has long been recognized as an important step in European antitrust legislation.[35] Nevertheless, no necessary registration for cartels was established, whereas notification conditions for mergers were very well developed. In the end, the High Authority of the ECSC authorized the majority of the cartels and mergers put before it in the 1950s. Instead of the authority developing into a strong supervisory body, the states largely regulated these issues on an intergovernmental basis.[36] According to Tobias Witschke, the High Authority thus merely took on the role of informally legitimizing national and industrial decisions to reconcentrate industry despite the anti-cartel and merger provisions of the Paris Treaty.[37]

Shortly before the treaty's ratification, the German trade unions achieved one of their central antitrust objectives: the legal establishment of parity co-determination for the trade unions in the coal and steel industry, which had already been practiced since the time of occupation in the Montan Co-determination Act of 1951. It established parity co-determination in the supervisory board for big coal and steel companies. The loss of its position in the coal and steel industry had previously been one of the DGB's biggest fears in competition legislature. The German ratification of the Paris Treaty followed in June 1952. After this, a remarkably rapid legislative procedure for the *Works Constitution Act* was initiated, which limited the parity to the coal and steel industries. Horst Thum developed the thesis in 1982 that the DGB had bought its approval of the Co-determination Act for coal and steel by agreeing to Adenauer's foreign policy, but that it had stabbed the DGB in the back via the Works Constitution Act.[38] It is generally accepted that Adenauer did not confront the DGB with the Works Constitution Act, which was delayed until the adoption of the ECSC. However, the available sources show that the DGB's commitment to the West was not only requested by Adenauer but also clearly part of the DGB's program. The Works Constitution Act was seen as a great defeat for the DGB and lead to Christian Fette being voted out of office and to a change of policy by the DGB under a new elected chairman, Walter Freitag. Partially as a result, the IG Metall gained a much stronger weight within the DGB, prompting a reorientation of policy toward the ECSC as illustrated in a letter Freitag wrote to Jean Monnet in August 1953. Freitag wrote that the ECSC 'created a cartel and syndicate in Western Europe of a size which had not existed before' and called for co-determination of the German trade unions to be extended into European institutions. He also demanded that the planned unbundling of coal sales (DKV) should be re-examined, as this unbundling would 'affect the vital interests of the German people, in particular the fate of millions of workers employed in industry.' This correspondence reflects the diverging interests between IG Metall and IG Bergbau on the Ruhr coal sales syndicate.[39] Initially, Freitag caused the DGB to lose most of its pro-European spirit, but after IG Metall gained a significantly higher representation in the institutions, IG Metall was able to develop a more conciliatory note during the 1950s. In 1957, finally, IG Metall even stated in its annual report that 'the activities of the ECSC had contributed to improving economic and social conditions.'[40]

Discussions within the DGB on the German cartel law

Although the Josten draft presented in 1949 had been defeated mainly due to pressure from industry, it became the basis for a new draft law presented in May 1951. After receiving expert opinions and repeated consultations between the Federal Government and interest groups, a revised draft law emerged in the spring of 1952 following fierce negotiations with the Allied powers. It was submitted to the Bundesrat, and then to the Bundestag in June 1952 for deliberation. The draft law once again provided for a fundamental ban on cartels and monopolies, but now mentioned exceptions for branded goods, licensing rights and sea transport. The new draft, based on the influence of expert groups and above all the BDI, provided significantly more exceptions to the prohibition principle. The DGB was skeptical of this draft. There were 'strong concerns' about the law's rationale, as the trade union considered freedom of competition through the abolition of economic power an 'illusion.' It was generally doubtful whether the 'suitability of the liberal economic system' was viable on the basis of Germany's experience. In addition, the principle of prohibition was generally opposed, as it also concerned 'economically valuable mechanisms.' Progress on the first draft was noted, for example, in the areas of trademark articles and planned criminal proceedings, but there was still no trade union co-determination or public access to the registers. Furthermore, 'resale price maintenance,' a form of vertical price restriction in which companies fix the resale prices of products they sell to retail shops and companies, was still allowed. The DGB took a consumer view on this issue and demanded that this form of price maintenance, which had been banned in former plans, also be prohibited. Trade unions also addressed branded goods or trademarks. These should be exempt from the competition rules. For a long time, however, it remained unclear how the law would define these 'branded articles.' The DGB feared that an ambiguous wording could be used by companies to circumvent the law. The new regulation with clear guidelines on how trademarks should be defined was seen as a clear step forward.[41]

The BDI also submitted its own disruptive counter-proposal to the pre-parliamentary debate in 1953, which reversed the discussion process and advocated the abuse principle, that is, it would allow cartels in principle and place the burden of proof of abuse on the state. Due to numerous requests in the Economic Policy Committee in the Bundestag and broader controversies in economic circles, the discussed law was never put to a vote.[42]

Meanwhile, a re-evaluation of competition policy took place in the economic department of the DGB, as is made clear in a note from 1952. The text is very critical that the federal government seemed to be taking the view that 'it is sufficient to eliminate the cartels and monopolies in order to enforce the market automatism of free competition and to prohibit new forms of competition.'[43] The note states that since the publication of *The Illusion of Free Competition*, the DGB had been of the opinion that the abuse principle was preferable to a ban. However, the note argues that such a separation into 'either-or' situations was problematic, since a free economy cannot function without planning elements, and a planned economy can never function completely without competition. However, according to a DGB memo, the Federal Government did not share this view, but rather appeared to echo US preferences: 'There is no question that the views that were decisive in the Allied unbundling policy, especially American ones, played a not insignificant role and were reflected in the government draft.'[44] However, this slow shift toward a more differentiated debate initially took place internally. The next major public statement of the DGB was in April 1953, in connection with a new draft that had been developed in cooperation with interest representatives. It reaffirmed the DGB's view from 1950, stating that 'a completely free competitive economy is utopian.' Instead, cartels and monopolies are not assessed completely negatively: 'A general ban on cartels would be appropriate if it were possible in principle to do without cartels.' However, this was decidedly not the case. Instead, the DGB argued against prohibiting market-dominating companies because the risk of abuse would be compensated by their advantages.[45] In the DGB's view, cartels could serve to 'stabilize employment levels,' offer 'effective protection against loss of capital and capital shortfalls,' are 'an important condition for specialization, mass production and increased productivity,' 'make it easier to recognise and prevent the abuse of preferential economic positions' and, above all, a cartel regime such as the one envisaged 'unnecessarily complicates the development or training of advanced forms of economic organization.' In order to keep administrative work to a minimum, an abuse regulation was therefore preferable.[46]

The annual report prepared for the DGB Federal Congress in 1954 concludes that the decisive question was not that of a prohibition or abuse regulation, but that 'the main problem is likely to lie with the tasks and powers of the cartel authority.'[47] Above all, the cartel authority must be capable of acting independently and be endowed with sufficient power.[48] We see here that, within the trade union movement, the DGB's relativizing view of favoring an abuse regulation and positively evaluating economic concentrations was being repeatedly put to the test in the 1950s. Letters calling for investigations were received by the DGB executive in which national districts and individual trade unions complained about restrictive business agreements operating allegedly to the detriment of consumers. In some cases, positive reference was made to Allied decartelization laws, which was rather remarkable given how opposed the trade unions had been to them in the 1940s.[49]

In 1954, a long-awaited clarifying discussion took place between the DGB and the federal government on the subject of antitrust law. Alfred Müller-Armack, one of the most important figures in developing the idea of a 'social market economy,' represented the Federal Ministry of Economics, and Kurt Hirche and Kurt Weighardt the DGB. Müller-Armack tried to convince the trade unionists of the merits of the prohibition principle, arguing that it was 'politically and practically better,' while the term 'abuse' was difficult to define and proving its existence was much more difficult in practice. The DGB officials, by contrast, argued that this would result in an 'ineffective cartel authority,' which could endanger the competitiveness of the entire economy. The two sides could not reach an agreement because of their fundamentally contradictory economic views, but concluded that they both wanted to prevent an ineffective competition authority.[50]

Franz Grosse, formerly a DGB member of the German delegation to the ECSC negotiations, criticized the work of the High Authority in 1956. He critiqued some ECSC policies, and argued that the High Authority would have to widen supervisory authority over the entire energy and oil industries and refrain from experiments such as the dissolution of the Ruhr cartels. He demanded a pragmatic approach: 'It would be better to say openly that under the current conditions the Treaty is not feasible in a whole series of its provisions.' In his opinion, this would serve the ECSC better than 'sticking rigidly to individual articles and paragraphs and trying desperately to put them into practice under all circumstances.'[51]

The 1957 German cartel law and the EEC Treaty

After the failure of the plans for the European Defense Community (EDC), the Messina conference opened a new period of European integration. Initially, there was no great pressure to establish new competition rules, firstly, because everyone was aware of the failure of the ECSC rules in practice, secondly, because national competition laws were scarce, and, thirdly, because the influence of US demands for anti-cartel rules was diminishing. Nevertheless, it became increasingly clear that a common market would require provisions to regulate competition and that the German discussion on a national competition law would have an influence on the competition rules.[52] Under the leadership of the Belgian politician Paul-Henri Spaak, a government committee was set up in the summer of 1955 to monitor and coordinate the preparatory work for new integration treaties. The Spaak Committee based its discussions on the European competition rules developed on the basis of national traditions, European Political Community (EPC) planning and ECSC competition rules, the Havana Charter provisions, GATT discussions and the Council of Europe resolutions on cartels. It was agreed relatively quickly that measures distorting competition, unfair competition practices and distortions of effective competition should be prevented. Cartels distorting competition should therefore be prohibited.[53] National attitudes toward antitrust policy differed widely.

The French and Italian sides favored a system of administrative discretion and an abuse-clause, while German representatives insisted on a tough ban on cartels.[54] The French side also preferred a harmonization of national legislation, while the German side preferred a European framework, not least because of its own national discussions on competition law. At first, these positions seemed incompatible, also because the French side was more critical of a further deepening in this area. As Laurent Warlouzet points out, the negotiations on the competition articles of the Treaties of Rome were clearly marked and shaped by this contradiction.[55]

The ICFTU welcomed the fundamental idea of enhanced European integration at a regional conference in May 1956, where it called for the planned projects to include control bodies with far-reaching powers and competences, unlike the ECSC. These shall above all 'become organizations at the service of the general interest and not the instrument of private interest.' Only the lack of trade union participation in the negotiations was criticized.[56] Elsewhere, the chairman of the ICFTU's European regional organization, Walter Schevenels, specifically welcomed an international system of competition regulation. On the basis of the Havana Charter, he demanded an international charter, that is, international control, which would prevent monopolies, cartels and practices that restricted competition.[57]

Spaak's final report provided for restricting companies and state actions distorting competition through binding competition rules. It identified distortions of competition via monopolies and cartels as clear obstacles to the common market.[58] A compromise was reached with the new French socialist government in office after a proposal by the future European Economic Community (EEC) Commissioner Hans von der Groeben, which left its interpretation to the future supranational authorities: Article 85 initially formulated the prohibition principle in the first paragraph to ban price-fixing, tie-in practices and market sharing, but also included an exception rule in the third paragraph, for practices that did not cause demonstrable harm or that promoted common interests.[59] With this, the EEC Treaty laid the foundations for a comprehensive common European competition policy. Cartels should be treated according to the principle of prohibition with exceptions for individual cases. The Commission was given extensive supervisory and investigative powers, without initially having strong sanction mechanisms at its disposal.

Despite repeated requests and attempts at intervention, the DGB, unlike during the Schuman Plan negotiations, did not participate directly in negotiations on the Common Market and Euratom, due to its worsening relationship with the Christian Democratic government and Adenauer's determination not to allow the participation of interest groups that might derail the negotiations. The DGB and ICFTU therefore had to rely on informal and public statements to exert influence. Initially, they primarily tried to expand trade union participation in the negotiations. The DGB repeatedly complained about its exclusion, demanding 'No Euratom without the trade unions.'[60] In a statement on the final treaty draft, the ICFTU considered the common market to be a decisive step toward the unification of Europe and welcomed it particularly as an opportunity to develop international competition policy. The planned organization was seen as a concrete objective to strengthen the European economy by inter alia stimulating competition, rationalizing the division of labor and promoting mass production. To achieve this, the trade unions called for a more democratic and supranational treaty, which should include greater involvement of the trade unions in the consultative Economic and Social Council.[61] It is noteworthy that the ICFTU and the DGB, however, were committed to restoring intra-European and international competition and did not criticize the treaty's cartel and competition provisions.

The DGB had also been confronted with new developments within Germany, as the dispute over a national competition law simmered on. Under the clear influence of the BDI, a new legislative proposal was drafted, which in the meantime included various exceptions. It was presented to the Bundestag in March 1955. The draft was discussed and revised in more than 80 meetings of the Economic Committee of the Bundestag.[62] A breakthrough in the negotiation of the German Competition Act (GWB) occurred in July 1954 at the latest. After Erhard had repeatedly pleaded with the BDI, DGB and other interest groups for a hard antitrust law based on the prohibition principle, a discussion with representatives of industry took place at Petersberg. For the first time, the BDI's united front against the prohibition principle was broken. Parts of industry came out in a letter against the line of the BDI and in favor of the strict antitrust law. Although the letter was condemned by the BDI, internal division finally made it possible to negotiate a ban on cartels on the basis of the prohibition principle.[63]

Inside the DGB, the antitrust dispute also became increasingly discursive. A letter from Viktor Agartz, head of the Wirtschaftswissenschaftliches Institut (WWI), to Ludwig Rosenberg, head of the economic policy department of the DGB, makes clear how controversial a new orientation toward a pragmatic reversal inside the DGB was. Complaining about the change of direction, Agartz demanded that the DGB revert back to its previous position, quoting the DGB's 1950 brochure that, 'the cartel problem cannot be seen in isolation from today's economic order and the current economic system.'[64] The discussion apparently continued within the DGB executive board and above all in the intellectual exchange with the SPD. This is clearly stated in a Rosenberg letter from June 1955, in which he wrote about the 'difficulties' the antitrust legislation raised for the trade unions. The DGB would have to exchange views once again with 'the party,' as it was more sensible to 'comment on individual questions and no longer on the entire problem.'[65] Obviously, there were profound differences in the perception of the cartel problem between the DGB and the SPD. The basic demands for a clearer definition of exceptions, greater publicity for decisions and registers and, above all, for the prevention of retail price maintenance remained.

Following this, the DGB gradually changed its position on competition policy – also as the pressure grew from consumers against economic concentrations in a wide variety of economic sectors such as potash production or mining. In 1955, to name an example, the DGB executive board reacted to massive criticism from consumer associations against a 'film fee' to be levied, that is, a special payment to cinema box offices for a film cartel to be created, with the statement that it was 'a dangerous start to a conditions cartel which could easily be joined by other branches of industry. The DGB has always opposed the formation of cartels.'[66]

To return to the cartel law, the SPD parliamentary representation requested that the DGB take a position 'on details of the draft law.' The previous statements had already led to a parliamentary discussion on maximum price fixing. The DGB's view that an abuse principle should be established, however, remained controversial. It was 'necessary to define the concept of abuse more precisely in order to reaffirm our previously expressed opinion that the Competition Act should be structured as an abuse law.'[67] In any case, the DGB continued to insist in public that a cartel authority must continue to allow certain economically sensible cartels. The 1956 annual report, for example, asserts that the DGB had not been prompted to 'deviate from its originally expressed views.' In the responsible Allied commission, the DGB asked above all about the impact on workers, questioned the price structure from the consumer's point of view and doubted that the cartel would be monitored properly without a Cartel Office or the publication of a register. Under certain circumstances, however, cartel formation continued to be 'economically healthier' in its view.[68]

From June 1956, responsibility for cartel issues within the Economic Department of the DGB directed by Rosenberg was transferred to Gerhard Kroebel, DGB economic expert and member of the Economic Policy Committee of the SPD Party Executive Committee. This key economic advisor of the German members of the European Economic and Social Committee, at that time, also dealt with working time, economic cycles and education. Interestingly, Kroebel wrote a letter on the controversial discussion of antitrust legislation and referred to the publications of the DGB in earlier years:

> At that time, our position – with the cooperation of Dr. Agartz – was based on the so-called principle of abuse. It will still be remembered from the discussions at that time that the opinions of our colleagues were not uniform and today one often has the impression that the general opinion tends towards the principle of prohibition. Apart from the fact that, in my opinion, both overvalued alternatives do not exhaust the possibilities of combating abuse – the so-called prohibition principle ultimately also amounts to such a line – the current question is whether it is at all opportune for the trade unions to be heard in the concert of the business associations.[69]

Kroebel's comments thus demonstrate very well that there had been a change of opinion within the DGB and that tactics must therefore also be adapted vis-a-vis forthcoming legislation. In the letter, however, he admitted that it would make more sense for practical reasons to wait for the legislative discussion to begin before making clear demands, 'Not to mention whether or not we stick to our previous position.'[70] This view was confirmed at the DGB Federal Congress in October 1956. The increasing private monopolization of the economy worried the congress, so the Executive Board included a paragraph on antitrust in its resolution on General Economic Policy, where it demanded an 'early adoption of an effective antitrust law' with the support of key industry associations, which was adopted.[71]

In the context of the introduction of various draft laws and consultations with associations and interest groups, the adoption of the GWB was delayed until July 1957. Discussions on the antitrust law even led the CDU/CSU faction to turn away from the principle of prohibition. On several occasions, most recently in March 1957, its parliamentary group published a statement in which it no longer categorically ruled out the abuse principle.[72] As a categorical defense, the DGB then developed striking new notes defending an increasingly hard legislative initiative based on the principle of prohibition. In March 1957, for example, the DGB criticized the CDU/CSU for the current proposal, which on the one hand would continue to allow retail price maintenance and on the other would soften the principle of prohibition by way of exemptions. The DGB argued that the proposal left too much scope for discretion.[73] The Bundestag passed a revised law on July 3, 1957. The DGB now openly advocated a tough law and the principle of prohibition. On July 5, 1957, the DGB published a press release defending Erhard's original law:

> A genuine anti-cartel law should not only establish free competition according to the unanimous will of the Federal Minister of Economics, the Bundestag opposition and the German Trade Union Federation, but should also protect it from those forces that abuse their economic power to the detriment of consumers.[74]

With the current law, however, this was no longer the case, especially since the principle of prohibition has been abandoned and the 'door and gate' is opened through exceptions to price fixing. The DGB expected changes to the 'unsatisfactory new law.'[75] The GWB came into force at the same time as the Rome Treaty on 1 January 1958 and replaced the Allied decartelization regulations, containing a very strict cartel law in European comparison.

After the signing of the Treaty of Rome, the 'Common Market Committee' within the DGB examined its likely effects on the German market in preparation for its work in the European Economic and Social Committee. This Committee was particularly interested in the antitrust issue. On the one hand, the Committee criticized the fact that within the treaty, different perspectives on cartels would exist in parallel and, on the other hand, that the interpretation of these differences could have clear effects, for example, on real wages. Interestingly, it regretted that the DGB had not yet dealt with the cartel problem. It was therefore decided to make the issue more tangible in the DGB by clarifying the effects of the agreement on the trade unions.[76] The report finally submitted by the Committee recommended that the DGB, in view of its effects on intergovernmental trade, accept the principle of prohibition and thus interpret Articles 85 to 87 in such a way that they only permit cartels in certain circumstances.[77] The SPD was also constructively involved in the negotiations on German and European antitrust law. Schröter, for example, points out in his chapter of this anthology that Erhard's tough cartel law was supported by large sections of the SPD from at least 1954. For example, in the 1954 Bundesrat vote, only SPD members supported Erhard and the SPD had worked against excessively large exemptions in the debate on the competition law. The negative vote of the SPD against the 1957 law on competition was due to excessively large exemptions and the perceived ineffectiveness of the proposed cartel law.

Disputes over the antitrust law arose again when a regulatory regime to enforce the cartel provisions came under intense discussion in the early 1960s. The European Commission's draft to concretize European antitrust legislation aimed to resolve the contradiction between Articles 85 and 87. In addition to a generally strong European antitrust policy, which the DGB had already pursued in the context of the GWB, the DGB was striving for a number of specific objectives in the debate. Firstly, it wanted to ban resale price maintenance in the new regulation and extend the competence of the regulation to all kinds of economic concentrations. This is clear in a newsletter from the economic department of the DGB[78] and in the position that the DGB took at the European level in the ICFTU, where it also called for the integration of a ban on retail price maintenance into the regulation and for reviews of diverse forms of economic concentrations.[79] Secondly, the DGB demanded an independent cartel office with its own supranational powers.[80] Revealingly, the DGB even went so far as not to include trade unions in the decisions of such an office so as not to hinder the decision-making capacity of the body, thus a powerful antitrust office appears to have taken priority over political co-determination. The third issue to be discussed within the DGB was the extent to which national implementations of European law should be monitored. An employee of the economic department of the DGB, Wilhelm Merl, asserted here that minimum rules should be required for the exercise of Articles 85 and 86 in order to prevent differences of interpretation in the Member States. Interestingly, he points out that the hard competition laws must not be undermined by more lenient interpretations of European law; competitiveness in Germany must therefore not be jeopardized.[81] In addition, the DGB advocated that the procedure and register be as transparent as possible and accessible to the public. The DGB promoted these positions at the European level, which can be seen in references to 'several meetings in Brussels' during this period.[82]

In addition to these meetings, the DGB was coordinating its actions with the Bundeskartellamt, which took a similar view and, in view of German law, also pushed for a tough European regulation.[83] In connection with its cooperation with the Bundeskartellamt, Merl also questioned the DGB's cautious view of the Bundeskartellamt: Merl derived from the experience of the DGB since its foundation that neither a planned economy nor unbridled competition were ideal economic systems, which is why he recommended concentrating on concrete economic policy goals by balancing between both systems. From this, he now deduced that the Bundeskartellamt had to be seen as a helpful 'instrument.' It was now necessary to work to reduce the number of exceptions to the GWB and to abandon its 'cautious' position on the Cartel Office. Instead, the DGB should now 'call oneself even more the guardian of competition than before – together with the office,' which would certainly also 'meet with a positive response from the Bundeskartellamt.'[84] Merl's internal discussion paper shows a competition policy discussion in the DGB economic department that is shaking the cornerstones of antitrust policy to date, although based on earlier internal debates. Instead of an idealistic, competition-critical attitude, Merl called on the DGB to commit itself to a competition-oriented policy as long as it helped achieve economic policy goals. The demand to declare oneself the 'guardian of competition' means a clear break with the brochure a few years earlier. It is interesting, however, that Merl clearly argued from the consumer's point of view and with the purpose of developing a political framework for action, thus incorporating arguments from the previous position.

After the first draft of the Council regulation was published during the negotiations in Brussels, the discussions within the DGB culminated in a publication that affirmed the DGB's position. It welcomed that an implementing regulation was now to replace national authorities with EEC law and so the patchwork of different national regulatory systems would be dissolved. It also confirmed that Article 85, which is based on the principle of prohibition, was preferred to Article 86. The statement then considers the individual planned articles and criticizes above all weakly formulated articles, which might permit a circumvention of the German law by means of a European detour. In principle, the document gives a positive assessment of the Implementing Regulation, in particular because of its harsher interpretation, based on Germany's strict law. However, the lack of transparency and publicity of the decisions is assessed negatively.[85] An internal document written shortly afterward noted that the DGB was also satisfied that retail price maintenance fell under the new regulation. The question of the obligation to register cartels, that is, a hard interpretation, was also discussed in the Economic and Social Committee, which was partly composed of trade unionists. The Economic Policy Division of the DGB noted that the trade unions in Europe are 'practically the only ones' who were advocating such a hard regulation. One had to assert oneself in this question against employers, above all the French side and against the 'German cartel lobby.' The trade unions must, the document asserted, 'vigorously put a stop to these efforts.'[86] The dissolution of the national patchwork and the unresolved contradictions in the EEC Treaty demanded by the DGB was to take place in February 1962 via Regulation 17/62. As demanded by the trade unions, a general prohibition was based on Article 85 that accorded with the German model. However, the regulation provided for non-publication of the decisions, which was contrary to the DGB demands. A far-reaching publicity and an involvement of the trade unions were excluded.[87] In the next years, the Bosch-De Geus and Grundig-Consten cases at the European Court of Justice strengthened the regulation in practice. In 1963, when the DGB published a new program of principles, it was clear that the DGB had completely abandoned its earlier ambivalence on questions of cartels and competition: 'Every economy, that is oriented toward competition, needs economic planning.' It is therefore necessary to restrict or prevent 'the formation of cartels, monopolies and oligopolies,' which was why the DGB considered the 'principle of prohibition' absolutely necessary.[88]

The importance of different interest groups for the development of this regulation is the subject of ongoing discussion in historiographic research. The importance of the regulation is also underlined in this chapter, as can be seen, for example, from the fact that the previous laws were criticized several times and that trade unionists were demanding that institutions regulating competition be granted more capacity to act. However, the conclusion that German ordoliberalism was the only significant influence over this regulation appears to be greatly exaggerated. It turns out that not only ordoliberalism but also various networks, like the European trade unions, exerted influence, developed a concrete competition policy and succeeded in implementing elements of their visions through their contacts and public relations. Frank Pitzer also argues that the compromise solution of the implementing regulation showed that Germany was prepared to make larger compromises after the GWB was passed. The exceptional areas of the GWB could also be accepted at the European level as long as German antitrust legislation was not affected.[89] Sigfrido M. Ramírez Pérez and Sebastian van den Scheur in particular have relativized the influence of ordoliberalism and highlighted the influences of a New Keynesian orientation during this period.[90] Shaev points in this direction in his chapter of this book analyzing the Socialist Group in the European parliament, which held intensive discussions with European representatives and economic experts on the issue of cartels, warned against a 'Europe of monopolies and cartels' and therefore advocated a strong antitrust policy. On the one hand, they thus remained direct supporters of the Commission and, on the other hand, they become an important factor in pushing for supranational enforcement powers to carry out the objectives Regulation 17/62, like Shaev also shows in his chapter in this publication. By examining DGB internal discussions over more than a decade, this section shows that trade union discourses were much more contested and less pro-cartel than previously presented. One can no longer speak of a hegemony of ordoliberalism, at least for the period leading up to 1962, since many other networks left their traces on the European framework as demonstrated in other chapters of this book. Especially on the question of the interpretation of Regulation 17/62, it becomes clear that trade unions advocated a model that would guarantee the greatest possible transparency and practical assertiveness – dimensions that they thought would have led to a stronger regulation.

Conclusion

This chapter examines how the DGB's view of German and European antitrust policy developed from 1949 to 1962. It is framed in both historical national and European contexts, without simplifying dissenting voices and ambivalent attitudes. It shows first of all that the DGB initially advocated a permissive antitrust policy after its foundation, that is, it emphasized the benefits of concentrations of power in the economy and argued in favor of an abuse regulation instead of a prohibition regulation. Firstly, this initial attitude can be explained by recourse to interwar discussions. Even though, as current research shows, tendencies toward an aggressive anti-cartel policy can be discerned in the trade unions (e.g. in the DMV)[91] for a long time, there was a restrained, sometimes even cartel-friendly theoretical discussion in the socialist movement. Secondly, this was also due to the special economic situation after the Second World War, in which trade unions were rooted above all in the coal and steel industries that were the most heavily cartelized in the German economy. The DGB therefore had a natural interest in maintaining these economic concentrations in order to safeguard its own participation. However, some of the DGB's constituent unions had an interest in breaking up cartels in other economic sectors. Especially, the mining trade union saw the anti-cartel and competition laws as a way to break up the old hegemony of German steel over German coal but they became concerned when Jean Monnet announced his plan to break up the coal syndicates themselves. Thirdly, this was also due to the DGB's economic-theoretical concepts. The DGB's demands referred to the socialization of key industries or, at least, the inclusion of trade unions in co-determination bodies for most companies. These goals, it seemed, would not have been possible if a consistent competition and unbundling policy had been implemented.

Not even 10 years later, this view had completely changed. During the debates for the German cartel law and the Treaties of Rome, the DGB supported a hard regulation on the basis of a prohibition principle at national and European levels that would contain as few exceptions as possible and that should be implemented by an authority that would be as independent and powerful as possible. Ultimately, the DGB even discussed whether it should present itself alongside the cartel authorities as the 'guardian of competition.' This change can be traced back to a number of factors that I have analyzed in this chapter. First, the DGB had to give up most parts of its socialization and co-determination plans following the adoption of the Work Council Constitution Act, which categorically excluded the expansion of co-determination of the coal and steel industry to other industries (the DGB had called e.g. for an extension to the chemical industry and the railway). Such an extension was still often demanded, but seemed unattainable. Thus, one of the main reasons for the soft cartel view became outdated. Second, even within the DGB, the American influence on antitrust legislation was being discussed. How strong this influence actually was can hardly be proven beyond doubt. The fact that the DGB explicitly mentions this external influence in its own documents, however, points to a greater significance. Thirdly, experience with the relatively weak ECSC cartel competence, ultimately determined by national directions, certainly had an influence on the turnaround. Fourthly, there is evidence of consultations between the federal government and the DGB on the one hand and representatives of supranational European institutions on the other, in which active attempts were made to convince the DGB of a hard cartel line. Fifthly, it can be seen that individual trade unions had already taken harder positions in individual cases, such as the film cartel, the potash cartel and also in the case of the miners' union in the coal and steel cartel, which was ultimately also noticed in the Executive Board.

From a trade union perspective, an active economic policy at that time was to be understood as a combination of elements of liberal competition and economic planning that would include the creation and enforcement of strong national and European competition regulations. As Karin van Leeuwen points out in her chapter on Dutch social democracy, competition policy was also understood by socialist forces as an instrument of labor market and welfare policy, especially in the 1950s and 1960s, based on concepts of 'ordering' the market. Trade union development must also be seen in this light. Initially, the DGB tried to remove economically sensible cartels from the legislation. It saw cartels as a link between economic planning and liberalism, through which planning elements could be integrated into economic policy. Moreover, it did not want to jeopardize the concept of a 'democratic economy,' which provided for the socialization of key industries and co-determination of trade unions in companies. However, when the concrete plans became unattainable under the Works Constitution Act and the market economy asserted itself as West Germany's economic system, the everyday interests of consumers and the media came to the fore, which increasingly rejected cartels. Moreover, the opinion-forming process within the DGB did not take place abruptly, but was characterized by internal disputes within the Executive Board, with individual trade unions and individuals and, above all, by long lines of tradition in the cartel discussion. The DGB underwent a slow yet thorough process of internal change, which ultimately transformed the Confederation into an advocate of a strong antitrust office in a competitive economic policy. A sudden and uncontroversial change of direction by German Social Democrats, and especially the German trade unions in this question after the Second World War, as it is often constructed, cannot withstand a multi-causal and multi-perspective methodology, as Schröter shows in his chapter. All the more interesting is the assessment that the European socialist and social-democratic bodies, which by and large had pursued an ambivalent competition policy during the interwar period and in some cases even after the Second World War, were to become an important proponent for tough antitrust policies in the course of the negotiations on the Treaties of Rome, that is, they supported as independent and efficient an antitrust authority as possible on the basis of a comprehensive and strict catalogue of laws. This influence, which at European level can definitely be seen in Shaev's chapter, contradicts a one-sided, even strongly nation-centered view of a conflict between ordoliberalism and economic interests. Rather, it must be said in a more differentiated way that the socialist-social-democratic-bodies, as interest groups, wanted to exert a clear influence on European competition policy and demonstrably they did so. This argumentation is also followed by this chapter, in which a complex and differentiated cartel discussion within the DGB is traced on the basis of internal DGB documentation and ICFTU sources. In the context of this publication, an overall picture emerges for the period between 1949 and 1962, in which the DGB, as a decidedly social-democratic and, at least in its early days, largely independent factor in the European system, set important impulses into motion in German and European competition policy, developed its own objectives and, in an internal, thoroughly contested opinion-forming process, developed into a clearly competition-oriented economic actor.

Notes

1 Wolfram Kaiser and Johan Schot, *Writing the Rules for Europe* (New York: Palgrave Macmillan, 2014); Heike Schweitzer and Kiran Klaus Patel, "EU Competition Law in Historical Context," in Kiran Klaus Patel and Heike Schweitzer (eds.), *The Historical Foundations of EU Competition Law* (Oxford: Oxford University Press, 2013), 207–230.

2 Lutz Niethammer, "Defensive Integration – Der Weg zum EGB und die Perspektive einer westeuropäischen Einheitsgewerkschaft," in Ulrich Borsdorf (ed.), *Gewerkschaftliche*

Politik: Reform aus Solidarität. Zum 60. Geburtstag von Heinz O. Vetter (Cologne: Bund, 1977), 567–596.

3 Heinz-Jürgen Axt, "Westeuropäische Integration, Nationalstaat und Arbeiterbewegung," in Frank Deppe (ed.), *Arbeiterbewegung und westeuropäische Integration* (Cologne: Pahl-Rugenstein, 1976), 98–141.

4 Jürgen Mittag (ed.), *Mitteilungsblatt des Instituts für soziale Bewegungen 42. Deutsche Gewerkschaften und europäische Integration im 20. Jahrhundert* (Bochum: Klartext, 2009).

5 Rainer Fattmann, *Für ein soziales Europa. Der Agrar-, Lebensmittel- und Tourismusbereich in der europäischen Gewerkschaftspolitik seit der Gründung der europäischen Wirtschaftsgemeinschaft* (Münster: Dampfboot, 2013).

6 Yves Clairmont, *Vom europäischen Verbindungsbüro zur transnationalen Gewerkschaftsorganisation. Organisation, Strategien und Machtpotentiale des Europäischen Metallgewerkschaftsbundes bis 1990* (Stuttgart: Franz Steiner, 2014).

7 Brian Shaev, "Workers' Politics, the Communist Challenge, and the Schuman Plan: A Comparative History of the French Socialist and German Social Democratic Parties and the First Treaty for European Integration," *International Review of Social History* 61, 2 (August 2016): 251–281.

8 Hartmut Bechtold, *Die Kartellierung der deutschen Volkswirtschaft und die sozialdemokratische Theorie-Diskussion vor 1933* (Frankfurt am Main: Haag + Herchen, 1986), 248; Tony A. Freyer, *Antitrust and Global Capitalism* (New York: Cambridge University Press, 2007), 246–260.

9 David J. Gerber, "Constitutionalizing the Economy: German Neo-Liberalism, Competition Law and the 'New' Europe," *American Journal of Comparative Law* 42, 25 (January 1994): 25–84, 63.

10 Dokument 251, 21 August 1946: "Entschließung der Gewerkschaftskonferenz der britischen Zone zur Beseitigung der Monopole. Protokoll der Gewerkschaftskonferenz der britischen Zone vom 21. bis 23. August 1946 in Bielefeld" (Bielefeld, 1946), 23, in: Hermann Weber and Siegfried Mielke (eds.), *Quellen zur Geschichte der deutschen Gewerkschaftsbewegung im 20. Jahrhundert. Gewerkschaften in Politik, Wirtschaft und Gesellschaft 1945–1949*, vol. 7 (Cologne: Dietz, 1991), 726–727.

11 *Ibid.*

12 Deutscher Gewerkschaftsbund (ed.), *Protokoll zum Gründungskongress des Deutschen Gewerkschaftsbundes in München, 12.–14. Oktober 1949* (Düsseldorf: Bund, 1949), 202.

13 Gerber, "Constitutionalizing the Economy."

14 19 December 1949: "Sitzung des Bundesvorstandes," in Jakob Kaiser (ed.), *Quellen zur Geschichte der deutschen Gewerkschaftsbewegung im 20. Jahrhundert Bd. 11. Der Deutsche Gewerkschaftsbund 1949 bis 1956* (Bonn: Dietz, 1996), 17–28.

15 Lisa Murach-Brand, *Antitrust auf deutsch. Der Einfluß der amerikanischen Alliierten auf das Gesetz gegen Wettbewerbsbeschränkungen (GWB) nach 1945* (Tübingen: Mohr-Siebeck, 2004), 110.

16 Frank Pitzer, *Interessen im Wettbewerb. Grundlagen und frühe Entwicklung der europäischen Wettbewerbspolitik 1955–1966* (Stuttgart: Franz Steiner, 2009), 108.

17 David J. Gerber, *Law and Competition in Twentieth Century Europe: Protecting Prometheus* (Oxford: Oxford University Press, 2001), 273.

18 Pitzer, *Interessen*, 105.

19 *Ibid.*, 158; Brigitte Leucht, "Transatlantic Policy Networks in the Creation of the First European Anti-Trust Law: Mediating between American Anti-Trust and German Ordo-Liberalism," in Wolfram Kaiser et al. (eds.), *The History of the European Union. Origins of a Trans- and Supranational Polity 1950–72* (London: Routledge, 2009), 56–73.

20 Murach-Brand, *Antitrust*.

21 Gerber, *Constitutionalizing*, 64.

22 Pitzer, *Interessen*, 109.

23 Rolf Wagenführ, "Unsere Stellungnahme zum Monopolproblem," *Gewerkschaftliche Monatshefte* 1, 3 (March 1950): 103–105.
24 Wirtschaftswissenschaftliches Institut (ed.), *Die Illusion des freien Wettbewerbs. Die Stellungnahme der Gewerkschaften zum Gesetz gegen Wettbewerbsbeschränkung* (Cologne: Bund, 1950), 6.
25 *Ibid.*, 43–52.
26 Archive of Social Democracy (ADSD), Bonn, 5 DGAN 22, Letter to the Members of the Bundestag and Bundesrat, subject "Gesetz gegen Wettbewerbsbeschränkungen," 19 May 1950, 5 DGAN 22.
27 Bernd Bühlbäcker, *Europa im Aufbruch. Personalpolitik deutscher Parteien und Verbände in der Montanunion 1949–1958* (Essen: Klartext, 2007), 72.
28 Bernd Bühlbäcker, "Debatten um die Montanunion: Gewerkschaften und europäische Integration in den 1950er Jahren," in Jürgen Mittag (ed.), *Mitteilungsblatt des Instituts für soziale Bewegungen. Deutsche Gewerkschaften und europäische Integration im 20. Jahrhundert* (Essen: Klartext, 2009), 43–62, here 56.
29 Robert Schuman, "Declaration of 9th May 1950 Delivered by Robert Schuman," *European Issue* 204 (10 May 2011): 2.
30 Severin Cramm, "Im Zeichen der europäischen Integration. Zur Rolle des DGB in den EGKS-Verhandlungen 1950/1951," in *Arbeit – Bewegung – Geschichte. Zeitschrift für historische Studien* 15, 2 (May 2016): 78–96.
31 Karl Lauschke, "Zwischen Mitbestimmungs- und Europapolitik: Die IG Metall und die Anfänge der europäischen Integration," in Jürgen Mittag (ed.), *Mitteilungsblatt des Instituts für soziale Bewegungen. Deutsche Gewerkschaften und europäische Integration im 20. Jahrhundert* (Essen: Klartext, 2009), 89–102; Jelena Jojević, "Nachholende Europäisierung? Reaktionen und Strategien der IG Metall gegenüber der Montanunion in den 1950er Jahren," in *Ibid.*, 103–122.
32 Sitzung des Beirats der IG Metall vom 10./11. Mai 1951, Jojević, "Nachholende Europäisierung?" 103.
33 11/12 March 1951: Sitzung des Bundesvorstandes, in: Josef Kaiser (ed.), *Quellen*, 152.
34 Pitzer, *Interessen,* 158.
35 Freyer, *Antitrust,* 272–273.
36 Laurent Warlouzet, "The Rise of European Competition Policy, 1950–1991: A Cross-Disciplinary Survey of a Contested Policy Sphere," *EUI RSCAS* 10, 80 (2010): 7.
37 Tobias Witschke, *Gefahr für den Wettbewerb? Die Fusionskontrolle der Europäischen Gemeinschaft für Kohle und Stahl und die "Rekonzentration" der Ruhrstahlindustrie 1950–1963* (Berlin: Akademie, 2009).
38 Horst Thum, *Mitbestimmung in der Montanindustrie. Der Mythos vom Sieg der Gewerkschaften* (Stuttgart: De Gruyter, 1982), 110–115.
39 AdsD, 5 DGAI 19, Letter from Walter Freitag to Jean Monnet, 4 September 1953.
40 Vorstand IG Metall, *Geschäftsbericht 1956/1957 des Vorstandes der Industriegewerkschaft Metall für die Bundesrepublik Deutschland* (Frankfurt am Main: IG Metall, 1956), 136; Jojević, "Nachholende Europäisierung?" 103.
41 AdsD, 5 DGAN 457, Stellungnahme des DGB zum Gesetzesentwurf gegen Wettbewerbsbeschränkungen vom 13 September 1951, 1.
42 Pitzer, *Interessen*, 108; Bundeskartellamt (ed.), *60 Jahre Bundeskartellamt* (Bonn: Self-Publishing, 2018), 9.
43 AdsD, 5 DGAN 457, Aktennotiz von Weighardt an Stenzel vom 25 June 1952, 1.
44 *Ibid.*, 2.
45 Board of the DGB, "Stellungnahme der Gewerkschaften zum Kartellgesetzentwurf," *Wirtschaft und Wettbewerb* (1953): 376–378, here 377.
46 *Ibid.*
47 Bundesvorstand des Deutschen Gewerkschaftsbundes (ed.), *Geschäftsbericht des Deutschen Gewerkschaftsbundes 1952–1953* (Cologne: Bund, 1954), 377.

48 *Ibid.*, 374–378.
49 Several letters from 1950 to 1954, AdsD, 5 DGAN 459.
50 AdsD, 5 DGAN 459, Minutes of the Meeting Held on 8 July 1954 at the Federal Ministry of Economics and Technology on Antitrust Legislation, 8 July 1954, 1.
51 Franz Grosse, "Montan-Union funktioniert so nicht," *Neue Ruhrzeitung* (2 April 1956): 5–8.
52 Laurent Warlouzet, "Competition Policy in the EEC," in Susana Fellman and Martin Shanahan (eds.), *Regulating Competition. Cartel Registers in the Twentieth-Century World* (Oxon; New York: Routledge, 2016), 48–65, here 50.
53 Pitzer, *Interessen,* 168–197.
54 Freyer, *Antitrust,* 279.
55 Warlouzet, "Competition Policy," 51.
56 Institute of Social History (IISH), Amsterdam, 1311, Report on the Regional Conference, 22 May 1956–24 May 1956, 1311.
57 IISH, 1310, Draft Program of Trade Union Action Aimed at Facilitating European Co-Operation and Integration, 4 April 1956.
58 Pitzer, *Interessen,* 168–197.
59 Warlouzet, "Competition Policy," 52.
60 "Euratom nur mit DGB! Forderung des DGB und der freien Gewerkschaftsinternationale zu den EURATOM-Verhandlungen," *Welt der Arbeit* (11 January 1957), from: 1281b, Institute of Social History (IISH), Amsterdam; AdsD, 5 DGAN 168, Letter of the Board of Directors, 12 September 1956.
61 AdsD, 5 DGAN 753, Stellungnahme der Gewerkschaften zum Vertrag des Gemeinsamen Marktes, 18 January 1957.
62 Pitzer, *Interessen,*114.
63 Volker Berghahn, *Unternehmer und Politik in der Bundesrepublik* (Frankfurt am Main: Suhrkamp, 1985), 178–179.
64 AdsD, 5 DGAN 460, Letter from Agartz to Rosenberg, subject "Kartellproblem – Marktwirtschaft," 9 March 1955.
65 AdsD, 5 DGAN 460, Letter from Rosenberg to Hirche, 6 June 1955.
66 AdsD, 4 DGAN 459, Statement on the Filmgroschen, 25 June 1955, 5 DGAN 459, Archive of Social Democracy (ADSD), Bonn.
67 AdsD, 5 DGAN 460, Letter from Hirche to the Board, Subject Cartel Law, 13 July 1955.
68 Bundesvorstand des Deutschen Gewerkschaftsbundes (ed.), *Geschäftsbericht des Deutschen Gewerkschaftsbundes 1954–1955* (Cologne: Bund, 1956), 369–372.
69 AdsD, 5 DGAN 460, Letter from Kroebel to Kühne, 14 September 1956.
70 *Ibid.*
71 Deutscher Gewerkschaftsbund (ed.), *Protokoll 4. Ordentlicher Bundeskongress Hamburg* (Cologne: Bund, 1956), 730.
72 Berghahn, *Unternehmer*.
73 AdsD, 5 DGAN 268, Statement of the DGB "Die Erklärung der CDU/CSU-Bundestagsfraktion befriedigt nicht," 19 March 1957.
74 AdsD, 5 DGAN 457, Statement of the DGB "DGB zum Kartellgesetz," 5 July 1957.
75 *Ibid.*
76 AdsD, 5 DGAN 148, Minutes of the Meeting of the Committee "Gemeinsamer Markt," Subject Kartellfragen im Gemeinsamen Markt, 24 June 1958.
77 AdsD, 5 DGAN 148, Report "Kartellfragen im Gemeinsamen Markt," 24 June 1958.
78 AdsD, 5 DGAN 253, Circular Letter of Rosenberg, Subject "VERBRAUCHERFRAGEN hier: Verbraucherinteressen innerhalb der Europäischen Wirtschaftsgemeinschaft," 9 February 1960.
79 AdsD, 5 DGAN 298, Letter from Rosenberg to Buiter, 25 October 1960.
80 AdsD, 5 DGAN 253, Letter from Buiter to von der Groeben, 10 October 1960.

81 AdsD, 5 DGAN 253, Circular Letter from Merl, Subject "Aussprache über gewerkschaftliche Grundsätze zur Kartellpolitik," 3 February 1960.
82 *Ibid.*
83 AdsD, 5 DGAN 704, Letter from Sohn to Becker, Subject Article of Fritze on European Cartel-Policy, 28 November 1960.
84 AdsD, 5 DGAN 253, Circular Letter of Merl, Subject "Aussprache über gewerkschaftliche Grundsätze zur Kartellpolitik," 3 February 1960.
85 AdsD, 5 DGAN 253, Statement of the DGB "Entwurf einer Ersten Durchführungsverordnung zu den Artikeln 85 und 86 des Vertrages zur Gründung der Europäischen Wirtschaftsgemeinschaft," 30 January 1961.
86 AdsD, 5 DGAN 564, Meeting of the "Arbeitskreis Kartellpolitik," 22 November 1963.
87 Warlouzet, "Competition Policy," 52–53.
88 AdsD, 5 DGAN 564, Meeting of the "Arbeitskreis Kartellpolitik," 22 November 1963, 1.
89 Pitzer, *Interessen,* 444.
90 Sigfrido M. Ramírez Pérez and Sebastian van de Scheur, "The Evolution of the Law on Articles 85 and 86 EEC," in Kiran Klaus Patel and Heike Schweitzer (eds.), *The Historical Foundations of EU Competition Law* (Oxford: Oxford University Press, 2013), 19–53, here 52–53.
91 Brian Shaev, "From Cradle to Grave: The German Trade Union Federation's Wage, Welfare, and Competitiveness Program for the Weimar Republic," in Lucia Coppolaro and Lorenzo Mechi (eds.), *Free Trade and Social Welfare: Explorations in the Long Twentieth Century* (London: Routledge, 2020), 30–51.

Bibliography

60 Jahre Bundeskartellamt edited by the Bundeskartellamt. Bonn: Self-publishing, 2018.

Axt, Heinz-Jürgen. "Westeuropäische Integration, Nationalstaat und Arbeiterbewegung." In *Arbeiterbewegung und westeuropäische Integration* edited by Frank Deppe. Cologne: Pahl-Rugenstein, 1976, 98–141.

Bechtold, Hartmut. *Die Kartellierung der deutschen Volkswirtschaft und die sozialdemokratische Theorie-Diskussion vor 1933.* Frankfurt: Haag + Herchen, 1986.

Berghahn, Volker. *Unternehmer und Politik in der Bundesrepublik.* Frankfurt: Suhrkamp, 1985.

Board of the DGB. "Stellungnahme der Gewerkschaften zum Kartellgesetzentwurf." *Wirtschaft und Wettbewerb,* (1953): 376–378.

Bühlbäcker, Bernd. "Debatten um die Montanunion: Gewerkschaften und europäische Integration in den 1950er Jahren." In *Mitteilungsblatt des Instituts für soziale Bewegungen. Deutsche Gewerkschaften und europäische Integration im 20. Jahrhundert* edited by Jürgen Mittag. Essen: Klartext, 2009, 43–62.

Bühlbäcker, Bernd. *Europa im Aufbruch. Personalpolitik deutscher Parteien und Verbände in der Montanunion 1949–1958.* Essen: Klartext, 2007.

Clairmont, Yves. *Vom europäischen Verbindungsbüro zur transnationalen Gewerkschaftsorganisation. Organisation, Strategien und Machtpotentiale des Europäischen Metallgewerkschaftsbundes bis 1990.* Stuttgart: Franz Steiner, 2014.

Cramm, Severin. "Im Zeichen der europäischen Integration. Zur Rolle des DGB in den EGKS-Verhandlungen 1950/1951." *Arbeit – Bewegung – Geschichte. Zeitschrift für historische Studien,* 15, 2 (May 2016): 78–96.

Die Illusion des freien Wettbewerbs. Die Stellungnahme der Gewerkschaften zum Gesetz gegen Wettbewerbsbeschränkung edited by the Wirtschaftswissenschaftliches Institut. Cologne: Bund, 1950.

Fattmann, Rainer. *Für ein soziales Europa. Der Agrar-, Lebensmittel- und Tourismusbereich in der europäischen Gewerkschaftspolitik seit der Gründung der europäischen Wirtschaftsgemeinschaft*. Münster: Dampfboot, 2013.
Freyer, Tony A. *Antitrust and Global Capitalism*. New York: Cambridge University Press, 2007.
Gerber, David J. "Constitutionalizing the Economy: German Neo-liberalism, Competition Law and the 'New' Europe." *American Journal of Comparative Law* 42, 25 (January 1994): 25–84.
Gerber, David J. *Law and Competition in Twentieth Century Europe: Protecting Prometheus*. Oxford: Oxford University Press, 2001.
Geschäftsbericht 1956/1957 des Vorstandes der Industriegewerkschaft Metall für die Bundesrepublik Deutschland edited by the Vorstand IG Metall. Frankfurt: IG Metall, 1956.
Geschäftsbericht des Deutschen Gewerkschaftsbundes 1952–1953 edited by the Bundesvorstand des Deutschen Gewerkschaftsbundes. Cologne: Bund, 1954.
Geschäftsbericht des Deutschen Gewerkschaftsbundes 1954–1955 edited by the Bundesvorstand des Deutschen Gewerkschaftsbundes. Cologne: Bund, 1956.
Grosse, Franz. "Montan-Union funktioniert so nicht." *Neue Ruhrzeitung*, 2 April 1956: 5–8.
Jojević, Jelena. "Nachholende Europäisierung? Reaktionen und Strategien der IG Metall gegenüber der Montanunion in den 1950er Jahren." In *Mitteilungsblatt des Instituts für soziale Bewegungen. Deutsche Gewerkschaften und europäische Integration im 20. Jahrhundert* edited by Jürgen Mittag. Essen: Klartext, 2009, 103–122.
Kaiser, Wolfram and Johan Schot, *Writing the Rules for Europe: Experts, Cartels, and International Organizations*. New York: Palgrave Macmillan, 2014.
Klaus Schönhoven and Hermann Weber (eds.). *Quellen zur Geschichte der deutschen Gewerkschaftsbewegung im 20. Jahrhundert. Der Deutsche Gewerkschaftsbund 1949 bis 1956*, vol. 11. Cologne: Bund, 1996.
Lauschke, Karl. "Zwischen Mitbestimmungs- und Europapolitik: Die IG Metall und die Anfänge der europäischen Integration." In *Mitteilungsblatt des Instituts für soziale Bewegungen. Deutsche Gewerkschaften und europäische Integration im 20. Jahrhundert* edited by Jürgen Mittag. Essen: Klartext, 2009, 89–102.
Leucht, Brigitte Leucht. "Transatlantic Policy Networks in the Creation of the First European Anti-Trust Law: Mediating between American Anti-Trust and German Ordo-Liberalism." In *The History of the European Union. Origins of a Trans- and Supranational Polity 1950–72* edited by Wolfram Kaiser et al. London: Routledge, 2009, 56–73.
Murach-Brand, Lisa. *Antitrust auf deutsch. Der Einfluß der amerikanischen Alliierten auf das Gesetz gegen Wettbewerbsbeschränkungen (GWB) nach 1945*. Tübingen: Mohr-Siebeck, 2004.
Niethammer, Lutz. "Defensive Integration – Der Weg zum EGB und die Perspektive einer westeuropäischen Einheitsgewerkschaft." In *Gewerkschaftliche Politik: Reform aus Solidarität. Zum 60. Geburtstag von Heinz O. Vetter* edited by Ulrich Borsdorf. Cologne: Bund, 1977, 567–596.
Pérez, Sigfrido M. Ramírez and Sebastian van de Scheur. "The Evolution of the Law on Articles 85 and 86 EEC." In *The Historical Foundations of EU Competition Law* edited by Kiran Klaus Patel and Heike Schweitzer. Oxford: Oxford University Press, 2013, 19–53.
Pitzer, Frank. *Interessen im Wettbewerb. Grundlagen und frühe Entwicklung der europäischen Wettbewerbspolitik 1955–1966*. Stuttgart: Franz Steiner, 2009.
Protokoll 4. Ordentlicher Bundeskongress Hamburg edited by the Deutscher Gewerkschaftsbund. Cologne: Bund, 1956.
Protokoll zum Gründungskongress des Deutschen Gewerkschaftsbundes in München, 12–14. Oktober 1949 edited by the Deutscher Gewerkschaftsbund. Düsseldorf: Bund, 1949.

Quellen zur Geschichte der deutschen Gewerkschaftsbewegung im 20. Jahrhundert. Gewerkschaften in Politik, Wirtschaft und Gesellschaft 1945–1949, vol. 7 edited by Hermann Weber and Siegfried Mielke. Cologne: Dietz, 1991.

Quellen zur Geschichte der deutschen Gewerkschaftsbewegung im 20. Jahrhundert, vol. 11 edited by Jakob Kaiser. Bonn: Dietz, 1996.

Schuman, Robert. "Declaration of 9th May 1950 Delivered by Robert Schuman." *European Issue* 204, 10 May 2011.

Schweitzer, Heike and Kiran Klaus Patel. "EU Competition Law in Historical Context." In *The Historical Foundations of EU Competition Law* edited by Kiran Klaus Patel and Heike Schweitzer. Oxford: Oxford University Press, 2013, 207–230.

Shaev, Brian. "From Cradle to Grave: The German Trade Union Federation's Wage, Welfare, and Competitiveness Program for the Weimar Republic." In *Free Trade and Social Welfare: Explorations in the Long Twentieth Century* edited by Lucia Coppolaro and Lorenzo Mechi. London: Routledge, 2020, 30–51.

Shaev, Brian. "Workers' Politics, the Communist Challenge, and the Schuman Plan: A Comparative History of the French Socialist and German Social Democratic Parties and the First Treaty for European Integration." *International Review of Social History* 61, 2 (August 2016): 251–281.

Thum, Horst. *Mitbestimmung in der Montanindustrie. Der Mythos vom Sieg der Gewerkschaften*. Stuttgart: De Gruyter, 1982.

Wagenführ, Rolf. "Unsere Stellungnahme zum Monopolproblem." *Gewerkschaftliche Monatshefte* 1, 3 (March 1950): 103–105.

Warlouzet, Laurent. "Competition Policy in the EEC." In *Regulating Competition. Cartel Registers in the Twentieth-Century World* edited by Susana Fellman and Martin Shanahan. Oxon/New York: Routledge, 2016, 48–65.

Warlouzet, Laurent. "The Rise of European Competition Policy, 1950–1991: A Cross-Disciplinary Survey of a Contested Policy Sphere." *EUI RSCAS* 10, 80 (2010).

Witschke, Tobias. *Gefahr für den Wettbewerb? Die Fusionskontrolle der Europäischen Gemeinschaft für Kohle und Stahl und die "Rekonzentration" der Ruhrstahlindustrie 1950–1963*. Berlin: Akademie, 2009.

5 "The economy is our destiny"

Socialists and the birth of European competition law, 1950–1962

Brian Shaev

Introduction

In 1958, the year the European Economic Community (EEC) opened, the community's socialist parties met to craft a united approach to the economic dimensions of European integration. Before them lay a document by a German economic expert that introduced a lengthy section on cartels and competition with the phrase, "The economy is our destiny."[1] The use of such grandiloquent language to introduce an area of law often considered technical, even tedious, was no accident. The transfer of sovereign regulatory powers over such a core feature of economic policy from national governments to supranational institutions captivated for several years the attention of socialist economists as well as politicians operating in international spheres. There followed a long series of meetings and conferences in which a transnational group of socialists and social democrats debated their ideal vision for a supranational system to regulate competition in a European common market.

Analyzing the extensive debates that took place on cartels and competition among socialists in the early years of the European communities sheds new light on the transformation of postwar social democracy in Western Europe and on the political context in which European competition policy began. Perhaps the most controversial subject that divided socialist parties during the Schuman Plan debates, cartels and competition policy are a valuable case study through which to analyze inter-party conflict, transnational cooperation between parties, and the political cohesion of one of the main party groups in the early European parliamentary assemblies. Furthermore, socialists (and political parties in the broad sense) are largely absent and marginalized within scholarly narratives of the "origin story" of European competition policy. Older literature like that of David Gerber argues that this policy was the singular achievement of a group of right-wing ordoliberals determined to refashion the postwar economic order in their image. Anselm Küsters' recent dissertation also analyzes German and European competition policy through an exclusive ordoliberal lens.[2] Other literature, in particular the studies of Lorenzo Pace and Katja Seidel, Sylvie Hambloch, Frank Pitzer, and Laurent Warlouzet, emphasize the international contest between national governments, in particular between France and Germany, to explain the emergence of European competition policy in the 1950s–1960s.[3] Transnational politics and parties play

DOI: 10.4324/9781351010573-5

little to no role in existing accounts of the formulation of EEC Regulation 17/62, the foundation stone for European competition law, though Warlouzet has recently acknowledged center-left support for the development of early European competition policy.[4]

Writing the transnational politics of competition into the broader context out of which emerged Regulation 17/62 reveals that ordoliberal thought did not hold a monopoly among political philosophies pushing for a strong regulatory framework to regulate cartels and competition. If ordoliberalism was the only significant frame of economic thought associated with building strong supranational regulatory powers for the European Commission, then it makes little sense that it was a transnational group of socialist politicians, and not Christian democrats or liberals, who were the most avid defenders of Commission proposals in 1959–1961. Yet, as this chapter demonstrates, it was the socialists who most consistently pushed, first, the High Authority of the European Coal and Steel Community (ECSC), and then the European Commission, to rigorously enforce the anti-cartel powers granted to them by European treaties. The transnational Socialist Group achieved cohesion on the question of cartels despite deep divisions rooted in the postwar politics of national reconstruction, as discussed in the chapter's opening analysis of political debates in France, Germany and the Netherlands in 1948–1951. A focus on these three countries is the most promising path for highlighting national priorities because there was no significant postwar cartel legislation proposed in Belgium, Italy or Luxembourg before the opening of the ECSC. Although concentrations and mergers proved a more elusive subject for socialists to find consensus in this period, the Socialist Group formulated the clearest and most comprehensive position of the party groups in favor of an ECSC supranational competition policy and, then, a few years later, in the EEC.

The socialist anti-cartel vision that emerged in the 1950s was not rooted in an idealized image of the virtues of free competition, a concept that underlies ordoliberal thinking. Rather socialists viewed competition policy not only as a means of protecting consumers, a traditional socialist concern discussed in preceding chapters, but also as a way to gain public oversight or control over concentrations of economic power they presented as growing political threats looming over democracy at both national and European levels. This vision continued to favor nationalizations in certain sectors, despite the increasingly market-oriented policies of post-Bad Godesberg German social democracy, and elements of planning at the European level. Furthermore, it wanted to subordinate competition policy to broader political and economic goals, including employment stability, an expansionist public-directed economic policy and social welfare. Though there was some internal dissent, the party group declared that such goals need not conflict with their support for a cartel ban and a rigorous supranational application of Articles 85 and 86 of the Treaties of Rome. Hence, as this chapter demonstrates, there was an alternative social-democratic conception of competition to that of ordoliberalism, one that contributed substantial political support to the Commission in its efforts to develop a strong community competition policy as embodied in Regulation 17/62.

The politics of reconstruction and the cartel question, 1948–1951

On the surface, socialist party positions on the "cartel question" in 1948–1951 appear to represent clear-cut national or regional interests. Cartels were subordinated to the high-order conflicts shaping international relations within the Western bloc: the geopolitical and economic logics of postwar reconstruction and competing conceptions of the role that the newly founded West German state should play within it. The French Socialist Party (SFIO) supported the anti-cartel foreign policy promoted by the French government with the purpose of constraining or, for some, destroying, the heavily cartelized Ruhr heavy industry, which they held responsible for German militarism and for the inability of French industry to compete on European and world markets. The Dutch Labor Party (*Partij van de Arbeid*, PvdA), like the Dutch coalitional government they led after 1948, did not have the insistent, sometimes desperate, geopolitical ambition of their French colleagues to tame the West German economy. Rather they viewed West German recovery as integral for their own national prosperity. They did, though, share the view that German cartelization was a traditional means by which the Ruhr coal sales syndicate discriminated against foreign metal industries, by selling discounted coal to German steel and iron companies, a practice known as "double-pricing." By contrast, German social democrats thought that the cartelized industrial structure linking coal, steel and manufacturing in the Ruhr was an indispensable guarantor of jobs and wages. Furthermore, they conceived of French proposals for an Allied anti-cartel law as a continuation of a vengeful and counterproductive French postwar policy that sought economic and political hegemony in Western Europe by means of economic discrimination against Ruhr industry and the exploitation of Ruhr miners for French industrial ambitions.

The catalyst for the SPD's decision to publicly oppose the Schuman Plan in the fall of 1950 was Jean Monnet's decision to demand that the ECSC High Authority be invested with legal powers to break up coal and steel cartels.[5] By targeting the Ruhr coal sales syndicate for dissolution, the Paris Treaty now appeared to threaten not only the Ruhr's vertical integration economy between coal, steel and manufacturing and horizontal integration in the steel industry (famously embodied by the interwar Vereinigten Stahlwerke) but also the horizontal integration structures of the German coal industry as well. Cartels became the most controversial issue of the Schuman Plan negotiations, as Severin Cramm discusses as well, bogging down progress until German Chancellor Konrad Adenauer, under U.S. pressure, capitulated to Monnet in April 1951. In the winter of 1950–1951, the SPD launched a caustic campaign against the Schuman Plan, in which it publicized a litany of complaints that focused on what it claimed were the discriminatory features of a community designed to permanently shackle German industry. Behind the scenes, French socialists, who came out in support of the Schuman Plan in June 1950, sought clarity on the SPD's position. This outreach led to a bilateral meeting in June 1951 between party leaders Guy Mollet and Kurt Schumacher, the results of which Mollet reported back to the SFIO national executive. The meeting was quite cordial, Mollet said, but,

> It is very apparent that the problem for them is essentially one of domestic policy. Schumacher declared that the SPD favored cartelization and the

> maintenance of double-pricing for coal. I responded to him that a common position with us was impossible if it included a defense of cartelization and double-pricing. At that moment Schumacher expressed a desire that the discussion cease.[6]

With this context in mind, one can hardly imagine a policy field less propitious for transnational socialist cooperation than the "cartel question." Yet, when the focus shifts from international to domestic politics and to intra-party discussions, this straightforward narrative is significantly transformed in a manner that allows us to appreciate why socialists were able to cooperate on the cartel issue after 1953 to an extent, despite some disagreements, that may otherwise have seemed impossible in 1950–1951. First, it bears emphasizing that the French Socialist Party demanded an anti-cartel policy not only for West Germany but for France as well. The SFIO was the most anti-cartel of the larger French political parties in 1948–1951, which found concrete expression in the party's unsuccessful proposal for national anti-cartel legislation. In 1948, SFIO economist and former economic minister André Philip told the French National Assembly,

> Prices should be fixed by the nation or by free competition. But what no one can tolerate is that a directed economy, escaping the hands of the state, passes into the hands of professionals. . . . I believe that we must establish legislation for cartels that creates either a cartel tribunal, like there was formally one in Germany, or an administrative commission like the Federal Trade Commission in America.[7]

Philip, who Ramírez Pérez argues had a decisive influence on the shape of the ECSC Treaty's competition articles, remained consistent in the next years, telling the SFIO's national executive in January 1951 that "[t]he fight against protectionism, the destruction of cartels must be at the forefront of socialist action."[8] On the initiative of SFIO deputy Albert Gazier, the National Assembly's Commission for Economic Affairs passed a resolution by a vote of 14 to 11 in December 1948 calling for "the preparation of an anti-trust law" to decrease prices.[9] Cartels came up again during a debate on economic policy in the SFIO national executive in April 1951, the month the ECSC Treaty was signed. An executive member said that, "the government is afraid to attack industrial and commercial ententes," but "it is necessary . . . [to] proceed to a direct attack on economic concentrations." Mollet replied,

> As for economic and commercial ententes, this is part of the proposals defended by the socialist ministers who have obtained the accord of the other parties for a vote on a proposed law before the end of the legislative session.[10]

Hence when Philip, for instance, proposed in 1948

> a European legislation for cartels and the creation of an inter-European organism, be it administrative, or judicial . . . to watch over the cartels and

> coalitions that inevitably and, as it is to be wished, are going to tend to surpass national borders,

the socialist position he advocated applied to both domestic and foreign policy.[11] The French National Assembly finally passed an antitrust law in 1953 that subordinated competition policy to price policy, a pattern we see also in postwar Finnish competition policy in Susanna Fellman's chapter.

Looking at national contexts casts a different light on the Dutch Labor Party as well. Perhaps the most significant nomination made by the PvdA to the ECSC Common Assembly was Gerard Nederhorst, who chaired the Social Affairs Committee from 1953 to 1962 and was delegate in the Common Market Committee (from 1958, the Internal Market Committee), charged with cartel policy, as well. By 1948, Nederhorst had already established himself as one of the firmest advocates of a national anti-cartel law in the Dutch parliament (see Karin van Leeuwen's chapter for the context of Nederhorst's position within the PvdA). In a wide-ranging speech in February 1948, he criticized delays in the creation of a cartel law and state deference to business' right to secrecy, stating that publicizing this information was necessary to determine whether cartels operated in the general interest as they claimed.[12] Nederhorst's colleague, Ko Suurhoff, trade union official and later minister and PvdA chair, followed up the next day stating that it was "regrettable that the [government] had rejected the publication of . . . the cartel register," which had been introduced during the German occupation of the Netherlands and to which "the people's representatives have every right."[13] The newly appointed Dutch economic minister from the Catholic Party (KVP), Jan van den Brink, replied to Nederhorst's urging of a "trust- and cartel law" that "I can see no need for this at the moment."[14] Almost two years later, a debate on cartels in the Dutch parliament broke down again along the same lines. Van den Brink compared cartel agreements between separate companies favorably to the benefits of his marriage contract with his wife.[15] In September, VVD (liberal) deputy and future member of the ECSC Assembly, Henk Korthals, stated that "cartel agreements can be very favorable for the economy."[16] Nederhorst, for his part, again called for the publication of the cartel register, saying, "I still do not see why every Dutch person is not allowed to know when there are real price agreements [between businesses] and when not."[17] Though he did not support the automatic dissolution of cartel agreements, he argued that, to avoid a ban, the government must determine that any such agreements resulted in lower, rather than higher, prices. As van Leeuwen demonstrates, the PvdA supported the 1956 Dutch Economic Competition Act in alliance with Dutch neoliberals, which has parallels with the tacit alliance between German ordoliberals and social democrats from the mid-1950s in favor of more regulation of competition.[18]

The surprise inclusion of supranational anti-cartel powers in the Schuman Plan negotiations led the SPD to oppose the treaty because (1) as the center of the community's coal and steel industries, a sectoral anti-cartel law seemed inherently discriminatory against Germany; (2) it thought that a French-led High Authority would exacerbate this inherent imbalance by implementing the treaty in a further discriminatory manner; and (3) Ruhr-based politicians like Dortmund Mayor Fritz Henssler saw cartels as necessary to maintain employment, wages and economic stability in the Ruhr. Beneath the surface, however, SPD cartel policy was increasingly ambivalent and in flux, as Harm G. Schröter shows in his chapter, as was that of the German Trade Union Confederation, as Cramm demonstrates. In November 1949, the SPD executive's political-economic committee held an experts meeting to advise the party's position on cartels. Paul Bleiss, a coal expert from the Ruhr and SPD deputy, said that "if one wants an economy steered by the state, one needs large economic units," while Fritz Baade, economist at the Kiel World Economics Institute, argued that "the concentration process of the capitalist economy is unavoidable and one should not forbid it but rather step-by-step take it under [state] supervision." The protocol records that "all the speakers were more or less in favor of concentration, but with public supervision."[19] When the Bundestag began debating a cartel law in February 1950 to replace Occupation Law 75, the SPD tapped Erik Nölting, Economic Minister of North-Rhine-Westphalia, to present the SPD's position. Nölting warned against dropping "an atomic bomb" on all monopolistic organizations and replacing them with "a ruinous competition of annihilation." Doing so would turn the economy into a "football field" in which price wars would result in business closures and job losses. The SPD therefore opposed a cartel ban and instead favored a law in which cartels would have to publicly register. A monopoly office and council would assess whether cartels were "guaranteeing the best possible supply for the market" and thereby operating in the general interest of the German economy. This SPD position came under attack from all sides as cartel-friendly (*kartellfreundlich*), an embarrassing charge Nölting rejected as "absurd."[20] Opponents spoke of an unholy alliance of social democrats with large business interests.

Two and a half years later, German Economic Minister Ludwig Erhard presented a cartel bill to the Bundestag based on the banning principle, calling the bill "the crown of our economic market order." Joachim Schöne, SPD deputy from the Ruhr and shortly after representative in the ECSC Assembly, had the unlucky task of presenting the SPD's amorphous position in the Bundestag. The SPD supported a cartel bill based on the "abuse" principle that would distinguish between "appropriate" and "inappropriate" economic power, with the former to be accepted but brought under public supervision. The party remained open though to possibly supporting a cartel ban once the government presented the final bill.[21] As the SPD slowly came to terms in the early 1950s with its failure to achieve socialization in the postwar German economy, internal divisions on cartel policy increasingly came to the fore. In November 1952, the SPD's Political-Economic Committee met again but "the back and forth among those present result[ed] in neither a decision for a ban, nor for abuse legislation."[22] The committee instead recommended that the party adopt a tactic in the Bundestag to delay final discussion on cartel legislation until after the 1953 federal election. By 1957, though, Schröter and Cramm show that German social democrats and trade unionists had become defenders of a strong form of state regulation of competition. They opposed the 1957 German Act against Restraints on Competition, the strongest competition law to date in Europe, as too weak to control concentration movements in the economy.

Cartels, the socialist party group and the opening of the ECSC, 1952–1955

When the ECSC opened in 1952–1953, cartels were the most divisive issue facing socialist deputies who gathered to represent their parties in the transnational Common Assembly. The SPD vigorously opposed proposals for European defense integration, in contrast to the PvdA and SFIO leaderships that supported it, but the ECSC's sectoral economic focus allowed socialists to exclude such high-order geopolitical issues from their daily work.[23] Socialists brought cartel policies they had forged in postwar domestic contexts into the assembly, creating the potential for a deep-rooted inter-socialist conflict that could have undermined the group's goal of fostering clear transnational positions on European integration. The issue was even more fraught because cartels and competition were the fields over which the Paris Treaty granted the strongest legal powers to the supranational community. That the Socialist Group succeeded in, first, containing such conflicts within reasonable bounds in 1953–1955 and, second, forging a relative consensus on cartel issues in 1955–1957 was no mean feat given the important economic interests at stake. Their success reflected the hard work of a group of politicians who were determined not to allow national differences to destroy the mandate passed down by the national parties that they build the most disciplined and cohesive political group in the early European assembly.

Conflict centered at first around the fate of the Ruhr's sales syndicate, which had long been the focus of Dutch and French concerns. The six organizations that made up the Ruhr sales syndicate (GEORG) operated in practice almost exactly as had its predecessor, the unitary Deutschen Kohle-Verkaufs-Gesellschaft (DKV). More than half of the early community's coal purchases occurred through this organization.[24] After an initial effort to break up the DKV in 1953, Monnet signaled in the spring of 1954 that he would seek a compromise solution with Ruhr industry. Ruhr coal companies took advantage of this breathing room to fortify a policy of intransigent non-cooperation, a position supported by the German government.

The conflict over cartels could not simply be papered over in internal socialist group meetings or in the Common Market Committee, the assembly's forum for discussing cartel policy. Already in 1953 Nederhorst accused the High Authority of permitting the recreation of cartels, and complained that Dutch consumers were still unable to buy coal directly from production sites.[25] In January 1954, he went further, telling the Common Market Committee that the High Authority's cartel policy was "compromis[ing] the prestige of the Community."[26] In April, he said, "the High Authority fears the power of cartels and [has been] obliged to cede to their demands," warning that "Dutch public opinion is particularly sensitive to this question."[27] By contrast, Schöne, also a committee member as well as president of the Investment Committee, encouraged the High Authority to take account of domestic economic consequences in formulating its cartel policy, in particular by considering any indirect, and not just direct, repercussions it would likely have on employment.[28] Repeatedly Schöne stated that free competition in the sale and purchasing of coal was economically impossible. He therefore welcomed the remarks of the Christian-democratic Commissioner Franz Etzel that a cartel ban was "not an end to itself." He also expressed his happiness in October that the High Authority would not "establish a [anti-cartel] dogma, but rather proceed in a pragmatic fashion."[29]

Disagreements among socialists on cartels gave impetus to some rather colorful remarks. Herbert Wehner, an important SPD politician, provided a positive portrait of cartels in his speech to the Common Assembly plenary in June 1955,

> It is understood that [ententes and cartels] are a priori, execrable, diabolical, and the treaty writers imposed a major excommunication against them.
>
> But one sees also that after three years the High Authority has had some trouble directing the lightning of this excommunication. One begins to perceive that cartels are, in industries such as ours, a necessary phenomenon, a reflex of the organism to avoid even worse disorders and the issue before us like with all natural phenomena is not to rise up and condemn it, but to discipline and regulate.[30]

Not to be outdone, PvdA deputy Paul Kapteyn recalled how Dutch ambitions in the 1930s to create an outlet in Strasbourg to sell coal were stymied by cartelized interests in Ruhr coal.[31] Remarking on GEORG, he said,

> Sometimes I am moved by the picture one draws of the benefits that the cartel renders to humanity. I have often asked myself if we have been victims of a frightful misunderstanding and whether our Common Assembly is not home to a dragon with numerous heads that, from all its mouths, spits fire on the saint and noble Saint Georg.
>
> (Smiles)
>
> That said . . . one can ask oneself whether a cartel of this nature is really so innocent.[32]

In a more extensive metaphor, he swept the Assembly's gaze back to the middle ages, criticizing the High Authority's leniency toward GEORG by recalling the "Pyrrhus victory" of William the Conqueror's Norman invasion of England,

> Like the Manchu victory in China led them to assimilate with the Chinese people, so were William the Conqueror and his men absorbed into the English people and so were bastardized the great sounding French names.
>
> A Beauchamps became Beachen, a Beaufort became Bedfort or something like that.

> I strongly fear . . . that the family names of the members of the High Authority will bastardize one day and become Georgevitch or something like that.
>
> (Laughter)[33]

Despite these contrasting remarks, socialists were already proving far more flexible in adjusting their stances on the cartel issue by 1955 than one might expect given their underlying disagreements. In two detailed policy reports in 1954, the SFIO delegation stated, "It does not appear to be demonstrated that the [coal] export cartel harms the general interest," a comment that reflected also the changing economic context that coal, scarce in 1948–1950, had become cheap and plentiful.[34] Albert Gazier conceded that a centralized Ruhr sales cartel was perhaps preferable to the "anarchy" that would result from de-cartelization. Nevertheless, in their view, GEORG posed the potential to harm community interests and therefore must be subordinated to the supervision and controls of the High Authority, which should be charged with monitoring its activities. This position provided the basis for developing a relatively strong socialist consensus on cartel policy in the ECSC's opening years.

That the SPD noticed that the cartel-busting High Authority was proving to be a hesitant, even lame enforcer of the treaty's anti-cartel provisions facilitated this emerging socialist consensus. Heinrich Deist, recently appointed to the SPD's ECSC delegation, wrote to Schöne and Kreyssig in October 1954 that the High Authority was taking account of German views and had "without limitation recognized the particular situation of the Ruhr basin."[35] SPD deputies, in consulting *IG Bergbau*, found that the miners' union, while relieved that GEORG had in essence been preserved, now worried that employers would escape public supervision and accountability.[36] Furthermore, as Tobias Witschke and others have demonstrated, rather than enforcing its legal powers to maintain the Allied deconcentration of German steel, if anything the High Authority assisted its reconcentration in the 1950s by not prohibiting a single merger that came before its authority.[37]

In 1955, socialists came together around a common position that was the most cohesive among the three political groups in the assembly, and the most critical of the High Authority's laxity toward cartels. They had relative autonomy at the time to do so, as the transnational trade union movement forfeited its opportunity to influence socialist debates, telling the Socialist Group's Economic and Social Affairs Working Group in April 1955 that "trade unionists cannot indicate a direction [on cartels] for the Socialist Group."[38] SPD deputies, conscious now that fears of the High Authority using Articles 65 and 66 to discriminate against German economic interests were unfounded, dropped the defensive crouch they had adopted within the Socialist Group. Schöne told the meeting, "It is a fact that many industrialists are delighted by the existence of the High Authority because they can form the cartels that they wish under its shadow." The month before, he and Nederhorst argued to the Common Market Committee that it was preferable that states or the High Authority have the authority to fix coal prices, rather than cartels.[39] Mollet explicitly sanctioned the group's decision to adopt an aggressive policy, telling the

Socialist Group in May that "the High Authority has lacked courage on the question of cartels."[40] Kreyssig, for his part, remarked that without a "public institution" the community would find itself operating a "policy of cartels."[41] Following remarks by Nederhorst, Schöne and the Belgian Henri Fayat, the Socialist Group noted that there was now "unanimity in regards to the question of cartels" to call for a public controlling mechanism under the supranational executive.[42] This unanimity built on the Economic and Social Affairs Working Group's conclusions. The SPD archive contains a blueprint in April 1955 for how transnational socialist cartel policy was stronger than the High Authority's proposals:

Differences between our [Proposal] and the HA [High Authority] Proposal [on regulating cartels]

Our Proposal	HA Proposal
Real Supervisory functions	Ineffective advisory functions
International occupation with HA-representatives	National committee without HA-Participation
Greatest amount of publicity	Compromised Non-publicity
Lasting HA-Supervision over production	Supervision only in crisis and shortage situations (not in normal situations)
Expanded areas of competence for committee	Only employment questions for committee
Positive policy for cartel question	Negative method of mere review of existing cartels and sorting out of allowed and forbidden practices
Danger: In place of national cartels comes an international super cartel! This requires our immediate activity (Schöne, SPD)	
Conclusion: The new cartel is nontransparent, un-supervisable, worse! (Deist, SPD)[43]	

On the basis of this consensus, the Socialist Group became the most organized and hostile faction in the Common Assembly to the High Authority's permissive policy on cartels. Nederhorst warned the High Authority in June 1955 that the German coal sales syndicate would try to take advantage of the "European relaunch" in the summer of 1955 to perform an end-run around community efforts to regulate and reorganize its activities. Schöne concurred, regretting the supranational executive's "overly restricted powers" that "constricts the High Authority to a kind of inactivity and neutrality" on cartel issues.[44] When, in November 1955, the High Authority announced that it would split GEORG into three organizations, the Socialist Group unambiguously rejected the decision as too weak. Heinz Potthoff, a German trade unionist and ECSC Commissioner, defended the High Authority's decision in a meeting with the Socialist Group but his words fell on deaf ears. Kapteyn, Nederhorst, Schöne and the newly appointed French Socialist Étienne Weill-Raynal took turns denouncing the High Authority's decision.[45] Nederhorst then presented the Socialist Group's position to the ECSC Common Assembly. "It is necessary, he told the plenary, "to substitute the existing organizations with new organizations the functioning of which will be as public as possible . . . and [that] must be supervised . . . in a permanent manner by the High Authority."[46]

Concentrations, state-owned enterprises and socialist views on competition

Despite lingering differences, in 1956, the Socialist Group synthesized an anti-cartel policy that, unlike the anti-cartel law emerging under Erhard's influence in Bonn, was not predicated on the principle of free competition. In internal meetings in February to June, Schöne insisted that the coal sector be permanently subjected to public manipulation rather than competition. Public authorities, therefore, not cartels, should mandate coal prices. Deist said that socialists must demand a "very strict public control" and obligatory publicity for cartels.[47] The ECSC should strip cartels of the power to set prices and grant the power, instead, to the High Authority. Dutch members Nederhorst and Kapteyn agreed with Schöne. Willi Birkelbach, SPD deputy and later president of the Socialist Group, confirmed his colleagues' view that Article 65 must be enforced. However, Schöne objected to using the word "liquidate" in reference to the Ruhr coal sales syndicate.[48] Rather, a publicly managed replacement should come into effect at the same time as the cartel's dissolution to prevent chaos on the coal market. Still, the German delegates joined their colleagues in rejecting the High Authority's decision to create three superficially independent coal sales companies. The High Authority's policy was little more than a farce: the three companies were housed in neighboring offices, shared a common mail box, and, in the next years, simultaneously announced coordinated price increases. Schöne remarked that, if the High Authority's decision stood, it "will be a capitalist authority that cannot any longer have the confidence of socialists." As "we are dealing here with a fundamental question," he reiterated his proposal that socialists make use of the only formal power they had within the Common Assembly, the right to censure the High Authority. That the Socialist Group came close to launching a censure motion in June 1956, the most politicized event in the young assembly's history, demonstrates the acrimonious relations socialists had with René Mayer, the new business-oriented High Authority President.[49] Though a censure motion would have been doomed to fail without support from Christian democrats or liberals, the socialist offensive is indicative of the group's success in crafting common positions, in particular in the fraught area of cartels, despite the unpromising setting in which such discussions began. The consensus was confirmed in January 1957 when, in preparation for the First Congress of Socialist Parties of the European Communities, the Socialist Group met with leading national political figures, including PvdA parliamentary leader Jaap Burger (soon after PvdA leader), the future Dutch prime minister Joop den Uyl and Belgian socialist René Evalenko. These prominent national figures explicitly approved the group's cartel policy.[50]

In 1956, the Socialist Group also reached a compromise on another competition-related issue that divided its constituent parties, the application of Community competition rules to the *Association technique d'importation charbonnière* (ATIC), a nationalized French organization that had a monopoly over coal imports into France. As the High Authority began its inquiry into GEORG, it also opened a formal process against ATIC in what many speculated was a politically savvy move to present the appearance of balance. French Socialists lined up with other

French delegates in the Assembly in support of ATIC. At first, Dutch and German delegates showed little sympathy for the French position. Schöne told the Common Market Committee in 1954 that he saw no difference between public and state cartels, stating that "in his view, the economic function and the effects are identical in both cases."[51] In February 1956, Dutch and Belgian socialists raised concerns that ATIC had the potential to discriminate on the basis of nationality in contravention of community law.[52] Dutch socialists in particular were concerned that publicly owned enterprises and national state aid could economically disadvantage small countries within the Common Market, as large countries had greater resources with which to aid their own industry.

In response, French socialists launched a campaign to convince their socialist colleagues to defend the nationalized body. In November 1955, a French socialist said comparing GEORG to ATIC was like "comparing a mouse to an elephant."[53] The SFIO submitted several documents to the group asserting that ATIC was an essential component of French economic policy, that it operated in the interest of consumers, and that attacks against it were part and parcel of a "liberal ideology" to roll back postwar nationalizations.[54] The SFIO's insistence bore fruit. Schöne said in February 1956 that ATIC's dissolution would result in a "mess and complete disorder."[55] In June, Nederhorst and Belgian socialist August de Block agreed with their French colleagues that ATIC "is not a cartel."[56] The faction took up the French proposal that, instead of dissolving ATIC, its framework should instead be extended to the entire community, with Kreyssig in December envisaging it as a move toward the "Europeanization," rather than "nationalization" of coal imports. The next year, Nederhorst complained that, "in general," the High Authority "is reacting more vigorously against governments than against businesses."[57] This consensus allowed the Luxembourg socialist Michel Rasquin to announce at the First Congress of Socialist Parties of the European Communities in January 1957:

> The difference between a private cartel and a state cartel is the following:
>
> 1) When the High Authority faces nationalized coal it faces a government; and
> 2) French coal faces domestic public opinion and cannot act in the same fashion as a private cartel.[58]

After the divisive issues related to Article 65 on cartel policy and its potential application to state-owned enterprises, the most significant feature of ECSC competition policy was the implementation of Article 66, which allowed the High Authority to ban economic concentrations that created "artificial" market conditions, though the treaty only applied to concentrations agreed to after the treaty came into effect. Socialists generally had a more favorable opinion at the time of concentrations than they had of cartels, considering them economically necessary for rationalization, economies of scale and competitiveness on foreign markets. Nonetheless, they again insisted on strict public oversight. Deist, from 1958 chair of the SPD central committee's political-economic committee and crafter of the economic section of the 1959 Bad Godesberg party program, began propagating a narrative about the growing threat that the economic accumulation of power in private hands posed for political democracy. This narrative merged the SPD's shift toward an anti-cartel policy in German domestic politics in the mid-1950s, discussed in Schröter's chapter, with the transnational Socialist Group's effort to craft a policy on the competition articles of the Treaties of Rome.

Community policy on concentrations got off to a slow start. Fayat was appointed by the Common Market Committee to write the first parliamentary report on concentrations. In December 1956, he told the committee that he thought that political objectives should be granted priority in the forging of community policy on concentrations. At the same meeting Schöne complained that it was not clear "what criterion [the High Authority was using] to determine the existence of an oligopoly in the market" and that "also in regards to concentrations, we would like to see a more active policy."[59] Several months later, Kreyssig told the Socialist Group that he thought it "dangerous" that the community executive had not developed its own ideas on concentrations and was using the crude measure of production percentages rather than assessing whether a business had acquired a dominant market position. Each case, in his view, required a "special inquiry" and he criticized the High Authority for being disinclined to exercise a "permanent control."[60] Deist supported Kreyssig's position.

With the opening of the EEC approaching, Deist authored a report on concentrations in the German economy that addressed the challenge of forging a community policy on competition in a general common market beyond the coal and steel sectors. He highlighted that concentrations were proceeding apace in all sectors of the German economy but emphasized that they were comparable to economic developments in the UK and the United States. In the steel sector, he acknowledged the "restoration of the oligopolistic market structure in its form before 1945 or even 1939 in the Ruhr basin and the failure of the attempt to re-establish some form of natural competition." The problem was not economic concentrations as such, which were "necessary in modern economies," but rather that "market power means the power to more or less impose one's will on others by means of superiority on the market," and this "economic power of business is in addition very often – the larger a concentration of businesses is – political power" that "offers possibilities for abuse of power at the heart of the democratic state." Three solutions were on offer: (1) "unleashing public control" accompanied by publicity; (2) "supporting or reinforcing weaker parties on the market," countervailing forces such as "consumer cooperatives or economic outsiders"; or (3) "paralyzing the organs that exercise economic power" by means of workers co-determination or other forms of power sharing.[61]

When Deist presented the report to the Socialist Group's Working Group on Economic and Social Questions in January 1958, he provided a policy and language on concentrations around which his international colleagues could rally. In German domestic politics, the concentration movement was considered a legitimate recovery effort from the irrational and punitive postwar Allied de-cartelization program but, Deist admitted, "from an economic point of view, it has certainly surpassed its objective."[62] After praising Fayat's report, he took a page from political philosophy, asserting that concentrations "are above all the accumulation of power [that] establishes relations of subordination of man to man." Kapteyn and Lapie explicitly praised Deist's remarks, while the Belgian Alfred Gailly emphasized the problem's importance and Gilles Gozard (SFIO) insisted on the necessity of publicity. The Common Assembly passed a resolution on concentrations in June 1958 that, on the socialists' initiative, demanded that the High Authority "take note of the eventual political repercussions of the movement towards concentrations."[63] In the next years, socialists united to insist that Community policy on mergers be based not only on economic but also on political criteria. In May, Deist criticized the High Authority for not "distinguishing between concentrations carried out due to technical goals [from] concentrations creating dominant market positions and acquiring political influence," while Nederhorst "also thinks that the Socialist Group should emphasize the political dimensions of concentrations."[64] This position led the group into conflict in 1959 with representatives of the High Authority. Facing a proposed merger of Krupp and Bochumer Verein, Nederhorst insisted in the Internal Market Committee that the "importance of a business concentration cannot be measured solely on the basis of statistics and technical considerations because there can be created a power susceptible to being used in a dangerous manner that cannot be expressed in numbers" and the High Authority's proposal "has an excessively technical and abstract character [that] does not remedy dangers of a political nature inherent to the concentration in question." Kreyssig shared Nederhorst's view that the High Authority should consider "the political aspects presented by concentrations," but High Authority representatives rejected this position on legal grounds, asserting that this would open it to charges of operating in an "arbitrary manner." Rather, they said, "It is up to governments to prevent such a danger."[65]

Though socialists had agreed to broad principles on concentrations, the large-scale mergers proposed first between Krupp and Bochumer Verein and then, even more significantly, between Thyssen and Phoenix-Rheinrohr, tore open old wounds from the early 1950s that socialists had largely succeeded in stitching over. Deist's international colleagues now mobilized his own rhetoric to denounce these reconcentration initiatives. Georges Bohy, a Belgian socialist, published an article in February 1960 titled "Democracy Beware!" in which he responded to media reports about the successful lobbying efforts the Thyssen family had personally conducted with Chancellor Adenauer to receive German permission for the merger. Bohy wrote, "I underscore that if financial groups can exercise such pressure on a government formed out of universal suffrage then democracy . . . is itself in danger, a danger of paralysis, a danger of impotence and deviance, a danger of being a phantom, an immense fraud."[66] This rhetoric achieved pride of place in an internal socialist report on concentrations that Nederhorst authored the next month. It highlighted the "political danger of concentrations of excessive size aimed against democracy," and warned darkly that in France, Germany and Italy, the largest countries in the Community, "the conservative parties are under the financial dependence of the concentrated economy."[67] At the end of his ten-page report, he demanded that either national governments buy Krupp out or the concentration be placed "under international administration with its responsibility entrusted to the High Authority," akin to proposals for "international socialization" that French socialists had advocated for Ruhr industry in the 1940s.[68]

This position placed German Social Democrats on the defensive. In December 1959, the Working Group on Economic and Social Questions met to discuss Thyssen-Rheinrohr's recent merger proposal. It was a tense meeting, as Deist and Kreyssig took Nederhorst to task for getting out ahead of the Socialist Group in his criticism of the merger, while French Socialist Henri Darras joined Nederhorst in questioning his German colleagues' claim that the merger was in the general interest.[69] Deist warned against discriminating against German businesses, citing a study by Günther Sieber that claimed that mergers in the steel industry were a Europe-wide, and not German-specific, phenomenon. In May 1960, Nederhorst published an article in a Dutch socialist newspaper, claiming

> On the German side a united front pressures for approval [of the Thyssen-Rheinrohr merger]. The Socialists of other countries and a portion of the Christian Democrats and some of the left-liberals from France for their part seek to counter the danger of a return of the prewar "Vereinigten Stahlwerke."[70]

A 1963 letter from Deist to Kreyssig makes clear his position, "You know that for more than ten years, since my days on the steel holding society [DKBL], I have considered and publicly said that this merger is necessary for technical and economic reasons."[71] At the December 1959 meeting, Deist defended the merger on economic grounds and sought to pose general principles for a socialist merger policy that, though they could not overcome socialist divisions on mergers in German steel, contributed to the general position the group adopted. Mergers, Deist argued, should have to submit themselves to four conditions, rather similar to the five "obligations" agreed by the Socialist Group in March 1960. These were: (a) cost savings brought about by mergers must benefit consumers, (b) public opinion must be regularly notified through publicity, (c) the executive must be informed of the exact conditions in which prices are formed and (d) businesses must notify the executive of any subsequent investment plans.[72]

Socialists, the common market and the birth of European competition policy, 1958–1962

Socialist Group members praised the inclusion of competition articles in the Treaties of Rome and thought they provided a suitable, if perhaps insufficient, basis upon which to build a supranational regime for regulating competition. The EEC Treaty's Article 85 banned cartels affecting intra-EEC trade with exemptions based on the German government's demand; Article 86 banned abuses of dominant market positions based on the socialist-led French government's preference; and Article 90 created a special status of "services of general economic interest," including publicly owned companies, that partially fell under EEC competition rules and were partially exempt, also reflecting here the socialist-led French government's point of view. In internal meetings in May 1957, after the treaties had become public but before their ratification, Schöne called competition rules "indispensable" and praised the wordings of the two articles, though he criticized that it was not clear who would be charged with determining if abuse had occurred and assigning sanctions. All in all, he concluded that "the dispositions for competition rules are sufficient."[73] Kapteyn and Nederhorst were more critical, arguing that the articles were not strict enough vis-a-vis already existing cartels and asserting that a supranational organization should also be invested with powers to make positive proposals including creating public organizations that would replace cartels. In Nederhorst's view, it was unclear whether the treaty provided such powers.

As national treaty ratifications took place over summer, the Socialist Group held its second congress with national party representatives. Hein Vos presented a report that highlighted the treaty's ambiguity concerning whether Article 85 represented a cartel ban. He concluded that such ambiguity "reflects precisely the internal confusion of liberalism." Socialists, he wrote, should state that "collaboration between entrepreneurs and businesses" was necessary for price and employment stability but "must be rigorously controlled" by a "public organization that includes workers representatives." He thought that the articles on public monopolies would prove of little importance because competition rules were to apply only to cross-national trade, while the state aid articles "appear . . . flexible enough for us to propagate our social conception of the community and, if possible, to modify its structure without violating the Treaty."[74] State aid was somewhat controversial within the group but generally, socialists permitted it if it contributed to other goals. Nederhorst, for instance, regretted that a larger scope was not carved out for state aid in the ECSC Treaty's revision because it could be used to keep coal prices down.[75] Schöne, by contrast, welcomed the EEC Treaty's Articles 92 to 94 banning state aid in principle but explained vaguely that "socialists envision substituting state aid policy with a dynamic economic policy" by community executives, implying a form of supranational planning.[76]

In the summer of 1958, the German Christian democrat Hans von der Groeben, newly appointed as the EEC's first commissioner for competition, began discussions with what was now renamed the Internal Market Committee on Commission efforts to implement the competition articles of the Treaties of Rome, a lengthy effort that eventually culminated in Regulation 17/62, finally published in January 1962. In these early debates, Nederhorst urged von der Groeben on multiple occasions to adopt a policy of publicity and strict executive oversight of cartels and mergers, suggesting using the United States as a model.[77] Vos' report for the October 1958 Socialist Congress also promoted a strong supranational competition policy, stating, "The intervention of public powers is necessary when competition is too strong as well as when it is too weak," noting that "competition has lost a lot of significance in today's economic and social system such that one needs recourse to public powers . . . to protect the precious vestiges of competition on the (current and future) European markets," a remark that, though distinct, comes closest of the socialist statements examined for this period to resembling ordoliberal arguments by emphasizing a need to protect competition.[78] In December, Kapteyn said that "cartels represent the greatest danger for the Common Market" and "the Socialist Group absolutely must act."[79] By 1959, the Socialist Group had coalesced around a more rigorous supranational policy to regulate competition in the EEC than the transnational liberal and Christian democratic groups.[80] In this context, the Socialist Group became the principle parliamentary ally of the European Commission in its effort to establish strict limitations on cartel practices in the common market.

In September 1959, Kreyssig intervened in his capacity as vice president of the Internal Market Committee to insert a paragraph into the committee's resolution on "The Rules of Competition" that demonstrates the hard-line position socialists had formulated on Articles 85 and 86. The paragraph reads:

> Your committee asks with insistence that the EEC Commission examine with particular attention the degree to which the effects of measures of tariff disarmament and the progressive suppression of quotas are destroyed by concentrations, ententes and other measures with equivalent effect concerning entire branches of industry. On this subject, the EEC Commission must above all carefully follow the practices of export ententes. In addition, it must take care that the abuse of economic power that could result or that has already resulted from geographic ententes, parceling of markets, discriminatory or boycott measures not cause the consumer to lose the benefits of the Common Market.[81]

In delivering the Socialist Group's position later that month to the assembly's plenary session, Kreyssig warned that "the number of these organizations, cartels, syndicates, ententes and other creations of this genre is much larger than we previously thought." "The Europe of Six," he continued, "we all know well, is characterized by an extraordinary multitude of powerful monopolistic groups. . . . The Federal Republic . . . is in the process of becoming again, by means of trusts, ententes and other measures, a classic country of cartels," while economic concentration in France was "extraordinarily strong" and Benelux was, quoting *The Economist*, "a cartel Mecca." Turning to Pieter VerLoren van Themaat, von der Groeben's subordinate, PvdA member and first director general of competition (see van Leeuwen's chapter for VerLoren van Themaat's role in early EEC competition debates), Kreyssig praised the "excellent conference" VerLoren had held in May in Milan. He read several passages from VerLoren's speech and then continued, "I will say in the name of my group that it should be well understood that if the EEC Commission energetically applies these [anti-cartel] measures . . . it can count on the support of the Socialist Group." Making clear that this was no partisan gesture, he then turned to von der Groeben, and quoted several passages from the "remarkable conference" he had held in Ratisbonne, concluding that his comments "are perfect!

Here is a new thesis [on competition], an excellent thesis!" With satisfaction, he concluded, if

> this declaration of a member of the Commission truly reflects the policy that the Commission of the European Economic Community will lead in this area, we will have already made a step forward and will be, it seems to me, on the right path to creating a European order.[82]

As van Leeuwen argues, the terms "order" and "ordering" were not exclusive to ordoliberals but rather were regular features of social-democratic economic discourse in the 1950s as well. Cramm also shows that Rolf Wagenführ, a German trade unionist hired to the ECSC's statistical office, advocated for an "ordering of the market." Lest anyone mistake Kreyssig for an ordoliberal in disguise, he then talked about the need for economic planning at the European level.

The creation of a strong supranational competition policy thus became a central demand of the Socialist Group in the EEC's opening years. A March 1960 document of the socialists' Cartel and Merger Working Group warns, "The creation of a more vast economic space . . . reinforces tendencies to concentration . . . [resulting in] an oligopoly." Furthermore, "Socialists fear rightly that the [recently agreed] acceleration of the implementation of the Common Market will provoke the accelerated creation of ententes, secret agreements between businesses and concentrations." Therefore, "it is necessary to accelerate the interpretation of Articles 85 and 86 [and] the elaboration of a regulation or directive to apply the principles contained in Articles 85 and 86." As for concerns about potential problems arising from excessive haste on the part of the Commission, the document concluded that "it is more opportune to proceed immediately and to create difficulties for the constitution of ententes and other private agreements than to be obliged later to fight against them in much more difficult circumstances." It called for granting the "EEC Commission much larger competence" in the manner, in particular by obliging businesses to register all ententes and cartels with the Commission.[83]

The Socialist Group's firm determination to build a supranational system for regulating competition comes out especially in its members' reaction to British-inspired negotiations for a free trade zone in 1958–1959 as well as to the British application to join the EEC in 1961. A close partnership with the United Kingdom, including dogged support for UK accession, was a consistent goal of European socialists up to the UK's accession in 1973 and held a privileged status within socialist policy on European integration. Therefore, it is all the more notable that the Socialist Group considered an accord on competition policy to be an essential component of any EEC agreement with the UK. The Socialist Group's internal report of October 1958 stated, "As for the Free Trade Zone, it will be necessary to define common rules of competition."[84] Dutch labor politicians were particularly concerned that an alliance of German liberals and industrial interests might use the free trade zone negotiations to destroy the bases for a supranational economic policy. In an internal PvdA meeting, Nederhorst stated,

> [German industry] sees in the free trade zone a means to escape these constricting controls. [German Economic Minister] Erhard parades his liberal ideals around but he really means in this way to loosen the supervisory and supranational grip. On the other hand one wishes for bonds among businesses in the form of trusts and cartels that can evolve as freely and easily as possible. This is the great political danger at this time and it is no coincidence that these political liberals under the strong involvement of industrial interests continue to actively oppose European integration in every possible way and have shown themselves powerful advocates that have as quickly as possible gone over to the ideals of the free trade zone.

To this, the soon-to-be Director General VerLoren van Themaat replied, "German industry expects from the free trade zone a weakening of the cartel policy."[85] The exchange is all the more remarkable as Erhard is understood to be an avid promoter of anti-cartel policies at domestic and European levels and an inspiration for the strict competition regime embodied by EEC Regulation 17/62. It appears from these quotes that Nederhorst and perhaps also VerLoren did not perceive Erhard's position in this way. An agreement between a UK-led free trade zone and the EEC fell apart in 1958 amid British-French squabbling but concerns that negotiations with the UK could weaken a competition policy in the process of formation resurfaced with the British application to join the EEC in 1961. Socialists made agreement on rules of competition a precondition (among others) for accession negotiations. Socialist Group President Birkelbach told the group in May 1961,

> The treaties creating the European Communities contain a solid core of dispositions (for example, majority voting in the Council, institutions, competition rules and a common policy in matters of external trade), subjects on which no negotiation that aims at weakening them may be envisioned, even with Great Britain. For the other parts of the treaties, the Six should show themselves disposed to negotiate.[86]

In September 1961, Nederhorst delivered this message directly to UK Labour Party officials who joined a Socialist Group meeting to discuss the British application. He said, "The liberalization of trade is . . . irrevocably tied to the creation of a common policy in the matter of ententes and concentrations as well as to a control of all concentrations of economic power." Furthermore, "It is no longer possible to control international concentrations of economic power at the national level [and] [t]hat is why control is indispensable at the European level."[87]

In 1959–1961, the Socialist Group engaged in a particularly intense period of consultations with economic and legal professors, national politicians, European commissioners and external lobby groups to formulate its position on supranational rules of competition. These conversations reinforced the group's move toward more restrictive policies on cartels. An association of socialist-aligned consumer cooperatives wrote to the Socialist Group calling for "a legal protection regime against all restrictions on competition practiced in production and distribution by monopolies, cartels and private trusts," and demanding that "Article 85 be applied in all its rigor" using the banning principle, in which cartels and ententes would have to demonstrate that "they operate in the interests of all consumers, including the final consumer" to gain exception from the ban.[88] In May 1960, the European Labor Committee invited socialist party officials and representatives of the Socialist Movement for a United States of Europe (MSEUE), a federalist organization, to a summer conference to discuss "the power of cartels and concentration in the European countries of the Common Market," as also discussed in Ramírez Pérez's chapter. Warning of the "concrete reality" of a "Europe of monopolies and cartels," it called on socialists to examine measures adopted at state and European levels and "elaborate, if necessary, a true antitrust policy for the Europe of Labor."[89] The resolution of the July conference called for a strong supranational anti-cartel policy from the standpoint of "a continuous, harmonious and regionally balanced European growth policy, a policy of full employment and social progress through planning and a coordination of investment."[90] That same month the Action Committee for the United States of Europe, the pro-integration organization founded by Jean Monnet in which socialists held prominent roles, published a resolution on the "Supervision of treaty-violating agreements and abuses of power by EEC institutions." The resolution proposed a "Commission registry of cartels and mergers" and the "granting of adequate full investigative powers to the Commission."[91]

In 1960, the Socialist Group's Cartels and Mergers Working Group held a series of intensive meetings as the Commission prepared its regulation. In March, Robert Marjolin, vice chair of the European Commission who was close to the French Socialist Party, updated the Socialist Group on the Commission's progress. He called attention to "the danger forming in Europe due to these cartels" and "even more dangerous perhaps the political power [that] these accords and concentrations will give businesses to counterbalance the existence of a European political power." When the time came to "engage the battle with [national governments]," he said, "we will need your help."[92] On occasion, the meetings included outside figures, such as Günther Sieber and André Marchal, French law professor who had delivered a report on "Cartels and Concentrations in the Common Market" at conferences in 1959. In June 1960, Fayat suggested adopting a policy based on the abuse principle that would examine: (1) "the disadvantage to consumers or other producers" and (2) "political purposes (danger to democracy)."[93] Dutch labor politician A.A. van Ameringen played an outsized role in the discussions, adding in October that "security in the employment field" should be added to "consumer interests" as a core factor in determining policies on cartels.[94] Moving beyond coal and steel, socialists emphasized the role of cartels in the automobile, chemical, paper and electronics industries. Schöne placed a large focus on financial concentration, and other socialists expressed worries that small numbers of people sat on many management boards and held large numbers of shares in multiple industries or companies within one industry.[95] There remained some internal disagreements among socialists. For instance, SFIO executive member Jacques Piette urged a less restrictive policy, especially on concentrations and, like Fayat, supported the abuse rather than banning position.[96] Socialists agreed though on the necessity of publicity. In his report to the working group, Evalenko suggested that the following principles guide socialist policies:

> It is self-evident that the Communities must maintain their corresponding control powers, especially as it concerns the effects of cartels and mergers. The productive costs and the sales price must be made known and verified by the Community.
>
> In each antitrust-law not just the juridical aspects, but the economic and social factors are the most important. On this basis above all must the advantages and disadvantages of merger plans or already achieved mergers be judged.[97]

In the extensive European parliamentary debates on the Commission's proposed regulation that took place in 1961, socialists consistently represented the most anti-cartel and pro-supranational position of the party groups. Cramm shows that the German Trade Union Confederation also adopted this position in the lead-up to Regulation 17/62. In a marathon session of the Internal Market Committee in February, socialists supported von der Groeben's call for obligatory registration and publicity of cartels against the views of the committee's rapporteur, Alfred Deringer, a German Christian democrat close to the ordoliberal Freiburg School of economics.[98] The leading liberal members on the committee wanted to weaken the Commission's powers and warned against the bureaucratic tendencies inherent therein. In response, PvdA deputy Siep Posthumus encouraged von der Groeben not to cede to industrial lobby pressures and Kreyssig supported the Commission's proposal to proceed with the banning principle.[99] The disagreement in the committee continued in April, when Deringer noted that a majority supported the Socialist Group's position in favor of obligatory notification.[100] Furthermore, Posthumus sided with von der Groeben in an unsuccessful attempt to change a paragraph of the committee's report to place more burden of proof on businesses, rather than on the Commission in determining whether a business held a market-dominating position.[101] In July, the committee approved Deringer's report, which included an obligation of notification, against the votes of most of the committee's liberal members.[102]

A united Socialist Group was not satisfied with the report when it was submitted to the full assembly for approval in October.[103] Noting that "their attachment to a strict application of the treaty" but also their willingness to compromise to reach a "quasi-unanimity on the Internal Market Committee," the group concluded that the "effort to reach a common position has been in vain" and called for amending the resolution to include the "obligatory declaration" of cartels and that "the absence of any retroactive authorizations be restored," proposals that had been included in the Commission's draft regulation.[104] This resulted in what Pitzer has described as "an especially extensive and controversial debate in the parliament" in

October 1961.[105] The Socialist Group tabled a series of amendments to restore the Commission's language and policies to the parliament's resolution, its final say on cartel and competition policy before the promulgation of Regulation 17/62 in January 1962.[106] Thus, the Socialist Group confirmed its status as the Commission's most earnest defender in the 1961 parliamentary debates on EEC competition law.

Conclusion

Not only was the Socialist Group an important protagonist in the political origins of Regulation 17/62, the birth of European competition policy, as this contribution has shown, but also a center-left government including the Belgian Socialist Party made a decisive contribution to the regulation's success by switching the Belgian government's position toward supporting the banning principle. Without this shift in power in the 1961 Belgian election, Laurent Warlouzet argues that the banning principle (supported by the Socialist Group and ordoliberals alike) might have been dropped from the regulation.[107] At the same time, socialists in the European Parliament, including Birkelbach, Kreyssig and Nederhorst, intervened to insert chapters on cartels and competition policy in a common socialist program on European integration that resulted from extended consultations between the socialist parties in 1961.[108] After painstakingly building a transnational socialist consensus on cartels and competition in the ECSC Common Assembly in the 1950s and despite some continued disagreement about policies toward concentrations and state aid, Socialist Group politicians were able to make clear contributions to the transnational conference.

In 1962, over 100 socialists gathered in Paris for the Fifth Congress of Socialist Parties of the Member Countries of the European Countries. Its purpose was to debate and approve a "Programme for Common Action" and "A Socialist Policy for Dealing with Economic Power in the European Community," the latter of which had been crafted by the Socialist Group's Cartels and Mergers Working Group. It formulated socialist policy on cartels as follows:

> Since the institutions of the European communities may come into difficulty due to their insufficient authorities, the Socialist Group has expressed support for a banning system within the European area. Within this system the party that wishes to breach the ban must demonstrate the correctness of their course of action; the business must therefore provide evidence.

The socialist policy report went on to state, "The Socialist Group has successfully pushed for a larger degree of registration. In this way the group has also successfully achieved an obligation of publication."[109] Hence, the crowning moment in transnational socialist efforts to achieve consensus on European policy in the early 1960s confirmed the Socialist Group's position as loyal supporter of the European Commission in its determination to create a powerful supranational regulatory framework to regulate cartels and competition. It would remain so over the next decades, as socialists railed against a "Europe of cartels" and pushed for national and supranational forms of merger control regulation, which succeeded in West Germany but failed at the European level in the early 1970s.[110]

Notes

1 International Institute of Social History (IISH), Amsterdam, Federatie van de Socialistische partyen Europese Gemeenschap (FSPEG)-4, Anmerkungen zu einer Konferenz der sozialistischen Parteien des Europa des Sechs.
2 Anselm Küsters, "The Making and Unmaking of Ordoliberal Language: A Digital Conceptual History of European Competition Law," PhD dissertation, Johann Wolfgang Goethe University, 2022.
3 Lorenzo Federico Pace and Katja Seidel, "The Drafting and the Role of Regulation 17: A Hard-Fought Compromise," in Kiran Klaus Patel and Heike Schweitzer (eds.), *The Historical Foundations of EU Competition Law* (Oxford: Oxford University Press, 2013); Sibylle Hambloch, *Europäische Integration und Wettbewerbspolitik: Die Frühphase der EWG* (Baden-Baden: Nomos, 2009); Frank Pitzer, *Interessen im Wettbewerb: Grundlagen und frühe Entwicklung der europäischen Wettbewerbspolitik 1955–1966* (Stuttgart: Franz Steiner, 2009); Laurent Warlouzet, "The EEC/EU as an Evolving Compromise between French Dirigism and German Ordoliberalism (1957–1995)," *Journal of Common Market Studies* 57, 1 (2019): 77–93.
4 Laurent Warlouzet, *Governing Europe in a Globalizing World: Neoliberalism and Its Alternatives Following the 1973 Oil Crisis* (London: Routledge, 2018), 159.
5 Brian Shaev, "Workers' Politics, the Communist Challenge, and the Schuman Plan: A Comparative History of the French Socialist and German Social Democratic Parties and the First Treaty for European Integration," *International Review of Social History* 61, 2 (August 2016): 251–281.
6 Office Universitaire de Recherche Socialiste (OURS), Paris, SFIO Comité directeur, 27 June 1951.
7 *Journal Officiel de la République Française, Débats parlementaires (JO)*, 6 July 1948, 4351.
8 Matthias Kipping, *Zwischen Kartellen und Konkurrenz: Der Schuman-Plan und die Ursprünge der europäischen Einigung 1944–1952* (Berlin: Duncker & Humblot, 1996), 37.
9 *Ibid.*, 72.
10 Archive d'histoire contemporaine, Paris, Groupe parlamentaire socialiste, 5 April 1951.
11 *JO*, 6 July 1948, 4351.
12 *Tweede Kamer, Vergadering*, 10 February 1948, 1344.
13 *Tweede Kamer, Vergadering*, 11 February 1948, 1386.
14 *Ibid.*, 1391.
15 *Tweede Kamer, Vergadering*, 25 January 1950, 200.
16 *Tweede Kamer, Vergadering*, 21 September 1950, 24.
17 *Ibid.*, 21.
18 Brian Shaev, "International Cartels in the Political Origins of German Competition Policy, 1949–1953," in Susanna Fellman and Martin Shanahan (eds.), *A History of Business Cartels: International Politics, National Policies, and Anti-Competitive Behaviour* (New York: Routledge, 2022), 83–102.
19 Archiv der sozialen Demokratie (AdsD), Bonn, Erich Potthoff 31, Protokoll der Tagung des Wirtschaftspolitischen Auschusses beim Vorstand der Sozialdemokratischen Partei Deutschlands am 25. und 26 November 1949.
20 *Verhandlungen des deutschen Bundestages*, 27 January 1950, 983–1003.
21 *Verhandlungen des deutschen Bundestages*, 26 June 1952, 9749–9756.
22 Ergebnis-Protokoll Tagung des Wirtschaftspoltischen Auschusses beim PV am 20. November 1952 Gesetz gegen Wettbewerbsbeschraenkungen (Anti-Kartellgesetz), Karl Schiller-104, Bundesarchiv Koblenz.

23 Brian Shaev, "Nationalism, Transnationalism and European Socialism in the 1950s: A Comparison of the French and German Cases," *History of European Ideas* 46, 1 (2020): 41–58.
24 Ursula Rombeck-Jaschinski, *Nordrhein-Westfalen, die Ruhr und Europa: Föderalismus und Europapolitik, 1945–1955* (Essen: Klartext, 1990), 147–150.
25 Historical Archives of the European Parliament (HAEP), Luxembourg, MACO-195311130010FR, 13 November 1953.
26 HAEP, MACO-195401130010FR, 3 January 1954.
27 HAEP, MACO-195404130010FR, 13 April 1954.
28 HAEP, MACO-195304190010FR, 19 April 1953; HAEP, MACO-195306090010FR, 9 June 1953.
29 HAEP, MACO-195410270010FR, 27 October 1954.
30 Archive of European Integration (AEI), Pittsburgh, Ceca. Débats de l'Assemblée Commune, 24 June 1955, 618.
31 For a history of the Ruhr coal syndicate's operations on the Dutch market during this period, see Eva-Maria Roelevink, *Organisierte Intransparenz: Das Kohlensyndikat und der Niederländische Markt, 1915–1932* (Munich: C.H. Beck, 2015).
32 AEI, Ceca. Débats de l'Assemblée Commune, 22 November 1955.
33 AEI, Ceca. Débats de l'Assemblée Commune, 19 June 1956.
34 AdsD, Gerhard Kreyssig (GK) 116, Vorschlag Gazier, La Question des cartels dans la CECA. Projet de résolution.
35 AdsD, GK-116, Deist letter to Schöne and Kreyssig, 25 October 1954.
36 AdsD, GK-116, Imig on *IG Bergbau* letterhead to Deist, Kreyssig and Schöne, 26 November 1954. See also AdsD, GK-118, October 1955, Vertraulich! Betr. Gemeinschaftsorganisation Ruhrkohle Arbeitsunterlage.
37 Tobias Witschke, *Gefahr für den Wettbewerb? Die Fusionskontrolle der Europäischen Gemeinschaft für Kohle und Stahl und die "Rekonzentration" der Ruhrstahlindustrie 1950–1963* (Berlin: Akademie, 2009).
38 Historical Archives of the European Union, Florence, Groupe socialiste au Parlement européen (GSPE)- 591, Compte-rendu analytique de la réunion du sous-comité des affaires économiques et sociales, 21 March 1955.
39 HAEP, MACO-195503140010FR, 14 March 1955.
40 HAEU, GSPE-591, Compte-rendu analytique de la réunion du groupe socialiste, 9 May 1955.
41 HAEU, GSPE-591, Compte-rendu analytique de la réunion du sous-comité des affaires économiques et sociales, 20 June 1955.
42 HAEU, GSPE-591, Compte-rendu analytique de la réunion du groupe socialiste, 12 May 1955.
43 AdsD, GK-117, Abschrift Bericht über die Sitzung der Arbeitsgruppe "Wirtschafts und Sozialfragen" der sozialistischen Fraktion in der Gemeinsamen Versammlung der EGKS, 19 April 1955.
44 HAEP, MACO-195507150010FR, 15 July 1955.
45 HAEU, GSPE-592, Kurzgefasster Bericht über die Sitzung der Arbeitsgruppe für Wirtschafts- und Sozialfragen, 12 November 1955.
46 AEI, Ceca. Débats de l'Assemblée Commune, 22 November 1955, 54.
47 HAEU, GSPE-593, Compte rendu analytique de la réunion du Groupe de Travail pour les affaires économiques, 17 et 18 February 1956.
48 HAEU, GSPE-594, Compte rendu analytique de la réunion du Groupe de Travail pour les affaires économiques economiques et sociales, 16 juin 1956.
49 Brian Shaev, "Flowers but no Bouquet: The Common Assembly's Relations with the High Authority of the European Coal and Steel Community under Presidents Jean Monnet and Ren Mayer, 1952–1956," in *New Europe College Yearbook 2014–2015* (2016), 349–369.
50 IISH, FSPEG AG5-12, Compte rendu analytique: 1ere Partie, 25 January 1957.
51 HAEP, MACO-11170010FR, 17 November 1954.

52 HAEU, GSPE-593, Compte rendu analytique de la réunion du Groupe de Travail pour les affaires économiques, 17 et 18 February 1956.
53 HAEU, GSPE-592, Compte rendu analytique de la réunion du Groupe Socialiste, 23 Novembre 1955.
54 HAEU, GSPE-593, L'A.T.I.C. (Association Technique d'Importation Charbonnière). Un point de vue français; HAEU, GSPE-594, L'Association Technique de l'Importation Charbonnière (ATIC) et la réglementation française du commerce d'importation des charbons, October 1956.
55 HAEU, GSPE-593, Compte rendu analytique de la réunion du Groupe de Travail pour les affaires économiques, 17 et 18 February 1956.
56 HAEU, GSPE-594, Compte rendu analytique de la réunion du groupe socialiste, 18 June 1956.
57 HAEU, GSPE-597, Compte rendu de la réunion du groupe socialiste, 14 May 1957.
58 IISH, FSPEG A5-12, Compte rendu analytique: 1ere Partie, 25 January 1957.
59 HAEP, MACO-19561217001OFR, 17 December 1956.
60 HAEU, GSPE-597, Compte rendu analytique de la réunion du Groupe de Travail pour les affaires économiques et sociales, 12 April 1957.
61 HAEP, AC-0026-57-mai0040FR, Heinrich Deist, Mouvement de concentration dans l'économie allemande, 1 October 1957.
62 HAEU, GSPE-600, Compte rendu analytique de la réunion du Groupe de Travail pour les affaires économiques et sociales, 10 January 1958.
63 HAEU, GSPE-602, Pierre-Olivier Lapie, Rapport sur l'activité du Groupe Socialiste de l'Assemblée commune de la C.E.C.A.; Journal official, Assemblée commune, Résolution sur le problème des concentrations d'entreprises dans la Communauté, 27 June 1958 444.
64 HAEU, GSPE-601, Compte rendu analytique de la réunion du Groupe de Travail pour les questions économiques et sociales, 2 May 1958.
65 HAEP, MACO-195902200020FR, 20 February 1959.
66 HAEU, GSPE-608, Georges Bohy, "Alerte à la démocratie!" *Le Peuple*, 18 February 1960.
67 HAEU, GSPE-608, Nederhorst, Document de Travail pour la réunion du 24 mars 1960, Points de vues socialistes concernant le phénomène des concentrations, 10 March 1960.
68 Brian Shaev, "Estrangement and Reconciliation: French Socialists, German Social Democrats and the Origins of European Integration, 1948–1957," PhD dissertation, University of Pittsburgh, 2014, 83–138.
69 HAEU, GSPE-607, Groupe de travail pour les questions économiques et sociales. Compte rendu de la réunion du 7 décembre 1959.
70 G.M. Nederhorst, "Kartelvorming," *Paraat*, 7 May 1960.
71 AdsD, GK-154, Deist to Kreyssig, 24 June 1963.
72 HAEU, GSPE-608, Groupe de travail: ententes et concentrations. Projet en vue de la discussion sur les lignes directrices d'une politique socialiste vis-à-vis du problème des concentrations d'entreprises, 1 March 1960.
73 HAEU, GSPE-599, Compte rendu de la réunion du groupe de travail pour les questions économiques et sociales, 21 May 1957.
74 IISH, FSPEG, A13-18, H. Vos, Bericht über den Vertrag zur Gründung der Europäischen Gemeinschaft, 4 June 1957.
75 HAEU, GSPE-600, Compte rendu de la réunion du Groupe socialiste du 11 janvier 1958.
76 Compte rendu analytique, Iere Partie, 25 January 1957, GSPE-596.
77 HAEP, MACO-19580717001OFR, 17 July 1958.
78 HAEU, GSPE-602, H. Vos, Problèmes de la zone de libre échange, 18–19 October 1958.
79 HAEU, GSPE-603, Compte rendu des réunions, Groupe de travail pour les affaires économiques et sociales, 13 December 1958.

80 Sandro Guerrieri, "The Genesis of Supranational Representation: The Formation of Political Groups at the Common Assembly of the ECSC, 1952–1958," in Lucia Bonfreschi et al. (eds.), *European Parties and the European Integration Process, 1945–1992* (Brussels: Peter Lang, 2015), 393–410, here 403–404.
81 HAEP, MACO-09100020FR, HAEP, 10 September 1959.
82 AEI, Ceca. Débats de l'Assemblée Commune, 23 September 1959.
83 HAEU, GSPE-608, Document de travail pour la réunion du 24 mars 1960. Les socialistes et les concentrations de puissance économique dans la Communauté économique européenne.
84 HAEU, GSPE-602, Pierre-Olivier Lapie, Rapport sur l'activité du Groupe Socialiste, 18–19 October 1958.
85 Archief nationaal, The Hague, Marinus van der Goes van Naters-58, Koos Vorrink Institut ter bestudering van international vraagstukken Partij van de Arbeid. Vertrouwelijk. Verslag van de conferentie inzake de Vrijhandelszone, gehouden op zaterday 2 mai.
86 HAEU, GSPE-610, Procès-verbal de la réunion du groupe socialiste, 10 May 1961.
87 HAEU, GSPE-611, Compte rendu analytique de la réunion du groupe socialiste, 5–6 September 1961.
88 HAEU, GSPE-606, Document d'information, 1959.
89 OURS, 27APO3, Enrique Gironella Letter, 27 May 1960.
90 AdsD, GK-152, Comité Européen du Travail. Aussprache über die Macht der Kartelle und Konzentrationen in den Europäischen Ländern des Gemeinsamen Marktes (Brüssel, 5, 6 und 7, Juli 1960). Schlussfolgerungen.
91 AdsD, GK-158, Aktionskomitee für die Vereinigten Staaten von Europa. Entschliessung III, 11 July 1960.
92 HAEU, GSPE-608, Confidentiel. Resumé de l'exposé du camarade R.M. concernant les recommendations de la commission de la C.E.E. visant l'application accélérée du traité, 25 March 1960.
93 AdsD, GK-158, Kurzbericht der Sitzungs der Arbeitsgruppe Kartelle und Zusammenschlüsse, 8 June 1960.
94 AdsD, GK-158, Kurzbericht der Sitzungs der Arbeitsgruppe Kartelle und Zusammenschlüsse, 7 October 1960.
95 *Ibid.*
96 OURS, 27APO3, Piette to Fernand Georges, 12 October 1961.
97 AdsD, GK-158, René Evalenko, Arbeitsdokument für die Sitzung vom 7. Oktober 1960.
98 Pace and Seidel, "The Drafting and the Role of Regulation 17," 73–74.
99 HAEP, MACO-196102240010FR, HAEP, 24–25 February 1961.
100 HAEP, MACO-19610411100020FR, HAEP, 11 April 1961.
101 HAEP, MACO-196105260010FR, 26 May 1961.
102 HAEP, MACO-196107110010FR, 11 July 1961.
103 AEI, Débats, Assemblée Parlementaire, Européenne, 19 October 1961, 19 July 1961, 182.
104 HAEU, GSPE-612, Document d'information concernant la consultation demandée a l'Assemblée parlementaire européenne par le Conseil de la CEE sur un premier règlement d'application des articles 85 et 86 du traité de la CEE.
105 Pitzer, *Interessen im Wettbewerb*, 390.
106 HAEP, MACO-610120FR to 610190FR, Documents de séance, 19 October 1961, amendments 11–12, 14–18.
107 Laurent Warlouzet, "Towards a Fourth Paradigm of European Competition Policy? A Historical Perspective (1957–2022)," in Adina Claici et al. (eds.), *The Transformation of European Competition Law – Next Generation Issues* (Alphen: Kluwer, 2023), 33–52.
108 HAEU, GSPE-611, Compte rendu analytique de la réunion du groupe socialiste, 5–6 September 1961.

109 IISH, FSPEG-5, Bericht über die Tätigkeit des Verbindungsbüros der sozialistischen Fraktion des Europäischen Parlaments (16. April 1960–14. Oktober 1962) von Willi Birkelbach.

110 Aurélie D. Andry, *Social Europe, the Road not Taken: The Left and European Integration in the Long 1970s* (Oxford: Oxford University Press, 2022); Brian Shaev, "International Cartels."

Bibliography

Andry, Aurélie D. *Social Europe, the Road Not Taken: The Left and European Integration in the Long 1970s*. Oxford: Oxford University Press, 2022.

Guerrieri, Sandro. "The Genesis of Supranational Representation: The Formation of Political Groups at the Common Assembly of the ECSC, 1952–1958." In *European Parties and the European Integration Process, 1945–1992* edited by Lucia Bonfreschi et al. Brussels: Peter Lang, 2015.

Hambloch, Sibylle. *Europäische Integration und Wettbewerbspolitik: Die Frühphase der EWG*. Baden-Baden: Nomos, 2009.

Kipping, Matthias. *Zwischen Kartellen und Konkurrenz: Der Schuman-Plan und die Ursprünge der europäischen Einigung 1944–1952*. Berlin: Duncker & Humblot, 1996.

Küsters, Anselm. "The Making and Unmaking of Ordoliberal Language: A Digital Conceptual History of European Competition Law." PhD dissertation, Johann Wolfgang Goethe University, 2022.

Pace, Lorenzo Federico and Katja Seidel. "The Drafting and the Role of Regulation 17: A Hard-Fought Compromise." In *The Historical Foundations of EU Competition Law* edited by Kiran Klaus Patel and Heike Schweitzer. Oxford: Oxford University Press, 2013.

Pitzer, Frank. *Interessen im Wettbewerb: Grundlagen und frühe Entwicklung der europäischen Wettbewerbspolitik 1955–1966*. Stuttgart: Franz Steiner, 2009.

Roelevink, Eva-Maria. *Organisierte Intransparenz: Das Kohlensyndikat und der Niederländische Markt, 1915–1932*. Munich: C.H. Beck, 2015.

Rombeck-Jaschinski, Ursula. *Nordrhein-Westfalen, die Ruhr und Europa: Föderalismus und Europapolitik, 1945–1955*. Essen: Klartext, 1990.

Shaev, Brian. "Estrangement and Reconciliation: French Socialists, German Social Democrats and the Origins of European Integration, 1948–1957." PhD dissertation, University of Pittsburgh, 2014.

Shaev, Brian. "Flowers but no Bouquet: The Common Assembly's Relations with the High Authority of the European Coal and Steel Community under Presidents Jean Monnet and Ren Mayer, 1952–1956." *New Europe College Yearbook 2014–2015* (2016): 349–369.

Shaev, Brian. "International Cartels in the Political Origins of German Competition Policy, 1949–1953." In *A History of Business Cartels: International Politics, National Policies, and Anti-Competitive Behaviour* edited by Susanna Fellman and Martin Shanahan. New York: Routledge, 2022, 83–102.

Shaev, Brian. "Nationalism, Transnationalism and European Socialism in the 1950s: A Comparison of the French and German Cases." *History of European Ideas* 46, 1 (2020): 41–58.

Shaev, Brian. "Workers' Politics, the Communist Challenge, and the Schuman Plan: A Comparative History of the French Socialist and German Social Democratic Parties and the First Treaty for European Integration." *International Review of Social History* 61, 2 (August 2016): 251–281.

Warlouzet, Laurent. "The EEC/EU as an Evolving Compromise Between French Dirigism and German Ordoliberalism (1957–1995)." *Journal of Common Market Studies* 57, 1 (2019): 77–93.

Warlouzet, Laurent. *Governing Europe in a Globalizing World. Neoliberalism and Its Alternatives Following the 1973 Oil Crisis*. London: Routledge, 2018.

Warlouzet, Laurent. "Towards a Fourth Paradigm of European Competition Policy? A Historical Perspective (1957–2022)." In *The Transformation of European Competition Law – Next Generation Issues* edited by Adina Claici et al. Alphen: Kluwer, 2023.

Witschke, Tobias. *Gefahr für den Wettbewerb? Die Fusionskontrolle der Europäischen Gemeinschaft für Kohle und Stahl und die "Rekonzentration" der Ruhrstahlindustrie 1950–1963*. Berlin: Akademie, 2009.

6 Ordering through competition? Pieter VerLoren van Themaat and social-democratic thinking about competition in the early postwar Netherlands, 1940s–1960s

Karin van Leeuwen

Introduction[1]

In May 1958, Pieter VerLoren van Themaat arrived in Brussels to take up the post of director general for competition (DG IV) in the newly established European Economic Community (EEC). Building upon ten years of experience in the Dutch Ministry of Economic Affairs, where setting up a new competition policy had been one of his key responsibilities, VerLoren van Themaat held a clear idea of the shape this new supranational competition policy was to take. Trusting his ideas to paper for his new superior, European Commissioner for Competition Hans von der Groeben, VerLoren sketched a competition policy that took what he referred to as a "medium course": promoting free competition in general, while allowing for restrictions where this served the interest of the Community.[2] With his recommendations, VerLoren distanced himself from the dominant approach to competition in Von der Groeben's Germany, where ordoliberal thinking had inspired a market-oriented policy that principally rejected all restrictions of free competition, including restrictions caused by business practices and dominating market positions. Instead, VerLoren presented himself as a proponent of the Dutch competition policy he had helped shape in the previous years. Unlike the German policy, this Dutch policy took a different, more moderate approach, only banning those restrictions that were contrary to public interest.[3]

In their analysis of the evolution of EEC competition policy, Sigfrido M. Ramírez Pérez and Sebastian van de Scheur introduced VerLoren van Themaat as one of the key proponents of what they labeled a "Keynesian approach to competition. With its "emphasis on public interest values," its "more tolerant stance towards cartels and state aid," and its "facilitating" approach to cross-border concentrations, this Keynesian conception of competition policy in the late 1950s presented an important, but often overlooked alternative to the ordoliberal approach to European competition policy, they argue.[4] This chapter, by placing VerLoren van Themaat's writings on and contributions to Dutch and European competition policy in the context of Dutch early postwar competition debates, confirms that, indeed, such an alternative conception of competition policy existed in the Netherlands, of which VerLoren van Themaat was a central protagonist. Exploring the

DOI: 10.4324/9781351010573-6

roots of VerLoren van Themaat's thinking, it aims to contribute to the more contingent and historicized understanding of European competition policy that has recently been developed.[5]

Due to his double role as civil servant and active member of the social-democratic party *Partij van de Arbeid* (PvdA), two contexts matter in particular to understand VerLoren van Themaat's thinking. In this chapter, both will be explored by analyzing and comparing archival and published sources from these two roles. In the first place, VerLoren represented an important evolution in social-democratic thinking, which is further explored in the second section of this chapter. Although competition policy did not figure prominently in postwar Dutch social-democratic thinking, internal ideological discussions suggest how, within the PvdA, classical socialist perceptions of anti-cartel policy as a weapon against power concentrations of businesses and undesired increases in consumer prices gradually were replaced by a more instrumental understanding of competition, in which competition policy, along with other economic policies, was to be used as an instrument *ordering* market functioning.

An important background to this ideological shift – and to VerLoren van Themaat's thinking – is the broader context of Dutch postwar economic policy that was shaped by government coalitions in which the PvdA shared power with confessional (Catholic, Protestant and Calvinist) parties from 1946 until 1958. The first section maps this context by reviewing earlier competition legislation developed in the 1930s as well as the more general developments in Dutch economic policy after 1945. Thereby, it will offer a fresh take on the pre-history of what in the literature repeatedly has been referred to as the case of a "cartel paradise."[6] Indeed, in the Netherlands, competition arrangements were allowed to flourish, especially once the new 1956 Economic Competition Act (*Wet economische mededinging*, WEM) entered into force. In early postwar Europe however, this was hardly exceptional. Like in other European states, the Dutch essentially adhered to what Gerber has referred to as the "administrative model" of competition policy: policies in which government officials played a central role and were "authorized to take measures against powerful firms whose restrictions on the competitive process were seen as harmful to society."[7]

As the first section will illustrate, a competition policy that only banned "harmful" competition practices very much fit the broader compromise on economic policymaking the PvdA and its confessional coalition partners had worked out for the Netherlands in the early postwar years.[8] In this essentially neocorporatist system, cooperation and coordination between companies was encouraged. Typical for the Dutch system, however, is that decision-making on social and economic matters more broadly was to follow from negotiations between social partners and the government – a clear concession to the PvdA's statism. Thus, the system provided the government with a means to "order" the economy, which marked an important difference with German ideas of "organized capitalism," which only regarded cooperation between companies.[9]

How both this broader context of Dutch economic policy and social-democratic ideas fed into the actual shaping of the legal text of the 1956 Economic Competition

Act and the negotiation and ratification of the 1957 EEC Treaty is analyzed in third and fourth section, respectively. In both sections, VerLoren van Themaat's contributions from behind the scenes will be compared with the interventions of PvdA deputies in parliament. A short final section will review the findings in the light of VerLoren van Themaat's later interventions in Dutch competition policy as the "expert from Brussels."

I. Crisis, war and cooperation: cartel legislation before 1950

Although the Netherlands at the opening of the twentieth century was marked by a high degree of economic liberalism, its earliest competition policies were anything but rooted in (ordo)liberal thinking. Following the path of many small states that after the First World War were confronted by policies restricting the international trade upon which their economies were highly dependent, economic intervention rather developed ideologically along the lines of democratic corporatism, leaving the responsibility for decisions that could not be left to individual companies to a dialogue of workers and businessmen.[10] With regard to competition, the centrist coalitions of confessional parties governing the Netherlands throughout the entire interwar period long persisted in the expectation that the open economy itself was to ensure that cartels did not gain root too deeply on Dutch soil – an expectation that, as Eva-Maria Roelevink's work on the German coal sales syndicate has illustrated, was not always realized.[11] Meanwhile, Dutch multinational companies, confronted with the protectionism emerging throughout Europe after the First World War, actively used competition-restricting agreements as well as mergers in order to keep up with their U.S. and German competitors that operated from much larger home-markets.[12] Only in the mid-1930s, when businesses urged the government to protect the domestic market from overheated competition that already had a ruinous impact on both profits and employment, did the Dutch government abandon its policy of non-intervention. The Business Agreements Act (*Bedrijfsovereenkomstenwet*) issued in response to these demands with the support of a broad parliamentary majority, however, left most decision-making in the hands of businesses and their collaborative organs.[13]

As an emergency act that was to diminish competition where it harmed public interest, this 1935 Business Agreements Act allowed the government to regulate cartels and even force membership upon uncooperative firms. Due to a strong adherence to principles such as free enterprise and self-regulation, however, the act did not allow the government to initiate such regulations. Depending on businesses to take the initiative, only a small number of cartels were formed under this act – which obviously did not reflect the number of informal competition agreements taking shape in these years.[14]

Not until it started preparing for a possible outbreak of war in 1939 did the then confessional-socialist coalition impose a further organization of the economy in which government officials were to take a more active role. Introducing offices administrating trade for each branch of industry, sectoral business organizations that already had emerged in the previous years were now to be joined by government officials controlling whether agreements concluded within these branches regarding production, prices and distribution sufficiently served the "general interest." At this stage, for example, the business-led "central office for metal industry" (*Kernbureau voor metalen*, 1938–1939) was transformed into the "government office for metal industry" (*Rijksbureau voor metalen*, 1939–1940) – the office that the German occupational government in 1940 converted into the *Rijksbureau voor IJzer en Staal* where VerLoren van Themaat started his professional career. By that time, however, the German occupation had completely locked off the Dutch market from foreign competition while markets had become completely state-controlled. In the field of competition policy, the 1935 act was replaced by the 1941 German-imposed Cartel Decision (*Kartelbesluit*), providing the legal grounds for a stricter regime with regard to cartels, introducing a cartel register and giving the Ministry of Economic Affairs the authority to dissolve cartels without further consultation.[15]

Immediately after the war, both the far-reaching competences of governmental planning offices and the authorities of the Ministry under the 1941 Cartel Decision were left unaffected, even though the lack of public support for this "German" law curbed the effective use of many elements that went beyond the 1935 law.[16] At the same time, wages and prices were still regulated. Also, in 1948, when, following on signs of economic recovery, many regulations introduced during the German occupation were abolished, not much change was to be observed in the field of cartel policy. As VerLoren van Themaat described in 1952, many of the cartel arrangements that had emerged in the 1930s as "Kinder der Not" (children of necessity) remained in place, even though they had lost their original purpose. While international competition still was minimal due to regulation of imports and exports, these competition arrangements conveniently secured efficiency and profits for their "parents."[17] Indeed, according to the data collected by the Ministry of Economic Affairs, in 1948, no less than 513 cartel practices were registered, growing to around 2,000 (national and local) practices in 1955. Moreover, the Ministry calculated that in 1952, up to 56% of the average Dutch household's expenditure was affected by registered cartels, mostly in food, but also in non-food items.[18]

Both the data published by the Ministry and VerLoren van Themaat's observations served to support the draft bill on competition that in 1953 would be sent to parliament. While the objective to develop legislation on "cartels and trusts" already figured in the program of the first democratically elected government in July 1946, the elaboration of such legislation would not start until 1948, after another round of elections had re-confirmed the wide public support for the confessional-red government coalition that would eventually remain in power until 1958.[19] Obviously, in the immediate postwar years, solving the shortage of goods and reviving domestic industry had been more important concerns for the department of Economic Affairs. Competition legislation, however, also had been held up by the development of the *Publiekrechtelijke Bedrijfsorganisatie* (PBO), a system of tripartite peak organizations in which labor, employers and government either in a certain industry or in certain commodities cooperated, whereby they could obtain self-regulatory authority. This system followed from the diverging ambitions of the coalitional partners PvdA and KVP to "renew" society at large and economic policymaking more in particular. Only when the PBO bill (the 1950 Industrial Organization Act, *Wet op de bedrijfsorganisatie*) was sent to parliament in June 1948 did the drafting of a new competition act start.

While the neocorporatist PBO system would deeply influence debates on this draft competition bill, the bill itself mainly resulted from difficulties in following up the various requests the Ministry received from the late 1940s onward to act against specific cartels.[20] In parliament, moreover, in particular, PvdA-representative Gerard Nederhorst had relentlessly reminded the coalition of its promises in this regard, fearing that otherwise the transformation of postwar planning into the new PBO system would allow business leaders to transform their previous agreements into corporatist forms of collaboration without any serious intervention from the government or workers.[21] As Shaev's chapter demonstrates in more detail, Nederhorst took a firm stance on competition, arguing that publication of the cartel register in the short term should already lead to a stricter control by shining light on the extent to which cartels benefited the public interest they claimed to serve. The next section will show that, while Nederhorst's "traditional socialist" concerns regarding the protection of consumers and the power of cartels indeed paved the way for a more active intervention of the Dutch social democrats in this matter, the PvdA soon took a more Keynesian turn, in which competition policy was to fit into a broader cyclical policy.

II. "Ordering" through competition: social-democratic thinking

Criticizing the delay in setting up a more active cartel policy, Nederhorst in the late 1940s proved himself representative of the traditional, socialist wing of the "Labor party" (*Partij van de Arbeid*, PvdA) that had been established in 1946 to "break through" prewar boundaries between the socialist *Sociaaldemocratische Arbeiders Partij* (SDAP) and workers voting for confessional parties. In the 1930s, Nederhorst had been part of the committee writing the *Plan van de Arbeid* ("Plan for Labor"), which, inspired by a quite similar "Plan" developed in Belgium by Hendrik de Man, claimed that the economic crisis and rising fascism had to be answered by an active economic policy of extensive public works, industrialization and an ordering of economic life into corporatist organs led by a central economic council.[22] The *Plan* marked a crucial step in transforming the SDAP from a party aiming at full socialization into a potential coalition partner in the late 1930s. And in the early postwar PvdA-catholic coalition government, the *Plan* served as an important source of inspiration for the interventionist economic policy that before 1940 had been unthinkable, but five years later was almost self-evident as an underlying principle of postwar welfare-state coalitions, as well as an important guideline for the PvdA in setting up the PBO-system.[23]

Yet, by holding on to the ideal of a planned economy well into the 1950s (if not beyond), Nederhorst, the PvdA's main spokesman on economic matters, increasingly represented a minority position among his peers. As would be articulated in the 1951 report *De weg naar vrijheid* ("The road to freedom"), the PvdA shortly after the war gradually abandoned its prewar ideals on more direct government intervention. Historians have traditionally explained this shift away from classical socialism as a consequence of the PvdA's aim to "break through" societal (and electoral) cleavages – an aim that well into the 1950s resulted in a strong preference for compromise and national unity[24] – as well as through French "personalist" ideas that during the war had introduced individual freedom as a central value in Dutch social-democratic thinking.[25] As the title chosen for the 1951 report indicates, however, its more immediate cause seems to have been the contemporary discussion on economic theory, and Friedrich Hayek's neoliberal critique of the dangers of economic planning more in particular.[26]

With regard to economic governance, *De weg naar vrijheid* presented yet another important step in replacing the ideal of socialization by a preference for "ordering," meaning that production was to be arranged according to government guidelines without transferring ownership to the government.[27] This increased government intervention was to prevent concentrations of economic power, while instead promoting democracy also in the economic sphere. This required an extensive economic legislation, concerned, for example, with establishment, investment policy and production policy, while, according to the report, competition law could also become instrumental to achieving broader economic policy goals.[28] This more instrumentalist view on competition was confirmed in 1952 by Joop den Uyl, the director of the PvdA's scientific bureau and its chief ideologist, who claimed that "even in a fully socialized economy, competition can actually fulfil a useful function" – an idea "with which socialists still have to familiarize themselves."[29]

Interestingly, the words used by Den Uyl strongly resemble those of a still relatively anonymous party member who, as an expert on competition law, had been invited to write a memorandum on competition in preparation for the *De weg naar vrijheid* report. Confronting leading party members, amongst whom was Nederhorst, with their own stereotypes, this civil servant remarked how, "in society at large and among social democrats in particular, cartels often were in disrepute." "However." he continued, "in practice cartels could both protect workers' jobs in times of crisis, while in quieter times they might indeed exploit consumers by fixing prices." Thus, VerLoren van Themaat concluded, a sound competition policy should not aim at banning competition agreements altogether, but rather at managing them.[30]

In his memorandum, VerLoren van Themaat, who himself later claimed to have been inspired to become a socialist mainly by the 1935 Plan, distanced himself from some of that Plan's most prominent authors, such as Nederhorst and former minister of Economic Affairs Hein Vos, who was an active participant in transnational socialist discussions on cartels in the European communities and a deputy in the parliamentary assembly of the Council of Europe.[31] It was probably their influence that steered the eventual 1951 report back to a more restrictive approach to cartels, placing the main discussion of the issue in the chapter on "economic concentrations" while arguing for a policy in which cartels had to acquire permission before being formed. VerLoren's suggestion to use competition policy as an instrument for "ordering" economic life, however, which closely resembled the broader approach to economic policy of the eventual report, was consequently reflected in the above-cited Den Uyl article. Thus, slowly, Dutch social-democratic thinking embraced the idea that competition policy needed to be inspired by not only concerns regarding the concentration of economic power but also the interests of consumers such as had been voiced by Nederhorst in the late 1940s. To these objectives, it added the aim of using competition policy to provide the government with an extra instrument to steer economic developments, and thus to regulate capitalism. In 1954, translating these aims into a future European competition policy, prominent social democrats argued that competition law should leave sufficient room for actual policymaking by the competent authorities. Furthermore, this policymaking was to be subjected to democratic, therefore, political control.[32]

From the mid-1950s onward, the emphasis in Dutch social-democratic thinking on economic policy further shifted to notions of freedom. In 1956, Den Uyl wrote, citing the influential German SPD ideologist and economist Karl Schiller, that the PvdA was to encourage "competition where possible, planning where necessary."[33] And in 1957, a report issued by the *Nederlands Verbond van Vakverenigingen (NVV)*, the workers union most closely associated to the PvdA, stated that allowing space for individual preferences with regard to profession and consumption was held to be a central consideration in economic policymaking.[34] As the next section will discuss in more detail, this further shift brought social democrats even closer to finding common ground with their confessional coalition partners over a new competition law.

III. Social democrats and the 1956 *Economic Competition Act*

Presenting the bill for an "Economic Competition Act" (*Wet Economische Mededinging, WEM*) to parliament in 1953, the then Minister of Economic Affairs Jelle Zijlstra placed much emphasis on the continuity of the proposal with regard to the present law. In the explanatory memorandum, he claimed that the government "continued to accept the basic principles of its 1935 act as right . . ., that both too much restriction of economic life, as well as too much freedom, are harmful for prosperity."[35] For insiders, it was clear that this stress on continuity was a deliberate choice.[36] In the previous five years, the foundations of the new law had been discussed in rather fundamental terms both within the department and in the consultation of the *Sociaal Economische Raad* (SER, Social Economic Council), the advisory body at the top of the tripartite PBO system in which employers, Labour, government and independent experts were represented. In the eventual bill, the general principles of the 1930s bill were indeed preserved. The actual instruments it contained, however, very much reflected the evolution that had since occurred in the practical use of cartels, as well as the shift in thinking on economic policy.

In spring 1948, upon finishing his work on the PBO legislation, the then 32-year-old VerLoren van Themaat started to issue memoranda to his superiors asking for instructions regarding the yet unfulfilled promise of developing cartel legislation. Meanwhile, he also initiated an extensive review of both standing Dutch competition legislation as well as practices and planned legislation from abroad.[37] As was reflected in these early policy documents, attention to cartel policy in the years around 1948 resulted at least partly from a fierce U.S. anti-cartel campaign accompanying the Marshall aid that started to have its impact. Yet, the "American" approach to competition was fiercely rejected both in these internal discussions in the Ministry and in academic circles.[38] Already in 1935, the Rotterdam economics professor Frans de Vries – at the time the main specialist – had publicly criticized U.S. competition law and its underlying belief in the functioning of free competition, an assessment he would repeat in an academic lecture in 1948.[39] That the policymakers within the Ministry of Economic Affairs agreed with De Vries was demonstrated when they managed to soften U.S. proposals for the Havana Charter, which was intended to establish a new International Trade Organization in 1948 – the Dutch prevented the clauses on the authority of this ITO to investigate transnational cartels from being phrased too specifically.[40] The failure of the U.S. Congress to ratify this Charter did not protect Dutch multinational companies from U.S. antitrust action, however, as multinationals such as Royal Dutch Shell and N.V. Philips experienced in the late 1940s.[41]

Unlike the U.S. example, the British draft bill on competition was cited favorably during the internal discussions on a new competition law, in particular by VerLoren van Themaat. In general terms, VerLoren supported a continuation of the prewar casuistic Dutch policy, allowing the decision to ban or approve cartels to depend on the demands of the time and society in which it operated. In legal terms, this casuistic approach rested on the term "general interest," which served as a precondition for anticompetitive arrangements to be approved – and, from 1951 onward, also to ban unfavorable cartels.[42] In the British example, VerLoren particularly appreciated the intention to involve parliament in the decision-making on anti-cartel measures. When he found colleagues arguing that such a procedure would endanger the legal security of businesses, VerLoren replied that it was necessary to protect consumers rather than producers. Aligning with his social-democratic-inspired understanding of the PBO as a system for economic "ordering," competition policy for VerLoren van Themaat clearly was a matter of (broader) economic policy, and not a purely legal question.[43]

In the discussion that followed the publication of the draft bill in 1950, legal security was already a key point of discussion. While the continuation of the casuistic prewar policy in general met with broad agreement,[44] the central concept that should guide this policy – that of "general interest" raised more discussion. Studying the legal consequences of the rapid expansion of social and economic law, a prominent lawyers' organization emphasized that this concept was impracticable in court, unless judges were to evaluate policy content.[45] Similar criticisms were raised by two economists, one of whom, A.A. van Ameringen, would also be actively engaged in the preparation of the PvdA's 1951 *De weg naar vrijheid* report and in later transnational socialist discussions on European competition policy.[46] As VerLoren would soon demonstrate, Van Ameringen and Brabers' harsh evaluation of what they considered mainly a tool to control "economic power" was in many respects ill-informed.[47] The concerns they raised with regard to the legal security of the procedure were, however, much quoted, such as in the many petitions sent to parliament by employers organizations and chambers of commerce. Moreover, they were seconded by the SER, the advisory body which at the time was chaired by cartel specialist Frans de Vries. Unlike other critics of the draft bill however, the SER did not favor suggestions such as opening an appeal procedure on decisions to bind, dissolve or modify cartel agreements. Instead, the SER suggested enhancing legal security by making the decision-making procedure more public.[48]

After Zijlstra took over the Ministry of Economic Affairs in 1952, preparing a response to this 1951 SER report was his first contribution to the draft *WEM*. As professor of economics, Zijlstra was generally known to be a supporter of the market economy, stating in his first general policy outline that he aimed to focus economic policy on the principle of consumer freedom and business interests.[49] Within the orthodox-protestant ARP however, Zijlstra represented a young generation in favor of a more active cyclical policy, thus distancing himself from the liberal policies of the party's interwar leader Colijn.[50] As a consequence, he had no problem accepting a suggestion made by the SER to strengthen the instrument of competition policy by adding to the bill a new provision allowing the minister to generally ban specific kinds of competition agreements such as price agreements at once.[51] In other respects, such as the SER's suggestions with regard to legal security, Zijlstra simply followed the decisions made by his predecessor. In the case of legal security, this meant that the SER's suggestion to make the procedure more public was turned down with the argument that such reform would deprive the government of its final responsibility for cartel policy.[52]

Thus amended, Zijlstra presented his bill to parliament in November 1953.[53] Due to the many requests and reports prepared by employers' organizations and the like, written preparations for the debates took no less than two years, one year of which was spent by the department preparing a detailed report of all information known about competition arrangements and their impact on the Dutch economy.[54] With many issues already smoothened in this phase, two main concerns were left for the parliamentary discussions in March 1956. The first regarded the involvement of the PBO in competition policy – a request that Zijlstra already had encountered in the Council of Ministers several years earlier.[55] Here, Zijlstra secured a compromise that kept the main responsibility for competition policy at his department, allowing it to continue its role in safeguarding the coherence of this "essential" element of economic policy.[56] Presumably, Zijlstra thereby benefited from the fact that the PBO system already appeared to develop less favorably than expected, covering only a few business sectors. The second issue, more controversial in the public debate, regarded the legal security of the businesses possibly affected by cartel policy.[57] On this issue, Zijlstra had to give in and agree with the preparation of an amendment bill that was to provide for an appeals procedure to improve the legal security of affected businesses.[58]

During the long and elevated discussions on the desirability of such an appeals procedure, Zijlstra could count on the PvdA for support – to a certain extent. Nederhorst, who found himself speaking again on the subject due to an illness of the PvdA's original spokesman, warmly welcomed the bill in general terms, claiming that in practice, the "abuse system" proposed in the bill did not differentiate too much from the prohibition system as it was applied by the German "neo-liberalistic" (sic) minister Ludwig Erhard, now that the latter in practice also had to allow cartel practices to some extent. Similarly, Nederhorst added, the European Coal and Steel Community (ECSC) cartel prohibition in practice did not ban cartels, but rather controlled their impact. Nevertheless, he argued, the choice for an abuse system meant that competition policy would become "an important instrument for the minister to engage in cyclical policy."[59] Such a use of competition policy in favor of broader economic policy goals did not, however, allow a uniform application of set rules, Nederhorst continued, thereby apparently supporting Zijlstra's defense against an appeals procedure.[60] Nonetheless, a bit further in the debate, even the PvdA defended such a procedure, albeit limited to cases of procedural injustice.[61] Apparently, as had also been demonstrated by publications of prominent PvdA official and later minister of Justice Ivo Samkalden, the social democrats could not stay aloof from concerns about individual rights, not even when this mainly concerned business owners.[62]

With the PvdA thus moving in a more "liberal" direction, it must have been surprised to find Zijlstra moving in the other direction. Asked by Nederhorst whether he would not use the policy instruments the new law offered in a too "neoliberalist" (sic) direction, the minister had replied by discerning various definitions of neoliberalism, one of which he immediately rejected: the ordoliberal ideal of free competition facilitated by state regulation. Alternatively, Zijlstra claimed to support a "healthy competition" that, based on a "balance of economic power," would eventually facilitate not only political democracy but also a "consumer democracy." Implicitly referring to the ideological development in social-democratic thinking in which notions of freedom and the interests of consumers had also gained ground, Zijlstra concluded that these ideas might just as well be called "neosocialist," as in some aspects, this was hard to discern from the neoliberalism he had just sketched.[63]

Indeed, in comparison to confessional, neocorporatist aims – preferring either non-regulation or, alternatively, regulation within the PBO's – social democrats and neoliberals did share a preference for regulation at the state level. And indeed, the eventual *Wet Economische Mededinging* very much reflected the evolution of social-democratic thinking on competition, which toward the end of the 1950s tended to increasingly appreciate individual freedom next to its Keynesian ideas of "ordering" the economy by means of cyclical instruments. Especially in the early stage of drafting, the hand of VerLoren van Themaat was clearly visible in the draft bill, for example, in the emphasis placed on the concept of "general interest" that was crucial for allowing competition policy to be used instrumentally. However, as VerLoren van Themaat emphasized in one of his many publications on the matter, the *WEM* also fit neocorporatist tendencies in Dutch confessional politics, to the extent that cooperation between businesses was to be approved, and even preferred over steering by the central government, as long as it served the "general interest."[64]

As one of the last "confessional-red" compromises in economic legislation – the coalition would break apart in 1958, giving way to a period of confessional-liberal coalitions – the prospects for the law were anything but perfect. Stripped of much of its political potential by the appeals procedure, the *WEM* was soon considered a "disappointment" by Zijlstra, who kept a close eye on it as minister in subsequent cabinets until 1967.[65] Indeed, until 1980, only two cartel agreements were formally suspended. Moreover, the informal way of steering, in which legal instruments such as suspension and prohibition of anticompetitive arrangements were mainly used to start negotiations with businesses involved in cartel practices (the manner in which competition policy in fact developed at the European level), was not used as much as had been suggested in the parliamentary debates.[66] In the meantime, the ideas that had inspired the *WEM* also guided Dutch policy with regard to European competition policy, which defended the potential use of competition policy for "ordering" the new common market.

IV. "Ordering" Europe? Dutch social-democratic ideas on European competition

Already in 1954, in a special "European" issue of the PvdA's scientific journal *Socialisme en democratie*, several leading Dutch social democrats had discussed "liberalization" and competition on the European level. Here, PvdA representative in the ECSC's Common Assembly Paul Kapteijn, among others, indicated that, as a democratic control mechanism was lacking on the European level, he favored a less "ordered" regime in economic policy than on the national level.[67] In a post-scriptum, Nederhorst, one of Kapteijn's associates in the ECSC Assembly, added that, while he favored ordering in the national context, on the European level, he preferred to stimulate competition, as this level already knew too much "ordering by businesses." As Shaev's chapter demonstrates, both Kapteijn and Nederhorst tended to be very critical of German cartels in particular, which they deemed to have gained ground in the ECSC. Implicitly referring to these powerful cartels, Nederhorst added that, on the European level, a "democratic ordering" of economic policy would only be possible after a phase of "liberalization."[68]

Throughout the 1950s, the positioning of Dutch social democrats with regard to European competition policy was often marked by a differentiation between the national and European levels. With regard to the ECSC, PvdA politics thereby hardly differed from official government policy, which in spring 1954 even filed a procedure at the European Court of Justice in order to contest the establishment of maximum coal prices by the High Authority, which the Dutch government considered a "disguise of existing cartels."[69] In its evaluation of the competition clauses in the EEC, the PvdA held a similar viewpoint. In the ratification debates, Nederhorst argued that the cartels and concentrations of economic power active on the European level should not be confused with the rather small and innocent anti-competition arrangements in the Netherlands. As a consequence, he could very well imagine that a common European policy was to be different, and stricter, than the Dutch legislation he had supported just a year earlier.[70] This time, however, Nederhorst found himself opposed to most other parties as well as to minister Zijlstra.

Interestingly, the "Dutch" competition policy Zijlstra and his colleagues claimed to defend against the stricter model promoted in the EEC Treaty bore the marks of the Keynesian, instrumentalist understanding of competition policy as embodied by the *WEM*. Already during the negotiations of the EEC Treaty, the Dutch government had actively defended what it referred to as the "European" model of competition policy – an abuse system, based on administrative control – against unwanted "U.S." influences leading to a prohibition system upheld by courts.[71] Most of these concerns mainly regarded the protection of the national system. Some reports – such as the SER evaluation of the Spaak report – explicitly added that the treaty clauses should allow competition policy to be used as a cyclical policy similar to Articles 58, 59 and 61 of the ECSC Treaty.[72] Internally, such concerns had already been voiced since the publication of the Spaak report in the spring of 1956. Yet, when in November 1956 Dutch negotiators sharply rejected German proposals for a prohibition system, this caused "quite some upheaval."[73] Standing alone in their opposition against the German delegation, the Dutch negotiators consequently had agreed on finding rather vague provisions for the treaty, which would leave sufficient room for the later legislation to take either of the two ways.[74] The evidence here challenges an existing account that the primary conflict in the negotiations was between the German ordoliberal and French *dirigiste* traditions.[75]

The eventual phrasing of the clauses in the treaty, which to Dutch eyes closely resembled German legislation, did not satisfy the Dutch government.[76] In the parliamentary debates on the ratification of the EEC Treaty, the competition provisions even turned out to be some of the most contested parts of the treaty.[77] Holding on to earlier agreements, Minister Zijlstra reassuringly claimed that the treaty was yet to be elaborated in legislation, whereby he would defend the Dutch, or rather, "European" approach. Moreover, Zijlstra added that differences between the Dutch and the EEC clauses were of a rather gradual nature.[78]

As had been pointed out in an alarming publication of corporate lawyers P.W.L. Brijnen and H.W. Wertheimer in 1957, Dutch businesses had good reason to be concerned about the competition clauses in the EEC Treaty.[79] In the Dutch constitutional setting, these clauses presented an immediate challenge for the execution of Dutch policy with regard to transnational competition agreements such as those between German industries and their Dutch sales representatives. In Article 85, the EEC Treaty appeared to place an immediate ban on such cartels. The wording of the article allowed for direct applicability, which in the Dutch constitutional setting meant that it could already be invoked in court cases dealing with the (in)validity of competition agreements as soon as the treaty was ratified.[80] The uncertainty created by the contradictory orientation of the treaty articles on the one hand and national law on the other hand eventually was "solved" by passing a special law leaving the enforcement of national and EEC rules to the discretion of the Minister of Economic Affairs.[81] While this solution did not suffice to guarantee legal security to companies involved in transnational competition agreements, it also gave no assurances for the direction the new European competition policy was to take.

In the turmoil caused by the new treaty clauses on competition in the Dutch parliament, the PvdA was remarkably silent. Apart from Nederhorst's remarks on the need for a stricter competition policy at the EEC level, the PvdA concentrated its contribution on the other parts of the treaty. Earlier, VerLoren van Themaat, who according to his own account had only been indirectly involved in the drafting of the clauses, had defended a similar position with regard to the further development of European cartel policy.[82] In an academic article, VerLoren described the difference between national and European policy as being basically of a procedural kind. According to him, the best guarantee for a European policy to be impartial and non-discriminatory might very well lay in a prohibition system rather than an abuse system. Moreover, he added that, in this context, a court possibly also was to be given a prominent role – something he had fiercely rejected in the Dutch context.[83] Thus, in agreement with his political associates in the PvdA, VerLoren argued for separating ideas on national competition policy from ideas on competition legislation at the supranational level.

Nonetheless, when, a year later, VerLoren found himself heading the directorate general charged with designing the new European competition regulations – a task he himself had claimed should be done "unprejudiced by national constructions, finding those constructions that guarantee the best equilibrium between policy considerations, avoidance of unnecessary administrative tasks and legal security" he actually did bring some Dutch influences to Brussels.[84] As has been previously noted, these influences in the first place comprised his practical experience with developing a competition policy on the basis of a case-by-case approach, rather than a strict ideological view on competition. As in the early 1950s in The Hague, VerLoren began by setting up an office of investigators and starting test cases in order to gradually develop a clearer understanding of what could and could not be allowed.[85]

Secondly, inspired by his social-democratic background, VerLoren also continued to regard competition policy as an instrument of economic policy more broadly – even though the EEC's limited competences did not allow the Commission to pursue a fully-fledged cyclical policy. In the short term, its scope could be limited to promoting competition within the common market. Thereby, the instrument of competition policy was to play a much more central role than on the national level, where a detailed system of cyclical and structural policies on prices and settlements, for example, provided greater instruments for economic policy.[86] This broader aim explains why VerLoren recruited economists as well as lawyers for the new directorate general: for him, competition policy built an integral part of a broader economic policy with both structural and cyclical elements, including aims such as price stability and a "rational" distribution of employment and resources.[87] As Shaev's chapter shows, these ambitions for a supranational economic policy aligned very well with the ideas the Socialist Group promoted in the European Parliament.

Conclusion

In September 1960, VerLoren van Themaat was invited to The Hague to address an audience of Dutch lawyers on the occasion of the founding of the Dutch Association for European Law (*Nederlandse Vereniging voor Europees Recht*, NVER). Sketching the early developments of European economic integration, VerLoren put great emphasis on the central role of free competition in advancing this integration. Turning to actual legislation, he pointed out that this regarded not only the cartel regulations that would soon be published but also EEC policies with regard to tax harmonization, anti-dumping measures and legislation concerning the opening of new businesses. With regard to cartel policy more in particular, VerLoren, backing a recent critical intervention of his political associate Samkalden in parliament, argued that the Dutch government should be less reluctant in "synchronizing" its domestic legislation to the demands of "European legal development."[88] Concluding with a call upon his audience to actively contribute to this "synchronization," VerLoren must have left some of his listeners with the impression that he had been fully converted to the very German, ordoliberal approach to competition he had only years ago helped Zijlstra to resist. Yet, drawing from the explorations into Dutch social-democratic thinking on competition summed up earlier, the *instrumental* and hence contextual understanding of competition policy in this 1960 speech shows considerable consistency with the intentions behind the 1956 law VerLoren had helped create – even when the actual actions he called for challenged the application of this law.

As this chapter has demonstrated, the instrumental approach to competition policy propagated by VerLoren also influenced social-democratic thinking on competition policy in the postwar Netherlands in important ways. Until the late 1940s, social-democratic interventions on cartel issues had mostly been inspired by more traditional concerns about the unwanted power of business concentrations and the rise of consumer prices. The 1950s however witnessed the emergence of competition policy as an instrument for government to influence economic performance with regard to goals such as employment stability and welfare levels. This change not only reflected an ideological evolution of social-democratic thinking inspired by personalism among other ideas but was also closely intertwined with the political situation of the PvdA as a partner in successive "confessional-red" government coalitions for most of the 1950s. Having substituted ideals of socialization through the realization of the PBO-system – a tripartite version of the neocorporatist ideal of sectoral self-organization – social democrats sought to define competition policy as an alternative means for the government to "steer" economic policy. Thus, debating a new competition law, they aimed to safeguard the responsibility for defining policy goals for central government authorities, which were to be controlled by a democratic, political organ only. In practice, this meant that the PvdA favored proposals to define the aim of competition policy in very general terms of "public interest" while rejecting judicial control of its execution.

In the development of the 1956 Dutch competition law, the *Wet Economische Mededinging*, this Keynesian understanding of competition policy as an instrument of counter-cyclical policy had a major impact. Broadly shared within the "confessional-red" government coalition, this understanding moreover also inspired the positioning of the Dutch government with respect to the parallel elaboration of competition policies on the global and European level. Taking pride in having already defended a "European," administrative-based conception of competition policy against "U.S.," antitrust influences in the context of the Havana Charter in 1948, the Dutch government left its traditional position somewhat with regard to the ECSC, where it favored a stricter policy with regard to the German coal sales syndicate that had dominated Dutch markets already for decades. Thereby, the Dutch government's view closely resembled the approach of prominent social democrats, who also took a firm position vis-a-vis the powerful German cartels. With regard to the EEC negotiations, social democrats and the Dutch government differed. While the latter again emphasized the Dutch preference for a "European" competition policy as opposed to German ordoliberalism, PvdA politicians now moved toward a more transnational position, emphasizing that the EEC context was totally different from national cartel issues. As VerLoren's 1960 speech illustrates, Dutch social democrats came to favor a stricter European competition policy as an instrument to stimulate transnational trade and protect the Dutch economy from the pernicious impact of foreign – German – cartels in a European common market.

Unlike in ordoliberal thinking, where competition is an aim in itself, competition policy for VerLoren remained an instrument of economic policy alongside many others. The extent to which this guided his thinking may be illustrated by the fact that VerLoren decided to leave his Brussels office when the directorate general he was responsible for lost its "other" portfolios concerning tax policy and harmonization in 1966. In his understanding of economic policy, which he consequently continued to carry out as professor in social and economic law in Utrecht, this rearrangement of portfolios threatened the coherence of the competition policy he had in mind for the EEC.[89] In his later career, publications on themes such as coordination, planning and ordering of economic policy persistently emphasized a similar broad approach of competition policy as one of many "ordering" instruments.[90] For researchers aiming to better understand social-democratic thinking about competition, it seems equally important not to restrict themselves to ordoliberal definitions that in later decades came to dominate European and national policies. As this chapter has laid out, VerLoren van Themaat's work offers an excellent starting point for further explorations of such alternative conceptions of competition.

Notes

1 The author wishes to thank the editors and Bram Mellink, Merijn Oudenampsen and Naomi Woltring for their valuable comments in preparation of this chapter.
2 Note "Wettbewerbspolitik," 25 May 1958, originally in Von der Groeben's private papers, as quoted in Katja Seidel, *The Process of Politics in Europe: The Rise of European Elites and Supranational Institutions* (London: I.B. Tauris, 2010), 134 and in Sigfrido Ramírez Pérez and Sebastian van de Scheur, "The Evolution of the Law on Articles 85 and 86 EEC," in Kiran Klaus Patel and Heike Schweitzer (eds.), *The Historical Foundations of EU Competition Law* (Oxford: Oxford University Press, 2013), 27–28.
3 B. Bouwens and J. Dankers, "The Invisible Handshake. Cartelization in the Netherlands, 1930–2000," *Business History Review* 84, 4 (2011).
4 Ramírez Pérez and Van de Scheur, "The Evolution of the Law on Articles 85 and 86 EEC," 21, 28–29.
5 See the aforementioned Kiran Klaus Patel and Heike Schweitzer (eds.), *The Historical Foundations of EU Competition Law* (Oxford: Oxford University Press, 2013).
6 This term was minted in H.W. de Jong, "Het kartelparadijs: punten van bezwaar," *Economisch-statistische Berichten* 77, 2 (1990) and returns as "cartel haven" in for example

Adrian Künzler and Laurent Warlouzet, "National Traditions of Competition Law," in Kiran Klaus Patel and Heike Schweitzer (eds.), *The Historical Foundations of EU Competition Law* (Oxford: Oxford University Press, 2013), 91 and – less directly – in Lilian T.D. Petit, Jarig van Sinderen and Peter A.G. van Bergeijk, "How the Tortoise Became a Hare. On the Initial Sclerosis and Ultimate Modernisation of Dutch Competition Policy," in Susanna Fellman, Peter Sandberg and Martin Shanahan (eds.), *Regulating Competition: Cartel Registers in the Twentieth-Century World* (London: Routledge, 2015) who use the image of a "tortoise." See for a critical discussion Wendy Asbeek Brusse and Richard Griffiths, "Paradise Lost or Paradise Regained? Cartel Policy and Cartel Legislation in the Netherlands," in Stephen Martin (ed.), *Competition Policies in Europe* (Amsterdam: Elsevier, 1998), 35.

7 David J. Gerber, *Law and Competition in Twentieth Century Europe: Protecting Prometheus* (Oxford: Oxford University Press, 1998), 174.

8 On the close links between the Dutch consultative model of policymaking ("poldermodel") and its competition policies, also see, for example, Bouwens and Dankers, "The Invisible Handshake" and Petit, Van Sinderen and Van Bergeijk, "How the Tortoise Became a Hare."

9 Martin Höpner, "Sozialdemokratie, Gewerkschaften Und Organisierter Kapitalismus, 1880–2002," MPIfG Discussion Paper, Max Planck Institute for the Study of Societies, 2004. https://econpapers.repec.org/paper/zbwmpifgd/0410.htm.

10 Peter J. Katzenstein, *Small States in World Markets: Industrial Policy in Europe* (Ithaca: Cornell University Press, 1985).

11 Eva-Maria Roelevink, *Organisierte Intransparenz: Das Kohlensyndikat und der Niederländische Markt, 1915–1932* (München: Beck, 2015).

12 The four big multinationals were Philips, AKU, Shell and Unilever: Bram Bouwens and Joost Dankers, *Bedrijfsleven in Nederland in de Twintigste Eeuw. Tussen Concurrentie En Concentratie* (Amsterdam: Boom, 2012); for case studies, see Pål Thonstad Sandvik and Espen Storli, "Big Business and Small States: Unilever and Norway in the Interwar Years," *The Economic History Review* 66, 1 (2013); and Harm G. Schröter, "Easy Prey? Firms Based in Small Nations and International Cartels, 1919–1939," *Scandinavian Economic History Review* 60, 2 (2012).

13 Bouwens and Dankers, "The Invisible Handshake," 755.

14 Only 45 requests for binding agreements were filed, of which 15 were granted. Further, three requests were submitted to declare agreements non-binding, all of which failed. Petit, Van Sinderen and Van Bergeijk, "How the Tortoise Became a Hare."

15 Bouwens and Dankers, "The Invisible Handshake," 756–757.

16 *Handelingen Tweede Kamer* (proceedings of Second Chamber, hereafter: *HTK*) 1947–1948 B 600 X 6, 11; National Archives, the Netherlands (NL-NA), Economische Zaken/Centraal Archief (EZ/CA), 2.06.87, inv. no. 4097, "Nota betreffende een wet tot vervanging van het kartelbesluit," 10 January 1950.

17 P. VerLoren van Themaat, "Het Kartelbeleid sinds de Bevrijding," *Sociaal-Economische Wetgeving* 1, 5 (1952): 132.

18 Wendy Asbeek Brusse and Richard T. Griffiths, "Early Cartel Legislation and Cartel Policy in the Netherlands. In Memoriam," *Acta Politica* 32, 4 (1997). Original data in NL-NA, EZ/CA, 2.06.87, inv. no. 4099; reproduced in *HTK* 1953–1954 B 3295 no. 8–9, "Benadering van het gedeelte van het huishoudbudget waarop invloed wordt uitgeoefend door kartels," 10 March 1952.

19 *Handelingen Verenigde Vergadering* (proceedings of the United Chambers) 1946-II, 2.

20 NL-NA, EZ/CA, 2.06.87, inv. no. 4097, Memorandum P. VerLoren van Themaat to Woudstra, 1 December 1948. For an overview of the interventions of the Ministry, see idem, inv. no. 2401, "Rapport inzake kartelvorming in het Nederlandse bedrijfsleven en de overheidsbemoeiing met bedrijfsregelingen in de periode 1945–1953."

21 *HTK* 1947–1948 B 600 X 4, 1; *HTK* 1947–1948, 1336, 1338. Also see G. Nederhorst, "De vakbeweging en de regeringspolitiek," *Paraat* 3, 28 (1948): 2.

22 F.J. Ter Heide, *Ordening en verdeling: besluitvorming over sociaal-economisch beleid in Nederland, 1949–1958* (Kampen: Kok Agora, 1986), 25.
23 Ter Heide, *Ordening en verdeling*, 25–29; J.M.M.J. Clerx, "Economische expansie door liberalisatie," in P.F. Maas (ed.), *Het Kabinet-Drees-Van Schaik (1948–1951)* (Nijmegen: Centrum voor Parlementaire Geschiedenis, 1991).
24 Bram Mellink, "Tweedracht maakt macht. De PvdA, de doorbraak en de ontluikende polarisatiestrategie (1946–1966)," *BMGN – Low Countries Historical Review* 126, 2 (2011).
25 Bart Tromp, *Het sociaal-democratisch programma. De beginselprogramma's van de SDB, SDAP en PvdA 1878–1977* (Amsterdam: Bert Bakker, 2002), 243.
26 Friedrich Hayek, *The Road to Serfdom* (London: Routledge, 1944). I thank Bram Mellink and Merijn Oudenampsen for this valuable insight.
27 Hein Vos, *De weg naar vrijheid: een socialistisch perspectief* (Amsterdam: De Arbeiderspers, 1951), 34–35.
28 Tromp, *Het sociaal-democratisch programma*, 295–299; Ter Heide, *Ordening en verdeling*, 189.
29 J.M. den Uyl, "Heroriëntering van het socialisme," *Socialisme en Democratie* 9, 5 (1952): 282.
30 International Institute for Social History (IISH), Den Uyl archive, ARCH01509, inv no 149, P. VerLoren van Themaat, "Van ondernemersovereenkomstenwet tot voorontwerp van Wet economische mededinging. De evolutie in de ondernemerswereld sinds 1935" (undated). Also see IISH, PvdA archive, ARCH01125, inv. no. 1505, P. VerLoren van Themaat, memo for the PvdA "werkgroep voor economische aangelegenheden" (undated, probably 1947–1948).
31 P. VerLoren van Themaat, "Waarom ik 50 jaar geleden deelnam aan de oprichting van de PvdA en er nog steeds lid van ben," *Socialisme en Democratie* 53, 5 (1996). Vos had hired VerLoren van Themaat at his department and probably also introduced him in the PvdA committee preparing *De weg naar vrijheid.*
32 "Economische integratie. Verslag van een gesprek tussen P.J. Kapteyn, J.J. van der Lee, I. Samkalden, J. Tinbergen en J.M. den Uyl. Met een naschrift van G.M. Nederhorst," *Socialisme en democratie* 11, 11 (1954): 662.
33 J.M. den Uyl, "Theorie en beweging," *Socialisme en Democratie* 13, 2 (1956): 154.
34 Ter Heide, *Ordening en verdeling*, 199.
35 *HTK* 1952–1953 B 3295 no. 3.
36 NL-NA, EZ/CA, 2.06.87, inv. no. 4098, P. VerLoren van Themaat, "Het wetsontwerp". Internal memorandum (March 1953).
37 NL-NA, EZ/CA, 2.06.87, inv. no. 4097, Minutes "Kartelbespreking afdeling bedrijfsorganisatie," 9 June 1948 and further and memorandum P. VerLoren van Themaat to Woudstra, 8 July 1948.
38 Asbeek Brusse and Griffiths, "Early Cartel Legislation," 391; on the U.S. pressure also NL-NA, EZ/CA, 2.06.87, inv. no. 4097, memorandum P. VerLoren van Themaat to Secretary of State, 22 December 1949.
39 Albert Mulder and M.R. Mok, *Kartelrecht* (Alphen aan den Rijn: Samsom, 1962), 28. It concerned F. de Vries, "Regeling of vrijheid," *Jaarboek der Nederlandsche Handelshoogeschool* 11 (1934–35); and idem, "Wettelijke bestrijding van de concentratie van economische macht in de Verenigde Staten van Amerika," *Jaarboek der Koninklijke Nederlandsche Akademie van Wetenschappen* (1947–1948).
40 NL-NA, EZ/CA, 2.06.87, inv. no. 4097, memorandum P. VerLoren van Themaat to Woudstra, 8 July 1948.
41 NL-NA, EZ/CA, 2.06.87, inv. no. 2396, "Rapport Werkgroep maatregelen anti-trustprocedure," 1952.
42 NL-NA, EZ/CA, 2.06.87, inv. no. 4097, minutes "Kartelbespreking afdeling bedrijfsorganisatie" 22 July 1948. In 1951, a temporary Business Regulation Suspension Act

(*Wet Schorsing Bedrijfsregelingen*) replaced previous legislation allowing the ministry to respond to complaints more effectively and at the same time actively search for unwelcome business agreements.

43 NL-NA, EZ/CA, 2.06.87, inv. no. 4097, minutes "Kartelbespreking afdeling bedrijfsorganisatie," 22 July 1948 and 27 October 1948 and memorandum VerLoren van Themaat "Nota betreffende een wet tot vervanging van het kartelbesluit," September 1949.

44 See for an overview I. Samkalden, "Het Wetsontwerp Economische Mededinging," *Sociaal-Economische Wetgeving* 2, 2 (1953): 641.

45 S.O. van Poelje and C.H.F. Polak, *Het Begrip "Algemeen Belang" in de Verschillende Onderdelen van Het Administratieve Recht: Prae-Adviezen* (Haarlem: Tjeenk Willink, 1950).

46 A.A. van Ameringen and J.L.P. Brabers, "Voorontwerp Economische Mededinging," *De Naamlooze Vennootschap* 28, 11 (1951).

47 P. VerLoren van Themaat, "Tweesnijdende Zwaarden En Tweesnijdende Critieken. Met Naschrift door A.A. van Ameringen en J.L.P. Brabers," *De Naamlooze Vennootschap* 29, 2 (1951). VerLoren also privately wrote to Van Ameringen to refute the latter's assumed misunderstanding of the inspiration for the bill: NL-NA, EZ/CA, 2.06.87, inv. no. 4098, letter 22 February 1951.

48 Sociaal-Economische Raad, *Advies betreffende het voorontwerp Wet economische mededinging* (Den Haag, 1953).

49 *HTK* 1952–1953 3210–3220, reproduced in G. Puchinger, *Dr. Jelle Zijlstra: gesprekken en geschriften* (Naarden: Strengholt, 1978), 241–249.

50 Ter Heide, *Ordening en verdeling*, 192–193. His biographer Jonne Harmsma presents Zijlstra as pragmatic politician rather than dogmatic theorist: *Jelle zal wel zien. Een eigenzinnig leven tussen politiek en economie* (Amsterdam: Prometheus, 2018).

51 This regarded the so-called "categorale onverbindendverklaring." Compare NL-NA, EZ/CA, 2.06.87, inv. no. 4098, memorandum "Ontwerp Wet economische mededinging," 29 February 1952 with idem, memorandum 30 January 1953.

52 NL-NA, EZ/CA, 2.06.87, inv. no. 4098, memorandum "Ontwerp Wet economische mededinging," 29 February 1952; and idem, inv. no. 2397, minutes discussion "Wet economische mededinging" with minister A.H.M. Albregts, 29 February 1952.

53 *HTK* 1953–1954 B 3295, no. 2.

54 *HTK* 1953–1954 B 3295, no. 7–9.

55 NL-NA, Algemene Zaken/Kabinet Minister-President (AZ/KMP), 2.03.01, inv. no. 929, Minister of Economic Affairs to Council of Ministers, 29 July 1953; NL-NA, Ministerraad (MR), 2.02.05.02, Minutes Council of Ministers 03-08-1953; NL-NA, EZ/CA, 2.06.87, inv. no. 4098, VerLoren van Themaat to Secretary-General, 26 September 1953.

56 *HTK* 1955–1956 at 3760, 3764.

57 For an authoritative voice in the public discussion on this issue, see the memorandum sent by the three employers' organizations to parliament in 1954 and 1955: NL-NA, EZ/CA 2.06.87, inv. no. 2397, *Nota van het Verbond van Nederlandsche Werkgevers, het Katholiek Verbond van Werkgeversvakverenigingen, het Verbond van Protestants-Christelijke Werkgevers in Nederland inzake het ontwerp van Wet houdende regelen omtrent de economische mededinging (Zitting 1954–1955, stuk 3295).*

58 *HTK* 1956–1957 B 4762 no. 2. Delayed by this amendment bill, the WEM only entered into force in 1959.

59 *HTK* 1955–1956 at 3720.

60 *HTK* 1955–1956 at 3721.

61 *HTK* 1955–1956 at 3746–3747. Spokesman on this point was lawyer Kees ten Hagen.

62 I. Samkalden, "Economische mededinging," *Sociaal-Economische Wetgeving* 3, 5–6 (1955). Samkalden certainly could not count on the support of the entire PvdA, though, as a memorandum written for PvdA prime minister Drees suggests: NL-NA, AZ/KMP 2.03.01, inv. no. 929, Memorandum J. Middelburg, 3 January 1957.

63 *HTK* 1955–1956 at 3760.
64 VerLoren van Themaat, "Het Kartelbeleid," 147–148.
65 J. Zijlstra, *Per slot van rekening: memoires* (Amsterdam: Contact, 1992), 46.
66 Asbeek Brusse and Griffiths, "Paradise Lost," 22–23; P. VerLoren van Themaat, "Het Kartelbeleid in de eerste ambtsperiode van Minister Zijlstra," *Sociaal-Economische Wetgeving* 5, 1 (1957): 1–24.
67 "Economische integratie," 662. The participants were Joop den Uyl, Ivo Samkalden, Paul Kapteijn en Niko Tinbergen. The latter two favored a more liberal European regime, while Samkalden argued for a kind of European parliament.
68 "Economische integratie," 664–666.
69 NL-NA, EZ/CA, 2.06.87, inv. no. 3473. Zijlstra to J. Monnet 16 March 1954. This resulted in ECJ case 6/54 Kingdom of the Netherlands v High Authority of the ECSC. *European Court Reports* (1954–6): 103.
70 *HTK* 1957–1958, 70.
71 NL-NA, AZ/KMP, 2.03.01, inv. no. 2848, Memorandum C.L.W. Fock for Drees 15 April 1956; NL-NA, MR, 2.02.05.02, Minutes Council of Ministers 16 April 1956.
72 NL-NA, Ministerie van Buitenlandse Zaken (BuZa), 2.05.118, inv. no. 18780, SER – Commissie Europese Economische Integratie. "Advies inzake de regeling van de concurrentie op de gemeenschappelijke markt," 15 November 1956; NL-NA, AZ/KMP, 2.03.01, inv. no. 2848, "Lijst van de belangrijkste Nederlandse bezwaren t.a.v. de tekst van het rapport-Spaak," 15 September 1956.
73 NL-NA, BuZa, 2.05.118, inv. no. 18794, "Weekbericht 15," 12–16 November 1956.
74 NL-NA, BuZa, 2.05.118, inv. no. 18794, Nederlandse delegatie. "Conclusies van de delegatiebespreking op 23 November 1956."
75 Laurent Warlouzet and Tobias Witschke, "The Difficult Path to an Economic Rule of Law: European Competition Policy, 1950–91," *Contemporary European History* 21, 3 (2012): 447.
76 NL-NA, MR, 2.02.05.02, Minutes Council of Ministers 18 March 1957.
77 *HTK* 1956–1957, 19–174. Hambloch, however, seems to overstate the importance of the subject suggesting that several parties threatened not to ratify the EEC treaty because of the competition arrangements. Cf. S. Hambloch, "Europäische Integration am Beispiel der Wettbewerbspolitik in der Frühphase der Europäischen Wirtschaftsgemeinschaft," Habilitationsschrift, Universität Siegen, 2007, 101.
78 *HTK* 1956–1957, 119–120. Warlouzet and Witschke confirm Zijlstra's suggestion that "the question of legal doctrine and its institutional implementation was left open and subject to future regulation": "The Difficult Path to an Economic Rule of Law," 447.
79 P.W.L. Brijnen and H.W. Wertheimer, "De interpretatie van de kartelbepalingen in het Europese Economische Gemeenschap-verdrag," *Sociaal-Economische Wetgeving* 5, 9 (1957). The authors were in-house lawyers of the Dutch multinationals *Bataafse Petroleum Maatschappij* (BPM, currently part of Shell) and N.V. Philips respectively.
80 Brijnen and Wertheimer, "De interpretatie," 257. See Karin van Leeuwen, "Paving the Road for Legal Revolution. The Dutch Origins of the First Preliminary References in European Law (1957–1963)," *European Law Journal* 24, 6 (2018).
81 *HTK* 1956–1957, Bijl. 4778, no. 1–2.
82 P. Verloren van Themaat, "Einige Betrachtungen über die Entwicklung der Wettbewerbspolitik in Europa vor und seit dem Zustandekommen der Verordnung 17/62," in *Europarecht, Kartellrecht, Wirtschaftsrecht: Festschrift für Arved Deringer* (Baden-Baden: Nomos, 1993), 398–415, 399.
83 P. VerLoren van Themaat, "De Kartelpolitiek in de Europese Economische Gemeenschap," *Sociaal-Economische Wetgeving* 5, 7–8 (1957).
84 VerLoren van Themaat, "De Kartelpolitiek in de Europese Economische Gemeenschap," 233.
85 Lorenzo Federico Pace and Katja Seidel, "The Drafting and the Role of Regulation 17: A Hard-Fought Compromise," in Kiran Klaus Patel and Heike Schweitzer (eds.),

The Historical Foundations of EU Competition Law (Oxford: Oxford University Press, 2013).

86 P. VerLoren van Themaat, "Europese sociaal-economische wetgeving," in Ivo Samkalden and C.J. Oort (eds.), *Sociaal-economische wetgeving in nationaal en Europees verband* (Deventer: Kluwer, 1966), 38.

87 Katja Seidel, "DG IV and the Origins of a Supranational Competition Policy: Establishing an Economic Constitution for Europe," in Wolfram Kaiser, Brigitte Leucht and Morten Rasmussen (eds.), *The History of the European Union: Origins of a Trans- and Supranational Polity, 1950–72* (Abingdon: Routledge, 2009), 135. In his 1968 inaugural speech VerLoren highlighted the importance of cooperation between lawyers and economists in order to avoid focusing too much on legal procedures only: P. VerLoren van Themaat, *Het coördinatiebeginsel als coördinerend beginsel van het sociaal economisch recht: macro-juridische verkenningen?* (Deventer: Kluwer, 1968).

88 Archive NVER, The Hague (private), Speech VerLoren van Themaat at NVER founding meeting 24 September 1960. For Samkalden, see *HTK* 1959–1960, 1163.

89 J. van der Harst and N. Betlem, Interview Pieter Verloren Van Themaat, 13 February 2004. https://archives.eui.eu/en/oral_history/INT744.

90 An overview of his work was published in P. VerLoren van Themaat, R. Barents and M.R. Mok (eds.), *In Orde: Liber Amicorum Pieter VerLoren van Themaat* (Deventer: Kluwer, 1982).

Bibliography

Ameringen, A.A. van and J.L.P. Brabers, "Voorontwerp Economische Mededinging." *De Naamlooze Vennootschap* 28, 11 (1951): 181–190.

Asbeek Brusse, Wendy and Richard Griffiths. "Paradise Lost or Paradise Regained? Cartel Policy and Cartel Legislation in the Netherlands." In *Competition Policies in Europe* edited by Stephen Martin. Amsterdam: Elsevier, 1998, 15–39.

Asbeek Brusse, Wendy and Richard T. Griffiths. "Early Cartel Legislation and Cartel Policy in the Netherlands. In Memoriam." *Acta Politica* 32, 4 (1997): 375–405.

Bouwens, B. and J. Dankers. "The Invisible Handshake. Cartelization in the Netherlands, 1930–2000." *Business History Review* 84, 4 (2011): 751–771.

Bouwens, Bram and Joost Dankers, *Bedrijfsleven in Nederland in de Twintigste Eeuw. Tussen Concurrentie En Concentratie*. Amsterdam: Boom, 2012.

Brijnen, P.W.L. and H.W. Wertheimer. "De interpretatie van de kartelbepalingen in het Europese Economische Gemeenschap-verdrag." *Sociaal-Economische Wetgeving* 5, 9 (1957) 253–257.

Clerx, J.M.M.J. "Economische Expansie Door Liberalisatie." In *Het Kabinet-Drees-Van Schaik (1948–1951)* edited by P.F. Maas. Nijmegen: Centrum voor Parlementaire Geschiedenis, 1991, 359–528.

"Economische integratie. Verslag van een gesprek tussen P.J. Kapteyn, J.J. van der Lee, I. Samkalden, J. Tinbergen en J.M. den Uyl. Met een naschrift van G.M. Nederhorst." *Socialisme en democratie* 11, 11 (1954): 653–666.

Gerber, David J. *Law and Competition in Twentieth Century Europe: Protecting Prometheus*. Oxford: Oxford University Press, 1998.

Hambloch, S. *Europäische Integration am Beispiel der Wettbewerbspolitik in der Frühphase der Europäischen Wirtschaftsgemeinschaft*. Siegen: Habilitationsschrift Universität Siegen, 2007.

Harmsma, Jonne. *Jelle zal wel zien. Een eigenzinnig leven tussen politiek en economie*. Amsterdam: Prometheus, 2018.

Hayek, Friedrich. *The Road to Serfdom*. London: Routledge 1944.
Heide, F.J. ter. *Ordening en verdeling: besluitvorming over sociaal-economisch beleid in Nederland, 1949–1958*. Kampen: Kok Agora, 1986.
Höpner, Martin. "Sozialdemokratie, Gewerkschaften Und Organisierter Kapitalismus, 1880–2002." *MPIfG Discussion Paper*, Max Planck Institute for the Study of Societies, 2004. https://econpapers.repec.org/paper/zbwmpifgd/0410.htm.
Jong, H.W. de. "Het kartelparadijs: punten van bezwaar." *Economisch-statistische Berichten* 77, 2 (1990): 921–927.
Katzenstein, Peter J. *Small States in World Markets: Industrial Policy in Europe*. Ithaca: Cornell University Press, 1985.
Künzler Adrian and Laurent Warlouzet. "National Traditions of Competition Law." In *The Historical Foundations of EU Competition Law* edited by Kiran Klaus Patel and Heike Schweitzer. Oxford: Oxford University Press, 2013, 89–124.
Leeuwen, Karin van. "Paving the Road for Legal Revolution. The Dutch Origins of the First Preliminary References in European Law (1957–1963)." *European Law Journal* 24, 6 (2018): 408–421.
Mellink, Bram. "Tweedracht maakt macht. De PvdA, de doorbraak en de ontluikende polarisatiestrategie (1946–1966)." *BMGN – Low Countries Historical Review* 126, 2 (2011): 30–53.
Mulder, Albert and M.R. Mok. *Kartelrecht*. Alphen aan den Rijn: Samsom, 1962.
Nederhorst, G. "De vakbeweging en de regeringspolitiek." *Paraat* 3, 28 (1948): 1–2.
Pace, Lorenzo Federico and Katja Seidel. "The Drafting and the Role of Regulation 17: A Hard-Fought Compromise." In *The Historical Foundations of EU Competition Law* edited by Kiran Klaus Patel and Heike Schweitzer. Oxford: Oxford University Press, 2013, 54–88.
Patel, Kiran Klaus and Heike Schweitzer (eds.). *The Historical Foundations of EU Competition Law*. Oxford: Oxford University Press, 2013.
Petit, Lilian T.D., Jarig van Sinderen and Peter A.G. van Bergeijk. "How the Tortoise Became a Hare. On the Initial Sclerosis and Ultimate Modernisation of Dutch Competition Policy." In *Regulating Competition: Cartel Registers in the Twentieth-Century World* edited by Susanna Fellman, Peter Sandberg and Martin Shanahan. London: Routledge, 2015, 66–87.
Poelje, S.O. van and C.H.F. Polak. *Het Begrip "Algemeen Belang" in de Verschillende Onderdelen van Het Administratieve Recht: Prae-Adviezen*. Haarlem: Tjeenk Willink, 1950.
Puchinger, G. *Dr. Jelle Zijlstra: gesprekken en geschriften*. Naarden: Strengholt, 1978.
Ramírez Pérez, Sigfrido and Sebastian van de Scheur. "The Evolution of the Law on Articles 85 and 86 EEC." In *The Historical Foundations of EU Competition Law* edited by Kiran Klaus Patel and Heike Schweitzer. Oxford: Oxford University Press, 2013, 19–53.
Roelevink, Eva-Maria. *Organisierte Intransparenz: Das Kohlensyndikat und der Niederländische Markt, 1915–1932*. München: Beck, 2015.
Samkalden, I. "Economische mededinging." *Sociaal-Economische Wetgeving* 3, 5–6 (1955): 172–182.
Samkalden, I. "Het Wetsontwerp Economische Mededinging." *Sociaal-Economische Wetgeving* 2, 2 (1953): 641–650.
Schröter, Harm G. "Easy Prey? Firms Based in Small Nations and International Cartels, 1919–1939." *Scandinavian Economic History Review* 60, 2 (2012): 146–164.
Seidel, Katja. "DG IV and the Origins of a Supranational Competition Policy: Establishing an Economic Constitution for Europe." In *The History of the European Union: Origins*

of a Trans- and Supranational Polity, 1950–72 edited by Wolfram Kaiser, Brigitte Leucht and Morten Rasmussen. Abingdon: Routledge, 2009, 129–147.

Seidel, Katja. *The Process of Politics in Europe: The Rise of European Elites and Supranational Institutions*. London: I.B. Tauris, 2010.

Thonstad Sandvik, Pål and Espen Storli. "Big Business and Small States: Unilever and Norway in the Interwar Years." *The Economic History Review* 66, 1 (2013): 109–131.

Tromp, Bart. *Het sociaal-democratisch programma. De beginselprogramma's van de SDB, SDAP en PvdA 1878–1977*. Amsterdam: Bert Bakker, 2002.

Uyl, J.M. den. "Heroriëntering van het socialisme." *Socialisme en Democratie* 9, 5 (1952): 273–282.

Uyl, J.M. den. "Theorie en beweging." *Socialisme en Democratie* 13, 2 (1956): 154–159.

VerLoren van Themaat, P. "De Kartelpolitiek in de Europese Economische Gemeenschap." *Sociaal-Economische Wetgeving* 5, 7–8 (1957): 224–234.

VerLoren van Themaat, P. "Einige Betrachtungen über die Entwicklung der Wettbewerbspolitik in Europa vor und seit dem Zustandekommen der Verordnung 17/62." In *Europarecht, Kartellrecht, Wirtschaftsrecht: Festschrift für Arved Deringer*. Baden-Baden: Nomos, 1993, 398–415.

VerLoren van Themaat, P. "Europese sociaal-economische wetgeving." In *Sociaal-economische wetgeving in nationaal en Europees verband* edited by Ivo Samkalden and C.J. Oort. Deventer: Kluwer, 1966, 37–51.

VerLoren van Themaat, P. *Het coördinatiebeginsel als coördinerend beginsel van het sociaal economisch recht: macro-juridische verkenningen?* Deventer: Kluwer, 1968.

VerLoren van Themaat, P. "Het Kartelbeleid in de eerste ambtsperiode van Minister Zijlstra." *Sociaal-Economische Wetgeving* 5, 1 (1957): 1–24.

VerLoren van Themaat, P. "Het Kartelbeleid sinds de Bevrijding." *Sociaal-Economische Wetgeving* 1, 5 (1952): 129–153.

VerLoren van Themaat, P. "Tweesnijdende Zwaarden En Tweesnijdende Critieken. Met Naschrift door A.A. van Ameringen en J.L.P. Brabers." *De Naamlooze Vennootschap* 29, 2 (1951): 22–33.

VerLoren van Themaat, P. "Waarom ik 50 jaar geleden deelnam aan de oprichting van de PvdA en er nog steeds lid van ben." *Socialisme en Democratie* 53, 5 (1996): 315–318.

VerLoren van Themaat, P., R. Barents and M.R. Mok (eds.). *In Orde: Liber Amicorum Pieter VerLoren van Themaat*. Deventer: Kluwer, 1982.

Vos, Hein. *De weg naar vrijheid: een socialistisch perspectief*. Amsterdam: De Arbeiderspers, 1951.

Vries, F. de. "Regeling of vrijheid." *Jaarboek der Nederlandsche Handels-hoogeschool* 11 (1934–35): 87–117.

Vries, F. de. "Wettelijke bestrijding van de concentratie van economische macht in de Verenigde Staten van Amerika." *Jaarboek der Koninklijke Nederlandsche Akademie van Wetenschappen* (1947–1948): 133.

Warlouzet, Laurent and Tobias Witschke. "The Difficult Path to an Economic Rule of Law: European Competition Policy, 1950–91." *Contemporary European History* 21, 3 (2012): 437–455.

Zijlstra, J. *Per slot van rekening: memoires*. Amsterdam: Contact, 1992.

7 Social democracy and the foundations of European competition policy and law, 1950–1973

Sigfrido M. Ramírez Pérez

Introduction

Myths about the past are difficult to deconstruct, particularly when are pertinent to the ideological struggles of the present. The active building of memory about European competition by ordoliberal scholars, together with their supposed ideological hegemony regarding recent debates about European economic policies, has supported a widespread belief in the neoliberal origins of European competition law and policy. More than two decades after the legal historian, David Gerber, gave ordoliberalism the central role in European competition law, a young historian, Quinn Slobodian, has recently continued to attribute to this German-speaking variety of neoliberals an undeserved political and intellectual hegemony about the origins of European competition law.[1] As explained in the introduction of this book, the new legal history of European integration had, however, already put the record straight after EU lawyers and political economists corrected this clear overstatement.[2] In particular, a collective book edited by historians and legal scholars corrected this misrepresentation by showing the existence of a dominant Keynesian conception of competition in this early period.[3] However, as the myth still appears to be alive, even though some of its foundations have been seriously weakened, this article aims to present the Keynesian foundations of EU competition policy during the first two decades of its birth and development by focusing on the social-democratic roots of EU competition policy and law.

It should be clarified from the outset that German ordoliberals were, indeed, influential in the birth of European competition law, and made every effort to shape the new rules on competition. However, this did not amount to a dominant influence on the competition articles of the founding treaties, which the most recent literature has now openly rejected. In reality, the clauses in the founding treaties derived from the French Keynesian experience, whereas the German ordoliberal conceptions were more influential in shaping the first Council regulation dedicated to control cartels, namely Regulation 17/62. This regulation allowed for a possible implementation of European competition policy in an ordoliberal direction, but it did not preclude or constrain policy decisions, which potentially, and de facto, could be inspired by other conceptions and policy objectives.[4] Expanding on a previous argument by political economists, we suggested that in opposition

DOI: 10.4324/9781351010573-7

to ordoliberalism there was a competing "Keynesian" conception referring to the postwar consensus on economic policy, which dominated in Europe until the 1970s. This was the period of embedded capitalism based on the constitutional principles which had been at the basis of the Welfare State. Nothing could be more counter-intuitive than concluding that a small network of intellectuals and technocrats with German ordoliberal origins could have imposed their views on what were the guiding hegemonic ideas and practices of the Golden Age of European capitalism: the Keynesian approach to competition policy and law. This alternative conception of competition at the service of the mixed economy and planning triumphed in this early period in the law and politics of European competition because it derived from the economic thinking shared by the dominant political ideologies involved in European competition. Christian-Democrats and Socialists believed in an organized economy at the service of the Welfare State, where competition policy could be used to serve other larger economic policy objectives and was not an aim in itself.[5]

The current chapter departs from this previous research by focusing on the contribution and conceptions of European Socialists to European competition policy and law. This contribution was undoubtedly plural and had as well some political and institutional limitations. Unlike the proponents of the "Ordoliberal" thesis, we do not take for granted that social democrats were the only prevalent force in shaping competition law and policy. In this early period of European integration, the political system of the European Communities was just in its beginnings, and other institutional actors and political forces also played an important role. More precisely, this included the European Court of Justice for the institutional actors, and Christian-Democrats, who were the dominant political force in government at European level. Therefore, this is neither a narrative just about success, but also about failures and roads not taken. These are the more necessary as in times of crises, such as the one we are now experiencing, the appetite for reforming the European competition regime increases. This creates a need to take stock of past experiences in all their complexity and not with overarching simplifications.

This chapter presents the socialist conceptions of European competition policy and law by reconstructing some of its key episodes at the European and national levels, from the first discussions about competition articles from the Treaties of Paris (1951) and Rome (1957) up to 1973. That was the year when the European Commission presented for approval the project regarding the first regulation about the abuse of dominant position. This was one of the crucial elements that social democrats had been pushing for since the origins of European integration, on the basis of its historical aim to break private monopolies. The first section will discuss the French socialists who were involved in the debates on competition in the negotiations of the Treaty of Paris instituting the Coal and Steel Community. The second section will explore the period 1955 to 1962 to examine the ways in which socialists in the government pushed in favor of competition articles in the Treaty of Rome, and the subsequent first Regulation 17/62, by paying attention to the debate among supranational actors. This includes the creation of the network of the European Left (*Gauche Unie*), bringing together political leaders with trade unionists and chief executive officers (CEOs) of state-owned companies, with the aim of defining a European understanding of competition policy and law. The third section will focus on the actions of social-democratic civil servants and European Commissioners in what was the most advanced debate of the time: a Council regulation to supervise the abuse of dominant positions. This regulation, which was a priority for the Keynesian approach, was approved by the European Commission in 1973 but put on hold by the Council of Ministers after wide-ranging consultation and discussion in institutional, political and academic circles. The chapter will conclude with the key elements characterizing the social-democratic conceptions of European competition policy and law during these first decades of European integration.

The French socialists and the articles on competition law of the ECSC (1949–1955)

The final shape of the section of the Treaty of Rome dedicated to competition was the result of tough negotiations between member states. If it is now generally accepted that German conceptions did not triumph, renewed attention has been focused on the French and Dutch conceptions of competition, which were put forward by socialist leaders. Before the treaty negotiations, they had been in government and had already discussed and approved national competition laws. On the other hand, Italy, Belgium and Luxembourg did not have national laws regarding competition and any European agreement would have directly impacted them. According to the most recent research, it was the French tradition of competition policy that predominated in treaty negotiations, and it cannot be concluded in any way that the Treaty of Rome directly transferred traditional ordoliberal conceptions to the European level.[6]

The first precedent was, therefore, the French Law 9951, approved on 10 July 1952, which did not, in principle, forbid cartels or dominant position per se, but only their abuse, contrary to the ordoliberal principle of forbidding cartels. The French law allowed for an evaluation of their effect upon the economy and prohibited them if they were found to have completely removed any competition in the market. A Decree of 9 August 1953 defined that good cartels were those that would bring specific advantages to competition such as improving or contributing to economic progress by rationalization or specialization. This French precedent requires some clarification as to its origins and its interaction with the debate about European competition rules.[7] This refers to three experiences with competition policy that had some influence in France. First, the American experience, which had been discussed in the framework of the Marshall Plan and the Organization for European Economic Cooperation (OEEC). More importantly for socialists, the Labour Party, in government in Britain, had approved national laws against monopolies and mergers (1948), and later on cartels (1956). However, the most relevant had been the competition clauses of the European Coal and Steel Community, which were in fact closely linked to the French debates.

Scholarly research about the origins of the competition clauses of the Treaty of Paris makes it clear that German ordoliberalism was of little influence, and it was instead the French option, which triumphed in the Treaty of Paris. For Witschke, this is indubitably demonstrated by the fact that not only did the German delegation reject the new articles on competition – Articles 65 (antitrust) and 66 (merger control) – as suggested by the French delegation at the end of October 1950 – but also they blocked the conclusion of the negotiations on this point for several months. Opposition to the inclusion of competition rules in the treaty included that of Ludwig Erhard, the Minister of the Economy, who also failed to pass an antitrust law in Germany in 1950.[8]

More debatable is the role played by the US experience to put pressure on the European Coal and Steel Community (ECSC) negotiations by the State Department and some influential legal advisers, such as the US diplomat, Georges Ball, and Robert Bowie, professor at Harvard and legal adviser of the US High Commissioner for Germany. According to Brigitte Leucht, both advisers intervened directly in this part of the negotiations, having a decisive influence on the final texts of the articles for competition, even though it is not possible to demonstrate to what extent the memorandums sent by these two American lawyers impacted the final form of the articles on competition.[9] On his part, Witschke put into question their influence on the articles of the treaty on the basis that the actual rules included elements, which were very far from US antitrust law. This included, for example, public pricing that allowed for a portioning of markets, and also the introduction of criteria for improving competitiveness in assessing mergers, going beyond the evaluation of strict market power. Matthias Kipping had already made clear that if the direct intervention of the US administration in the negotiations was well known, this was not enough to explain the introduction of competition articles in the Treaties at the request of France, which was instead guided by domestic concerns.[10]

Competition articles in France originated from Jean Monnet, who in 1949 had already attempted to pass a competition law in France to break national cartels. These had remained in place after the fall of Vichy France in the form of Organization Committees from the Ministry of Industry. In the opinion of Monnet and his team at the Planning Commissariat, which included the French negotiators of the treaty, the Socialist technocrats, the economist Pierre Uri and the engineer Etienne Hirsch, the steel cartel and other cartels in raw material sectors blocked the development of French industry. Therefore, the need to introduce competition rules in France could count on the support of steel consumers from the mechanical industry such as Pierre Lefaucheux, president-CEO of the nationalized automobile company Renault, who was concerned about international competitiveness. In political terms, the key support came from the former minister of economy and finances, André Philip, who had argued in favor of European competition laws as early as in 1949. In Kipping's point of view, his role as French Socialist Party (SFIO) leader was politically crucial for the later acceptance of the Treaty of Paris in the National Assembly. Philip had participated in led the negotiations on behalf of the Foreign Affairs Commission of the National Assembly, and was later in charge of the report which recommended the approval of the treaty at the Economic and Social

Council, which represented social and economic actors in the legislative process.[11] This French socialist tradition of competition policy and law has, however, been seriously neglected by the most recent literature on European competition policy and law. It is time to reconsider this tradition, as it was more relevant for the history of European competition than any ordoliberal or American influences.

The French debate on competition had started during the interwar period, in the discussions around the Flandin-Marchendeau bill of January 1935. Before that date, all cartelization was considered illegal according to Article 419 of the Penal Code of 1810, but the jurisprudence approved those cartels, which did not result in abuses. This article was modified by the Colrat-Dior law of 3 December 1926, which defined the limits of legal combinations, but rejected creating an administrative supervision with compulsory registration. Following the League of Nations inquiry on cartels of 1930, there was a failed attempt to elaborate a specific competition law with the Reynaud-Rollin bill at the Senate of 3 March 1932 aiming to create a consultative committee for combinations (ententes). The 1935 bill was, therefore, the starting point for a political debate, which took place within the context of the crisis of the 1930s, following the request by employers wanting a legal framework to be able to organize their combinations with the support of the government and to be supervised by arbitration committees to solve conflicts in their application. The SFIO representative in that debate in the National Assembly, Paul Ramadier, later Minister of Economy during the negotiations of the Treaty of Rome, accepted such a scheme provided that the combinations included the participation of workers and labor collective agreements. The main point for the French socialists was to prevent a corporatist organization organized by the employers without trade union participation. Considering the inclusion of some of these proposals, the bill was approved in the National Assembly, but blocked in the Senate at the request of the employers, for whom the approved bill went too far from their original intention and opened the way to state intervention and planned economy. The fact that the government had to proceed to control cartels with ad-hoc laws kept the debate open. However, there was no definitive legal conclusion before the end of the Vichy regime, where cartelization was compulsorily organized and coordinated by the Ministry of Industry to cope with the war economy.[12]

Claude Didry and Fréderic Marty have recently confirmed Kipping's thesis that in postwar France, the attempt to dismantle combinations did not aim to defend the market order, but was rather an attempt to modernize the industrial sector, and an instrument of industrial policy on the part of the French administration and the leaders of nationalized companies.[13] These state-owned companies had been expanded substantially during the Liberation of France in competitive sectors such as the automobile (Renault) but also in oligopolistic sectors such as the coal (Charbonnages de France) or electricity sectors (Electricité de France-EDF). The action of these companies became crucial in the European competition law debate as they were fully aware of the importance of cartels in the French economy. The first place where the creation of a new competition law was clearly discussed was, unsurprisingly, at the Planning Commissariat directed by Jean Monnet. This occurred in September 1948 during the meetings of its working group for productivity led by Jean Fourastié, departing from a report elaborated by the MRP Senator, André Armengaud. During the meetings, it was made clear that the major problem was not just cartels, which could have a positive impact on the specialization of production. It was rather that the administration had to control them because without legislation against concentrations, companies might take advantage of their market power. The other institution from where a request for a competition legislation emanated was the National Assembly at the request of Socialist Members of Parliament. As early as December 1948, the former Secretary of State for Finances and Economic Affairs, Albert Gazier, successfully put forward a resolution to the economic committee of the National Assembly asking for antitrust legislation to reduce prices and the excessive profit of companies operating in combinations. It also requested the creation of courts in charge of persecuting and removing cartels who broke past agreements. Even if this first resolution was not followed up by legislation, the place of contact of both initiatives took place in a meeting between the Socialist President of the Republic, Vincent Auriol, and Jean Monnet in March 1949, where the planning commissioner expressed the urgency for such a legislative initiative. The problem, though, was that there was opposition from the Ministry of Finances and of the Economy, which wanted to promote a law distinguishing between good and bad combinations, whereas the draft bill elaborated by the Planning Commissariat in April suggested the principle of a total ban on cartels, following the advice of Paul Reuter, the law professor who was co-drafter with Etienne Hirsch of the Monnet note, which gave way to the Schuman Plan.

It was precisely in April 1949, when the former Minister of Economy and Finances from the SFIO, André Philip, suggested a European framework for such a law during the Economic Conference of the European Movement in Westminster.[14] This long-serving president of the Movement for the Socialist United States of Europe (MSEUE) introduced this proposal in the subcommittee of Industrial Production even though the final proposal was watered down by the economic Committee members, which included liberal and Christian-democratic politicians, as well as representatives of large businesses. Philip proposed not only a strict prohibition of cartels but also the creation of a European Authority for Steel in order to assure cheap prices to mechanical industries. Following the example of the French Planning Commissariat, this sectoral agency would be able to take autonomous decisions for this strategic sector for the European economy. In various settings, the former minister had accused the steel cartel in France of having maintained high prices for industry thereby aggravating the crisis in the 1930s. In Kipping's opinion, contact between Monnet and Philip had been maintained, corroborated by the Planning Commissariat proposal for a competition law in those months. However, this common position in favor of strict regulation of competition at the French and European levels was not initially successful, despite the support of the Socialist MPs in the National Assembly. The Christian-Democrat Minister in charge of Economic Affairs, Robert Buron, had prepared an antitrust law, which distinguished between good and bad combinations, punishing only abuses, as French Christian-Democrats were in favor of cartel agreements, even with compulsory affiliation. Therefore, the Buron law presented on 12 May 1950 by the Minister of Finances,

Maurice Petsche, collapsed politically when the Economic and Social Council rejected it in June, arguing that the creation of the Higher Council for Combinations lacked accountability, and introduced an exceptional jurisdiction with the setting up of a High Council for Cartels in charge of overseeing its functioning.

Following their defeat in May to pass a strict competition law in France due to the opposition of the Christian-Democrats, the French socialists modernizers saw in the Schuman plan an opportunity to solve this domestic problem, aside from tackling the Ruhr question, which included the discriminatory prices on coal and steel applied by German suppliers. It is, therefore, not surprising that from day one, Monnet asked to make clear to the Americans that the Schuman Plan did not want to recreate a European steel cartel, asking his right-hand man, the Socialist Pierre Uri, to write a note on this matter.[15] This note represented the original intention, which informed the Schuman Plan, and for this reason, it is important to analyze it in some detail. The Schuman Plan was anti-cartel in its final objectives, which was not to maintain price agreements to freeze market structures, but rather to increase production and productivity by the enlargement of markets, improvement of methods and rationalization of production. The new international organization would also make public its activity, unlike behind-the-door cartels, and be directed by "independent personalities bringing together their technical qualification with the general interest, being publicly accountable at any time." The most relevant, though, was that the new organization might use cartel-like methods of distribution of markets or supplies. This was presented only as a transition measure destined to smooth the re-adjustment of activities at a lower cost, and it would not permanently eliminate competition. However, contrary to cartels whose fundamental feature was to serve the private employer by generating profits, the new organization would take responsibility for these two industries not just because of their economic impact on national economies but also to preserve the political relations between all countries. More broadly, it aimed at increasing growth and the standard of living of all countries concerned, and not just of the workers employed in both strategic sectors. This last point revealed the crucial political nature of the project because it would be through these concrete results that the new organization would gain authority with the member states. In economic terms, this political intervention amounted to the creation of perfect competition, but in a publicly managed way to avoid being blocked by cartel members. The tone of this Uri's note showed that it was clearly addressed to US decision-makers and public opinion. It aimed to dispel their mistrust about the resurrection of European cartels, even if the Marshall Plan Administration (ECA) had already concluded in various inquiries at the end of 1949 that cartels were already fully active in France, but recognizing that French reformers had chosen to curb monopoly by nationalizations rather by antitrust legislation.[16] According to Kipping, Monnet confirmed this anti-cartel nature of the Schuman Plan to the Labor government in his visit to Britain on 15–16 May where he met all major ministers, and in particular his homologue at the Economic Planning Board, Sir Edwin Plowden.[17]

However, as the negotiations on the competition clauses of the treaty did not progress over the summer of 1950, Monnet urged the head of delegations to provide some results by 4 October 1950. He clarified that for the French delegation, all cartels had to be forbidden in principle and past agreements would be automatically void. Only specialization agreements or mergers might be authorized by the High Authority of the ECSC if they had as their objective the increase of productivity and the rationalization of production. He promised to provide the negotiators with two proposals which were submitted for discussion at the end of the month, on 27 October. These are the origins of the two articles on competition which reinforced the previous points with an additional request to limit monopolies. No firm could own a share of more than 10% in a competing firm and introduced a maximum threshold for authorizing a merger of a maximum market-share limit of 20% in the common market in coal and steel. Such stringent thresholds were softened by giving the High Authority the discretionary power to provide exemptions. In the final proposals made by France on 7 December 1950, they obtained the support of Italy and the Netherlands, while Belgium, Luxembourg and Germany were opposed to these competition clauses in the Treaties.

The negotiations were blocked until February 1951, after Monnet had given an ultimatum in January to the German negotiator, Walter Hallstein: if these competition clauses were not accepted, the conference would be over. The German and the Belgian delegations argued that the clauses might alienate the companies concerned and the ratifications in their country might be in danger. Most research agrees that the Americans put pressure on them to convince them to take such risk, even if they obtained some concessions in the subsequent negotiations to finalize the treaty: on the one hand, a limitation of the discretionary powers of the High Authority to grant exemptions, if certain criteria were met, and on the other hand, the exemption of past concentrations from authorization.[18] The French had already removed the 20% clause on more flexible conditionality to authorize mergers: the resulting merger would neither result in an increase of market power able to determine prices, nor the control of production and distribution in an important share of the market, and it would also improve the production and distribution of products. The major concession, however, to the Germans was the non-discrimination clause, which permitted that all decisions on concentrations would also consider the existence of other companies of the same nature in other member states. According to Witschke, this clause was ambiguous and fundamental in the arguments to convince the French and German legislators to ratify the treaty, which was quickly signed in March 1951 and formalized in April of that year.

The latest literature confirms that beyond the pressure and contribution of the Americans to the success of the negotiations about competition clauses, the French had their own political reasons and ideas about competition. Furthermore, the differences from the US antitrust experience were as important, so that the treaty articles cannot be considered a simple transfer of the antitrust ideas of the New Deal. The origins came rather from the influence of André Philip, who became key on the path toward ratification of the treaty in France, following the failure in 1950 of the various parliamentary initiatives for a competition bill presented on behalf of the SFIO by Albert Gazier, at the National Assembly on 8 June, and in the Senate by the Republican André Armengaud on 22 June.

The direct filiation of the Schuman Plan and the previous proposals led by Philip in the framework of the European sphere were publicly revealed by the French socialist in his report to the Economic and Social Council, where he recommended the approval of the treaty. He presented the Treaty of Paris as the first materialization of the Westminster resolution of 1949, where the European Movement, under his initiative, had suggested a coordination plan in basic industries, including not just coal and steel, but also electricity and transport. He also pointed out that the three bodies suggested (the High Authority, the Consultative Tripartite Committee and the one representing professional organizations) were also included in the treaty. The only difference was that industrial combinations between public and private companies in the same sector would not enjoy of a delegated role to implement European planning, which was to be carried out, instead, by the High Authority. He underlined the direct precedent of his own report on the European Steel Industry adopted at the end of 1949 by the Economic Committee of the Assembly of the Council of Europe. In that report, he suggested creating a planning authority with investigative powers, and without delegation of powers. From the steel sector, it would later expand into other key sectors (coal, oil, electricity and transport). Last, but not least, he made clear that after the announcement of the Schuman Plan, the sub-committee for Industry of the same Assembly had taken a public position in favor of the creation of the High Authority of Coal and Steel. This authority would receive powers delegated by states and companies, not only to plan but also to intervene in this sector with the creation of European firms by encouraging combinations or mergers politically directed to serve the European general interest. In his opinion, this was exactly what the ECSC was about, as it created a supranational ("not international") regime where "the country members of the Community conform a single State".[19]

Regarding the articles on competition, Philip also made it clear in his report that this was an unprecedented step forward for regulating capitalism as no member state yet had such a novel policy. In the negotiations concerning the first article on cartels (Article 65), two methods had been discussed: either the High Authority was informed and delivered a previous authorization or a general declaration made all cartel agreements illegal per se. The negotiators had agreed to ban all those concerted practices that directly or indirectly controlled production and investments, fixed prices and allocated markets. However, some combinations with positive impacts on costs or productivity could be authorized by Article 66(2) on the condition that they aimed toward these objectives and would not result in dominant positions in the common market. Indeed, it was Article 66 on mergers, which retained the interest of the socialist leader, who pointed out that contrary to the absolute ban, here the principle chosen had been the previous authorization of future concentrations by the High Authority, which would evaluate the monopolistic risks with flexibility. He reassured the French that Article 83 clarified that nationalized sectors, or companies such as Charbonnages de France, could be kept in public hands as the treaty did not preclude the type of property of the firms. However, the treaty safeguarded the elimination of any competition in the common market, in case a monopoly affected not only production but also sales and imports into its domestic market. Further proof of the relevance and breadth of competition clauses was that the employers' associations contested these articles and aimed to restrict them by asking to remove the ban principle for any type of cartel, favoring an authorization principle only for those agreements that would be contrary to the general objectives of the treaty. Furthermore, they wanted to strip the High Authority of its "abusive power" and suggested that representatives of the industries would decide under the supervision of the High Authority, who might forbid them only if abuses were demonstrated, and under the control of the Court of Justice. Such serious amendments to the competition rules would weaken the High Authority's capacity to break hidden combinations, and the Court would not be suitable to pass judgment on the economic evaluation made by the HA, changing its true nature of Administrative Court, similar to the French *Conseil d'Etat*.[20]

Could Philip's statements of direct filiation be considered credible? In our opinion, this is the case, as it came about at a moment in which the success of the Treaty of Paris was not yet guaranteed, and the direct support by French socialists to the ECSC project created a direct clash with the most important socialist party in government, the Labour Party, which had attacked the creation of the ECSC as a conservative device at the service of private monopolies. Philip's aggressive defense of the ECSC explained clearly that he considered this first step for European integration a creature of French socialism. In his article "Socialism and European Union," he made clear that despite being the president of the Socialist Movement for the United States of Europe, he elaborated a personal reply to the public position of the Labour Party against any type of European integration based on the supra-national principle. Considering that this lawyer and economist had written his doctorate about the Labour Party, and spent years in Britain, it was quite evident his anger at what he considered "a very hard hit against all socialist parties of the European Continent." In this reply, he made clear that the enemy of the working class were capitalist monopolies, which were fortified behind protectionist devices like those devised by the British government with the excuse of protecting nationalized companies. More precisely, cartels were removing competition by maintaining high prices and inflation, which exploited the consumer. The earnings obtained from such monopolistic positions extracted profits from workers by reducing their real wages to nothing, even if some of these profits were distributed to "some working-class corporatist groupings." This was the economic and political reasoning behind the support for competition rules by French socialists, who considered them compatible with nationalized industries and a planned intervention in the economy, but not with the protectionism, which the Labour Party was advocating in a nationalistic manner.[21]

After parliamentary approval in France of the ECSC Treaty, the French government failed to approve its own competition bill in the National Assembly during 1952. It had to wait until August 1953 when the radical-socialist minister of economy and finances, Edgard Faure, profited from the exceptional powers obtained by the Laniel government to pass a governmental decree "anti-trust regulating professional combinations and resuming free competition." This executive act (Decree 53–704) was made to complement an earlier regulation dealing with price control

(Ordinance 45–1483) subordinating competition to this other objective of economic policy. This regulation took as a basis the abuse principle, with a form of governance, which gave all powers to the French administration, and more precisely to the Directorate for Prices of the Ministry of Finances. The director of that service, Louis Rosenstock-Frank, from whom this decree originated, knew well the corporatist traditions and the New Deal experience.[22] This new regulation distinguished between forbidden (those blocking the reduction of prices or favoring their increase) and authorized cartels (those combinations that aimed to improve distribution and economic progress through rationalization or specialization). It created a Technical Committee for Combinations with a consultative role for the Minister, who maintained the discretionary power to ban or authorize the combinations even if it did not impose their compulsory registration. It explicitly excluded monopolies and abuse of dominant position without touching upon mergers, which had been the most original contributions of the Schuman Plan.[23]

From the Spaak report to the Treaty of Rome and Regulation 17/62 (1955–1962)

European socialists became central actors of the Treaties of the European Economic Community (EEC) and Euratom from the Messina Conference of 1955 up to their signature and ratification in 1957. Following the failure in the French Parliament of the European Defense Community (EDC) in 1954, the ECSC governments asked in Messina the minister of foreign affairs of Belgium, the Socialist leader Paul-Henri Spaak, to preside over an intergovernmental conference to relaunch the negotiations. This EDC Treaty collapsed in the French National Assembly precisely because of the split of the SFIO, which provided a majority in the Chamber to the political parties opposed to this new Treaty. This was done despite the efforts of SFIO's secretary general, Guy Mollet, who publicly supported the supra-nationality principle of the ECSC following Philip's proposal of further sector integration in transport and energy. This was the preferred model for Jean Monnet, but also for Spaak who included these proposals in his report published on 21 April 1956, drafted by a German-French tandem: on the one hand, the Socialist Pierre Uri, who had kept serving Monnet as chief economist of the High Authority of the ECSC; and, on the other hand, the future European commissioner for competition, the ordoliberal Hans von der Groeben, who had been put in charge of the ECSC in the German Ministry of Economics directed by Ludwig Erhard. Both men were fully aware of the importance of competition articles, nonetheless, because in Germany, there was a simultaneous political debate about the new competition law, whereas Uri had had experienced the practical limits of the competition articles included in the ECSC.

The Spaak report included competition clauses in its Title Two, under the heading of Common Market policies, making clear that competition policy aimed to "correct or complete the automatic functioning of market with the use of rules, procedures and common actions." Its objectives were a higher rationalization of production, an increase in the standard of living and economic growth. The report distinguished between the competition rules applied to companies and those applied to states. For companies, the first concern was to avoid discrimination due to dumping practices. Therefore, it would be necessary to control abuses and harmonize these practices before their elimination by the end of the transitory period, when European-wide anti-dumping rules would be elaborated toward third countries. The core of the competition policy was presented as a struggle against monopolies, deriving from their large size and cartel agreements, whereas the treaty had to present only basic rules restricted to inter-state trade, leaving the competency of controlling national cartels to member states. These basic rules had to be precise enough to allow the European Commission to prepare general regulations for their execution that would need to be approved by the Parliamentary Assembly. The report favored drafting specific rules for merger control and to ban abuses of dominant positions by a company or a combination of various companies in three precise monopolistic practices or de facto situations: market-partitioning cartels; combinations against productivity gains by production-sharing or slowing down technical progress; and the monopolistic domination in one product by one company. The exclusive competency of the European Commission to instruct these decisions would be subjected to appeal at the European Court of Justice, but with a previous procedure of conciliation and arbitration by a Consultative Committee on Combinations and Discriminations. If there were disagreement, the case could be appealed within a period of two months by the member states or the Commission to the European Court of Justice, which would have a specialized chamber composed not only of jurists but also of "economic and technical experts." It is likely that these proposals emanated from Uri, not only due to the preference for a supranational control of the process but also because of the presence of economists in the Court, and the creation of a consultative committee, which directly came from the French competition experience.

The more ordoliberal imprint is visible in the demand to apply these rules at first to state administrations and state companies with tight control on the use of state aids, to which a whole section of the competition policy proposals was dedicated. This was attenuated, however, by the rejection of a general ban on state aids, and a consideration of authorization according to their positive economic effect and utility for the success of the common market, pointing to positive help such as regional aids for development. Member states would be obliged to notify all aid to firms or sectors to the Commission, which would also decide on their compatibility with the common market under the control of the Court of Justice.[24] Contrary to what is generally assumed, the German ordoliberal influence looked very much diminished in comparison with the French approach and the influence of the ECSC experience, as the Spaak report also suggested including a clause for merger control and concentrations in the treaty.

The Spaak report was received with great concern in the French Economic Council, whose formal opinion had been required by the new Radical-Socialist government presided over precisely by Guy Mollet. The Council discussed the question in July 1956 and approved an opinion in the report elaborated by Jean

Deleau, a representative of the agricultural group. The major criticism concerned the principle of economic liberalization as an end in itself rather than as a means for growth. Competition policy figured as the first position that the Council members favored as the legitimate reason for integration, namely, "a common economic policy" agreed by all member states. During the debate of the report, the trade union CFTC (French Confederation of Christian Workers) successfully suggested that Article 83 of the ECSC Treaty be reinstated, which left open the choice for each member state to decide upon the limits of property rights in their economy. Council opinion also asked the French government to take care that the application of competition rules did not limit legitimate state aids and an explicit clause to guarantee the protection of the legal structures of the French public economy.[25] The newly formed Radical-Socialist government led by Guy Mollet and the Minister of Foreign Affairs, Maurice Faure, introduced these two questions from the start of the treaty negotiations. These were coordinated on the French side by another SFIO economist coming from Monnet's Planning Authority, Robert Marjolin, a former secretary general of the OEEC, and had as main advisor for the economic aspects of the negotiations, Alexandre Verret, CEO of the state-owned company Charbonnages de France.

All accounts of the negotiations agree now that the abuse principle consecrated in the article dedicated to combinations (Article 85) resulted in a victory for the French ideas, despite its ambiguous drafting, which put forward that combinations were banned in principle, but with broad exemptions. This ambiguity permitted leaving the question open for further negotiations between member states within three years in the form of a future Council regulation. Most of the literature has generally focused on this article and paid less attention to the anti-monopoly clause on abuse of dominant position (Article 86), or to the provision on state firms and public monopolies (Article 90), dumping (Article 91) and state aids (Articles 92–94). This is one of the main reasons why it is incorrect to use the narrow term of antitrust as a synonym of European competition rules, as is used sometimes in the literature by comparing it with US competition. The treaty section on competition policy included much more than combinations, even if this was the main type of agreement dealt with by the European Commission, which became responsible for making legislative proposals and the concrete application of this multi-faceted economic policy.

Contrary to some superficial analyses, the French socialists successfully managed to introduce their proposals in the negotiations dealing with competition policy.[26] According to the most documented analysis until now, France achieved most of its aims in this matter. At first, the treaty did not deviate from its own competition regulation by punishing only the abuse of combinations and dominant positions, and not a strict ban. This strict ban had been the original position that the German government was advocating in the parallel negotiations of its own domestic law for cartels, whereas it was very permissive on concentrations, without any regulation on merger control. It has been argued that in spite of this success, competition clauses were not very important in the negotiations or that they were left so open in its interpretation that nobody could claim that its position had triumphed.[27]

This appears to be an overstatement for two reasons: first, because each delegation had a position of departure for the negotiations and put on the table their proposals, with the obvious aim of making it acceptable to the other delegations; and second, because competition regulations were followed with great concern by economic and social forces whose support for the treaties was crucial for their ratification in member states.[28]

The initial French proposal for the negotiation was that cartels and monopolies would be treated in the same article, and that even if forbidden in principle, they would include large and flexible exemptions related to the improvement of production, distribution and promotion of technical and economic progress. These competition rules would be confined to the European dimension, leaving national cartels and monopolies exempt from European competition rules. This left enough margin for political decisions by member states such as in the initial French proposal, and the European Commission would be playing a simple administrative role of supervision and proposals for a future policy harmonization. Not surprisingly, the key role would be played by the Council of Ministers, deciding by qualified majority on punishing those infractions, following the Commission's proposals. For their part, Italy and the Netherlands suggested a supranational governance leaving the harmonization of national laws to the Commission and not to national parliaments, as had been suggested by the German delegation. The two countries also urged that the rules be directly applicable without waiting for a future general regulation to execute them, in order to avoid uncertainty for undertakings. They attributed to the Court of Justice the key role of controller of the Commission's decisions. The Germans went even further in this direction, as after the approval of the regulations for competition by the Council by qualified majority, they also gave the Court the competency to instruct cases and take final decisions, taking them away from the hands of the Commission. The Germans also remained more lenient on the abuse of dominant position in relationship to the French delegation, which had made of it an important proposal.[29]

It was precisely on this point of the abuse of dominant position that the French delegation tried to go the furthest. This was a demand expressed by French industrialists, including CEOs from nationalized companies such as Pierre Dreyfus, President of Renault. Like Mollet, Philip and Marjolin, he was a former member of the interwar SFIO's fraction "Révolution Constructive," favorable to planning and state-owned companies to solve the crisis of the 1930s. This high-civil servant from the Ministry of Industry sent various memorandums to Marjolin, asking to develop in this article a Special Committee dedicated to controlling direct foreign investments from outside the Common Market, namely, from US multinational companies. It would be authorized to examine the ways to reset fair competition between them and European companies, considering only those where European shareholders owned at least 77% of the capital. Dreyfus suggested considering a dominant position when a company controlled more than 25% of the European market, putting limits to their expansion. Marjolin replied that such a proposal was blocked by Germany and Belgium, which were fiercely against controlling US foreign direct investment (FDI), as they hosted important European subsidiaries.

However, as Marjolin declared later to Renault's workers in a speech to support the ratification of the Treaty of Rome, the French had obtained the inclusion in the Treaty of Article 86, which could be used against monopolistic situations, and of Article 226, a safeguard clause to protect any industrial sector from an abnormal upsurge in US imports. Dreyfus used these two arguments to openly support the ratification of the treaty against his close friend and Radical-Socialist leader, Pierre Mendes-France.[30]

Dreyfus and other CEOs of state-owned companies also had other good reasons to be satisfied with the treaty. France succeeded in inserting the requests of the Economic Council, namely, Article 37 to safeguard state monopolies, but more importantly Article 90, which transposed into the treaty the French legal distinction between state-owned companies in competitive sectors such as Renault, to which the competition rules were also applied, and those providing services of economic public interests, exempted from respecting them. At the pinnacle of success, like in the ECSC Treaty, Article 222 stated that the treaty was neutral in the question of property rights of member states, allowing future nationalizations to be decided by a member-state without being contrary to the treaty. Recent research has considered these articles an operational compromise between ordoliberals and the partisans of the public economy. However, if we include in the picture that for the public sector the point of departure was the Spaak report, there is little doubt that this was a successful victory of the French socialist government over German ordoliberals. The German strategy had to wait for a better opportunity in the debate on the Council regulation planned within three years, which was one of its original proposals. In the meanwhile, they forcefully advocated for the direct applicability of the articles as they had approved their own domestic law and three member states did not have a competition law, including Italy, Belgium and Luxembourg.[31]

As the Germans failed to transfer their own model of competition into the Treaty of Rome, most research had concluded that they were partially successful with Regulation 17/62, which dealt with clarifying Article 85 dealing with cartels. This unanimity had to be moderated by the fact that they did not manage to include an independent authority, such as the German Cartel Office, which was able to make decisions independent of political influences.[32] Even worst, the new commissioner of competition, Hans von der Groeben, had to accept some political control on the part of the member states, with the acceptance in Regulation 17/62 of a consultative committee of cartels and dominant positions. It was compulsory for the European Commission to consult this intergovernmental committee before making any legal decision, and its members were civil servants representing their governments, and not technical experts as in the US Federal Trade Commission. It was precisely the creation of such a consultative European Federal Trade Commission that the CEOs of European and American multinational corporations, sitting in the working group for competition rules of the International Chamber of Commerce (ICC), had requested in a high-level meeting with von der Groeben and the new director general for competition, the Dutch Laborite Pieter VerLoren van Themaat, who had reminded them that it was not legally possible to exclude member states entirely from the decision-making process.[33]

There has been a recurrent flow of analysis focusing on the importance of ordoliberal networks in legal and economic debates after the Treaty of Rome, but not much has been said about those of Social-democracy and other supporters of the Keynesian conception of competition policy, such as VerLoren van Themaat, the German Trade Union Confederation (*Deutscher Gewerkschaftsbund*, DGB) and Social Democratic Party of Germany (*Sozialdemokratische Partei Deutschlands*, SPD), and the Socialist Group in the European Parliament, analyzed in other chapters of this book. This alternative conception reflected the ideological adherence of Social democrats, Social Christians and Christian democrats to state-owned companies, planning and neo-corporatism as an economic coordination mode on behalf of the democratization of markets previously dominated by cartels and monopolies. This "Keynesian post-war consensus" in the field of competition implied three features, which distinguished them from Ordoliberals: the subordination of competition policy to industrial and social objectives; the tolerance toward state aids and some cartels based on increasing productivity and economic growth; and last, but not least, the special preference for merger control in order to avoid the creation of private monopolies, which could take advantage of their dominant position.[34] The second part of this chapter will discuss their doctrine and action in the first decade after Regulation 17/1962, in order to provide some light upon their own proposals and participation in the definition of European competition policy during the 1960s.

Socialists' doctrine in action: planning, state firms and control of monopolies (1959–1974)

After the ratification of the Treaty of Rome, the discussion about the concrete application of competition rules created lot of concern within the ranks of the newly created European Committee of Labour (ECL). This Committee was an initiative of André Philip and his right-hand man in Paris, the Spanish émigré from the Spanish Trotskyist party, POUM, Enric Adroher. Known in France as Henri Gironella, he was, at that time, the secretary general of the Socialist Movement for the United States of Europe (MSEU), presided over by Philip since its foundation in 1949. At the beginning of 1959, both socialists suggested to the International Executive Committee of the MSEU the creation of the ECL as a new European association bringing both the members of the MSEU from EEC countries, and those non-socialist pro-Europeans coming from Christian-Democracy and European trade unionism in order to create the embryo for a European Labor Movement. The first reason was to counter the "liberal offensive in Europe which is being materialized by the creation of a large number of cartels, as far as economic combination is concerned (more than 500 only in January according to some sources)," and other austerity measures, which risked stopping economic growth and create recession and unemployment. More broadly, they aimed to federate beyond the narrow banner of socialism to stop the conservative turn taken by European affairs.[35]

During its founding congress in Paris in February 1960, the ECL agreed as a first objective to prepare a common position about cartels, monopolies and merger control and European integration. To that aim, they organized a programmatic conference in July of that year in Brussels. The guest speakers were lawyers and economists coordinated by the French Professor from the University of Nancy, Jacques Houssiaux, a protégé of Professor André Marchal. Both French economists were regularly consulted by the directorate general for competition and the legal service, as Marchal was also the brother-in-law of the head of the legal service of the Commission, Michel Gaudet, who probably knew the arguments developed by Marchal in his contribution to the conference.[36]

Marchal confirmed the ambiguity of the treaty drafters on competition rules, which in his view did not define a clear general policy as had been done in the ECSC Treaty, with practical rules about how to deal with cartels, concentrations and monopolies at the European level. The first reason was the ambivalent nature of the EEC, which resulted from a compromise between "the partisans of a Liberal Europe and those in favor of an Integrated Europe." Their final objectives were different: for the former, the inspiration was an intergovernmental international division of labor, whereas the latter bet on supranational integration. For liberals, the market mechanism would integrate economies, whereas for integrationists, the key role was played by common institutions and common policies, as shown by the differences between the EEC and the Free Trade Zone negotiated at the OEEC level. For European liberals, any distortion to free circulation and competition had to be removed, and consequently, combinations and concentrations had to be banned. For European federalists, this opposition was more nuanced and pragmatic, as both economic phenomena might be useful to favor integration by creating solidarity networks across borders. In his presentation, Marchal developed the two kinds of competition policies that each of these political options would favor. Let us focus here on the one that represented the Keynesian perspective that he supported. For this approach, European combinations created irreversible economic ties favoring European unity and solidarity. However, they had to be flexibly controlled, unlike the rigid regulations introduced in the ECSC Treaty, and most national regulations, which condemned as principle combinations and concentrations. The Treaty of Rome had left this issue open, allowing for the alternative policy, which Marchal advocated. The first way to control combinations and monopolies to make them acceptable was by encouraging at the European and national level the creation of "countervailing powers." This concept, elaborated by the American economist John Kenneth Galbraith, included trade unions and collective consumers such as the cooperative movement in Sweden or public administrations. However, these collective actors were not sufficient to control them and both European institutions and member states had to exercise direct control over private economic power with a flexible control based on economic and political considerations. To that aim, he recommended creating a consultative European Administrative Court made of experts, which would evaluate beyond legal considerations on behalf of the general interest. In short "a kind of European Planning Commissariat," which would decide the level of acceptable competition on the basis of a "dynamic and realist conception" of competition, ultimately controlled by political power on behalf of social progress and harmonious growth, instead of the static and regressive conceptions of undistorted competition typical of liberal conceptions of competition, as the constitutive basis for an economic order.

Houssiaux, who not only introduced the debate but also drafted the conclusions and political proposals made by the participants to this conference, formulated a precise definition of the social-democratic proposals on this point. He suggested that such a consultative European Planning Commissariat would be created by the directorate general for competition, including independent personalities, but also trade unionists and consumer representatives. Its role would be to provide opinions published in an annual report addressed to the Parliamentary Assembly and the Social and Economic Committee to inform the public with regular economic data and reports about industrial sectors in order to ensure "market transparency which is required for having true democracy and efficient action." The major common conception was that any anti-competitive practice was not "per se" damaging, but all depended on the effect of these practices, which had to be evaluated case by case. Moreover, the effects had to be evaluated not in abstract terms, but in relationship to social and economic-policy objectives. These objectives for the European Community had to be those of "stable, harmonious and regionally balanced growth conducive to full employment and social progress by means of planning and coordination of investments." For the future Council regulation required by the treaty, he made two proposals: on the one hand, cartels (Article 85) were, in principle, to be treated with suspicion, deserving a general ban, and on the other hand, regarding mergers, it was crucial to monitor and control them, given the risks that they implied also in political terms. These three principles (banning, monitoring and control) required a right of inquiry into firms or sectors, which had to prove that they were not using damaging practices. Such inquiries had to produce efficient decisions to be taken not just based on technical or formalistic criteria, but at the service of economic and social objectives, with the aim that incriminating practices were effectively and durably stopped. Regardless of its failures, the experience of the ECSC had to be taken as a point of departure. However, the major objective of the new EEC competition policy had to be the harmonization of national legislation, considering that dominant positions in member states could produce European effects. In any case, the common position of the experts concluded that any efficient struggle against prejudicial forms of combinations and concentrations required

> the creation of political and economic powers at the European level able to oppose and dominate private powers, and the unity of trade unions and political forces of the European left to impose a policy of planned growth. To confront the organization of business forces at the European level, workers and consumers should get quickly and efficiently organized at this same level.[37]

The list of distinguished participants at that meeting suggests that it was a success. The Belgian participants were the president of the Socialist trade union, FGTB, Dore Smets, the member of the European Parliament, Professor Fernand Dehousse, and politicians such as the Socialist Party of Belgium (PSB) president,

Leo Collard. From the Netherlands were Paul J. Kapteyn, a lawyer specializing in transport from the Labour Party, who presented a piece on the ECSC experience on behalf of the head of the Social Affairs Committee in the European Parliament, the MEP Gerhard Nederhorst. From Germany, Joachim Schone from the SPD presented a paper, and Johannes Sauermann from the IG Metall and Karl Kuhne from the Public Service Union from the DGB attended. The French SFIO sent to the meeting the right-hand man of Guy Mollet, Jacques Piette, but trade unionists from CGT-F.O. and the C.F.T.C., together with experts such as Bernard Clement, head of combinations at the Technical Commission for Competition of the French Ministry of Economy and Finances, also participated. The Italian participation included members of the socialist trade union UIL, and of the two Socialist Parties, PSI (Mario Zagari) and PSDI (Luigi Preti), whereas the Socialist Workers Party of Luxembourg was represented by the Secretary General of the Socialist Fraction in the European Assembly, Fernand Georges. Other international guests included Walter Freitag, secretary general of the European section of the International Confederation of Free Trade Unions (ICFTU) and Robert Van Schendel, secretary general of the European Movement.[38]

The successful action of Philip and Gironella with this first conference showed the relevance that competition had for European left-wing leaders. In the summer of 1960, they quickly launched two European programmatic “confrontations”: one on the public sector in Europe, and a second one on European Planning. The idea came from Paul-Henri Spaak at an informal meeting with the CEOs of French nationalized companies like EDF and Renault. The French public managers agreed to participate on the condition that their European counterparts also accepted.[39] The initiative was strongly supported by the former European Commissioner, the Italian Christian-Democrat Giuseppe Petrilli, in his new role as president of the Instituto per la Ricostruzione Industriale (IRI), the largest state-owned holding of the country. Spaak involved his socialist comrade Georges Rogissart, CEO of the National Society for Industrial Credit of Belgium (SNCI). This conference took place in the headquarters of Euratom in Brussels at the beginning of December 1961 hosted by the president of Euratom, Etienne Hirsch. The major practical conclusion of this other meeting was the creation of a permanent working group of public sector companies assisted by a Secretariat who would oversee the next steps for setting up a European grouping.[40] This was the informal creation of the European Centre for Public Enterprises (CEEP), which organized a second conference in October 1962 in Rome. André Philip delivered the opening speech in his new role as secretary general of the European Left Movement, which had succeeded the MSEU in February 1961, with the appointment of Spaak as its President. Gironella was also in Rome, and following the conference was appointed secretary of the new CEEP, even though he was still in charge of organizing the last CET Conference on European Planning in Paris, where Etienne Hirsch launched the proceedings. Gironella remained in this strategic position until 1965, when the CEEP was formally founded in Belgium as an association, presided over by Rogissart, and moved to Brussels. This new European interest group received public endorsement in November 1965 in a meeting with Walter Hallstein, who was accompanied by its supporters in the European Commission: Robert Marjolin in charge of Economic policies, the Social Christian Lambert Schaus from Luxembourg, who was commissioner for transport policy, and the Italian Social Democrat Lionello Levi-Sandri, in charge of the Social Affairs portfolio.

According to Melanie Vay, the early years of CEEP were seriously shaken by the differences between its German section and the other sections with regard to the question of whether it was necessary to clarify the exact content and limits of Article 90 in the Treaty of Rome. Whereas the German section feared that it was necessary to clarify this point with the European Commission in order to make clear the limits of the application of all other competition rules to public companies, the other sections preferred not to go too far in this direction. They trusted that the Council of Ministers would be responsible for this, in spite of the provocations of Hans von der Groeben at the CEEP conference in Berlin where he showed his political objective of not giving any special treatment to public enterprises as far as competition rules were concerned. In any case, by the end of 1965, the German ordoliberal commissioner for competition had not done much against public enterprises during his mandate, apart from showing his hostility toward their simple existence.[41]

This provocation might be interpreted as a sign of frustration, as VerLoren van Themaat had to apologize to the CEEP members for the misinterpretation of the words of the Commissioner on the eve of the meeting of November 1965 with Hallstein, and the other Commissioners, who closely monitored the action of the German commissioner within the subgroup of Commissioners in charge of competition matters. Marjolin's supervision had been clear and straightforward from the first day as the competition portfolio was originally destined for the French Socialist. However, Erhard had struggled to take it out from his larger portfolio of economic policies, even if this was compensated for by the appointment as director general of a social democrat like Pieter VerLoren van Themaat, supported by the Dutch Commissioner Sicco Mansholt. On the actual performance of the directorate general for competition during the two-mandates (1958–1967) in which it was led by von der Groeben, it seems clear that there was a lot of talk about ordoliberal doctrines and legal conferences. But there was limited capacity to confront existing cartels, and definitively not much either to control state aids, public enterprises, monopolies or mergers, which had boomed following the progressive creation of the common market. Most of the historiographical literature systematically overstate the concrete achievements of DG IV during the years directed by von der Groeben, considering it as a kind of golden age of ordoliberalism. As explained elsewhere, we do not share this interpretation, as there is evidence of open conflict in the directorate general, where ordoliberals around von der Groeben's office remained isolated, as well as conflict with member states and other commissioners.[42]

Following the end of the second Hallstein Commission, and the merging of the European executives in 1967, Hans von der Groeben remained in the Commission, but was significatively removed from his portfolio, which went to a much more experienced politician and lawyer, who precisely adhered to the Keynesian doctrine in competition matters: the Dutch Social Catholic, Emmanuel (Maan) J.A.

Sassen, who came from the Euratom executive. The German, though, managed, as compensation, to obtain the position of director general for his former chief of staff, Ernst Albrecht, who substituted VerLoren van Themaat, who had left for an academic position in the Netherlands. However, the political direction shifted, however, clearly toward Keynesian concepts, in open rupture with the ordoliberal ideas held by von der Groeben. This included rejecting the restrictive and negative connotation of "antitrust" on behalf of another dynamic of economic efficiency, industrial policy and competitiveness of European firms and companies. Furthermore, the new Dutch Commissioner made clear that in his view competition policy did not have an autonomous existence, but was instead part of general economic policies, which had to be decided by a political institution like the European Commission, and monitored by the European Parliament, without delegating this to a technical body such as a European cartel office similar to the German model.[43]

As the common market neared completion, the priority became merger control and abuse of dominant positions. The commissioner introduced this new policy in May 1968 in a speech delivered in Frankfurt to the Gotha of European industrialists of leading multinational corporations.[44] This "new and dynamic competition policy at the scale of the European common market and of the position of European industry in the world" aimed directly to reply to the famous "défi américain" by the French publicist Servan-Schreiber with "a European challenge." Sassen made clear that the application of Articles 85 and 86 of the Treaty of Rome to concentrations and industrial cooperation would not be based in pure legal objectives, but informed by the economic realities in each industrial sector. Furthermore, concentration and oligopolies were not to be forbidden through principle, if they preserved "efficient competition in the market." This was going to be the criteria of the European Commission to authorize agreements and concentrations, using Articles 85 and 86, even if the EEC didn't have, unlike the ECSC, a specific article on merger control. The new commissioner made clear that there would not be a general criterium for optimum size, but it would be variable per sector, and therefore economic power would be evaluated in each concrete case. The Commission's proposal to encourage European firms to benefit from the common market was for the Council to approve specific legal statutes for European companies, and the fiscal harmonization of direct taxes in favor of European concentrations.[45]

This new direction of competition policy was clearly Euro-mercantilist, as it encouraged mergers between European multinationals in order to avoid only American companies benefitting from the newly unified market. The occasion to show the teeth of the Commission, in relation to merger control, took place with the famous decision taken on 9 December 1971 on the basis of Article 86 in the Continental Can case involving this US multinational. This decision, however, was adopted by the successor of Sassen, his fellow Social-Christian democrat, Albert Borschette, who had chosen as director general the German Social Democrat Willy Schlieder. A former lawyer in the DGB headquarters, Schlieder started his career in 1961 in the directorate general for competition, before becoming head of the private office of the man of Willy Brandt in Brussels: the vice president of the Commission, Wilhelm Haferkamp, in 1967. It was no coincidence that with two tenants of the Keynesian approach in the driving seat of competition, they started dealing with the development of Article 86. After all, the control of abuse of dominant positions had been the priority of social democrats, as we saw in previous sections.

The legal basis for proper control was weak, considering that there was not a specific treaty chapter on merger control. The application of Article 86 to the control of concentrations was risky and limited to the control a posteriori of mergers, even if the European Court of Justice ultimately validated the indirect use of this article for such purposes. Therefore, Borschette and Schlieder decided that the moment was ripe for launching a Council regulation like Article 17/62 invoking the attribution of new powers to the Commission in merger control on the basis of Article 235 of the treaty. This article allowed more competencies to be given to the EEC, if there was an unanimous agreement by the member states. The legislative proposal was submitted in July 1973 and its content was similar to Keynesian reasoning: the European Commission would be able to block all mergers of a certain size if they hindered competition, but was also allowed to grant exemptions on the basis of reaching a higher objective in the common interest of the community, maintaining political flexibility to decide on a case-by-case basis. In this way, competition could again be subordinated to other objectives and, in that context, to industrial policy objectives. This Euro-mercantilist turn received a hostile reception from multinational corporations represented by the International Chamber of Commerce (ICC) and the European employers' federation (UNICE), which would have preferred, like the ordoliberals, to have the cases considered by an independent agency and not by a political body like the Commission. On the contrary, the proposal received the full support of the center-left majority in the European Parliament and in the European Social and Economic Committee. However, this support was insufficient as a large majority of member-states in the Council opposed the regulation, except for one of the new EEC members, the UK, which had just elected in 1974 a new Labour government.[46]

The European regulation was similar to a contemporary national regulation, which had been approved in in Britain with similar objectives: the Fair Trading Act of 1973. This new regulation instituted the creation of an Office of Fair Trading to oversee mergers and did not require compulsory notification, contrary to the European regulation. But, as in the Commission's proposal, it was for the Minister of Industry and Trade to decide upon sending the cases to the Monopolies and Merger Commission. This consultative body existed already under the previous 1965 Monopolies and Merger Act, which had been approved, at the time, by a Labour government with the support of the Trade Union Congress (TUC) and opposed by the employer's association CBI. As in the European merger, the criteria for a political decision was not competition as such, but general public interest criteria like consumer protection, export volumes and employment.[47] Schlieder, described by the British as a "good Brandt place-man", was perfectly aware of the British debate, as the Department of Trade and Industry informed him before sending the bill to parliament in November 1971, in order to check its compatibility with the treaty before accession. In the meeting held in Brussels, Schlieder confirmed that this new legislation was not in conflict with European competition law.[48]

Encouraged by this parallel development in member states, the legislative proposal of the Commission for merger control gained Gironella's approval after consulting the members of the CEEP and that also the newly founded European Trade Union Confederation (ETUC). Both gave it a green light with a positive vote of their representatives in the European Social and Economic Committee, whose consultation had been expressly requested by the President of the Commission, François-Xavier Ortoli, to strengthen its legitimacy, given that the ICC and UNICE opposed to this regulation. Let's analyze in turn some of the arguments put forward by the key holders of the Keynesian and social-democratic approaches to competition policy in order to single out their views on merger control.

The CEEP made clear its general agreement with the overall policy objective of the Ortoli Commission to conciliate the creation of European champions of continental size while maintaining control over their impact in economic sectors. This was necessary as there had been important mergers made either on a national basis but with European impact, or by take-overs from non-European companies. Therefore, they agreed that effective competition in the Common market had to be preserved as part of the general imperative of European policy for economic development. There was, however, a danger of conflict between the new regulation and the existing merger control regulations at the national level, and therefore, it suggested a simultaneous harmonization with national legislation. On the legal controversy of using Article 235, the public enterprises recalled that the states had expressly decided not to include a merger control like in the ECSC Treaty, and therefore there was a danger that strong opponents might request, instead, a treaty amendment. In any case, the CEEP made clear its favorable support for merger control, including prior control, but on the principle that notifications were not compulsory, but left to the initiative of the undertakings involved in the merger. The major reason was to avoid that this becoming a principle of interdiction, as in Article 85, even if there were distinctions between good and bad mergers.

Gironella made it explicit to the Commission that this issue divided the members of the CEEP and therefore if the Commission wished to maintain the compulsory notification principle, some changes had to be made to the exemptions suggested. At first, the minimum thresholds on turnover for compulsory notification had to be substantially reduced, as the suggested absolute limit was similar to national regulations dealing with national mergers and many large European companies would be exempted. The ideal solution would be to take a dynamic approach with a periodical review of the threshold. The second was that a particular attention to the banking sector, which they found necessary to include, not only when banks and investment firms became shareholders by capital increase but also by short-term placement in the stock market. The last comment by the CEEP included broadening the justification for the authorization of a merger, which might limit effective competition. Instead of declaring the merger "indispensable" for the fulfillment of an objective considered a priority on behalf of the general interest of the Community, it would suffice that the merger would be "beneficial" for reaching such a policy objective. Last, but not least, public enterprises agreed that the regulation had not created any specific element concerning them because "public enterprises are like any other enterprise, notwithstanding the reserves included in Article 90 of the Treaty." They advocated for mentioning Article 90 in the regulation, even if in case of conflict, the treaty would prevail. Along these lines, Gironella confirmed that public enterprises might also become more concentrated in cases of transnational cooperation, particularly in the management of public services, but he recalled that in oligopolistic markets, public enterprises constituted a "countervailing power." The utility of such a central concept was not redundant in the framework of the oil crisis and confirmed the affinity between the CEEP and the European Commission led by President Ortoli.[49]

The newly created ETUC also gave clear and public support to the draft regulation. Being the result of the merger of the European Confederation of Free Trade Union (ECFTU) with other trade unions (Christians and communists), the detailed position reflected the one adopted already in 1970. In that year, the ECFTU had dedicated a large part of its Annual Assembly to the social and economic problems created by the concentration of undertakings. It had concluded that not only the existing Treaties provided the necessary legal basis but also it was imperative to claim a preventive control on them. This was more urgent than ever as the process had accelerated, and EEC enlargement would make it even more intensive. That said, the competition articles were not enough to "guarantee an effective competition within the Common Market" and, therefore, they found "imperative and justified to take Article 235 of the Rome Treaty" as an additional basis. It also approved the Commission's flexible proposal, which was "neither based on a rigid principle of prohibition, nor on a vague principle of abuse." However, this required having the necessary organization and manpower to supervise and control "carefully and permanently all the processes of concentration."

For European trade unionists, the political initiative of the Commission was to seize the invitation made by the European Council in its October 1972 Paris Summit for the "elaboration of provisions ensuring that the concentrations affecting undertakings of the Community are in agreement with the economic and social objectives of the Community." They approved the right of the Commission to intervene in any concentration and not just in those of compulsory notification, regardless of whether they exceeded the threshold of the obligation of notification. However, this did not mean that there should be a prejudice against concentrations and "refusing ex officio" any concentration. Such concentrations were an inevitable process, which in general could have favorable implications for workers and consumers, but they needed to be controlled in their objectives and to respect competition rules. It was to ensure such an efficient control that the ETUC welcomed the urgent approval of positive opinions of this new regulation in the European Parliament and the Social and Economic Committee. As at this point amendments were still possible, it made a series of detailed proposals for improvements with particular attention on the protection of workers in cases of concentration. They particularly requested that trade unions enjoy the same rights to give their opinion as the associations of the enterprises concerned, and that an information and consultation procedure was carried out before the enterprises concerned took a decision, in such a way that workers were effectively protected. Last, but not least, the European Commission had to inform and consult the trade unions of the company, the ETUC and the European trade union federations of the sector concerned. Most originally, the ETUC also opened the door to creating an independent "Community Authority" for the control and supervision of concentrations, creating in this way the embryo of "a cartel bureau at Community level," which would also consult trade unions before taking any decisions in an independent manner.[50] This proposal following the British model was most likely the initiative of the secretary in charge of the issue at the ETUC, Walter Braun, who surely had in mind the simultaneous discussion in Germany proposed by the SPD on this issue.[51]

These amendments very clearly put on the table the social-democratic conceptions of competition policy and law. The fine-tuning with Schlieder went so far that he worked on a speech for a meeting of Commissioner Borschette with the ETUC in November 1974. The aim was to clarify some points, but also to thank them personally for their public support in a context in which the economic crisis made it politically difficult to reach unanimity, even when the draft also got the support of the European Bureau of Consumers Unions (*Bureau Européen des Unions de Consommateurs*, BEUC), the European Community of Consumer Cooperatives, the European grouping of saving banks and the Liaison Committee of small and middle industrial enterprises. The hostility of the European lobby of the Chambers of Commerce and Industry, the UNICE and the ICC were all directed against the obligation of prior compulsory notification. The commissioner made it clear to the ETUC that European competition policy was considered realistic and efficient with regard to the general interest of the Community, which included the economic interest not only of undertakings but also of workers and consumers. DG competition was at the avant-garde of the application of competition policy to multinational companies, as reported to the High-Level Group appointed by the UN to examine the problem of multinational companies, which included the former president of the Commission, the social democrat, Sicco Mansholt. The number of cases involved mostly US multinationals such as Continental Can or Commercial Solvents Corporation for Article 86, but of course most previous cases had been developed through Article 85 and also applied to European companies. On the legal basis confirmed by the European Court of Justice, the Commission was instructing other cases (I.B.M., Hoffman-La Roche, United Fruit) with a particular inquiry against some of the Oil majors. But this "application of competition law in a full, uniform and non-discriminatory manner within the common market" was not enough to control multinationals, which were also the origin of price increases motivated by collusions of all kinds. As concentration processes accelerated, the political choices were clear: Did the Community want a new regulation or not? The Council working group in charge of the matter was not going in a positive direction as various member states had invoked questions of principle such as the use of Article 235, or their potential conflict with national competition laws and their own industrial, regional or social policies.

In the opinion of the Commissioner and his director general, this last point had already been solved with an amendment introduced to take into consideration "the priority objectives of the Community," whereas regarding the coherence with national policies, this was a general problem in all policies, and the Community could not refrain from taking action in cases of serious divergences between European and national policies. In any case, the major issue at stake was the request of some member states to have the guarantee of participating in the application of the regulation beyond their consultative role in the Advisory Committee provided by Regulation 17/62. This included a compulsory opinion before any decision and some solutions to go further were possible, such as the system of Article 93 in state aids, which required unanimous agreement in the Council in exceptional cases; or Regulation 1017/68, which applied competition rules to transports in which the Council had a role. But the Commission opposed losing its central role with a co-decision in the form of a "management committee." This would imply sharing exclusive competencies with member states, which would be able by a qualified majority to change the decision taken by the Commission. Coming to the more contentious matter, prior control, the Commission made it clear that the alternative was much less efficient. This was particularly in terms of the negative economic and social consequences linked to the possible de-concentration in negative cases of clearing, not to mention legal insecurity. On this point, most member states seemed to agree even when this was the main matter of opposition from business lobbies. The Commission would not change this point, even if there were some adjustments to the concrete format. Finally, in the opinion of the commissioner, the consultation of trade unions as requested by the ETUC was acceptable for the Commission, which could consult interested parties and take into consideration the social effects of a merger. In any case, if the Draft Regulation were not successful, as was ultimately the case, the ETUC was ensured that Article 86 was already a useful point of support to monitor mergers, despite its evident limitations, so the final policy choice for the Commission was not choosing between "anything or nothing".[52]

Conclusion: the central tenets of the social-democratic approach for European competition

In the mid-1970s, the social-democratic perspective envisaged important progress in relationship to merger control. The ECSC article that had been put forward by Philip, Monnet and Uri back in 1950 was the actual model for the merger control regulation launched by the European Commission two decades later, as was rightly pointed out at the Consultative Council of Competition by the French representative, who was none other than the same Bernard Clement who had participated ten years earlier at the Conference organized by André Philip and Gironella in Brussels.[53] Such a valiant attempt was to a large extent the work of Schlieder's knowhow, because this former DGB lawyer had spent most of his career in the Commission at the directorate general for competition.

The window of opportunity had opened in the context of the Commission wanting to make competition an instrument able to support European champions and at the service of the social and economic policies of the Community. This was coherent with its long-term conception of using competition policy as a means for other objectives and guided by political decisions and not just a simple technical application of norms to protect competition as such. Obtaining a political space for democratic executives to control the power of capitalist oligopolies was what the British and German merger control regulations also wished to achieve. Indeed, if the merger control stagnated in the Council corridors for more than a decade, this was exclusively due to member states rejection in times of economic crisis. It is right to point out that member states and large companies feared that any other policy goal, outside of competition policy, could be decided by the Commission as the basis to block mergers, because this would imply an important cession of economic sovereignty with political consequences as Marchal had brilliantly argued with federalist spirit.

However, as we explained throughout this chapter, this was the doctrinal position that André Philip and other European socialists had designed 20 years earlier: competition policy was at the service of larger objectives, the first being an integrated European polity at the service of social progress. It is widely acknowledged that the economic crisis of the 1970s reinforced nationalist solutions, which made politically unfeasible the approval of any European merger control at a time when member states were protecting their own national industries from industrial restructuring. The historical moment of the economic crisis turned out to be unfavorable for the creation of a legal basis for a euro-mercantilist and social resolution as advocated by Social democrats for nearly three decades. But this partial failure did not put an end, yet, to the Keynesian conception of competition and its social-democratic supporters, who were able to rely on other legal bases to expand their own priorities in competition policy for their own political purposes, as Schlieder explained to the ETUC, and as confirmed by other chapters of this book.[54]

Notes

1 David J. Gerber, *Law and Competition in Twentieth Century Europe: Protecting Prometheus* (Oxford: Clarendon Press, 1998); Quinn Slobodian, *Globalists: The end of Empire and the Birth of Neoliberalism* (Cambridge: Harvard University Press, 2018).

2 Pinar Akman and Hussein Kassim, "Myths and Myth Making in the Institutionalization and Interpretation of EU Action: the Case of EU Competition Policy," *Journal of Common Market Studies* 48 (2010): 111–132; Huber Buch-Hansen and Angela Wigger, *The Politics of European Competition Regulation: A Critical Political Economy Perspective* (London: Routledge, 2011).

3 Kiran K. Patel and Heike Schweitzer (eds.), *The Historical Foundations of EU Competition Law* (Oxford: Oxford University Press, 2012).

4 Anselm Küsters, "The Making and Unmaking of Ordoliberal Language: A Digital Conceptual History of European Competition Law," PhD dissertation, Goethe University Frankfurt am Main, 2022.

5 Sigfrido M. Ramírez Pérez and Sebastian van de Scheur, "The Evolution of the Law on Articles 85 and 86 (Articles 101 and 102 TFEU): Ordoliberalism and its Keynesian Challenge," in K. Patel and H. Schweitzer (eds.), op. cit., 19–53.

6 Lorenzo Federico Pace and Katja Seidel, "The Drafting and the Role of Regulation 17: A Hard-Fought Compromise," *Ibid.*, 54–88. This extent has also been confirmed by the latest research by Anselm Küsters, op. cit.
7 Adrian Kuenzler and Laurent Warlouzet, "National Traditions of Competition Law: A Belated Europeanization through Convergence?" *Ibid.*, 89–125.
8 Tobias Witschke, "The Evolution of a 'Protoplasmic Organisation'? Origins and Fate of Europe's First Law on Merger Control," in Fernando Guirao, Frances M.B. Lynch and Sigfrido M. Ramírez Pérez (eds.), *Alan S. Milward and a Century of European Change* (New York; London: Routledge, 2012), 317–333.
9 Brigitte Leucht, "Transatlantic Policy Networks in the Creation of the First European Anti-trust Law: Meditaing between American Anti-Trust and German Ordo-Liberalism," in Wolfram Kaiser, Brigitte Leucht and Morten Rasmussen (eds.), *The History of the European Union. Origins of a Trans-and sUpranational Polity 1950–1972* (Abingdon: Routledge, 2009), 56–73.
10 Mathias Kipping, *La France et les origins de l'Union Européenne: Intégration économique et compétitivité international* (Paris: Comité pour l'histoire économique et financière, 2002).
11 Mathias Kipping, "Concurrence et competitivité: Les origines de la legislation anti-trust française après 1945," *Études et Documents* VI (1994): 429–455.
12 Alain Chatriot, "Les ententes: débats juridiques et dispositifs législatifs (1923–1953): la genèse de la politique e la concurrence en France," *Histoire, économie et société* 1 (2008): 7–22.
13 Claude Didry and Frédéric Marty, "La politique de la concurrence comme levier de la politique industrielle dans la France de l'après-guerre," *Gouvernement et action publique* 4 (2016): 23–45.
14 Christian Chevandier and Gilles Morin (eds.), *André Philip: Socialiste, patriote, chrétien* (Paris: Comité pour l'histoire économique et financière de la France, 2005).
15 Historical Archives of the European Union (HAEU), Pierre Uri (PU), b.19, Negotiations of the Schuman Plan: anticartel nature of the future organization, 9 May 1950.
16 Kai R. Pedersen, "Re-Educating European Management: The Marshall Plan's Campaign Against Restrictive Business Practices in France: 1949–1953," *Business and Economic History* 25, 1 (1996): 267–274.
17 Kipping, *La France et les origins de l'Union Européenne*, *Ibid.*, 182.
18 Richard Griffiths, "The Schuman Plan Negotiations: The Economic Clauses," in K. Schwabe (ed.), *Die Anfänge des Schuman-Plans 1950/1951* (Baden-Baden: Nomos, 1988), 35–71.
19 HAEU, PU-b.37, Economic Council, Committee for Economic Affairs and Planning, Working Group for the study of the ECSC, Information Report by Mr. André Philip, 10 November 1951.
20 Idem.
21 Center for the Virtual Knowledge of Europe (CVCE), André Philip, *Socialism and the Union of Europe*. Reply to the Leadership of the Labour Party, Socialist Movement for the United States of Europe, 1950, 14.
22 Louis Franck, *697 Ministres: souvenirs d'un directeur général des prix, 1947–1962* (Paris: CHEFF, 1990).
23 Louis Franck, *La libre concurrence* (Paris: PUF, 1963).
24 AHUE-PU-b.53.Comité intergouvernmental crée par la Conférence de Messine, Rapport des chefs de délégation aux Ministres des Affaires Etrangères, Bruxelles, 21 April 1956. MAE 120f/56 (corrigé).
25 Melanie Vay, *La mise en problème européen de l'économie publique* (Paris: Dalloz, 2021), 36–41.
26 François Denord and Antoine Schwartz, "L'économie (très) politique du traité de Rome," *Politix* 23, 89 (2010): 35–56.

27 Laurent Warlouzet, "The Rise of European Competition Policy 1950–1991: A Cross-Disciplinary Survey of a Contested Policy Sphere," EUI Working Paper, RSCAS 2010/80, 8–9.
28 Sigfrido M. Ramírez Pérez, "The French Automobile Industry and the Treaty of Rome: Between Welfare State and Multinational Corporations 1955–1958," in Michael Gehler (ed.), *From Common Market to European Union Building: 50 Years of the Rome Treaties 1957–2007* (Wien; Köln; Weimar: Böhlau Verlag, 2009), 169–197.
29 AHUE, CM3/NEGO 236, Secrétariat du Groupe du Marché Commun "Memento interne de la réunion du 3 et 4 Septembre 1956," 7 September 1956 and "Tableau synoptique des projets d'articles soumis par les délégations concernant les règles de la concurrence applicables aux entreprises," 18 September 1956.
30 Sigfrido M. Ramirez Perez, "Anti-trust ou Anti-US? L'industrie automobile européenne et les origines de la politique de la concurrence de la CEE," in Eric Bussière et Michel Dumoulin (eds.), *Europe organisée, Europe du libre-échange? Fin XIXe siècle – années 1960* (Bruxelles: Peter Lang, 2006), 203–228.
31 Melanie Vay, op. cit., 77–87.
32 Laurent Warlouzet, "The EEC/EU as an Evolving Compromise between French Dirigism and German Ordoliberalism (1957–1995)," *Journal of Common Market Studies* 57, 1 (2019): 77–93.
33 Sigfrido M. Ramírez Pérez, Antitrust, op. cit.
34 Sigfrido M. Ramírez Pérez and Sebastian van de Scheur, "The Evolution of the Law," op. cit., 21.
35 Archives Université Catholique de Louvain (A-UCL) Raymond Rifflet (RR), b.97, MSEU, Bureau Executif International, 14 and 15 February 1959.
36 Idem, Comité Européen du Travail, Confrontations sur le pouvoir des monopoles et les cartels dans l'Europe du Marché Commun, Bruxelles, 5–7 Juillet 1960. Rapport d'André Marchal "Les ententes et les concentrations dans le Marché Commun". Introductory report used for the Study Days of the University of Caen on Mai 1959.
37 Idem, Letter of Gironella for information, Conclusions des travaux, 8 July 1960.
38 Idem, Confrontation sur les pouvoir des ententes et des concentrations dans l'Europe du Marché Commun, Organisations et personnalités participantes, Bruxelles 5–7 Juillet 1960.
39 Idem, Henri Gironella, Note sur l'organisation d'une confrontation sur le secteur public dans l'Europe du Marché Commun, 11 octobre 1960.
40 Idem, Jacques Germain, Réunion des organismes publics de la Communauté Européenne, Séance du Groupe de Travail du 19 Février 1962, Compte-rendu des décissions adoptées, Paris, 28 Fébruary 1962.
41 M.Vay, La mise en problème, Chapter 2.
42 Sigfrido M. Ramírez Pérez, Sebastian van de Scheur, op. cit., 30–31.
43 Sigfrido M. Ramírez Pérez, Sebastian van de Scheur, op. cit., 32–33.
44 Historical Archives of the European Commission (HAEC), Speeches collection, Sassen, Discours prononcé par le Commissaire Sassen, Francfort, 10 May 1968, 11.
45 Idem.
46 Hubert Buch-Hansen and Angela Wigger, *The Politics of European Competition Regulation* (Routledge: Abingdon, 2011), 70–72.
47 Hubert Buch-Hansen, "Rethinking the History of European Level Merger Control: A Critical Political Economy Perspective," PhD series, Copenhagen Business School, 2008, 129–130.
48 British National Archives at Kew, Public Record Office (PRO), FV60/65, EEC Competition Policy, Consultations with the Commission, Confidential note of a discussion with Herr Schlieder, 23 November 1971.
49 AHCE, BAC 71/1988, no. 5, Avis du Centre Européen de l'Entreprise Publique sur les Proposition de réglement CEE du Conseil relatif au contrôle des concentrations, Avril 1974. Letter from Gironella to Schlieder, 8 May 1974.

50 Idem, ETUC, Position on the Proposal for a Regulation of the Council on the Control of Concentrations between Undertakings, 12 December 1973. This proposal was the object of various exchanges between Schlieder and Braun, who called him "Colleague" and used in his letters the familiar "Du" as a clear sign of comradeship between trade unionists.
51 Brian Shaev, "International Cartels in the Political Origins of German Competition Policy, 1949–1973," in Susanna Fellman and Martin Shanahan (eds.), *A History of Business Cartels: International Politics, National Policies and Anti-Competitive Behaviour* (New York: Routledge, 2022), 83–102.
52 AHUE, BAC 71/1988, no. 5, Note de Schlieder pour M.Borschette, Projet d'un exposé pour la reunion du 5 Novembre 1974 avec la Confédération Européenne des Syndicats, 25 October 1974.
53 Idem, 24e conférence des experts gouvernementaux des États membres des Communautés Européennes en matière d'ententes, 2 July 1973.
54 Warlouzet, "The Rise of European," 15–17. The author is right to point out that ordoliberalism in European competition faded away during the 1970s. However, he takes his case too far when arguing that the failure of the regulation was mainly due to internal incoherencies of DG IV. The prevalent thesis in the literature is that external political constraints from member states were decisive for the failure of this regulation, as shown by Buch-Hansen and Wigger. In our view, unanimity was the most important barrier as the legal service of the Commission had confirmed that Article 235 was the adequate legal basis to go forward. AHCE, BAC 71/1988, no. 5, Note JUR/3051/72, Recours à l'article 235. Note of Walter Much, Gerard Olivier and Jochen Thiesing, 5 December 1972.

Bibliography

Akman, Pinar and Hussein Kassim. "Myths and Myth Making in the Institutionalization and Interpretation of EU Action: the Case of EU Competition Policy." *Journal of Common Market Studies* 48 (2010): 111–132.

Buch-Hansen, Hubert. "Rethinking the History of European Level Merger Control: A Critical Political Economy Perspective." PhD series, Copenhagen Business School, 2008.

Buch-Hansen, Huber and Angela Wigger. *The Politics of European Competition Regulation: A Critical Political Economy Perspective*. London: Routledge, 2011.

Chatriot, Alain. "Les ententes: débats juridiques et dispositifs législatifs (1923–1953): la genèse de la politique e la concurrence en France." *Histoire, économie et société* 1 (2008): 7–22.

Chevandier, Christian and Gilles Morin (eds.). *André Philip: Socialiste, patriote, chrétien*. Paris: Comité pour l'histoire économique et financière de la France, 2005.

Denord, François and Antoine Schwartz. "L'économie (très) politique du traité de Rome." *Politix* 23, 89 (2010): 35–56.

Didry, Claude and Frédéric Marty. "La politique de la concurrence comme levier de la politique industrielle dans la France de l'après-guerre." *Gouvernement et action publique* 4 (2016): 23–45.

Franck, Louis. *697 Ministres: souvenirs d'un directeur général des prix, 1947–1962*. Paris: CHEFF, 1990.

Franck, Louis. *La libre concurrence*. PUF: Paris, 1963.

Gerber, David J. *Law and Competition in Twentieth Century Europe: Protecting Prometheus*. Oxford: Clarendon Press, 1998.

Griffiths, Richard. The Schuman Plan Negotiations: The Economic Clauses." In *Die Anfänge des Schuman-Plans 1950/1951* edited by K. Schwabe. Baden-Baden: Nomos, 1988, 35–71.

Kipping, Mathias. "Concurrence et competitivité: Les origines de la legislation anti-trust française après 1945." *Études et Documents* VI (1994): 429–455.

Kipping, Mathias. *La France et les origins de l'Union Européenne: Intégration économique et compétitivité international.* Paris: Comité pour l'histoire économique et financière, 2002.

Kuenzler, Adrian and Laurent Warlouzet. "National Traditions of Competition Law: A Belated Europeanization through Convergence?" In *The Historical Foundations of EU Competition Law* edited by Kiran K. Patel and Heike Schweitzer. Oxford: Oxford University Press, 2012, 89–124.

Küsters, Anselm. "The Making and Unmaking of Ordoliberal Language: A Digital Conceptual History of European Competition Law." PhD dissertation, Goethe University Frankfurt-am-Main, 2022.

Leucht, Brigitte. "Transatlantic Policy Networks in the Creation of the First European Anti-trust Law: Mediating Between American Anti-trust and German Ordo-Liberalism." In *The History of the European Union. Origins of a Trans-and Supranational Polity 1950–1972* edited by Wolfram Kaiser, Brigitte Leucht and Morten Rasmussen. Abingdon: Routledge, 2009, 56–73.

Pace, Lorenzo Federico and Katja Seidel. "The Drafting and the Role of Regulation 17: A Hard-Fought Compromise." In *The Historical Foundations of EU Competition Law* edited by Kiran K. Patel and Heike Schweitzer. Oxford: Oxford University Press, 2012, 54–88.

Patel, Kiran K. and Heike Schweitzer (eds.). *The Historical Foundations of EU Competition Law*. Oxford: Oxford University Press, 2012.

Pedersen, Kai R. "Re-Educating European Management: The Marshall Plan's Campaign Against Restrictive Business Practices in France: 1949–1953." *Business and Economic History* 25, 1 (1996): 267–274.

Ramirez Perez, Sigfrido M. "Anti-Trust ou Anti-US? L'industrie automobile européenne et les origines de la politique de la concurrence de la CEE." In *Europe organisée, Europe du libre-échange? Fin XIXe siècle – années 1960* edited by Eric Bussière et Michel Dumoulin. Bruxelles: Peter Lang, 2006, 203–228.

Ramírez Pérez, Sigfrido M. "The French Automobile Industry and the Treaty of Rome: Between Welfare State and Multinational Corporations 1955–1958." In *From Common Market to European Union Building: 50 years of the Rome Treaties 1957–2007* edited by Michael Gehler. Wien-Köln-Weimar: Böhlau Verlag, 2009, 169–197.

Ramírez Pérez, Sigfrido M. and Sebastian van de Scheur. "The Evolution of the Law on Articles 85 and 86 (Articles 101 and 102 TFEU): Ordoliberalism and Its Keynesian Challenge." In *The Historical Foundations of EU Competition Law* edited by Kiran K. Patel and Heike Schweitzer. Oxford: Oxford University Press, 2012, 19–54.

Shaev, Brian. "International Cartels in the Political Origins of German Competition Policy, 1949–1973." In *A History of Business Cartels: International Politics, National Policies and Anti-Competitive Behaviour* edited by Susanna Fellman and Martin Shanahan. New York: Routledge, 2022, 83–102.

Slobodian, Quinn. *Globalists: The End of Empire and the Birth of Neoliberalism*. Cambridge: Harvard University Press, 2018.

Vay, Mélanie. *La mise en problème européen de l'économie publique*. Dalloz: Paris, 2021.

Warlouzet, Laurent. "The EEC/EU as an Evolving Compromise between French Dirigism and German Ordoliberalism (1957–1995)." In *Journal of Common Market Studies* 57, 1 (2019): 77–93.

Warlouzet, Laurent. "The Rise of European Competition Policy 1950–1991: A Cross-Disciplinary Survey of a Contested Policy Sphere." *EUI Working Paper*, RSCAS 2010, 80.
Witschke, Tobias. "The Evolution of a "Protoplasmic Organisation"? Origins and Fate of Europe's First Law on Merger Control." In *Alan S. Milward and a Century of European Change* edited by Fernando Guirao, Frances M.B. Lynch and Sigfrido M. Ramírez Pérez. New York/London: Routledge, 2012, 317–333.

8 Finnish social democrats and competition policy

From the first "cartel law" to the application for EU membership

Susanna Fellman

For most of the twentieth century up until new legislation in 1992, cartels were permitted to operate quite openly in Finland. Monopolies and other restrictive practices were also common. The first legislation to combat restrictive practices, called the "cartel law," was passed in 1957. This law was replaced by new legislation several times as it was considered ineffective for targeting harmful cartel agreements and their abuse of market power. But until the 1992 legislation, in reality, the authorities had little power to combat restrictive practices. Nevertheless, during the post–WWII decades, an awareness of the problems arising from restrictive practices grew, leading to a series of parliamentary debates and step-by-step revisions to competition law in an increasingly restrictive direction.

In this chapter, I will investigate how the Finnish Social Democratic Party considered the possible problems arising from cartels, trusts and monopolies and what role the party played in draft legislation aimed at regulating restrictive practices and firms with dominant market positions, and how their attitudes and policies changed over time. As in other European countries, the Social Democratic Party (SDP) was a strong political force in the postwar period, and this can also be observed when studying this policy area. However, it did not have such a hegemonic position as did the Swedish Social Democrats for example during these decades. Firstly, the Finnish left was more fragmented with one significant party on the far left, the People's Democratic League of Finland (*Suomen Kansan Demokraattinen Liitto,* SKDL), which was divided into two factions, namely a Euro-Communist majority wing and a pro-Soviet minority wing.[1] The Agrarian party (later the Center Party) also enjoyed strong support among large sections of society, reflecting the fact that Finland was still quite agrarian and also the strong non-socialist orientation in rural areas. The Finnish political "map" overall was quite fragmented and small splinter groups occasionally made the situation for the traditional parties difficult. From time to time, the SDP was also burdened by internal struggles. While the Social Democrats were often in government in the postwar period, as a rule, it was as part of various coalitions, often with the Center Party and, occasionally, the far left. In fact, as Mikko Kuisma and Magnus Ryner emphasize, this coalition became a hegemony in the Finnish postwar political landscape.[2] However, the SDP was certainly a key player in politics, especially during the era of consensus and compromise from the late 1960s to the 1980s. As I shall observe further in the text, the

DOI: 10.4324/9781351010573-8

SDP played a significant role in several of the reforms of competition legislation. Nevertheless, it did not always achieve its goals, and during some reforms, the party was in opposition.

The period of investigation extends from the process leading up to the cartel law in 1957 until the introduction of zero-tolerance legislation in connection with Finland's aims to participate in the European integration process. This was a turbulent period, as in a short period of time, the country went from aiming to sign an agreement to enter the European Economic Area (EEA) to deciding to apply for membership of the European Union.

The Finnish case provides some interesting perspectives, as the legislation was up for reform several times. The process can be described as one of "baby-steps." We can therefore study how the SDP perceived and at times acted for reforms and discern possible changes in its perceptions and strategies. I will show that the Finnish Social Democrats often promoted the necessity of a tightening of the legislation and the party was usually in power when initiatives for legislative reforms were put forward. Nevertheless, one should not overplay their eagerness in this area. As we shall observe later, the competition legislation was often secondary to other aims, in particular price monitoring and price regulation legislation among both the Social Democrats and organizations close to them, like the Central Organization of Finnish Trade Unions (*Suomen Ammattiliittojen Keskusjärjestö*, SAK). While the focus here is on the SDP, its internal discussions and the party's actions within parliamentary debates, its approach to competition legislation cannot be studied without also taking into account the trade unions and other associations with close connections to the party, in particular the left-wing consumer cooperative (*Kulutusosuuskuntien Keskusliitto*, the Central Union of Consumer Co-operatives, KK) and the more radical left (SKDL). Furthermore, various groups within the party often had divergent attitudes to competition legislation; consumer interest groups and employees in small cooperatives had different interests than workers employed in big export industries. The SDP had to accommodate this diversity of views. How the party representatives positioned themselves in the parliamentary debates depended not only on whether the SDP was in government or in opposition but also on the views expressed by the radical left.

Moreover, competition legislation as such attracted the attention of relatively few people within the party, and these primarily had connections to the cooperative movement. This was especially the case up to the 1970s. However, those engaged in the issue were key individuals in the party and influential to such an extent that we may consider them policy entrepreneurs who pushed the party to adopt policies to restrict anticompetitive business practices by means of legislation.

Nevertheless, the party's political goals with respect to price and competition policy changed over time. Especially in the 1980s, the SDP supported the idea of a less tolerant legislation. This occurred in conjunction with a general swing toward a more market-oriented way of thinking, when leading Social Democrats clearly shifted their focus toward a "Third Way" type of social democracy. This Third Way meant a greater acceptance of market-based solutions in the economy and the abandonment of the full employment target. In many countries, especially in Finland, the SDP now also tolerated cuts in social spending and policies to stimulate labor supply ("workfare"). This agenda was intended to save social democracy in a globalizing world, where traditional industrial jobs were disappearing. Nevertheless, according to Ryner, it differed from a "neoliberal" agenda as it still promoted, for example, traditional labor market policies and an extensive social security system to limit individual risks.[3]

Another issue that has to be taken into account is that pressure from interest groups was great in many policy areas, even in competition policy. The postwar period was marked by strong neo-corporatist features. One important reason for this were efforts to achieve some kind of "workable competition" – a competitive market situation that balanced the advantages for consumers of promoting competition against growth targets and the interests of businesses. At the same time, the aim was to make the interest groups "co-responsible partners." By involving them in policy formation and policy implementation, they were empowered to take responsibility for their decisions.[4] Since competition policy and legislation in many countries was quite a technical and bureaucratic policy area,[5] this also meant that this legislation often received little attention outside of small groups. Nevertheless, it is also important to look at the political level and political decision-makers, as ultimately legislation is a result of parliamentary processes and political parties pushing for reforms.

This research adds to our understanding of changes in the Social Democrats' economic policy agenda that occurred in the 1980s in particular, and the emergence of a "Third Way" form of social democracy. Competition policy became a wedge that opened up new perspectives for the Finnish SDP's attitudes toward economic policy more broadly. This field of regulation is therefore an excellent "window" through which to study changing views on the role of competition in the market economy in addition to the impact of political parties and policy entrepreneurs on competition legislation.

Some early but unsuccessful initiatives

During the (fairly) liberal interwar period, non-interference in business and freedom of contract were considered basic principles of commercial life, in which cartels were a legitimate way to organize economic activity. Many also thought of covenants between firms as bringing stability to the market, while the big export cartels were viewed as advantageous for a small, young nation, which had achieved independence only in 1917 and where industrialization was still in its prime. Cooperation instead of cutthroat competition was viewed by many to be a "more civilized" approach to capitalism.

Nonetheless, there were discussions about legislation to control and monitor restrictive trade practices, primarily inspired by the draft legislation in the other Nordic countries in the 1920s. Debates on the growing roles of trusts and combines were on the agenda in many other countries, and in international forums such as the League of Nations. Finnish economic and political thinkers were following these discussions and the awareness of the disadvantages of restrictive covenants for consumers and small independent firms grew. One of the most active groups in this debate was the left-wing consumer cooperative association *KK*, an ideological "umbrella" association for the "progressive" (i.e. left-wing) cooperative movement, commonly referred to as the E-movement (*E-liike*).[6] The KK had connections with the political left and in particular the Social Democratic Party. At the meeting of KK representatives in 1928, the association issued a statement in which it urged the state to take action to implement some kind of control over trusts, cartels and monopolies. KK's statement was based on a pamphlet published in 1927.[7] These initiatives did not lead to any concrete measures at the time, however. The political left was fragmented and weakened after the Civil War of 1918.

Swedish economic historian John Lapidus has discussed the quite permissive attitude of the Swedish Social Democrats toward cartels in the interwar period (see also his chapter in this volume for his discussion of a more recent period).[8] He argues that this was partly a result of a perception within the party leadership that cartels and monopolies would be easier targets for socialization than a multitude of smaller independent private firms. Birgit Karlsson argues further in this volume that interwar Swedish Social Democrats were concerned above all with efficiency and moved from a policy of socialization of production to a socialization of consumption. To what extent did such ideas influence Finnish policy debates on competition legislation? Did they exist among the Finnish Social Democrats as well? As will be shown, their views on both private big business and state ownership were important topics of debate and the nationalization of big business, in particular banks and insurance companies, was on the agenda, especially during the first decades after the war. State enterprises were also considered important for employment reasons, for example, and for promoting economic development, especially in poorer regions. Arguments for socialization of big business were included in the SDP's party programs, especially during the decades after the war. Their presence also continued in internal discussions much later but was tied to favoring competition legislation. Such arguments for restricting cartels and business collusion came primarily from the far left.

The first legislation, 1957: the KK and the social democrats on the move

After World War II, there was increasing awareness of the need to at least monitor the activities of cartels and monopolies and likewise to curb their most harmful effects. Concerns about the prevalence, power and negative effects of powerful cartels and of growing concentration in the Finnish market grew. It appears that the Finnish economy had experienced increasing cartelization during the first decades of the twentieth century.[9] Economic regulation during the war had also promoted cartelization and cooperation within many industries and in 1942, for example, KK director Jalmari Laakso expressed concerns about the growing concentration of wholesale and retail trade and its effects on consumers.[10]

The KK's demand for some form of control of cartels and monopolies was repeated again after the end of the war and in 1948 the association issued a new statement that cartels and monopolies ought to be put under government control at the association's meeting of representatives.[11] This time, the KK's efforts had an impact. In 1948, a committee to investigate the need for such legislation was formed. Similar legislation was introduced in many countries, in particular in Sweden, which led to an act in 1946 (see Karlsson in this volume). Moreover, this time, the KK had the "ear" of the government, a center-left coalition that included a social-democratic Minister for Trade and Industry, who was responsible for this issue.

The cartel committee, which consisted of legal experts and representatives of various interest groups, worked slowly; its report was not submitted until 1952.[12] The committee's work was hampered by internal conflicts, but it also did quite profound groundwork by studying competition legislation in other countries. Moreover, the decade after the war was marked by political instability and short-term governments, while many urgent economic and political questions dominated the agenda, for example, economic reconstruction and the burdensome war reparations payments to the Soviet Union.[13]

The committee's report included a proposal for an act, but as the committee stated, it was better to tread cautiously and first "wait and see" how such an act would sit with Finnish society. The proposed legislation was quite tolerant, primarily aiming at investigating the market situation and acquiring information about the existence of restrictive covenants and cartels on the Finnish market.

Again the process was fairly slow, and draft legislation was only put before Parliament in 1954. The government in charge had changed, but again it was a center-left coalition government, including the SDP, but led by a prime minister from the Agrarian Party. The draft legislation consisted of an act based on the anti-abuse principle, with the main object being to control and monitor the market situation by collecting information about the prevalence of restrictive covenants. Information about these covenants was to be compiled in a register, which was to be made public. Such registers existed in many other countries at the time.[14] It was proposed to ban two forms of restrictive covenants: bid rigging and resale price maintenance (with possibilities for derogations). Resale Price Maintenance (RPM) agreements were a form of restrictive covenant that many European countries banned early as they were often considered to be particularly harmful for consumers and, especially in small countries, these could very rapidly lead to a complete lack of competition in the distribution chain.[15] A Cartel Bureau to implement and maintain the register was to be established and placed within the Patent and Registry Office.

The SDP was one of the parties actively pushing for the first legislation. It was not the subject of extensive debates internally in the party, however. Many other issues were on the political agenda during the 1950s, and the party suffered from internal conflicts. Moreover, the committee consisted primarily of representatives of interest groups and therefore, prior to entering the parliamentary process, the debates had occurred partly outside the party's formal political activities.[16] People connected to the cooperative movement were active on the cartel issue, however. For example, Jalmari Laakso was a member of the committee and a moderate Social Democrat. Another key person was Väinö Tanner, who had been managing director of the consumer cooperative Elanto since 1915 (until 1956). Elanto was the largest and most significant cooperative retailer within the E-group. Tanner was also party leader between 1918 and 1926 and again during the period 1957–1963. He had been prime minister in 1926–1927, and a minister in the government several times in the interwar period and during World War II. He was sentenced to imprisonment after the war as part of the war responsibility trials against some leading political leaders, which Finland was forced to prosecute as part of the peace treaty. He was released in 1948, however, and returned to politics. Tanner was an ardent advocate of the cooperative movement and the cartel issue was close to his heart. During his imprisonment, Tanner translated the book *Cartels: Challenge to a Free World* (1944) by Wendell Berge into Finnish.[17] In the foreword to the Finnish language edition, Tanner stated that it was important for Finns to become familiar with the American experience with cartels and trusts and asserted that Berge was one of the best experts on the topic, having served as head of the Antitrust Division of the Department of Justice. Helle noted especially that Berge discussed that many people in the United States had initially considered trusts to be a good way to organize and rationalize production and to avoid cyclical fluctuations, but that the real negative effects eventually became clear to everyone. These combines had become powerful players with harmful effects on outsiders, consumers and workers. Moreover, their hostile attitudes toward the unions had made it urgent to combat their power. Nevertheless, Tanner also emphasized Berge's strong declaration in favor of protecting the freedom of American business from state interference. As Tanner was a key player in the party, we can assume he influenced the party's views significantly. As we will see next, one of those most active in the parliamentary debates was also a Social Democrat with close ties to the E-movement, Veikko Helle.

However, from studying party documents, it becomes evident that price issues and high inflation, in particular rising food prices, were the issues to which the SDP paid most attention. This was the case for the SAK as well. Rising consumer food prices were mostly considered to be results of unsuccessful price policies. Some of these problems were inherited from the strict wartime regulation of prices, which had led to market distortions. Many had become accustomed to a system of price and wage regulation and within SDP direct interference in market mechanisms was seen as the best way to fight price increases. On the other hand, this had led to growing tensions between the agrarian population and wage-earning workers. A system, in which agricultural prices were raised to compensate for wage increases, and vice versa, had developed. This system was meant to balance the interests of the two groups so that living standards would rise for both urban and rural populations. But one of these groups always considered itself disadvantaged and increases in food prices were consistently met with new wage demands.[18]

The role of capitalists and monopolists in price increases was frequently mentioned in the debates, but zero-tolerance competition legislation was not presented as a solution. In the 1950s, SDP members occasionally put forward demands for more effective ways to force entrepreneurs to lower their prices, but price policies were eventually to become more effective. The question of big business power and the nationalization of big monopolies was included in the party program in the late 1940s. For example, Emil Huunonen – a Social Democrat and a leading individual in SAK – mentioned in a 1949 pamphlet entitled "What does SAK want now" that the wave of concentration in big business was a threat and that monopolies should be taken over by the state.[19] The SAK's meeting of representatives made similar statements.[20] However, only the white-collar employee union (HTK) submitted a statement during a formal round of public comments to the Cartel Committee's report at this time. The SAK focused instead on improved price regulation and in general urged the state to take stronger actions against price increases in business.[21]

The cartel law in the parliamentary process

The draft legislation was as mentioned submitted to Parliament in 1954. A private member's bill from two Members of Parliament, Penna Tervo and Viljo Virtanen, was submitted at the same time. Tervo was Minister of Trade and Industry at the time and a Social Democrat active in the cooperative movement. This bill was similar to the government's draft legislation, but with a number of stricter formulations (resulting in fewer possibilities for derogations) and would have provided better tools for making more of the restrictive covenants public.

The draft legislation was not debated before it was submitted to the parliament's Commerce Committee for further consideration. Again, the process was slow and the bill stayed in committee for a long time. This was partly due to disagreements and partly to extensive work with many experts and interest group representatives. Intense lobbying occurred, led especially by representatives of business interest associations. Several dissenting opinions were also added to the draft legislation.[22] It came back to a plenum in 1956 with some slight modifications. In particular, the ban on RMP had been removed and replaced with a version in which a covenant could be dissolved if the authorities considered it "harmful."

The plenary debate was intense this time. Representatives of a small but colorful rural populist party were very active, as were the members of SKDL, who wanted more far-reaching legislation. They proposed that big business and monopolies ought to be placed under much stricter control. One representative stated that the draft legislation was so weak that conservative members would not even bother to discuss it. In fact, "monopolists and big business capitalists just laugh at the proposal."[23]

Conservative representatives (the National Coalition Party) did not participate very actively in the debate, although they did state that they objected to the ban on resale price maintenance.[24] Their argument was that the resale price maintenance made prices equal across the whole of Finland, which was most "fair" for consumers. If RPM were to be banned, those in more remote areas would have to pay more for the same goods and services as those in Helsinki because there was more competition in Helsinki than in rural areas. The conservatives and many of the business interest associations argued together that there were in fact few restrictive covenants in the Finnish market, and if there were such covenants, they were less harmful than the state enterprises. In fact, cartel collaboration was the only way they could compete with state enterprises.[25] Another aspect the business interests opposed was the idea of a notification system, as it would result in the disclosure of trade secrets. A representative for the Liberal Party stated that it was odd that "free competition" was to be promoted by state regulation.

One of the most active individuals in the debate was a leading Social Democrat, Veikko Helle. Since his youth, Helle had been active in the progressive cooperative movement in various positions of trust, at both local and regional levels, and he later became chairman of the supervisory board of KK.[26] As expected, Helle would have preferred the original version, which entailed a full ban on resale price maintenance, but was also willing to accept the more lenient version. Helle emphasized the urgent need for such a law and that it was important to conclude the matter quickly. He stated that "two governments [*coalitions including Social Democrats:* author's comment] had been required to get it this far."[27] He also noted that Finland was the only country in which government agencies did not even carry out investigations into the situation on the market and the existence of monopolies. This was not entirely correct, as there were countries that had not yet introduced any competition legislation. Finland was, however, quite late in Western Europe in doing so.[28]

The law, formally entitled the act on the Control of Practices Restricting Economic Competition [*Laki talouselämässä esiintyvien kilpailurajoitusten valvonnasta*] was finally passed in December 1957, nine years after the Cartel Committee had been formed. The legislation banned bid rigging, but resale price maintenance was only to be banned if determined to be "harmful." A system of notifications and a public register was established, to be managed by the new Cartel Bureau.

By looking at SDP internal party documents, it can be concluded that this legislation was not often discussed and it was an issue mainly for a few committed individuals within the SDP like Tanner, Helle and Tervo. However, when it was on the agenda, the party leadership considered it an important topic. For example, in the government program drawn up in 1956 for the following period in the government, the legislation was mentioned as a key issue.[29]

The 1964 legislation: the SAK mobilizes

The 1957 legislation was soon deemed unsatisfactory, by both the authorities and various groups, including the Social Democrats. One problem stressed by the authorities was the disinclination of businesses to notify their agreements to be included in the register. The authorities also had very few tools to interfere when agreements were suspected of being "harmful." In fact, they also struggled with interpreting the law, as it did not specify what "harmful" meant. Nor did the business community understand what "restrictive covenants" or "competition restrictions" (*kilpailunrajoitus*) meant. Resale price maintenance agreements were common and considered problematic, but as the definition of "harmfulness" was unclear, the legislation did not solve these problems. Another issue that put pressure on the legislation was Finland's signing the European Free Trade Agreement (EFTA) in 1961. This agreement had clear repercussions for the competition legislation, as restrictive practices were not to counteract the advantages flowing from the abolition of trade barriers.

In 1961, the government assigned a committee investigating economic regulation, which was already looking at the price regulation legislation, the task of suggesting changes to the existing legislation. This time the committee worked swiftly and came up with a report and a proposal in 1962. It was now suggested to ban resale price maintenance altogether. The primary goal was, however, to give authorities more power to interfere in cases of abuse. The authorities were to be reorganized and better staffed. The committee proposed that a negotiation procedure similar to the one existing in Sweden was to be introduced, such that in cases in which an agreement was suspected of having harmful effects, the cartel members or signatories to the agreement could be called in for negotiations with the authorities with the intention of removing certain clauses or dissolving the entire agreement. The law was to be called the Act for the Promotion of Competition and draft legislation was submitted to Parliament already later the same year.

This time, the government in charge was a non-socialist coalition government led by the Agrarian League. The legislative initiative was not broadly discussed internally in the SDP, although price policies and price regulation were on the agenda. On the other hand, the SAK was more alert this time and issued various statements. While the committee was still working in 1961, the SAK asserted that price and cartel controls were becoming increasingly important in the fight against price increases. The party concluded that, from workers' perspectives, the existing legislation was indeed ineffective, and it was too easy to conclude restrictive covenants, while consumers had only a weak "price awareness" (*hintatietoisuus*).[30] Party leaders attributed this to the long period with regulation. They had taken notice of the investigation by Ahti M. Salonen (1955) that asserted that the increasing concentration in the retail market was tending to drive consumer prices upward. Moreover, the SAK emphasized that the Cartel Bureau was a weak authority with too few instruments with which to intervene.[31] The 1957 law should be replaced with a less tolerant one. Later, when the proposal was up before Parliament, SAK argued that it was too lenient; it "did not live up to the expectation that had been set and to the goals of good legislation."[32] Their strong opinion was not so surprising bearing in mind that the government was a non-socialist one. The need for a more effective authority was an issue that the SAK also returned to later. Investigations into price and competition issues were to be improved and the registration procedure was to become more active.[33] Nevertheless, for the SAK, price regulation and price monitoring were the most important questions. In 1961, they stated, in a response to a consultative circular on the issue of price monitoring legislation, that the only effective way to dampen price increases was a proper price regulation. A system based solely on reporting prices would not be enough.[34]

The debate in Parliament primarily concerned how to make the authorities work more effectively, especially in relation to the introduction of a negotiation procedure. The Social Democrats were active and they advocated strongly for mandatory notification of all restrictive covenants by every entrepreneur and business on their own initiative. However, this was not in the original proposal and was not introduced in the final legislation. An unconditional ban on RPM was also necessary, according to the SDP. This time too, Veikko Helle was active in the debate. He stated, for example, that if more effective regulations concerning the notification of agreements were not introduced in the law, along with the introduction of a negotiation procedure and a ban on RPM, then it would be bombastic to call the law an Act for the Promotion of Competition.[35] Moreover, Helle and another Member of Parliament from the SDP also advocated strongly for a ban on boycotts, an issue that KK had discussed already in the 1920s.[36]

SKDL representatives had even more far-reaching suggestions, however. One representative regretted that he had expected to see a proposal that included a total ban on cartel agreements, instead of small, incremental changes.[37] The pro-Soviet faction among the Communists, led by Taisto Sinisalo, considered it highly problematic that private capitalist and state enterprises collaborated in cartels; state-owned enterprises were on the capitalists' "leash."[38] State enterprises were to be developed for the benefit of the people, and private monopolies and cartels were to be dissolved.[39] In spite of aiming for more far-reaching legislation than the government's proposal, Veikko Helle defended the bill against the most radical suggestions. It appears that the Social Democrats felt a need to distance themselves from the far left.

The conservatives objected to the tighter legislation and in particular to a total ban on RPM agreements and the expanded notification requirements. Hostility toward large state companies was again an argument that the conservatives used. The business associations appear to have resorted to lobbying also this time, which did not go unnoticed in Parliament; one Communist alleged that the conservatives and right wing as usual were using unfair methods outside Parliament (*ulkoparlamentaariset keinot*).[40] Nonetheless, the National Coalition Party appears to have been considering also competition regulation to be essential for a modern market economy. Its role was, for instance, stressed in its 1966 party program. The NCP was divided though on what a free market meant.[41]

Overall, the debates followed familiar pathways, but there were indications that a new view on the role of competition legislation as a tool for promoting a healthy market economy was emerging among some groups; one liberal representative stated that "competition legislation was an explicit way to position oneself on the side of a proper market economy" (*kilpailulainsäädäntö merkitsee selvää asettumista markkinatalouden kannalle*).[42]

The new law, titled the Act on the Promotion of Economic Competition [*Laki taloudellisen kilpailun edistämisestä* L 1964/1], was passed in December 1963 and enacted in 1964. Resale price maintenance was conditionally banned, that is, such agreements were declared illegal, unless it was explicitly declared by the businesses involved that their recommended price could be undercut through competition.[43] It became mandatory for trade associations or formal cartels to register their agreements on their own initiative. Businesses and entrepreneurs who had independently signed restrictive covenants had to report their agreements only on request, as before. Non-compliance with the notification requirement could result in fines. The negotiation procedure was introduced. The KK was disappointed again that no ban on boycotts had been introduced. In conjunction with the revised law, the Cartel Bureau became the Bureau for Freedom of Commerce (*Elinkeinovapausvirasto – Näringsfrihetsverket*), with a larger staff. A Council for Freedom of Commerce (*Elinkeinovapausneuvosto – Näringsfrihetsrådet*) was established, which had the power to initiate the negotiation procedure.

Competition policy to supplement more permanent price monitoring: developments in the 1970s

Within a few years, the legislation was again considered to be inadequate. The negotiation procedure in particular had been a disappointment. Some restrictive agreements had fallen under investigation, but no negotiation procedure had been initiated. Some entrepreneurs had removed restrictive clauses voluntarily, however. The ban on RPM agreements had worked fairly well, however, and a new system of list prices (*ohjehinta; riktpriser*) had become the standard. Nevertheless, Finnish markets tended to become more and more concentrated and the number of notifications to the register was still low.[44] The authorities also wanted to make the Finnish legislation similar to that of other Nordic countries as part of increasing economic cooperation in the Nordic area.[45]

Another reason behind the initiative to renew the legislation was an increasing recognition that problems with high inflation were in part due to the role of restrictive practices. SDP representatives stated that the lack of competition in the Finnish market was indeed problematic from the perspective of consumers and workers.[46] However, the SDP and the trade unions were especially dissatisfied with the lack of what they considered "effective" price regulation. Finland had had price regulation and price monitoring in some form since World War II, but it had been based on temporary legislation that had been renewed and expanded at regular intervals. The SDP and SAK called for more permanent legislation. However, they stated that a Price Monitoring Act also required competition legislation to counteract the price increases which were caused by monopolization and the lack of competition on the domestic market.[47] For the SAK as well as the SDP, the first priority was the Price Regulation Act, however.[48]

In October 1971, an SDP-led center-left coalition government established a new committee to oversee the need for both a new Price Monitoring Act and new competition legislation. The committee submitted its report including drafts for both new pieces of legislation in May 1972. In the draft competition legislation, there was some tightening concerning the reporting of restrictive agreements and harsher sanctions in cases of non-compliance. No new bans were proposed besides prohibiting resale price maintenance altogether.[49] One of the most significant reforms was to establish a completely new authority, to be called the National Board of Trade and Consumer Interests (*Elinkeinohallitus – Näringsstyrelsen*). This new Board was to administer these two policy areas (later also consumer protection) in order to foster a better synchronization of competition policy with price regulation. The Board was to consult with representatives from relevant businesses or industries and other experts. Its decision-making was to take place in "meetings" of the management of the Board once per week. However, important issues were to be assigned to "extended meetings" (*lisätty istunto)* at which interest group representatives were allowed to participate. It was also proposed to introduce a *Competition Ombudsman* (*Kilpailuasiamies – Konkurrensombudsman*) similar to Sweden's Competition Ombudsman (*Näringsfrihetsombudsman*) at the time. This Ombudsman was to initiate new measures that would promote competition. He/she was also tasked with investigating individual cases independently or in conjunction with the planned Board, initiating preparations for action for negotiation procedures.

Several committee members provided dissenting opinions on the committee's report. One point of criticism concerned the draft for a Price Monitoring Act. Business representatives and independent experts stated that if there was a need for price regulation, it should be temporary (*määräaikainen*).[50] The NCP objected strongly to the idea of a more permanent Price Monitoring Act throughout the parliamentary process. For both the SDP and SAK, however, it was important to push this legislative package forward. In the SDP's government program for the upcoming years, safeguarding the Price Monitoring Act was one of its first priorities and the legislation was repeatedly mentioned in internal discussions.[51] The administrative reform was also considered important, but the SDP expressed some doubts about it. The SAK was strongly in favor of the establishment of the new Board, most likely because significant influence was going to be granted to interest groups in the "extended meetings." In fact, the SAK had already lobbied for a new organization in early discussions in 1969 that would combine the implementation of the price and competition policies.[52] However, the SDP leadership feared a "bureaucratization" of the administration of the competition and price policies in which political influence would decrease.[53] The establishment of the Board with its extended meetings would introduce an even stronger corporatist aspect into competition and price policies.

The SDP-led coalition submitted the draft legislation to the Finnish parliament in November 1972 but, internally, the SDP leadership expressed worries about their fate. For example, in May 1973, Prime Minister Kalevi Sorsa (SDP) emphasized the importance of getting this legislation passed.[54] In the end, the process was swift and the debates in parliament quite brief. The National Coalition Party continued to object to the Price Monitoring Act and especially to make it more permanent. Both Acts passed, however. Resale price maintenance was totally prohibited and horizontal price agreements between individual entrepreneurs were also to be reported on the participants' own initiative. The possibilities for dismantling specific restrictive agreements were enlarged. Sanctions for non-compliance with notification requirements became harsher. The Price Monitoring Act (*Hintavalvontalaki* 156/74) was also passed, but in the end, it continued to be temporary legislation, to be renewed every four years. The SDP thus experienced a small defeat.[55]

The most important reform was the reorganization of the competition authorities. The new National Board of Trade and Consumer Interests and a new Competition Ombudsman were established. The Ombudsman's task was to cooperate closely with the Board. The creation of an Ombudsman in particular was considered representative of the Act's general purpose of fostering a more proactive competition policy. Moreover, a new Competition Council (*Kilpailuneuvosto – Konkurrensråd*) replaced the old Council for Freedom of Commerce.

A shift to a less tolerant attitude toward restrictive trade practices: the 1980s

This legislation was up for renewal again in the early 1980s. The Competition Ombudsman actively took the initiative this time. According to him, one of the problems with the current legislation was the lack of any kind of merger control and weak enforcement of controls against the abuse of dominant market positions. However, the legislation needed reform in several other respects as well to promote a healthier competitive market. It was suggested to make notification requirements mandatory for all entrepreneurs. Outside organizations also had an impact; for instance, in 1978, the Organisation for Economic Co-operation and Development (OECD) urged Finland to make the legislation more effective. Another motivation was that Sweden's competition legislation from 1953 was under review and the Finnish authorities kept abreast of developments across the border.[56] Another issue on the agenda, which came to divide the committee internally, was a proposal that banks and insurance companies should come under the competition legislation. Hitherto, the financial services industry had been exempted from competition legislation, motivated by the fact that it was regulated by separate banking and insurance legislation. These reforms were promoted by the SAK in particular, which made its positions clear in the statements and comments its members provided in relation to the proposals.[57]

A Social Democratic-led government, with Mauno Koivisto as prime minister, appointed a new committee in late 1980, which came up with a report and a draft proposal in 1982. Nevertheless, this time only minor readjustments to the existing Acts came about, the most important of which was that all restrictive agreements were to be notified on the entrepreneurs' own initiative. This meant that the number of restrictive agreements in the register grew significantly. The 1982 report is interesting to read as it shows a notable change in attitudes toward competition policy and its role in a modern market economy. A growing perception of the role of the price mechanism in the allocation of resources seems to have taken root and the promotion of competition as a way to increase consumer welfare was emphasized. The report was written at the same time as the Finnish economy was undergoing a rapid shift toward a more liberal market economy. Most notably, the strictly regulated financial markets were starting to be liberalized. Other reforms also came onto the agenda, for example, the privatization of state enterprises.

From statements and discussions within the SDP and SAK, it appears that they had become increasingly ardent supporters of harsh legislation. For example, the SAK emphasized that the authorities had a responsibility to more actively monitor and dismantle harmful agreements to protect consumers. They also urged a total ban on more restrictive practices, and the authorities, especially the Competition Council, were to be given more tools to intervene. They strongly urged that the banking and insurance industry also be covered by the competition legislation. Mergers and abuses of dominant market positions were to be more effectively and actively monitored. The SAK even stated that it was time for horizontal agreements (price and quota agreements) to be banned altogether. Moreover, the burden of proof concerning the "harmfulness" of a restrictive agreement was to be placed on the entrepreneurs and not on the authorities. This would mean that the entrepreneurs must be able to show that their restrictive agreements were not harmful.[58] Nevertheless, in one respect, the SAK did not want to give the market mechanism a stronger role: it strongly objected to getting rid of the price monitoring and price regulation system. As they emphasized in one statement, price stability was to be a matter for the authorities.[59] Nevertheless, as mentioned, no legislative reform occurred this time.

The 1988 legislation: steps toward less tolerant legislation and a new authority

After a few years, the legislation was up for discussion again. One of the main motivations for revising the legislation was price monitoring came to be seen as distorting markets with serious negative effects.[60] In the context of a more liberal economy, price regulation and price monitoring were increasingly considered to be outdated. The OECD had again urged the Finnish government to modernize its competition legislation and to make the authorities function more effectively.[61] In November 1985, an SDP-Center coalition government led by Kalevi Sorsa as prime minister appointed a new committee to oversee the competition and price monitoring legislation.

The committee submitted its report and draft legislation in 1987. It declared that price regulation was to be abolished and Finland's competition legislation was to be updated as it was not working well. The committee had even discussed competition legislation based on the prohibition principle, but considered that this was not the optimum solution at the time. The draft legislation was still based on the abuse principle, and no new bans were suggested. Better control of mergers and acquisitions was to be introduced, although full merger control was not yet on the agenda.

The main reform was to establish a new authority. The existing authorities were considered weak in effectively hindering restrictive practices. One reason was that the Board was highly influenced by interest groups and was in general based on an outdated administrative model. Instead, an independent authority to implement effective competition policy was to be established. In many other countries, independent competition authorities with far-reaching powers emerged during this period. Moreover, as price monitoring and regulation were to be abolished, part of the Board's tasks would disappear.

Draft legislation was put before the Finnish parliament on October 30, 1987. The government had changed after the committee had submitted its report; however, a new "red-blue" coalition government consisting of the Social Democrats, the National Coalition Party, and two small centrist parties had come to power. The new prime minister was Harri Holkeri and the Minister for Trade and Industry,

Pertti Salolainen, whose ministry was responsible for competition legislation, were both from the NCP. An independent legislative initiative concerning the prevention of monopolization, signed by three MPs from the SDP, was also submitted to parliament.[62]

This government coalition is an interesting one in Finnish political history because it was a coalition between social democrats and conservatives, but also because it left out the Center party, which had often been part of various coalitions with conservatives as well as with left-wing parties. The slogan of this government was "balanced structural change" (*hallittu rakennemuutos*) and one important aim was the modernization of the Finnish economy through structural reforms, including further liberalization of capital markets and the privatization of state-owned enterprises. Neither for the SDP nor for the NCP was such a coalition altogether easy, although social democrats and conservatives could agree on some issues. Both parties could be seen as representing urban Finland and the conservatives had become more of a wage-earner party due to the white-collarization of Finnish society; therefore it could increasingly accept the need for social aspects within the market economy. During the 1980s, the SDP increasingly adopted a "Third Way" agenda, that is, it accepted that letting the market mechanism work more efficiently and opening up the economy could also be in the interest of workers as well as reforms that promoted economic growth.[63]

A change in attitude toward competition policy and price monitoring is visible in SDP internal debates. Prior to the 1980s, the party had considered price regulation and price monitoring to be the key instruments to hinder price increases, but now an active competition policy for fighting inflationary pressures was emphasized. In fact, it was even seen as potentially better than the direct regulation of markets.[64] Overall, growing support for more "free market" competition can be observed in the party. At the party's annual general meeting in 1984, it was stated in a resolution that "society should encourage competition and individual capacities to come up with new ideas, and in particular small-scale entrepreneurship, while the growing power of monopolies and cartels is to be prevented."[65] In 1987, a new doctrinal program established these views as policies within the party. These policies were primarily driven by a new generation of key persons, in particular Paavo Lipponen (later Chair and Prime Minister) and Erkki Liikanen (Minister for Finance at the time).[66] Liikanen was the youngest member of parliament ever when he was elected in 1972 and experienced a long career in various positions (among others, minister of finance). Liikanen later became Finnish ambassador to Brussels, EU commissioner for Budget, Personnel and Administration and finally governor of the Bank of Finland, where he remained until his retirement in 2018. Lipponen also started his political career early and was, among other positions he held, political secretary to Veikko Helle, when Helle was minister of labor. Both were international in their orientation and architects behind the new orientation of the SDP in the 1990s. Liikanen belonged in his early career to the more leftist wing of the SDP, but in the 1980s, he supported reforms supporting a more market-based economic model.

Nevertheless, this period in government did not present an easy situation for the SDP. The party was under pressure and internally divided on many issues. For example, structural reforms concerning the labor market were on the agenda and this was a difficult issue for many, especially those with connections to the trade unions. There was also internal opposition to the plans to abolish price regulation and the role of state-owned enterprises was extensively debated. Lipponen and Liikanen considered gradual privatization to be a healthy development, but not everyone within the party supported privatization.[67] While popular and respected, internal tension of the SDP in the 1990s continued and, for example, Lipponen was publicly accused of "neoliberalism" by some party members, after continuing to pursue a tight economic policy to balance public finances in the aftermath of the 1990s economic crises. Liikanen describes how his suggestion to both decrease state ownership in big business and to limit the role of politicians and civil servants in state companies' boards of directors and supervisory boards met with resistance, both among civil servants and politicians and within the SDP.[68]

The new competition draft legislation was submitted to the Finnish parliament in April 1987. In the parliamentary debate, one social democrat, Reijo Lindroos, was very active. Lindroos emphasized the importance of a total ban on horizontal cartels. He was concerned that competition would become so "free" that monopolization would likely result and this problem would be even worse if the price monitoring regulation was to be abolished.[69] Lindroos also proposed transferring the burden of proof to entrepreneurs and business associations, which had been the SAK's proposal from the previous legislative initiative in 1982. The SAK also repeated this idea in their advisory opinions on the draft legislation.[70] According to Lindroos, the conservatives (and Salolainen) had stalled far-reaching competition legislation after lobbying from business interest organizations; he asked: Why were they not looking to their free-market idols Margaret Thatcher and Ronald Reagan this time? This was a dig at their partners in the government. According to Salolainen, in its present form, the legislation would be an important step forward. Though he maintained that Finland was not yet ready for zero-tolerance legislation, he emphasized that the new authority would mean more effective implementation of the legislation.[71] Judging from Lindroos' arguments, the SDP (and the SAK) would have preferred a different solution than Salolainen's proposal. Moreover, the SAK also strongly supported the continuation of the price monitoring legislation in their statement.[72]

The legislation, titled the Act on Competition Restriction [*Laki kilpailunrajoituksista* L709/1988], was passed in October 1987, with only a few minor changes from the original draft. The price regulation system came to an end and was replaced by an Act on Price Freezes (*Laki hintasuluista)*, which could be implemented in cases of emergencies. The existing Board was abolished and replaced with a new Finnish Competition Authority, which has been seen as an important step toward a much more active and effective implementation of competition policy in Finland.

Toward European integration and legislation based on the prohibition principle

However, it was not long before a new committee was appointed in May 1990 to assess the existing legislation and suggest potential areas for revisions. The same "red-blue" government was in fact still in power; in the 1980s, Finland had entered an era of fairly stable majority coalition governments. The need for oversight of the existing legislation was motivated by reforms under way in other Nordic countries, most notably in Sweden and Norway. Another task of the committee was to evaluate the work of the new Competition Authority. However, one important reason for reviewing the legislation was Finland's aim to participate more actively in the European integration process.[73] At the time, the Finnish government was preparing to fulfill the requirements for signing an agreement to become part of the European Economic Area (EEA). This legislative process, however, came to be influenced by the start of serious discussions of pursuing full membership in the European Communities.

In fact, since the late 1980s, a possible membership of the European Communities had been discussed, although this was not yet spelled out as an objective by the government.[74] The first years of the 1990s were also turbulent. The Berlin Wall had fallen in 1989 and the Soviet Union weakened and disintegrated rapidly in the early 1990s. This opened up new opportunities for Finland, especially in the foreign policy area and in its relation to the European integration process. On the other hand, the former Soviet Union was politically unstable and the outcome was unforeseeable, which made Finland's position sensitive. The Soviet Union had also been an important trade partner. The period was turbulent economically. Finnish growth figures in the 1980s had been favorable and the swift liberalization of the economy in the 1980s would indeed have long-term positive effects. But the economic situation in the late 1980s was beginning to look increasingly weak. In fact, liberalization had led to overheated financial and housing markets, with surging asset and housing prices, and increasing indebtedness in the private sector (firms and households). An international recession was looming, which led to weakening exports to the west. The significant trade with the Soviet Union disappeared in a very short period of time in late 1990–early 1991, which severely impacted some Finnish industries. When a recession struck with full power, a cascade of bankruptcies, skyrocketing unemployment figures and a crash in the housing market ensued. A severe economic down-turn and financial crises followed that lasted from 1991 to 1993. This downward spiral led to swiftly growing deficits in public finances.

In this context, the committee submitted its report in April 1991. The report stated that the 1988 Act had worked fairly well; a number of horizontal agreements had been dismantled and barriers to market entry had been lowered. On the other hand, more sophisticated forms of restrictive practices had emerged instead, while the merger control was not working well.[75] According to the report, the new authority had been quite successful and was equipped with better tools than it previously had; however, the sanctions system was still not deterring collusive practices in an effective way.[76]

The committee emphasized that the European Economic Area would not require the legislation to be completely harmonized with the EC legislation, but if the legislation was very different, the regulation of international trade and international business activities would become complicated.[77] Moreover, it underlined that there was in fact no hindrance to adopting legislation based on the prohibition principle with effective sanctions, and finally abolishing the problematic registration procedure. It was now considered "advisable" to promote a more competitive environment using prohibition legislation and the report included draft legislation based on the prohibition principle. The draft was also quickly submitted to the Finnish parliament in October 1991.

The government had changed since the committee was appointed, however. In the spring of 1991, general elections had been held and the Social Democrats ended up in opposition. The Center Party was a clear winner in the elections and a new center-conservative government with the chairperson of the Center Party, Esko Aho, as PM had been formed.

Also in the new government, Pertti Salolainen continued as Minister for Trade and Industry.[78] This time, he and his colleagues in the National Coalition Party actively pursued legislation based on the prohibition principle. The reason behind the party's (and the business lobby's) change of heart was the ongoing EEA negotiations: Finnish business was urging a swift integration with Western Europe. Moreover, there was also an ideological shift among the conservatives, who came to consider competition to be important for a healthy market economy.

The draft remained in the Parliament's Commerce Committee for some time; it was indeed transformative legislation. In addition, the parliament had many other issues on its plate: trying to deal with the severe economic down-turn, acute banking crises, other issues in relation to the integration process and a reformation of the Finnish Constitution. The Commerce Committee came back with its draft in April 1992.

The political environment had changed since the draft legislation had been submitted to parliament. By then, full membership in the European Union had become not only a realistic alternative but also the application for full membership in fact had already been submitted in March. Finland was here following Sweden, which had submitted its application in late 1991. The parliamentary debate was vigorous and a number of key SDP representatives were particularly active, including Paavo Lipponen and Matti Louekoski. They emphasized for example that they had already been arguing for prohibition legislation banning most restrictive practices in 1988.

The strictly zero-tolerance legislation was passed, banning restrictive agreements and imposing harsh controls of mergers and abuses of a dominant market position. The registration process also came to an end. In May 1992, the EEA agreement was signed, but as mentioned Finland's application for full membership of the EU had already been submitted. Sweden and Finland went on to become members of the EU in 1995.

SDP in opposition during a transformative phase

For the Social Democrats, this process was clearly different from in the case of many of their previous reforms, as they were now in opposition. On the other hand, they did not object to the draft legislation. Firstly, as discussed earlier, they had already proposed zero-tolerance legislation, so the new draft legislation suited their aims. For example, in 1990, the party leadership stressed in a memorandum that it should be a goal to get Finnish competition policy to the same level as in other European countries. The SAK had also indicated full support in their comments on the committee report for legislation based on the prohibition principle, and for the tightening of merger control and the control of abuses of dominant market positions. In fact, the SAK repeatedly emphasized that it had advocated less tolerant legislation for a number of years. Moreover, they urged the establishment of a special court for competition issues and continued to call for a reverse burden of proof (*käänteinen todistustaakka*) for firms suspected of upholding restrictive agreements.[79]

Another important goal was to lower food prices, and this was to be achieved by dismantling domestic monopolies and opening the borders for food and retail imports.[80] Lipponen also raised the issues of agricultural production and high food prices in the parliamentary debate, which, he emphasized, resulted from a weak competition policy and a lack of foreign competition.[81] Price regulation and price monitoring had been finally abolished in the 1980s, so competition policy and trade policy were now the main tools to achieve this. In fact, the SDP's program to prepare for possible negotiations to form a government in 1991 had placed consumer policies and new competition legislation high on the agenda.[82] The problems of protectionism and inefficiencies in domestic markets were discussed regularly in party documents and within the SAK.[83] As Paavo Lipponen once emphasized, no competition legislation would solve the problem of Finnish price levels unless the primary production and food industries faced competition both at home and from abroad.[84]

A belief that a lack of competition was the reason behind high consumer prices had gained ground in the party, fueling increasing support for a reliance on market mechanisms as solutions to high prices. People like Liikanen and Lipponen in particular propagated this view. In fact, the market mechanism was seen as potentially being the workers' best friend. After the Berlin Wall's fall, Liikanen, who had been one of the strategists behind tighter competition policy since the late 1980s, stated in internal discussions that "markets had beaten socialism 70–0."[85] However, the SDP leadership stressed that such policies ought to be combined with policies supporting equal opportunity and social security, that is, the goal was to promote a worker-friendly, social market economy. The party leadership also strongly supported the integration process and the application for membership of the EU. And this legislation was important for this goal. Nevertheless, the party leadership considered that, irrespective of EU membership, legislation based on prohibition and strong merger control should be seen as modern competition legislation.[86]

The SDP shifted quite rapidly toward what could be labeled a "Third Way policy" under the leadership of Paavo Lipponen. This shift was linked to the overall trend among many European Social Democratic parties during these decades. The changing nature of the working class, structural transformations and ideological and political shifts that were occurring in many Westerns societies paved the way for a "new" kind of social democracy. According to Finnish political historian Sami Outinen, the beginnings of this transformation of the Finnish SDP were already visible in the party's principles program (*periaateohjelma*) from 1978, when new policies concerning nationalization and socialization were adopted. For example, it was stated that the "market mechanism" was to be considered a natural part of the economy, although it was to be monitored strictly. Moreover, both private, market-based activities and planned, state-led undertakings could also run into problems.[87] Nevertheless, there were also limits to the SDP's "neoliberal" or "third-way agenda," especially when it came to social and labor market policies. Not everyone within the party was unanimously in favor of the new political agenda, as it caused problems for the social-democratic identity. For example, the positive attitude within the party leadership toward the gradual privatization of state enterprises was problematic for many grassroots members as previously mentioned. Any potential selling off of shares was to be carried out in a careful manner and "worked out on a case-by-case basis."[88] For example, the EEA was considered a good way by many to break up strong cartels and close old school networks. However, not everyone was equally positive toward the competition legislation, while the requirement for the EEA agreement was considered by some the latest link in a chain that had been "built up by the OECD, GATT, EFTA, and the IMF." International recommendations and agreements were still considered by many as placing limits on independent economic, social and employment policies.[89]

Although competition legislation was a recurring issue in the party's internal debates and considered important in the early 1990s, it was – as it had been many times previously – overshadowed by other significant issues, for example, the economic downturn and the extensive reforms that the center-right government began to introduce to balance the galloping deficits in public finances. The downward economic spiral also increased demands for labor market reforms and welfare retrenchment. The SDP and the SAK did not look upon these policy goals benevolently and the party put a lot of energy into opposing social welfare and labor market reforms. In 1995, Lipponen led the SDP to an election victory and became one of the longest-governing prime ministers in Finland (1995–2003).

Concluding remarks

Finnish competition legislation was a process of "baby steps." The political context in Finland favored a cautious stance: better first investigate before making any drastic decisions. The legislation – and the changes to it – has to be seen also in relation to transformations in the economic policy context. The Finnish economy evolved from a highly regulated top-down, economic model after the end of World War II toward a more liberal market economy in the 1980s. The stepwise transition in its regulation of competition reflects this process. Although the transition in the 1980s was very swift, the Finnish economy had been liberalizing in a stepwise manner since the mid-1950s.[90] As the committee report from 1987 had stated, the Finnish price regulation system had been balanced against other economic and political goals and phenomenon.[91]

These "baby steps" were also a result of the corporatist model, which meant balancing between various interests, and especially the strong objections that came from business interests made the outcomes from the legislative process weaker and led to more cautious compromises than the drafts originally proposed. The swift shift in the Finnish market economy in the 1980s – and in the SDP's perception of the role of competition and market forces – should not be underestimated. The committee report from 1991 emphasized the need for a liberalization of many market sectors, and made demands for new competition legislation.[92] Similar arguments are observed in the SDP debates. The general opinion in favor of zero-tolerance legislation was growing in the social-democratic community at large, while support for direct price regulation had lost ground. The register procedure as a tool for authorities to achieve some kind of "optimum competition" was increasingly questioned. Instead of aiming to regulate in a *dirigiste* manner, it was increasingly seen as preferable to promote well-functioning markets, where the market mechanism was allowed to work freely.

How did the SDP adapt to the changing market conditions and views on competition regulation? As earlier stated, Outinen argues that the Finnish social democrats began to adopt a "Third Way" ideology after 1978.[93] He also notes that the promotion of competition, of innovative thinking and of labor intensive entrepreneurship began with a party meeting in 1984.[94] A reading of the documents concerning competition policy supports the idea of a change in the SDP's agenda toward accepting and even promoting policies to advance competition and the role of the market mechanism from the mid-1980s, but not really earlier.[95]

This history has revealed that the SDP in general supported tightening competition legislation over a long period. It is important therefore to remember that support for a harsh competition policy might not only be the result of a shift to a "neoliberal" or "Third Way" approach. Support for zero-tolerance competition policy can be based on a pro-market view – as was increasingly the case from the 1980s – but it can also be based on a hostile attitude toward the private sector, in particular big business. This was the case in the 1950s and 1960s and even in the 1970s, although compromise thinking changed this gradually. Corporatist bargaining systems made employers and unions sit at the same negotiation table. Whether there was in fact a "third way," market-friendly shift already in the late 1970s would require more in-depth investigations. Nevertheless, it is safe to say that the ideological basis for the Social Democrats' support for a less tolerant policy did change over time, from a hostile attitude toward business to a pro-market agenda. Competition policy developed first as a tool of price regulation for the SDP; hence it was subordinated and complementary to other economic goals. But when price regulation fell out of fashion during the broad economic realignment of the 1980s, competition policy replaced price regulation for the SDP as a primary means of keeping prices down. This development was reinforced by the aims for accession to the EEA and later the EU. While the SDP's views were influenced by external factors and especially by the aim of participating in European integration in the early 1990s, the internal debates and tensions reveal the high importance of the domestic situation for policy formation.

Finally, what was the role of the SDP in the design of Finnish postwar competition legislation? Overall, the SDP and KK played significant roles in this legislation coming into being in the 1950s, while the 1970s reforms in particular were clearly a result of the vision of the SDP and SAK in an era of compromise thinking. During this period, the SDP was regularly part of various coalition governments (often agrarian-left wing, with or without the SKDL) and the party had a stable and strong role in Finnish politics. After World War II, the internal problems within the party had settled down. The unions had become increasingly influential in policy formation and implementation. Nevertheless, it is important to stress that up until the 1980s, the main target for both the unions and the SDP was to ensure a price regulation and price monitoring system, while competition policy was seen as supplementary to this.

As stated in the introduction, the SDP and their views on competition legislation form a propitious window through which to observe the party's views on markets, the market economy, and society more broadly. Its focus changed from paving the way for socialism in the 1950s – even by means of revolution – toward building a modern, prosperous industrial society through compromise thinking, bargaining and the implementation of a generous welfare state, and finally toward forming a modern responsible market economy by embracing the ideas of free markets in combination with responsible and active social and welfare policies.

Notes

1 The People's Democratic League of Finland (SKDL) consisted of the Communist Party, which was the main driving force, and left-wing socialists allied with them. Parliamentary politics was conducted under the name SKDL.

2 Mikko Kuisma and Magnus Ryner, "Third Way Decomposition and the Rightward Shift in Finnish and Swedish Politics," *Contemporary Politics* 18, 3 (2012): 325–342.

3 On the Third Way policies in the Nordic countries, see Magnus Ryner, "An Obituary for the Third Way: The Financial Crisis and Social Democracy in Europe," *Political Quarterly* 81, 4 (2010): 554–563; Kuisma and Ryner, "Third Way Decomposition"; Sami Outinen, "From Steering Capitalism to Seeking Market Acceptance: Social Democrats and Employment in Finland, 1975–1998," *Scandinavian Journal of History* 42, 4 (2017): 389–413.

4 P.C. Schmitter, "Still the Century of Corporatism?" in G. Lehmbruch and P.C. Schmitter (eds.), *Patterns of Corporatist Policy-Making, Sage Modern Politics Series 7* (California: Sage Publications, 1982), 296.

5 Susanna Fellman, "Creating the 1957 Cartel Law: The Role of Pressure Groups on Finland's Competition Policy and Cartel Registration," in Susanna Fellman and Martin Shanahan (eds.), *Regulating Competition: Cartel Registers in the Twentieth Century World, Routledge Explorations in Economic History* (Oxon; New York: Routledge, 2016), 48–65.

6 The letter "E" came from the word *edistyksellinen*, which means "progressive."

7 Sulo Suortti, *Osuuskauppaliikkeen suhde yrittäjäryhmiin* (Helsinki: Kuluttajaosuuskuntien Keskusliitto, 1927).

8 John Lapidus, "Why Such a Permissive Attitude towards Monopolistic Associations? Social Democracy up to the First Swedish Law on Cartels in 1925," *Scandinavian Journal of History* 38, 1 (2013): 65–88.

9 Ferdinand Alfthan, "Finländska karteller," *Ekonomiska Samfundets Tidskrift* VII, 2 (1921): 278–331; Ahti M. Salonen, *Tutkimus taloudellisesta kilpailusta Suomen nykyisessä yhteiskuntaelämässä* (Helsinki: Kulutusosuuskuntien Keskusliitto, 1955), 60–63.

10 Jalmari Laakso, *Ajankohtaisia osuuskaupallisia talouspoliittisia kysymyksiä* (Helsinki: Kuluttajaosuuskuntien Keskusliitto, 1942), 38–42.
11 Kuluttajaosuuskuntien Keskusliitto, "Monopolistiset yhtymät kuluttajien vaarana," in *Vuosikirja 1948* (Helsinki: KK, 1948), 470–473.
12 KM 1952: B33 *Kartellikomitean mietintö 1952: B33* (Helsinki, 1952).
13 See for details, Fellman, "Creating the 1957 Cartel Law."
14 Martin Shanahan and Susanna Fellman, "Cartel Registers around the World," in Susanna Fellman and Martin Shanahan (eds.), *Regulating Competition: Cartel Registers in the Twentieth Century World* (Oxon, New York: Routledge, 2016), 113–132.
15 For example, H.B. Thorelli, "Antitrust in Europe: National Policies after 1945," *University of Chicago Law Review* 26, 2, (1959): 222–236. Thorelli gives Denmark as an example, where the ban on RPM agreements had led to new forms of distribution.
16 For the debates, see Salonen, *Tutkimus taloudellisesta kilpailusta*, 151–159.
17 Wendell Berge, *Kartellit vapaan talouselämän uhkana* (Helsinki: Tammi, 1948).
18 Other factors also led to inflationary pressures, including frequent devaluations of the Finnish currency.
19 Emil Huunonen, *Mitä SAK nyt tahtoo? Suomen ammattiyhdistysten keskusliiton julkaisusarja no 17* (Helsinki: SAK, 1949), 114.
20 SAK, *Mitä SAK nyt tahtoo? SAK:n viidennen edustajainkokouksen julkilausuma sodanjälkeisestä kehityksestä ja päätöslauselma lähiaikojen toimintaohjeiksi* (Helsinki: SAK, 1949).
21 Salonen, *Tutkimus taloudellisesta kilpailusta*, 190–192.
22 See Fellman, "Creating the 1957 Cartel Law."
23 *Valtiopäiväkirjat 1956, pöytäkirjat* (VP 1956, pk), Enne 13 December 1956, 1900.
24 See parliamentary debates on 30 May 1956 and 13 December 1956.
25 Shanahan and Fellman, "Cartel Registers around the World."
26 "Veikko Helle," *Kansallisbiografia (The National Biography)*. Online source: https://kansallisbiografia.fi/kansallisbiografia/henkilo/3965 (downloaded 20 September 2018).
27 VP 1956, pk, Helle, 30 May 1956, 782.
28 *Ibid.*, Helle, 13 December 1956, 1896–1897.
29 SDP, Hallitusohjelma. Puoluetoimikunnan pöytäkirjoja, Liite 1, 1956. SDPn arkisto.
30 *SAK Vuosikirja 1961* (Helsinki: SAK, 1962), 25.
31 *SAK Pöytäkirja Suomen Ammattiyhdistyksen Keskusliitto r.y:n kahdeksannesta edustajakokouksesta Helsingistä 28 May–31 May 1961* (Helsinki: SAK, 1962), 25.
32 *SAK Vuosikirja 1962* (Helsinki: SAK, 1963), 39.
33 *SAK Vuosikirja 1963* (Helsinki: SAK, 1964), 51.
34 SAK, Lausunto, 3 July 1962 Kauppa- ja teollisuusministeriölle, lähete KD 452/165, 1961. Lausunnot. SAK arkisto.
35 VP 1963, pk, Helle, 15 November 1963, 1965.
36 *Ibid.*, Voutilainen, 15 November 1963, 1968; see Fellman, "Creating the 1957 Cartel Law."
37 *Ibid.*, Gröndahl, 12 March 1963, 301.
38 *Ibid.*, Sinisalo, 12 March 1963, 303.
39 *Ibid.*, Lindqvist, 15 November 1963, 1966.
40 *Ibid.*, Stenberg, 15 November 1963, 1970.
41 See Jouko Marttila, *Hillitty markkinatalous, Kokoomuksen ja SDP:n talouspoliittinen lähentyminen ja hallitusyhteistyö 1980-luvulla* (Helsinki: Helsingin Yliopisto, Valtiotieteellinen tiedekunta, 2016), 87–93.
42 VP 1963, pk, Ojajärvi, 15 March 1963, 351.
43 Kirsi Rissanen, *Kilpailu ja tavaramerkit: kilpailunrajoituslainsäädännön soveltaminen tavaramerkin yksilöimiin järjestelyihin, Suomalaisen lakimiesyhdistyksen julkaisuja A 131* (Helsinki, 1979), 39.

44 *Hinta- ja kilpailukomitean mietintö* KM 1972: B 52 (Helsinki: Kauppa- ja teollisuusministeriö, 1972), 44–46.
45 Fellman, "Creating the 1957 Cartel Law."
46 See, for example, "Suomen Sosiaalidemokraattisen Puolueen kuluttajapoliittinen ohjelma." Puoluehallituksen pöytäkirjan liitteet 1971, Liite 381/51. When the consumer program was discussed, some member of the party committee emphasized that it was good and socialist in its character and not so market-oriented as the SAK's consumer program was. Puoluehallituksen pöytäkirja 21 August 1971.
47 *SAK, Pöytäkirja Suomen Ammattiliittojen Keskusjärjestö r.y:n kymmenennestä sääntömääräisestä edustajainkokouksesta 29 June–2 July 1971* (Helsinki: SAK, 1972).
48 Sosiaalidemokraattisen puolueen eduskuntaryhmän toimintakertomus 1973. Puoluetoimikunnan pöytäkirjoja.
49 KM 1972: B 57,71.
50 KM 1972: B 57,76.
51 SDP, Puheenjohtajaryhmän esitys hallitusohjelmaksi 18 August 1972; SDP, Talouspoliittinen työryhmän esitys puoluetoimikunnalle, Liite no 380/58; SDP, Puoluetoimikunnan esitys puolueneuvostolle 15 November 1972. Liite 382/59. Puoluetoimikunnan pöytäkirjat 1972.
52 Olavi Väyrynen, *Hintavalvonnan vaiheita* (Porvoo: WSOY, 1990), 225.
53 SDP, Ehdotus Elinkeinohallituksen perustamisesta, heinäkuu 1971. Puoluetoimikunnan pöytäkirjat 1971.
54 SDP, Puoluetoimikunnan pöytäkirja 3 May 1973.
55 Väyrynen, *Hintavalvonnan vaiheita*, 199, 203.
56 *Kilpailutoimikunnan mietintö* KM 1982: 49 (Helsinki, 1982), 33.
57 SAK, Lausunto Kilpailutoimikunnan mietinnöstä (1982: 49) 3 February 1983. KM222/070/82; SAK, Lausunto Hallituksen esityksestä eduskunnalle laiksi taloudellisen kilpailun edistämisestä annetun lain muuttamisesta 4 October 1984. Lausunnot, SAK:n arkisto. The Labour Archives.
58 SAK, Lausunto hallituksen esityksestä eduskunnalle laiksi taloudellisen kilpailun edistämisestä annetun lain muuttamisesta. 4 October 1984.
59 SAK, Lausunto kilpailutoimikunnan mietinnöstä 1982: 49. 3 February 1983. KM 222/070/82.
60 *Kilpailu- ja hintakomitean mietintö* KM 1987: 4 (Helsinki: Kauppa – ja teollisuusministeriö, 1987), 1.
61 KM 1987: 4, 9.
62 *Kilpailulainsäädännön uudistamisesta, monopolisoitumisen estämiseksi.* Toivomusaloite no 309. 1987 (VP), 349.
63 On this, see Sami Outinen, *Sosiaalidemokraattien tie talouden ohjailusta markkinareaktioiden ennakointiin: työllisyys sosiaalidemokraattien politiikassa Suomessa 1975–1998* (Helsinki: Into, 2015), 190–193; On the rapproachment between the conservatives and the SDP, which preceeded this government, see Marttila, *Hillitty markkintalous.*
64 'The promotion of competition and removal of barriers to market entry are the only effective measures to lower food prices'. PM SDP:n Puoluetoimikunnan kokouksesta 24 May 1990. Puoluetoimikunnan pöytäkirjat. Liite 239.
65 Outinen, *Sosiaalidemokraattien tie*, 185.
66 *Ibid.*, 214–215.
67 *Ibid.*
68 See, for example, "Valtionyhtiöt ja niiden rooli riskirahoituksessa," speech held by Erkki Liikanen at Central Chamber of Commerce, Helsinki on November 16th, 1988. (Copy received from Liikanen by email on March 20, 2019).
69 VP 1988, pk, Lindroos 17 May 1988, 1442–1443.
70 SAK, Lausunto Kilpailu- ja Hintakomitean mietinnöstä 26 March 1987; 25 May 1987.

71 VP 1988, pkt, Salolainen 24 May 1988, 1494–1496.
72 SAK, Lausunto Kilpailu- ja Hintakomitean mietinnöstä 26 March 1987.
73 KM 1991: 15, 1–3.
74 See, for example, https://www.eduskunta.fi/FI/tietoaeduskunnasta/kirjasto/aineistot/eu/suomen-liittyminen-eu/Sivut/eu-jasenyyden-hakeminen.aspx (downloaded 20 November 2018).
75 *Kilpailulainsäädännön uudistaminen. Kilpailulainsäädännön uudistmistyöryhmän mietintö* KM 1991: 15, 2–3.
76 *Ibid.*, 82.
77 *Ibid.*, 39–40.
78 Some other draft legislation connected to this was submitted, most notably an Act on the Competition Council and one dealing with banking and insurance.
79 SAK, Lausunto 15 March 1991; Lausunto 7 June 1991. Viralliset kirjeet.
80 SDP, "Sinulle, Suomelle, Euroopalle – SDP: Tavoitteita vaalikaudelle 1991–1994." Puoluetoimikunnan pöytäkirjat. liitteet.
81 VP 1992, pk: Lipponen 24 April 1992, 1485.
82 SDP, Hallitusneuvottelut 1991 24 April 1991. Puoluetoimikunnan pöytäkirjat, liitteet.
83 SDP, Toimintakertomus 1989, 2. Puoluetoimikunnan pöytäkirjat, liitteet; SAK, Talouspoliittinen ohjelma 1991, 2.
84 SDP, Pöytäkirja puoluetoimikunnan kokous 31 January 1991.
85 Outinen *Sosiaalidemokraattien tie*, 228.
86 SDP, "Suomi käyntiin – ihmiselle töitä" 4 June 1992; SDP, Rakenne ja hallintotyöryhmä muistio 10 November 1992. Puoluetoimikunnan pöytäkirjat.
87 Outinen, *Sosiaalidemokraattien tie,* 182–183.
88 SDP, Kooste työryhmien raporteista 1992, 6. Puoluetoimikunnan pöytäkirjat.
89 Outinen, *Sosiaalidemokraattien tie*, 225.
90 See Susanna Fellman, "Growth and Investment: Finnish Capitalism, 1850–2005," in S. Fellman et al. (eds.), *Creating Nordic Capitalism – The Development of a Competitive Periphery* (Basingstoke: Palgrave-Macmillan, 2008), 129–217.
91 KM 1987: 4, 1.
92 KM 1991: 15, 87–89.
93 Outinen, "From Steering Capitalism."
94 Outinen, *Sosiaalidemokraattien tie*, 185.
95 Also other scholars have been somewhat critical toward Outinen's strong conclusion about the shift occurring so early. See Marttila, *Hillitty markkinatalous*, 20–21.

Bibliography

Alfthan, Ferdinand. "Finländska karteller." *Ekonomiska Samfundets Tidskrift* VII, 2 (1921): 278–331.

Berge, Wendell. *Kartellit vapaan talouselämän uhkana*. Helsinki: Tammi, 1948.

Fellman, Susanna. "Creating the 1957 Cartel Law: The Role of Pressure Groups on Finland's Competition Policy and Cartel Registration." In *Regulating Competition: Cartel Registers in the Twentieth Century World* edited by Susanna Fellman and Martin Shanahan. Oxon, New York: Routledge, 2016, 48–65.

Fellman, Susanna. "Growth and Investment: Finnish Capitalism, 1850–2005." ' In *Creating Nordic Capitalism – The Development of a Competitive Periphery* edited by Susanna Fellman et al. Basingstoke: Palgrave-Macmillan, 2008, 129–217.

Huunonen, Emil. *Mitä SAK nyt tahtoo? Suomen ammattiyhdistysten keskusliiton julkaisusarja no 17*. Helsinki: SAK, 1949.

Kartellikomitean mietintö KM 1952: B33. Helsinki, 1952.

Kilpailu- ja hintakomitean mietintö KM 1987: 4. Helsinki: Kauppa ja teollisuusministeriö, 1987.

Kilpailulainsäädännön uudistaminen. Kilpailulainsäädännön uudistamistyöryhmän mietintö KM. 1991.

Kilpailulainsäädännön uudistamisesta, monopolisoitumisen estämiseksi. Toivomusaloite no 309. 1987.

Kilpailutoimikunnan mietintö KM 1982: 49. Helsinki, 1982.

Kuisma, Mikko and Magnus Ryner. "Third Way Decomposition and the Rightward Shift in Finnish and Swedish Politics." *Contemporary Politics* 18, 3 (2012): 325–342.

Kuluttajaosuuskuntien Keskusliitto. "Monopolistiset yhtymät kuluttajien vaarana," *Vuosikirja 1948*. Helsinki: KK, 1948.

Laakso, Jalmari. *Ajankohtaisia osuuskaupallisia talouspoliittisia kysymyksiä*. Helsinki: Kuluttajaosuuskuntien Keskusliitto, 1942.

Lapidus, John. "Why Such a Permissive Attitude towards Monopolistic Associations? Social Democracy up to the First Swedish Law on Cartels in 1925." *Scandinavian Journal of History* 38, 1 (2013): 65–88.

Magnus Ryner, "An Obituary for the Third Way: The Financial Crisis and Social Democracy in Europe." *Political Quarterly* 81, 4 (2010): 554–563.

Marttila, Jouko. *Hillitty markkinatalous, Kokoomuksen ja SDP:n talouspoliittinen lähentyminen ja hallitusyhteistyö 1980-luvulla*. Helsinki: Helsingin Yliopisto, Valtiotieteellinen tiedekunta, 2016.

Outinen, Sami. "From Steering Capitalism to Seeking Market Acceptance: Social Democrats and Employment in Finland, 1975–1998." *Scandinavian Journal of History* 42, 4 (2017): 389–413.

Outinen, Sami. *Sosiaalidemokraattien tie talouden ohjailusta markkinareaktioiden ennakointiin: työllisyys sosiaalidemokraattien politiikassa Suomessa 1975–1998*. Helsinki: Into, 2015.

Rissanen, Kirsi. *Kilpailu ja tavaramerkit: kilpailunrajoituslainsäädännön soveltaminen tavaramerkin yksilöimiin järjestelyihin*. Helsinki: Suomalaisen lakimiesyhdistyksen julkaisuja A 131, 1979.

SAK, *Mitä SAK nyt tahtoo? SAK:n viidennen edustajainkokouksen julkilausuma sodanjälkeisestä kehityksestä ja päätöslauselma lähiaikojen toimintaohjeiksi*. Helsinki: SAK, 1949.

Salonen, Ahti M. *Tutkimus taloudellisesta kilpailusta Suomen nykyisessä yhteiskuntaelämässä*. Helsinki: Kulutusosuuskuntien Keskusliitto, 1955.

Schmitter, Philippe C. "Still the Century of Corporatism?" In *Patterns of Corporatist Policy-Making* edited by Gerhard Lehmbruch and Phillipe C. Schmitter. California: Sage Publications, 1982.

Shanahan, Martin and Fellman Susanna. "Cartel Registers around the World." In *Regulating Competition: Cartel Registers in the Twentieth Century World* edited by Susanna Fellman and Martin Shanahan. Oxon, New York: Routledge, 2016, 113–132.

Suortti, Sulo. *Osuuskauppaliikkeen suhde yrittäjäryhmiin*. Helsinki: Kuluttajaosuuskuntien Keskusliitto, 1927.

Thorelli, Hans B. "Antitrust in Europe: National Policies after 1945." *University of Chicago Law Review* 26, 2 (1959): 222–236.

Väyrynen, Olavi. *Hintavalvonnan vaiheita*. Porvoo: WSOY, 1990.

9 European Social Democracy, Community Competition Law and Industrial Policy during the crisis of the 1970s and 1980s

Dimitri Zurstrassen

Introduction

In October 1973, the beginning of the Yom Kippur War put an end to the golden age of European economies, the period of constant capitalist growth and full employment. The rise of oil prices following the introduction of an embargo on supply by the Arab members of Organization of the Petroleum Exporting Countries (OPEC) brought the industrialized countries into a period of stagflation, a mix of hyperinflation, low growth and high unemployment. In addition, shifts in the nature of global economic activity such as increased trade liberalization and integration of global financial markets led to an extension of international economic interdependence and of large transnational corporations. The consequences were a significant reduction of the ability of the state to regulate economic activity and the layoff of many workers. At the same time, the redistribution of comparative advantages around the world and the change in the geographical distribution of global demand threatened the future of European industry.

This "shock of the global"[1] and the end of postwar capitalist growth obliged European social democracy to rethink its economic policy strategy. Socialist parties could not rely anymore on full employment and high and rising wage levels to develop a welfare state based on the allocation of budget surpluses to public services. Globalization and the new economic situation questioned the ability of the state to pursue Keynesian demand management and macro-economic coordination policies promoted in Europe since the 1950s. In this debate, the rise of neoclassical ideas such as market liberalization and privatization of state-owned companies had a significant influence on European political parties, including those of the left. The social democrats analyzed in this chapter presented these measures as the only ones that could be applied in the new economic and social context of the 1970s and 1980s.

Another important restriction on social-democratic policymaking was the progressive development of Community competition law and industrial policy during this period. In order to regulate globalization and to face the crisis of European industry, European governments and influential commissioners created new Community instruments during the 1970s and 1980s to achieve industrial restructuring

DOI: 10.4324/9781351010573-9

and redeployment. The rise of Community industrial policy and competition law inevitably raised the question of complementarity or opposition between them. At the national level, these significantly restricted the ability of member states to formulate independent industrial policies in particular by controlling state aid and the restructuring of their industries.

Starting with a study of the competition and industrial policies promoted by socialist commissioners during the 1970s and following with an analysis of the industrial policies of the French and Spanish socialist governments in the steel sector in the first half of the 1980s, this chapter will analyze how European social democracy engaged with Community competition law and industrial policy during the crisis of the 1970s and 1980s. We argue in this chapter that throughout the 1970s, European social democracy contributed actively to the development of Community competition and industrial policies through the actions of their commissioners. Altiero Spinelli promoted a strong socially oriented industrial and competition policy to reach its political objectives, whereas Raymond Vouel tried to adapt Community competition rules to achieve industrial restructuring objectives. Also, we claim that socialist governments in the 1980s did not contest Community competition law and the rules imposed by the industrial restructuring programs despite initial attempts in the French case.

European Social Democracy and Community competition law and industrial policy in the Commission during the 1970s

The 1970s: a socialist decade in Western Europe

When the Ortoli Commission took office on 6 January 1973, socialist parties were in power in the majority of the European Community countries as leading governmental forces or coalition members, while they were also the largest political force in the European Parliament. The College of Commissioners for its part initially included four members coming from socialist parties[2] who had key portfolios in the management of the new economic crisis.[3] Even if the appointment of European commissioners was and still is the responsibility of national governments, this was the result of the application of a deliberate strategy elaborated by the Liaison Bureau of the Socialist Parties in the European Parliament to give socialist members of the European Commission strategic policy portfolios.[4] These commissioners participated, along with socialist ministers and members of the socialist group of the European Parliament, in meetings of the Socialist International, the Liaison Bureau of the Socialist Parties in the European Community (replaced by the Confederation of Socialist Parties in the EC in 1974) and the Socialist Group of the European Parliament, forming a wide network for the exchange of ideas and projects on policymaking in the European Community.[5]

Altiero Spinelli and the promotion of a progressive global Community industrial policy

Because of the effects of the economic and social crisis that emerged at the beginning of the 1970s, Community industrial and competition policies became one of the main topics of discussion among socialist leaders. The commissioner responsible for industrial and technological policy, Altiero Spinelli, was one of the most important personalities involved in these discussions in the early 1970s and was directly responsible for transforming them into concrete policy proposals. After three decades of activism in favor of European federalism, his nomination as commissioner enabled him, as mentioned in his *diario*, "to do something for Europe after having talked about it so much".[6] Industrial and technological policy was for him a key area of action given its important economic and social role and the initiatives of the Commission of the European Communities in this field since the mid-1960s.[7] As soon as he took office, Spinelli tried to insert the industrial policy proposals put forward by his predecessor in the so-called "Colonna memorandum on Community industrial policy"[8] into a broader framework by organizing a major conference on the foundations of Community industrial policy. The "Industry and Society" conference held in Venice from 20 to 22 April 1972 gathered members of civil society, political institutions, and trade unions to discuss environmental, regional and social requirements of industrial development.[9] The results of the conference aimed to develop proposals on industrial policy closer to socialist ideas.[10]

Presented by the European Commission in May 1973, the *Memorandum on Industrial and technological policy*[11] proposed the creation of a common industrial base as a key element for the realization of an economic and monetary union which constituted one of the priorities of the Ortoli Commission. To reach this objective, the document proposed, like the Colonna memorandum on industrial policy, the completion of the internal market, the opening of national public markets but also sectoral interventions for advanced and declined sectors. However, the new document included elements reflecting Altiero Spinelli's vision: the need for industrial development to be part of an overall policy for society aimed at improving quality of life, working conditions and the environment; the promotion of economic development oriented more toward the satisfaction of collective needs; and the fight against regional imbalances but also the defense of a balanced economic growth allowing a better allocation of resources.[12]

A new global socialist industrial policy had to be thus realized in conjunction with strong development, environmental and regional policies. The elaboration of a significant development policy had always been a priority for European Social Democracy. It was indeed one of the most important policy fields on the agenda of the Socialist International.[13] The presence of Claude Cheysson from April 1973 as European Commissioner for Development Policy and Cooperation represented for this purpose an opportunity. Upon his arrival at the Commission, Cheysson had a long experience in the French senior civil service, particularly in diplomatic networks. For the strengthening of Community regional policy, Spinelli could rely on the presence of George Thomson, the British commissioner for Regional Policy.

Member of the Labour Party, he developed strong policies to combat regional disparities in the Community during his mandate. His impetus notably led to the creation of the European Regional Development Fund in 1975.[14]

This collaboration with the other socialist commissioners was facilitated by the existence of numerous political structures. Spinelli participated as regularly as possible in the meetings of the Socialist Group in the European Parliament with the other socialist commissioners as well as in the congresses of European socialist parties.[15] Also, a working group presided by Spinelli and composed by the commissioners with a portfolio related to industrial policy issues, Wilhelm Haferkamp, Patrick Hillery, Albert Borschette and Finn Olav Gundelach was created at the European Commission level. This working group was mandated to establish an assessment of the existing problems and to prepare initiatives to be adopted by the Commission of European Communities in the field of industrial policy.[16] These interactions were essential to build the new progressive global industrial policy devised by the Italian commissioner.

These industrial policy proposals were in Spinelli's view fundamentally complementary with proposals for strengthening Community competition policy put forward at the time. Indeed, its development was strongly defended at in the early 1970s by the European center-left political class and trade unions with the aim of lowering prices for the working class and the power of multinationals in the context of rising inflation and increasing globalization of the world economy.[17] The 1973 memorandum on industrial and technological policy therefore stated that "industrial and competition policies pursued by the Commission complemented each other closely".[18]

One important issue in the field of competition policy for the socialist commissioners was the reform of state aid rules. In response to economic and social difficulties affecting their countries, European governments had massively intervened since the beginning of the crisis to save their companies, promote employment and ensure economic recovery. They used the provisions of Article 92 of the EC Treaty for this purpose, which authorized state aids aiming at addressing regional issues or promoting key industries in the Community. Although their granting was legal, the European Commission quickly feared that the proliferation of such aid could jeopardize the unity of the common market.

This was particularly the case for regional aid, which had increased significantly since the completion of the customs union in July 1968. In order to respond to this situation, the Commission had defined principles of coordination in 1971,[19] which were completed in 1973 after the accession of the UK, Ireland and Denmark to the European Communities.[20] However, these principles concentrated on the more developed regions of the Community and thus lacked the definition of schemes considering the specific problems of the other regions. To settle this question, the British socialist commissioner for regional policy George Thomson proposed as early as 28 June 1973 a communication to the Council. The aim was to make it easier for the most disadvantaged regions with the greatest needs to benefit from state aid.[21]

Spinelli was also interested in the modernization of state aid to achieve his political objectives. Of the existing means of action for developing an industrial policy at the Community level, he considered the control of state aid to be the most important.[22] He was concerned that the Commission of European Communities had never succeeded in obtaining from the member states prior notification of aid for industrial purposes and that the institution could not base its assessment of the scope of aid on any economic objective.[23] In order to address this deficiency, he recommended that the Commission set out a multi-annual plan of the Community's broad economic objectives, whose contribution to their completion would be a condition to authorize state aid.[24] Next, the Italian commissioner tried to use competition policy to limit the powers of multinational corporations. That is one of the reasons why he supported the opening of an investigation into a possible abuse of dominant position by IBM in 1974. In this case, the objective was also to support the creation of a European industrial champion in the IT sector.[25] Finally, antitrust law was applied to protect the environment by preventing polluting companies from gaining an unfair competitive advantage.[26]

Given this complementarity between competition and industrial policies in this period, the commissioners did not veto Spinelli's industrial policy proposals.[27] These reflections did not bring however the expected results because member states opposed these proposals.[28]

Willy Schlieder and Raymond Vouel's vision of Community competition policy

In May 1976, several personnel changes affected the composition of the Ortoli Commission. First, Spinelli's candidacy in the Italian parliamentary elections led to his replacement on 19 May by Henri Simonet as commissioner for industrial and technological affairs.[29] Next, Albert Borschette's health problems forced the European Commission to entrust his portfolio to George Thomson, the commissioner for regional policy. He would remain the competition commissioner until the Luxembourg government appointed a new candidate, Raymond Vouel, who took office on 19 July.[30]

Member of the Luxembourg Socialist Workers Party, Raymond Vouel became member of the Commission of the European Communities after a long career in politics. Elected as town councilor in Esch in 1963, he quickly joined the government as State Secretary for Public Health, Employment, Social Security and the Mining Industry in 1964. He became chairman of the Socialist Parliamentary Group in 1970 and served from 1974 in the government as Vice President and Minister of Finance until he became commissioner in July 1976. When he took office, he decided to keep the same team as his predecessor Borschette, headed by Robert Sunnen. The later was liberal leaning. Thus, for the first time, a Socialist commissioner had a liberal head of Cabinet, against the tendency in the Commission to have a head of Cabinet from the same political camp as the Commissioner.[31]

At the administrative level, DG IV was managed by Willy Christoph Schlieder during Vouel's mandate. The director general was a German lawyer and member of SPD. Before entering the Commission, he had been legal adviser to the Federal Directorate of the Confederation of German Trade Unions in the 1950s, and held various management positions in the Commission of the Communities from 1958 to 1967. In that year, he became chief of Staff of Commissioner Haferkamp, until he succeeded Ernst Albrecht at the head of DG IV in 1970. Schlieder was in favor of a strict respect of Community competition law, considering that "any protection resulting from state aids and concerted practices between companies were carrying the seeds of economic decadence and social disaster".[32] He defended however in the case of an economic crisis the flexibility of competition rules like the authorization of agreements between companies[33] or the acceptance of transitional state aids[34] but always limited in purpose and time.

This vision of the role of Community competition policy was shared by Raymond Vouel who advocated that competition policy should essentially have the task of maintaining or recreating the conditions for free competition between undertakings, and of prosecuting and penalizing any action that would jeopardize it.[35] This was to ensure the proper functioning of the market economy and to avoid protectionism.[36] Nevertheless, for him, competition policy did not mean the strict application of rules embodied in the treaties but a policy that must adapt when the economic and social situation required it.[37] This was especially true when market forces alone could not bring about the structural changes needed in times of crisis. However, any adaption of the rules should in no way, in his view, lead to a calling into question of the unity of the common market and consumers' freedom of choice,[38] and had to be in force for a short period of time and under very strict structural conditions.[39]

The Jenkins Commission: a broader and comprehensive strategy to address the structural crisis

Roy Jenkins replaced François-Xavier Ortoli as president of the European Commission in January 1977. He took office with solid political experience after serving as Home Secretary twice, Chancellor of the Exchequer and deputy leader of the British Labour Party. As former Chancellor, he acquired strong skills to elaborate a complete economic policy which made him well-prepared to deal with the effects of the economic and social crisis of the 1970s. He considered the stagflation affecting the Community since 1973 "one of the worst diseases which had affected the bloc since its beginnings".[40] To combat this, he thought that there was no alternative to formulating a disciplined community approach.[41] Reducing the high rate of unemployment, inflation and the widening gap between national economic performances were seen as closely interlinked and to be achieved through the formulation of more tightly linked economic and social policies.[42] The crisis was indeed the result of multiple intertwined causes and for reasons of efficiency, the new Commission wanted to deal with them simultaneously in order to align objectives on a Community basis.[43] The purpose was to provide a coherent framework for the efforts of member states to address the crisis, to use Community funds as a counterweight to the centrifugal forces leading to divergent economic performances between member states and to turn the Community into a major negotiating force in international economic affairs.[44]

The new College of Commissioners was composed of seven social-democratic members[45] with key responsibilities to manage the industrial crisis. The worsening of the economic and social situation forced the Commission to formulate a broader action strategy in which external, regional and social measures were reinforced and placed in line with one another. The gradual reduction of industrial overcapacity led to the development of social measures for reconversion and rehabilitation while a reform of the Regional fund was carried out to meet the needs of regions with the most serious structural problems. All this was accompanied by an active external policy to restrict non-Community imports.

These socialist commissioners had to collaborate on industrial policy with Etienne Davignon, the Commissioner for Industrial Affairs, Internal Market and Customs Union. Davignon was a Belgian Christian democrat who firmly defended the development of a strong Community industrial strategy to fight the crisis while avoiding national protectionism. Under his aegis, several action programs were adopted to tackle problems of overcapacity in the steel, textile and shipbuilding sectors.[46]

The multiplication of these sectoral Community policies raised questions of the legal basis of such interventions and the adaptation of competition law to meet its objectives. Aware that the economic and social situation called for a reform of competition rules that would support, in particular, the Community's industrial restructuring policies,[47] Raymond Vouel sought to achieve the results sought by Davignon and DG III at all costs without infringing Community law.[48] These discussions were intense as we will see in analyzing the debates around reforming state aid rules for sectoral interventions and the authorization of a crisis cartel in the synthetic fibers sector.

The reform of state aid rules for crisis sectors: competition law as a tool for industrial adaptation

The European Economic Community (EEC) Treaty's Article 92 prohibited in principle the granting of state aid when it distorted or threatened to distort competition in the Common market as provided for in European Coal and Steel Community (ECSC) Treaty Article 4. This prohibition was reduced in the EEC Treaty level by numerous exceptions such as state aid to promote the economic development of areas with an abnormally low standard of living or with serious underemployment. In view of these exceptions and to boost growth and employment, the Commission had accepted the granting of state aids by Member States without any structural counterpart in 1975 and 1976. From 1977, the Commission considered a reform of its rules in this area firstly concerning the granting of state aid in the steel industry and then, from 1978 onward, in other industries in crisis.

The objective was to build legal mechanisms to enable state aid law to be an instrument for the permanent adaptation of industry to pursue economic development. State aid was limited to sectors where they were considered vital and on the condition that firms make the necessary adjustments to increase their competitiveness.[49] This was an essential problem for Vouel, who was convinced that an effective discipline with regard to state aid was necessary in order, in particular, to preserve a certain equality of opportunity between the various member states for sectors in difficulty.[50] However, for his colleague Willy Schlieder, this new legal framework was only intended to apply to industries facing problems of exceptional gravity.[51] Also, he advocated that any approved national interventions should under no circumstances lead to increases in capacity or have the effect of restricting competition within the Common Market.[52]

This conception of the new competition rules conflicted with those of DG III (Industry and Internal Market) and DG XVI (Regional and Cohesion Policies). They were opposed to prohibiting any aid that led to overcapacity as a principle, arguing that this was part of a legal approach that did not take into account economic principles.[53] They were defending, for their part, that the Commission should analyze state aid on a case-by-case basis using economic criteria.[54] Another point of divergence was that the rules had to be applied only to industries facing catastrophic situations.[55] Contrary to this, DG III argued that there was a need for constant monitoring of sectors experiencing difficulties.[56]

The synthetic fibers crisis cartel case

Complementary to the reform of Community state aid law, the European Commission tried to adapt new rules on so-called structural crisis agreements. In the face of the deterioration of the situation of the "sectors in structural crisis" (shipbuilding, steel, textiles), Etienne Davignon took action to try to resolve the problems of these industries. In the synthetic fibers sector, intervention was particularly necessary because of decreasing demand, excess capacity, low prices and heavy financial losses.[57] To address these problems, Davignon defended the idea of a structural crisis cartel in the sector. Negotiations between the producers resulted in 11 companies signing a three-year agreement on 20 June 1978, including a plan to reduce production capacity and quotas. After its notification to the Commission on 14 July 1978, a strong legal and political discussion took place around the possibility of authorizing this crisis cartel under Article 85 (3) of the EEC Treaty. The debate focused on whether a crisis cartel could be used as an instrument to overcome the problems caused by structural overcapacity and to promote an industrial structure able to face world competition.[58]

While initially opposed to the idea of the formation of crisis cartels like the majority of his colleagues,[59] Raymond Vouel had to deal with a case put on the table of the Commission by Etienne Davignon who seemed, according to an official, more worried about real problems than legal orthodoxy.[60] With a view to the acceptance of this crisis cartel by the Commission, Davignon and Vouel elaborated a proposal for a Council regulation on crisis cartels based on Article 85 of the EEC Treaty.[61] The objective was to put in place a legal mechanism allowing companies from a determined sector in structural crisis to practice a concerted policy regarding prices and market shares.[62] The proposal was fundamentally inspired by the system provided by the Council Regulation (EEC) No 1078/68 of 19 July 1968, which allowed the European Commission to accept agreements between companies in the event of recognition by the Council of a "state of crisis".[63]

This proposal met with fierce opposition from some of the commissioners (Brunner, Haferkamp and Tugendhat), who opposed the principle of crisis cartels for doctrinal and economic policy reasons.[64] Despite this, Raymond Vouel continued to stand firm for the adoption of his proposal, which constituted for him the most efficient and fairest method to establish a restrictive crisis policy. The proposal could prevent the creation of particular cases as the Commission set the general conditions of the acceptance of crisis cartels by the Council independently of the situation of each sector while the use of Article 85(3) could multiply the requests for crisis cartels. His preferred solution remained, however, to continue to respect market rules, which in his opinion had proven their effectiveness. According to the commissioner, the authorization of crisis cartels had to be limited to avoid any temptation that the companies would not apply structural measures and remain uncompetitive.[65]

Finally, faced with a deep division on this issue inside the European Commission, Raymond Vouel proposed the provisional exclusion of this item from the Commission agenda in July 1978.[66] In the absence of an agreement on the adoption of a special Council regulation concerning crisis cartels, the issue of resolving the structural problems of the synthetic fibers industry without promoting crisis cartels remained. Raymond Vouel was in favor of a prohibition of the agreement if no new Council regulation was adopted. For his part, Etienne Davignon emphasized the need for the European Commission, if certain provisions of the agreement were not compatible with the EEC Treaty, to find a way to obtain an orderly capacity reduction at the European level in the framework of the legal text.[67]

In order to overcome the divergent views between Davignon and Vouel on this question, Roy Jenkins submitted to the College on 29 November 1978 a draft negotiating mandate to the directors-general of DG III, DG IV and the Legal Service to explore the possibility of adopting various measures to solve the problems of the synthetic fibers industry.[68] These included the adoption of an agreement for the reduction of capacity respecting Article 85 of the EEC Treaty but also for further cuts. This last proposal was refused by the socialist commissioners Haferkamp, Tugendhat, Vredeling and Vouel. It was impossible for them to accept a solution including the elaboration of individual recommendations of the European Commission to fix market rates or a production target by company and an agreement on capacity reduction. For Vouel, such a proposal was "incompatible with the competition policy and the economic system of the Community".[69] At the end, this provision was adopted by the College with a majority of eight votes against four.[70]

Southern European Democracy and Community industrial and competition law in the 1980s

European Social Democracy and the changing legal and political environment of the 1980s

The end of the 1970s and the start of the new decade brought considerable political changes to the European political landscape. In 1979–1985, new right-wing governments replaced socialist governments in several countries, notably in Belgium, Denmark, Germany and the UK. This succession of electoral successes of conservative forces reflected the growing acceptance of neoliberal ideas in Europe since the end of the 1970s. Deregulation, privatization, the containment of public spending and the fight against inflation became the new governments' priorities. At the same time, a new College of Commissioners under the presidency of the Liberal Prime Minister of Luxembourg Gaston Thorn took office in January 1981. It was formed by new personalities, notably Frans Andriessen responsible for competition and Karl-Heinz Narjes, with the internal market and industry portfolio. These latter figures were in favor of both the adoption of a market-oriented approach to Community competition and industrial policies.[71]

Nevertheless, this conservative tide did not affect the whole continent. In Southern Europe, the French Socialist Party (PS), the Italian Socialist Party (PSI), the Spanish Socialist Workers' Party (PSOE) and the Panhellenic Socialist Movement (PASOK) came into power after long periods in opposition. Faced with pressing economic and social problems, economic policy preferences differed within European social democracy between those in favor of adopting an expansionist economic strategy and those wishing to implement an orthodox one.

Since the Epinay Congress in June 1971, the French Socialist Party was defending an economic program of rupture with capitalism through the development of a strong planning and regulatory state. The inflationary spiral had to be contained by a mix of nationalizations and Keynesian stimulus policies.[72] This leftist strategy of the French Socialist Party was the consequence of its electoral competition and subsequent alliance with the French Communist Party. Discussions between the two formations led to the adoption of a common government program in 1972 in which nationalizations of key French companies had an important place. After the 1974 presidential elections, a lively internal debate raged between the Marxist and Keynesian sensibilities on the place to be given to state intervention in economic policy. At the Metz Congress in April 1979, a synthesis between the different approaches was carried out. Marxist and neo-protectionist elements were reintroduced in the party's texts, while the compatibility of the economic program with the rules of liberal capitalism was affirmed.[73] The content of the programmatic document "110 proposals for France" adopted for the 1981 presidential election campaign reflected this balance with proposals for economic recovery, nationalizations for the "reconquest of the internal market," the strengthening of the Planning Authority and new rights for workers.[74]

The economic ideology of the Spanish Socialist Workers' Party (PSOE) evolved differently during the 1970s. At the beginning of the political transition, the organization was following a leftist strategy to compete with the Spanish Communist Party (PCE) and other leftist groups.[75] After good results in the parliamentary elections of June 1977, the PSOE shifted from defending "revolutionary reformism" (non-dogmatic Marxism in favor of a non-capitalist society) to "democratic reformism".[76] This change in strategy was the result of the ongoing internal renovation process since the 1970s to modernize the party's image in order to attract moderate sectors of society and prepare the party's path to power.[77] The two socialist congresses of 1979 represented a crucial moment in this evolution, when it was decided to re-found the organization by abandoning Marxism as an ideological referent. The PSOE defined itself as a moderate political force upon which Europeanization, economic modernization and democratic consolidation depended.[78] This triple historical mission had to be achieved through the implementation of an agenda *por el cambio* adopted for the 1982 parliamentary elections.[79] Unlike its French counterpart, the PSOE did not seek to break with capitalism with this program but rather to be the party that would carry out Spain's economic modernization.[80] The failure of the French socialist experience played a major role in this shift toward a more market-oriented strategy. Although the PSOE program advocated the implementation of an expansionist policy based on government intervention to address the unemployment problem, the electoral program also contained orthodox economic references such as affirming the prevalent economic role of the market and the need to implement anti-inflation policies.[81]

These new macro-economic strategies had to be pursued in difficult conditions. The 1979 oil shock system led to a worsening of an already battered world economy. The major economic and social structural changes caused by an increasingly globalized economy continued and caused a significant decline in manufacturing employment in Europe. In addition, socialist governments had to cope with the burden of the economic legacy of their predecessors who had failed to address the crisis. Finally, these governments had to comply with a growing institutionalization of Community law. This implied that the socialist governments would respect the objectives of industrial restructuring policy and the new competition rules. Given the importance of the steel industry in Europe, the fact that it was at that time mainly made up of state-owned companies and the concentration of its workforce in particular regions, it was a test-case for the compatibility of social-democratic industrial policies with Community competition law.

Because of the gravity of the crisis in the steel sector and the existence of interventionist provisions in the ECSC Treaty, investment in the industry was carefully regulated. After several attempts by commissioners Altiero Spinelli and Henri Simonet to elaborate a crisis policy for the sector, the Commission launched the Davignon Plan in 1977 that included fixing mandatory minimum prices for three types of products and introducing voluntary production restriction systems on the basis of agreements between Eurofer and the Commission. The declaration of a manifest state of crisis in 1980 by invoking Article 58 of the ECSC Treaty transformed the voluntary system into a binding one with the imposition of mandatory quotas by the Commission of the European Communities.[82] In addition, because of increasing state aid to the steel industry and strong pressure from the German government,[83] the Commission derogated the principle of prohibition of state aid as established in the ECSC Treaty's Article 4 to control the granting of state aid to the sector in 1980. These competition rules constituted an important part of the European Commission's restructuring plan. The objective was to avoid distortions of competition inside the Community. This framework oriented the national policies because they were informed in advance of the industrial objectives, which they had to reach.

After the adoption of the first Steel Aid Code in 1980, the Commission strengthened the state aid control system by prescribing the progressive elimination of state aid within a defined time frame. Recipients had to have a coherent restructuring program, including capacity reductions and the restoration of competitiveness and financial viability. Complementary to this, state aid was authorized until 1 July 1983 and payments until 31 December 1985 with the exception of interest subsidies or payments for loan guarantees disbursed before this period.[84] The purpose of imposing this timeframe was to bring the exceptional action framework implemented to restructure and liberalize the sector to a gradual end.

The French socialist government and the limits of the strategy of reconquering the internal market

The election of François Mitterrand, candidate of the French Socialist Party as the first left-wing president of the Fifth Republic and the victory of his party in the 1981 parliamentary elections, represented a turning point in a Europe increasingly dominated by neo-liberal conservative forces. French Socialists were advocating a radical change in economic policy from that of their liberal predecessor, Valéry Giscard d'Estaing, who had adopted programs of fiscal reduction and tight monetarism to fight inflation with Raymond Barre as Prime minister. Their economic strategy was expressed in the *Programme Commun* signed by the French Communist Party, the Radical Party and the Socialist Party in 1972 and the *110 propositions* of the presidential socialist candidate François Mitterrand. In terms of industrial policy, the coalition promoted a radical change of course in relation to the Giscardian industrial policy of "picking and backing winners," which was producing, in their view, a dual economy characterized by the privatization of profits and the socialization of losses.[85] The fall in investment had to be fought by means of stimulating demand through reflation and applying a strong interventionist industrial policy including nationalization, recapitalization and restructuration of the means of production.[86]

The nationalization program was considered a central pillar in their industrial strategy as it allowed "to orientate production, carry out industrial reconversions, strengthen and adapt industrial structures to face international competition."[87] More concretely it could allow the development of industrial investment in France and bring societal changes, notably higher wages and the reduction of working time.[88] For this reason, the new French government, which included also Ministers from the French Communist Party and the Radical Party, proceeded to nationalize large banks as well as industrial groups and companies occupying strategic positions of the economy.

In addition to the planned nationalization of Sacilor and Usinor, Mitterrand had promised during his presidential campaign to apply a major expansionary policy of increasing steel production in order to mark a break with the measures taken by the Barre government. This was in order to satisfy steel workers and their families who were an important part of his electorate, but also due to the heavy symbolism represented by intervening in the sector.[89]

After the elections, the newly formed socialist government under Prime Minister Pierre Mauroy decided to quickly apply its state-led industrial strategy to regain control of the national market. The French steel industry was suffering from low productivity, obsolete technology and a chronically unviable financial situation despite having had already three rationalization plans in 1966, 1977 and 1978.[90] To remedy these problems, the Mauroy government decided first to grant Usinor and Sacilor, which represented 95% of the steel market, emergency aid to help sustain their immediate needs in August and September 1981. In order to do so, they took advantage of Article 6 of the Steel Aid Code of 1981, which allowed the government to grant emergency aid before submitting its restructuring program.[91] Additionally, the government converted FDES loans to Sacilor and Usinor into shared capital as part of its nationalization program, which was viewed as essential for conducting its socialist economic policy.[92] These actions were part of a new steel plan whose objectives were not just to rescue the two companies but also to help them modernize and restructure with the prospect of returning to competitiveness.[93]

These measures raised some concern from the European Commission, which feared the development of a steel restructuring policy at the national level.[94] Although Article 222 of the EEC Treaty stated that the legal text did not prejudice member-states' ownership regimes, the future behavior of the French state and its companies remained subject to the treaty's economic rules. These companies were prohibited from jeopardizing interstate trade in the internal market or adopting anticompetitive structures affecting it.[95] With respect to French state aid granted to their steel companies, the European Commission raised the problem of the absence of prior notification.[96] As a result, the European Commission decided to open an infringement procedure under the ECSC Treaty's Article 88 against France in December 1978 over the emergency aid granted to Usinor and Sacilor and the aid's conversion into capital. It cited the absence of sufficient information about the measures to assess their compatibility with the Steel Aid Code.[97] Nevertheless, more emergency aid granted by the Socialist French government to Sacilor and Usinor was authorized by the European Commission as it was considered essential to the survival of these companies and allowed them to avoid serious social problems pending a restructuring plan for the French steel industry.[98] After this decision, emergency aid could not be notified. Only functioning and investment aids could be granted by the member states on the condition that they were part of a restructuring program.[99]

Committed to an ambitious interventionist industrial policy with expansionist policies focused on investment,[100] the socialist government argued in 1982 that a strong competitive industry capable of producing 24 million metric tons of steel would be re-established within four years thanks to an important modernization program.[101] This production target was based on the most optimistic forecast for the evolution of the steel market in France set out in Pierre Judet's report. This was done in order to spare the opposition of the various social partners.[102] The Mauroy government informed the Commission of the restructuring program for the French steel industry on 30 September 1982. It included state aids to Sacilor and Usinor amounting to FR 26,220 billion (FR 8,273 billion of functioning aid and FR 17,947 billion of investment aid) for the period 1981–1982.[103] At the end of 1982, the Commission authorized the payment of investment aid amounting to FR 9,198 million, operating aid amounting to FR 5,639 million and aid to cover losses in 1981 (FR 4,914 million). However, the aid was to be granted under strict conditions: first, the reduction of Usinor and Sacilor's capacities, then the investment aid would be granted by the French government only on the basis of payments made by the companies for their investments. Also, Usinor and Sacilor would have to comply with the provisions to ensure that state aid was not used to compensate for losses resulting from non-compliance with the price provisions.[104]

The Commission's final decision on the program only came in June 1983. It considered the reduction in production capacity announced by the French government to be insufficient. Consequently, it requested that, in order for some of this aid to be compatible with common market rules, the companies had to reduce their production by a further 630,000 tons compared with a net reduction in hot-rolled product capacity proposed by the French government of 5,977,000 tons.[105]

However, despite its promises, the French government quickly admitted that the production level planned in the program was impossible to reach[106] and did not significantly stem the steel firms' losses.[107] As a result, the French government reduced its production target to 17.6 million metric tons for 1983 instead of the 24 million metric tons initially planned.[108] From 1982, the left-wing government gradually abandoned the national Keynesian economic strategy in force since 1981, by applying competitive disinflation policies to cope with the macroeconomic and monetary crisis.[109] On the industrial policy side, this evolution from expansionist to restrictive policies led to a progressive disengagement of the state marked by the abandonment of the strategy of promoting national champions and rescuing "lame duck" industries such as steel.[110] The European Community was to become the privileged level empowered to develop an industrial policy in the sectors of the future, particularly in the face of US and Japanese competition.[111]

This change of strategy was reflected in the adoption of the new steel plan by the French government in March 1984. The objective pursued by the latter was the modernization of the French steel industry through a significant reduction in production capacity and staff.[112] In accordance with this, the steel companies had to function in ten years' time as independent firms in competitive markets and thus no longer be dependent on government subsidies.[113]

The PSOE and the steel industry: Spain's accession to the Communities at any price

The result of the parliamentary elections held in October 1982 was a smashing victory for the PSOE, which won an absolute majority of 202 of the 350 seats in Congress. Its young secretary general, Felipe González, became prime minister. His election marked the beginning of a new era for Spain that featured democratic consolidation and the successful conclusion of the negotiations for joining the European Communities. Spain's accession was the government's primary political priority in order to make the transition to democracy in Spain irreversible.[114]

To fulfill this objective, the new government had to unblock several negotiation chapters left unsettled by its predecessors. One of the most important of these was the problem of the integration of the Spanish steel industry into the ECSC. Since 1978, industrial consultation had been established between the Commission and the Spanish Ministry of Industry and Energy to allow the exchange of information between the two parties for a better mutual knowledge of the respective industrial sectors. However, discussions were blocked due to the lack of results from the implementation of the restructuring plans for the Spanish steel industry.[115] With the arrival of the new government, the negotiations on this topic sped up so that they could be concluded in time for Spain's entry into the Communities on 1 January 1986.

The Spanish steel industry was suffering from several structural weaknesses when negotiations began in February 1979. As a result of decades of implementation of highly interventionist and protectionist industrial policies, the sector was subject to significant overcapacity, tariff protection and non-tariff barriers. In addition, it was one of the industrial sectors most affected by the oil shocks given its high energy dependence.[116] Finally, it was heavily subsidized by forms of state aid that were illegal under ECSC competition rules. To enable it to integrate into the Community and survive in free-trading conditions, the sector had to carry out an extremely costly restructuring process in terms of both capital and labor.[117]

The previous liberal governments of the Union of Democratic Centre (UCD) had made several attempts to resolve this situation by approving various conversion decrees in 1981 and 1982, but these focused on the financial reorganization of steel companies without carrying out the productive restructuring that was necessary.[118] Given the approach of Spain's expected accession date, this policy had to be implemented by the new socialist government in accordance with the steel restructuring policy pursued at the Community level. Otherwise, the government risked provoking pre-accession penalties.[119]

Upon its arrival in power, the recently elected government tried to integrate this policy into its new economic and industrial strategy. The fight against inflation and strengthening the competitiveness of industry were priority objectives of the government. In its view, this required promoting a major structural adjustment policy in traditional sectors as well as developing new sectors, activities and production lines[120] so as to catch up with other European economies.[121] The Socialists' plan to accelerate and transform Spain's crisis restructuring policy represented a major challenge. The application of adjustment measures could lead to significant job losses for workers who traditionally supported the PSOE. The sector was indeed a stronghold of the UGT (the General Union of Workers), the socialist trade union.

One month after taking office in 1983, the new minister of industry and energy, Carlos Solchaga, announced the elaboration of a White Paper on Industrial conversion and a royal decree law.[122] However, these documents were submitted later than planned so that they could not influence local elections held in May.[123] Their publication was accompanied by the approval of the Royal Decree Law 1853/1983 on the integral steel industry, which contained financial and labor measures for companies. In this decree, objectives of competitiveness and long-term viability were set for the first time since the beginning of the restructuring process. The socialist government thus abandoned its previous policy of remodeling of assets and adjusting productive specializations.

In parallel with the adoption of these measures, the PSOE decided not to build new facilities in Sagunto. As part of its attempt to develop a policy for the reindustrialization of the steel sector, the second UCD government, led by Leopoldo Calvo-Sotelo, had set up in 1982 a "Coordination Committee for Royal Decree 878/1981," whose task was notably to "direct reindustrialization plans to companies".[124] To apply this decree, the committee used the services of an external consultant, the Kawasaki Steel Corporation. Its report underlined "the need for the building of a steel plant near the sea if the Spanish steel companies wished to compete in the future on the international market" and indicated "that the fourth steel plant under construction in Sagunto could fulfil this function."[125] The report's content had not been well-received by the companies AHV, ENSIDESA and the trade unions. The companies feared that investments in improving their facilities would not be sustainable, while the trade unions denounced the social cost of the program. In the face of these criticisms, the Calvo-Sotelo government distanced itself from the report and the companies as well as the autonomous communities concerned were asked to formulate alternative proposals for the reindustrialization of the steel sector.[126]

Soon after its installation at the Moncloa Palace, the González government presented a plan to be discussed with companies and trade unions. It defended the building of two new steel installations by ENSIDESA and AHV and the modernization of their hot strip trains. As explained by Minister of Industry and Energy Carlos Solchaga, this choice resulted in the abandonment of the project to build a new hot strip train in Sagunto.[127] This proposal was formulated to meet two imperatives: firstly, the need to carry out a restructuring policy in the steel sector with the lowest possible social and political costs. For this reason, it was decided to close installations in the Valencia region rather than in the northern regions where steel employment was more significant.[128] Secondly, in order to conclude the negotiations with the Communities as soon as possible, the socialist government wanted to favor a solution that was more acceptable for the Community institutions.[129] The project to build a new hot strip train in Sagunto had been a concern for the Communities since 1978 because it could result in a considerable increase in the Spanish steel industry's production capacity.[130]

It is in this context that the new Spanish negotiating team attended the 17th EEC-Spain ministerial session in October 1983 determined to move forward with the accession negotiations. The socialist government could boast of having adopted major adjustment measures since coming to power. As a result, the Community institutions welcomed the provisions in favor of the steel industry taken thus far. These were, according to them, following

> the guidelines of Community steel policy as they provided for a substantial reduction in hot-rolled products capacity by 1986 (a reduction of ±15% in installed steel capacity in 1980), an ambitious investment plan for the sector

> without increasing production capacity (by the modernization of installations, rationalization of the production structure of steel companies) and a reduction in the workforce in 1986 of ±36% of workers in the sector as compared with 1980.[131]

This declaration was supplemented by a commitment by the Spanish government to "communicate to the Commission the detailed restructuring plans of each of the companies benefiting from public aid."[132]

The European Commission's position changed during the summer after the Spanish government sent its documents on steel restructuring. In a statement submitted in September, the Commission was complaining about the late delivery of information on Spain's steel restructuring (which was received by the Commission only at the end of August 1984) and consequently about the existence of "too many elements of uncertainty at this stage of the negotiations."[133] It is for this reason that the Commission considered the idea of "inserting a draft protocol in the instruments of accession in order to avoid distortions between the Community and Spanish steel industries."[134]

As expected, the Commission's draft was badly received by the Spanish government. The Minister of Industry and Energy, Carlos Solchaga Catalán, reacted by sending a letter on 17 September to Davignon, still European Commissioner responsible for Industrial Affairs. In the latter, Solchaga reminded the Commission of "the great efforts Spain had made to integrate [into] the Community, particularly through the development of a major restructuring policy" and that is why the country was complaining that "the treatment inflicted did not respond to the current challenges".[135] However, the PSOE government had no choice but to accept the measures imposed by the Commission in order to join the Communities in 1986.

These declarations led the Council of the EEC to grant an exploratory mandate to the Commission in October 1984. The conditions imposed on Spain were the following: the steel company restructuring plans could not permit the production capacity of hot-rolled ECSC products to exceed 18 million tons at the end of the transition period and had to be compatible with the general Community objectives set for steel production adopted before accession. Also, for a period of three years from the date of accession, Spain had the obligation to complete its steel industry's restructuring under the terms of the protocol. Finally, the transition's duration could be abrogated depending on the state of progress of the Spanish restructuring plans and the steel measures in force after accession.[136]

Lastly, it was agreed that the Spanish steel industry would apply the ECSC price system from accession while setting maximum quantities for Spanish exports to the EEC during the first three years after the country's accession. The Spanish steel industry's restructuring had to be completed within three years. At the end of this period, the production of hot-rolled products should not exceed 18 million tons to enable the Spanish steel industry to be incorporated into the ECSC and conform with the Steel Aid Code.[137]

Conclusion

In this chapter, we have analyzed how European Social Democracy engaged with Community competition law and industrial policy during the crisis of the 1970s and 1980s. As we saw, economic globalization and the subsequent crisis of the Keynesian state model of management in the 1970s forced European social democracy to rethink its political strategy to meet the social needs of workers. In this new context, the EEC became the privileged level of power to reach this goal. Taking advantage of the favorable political context, European social democracy tried through European commissioners and a wide network of associated European political organizations to develop an ambitious and progressive industrial policy at the Community level in the 1970s. Given the nature of the economic crisis, this Community policy was part of a general action program promoted by the Ortoli and Jenkins Commissions. A new Community industrial policy had to pursue two objectives: first, to manage and respond to the social consequences of industrial change, and second, to develop new European industrial and technological activities to cope with foreign competition.

This strategy was implemented in two phases. First, European social democracy took initiatives in this field through its commissioner Altiero Spinelli. Then, from 1977 onward, Socialists contributed to the development of an anti-crisis policy by supporting the policy proposals of Commissioner Etienne Davignon and by developing regional and social programs to mitigate the consequences of restructuring policies on workers and the afflicted territories.

These initiatives led to a reflection within the Commission on the interaction between Community industrial policy and competition law. During Altiero Spinelli's mandate, Community action in industrial policy was seen as complementary to competition policy. With the significant development of sectoral industrial policies from 1976, the balance between the two policies was increasingly called into question. To enable industrial restructuring to take place while preserving the unity of the common market, major reforms of Community competition law were envisaged by social-democratic commissioners. These reflections were led by two social democrats: Raymond Vouel, commissioner of competition from 1976 to 1981, and Willy Schlieder, director general of the DG IV. In the face of a serious crisis of the European industry, they tried to devise legal solutions to sectoral problems within the framework of the Common Market, to which they were particularly attached. However, according to them, these new rules had to have concrete objectives and a limited timeframe, in order to return to conformance with the general functioning of Community competition policy. This view conflicted with that of DG III and Industry Commissioner Davignon, who wanted a competition policy that put the interests of industry first, as we have seen with the cases of the state aid reform to help certain industries, and the crisis cartel in the synthetic fibers sector.

The strengthening of the Community's competition rules and industrial policy was a challenge for the socialist governments that came to power in the early

1980s. It significantly reduced their room for maneuvering in an unfavorable economic and political environment. In this context, the Mauroy government first tried to develop an expansionist industrial policy accompanied by nationalization measures to regain control of the French internal market. This strategy conflicted with Community competition rules and industrial policy, leading the Commission to reject the restructuring program for the French steel industry. Affected by a monetary and political crisis, as well as by a significant increase in the national external trade deficit, the French socialist government made a radical shift in its economic policy from 1983 by abandoning its Keynesian stimulus policy in favor of a competitive disinflation policy. This was accompanied by a new commitment from Mitterrand to develop an industrial policy at the Community level and thereby bring French industrial ambitions into compliance with Community competition rules.

The PSOE's conception of industrial policy was different from that of its French counterparts particularly because, prior to reaching power, the party had adopted a strategy of subordinating their economic modernization policies to its primary goal of acceding to the European Communities at any price. The government therefore accepted the conditions laid down by the Community institutions for the integration of Spanish industry into the Common Market. This was despite the deep structural problems in Spanish industry and the goal of limiting the social impact in some of its electoral strongholds.

There are several explanations for the position of European Social Democracy in favor of strengthening competition law as a complement to a Community industrial policy and the relative compliance of social-democratic governments with its rules during the crisis of the 1970s and 1980s. First, as mentioned earlier, Community competition law during the 1970s was seen by European social democracy as a tool to improve the situation of workers and control the power of multinationals. Secondly, the support of the European integration process by the socialist parties during the period[138] resulted in their governments accepting Community competition law while attempting to bring it into accord with other progressive policy objectives.

Notes

1 Niall Ferguson et al. (eds.), *The Shock of the Global. The 1970s in Perspective* (Cambridge: Belknap Press, 2011).
2 Wilhem Haferkamp, Henri Simonet, Altiero Spinelli and George Thomson.
3 Wilhem Haferkamp had the portfolio of Economy, Finance and Investment; Henri Simonet the portfolio of Taxation and Energy; Altiero Spinelli the portfolio of Industrial and Technological Policy while George Thompson held the portfolio of Regional Policy.
4 Christian Salm, *Transnational Socialist Networks in the 1970s. European Community Development Aid and Southern Enlargement* (Basingstoke: Palgrave Macmillan, 2016), 82–83.
5 Salm, *Transnational Socialist Networks in the 1970s.*
6 Altiero Spinelli, *Diario Europeo. 1970/1976* (Bologna: Il Mulino, 1991).
7 Eric Bussière, "Devising a Strategy: The Internal Market and Industrial Policy," in Eric Bussière et al. (eds.), *The European Commission. History and Memories of an Institution.* (Luxembourg: Publications Office of the European Union, 2014), 263–276;

Laurent Warlouzet, "Europe de la concurrence et politique industrielle communautaire. La naissance d'une opposition au sein de la CEE dans les années 60," *Histoire, économie & société* 1 (2008): 47–61.

8 *The Community's Industrial Policy*, Memorandum from the Commission to the Council. Luxemburg, Official Publications Office of the European Communities, 1970.
9 Conférence "Industrie et Société." Venise, 20–22 April 1972, AS-202, Historical archives of the European Union, Florence.
10 Lettera di Altiero Spinelli al Professore Francesco De Martino, AS-29, 25 May 1971, HAEU, Florence

11 Commission of the European Communities, *Pour la création d'une assise industrielle européenne. Communication de la Commission relative au programme de politique industrielle et technologique (présentée le 7 mai 1973*, supplement number 7 of the Bulletin of the European Communities, 1973.
12 *Ibid.*
13 Salm, *Transnational Socialist Networks in the 1970s*, 43.
14 Pierre Tilly, "Regional Policy: A Tangible Expression of European Solidarity," in Eric Bussière et al. (eds.), *The European Commission. History and Memories of an Institution. 1973–1986* (Luxembourg: Publications Office of the European Union, 2014), 345–347.
15 Lettera di Altiero Spinelli al professor Francesco De Martino, 25 May 1971, AS-29, HAEU, Florence; Lettre d'Altiero Spinelli à Mario Tanassi, 25 May 1971, AS-31, HAEU, Florence.
16 Minutes of the 328th meeting of the European Commission, 19 February 1975, COM(75) PV 328, Historical archives of the European Commission, Brussels.
17 Laurent Warlouzet, *Governing Europe in a Globalizing World. Neoliberalism and Its Alternatives Following the 1973 Oil Crisis* (Abingdon-on-Thames: Routledge, 2018), 159.
18 Commission of the European Communities, *Pour la création d'une assise industrielle européenne. Communication de la Commission relative au programme de politique industrielle et* technologique, 7 May 1973.
19 Régimes généraux d'aides à finalité régionale, 4 November 1971, JOCE C 111 (Communication de la Commission au Conseil).
20 Régimes généraux d'aides à finalité régionale, COM(73) 1110, 27 June 1973, HAEC, Brussels.
21 Session of 17 June 1976, 216, Archives of the European Parliament, Luxembourg.
22 Politique communautaire en faveur des mutations industrielles, SEC(75) 2103, 12 June 1975, HAEC, Brussels.
23 *Ibid.*
24 *Ibid.*
25 Arthe Van Laer, "The European Lilliputians Attacking IBM: Balancing Innovation and Competition in the European Commission's First Big Antitrust Case (1973–1984)," *Business History* 62, 5 (2018): 4.
26 John Pinder, "Altiero Spinelli's European Federal Odyssey," *The International Spectator* 42, 4 (2007): 577.
27 Thorsten Käseberg and Arthe Van Laer, "Competition Law and Industrial Policy. Conflict, Adaptation and Complementarity," in Kiran Klaus Patel and Heike Schweitzer (eds.), *The Historical Foundations of EU Competition Law* (Oxford: Oxford University Press, 2013), 175.
28 *Ibid.*, 175–176; Bussière, "Devising a Strategy: The Internal Market and Industrial Policy," 268.
29 Session of 6 July 1976, 6 July 1976, COM(76) PV 391, HAEC, Brussels.
30 Agence Europe, 19 and 20 July 1976, 4, AGE, HAEU, Florence.
31 Interview with Robert Sünnen by Ghijseppu Lavezzi, 25 February 2004, HAEU, Florence available here: https://archives.eui.eu/en/oral_history/INT739.

32 Willy Schlieder, "Politique européenne de concurrence et crise," in *Feduci, Séminaire de la Commission droit et vie des affaires de l'Université de Liège* (Paris: Editions du Moniteur, 1980), 66.
33 *Ibid.*, 67.
34 Note de Willy Schieder à Raymond Vouel. Sprechzettel. Secteurs en difficulté et politique de concurrence, 24 April 1978, BAC 83 1986 26, HAEC, Brussels.
35 Session of 16 September 1976, 232, Archives of the European Parliament, Luxembourg.
36 Projet d'intervention de Raymond Vouel au Collège des commissaires, 23 May 1978, BAC 40/1986 125, HAEC, Brussels.
37 Session of 16 November 1977, 207, Archives of the European Parliament, Luxembourg.
38 *Ibid.*
39 Session of 12 October 1978, 265, Archives of the European Parliament, Luxembourg.
40 Speech by Roy Jenkins in front of the European Parliament, 6 July 1977, HAEC, Brussels.
41 *Ibid.*
42 Speech of Roy Jenkins to the congress of the European Metalworkers' Federation in Amsterdam, 17 May 1977, HAEC, Brussels.
43 Discours de Henk Vredeling à Luxembourg, 27 June 1977, HAEC, Brussels.
44 Speech by Roy Jenkins in front of the Economic and Social Committee in Brussels, 23 June 1977, HAEC, Brussels.
45 Claude Cheysson, Antonio Giolitti, Wilhem Haferkamp, Roy Jenkins, Raymond Vouel and Henk Vredeling.
46 Bussière, "Devising a Strategy: The Internal Market and Industrial Policy," 272.
47 Session of 16 November 1977, 207, Archives of the European Parliament, Luxembourg; Session of 12 October 1978, 265, Archives of the European Parliament, Luxembourg.
48 Compte-rendu de l'entretien entre MM. Davignon et Vouel, 24 March 1977, BAC 10 1985 427, HAEC, Brussels.
49 Note from Schlieder to Vouel. Exchange of views on the Commission's sectoral aid policy, 2 June 1978, BAC 83 1986 26, HAEC, Brussels.
50 Session of 12 October 1978, 364, Archives of the European Parliament, Luxembourg.
51 Note pour Raymond Vouel de Willy Schlieder. Secteurs en crise, 21 March 1978, BAC 40/1986 125, HAEC, Brussels.
52 *Ibid.*
53 Note de Pierre Mathijsen à l'attention de Willy Schlieder. Secteurs en crise, 1978, BAC 83 1986 26, HAEC, Brussels; Document de la DG III de réflexion sur les aides d'État., 20 April 1978, BAC 88 1992 16, HAEC, Brussels.
54 *Ibid.*
55 Note pour Raymond Vouel de Willy Schlieder. Secteurs en crise, 21 March 1978.
56 Document de la DG III de réflexion sur les aides d'État, 20 April 1978, BAC 88 1991 16, HAEC, Brussels.
57 Richard Shaw and Susan Shaw, "Excess Capacity and Rationalisation in the West European Synthetic Fibre Industry," *The Journal of Industrial Economics* 32, 2 (1983): 151.
58 Note pour Claus-Dieter Ehlermann et Fernand Braun. Document de travail pour la 30ème conférence des experts gouvernementaux des Etats membres en matière d'ententes: Article 85 du Traité CEE et les crises sectorielles de structure, 25 April 1978, BAC 83/1984 425 (378), HAEC, Brussels.
59 Letter from Raymond Vouel to Roy Jenkins, 18 July 1978, HAEC, Brussels; Letter from Claus-Dieter Ehlermann to Crispin Tickell, 22 June 1978, BAC 40/1986 125, HAEC, Brussels.
60 Note à l'attention du Service Juridique. Compte-rendu du XXXIIème Séminaire de la Commission droit et vie des affaires de l'Université de Liège consacré aux aides et mesures de sauvegarde en droit international et économique, 24 October 1979, BAC 83/1984 425 (378), HAEC, Brussels.

61 René Joliet, "Cartelisation, Dirigism and Crisis in the European Community," *World Economy* 3, 4 (1981): 413.
62 Proposition de règlement (CEE) du Conseil au titre de l'article 87 paragraphe 2 du traité concernant l'exemption de l'article 85 paragraphe 1 des accords entre entreprises nécessaires à la réduction de surcapacités structurelles, 18 May 1978, COM(78) 224, BAC 83/1984 425 (378), HAEC, Brussels.
63 Note to Raymond Vouel from Willy Schlieder, 28 April 1978, BAC 466/1998 61, HAEC, Brussels.
64 Règlement d'exception-article 87 CEE (COM(78) 224). Résultats de la réunion spéciale des Chefs de Cabinet du mardi 23 mai 1978, 23 May 1978, COM(78) 224/2, BAC 83/1984 425 (378), HAEC, Brussels; Résultats de la réunion spéciale des Chefs de Cabinet du 2 juin 1978, 2 June 1978, BAC 83/1984 425 (378), HAEC, Brussels.
65 Aide-mémoire pour la proposition de règlement concernant les cartels de crise, 7 June 1978, BAC 466/1998 61, HAEC, Brussels.
66 Minutes of the 483rd Meeting of the European Commission, 2nd part, 26 July 1978, 26 July 1978, COM(78) PV 483, HAEC, Brussels.
67 Minutes of the 492nd Meeting of the European Commission, 2nd part, 8 November 1978, COM(78) PV 492, HAEC, Brussels.
68 Minutes of the 495th Meeting of the European Commission, 2nd part, 29 November 1978, COM(78) PV 495, HAEC, Brussels.
69 *Ibid.*
70 The President Jenkins, François-Xavier Ortoli, Finn Olav Gundelach, Lorenzo Natali, Claude Cheysson, Antonio Giolitti, Richard Burke and Etienne Davignon voted in favor while Wilhem Haferkamp, Henk Vredeling, Christopher Tugendhat and Raymond Vouel voted against the proposal. *Ibid.*
71 Warlouzet, *Governing Europe in a Globalizing World*, 156–179.
72 Matthieu Fulla, *Les socialistes français et l'économie (1944–1981). Une histoire économique du politique* (Paris: Les Presses Sciences Po, 2016), 241–242.
73 *Ibid.*, 367–370.
74 *Ibid.*, 385.
75 Albert Recio and Jordi Roca, "The Spanish Socialists in Power: Thirteen Years of Economic Policy," in Andrew Glyn (ed.), *Social Democracy in Neoliberal Times. The Left and Economic Policy since 1980* (Oxford: Oxford University Press, 2001), 174.
76 Antonio García Santesmases, "Evolución ideológica del socialismo en la España actual," *Sistema: Revista de ciencias sociales* 68–69 (1985): 62–69.
77 Richard Gillespie, *The Spanish Socialist Party. A History of Factionalism* (Oxford: Clarendon Press, 1989), 6; Juan Antonio Andrade Blanco, "Renuncias y abandonos en la evolución ideológica durante la transición a la democracia: una propuesta para el estudio del IX Congreso del PCE y el congreso extraordinario del PSOE," *Historia Actual Online* 8 (2005): 44.
78 Santos Juliá, *Los socialistas en la política española. 1879–1982* (Madrid: Taurus, 1996), 554; Sergio Gálvez Biesca, "Modernización socialista y reforma laboral (1982–1992)," PhD thesis, Complutense University of Madrid, 2012, 347.
79 PSOE, *Por el cambio. Programa electoral* (Madrid: PSOE, 1982).
80 Einar Berntzen, "Democratic Socialism in Spain, Portugal and Greece," in Lauri Karvonen and Jan Sundberg (eds.), *Social Democracy in Transition* (Dartmouth: Aldershot, 1991), 228.
81 Recio and Roca, "The Spanish Socialists in Power," 174–175.
82 Loukas Tsoukalis and Robert Strauss, "Community Policies on Steel 1974–1982: A Case of Collective Management," in Yves Meny and Vincent Wright (eds.), *The Politics of Steel. Western Europe and the Steel Industry in the Crisis Years (1974–1984)* (Berlin: de Gruyter, 1986), 211.

83 Laurent Warlouzet, "When Germany Accepted a European Industrial Policy: Managing the Decline of Steel from 1977 to 1984," *Jahrbuch für Wirtschaftsgeschichte* 58, 1 (2017): 154–156.
84 Commission Decision No 2320/81/ECSC of 7 August 1981, establishing Community rules for aids to the steel industry.
85 Kenneth Dyson and Stephen Wilks, *Industrial Crisis. A Comparative Study of the State and Industry* (Oxford: Martin Robertson, 1983), 187.
86 Rand Smith, *The Left's Dirty Job. The Politics of Industrial Restructuring in France and Spain* (Pittsburgh: Pittsburgh University Press, 1998), 70–71.
87 Parti communiste et socialiste français, *Changer la vie – Programme de gouvernement du Parti socialiste et programme commun de la gauche* (Paris: Flammarion, 1972).
88 Vivian Schmidt, *From State to Market? The Transformation of French Business and Government* (Cambridge: Cambridge University Press, 1996), 96–98.
89 Pascal Raggi, "François Mitterrand et la sidérurgie française," *Annales de l'Est* 1 (2018): 238.
90 Smith, *The Left's Dirty Job*, 159.
91 Christine Camdessus, *Les interventions financières des Etats en faveur de la sidérurgie dans la C.E.C.A.: l'exemple français* (Paris: Presses Universitaires de France, 1987), 96–97.
92 Pierre Mauroy, "Discours à l'Assemblée Nationale," 8 July 1981. http://archives.gouvernement.fr/villepin/IMG/doc/Discours_de_politique_generale_de_Pierre_Mauroy.doc.
93 Camdessus, *Les interventions financières des Etats*, 105.
94 Note d'Etienne Davignon à Gaston Thorn, 8 October 1981, BAC 83/1984 92 (92), HAEC, Brussels.
95 Sessions of 7 and 8 October 1981, PV(81) 620, HAEC, Brussels; Background brief pour la visite à Paris de Gaston Thorn. Projet de loi français de nationalisation, 30 September 1981, BAC 83/1984 92, HAEC, Brussels.
96 Visite à Paris du 9 octobre 1981. Background brief. Non-Observation by the French Government of its Obligations to Notify State Aids, 8 October 1981, BAC 83/1984 92 (92), HAEC, Brussels.
97 Bulletin of the European Communities. Commission, 12 1981, point 2.1.43, 34.
98 Commission of the European Communities, Eleventh Report on Competition Policy, 1981, 125.
99 Cfr. Article 5 of Decision 2320/81/ECSC of the European Commission, of 7 August 1981, Instituting Community rules for the aids to the steel sector.
100 Schmidt, *From State to Market?* 94.
101 Jack Hayward, "The Nemesis of Industrial Patriotism: The French Response to the Steel Crisis," in Yves Meny and Vincent Wright (eds.), *The Politics of Steel. Western Europe and the Steel Industry in the Crisis Years (1974–1984)* (Berlin: de Gruyter, 1986), 529; Smith, *The Left's Dirty Job*, 162.
102 Alexis B. Moraitis, "Transnational Depoliticisation and Industrial Policy: The European Commission and French Steel (1980–1984)," *New Political Economy* 25, 4 (2020): 562.
103 Camdessus, *Les interventions financières des Etats*, 99.
104 *Ibid.*, 99.
105 *Ibid.*, 100–101.
106 Smith, *The Left's Dirty Job*, 163.
107 Moraitis, "Transnational Depoliticisation and Industrial Policy," 562.
108 *Ibid.*, 562.
109 Frédéric Lordon, "The Logic and Limits of *Désinflation Compétitive*," in Andrew Glyn (ed.), *Social Democracy in Neoliberal Times: The Left and Economic Policy Since 1980* (Oxford: Oxford University Press, 2001), 116; Georges Saunier, "Le

gouvernement français et les enjeux économiques européens à l'heure de la rigueur 1981–1984," in *Comité pour l'histoire économique et financière de la France, Milieux économiques et intégration européenne au XXe siècle. La relance des années quatre-vingt (1979–1992)* (Paris: Institut de la gestion et du développement économique, 2007).

110 Schmidt, *From State to Market?* 127.

111 Commissariat Général du Plan, *Quelle Stratégie Européenne Pour la France dans les Années 80?* (Paris: Documentation française, 1983).

112 Raggi, "François Mitterrand et la sidérurgie française," 243.

113 Smith, *The Left's Dirty Job*, 166.

114 Roberto Mesa, *Democracia y política exterior en España* (Madrid: EUDESA, 1988), 68.

115 Rapport intérimaire de la Commission au Conseil au sujet de l'élargissement: mesures internes dans les deux pays candidats dans des secteurs particulièrement sensibles, 1 March 1983, COM(83) 115 final, HAEC, Brussels.

116 José Manuel Mateu de Ros and Miguel Valle Garagorri, "Algunas ideas en torno a la crisis siderúrgica," *Papeles de economía española* 4 (1980): 135.

117 *Ibid.*

118 Mikel Navarro Arancegui, "La política de reconversión en España: El caso de la siderurgia," PhD thesis, Deusto University, 1988, 134.

119 Note by Inger Nielsen, Head of the Delegation for the Enlargement Negotiations. Pre-accession disciplines in candidate countries, 29 April 1983, BAC 147 1991 89, HAEC, Brussels.

120 Carlos Solchaga Catalán, "La nueva política industrial española," *Economía Industrial* 229 (January–February 1983): 43.

121 Tom Gallagher and Alan M. Williams, *Southern European Socialism: Parties, Elections and the Challenge of Government* (Manchester: Manchester University Press, 1989), 199.

122 Arancegui, "La política de reconversión en España," 140.

123 *Ibid.*, 141.

124 *Ibid.*, 542.

125 *Ibid.*, 551.

126 *Ibid.*, 562.

127 Pablo Díaz Morlán, Antonio Escudero and Miguel Ángel Sáez García, "El desmantelamiento de la siderurgia integral del Mediterráneo español (1977–1984)," *Revista de Historia Industrial* 38 (2008): 178.

128 *Ibid.*, 178.

129 *Ibid.*, 179.

130 *Ibid.*, 174.

131 Declaration of the Spanish delegation concerning the ECSC chapter, CM5 ADH3 19.1, 18 October 1983, Archives of the Council of the European Union, Brussels.

132 *Ibid.*

133 Négociations d'adhésion avec l'Espagne. Chapitre CECA. Mesures transitoires dans le cadre de l'adhésion pour la sidérurgie espagnole, 7 September 1984, CM5 ADH3 65.38, Archives of the Council of the European Union, Brussels.

134 *Ibid.*

135 Letter from Carlos Solchaga to Etienne Davignon, 17 September 1984, Box 538, Archives of the INI, Madrid.

136 Note sur la restructuration de la sidérurgie espagnole: Mandat exploratoire à donner à la Commission, 29 October 1984, CM5 ADH3 29.10, Archives of the Council of the European Union, Brussels.

137 Matias Rodríguez Inciarte, "El acto de adhesión de España," *Papeles de Economía Española* 25 (1985): 34.

138 Georges Saunier, "Le gouvernement français et les enjeux économiques européens à l'heure de la rigueur 1981–1984"; Kevin Featherstone, *Socialist Parties and European Integration: A Comparative History* (Manchester: Manchester University Press, 1988).

Bibliography

Andrade Blanco, Juan Antonio. "Renuncias y abandonos en la evolución ideológica durante la transición a la democracia: una propuesta para el estudio del IX Congreso del PCE y el congreso extraordinario del PSOE." *Historia Actual Online* 8 (2005): 43–50.

Berntzen, Einar. "Democratic Socialism in Spain, Portugal and Greece." In *Social Democracy in Transition: Northern, Southern and Eastern Europe* edited by Lauri Karvonen and Jan Sundberg. Dartmouth: Aldershot, 1991, 219–242.

Bussière, Eric. "Devising a Strategy: The Internal Market and Industrial Policy." In *The European Commission. History and Memories of an Institution* edited by Eric Bussière et al. Luxembourg: Publications Office of the European Union, 2014, 263–276.

Camdessus, Christine. *Les interventions financières des Etats en faveur de la sidérurgie dans la C.E.C.A.: l'exemple français*. Paris: Presses Universitaires de France, 1987.

Commissariat Général du Plan. *Quelle Stratégie Européenne Pour la France dans les Années 80*? Paris: Documentation française, 1983.

Díaz Morlán, Pablo, Antonio Escudero and Miguel Ángel Sáez García. "El desmantelamiento de la siderurgia integral del Mediterráneo español (1977–1984)." *Revista de Historia Industrial* 38 (2008): 161–188.

Dyson, Kenneth and Stephen Wilks. *Industrial Crisis. A Comparative Study of the State and Industry*. Oxford: Martin Robertson, 1983.

Featherstone, Kevin. *Socialist Parties and European Integration: A Comparative History*. Manchester: Manchester University Press, 1988.

Ferguson, Niall et al. (ed.). *The Shock of the Global. The 1970s in Perspective*. Cambridge: Belknap Press, 2011.

Fulla, Matthieu. *Les socialistes français et l'économie (1944–1981). Une histoire économique du politique*. Paris: Les Presses Sciences Po, 2016.

Gallagher, Tom and Alan M. Williams. *Southern European Socialism: Parties, Elections and the Challenge of Government*. Manchester: Manchester University Press, 1989.

Gálvez Biesca, Sergio. "Modernización socialista y reforma laboral (1982–1992)." PhD thesis, Complutense University of Madrid, 2012.

García Santesmases, Antonio. "Evolución ideológica del socialismo en la España actual." *Sistema: Revista de ciencias sociales* 68–69 (1985): 61–78.

Gillespie, Richard. *The Spanish Socialist Party. A History of Factionalism*. Oxford: Clarendon Press, 1989.

Glyn, Andrew. *Social Democracy in Neoliberal Times. The Left and Economic Policy Since 1980*. Oxford: Oxford University Press, 2001.

Hayward, Jack. "The Nemesis of Industrial Patriotism: The French Response to the Steel Crisis." In *The Politics of Steel. Western Europe and the Steel Industry in the Crisis Years (1974–1984)* edited by Yves Meny and Vincent Wright. Berlin: de Gruyter, 1986.

Juliá Díaz, Santos. *Los socialistas en la política española 1879–1982*. Madrid: Taurus, 1996.

Käseberg, Thorsten and Arthe Van Laer. "Competition Law and Industrial Policy. Conflict, Adaptation and Complementarity." In *The Historical Foundations of EU Competition Law* edited by Kiran Klaus Patel and Heike Schweitzer. Oxford: Oxford University Press, 2013, 162–190.

Lordon, Frédéric. "The Logic and Limitis of *Désinflation Compétitive*." In *Social Democracy in Neoliberal Times* edited by Andrew Glyn. Oxford: Oxford University Press, 2001, 110–137.

Mateu de Ros, José Manuel and Miguel Valle Garagorri. "Algunas ideas en torno a la crisis siderúrgica." *Papeles de economía española* 4 (1980): 135–151.

Mesa, Roberto. *Democracia y política exterior en España*. Madrid: EUDESA, 1988.

Moraitis, Alexis B. "Transnational Depoliticisation and Industrial Policy: The European Commission and French Steel (1980–1984)." *New Political Economy* 25, 4 (2020): 552–571.

Navarro Arancegui, Mikel. "La política de reconversión en España: El caso de la siderurgia." PhD thesis, Deusto University, Bilbao, 1988.

Parti communiste et Parti socialiste français. *Programme commun de gouvernement du parti communiste et du parti socialiste*. Paris: Flammarion, 1972.

Pinder, John. "Altiero Spinelli's European Federal Odyssey." *The International Spectator* 42, 4 (2007): 571–588.

PSOE. *Por el cambio. Programa electoral*. Madrid: PSOE, 1982.

Raggi, Pascal. "François Mitterrand et la sidérurgie française." *Annales de l'Est* 1 (2018): 235–254.

Rodríguez Inciarte, Matías. "El acto de adhesión de España." *Papeles de Economía Española* 25 (1985): 28–44.

Salm, Christian. *Transnational Socialist Networks in the 1970s. European Community Development Aid and Southern Enlargement*. Basingstoke: Palgrave Macmillan, 2016.

Saunier, Georges. "Le gouvernement français et les enjeux économiques européens à l'heure de la rigueur 1981–1984." In *Milieux économiques et intégration européenne au XXe siècle. La relance des années quatre-vingt (1979–1992)*. Paris: Institut de la gestion et du développement économique, 2007, 106–146.

Schlieder, Willy. "Politique européenne de concurrence et crise." *Feduci, Séminaire de la Commission droit et vie des affaires de l'Université de Liège*. Paris: Editions du Moniteur, 1980, 65–68.

Schmidt, Vivian. *From State to Market? The Transformation of French Business and Government*. Cambridge: Cambridge University Press, 1996.

Shaw, Richard and Susan Shaw. "Excess Capacity and Rationalisation in the West European Synthetic Fibre Industry." *The Journal of Industrial Economics* 32, 2 (December 1983): 149–166.

Smith, Rand. *The Left's Dirty Job. The Politics of Industrial Restructuring in France and Spain*. Pittsburgh: University of Pittsburgh University Press, 1998.

Solchaga Catalán, Carlos. La nueva política industrial española. *Economía Industrial*, 229 (January-February 1983): 43–63.

Spinelli, Altiero. *Diario Europeo. 1970/1976*. Bologna: Il Mulino, 1991.

Tilly, Pierre. "Regional Policy: A Tangible Expression of European Solidarity." In *The European Commission. History and memories of an institution, 1973–1986* edited by Eric Bussière et al. Luxembourg: Publications Office of the European Union, 2014, 337–350.

Tsoukalis, Loukas and Robert Strauss. "Community Policies on Steel 1974–1982: A Case of Collective Management." In *Politics of Steel. Western Europe and the Steel Industry in the Crisis Years (1974–1984)* edited by Yves Meny and Vincent Wright. Berlin: de Gruyter, 1986, 186–221.

Van Laer, Arthe. "The European Lilliputians Attacking IBM: Balancing Innovation and Competition in the European Commission's First Big Antitrust Case (1973–1984)." *Business History* 62, 5 (2018): 837–857.

Warlouzet, Laurent. "Europe de la concurrence et politique industrielle communautaire. La naissance d'une opposition au sein de la CEE dans les années 60." *Histoire, économie & société* 1 (2008): 47–61.

Warlouzet, Laurent. *Governing Europe in a Globalizing World. Neoliberalism and its Alternatives following the 1973 Oil Crisis*. Abingdon-on-Thames: Routledge, 2018.

Warlouzet, Laurent. "When Germany Accepted a European Industrial Policy: Managing the Decline of Steel from 1977 to 1984." *Jahrbuch für Wirtschaftsgeschichte* 58, 1 (2017): 137–162.

10 The impossible social-democratic European competition policy, 1985–2000

Laurent Warlouzet

Introduction

European Economic Community/European Union (EEC/EU) competition policy became much stronger from 1985 onward. It benefited from various factors, from the rise of neoliberal ideas to the discredit of previous dirigiste policies.[1] During these decades, many social-democratic leaders played instrumental roles in implementing European economic policies. Thanks to newly available sources dealing with the period ranging from 1985 to 2000, this contribution will examine the contribution of social-democratic leaders within EEC/EU institutions to the evolution of competition policy. It argues that strong divisions existed first among the European commissioners, and second among the social democrats in the European Commission about the future of competition policy. Even the most powerful EEC/EU social-democratic leader, Jacques Delors, who presided over the Commission between 1985 and 1995,[2] struggled to impose his vision, and to contain the neoliberal drift of competition policy.

To unveil the intensity of this debate, this contribution will make use of the typology of economic policies to ease comparison. Such a typology is especially useful in the case of competition policy, sometimes presented by its supporters as a rather consensual technical area, whereas it has rather been a battlefield for opposed economic programs. More specifically, I contend that the analysis of European public policy in a comparative perspective requires recourse to a threefold typology, which I elaborated in *Governing Europe in a Globalizing World* for the years ranging from 1973 to 1986.[3] Each public policy can be associated with any of these three categories: socially oriented policies aim at reducing inequalities and protecting the weakest, neomercantilist ones prioritize support for national industries, and market-oriented ones promote the adoption of free-market mechanisms. Neoliberal policies are considered a radical version of the last category, when market-oriented measures triggered a significant retreat of the welfare state. This threefold typology is especially suited to competition policy: a socially oriented competition policy would aim at reducing inflation and limiting the power of powerful economic actors, whereas a neomercantilist one would protect national industries by tolerating state aids, cartels or monopolies, or by attacking foreign companies. A market-oriented competition policy would be associated with the exclusive promotion of

DOI: 10.4324/9781351010573-10

free-market rules, whereas its neoliberal variant would especially target welfare state measures such as state aids or privileges given to companies deemed of public interest. Crucially, a market-oriented philosophy would establish competition policy as a major field, independent from other economic domains, with its own yardstick of pure and perfect competition. Even if these categories were not used by contemporary actors, they are useful heuristic tools to establish a precise comparison across different states and decades.

This typology is especially useful to differentiate two groups among center-left EEC/EU leaders working in the European Commission from 1985 to 2000. On the one hand, Delors, supported by many of his fellow center-left commissioners, defended a comprehensive vision of competition policy, that synthesized socially oriented, neomercantilist and market-oriented visions. On the other hand, other social-democratic leaders in the 1990s did not share such misgivings. European commissioner Karel van Miert and director general Claus-Dieter Ehlermann, both social democrats, defended a reformed market-oriented competition policy. As a matter of fact, this was not a complete novelty, since in the 1970s two social democrats, commissioner Raymond Vouel and director general Willy Schlieder, struggled to promote a market-oriented competition policy, but they were defeated by the mighty neomercantilist commissioner Etienne Davignon.[4]

In terms of actors, this contribution is concentrated on the European Commission as it is the main actor charged with the implementation of EEC/EU competition policy rules, though mentions are also made of the European Parliament (EP) and the influence of member-states when it is helpful to understand the EEC/EU decision-making process.

Based on the exploitation of national and European archives, both written and oral, this contribution will examine the Delors period, when the president of the Commission strived both to strengthen competition policy and to resist its neoliberal drift, before moving to the 1990s, when van Miert and Ehlermann participated in the reform toward a mature market-oriented policy.

Delors: promoting competition policy and resisting the neoliberal drift

Under the chairmanship of Jacques Delors, competition policy became one of the flagship policies of the EEC/EU. On the one hand, the Commission managed to solve its old problem of backlog in the cartel area, and it became more assertive in the monitoring of state aids. On the other hand, it enlarged its scope to new fields such as the control of concentrations, thanks to the 1989 merger regulation,[5] and the liberalization of air transport[6] and of telecommunications.[7] This evolution was supported by a context favorable to market-oriented ideas. Market regulation through competition policy rules replaced direct state management of the markets through price policy and industrial policy in the 1980s, both at the European level and in many Western European countries, as Susanna Fellman shows in her chapter on Finland, for instance.[8] The Single Market program encapsulated in the 1986

Single Act also supported this dynamic, but it contains hardly any mentions of competition policy.

Therefore, it is argued that this favorable context was not sufficient in itself for the development of a strong competition policy at the EEC level. Another major, if often neglected factor, was the role played by the more assertive commissioners for competition, first Frans Andriessen (1981–85), and then within the Delors Commission, Peter Sutherland (1985–89) and Leon Brittan (1989–93). All of them were bolder than their predecessor Raymond Vouel, and belonged to center-right and right political parties. Andriessen and Sutherland belonged to political movements close to the Christian Democrats, whereas Brittan was a Tory and a hardcore Thatcherite.

In the mid-1980s, the development of EEC/EU competition policy took a neoliberal turn. Sutherland and Brittan changed the emphasis of the Commission from cartelbusting toward curtailing certain state interventions, such as state aids or the organization of certain sectors as monopolies or oligopolies protected by public law. Some of these economic interventions could be considered part of the welfare state in some countries, since they played a major role in terms of social, industrial and regional policies. Therefore, it is argued that "competition policy became in the 1980s the first neoliberal policy waged by the European Communities."[9] This neoliberal drift was especially acute under Brittan, who was an ideologue crusading for the righteousness of free markets against any state interventions.[10]

Jacques Delors had supported the strengthening of EEC/EU competition policy but not a neoliberal turn. The President of the Commission belonged to the French Catholic trade-union Confédération Française des travailleurs chrétiens (CFTC). A former civil servant in the Bank of France, he was responsible for social affairs in the French planning authority, before becoming the advisor for social affairs for the moderate Gaullist Prime minister Jacques Chaban-Delmas. He then joined the French Socialist Party (PS) and held his first political mandate in 1979 as A member of the EP, before becoming the minister of Economics and Finance of French socialist President François Mitterrand, in the government led by Pierre Mauroy from 1981 to 1984.[11]

Before becoming president of the European Commission in 1985, Delors had manifested a keen interest in the development of European competition policy. In 1976, Delors took part in the work leading to the so-called Maldague report entitled Problems of Inflation.[12] He cowrote large parts of the reports with two other economic experts, the British labourite Stuart Holland and the Italian academic Franco Archibugi. They published their reflections extensively in a book issued in 1978, which advocated for European planning.[13] It called "for action at national and Community levels to deal with the behaviour of meso-economic firms, in the structure of supply of goods and services, the formation of prices, in employment and in capital markets, where they now occupy a dominant position," for the setting up of "a committee of representatives of employer's organizations and trade unions . . . to advise the Commission's Directorate General for Competition on restrictive practices and further ways of containing multinational firms more effectively," and for "obliging exclusive distributors to make available their price lists and other conditions of sale for inclusion in a public register. Participation in an unauthorized restrictive price agreement should also be classified and penalized as an offence."[14] In other words, Delors and his two coauthors called for the strengthening of national and EEC competition policy in order to control "restrictive practices," which are covered by Article 85 EEC, and "dominant positions," which are dealt with in Article 86 EEC. They developed a socially oriented vision of competition policy, the main targets of which should be large companies, rather than state practices.

Delors' action to promote competition policy was also visible at the French level. As soon as 1981, he requested notes on German competition policy, which was considered a reference within the EEC.[15] Notwithstanding the opposition of part of the French civil service, he promoted reforms designed to strengthen French competition policy in 1982–1983.[16] In 1984, when he met the commissioner for competition Frans Andriessen, he requested a note from the Commission on the EEC debates on merger control, since he wanted to reform the French system of monitoring concentrations.[17]

Beyond Delors, many French socialists had defended the need to strengthen competition policy to curb the excessive powers of some private companies. Of course, the appellation "competition policy" was not always used, but the idea remained the same. As soon as 1925, the trade-unionist Léon Jouhaux and several officials from the International Labour Organization (ILO) were requesting an international control of cartels.[18] In 1946, when he came back from the United States, socialist leader and French head of government Léon Blum expressed his admiration for the antitrust policy which reduced the margins of private companies.[19] In 1952, several French socialists requested a more severe repression of illegal agreements between companies (called "ententes") in France, as also discussed in Brian Shaev's chapter, while socialist leader Guy Mollet demanded an efficient antitrust policy within the first European Community, the European Coal and Steel Community.[20] Later on, in 1965, Mollet made the same request for the EEC; otherwise, "trusts and cartels" would take control of the Common Market.[21] In 1988–1989, the French socialist governments of Michel Rocard and Pierre Bérégovoy supported the adoption of the EEC regulation to control concentrations, despite internal doubts among French officials that this might hinder industrial politics.[22] Eventually, the regulation was adopted in December 1989 when France held the rotating presidency of the Council, and after much pressure exerted by Paris on its partners to reach a compromise.

Beyond France, this social-democratic inclination to defend competition policy existed among many European leaders in the late 1970s and early 1980s. In 1977, the European Trade Union Confederation (ETUC) estimated that "[i]nflation should be controlled through stronger rules governing competition and through an active price policy and not through the lowering of overall demand."[23] Strikingly, competition policy was used as an argument against macro-economic austerity. In 1980, the ETUC renewed its claims to use competition policy to fight against inflation.[24] In 1982, the ETUC's call to strengthen competition policy was also linked to the whole debate over the democratization of large companies through the so-called Vredeling directive.[25] The ETUC argued that it was necessary to develop an EEC merger control, probably in order to increase the Community's leverage on large companies.[26] This concern was visible within the EP's Socialist Group too. In 1984, an internal report estimated that it was urgent to support the Commission "which must obtain the necessary resources actively to pursue the goal of competition policy," and that "bigger firms, in particular multinationals, should be prohibited from acquiring a dominant position on the market."[27] The same linkage between competition policy and the control of large companies was repeated in 1985.[28] The socialists clarified that they were not in favor of competition as a goal in itself. They rather wanted to promote competition policy in order to control large undertakings.

As a president of the European Commission, Jacques Delors supported the development of EEC competition policy in a general manner. In his programmatic speech of January 1985, he underlined the necessity to get rid of "the obstacles to healthy competition."[29] He stated that "competition can kill competition if the market does not permit fair contest between the different rivals," so it was necessary to harmonize national laws to a certain extent. Similarly, he called for a common industrial policy "instead of the costly and ineffective escalation of national aids and incentives." To sum up, Delors promoted free competition through a mixture of various instruments. He was in favor of state aid control, but not in order to eliminate any form of direct support for industry, as the neoliberals wanted. His aim was rather to improve industrial policies by Europeanizing them.

Another hint of Delors' general commitment to support the development of EEC competition policy is given by the famous White Paper "Completing the Internal Market" of 1985.[30] It was drafted under the responsibility of the British commissioner Arthur Cockfield and of the director general for the Internal Market Fernand Braun. This document was strongly backed by Delors, who, moreover, was close to Braun.[31] The White Paper contains at the end a paragraph asserting that

> a strong competition policy will play a fundamental role in maintaining and strengthening the internal market. . . . As the Community moves to complete the Internal Market, it will be necessary to ensure that anti-competitive practices do not engender new forms of local protectionism which could only lead to re-partitioning of the market.

However, beyond this general idea, the White Paper did not elaborate on the specific legal instruments to use, except in the field of state aid:

> As the physical and technical barriers inside the Community are removed, the Commission will see to it that a rigorous policy is pursued in regard to state aids so that public resources are not used to confer artificial advantage to some firms over others; An effective Community discipline will make it possible to ensure that available resources are directed away from non-viable activities toward competitive and job creating industries in the future.

But here too, the only precise recommendation was the necessity to carry out a state aid inventory. The Single Act Treaty transformed the White Paper into a binding treaty, but it ignored competition policy. The articles of the Rome Treaty dealing with this domain were not affected. Competition policy was mentioned only in relationship to other policies (such as cohesion policy in Article 130f-3). As a result, the rise of EEC/EU competition policy did not derive from a mechanical interpretation of the Single Act, but rather from the activism of commissioners Sutherland and Brittan.

As a French socialist, Delors was disturbed by the neoliberal tendencies of Commissioners in charge of EEC competition policy. This was true already under Sutherland. In recent testimonies, both Delors and Sutherland estimated that they got along well since they both shared an ambitious agenda for European integration, but they also recognized that specific conflicts had occurred over state aid.[32] One such instance concerned Boussac, the largest textile firm in France. The Commission targeted a huge state aid of circa FF 1 billion to the company, so the case was very sensitive. In 1985, Sutherland took over the procedure against the state aid granted to Boussac, which was launched by Andriessen in late 1984.[33] French officials argued that this mighty company was on the verge of bankruptcy. The aid was justified to avoid massive layoffs in regions of Northern and Eastern France crippled by the industrial crisis. Sutherland underlined that since Boussac was an exporting firm, and since the subsidies were granted without a matching restructuring plan, the aid was illegal.[34] The Irish commissioner was also motivated by the clumsiness of French officials, who blatantly ignored EEC rules on state aids and who were unwilling to disclose information.[35] Within the Commission, he proposed to request a massive repayment of FF 999 million by the company. This triggered a hostile reaction from François Lamoureux, a prominent member of Delors' cabinet and former member of the legal service of the European Commission, who estimated that there was an "unprecedented disagreement" within the Commission over it.[36] Lamoureux was a staunch socialist, who later became deputy head of Edith Cresson's cabinet, when she was the French prime minister of the socialist government (1991–2). Two issues sparked controversy within the Commission. First, many Commission officials contested DG IV's calculus of the illegal aid. DG III, following a neomercantilist reasoning, insisted on the need to take into account the intensity of Boussac's restructuring and the problem of international competition.[37] Second, the Irish commissioner contested evidence provided by a national government, an accusation that was extremely controversial from a political point of view. In the end, Sutherland secured the Commission's support to sanction the French government but he had to negotiate with it.[38] He settled for a compromise of FF 338 million.[39]

Sutherland bothered other social-democratic commissioners. This demonstrated that Sutherland's zeal in attacking national industrial policies was considered an affront to national welfare states in many countries, and that this was not just a matter of Jacques Delors being preoccupied by the French case. As a matter of fact, the Italian socialist Carlo Ripa di Meana accused Sutherland of being "too repressive towards European industry."[40] In July 1986, when the college of commissioners discussed Sutherland's draft directive aimed at imposing a more severe control of state aid to shipbuilding, he faced opposition from multiple commissioners, who all belonged to the center-left (with the exception of Christian democrat Lorenzo Natali): the Spanish socialist Manuel Marin (social affairs), the Italian socialist Carlo Ripa di Meana (institutions and culture), the Greek socialist Grigori Varfis (regional policy) and the British Labourite Stanley Clinton-Davies (transport).[41] All of them asserted that competition policy should also take into account social and neomercantilist aims.

The conflict between Delors and the neoliberal inflexions of EEC competition policy was also visible during his second mandate as president of the Commission when the competition portfolio was under Leon Brittan. The most famous conflict occurred in 1991 when Brittan decided to ban the merger between ATR and De Havilland, two aircraft companies.[42] The case was sensitive for a variety of reasons: from the institutional point of view, it was the first time that the Commission used its power to ban a concentration between companies since the merger regulation had been only recently adopted in late 1989. From the economic point of view, the merger made sense since other competitors of similar size existed in Europe, notably British Aerospace and Fokker notably, as well as others outside Europe. From the political point of view, this operation was hailed for symbolizing an EEC industrial policy in high technology aimed at creating European champions able to compete with the mightier US firms. Indeed, it was the Franco-Italian firm ATR, itself an example of European industrial cooperation, which bought its Canadian competitor De Havilland. However, Brittan opposed it on competition grounds: he adopted a narrow definition of the relevant market in order to demonstrate that the new companies would have a dominant position.[43] This decision was contested within the Commission, and it triggered reservations even within DG competition.[44] Delors supported the operation but he lost the vote within the college of commissioners, in which a coalition of mostly center-right commissioners prevailed.[45] Delors abstained when he realized that he would lose the vote, but he was clearly favoring the operation, which fitted well with his strong support for a neomercantilist EEC industrial policy in high technology.[46]

To conclude, while Delors was generally supportive of the strengthening of EEC policies in general, and of EEC competition policy in particular, he opposed the neoliberal drifts of Sutherland and Brittan, sometimes with the support of other social-democratic commissioners.

Van Miert and Ehlerman: modernizing competition policy

In the 1990s, the influence of EU competition policy continued to flourish. During this decade, two social democrats played major roles in shaping this policy, Claus-Dieter Ehlermann who was director general from 1990 to 1995, and Karel van Miert who was commissioner from 1993 to 1999. Both of them supported a strong and market-oriented EU competition policy, while at the same time launching the so-called modernization of competition policy.

The "modernization" process designates a series of reform, which completely overhauled EU competition policy in the first years of the 21st century.[47] It contains a procedural element, with the replacement of the ban by the abuse system concerning cartels, and a substantive element, with a growing use of economic thinking in order to complement the more legally driven approach.

Claus-Dieter Ehlermann had long been a prominent actor in the development of EEC/EU law in general, and of EEC/EU competition law in particular. Born in 1931, he studied law in Germany, but also in France and in the United States. From 1959 to 1961, he was the assistant to Hans Kutscher, a judge at the German constitutional tribunal. A social democrat, Kutscher later became a judge at the ECJ. Ehlermann was a social democrat too, who strived to promote Willy Brandt's European ideas.[48] Right after his stint with Kutscher, Ehlermann joined the European Commission's legal service. He became director general of the legal service from 1977 to 1987, before moving to the position of spokesperson for Delors, and finally director general for competition from 1990 to 1995. He was described by his colleagues as a mastermind of all the legal intricacies of EU law. For example, John Temple-Lang, himself a former competition lawyer from the legal service and DG IV asserted that:

> Claus Ehlermann was the most actively involved in the details, he was incredibly hard working and he liked to be absolutely in charge, as far as it was possible, of every case that came up for discussion at the Commission.[49]

Typically, Ehlermann ended his career by becoming law professor at the European University Institute in Florence, as well as the European expert for the World Trade Organization (WTO) Dispute Settlement Appellate Body.

As a director general of competition, Ehlermann's actions were not tainted by his social-democratic background according to his own testimony and to the retrospective analysis of his activities. His priority was the smooth implementation of the merger regulation adopted in 1989, which represented a huge challenge since it forced the Commission to decide quickly on complex and sensitive operations.[50] He also resumed the long-term tasks of his predecessors, namely streamlining cartel-busting by solving the backlog issue, reinforcing state-aid control, and liberalizing sectors previously shielded from competition, in particular telecommunications and air transport, but also energy and postal services.

Just before leaving the Commission, Ehlermann launched the so-called modernization process. On 5 January 1995, he sent a note to all his directors requesting a large debate on the future of EU competition policy. It should be informed by the imperative to tackle both old challenges, such as the backlog of cartel cases which was still looming, and new ones, such as the perspective of a massive enlargement to Central and Eastern European countries. According to him, "DG IV has to concentrate on what is essential and has to be done at the level of the EU. All the rest must either be left to member states or simply be neglected."[51] Most important for him was for the DG, and hence for the European Commission, to keep its intellectual leadership in competition policy matters. This was crucial in 1995, at a time when all EU member states now had functional competition policy authorities, whereas before the 1980s, most European states did not have any genuine interest in this field. This represented both an opportunity, as DG IV was then able to delegate more powers to these new actors to implement the Treaty of Rome, and a challenge, since those national institutions could potentially contradict the Commission's orientations. In addition, the Commission's monopoly to interpret and implement EU rules (bar the appeal to the European Court of Justice, ECJ) was put into jeopardy by the perennial debate over the creation of an independent "European cartel authority." This project was regularly put forward by many German experts, who considered the Commission too political a body to be entrusted with such a regulatory policy. Ehlermann himself discussed this development in an academic article.[52] This new body would likely have been modeled on the German Bundeskartellamt. The aim would have been to sever the link between the technical inquiry made by civil servants, and the political decisions of the College of commissioners.

The main point for Ehlermann was that DG IV should become more proactive. He recognized that the system set up by Regulation 17/62 "is the area of most of the external criticism and of profound internal frustration (cf. high number of pending cases, length of procedures, low number of formal decisions). At the same time, it occupies most of DG IV's staff (almost four directorates out of six)" meaning that most of the DG IV's energy was concentrated on treating self-declared agreements, instead of launching investigations to uncover hidden cartels, which are usually much more detrimental to free competition. However, Ehlermann considered that "the exemption monopoly of the Commission under art 85–3 should only be abandoned as a matter of last resort." He did not want to shed the institutional framework of Regulation 17/62, which was adopted under German influence in 1962. Instead, he preferred to improve it by an even greater recourse to block exemptions and by improving the economic analysis of DG IV. Ehlermann's brainstorming was also engineered by the perspective of ongoing negotiations for what became the Treaty of Amsterdam. The director general anticipated possible criticisms of EU competition policy. He envisaged potentially radical reforms:

> If this defense proved impossible, the Commission might, as a weapon of last resort, propose to amend Reg. 17/62 and allow article 85 para 3 to be applied in certain situations also by national courts and administrations. Such situations might be restrictions of competition which are formed in vertical relationships, like distribution agreements.

It is probable that Ehlermann considered horizontal agreements, like price cartels, to be more detrimental to competition and more complex to handle than distribution agreements, on which a large jurisprudence had existed since the 1960s. Other important officials in DG IV, such as Philip Lowe (the director of the "merger task force" from 1993 to 1995) or John Temple-Lang (the director of one of the cartel division from 1988 to 1995, and then telecommunications-media director from 1995 to 2000), wanted to drastically reform the system of Regulation 17/62.[53]

Commissioner Karel Van Miert continued this dual policy of both asserting a bold market-oriented competition policy on the one hand and modernizing it on the other hand. Van Miert was a prominent Belgian socialist as he chaired the Flemish Socialist Party (SP) after the confederal split of the Belgian Socialist Party (PSB) in 1978. After ten years as a member of the EP, he became commissioner for transport and consumer protection in the Delors II Commission in 1989. Then he occupied the function of competition commissioner from 1993 to 1999, in the Delors III Commission (1993–1995), and the Santer commission until 1999, with Claus-Dieter Ehlermann as director general until 1995, followed by another German, Alexander Schaub, who remained in this position until 2002.

In various testimonies, Van Miert appeared committed to implementing a market-oriented competition policy in a pragmatic manner, in contrast to the doctrinal neoliberalism of Brittan. This is what he asserted in his memoirs.[54] When he took up this position, Delors gave him the following roadmap: "I would like you to restore the credibility of competition policy' Delors told me. He therefore entrusted me will a precise mission: that I attack competition [policy] in a more pragmatic manner."[55] Later on in the book, Van Miert confirmed his compliance with the pro-market credo: "Of course, there remained much to do, for example in the matters of the liberalization of postal services, the modernization of railroads, the integration of financial services or even labor market flexibility."[56]

This vision is confirmed by the testimonies of his former collaborators. According to Director General Ehlermann:

> He [van Miert] was a socialist and he was used by Delors to defend his ideas against Leon Brittan [when van Miert was commissioner for transportation]. In the battles within the commission and between chiefs of staff, Jacques Delors often asked Pascal Lamy to do the dirty work of battling against the proposals of Leon Brittan. . . . What was truly surprising, shocking, was that we were all afraid because competition seemed at heart a devil to Karl van Miert that must be mastered, put in a corner. However, in the end Karel van Miert went through a total conversion. He became in my view from that point, I do not want to speak of his successors, the best or one of the best defenders of competition policy because a socialist who converts into a liberal is much better than a liberal who veers to the right like Martin Bangemann for example. Martin Bangemann was a German liberal but was practically a spokesperson for industry. What mattered as it concerns Karel van Miert, by contrast, were consumers, small and medium-sized companies. . . . He had nothing against large companies, he was just defender of the rules as they had been presented to him and he was a man of good sense.[57]

This view is confirmed by archival records from 1991, which demonstrate that Van Miert was opposed to Brittan's severe stance concerning state-aid control:

> DG IV continues to consult member-state experts on the project to allow the Commission to regulate aids by notifying balance sheets, loans, guarantees,

> profits, sales of companies to verify whether a public enterprise has the behavior of a private operator. Mr. Van Miert was disconcerted by the project. [M. Van Miert s'est ému de ce projet.][58]

DG IV wanted to increase its control of state-owned companies. As a commissioner for transport of Belgian origin, Van Miert was especially concerned by the fate of the Belgian flag-carrier Sabena. In 1990, when Brittan examined the possibility of prosecuting Sabena for abuse of dominant position, Van Miert vigorously defended it by underlining the necessity of taking into account not only competition policy rules but also EEC transport policy as a whole (that is to say neomercantilist and social concerns).[59]

When Van Miert became commissioner for competition in 1995 however, he fully defended his new policy. Van Miert's special advisor, the Belgian Jean Dubois, confirmed this impression:

> Here was a very left-wing socialist politician who became commissioner of competition after having been commissioner of transportation. He applied the rules of competition in an absolutely rigorous and impartial manner and he intervened energetically in the domain of state aids.[60]

Anne Houtman, a Belgian chief of unit, concurred with this assessment. She estimated that the style changed a lot between the cold and intellectual Leon Brittan, and the more diplomatic Karel van Miert, but that the substance remained the same.[61]

To sum up, Van Miert is presented as an efficient and pragmatic rule-enforcer, whose socialist background prevented him from leading a neoliberal crusade like Brittan, and from indulging in neomercantilist support for big business. As a matter of fact, the strengthening of market-oriented EU competition policy continued unabated in the 1990s, with three main areas of focus: the modernization of cartel enforcement, the regulation of service of general interest and the internationalization of competition law.

The "modernization" of EU competition policy took shape under Karel van Miert, even though the final decision was adopted under his successor Mario Monti. The Belgian commissioner promoted it through a 1997 Green paper and then a 1999 White Paper.[62] Van Miert also launched a comprehensive study on the notion of "relevant market" since this notion was at the heart of merger cases.[63] This work paved the way for Regulation 1/2003, which completely overhauled the system of cartel-busting. The notification procedure invented by Regulation 17/62 and the monopoly of the Commission over the interpretation of Article 85-3 EEC were abolished. National authorities were empowered as they became the first enforcers of competition rules, but they were encompassed in a European Competition Network (ECN) dominated by the Commission.

In parallel, Van Miert secured the adoption of the leniency directive in 1996.[64] Inspired by the US experience, this piece of legislation allows the first whistleblower of an illegal cartel to be cleared from any sanctions (or at least its sanction can be reduced). This reform was crucial since it rendered the notification system almost useless since the Commission gained a steady flow of information through denunciation. In parallel, fines increased.[65] This cannot be considered neoliberal since it reinforced the repression of private companies' illegal behavior to the benefit of the public purse, since more money flowed into the EU coffers.

The third and last branch of the modernization process was the "more economic approach."[66] EEC/EU competition policy had been accused of following a legalistic approach inspired by ordoliberalism, which ignored economic realities. Van Miert took this criticism into account when he promoted the shift from a "form-based" to an "effects-based" approach in particular through the new guidelines for vertical restraints published in 1999,[67] and through the 1999 Block Exemption Regulation. This development was accompanied by the development of economic expertise at DG IV (a unit traditionally dominated by lawyers), and by the rise of the yardstick of "consumer welfare." Van Miert strove to promote fairness by publishing the first "fining guidelines" in 1998.[68] They rendered the Commission policy more predictable.

The "service of general interest" was a thorny issue for a social-democratic competition commissioner. Promoters of socially oriented economic policies defend the exemptions from market rules for the provision of basic services to a large chunk of the population despite the higher costs in postal deliveries, in telecommunications, in air transport as well as in railways. However, in the 1990s, EU competition policy liberalized those sectors and considerably weakened the position of incumbent firms, which were often state-owned monopolies.[69] In his memoirs, Van Miert clearly asserted that there was no contradiction between attacking those companies and being a social democrat, since he thought that many of those enterprises often rendered a poor service and were plagued by vested interests.[70] Whereas under Brittan, there were regular fights with member states over prominent state-aid cases, van Miert strove to promote a less confrontational and more constructive approach.[71] In 1995, Ehlermann feared that some member states wanted to take advantage of the Treaty of Amsterdam's negotiations to curb the DG IV's power in this area, by creating independent sectoral authorities and/or by reasserting the exemptions of competition rules for services of general interest.[72] This fear did not materialize in the treaty, but it certainly motivated the Commission to adopt the first communication on services of general interest.[73] Van Miert was especially keen on that because this communication helped member states to understand the boundaries within which subsidies and privileges granted to companies could be authorized.[74] It was completed by the first regulations on state aids, a block exemption in 1998 and a procedure regulation in 1999.[75] The aim was both to render the Commission's policy fairer and more predictable, and to demonstrate the compatibility of socially oriented national economic policy with EU competition rules.

Lastly, van Miert had an impressive international record. Under his leadership, the Commission forced two mighty US giants, Boeing and McDonnell Douglas to reconsider their merger in 1997. In particular, Boeing had to relinquish exclusive agreement with airlines. This triggered tensions with the US government, as the European commission was accused of waging a neomercantilist policy to protect

Airbus. As a result, in 1998, a new bilateral agreement between the United States and the EU on the streamlining of the treatment of competition cases affecting both sides of the Atlantic was signed. It went further than the original 1991 EU/US Competition Cooperation Agreement.[76]

Van Miert went further by promoting the internationalization of competition rules. This issue was not new: the stillborn International Trade Organization negotiated in 1947 contained provisions against restrictive trade practices, and the debate bounced back and forth in the subsequent decades at the Organisation for Economic Co-operation and Development (OECD), the UN, the General Agreement on Tariffs and Trade (GATT) and then the WTO.[77] Following the 1994 GATT meeting in Marrakech which discussed this issue, Van Miert appointed three renowned international experts on competition and trade rules, Ulrich Immenga, Frédéric Jenny, and Ernst-Ulrich Petersmann, to draw up a report. Prominent experts from the Commission, such as Claus-Dieter Ehlermann and François Lamoureux were also invited to contribute. Later on, European experts took part in the project of drafting an international antitrust code.[78] In the end, US opposition to the Europeans' attempt at promoting a "managed globalization" condemned this venture.[79] Overall, this can be considered another symptom of van Miert's attempt to promote fair rules among economic actors through a market-oriented competition policy.

Beyond the Commission, social-democratic leaders also took part in the debate over competition policy within a second EU supranational institution, the EP. Overall, this institution had only very limited prerogatives in this field, bar the yearly discussion of the competition policy report. As a result, when the flagship reform prepared by van Miert, the modernization of competition rules, was discussed during the Plenary session of 18 January 2000, most speakers from the Party of European Socialists (PES) deplored the lack of powers of the EP in this area, rather than comment on the proposed modernization rules.[80] The German MEP Bernhard Rapkay loudly complained: "Parliament is a legislative body, but the fact that we have no more "than" the right of consultation in matters of competition law, of all things, is truly scandalous. Therefore, I would urge the Council and the Intergovernmental Conference to introduce the codecision procedure into legislation in this area."

In terms of substance, the PES's official position on this reform, expressed by the Spanish MEP Luis Berenguer Fuster, was rather positive. The modernization of cartel enforcement was mainly seen as a technical matter, aiming at increasing efficiency. Within the EP, the main social-democratic criticisms were directed at the state-aid control regimes, which were deemed too severe. Bernhard Rapkay defended state aids to Small and Medium companies in certain cases (R&D, environmental and regional policy). The Luxembourger MEP Jacques Poos also underlined:

> The main objective of the Union's competition policy cannot be to reduce the overall level of aid. This aid must be aligned with the objectives of the Union, particularly economic and social cohesion, sustainable development and research. The Commission must track down the illegal aid and aid that actually hinders the internal market. It would be a serious mistake to

> eliminate all public aid. The Internet is not a product of the market, but the result of research financed by the American army.

Poos articulated here a typical socially-oriented and neomercantilist vision of competition policy that was reminiscent of Delors'. Thus, it appears that Van Miert's modernization reform seems relatively consensual as it concerned mostly private companies through cartel enforcement. State-aid control was more controversial as it infringed on industrial, social and regional policies that were considered major parts of the welfare state in many EU states.

Conclusion

There was no common attitude among social democrats when confronted with the rise of competition policy in the 1980s and the 1990s. This is probably due to the fact that this domain was still secondary in most Western European countries. All the social-democratic leaders examined in this study accompanied the development of a market-oriented competition policy. This is especially true for the German director general, Ehlermann, whose national background is as important as his political backgrounds in explaining his positions. In West Germany, implementing a market-oriented competition policy has been considered a cornerstone of liberal democracy since the mid-1950s, even by many social democrats.[81] Commissioner van Miert, like its predecessor Vouel in the 1970s, loyally defended his portfolio and was progressively convinced by the preeminence of the market-oriented vision. Delors stood out because he had his own ideas about competition policy. He thought that it should synthesize market-oriented, socially oriented and neomercantilist features. His discourses demonstrate that he considered competition policy not an end in itself but a tool for other economic aims like controlling companies, the democratization of multinationals and other similar measures. His action in the ATR/De Havilland illustrated his strong commitment to a neomercantilist European industrial policy, which was not protectionist, but which could efficiently support European high-tech companies, like the US or the Japanese governments were doing during the same period. While Delors was probably the most influential social-democratic leader of the period within EEC/EU institutions, he did not manage to prevent the neoliberal drift, which was blatant under Brittan. The European Commission was the main forum of debate between different political visions of competition policy.

Recently, this debate over the features of a social-democratic competition policy has raged on. At the academic level, lawyer Ann Gerbrandy has urged EU competition policy officials to be more socially oriented.[82] In the political realm, frequent squabbles have arisen recently, in particular between the French government and European Commission. In 2013 and 2014, French Socialist and Minister of Industry Arnaud Montebourg and the Competition Commissioner Joaquín Almunia, who was also a socialist, exchanged a bitter public correspondence.[83] The French minister complained about the excessive neoliberal rigidity of EU competition policy, which threatened some prominent European companies. Paradoxically, Almunia's successor, the liberal Margrethe Vestager, has a much better image among French socialists initially (until the ban of the Alstom/Siemens merger in 2019) since she has pursued bold action against major US multinationals. In other words, a social-democratic European competition policy is still elusive in the 21st century.

Notes

1 On the history of EU competition policy in the late XXth century, see: Laurent Warlouzet, "Towards a Fourth Paradigm in European Competition Policy? A Historical Perspective," in Adina Claici et al. (eds.), *The Transformations of EU Competition Law – Next Generation Issues* (Alphen: Kluwer, 2023), 33–52. https://papers.ssrn.com/sol3/papers.cfm?abstract_id=4426768. See also: Michelle Cini and Lee McGowan, *Competition Policy in the European Union* (Basingstoke: PalgraveMacmillan, 2008); Hubert Buch-Hansen and Angela Wigger, *The Politics of European Competition Regulation. A Critical Political Economy Perspective* (London: Routledge, 2011); Tim Büthe, "The Politics of Competition and Institutional Change in European Union: The First Fifty Years," in Sophie Meunier and Kathleen R. McNamara (eds.), *Making History: European Integration and Institutional Change at Fifty* (Oxford: Oxford University Press, 2007), 175–194.

2 The fact that Delors was much more influential than most other presidents of the Commission is even recognized in studies adopting an intergovernmental angle: Andrew Moravcsik, *The Choice for Europe. Social Purpose and State Power from Messina to Maastricht* (Ithaca: Cornell University Press, 1998), 361–362. Historians of the European Commission tend to rate him as the most influential alongside Walter Hallstein.

3 Laurent Warlouzet, *Governing Europe in a Globalizing World. Neoliberalism and Its Alternatives Following the 1973 Oil Crisis* (London: Routledge, 2018); Laurent Warlouzet, *Europe contre Europe. Entre liberté, solidarité et puissance* (Paris: CNRS éditions, 2022).

4 This contest is examined in: Laurent Warlouzet, *Governing Europe*, op. cit., 113–114; see also: Laurent Warlouzet, "When Germany Accepted a European Industrial Policy: Managing the Decline of Steel from 1977 to 1984," *Economic History Yearbook/Jahrubuch für Wirtschafsgeschichte* 58, 1 (2017): 137–162.

5 On the adoption of this regulation, including an historiographical review of the literature, see: Laurent Warlouzet, "The Centralization of EU Competition Policy: Historical Institutionalist Dynamics from Cartel Monitoring to Merger Control (1956–91)," *Journal of Common Market Studies* 54, 3 (2016): 725–741.

6 Hussein Kassim and Handley Stevens, *Air Transport and the European Union. Europeanization and Its Limits* (Basingstoke: Palgrave Macmillan, 2010).

7 Mark Thatcher, *Internationalisation and Economic Institutions: Comparing the European Experience* (Oxford: Oxford University Press, 2007).

8 Warlouzet, *Governing Europe in a Globalizing World*, op. cit., 159–161.

9 *Ibid.*, op. cit., 156.

10 Jean Joana and Andy Smith, *Les commissaires européens. Technocrates, diplomates ou politiques?* (Paris: Presses de sciences-po, 2002), 132; EU archives, oral archives, interview of Anne Houtman by Laurent Warlouzet on 10 June 2016. Anne Houtman worked at DG Comp between 1987 and 1999, before moving to President Prodi's cabinet.

11 Jacques Delors, *Mémoires* (Paris: Plon, 2004).

12 Commission européenne, Report of the Study Group "Problems of Inflation," 3 March 1976, known as the "Maldague Report."

13 Franco Archibugi, Jacques Delors and Stuart Holland, "Planning for Development," in Stuart Holland (ed.), *Beyond Capitalist Planning* (Oxford: Basil Blackwell, 1978), 198.

14 *Ibid.*, 185, 196 and 197–198.

15 Archives of the French Ministry of Economics and Finance, B 65840, note DG concurrence, 25 June 1981; see also a reflection on the notion of dominant position inspired by the German model: note "calendrier des mesures prêtes ou à l'étude en matière de concurrence," 10 December 1982.

16 Archives of the French Ministry of Economics and Finance, B 65840, note, 26 August 1982; note "calendrier des mesures prêtes ou à l'étude en matière de concurrence," 10 December 1982; note on draft discourses of the Prime Minister "en vue de la sensibilisation de l'appareil d'Etat à la concurrence," 26 December 1983.

17 EU archives, European Commission, BAC 104/1993/152/51, note CEE on the Delors-Andriessen meeting of 1st March 1984.

18 Johan Schot and Wolfram Kaiser, *Writing the Rules for Europe. Experts, Cartels, and International Organizations* (Basingstoke: Palgrave Macmillan, 2014), 197–202.

19 David Spector, *La gauche, la droite et le marché* (Paris: Odile Jacob, 2017), 244.

20 *Ibid.*, 244.

21 Guy Mollet, "La construction européenne . . . vue par un socialiste français," *Documentation socialiste* 156 (April 1965).

22 Laurent Warlouzet, "The Centralization of EU Competition Policy," 725–741.

23 British national archives, T 390/98, advance Statement by the President of ETUC, European Council 25/26 March 1977.

24 International Institute of Social History, ETUC archives, 1480, ETUC declaration, note 19 November 1980.

25 On the "Vredeling directive" debate, see: Laurent Warlouzet, *Governing Europe in a Globalizing World*, op. cit., 67–74; Francesco Petrini, "Demanding Democracy in the Workplace: The European Trade Union Confederation and the Struggle to Regulate Multinationals," in Wolfram Kaiser and Jan-Henrik Meyer (eds.), *Societal Actors in European Integration. Polity-Building and Policy-Making, 1958–1992* (Basingstoke: Palgrave Macmillan, 2013), 151–172.

26 IISH, ETUC archives, 1482, note CES on a meeting between ETUC President Georges Debunne-President of the Commission Gaston Thorn, 18 June 1982.

27 EU archives, GSPE 74/405, report for the 13th Congress, 8–9 March 1984, Ernest Glinne, General Secretary of the Socialist Group in the EP.

28 EU archives, GSPE 75/1454, Work Programme of the Socialist Group, December 1985.

29 "The thrust of Commission policy," Statement by Jacques Delors, "President of the European Commission to the European Parliament and Extracts from His Reply to the Ensuing Debate, Strasbourg, 14 and 15 January 1985," in *Bulletin of the European Communities*, Supplement 1/85. This document is a translation of the original speech pronounced in French.

30 Commission of the European Communities, *Completing the Internal Market. White Paper from the Commission to the European Council*, Milan 28–29 June 1985, COM(85) 310, 14 June 1985.

31 EU archives, oral archives, interview of Jacques Delors by Vincent Dujardin, Lorenzo Mechi et Benedetto Zaccaria, 25 February 2016; Eric Bussière, "Devising a Strategy: The Internal Market and Industrial Policy," in Eric Bussière et al. (eds.), *The European Commission, 1973–86. History and Memories of An Institution* (Brussels: Publications Office of the European Union, 2014), 263–276.

32 EU archives, oral archives, interview of Peter Sutherland by Laurent Warlouzet on 8 September 2011, interview of Jacques Delors by Vincent Dujardin, Anne-Sophie Gijs, and Sophie Kaisin on 20 June 2017.

33 EU archives, European Commission, BAC 327/1994/159, note from the Director General to Sunnen, 11 October 1985; letter from Andriessen to Cryer, 28 November 1984.

34 EU archives, European Commission, BAC 327/1994/159, note Thies for Sunnen, 11 October 1985; note on a meeting with representatives of the French government, 18 October 1985.

35 EU archives, European Commission, BAC 327/1994/159, note Thies for Sunnen, 11 October 1985; BAC 408/1991/201, note on the Commission's meeting of 8 October 1986.
36 EU archives, European Commission, BAC 408/1991/201, note Lamoureux for Delors, 2 and 11 December 1986.
37 EU archives, European Commission, BAC 327/1994/160, note SG SEC(87) 1147/8, 13 July 1987; BAC 408/1991/201, note Lamoureux for Delors, 11 December 1986.
38 AEU, BAC 327/1994/159, minutes of the Commission meeting 17 December 1986.
39 Decision of the Commission n° 87/585/CEE of 15 July 1987 "relative aux aides accordées par le gouvernement français à un fabricant de textiles, d'habillement et de produits à base de papier Boussac Saint Frères."
40 EU archives, European Commission, BAC 327/1994/159, note Ripa di Meana to Sutherland, 16 December 1986.
41 EU archives, European Commission, BDT 323/93/210, note on the meeting of commissioner, 4 July 1986, note on the meeting of the chef de cabinet, 11 July 1986.
42 Mark Pollack, *The Engines of European Integration. Delegation, Agency, and Agenda Setting in the European Union* (Oxford: Oxford University Press, 2003), 292–299; Michelle Cini and Lee McGowan, *Competition Policy in the European Union* (Basingstoke: Palgrave, 1998), 129.
43 Frédéric Jenny, "Droit européen de la concurrence et efficience économique," *Revue d'économie industrielle* 63 (1993): 202–203; Catherine Goybet, "La CEE a-t-elle une politique industrielle?" *Revue du Marché Commun* 352 (1991): 753.
44 On the reservation of DG Competition: EU archives, oral archives, interview of Helmut Schröter by Laurent Warlouzet, 30 September 2016 (oral record); on the reservation of other DGs, see: EU archives, oral archives, interview of Martine Reicherts by Laurent Warlouzet on 14 December 2017. At that time, Helmut Schröter was a DG IV officials, and Martine Reicherts was the assistant to the Director-General for Internal Market and Industrial Affairs.
45 George Ross, *Jacques Delors and European Integration* (Cambridge: Polity Press, 1995), 178. According to him, Brittan won nine votes: himself, four liberals and conservatives (Andriessen, Schmidhuber, Christophersen, MacSharry), one non-affiliated (Dondelinger) and three socialists and socialdemocrats (Cardoso, Millan and Marin). He added that: "Manuel Marin, the swing vote, gave an utterly incomprehensible argument to explain himself, but seemed to have traded his vote for help from Brittan on a pending project to reorganize the European fishing fleet, an essential Spanish dossier."
46 On Delors' commitment to develop EEC industrial policy in high technology: Laurent Warlouzet, *Governing Europe in a Globalizing World*, op. cit., 192–194 and 200–202.
47 David J. Gerber, "Two Forms of Modernization in European Competition Law," *Fordham International Law Journal* 31, 5 (2007): 1235–1265.
48 EU archives, oral archives, interview with Claus-Dieter Ehlermann by Sigfrido M. Ramírez Pérez and Angel Viñas, 8 October 2010.
49 EU archives, oral archives, interview of John Temple-Lang by Laurent Warlouzet, 2 December 2016.
50 EU archives, oral archives, interview of Claus-Dieter Ehlermann by Laurent Warlouzet, 3 February 2017.
51 EU archives, PL 11, note Ehlermann, 5 January 1995, quoted in Laurent Warlouzet, "Competition Policy," in Eric Bussière et al. (eds.), *The European Commission, 1973–86* (Luxembourg: Publications office of the EU, 2019), 268–280.
52 Claus-Dieter Ehlermann, "Reflections on a European Cartel Office," *Common Market Law Review* 32 (1995): 471–486.
53 EU archives, Philip Lowe (PL)14, note Lowe to Ehlermann, 16 December 1994, quoted in Laurent Warlouzet, "Competition Policy," in *The European Commission*, op. cit.; Laurent Warlouzet, "The Difficult Quest to Implement Cartel Control: Grundig-Consten

(1966) and Philip Morris (1987)," in Bill Davies and Fernanda Nicola (eds.), *EU Law Stories. Contextual and Critical Histories of European Jurisprudence* (Cambridge: Cambridge University Press, 2017), 261–277.

54 Karel Van Miert, *Le marché et le pouvoir. Souvenirs d'un commissaire européen* (Brussels: Racine, 2000).

55 *Ibid.*, 42, translated from the original in French.

56 *Ibid.*, 267.

57 EU archives, oral archives, inteview of Claus-Dieter Ehlermann by Laurent Warlouzet, 3 February 2017, translated from the original in French.

58 EU archives, FL 562, note François Lamoureux to Jacques Delors, 12 February 1991, quoted in Laurent Warlouzet, "Competition Policy," in *The European Commission*, op. cit., translated from the original in French.

59 EU archives, COM(90) PV 1018, meeting of 27 June 1990, quoted in *Ibid.*

60 EU archives, oral archives, interview of Jean Dubois by Laurent Warlouzet, 16 February 2011.

61 EU archives, interview of Anne Houtman by Laurent Warlouzet, 10 June 2016.

62 *Green paper on vertical restraints in EEC competition policy*, COM(96) 721, 22 January 1997; *White Paper on modernisation of the rules implementing Articles 81 and 82 of the EC Treaty* – Commission programme 99/027, 28 April 1999; Council Regulation (EC) No 1/2003 of 16 December 2002 on the implementation of the rules on competition laid down in Articles 81 and 82 of the Treaty.

63 EU archives, BAC 189/00/430, note SG on the meeting of chef de cabinet of 3 October 1997: quoted in Laurent Warlouzet, "Competition Policy," in *The European Commission*, op. cit.

64 *Commission notice on the non-imposition or reduction of fines in cartel cases*, 96/C 207/04, 18 July 1996.

65 Martin Carree, Andrea Günster and Maarten Pieter Schinkel, "European Antitrust Policy 1957–2004: An Analysis of Commission Decisions," *Review of Industrial Organization* 36 (2010): 97–131.

66 Gerber, op. cit., 1247.

67 Gerber, op. cit., 1254–1255; *Communication pursuant to Article 5 of Council Regulation No 19/65/EEC of 2 March 1965 on the application of Article 81(3) of the Treaty to categories of agreements and concerted practices*, OJ C 270, 24 September 1999; *Council Regulation (EC) No 1215/1999 of 10 June 1999 amending Regulation No 19/65/EEC on the application of Article 81(3) of the Treaty to certain categories of agreements and concerted practices*, OJ L 148, 15 June 1999.

68 *Information from the Commission – Guidelines on the method of setting fines imposed pursuant to Article 15 (2) of Regulation No 17 and Article 65 (5) of the ECSC Treaty*, OJ C 9, 14 January 1998.

69 Thatcher, *Internationalisation and Economic Institutions*.

70 Van Miert, op. cit., 51–52.

71 EU archives, oral archives, interview of Anne Houtman by Laurent Warlouzet, 10 June 2016.

72 EU archives, PL 11, note Ehlermann, 5 January 1995, quoted in Laurent Warlouzet, "Competition Policy," in *The European Commission*, op. cit.

73 European Commission, *Communication on Services of general interest in Europe*, COM(96) 443, 11 September 1996.

74 EU archives, interview of Anne Houtman and of Jonathan Faull by Laurent Warlouzet, respectively on 10 June 2016 and on 25 November 2016. Under van Miert, Anna Houtman was chief of unit and Jonathan Faull was director in DG Comp.

75 Council Regulation (EC) No. 994/98 of 7 May 1998 on the application of Articles 92 and 93 of the Treaty establishing the European Community to certain categories of horizontal state aid; Council Regulation (EC) No. 659/1999 of 22 March 1999 laying down

detailed rules for the application of Article 93 of the EC Treaty; on these regulations, see: EU archives, oral archives, interviews of Anne Houtman and of Michel Petite by Laurent Warlouzet respectively on 10 June 2016 and on 23 June 2016.

76 The 1991 Agreement was encapsulated in the text 95/145/EC (Decision of the Council and the Commission of 10 April 1995 concerning the conclusion of the Agreement between the European Communities and the Government of the United States of America regarding the application of their competition laws); 1998 Positive Committee Agreement (Agreement between the European Communities and the Government of the United States of America on the application of positive comity principles in the enforcement of their competition laws of 4 June 1998).

77 Laurent Warlouzet, "La contribution européenne aux projets de régulation mondiale de la concurrence (1945–2005)," in Éric Bussière (ed.), *Régionalisme européen et gouvernance mondiale au XXe siècle* (Paris: Cahiers de l'IRICE, 2012), 105–116.

78 EU archives, interview of Jonathan Faull by Laurent Warlouzet, on 25 November 2016; Laurent Warlouzet, "La contribution européenne aux projets de régulation mondiale de la concurrence (1945–2005)," op. cit.

79 Rawi Abdelal and Sophie Meunier, "Managed globalization: doctrine, practice and promise," *Journal of European Public Policy* 17, 3 (2010): 350–367.

80 European Parliament website, minutes of the plenary session of 18 January 2001, consulted on 7 September 2018; one exception was the German MEP Christa Randzio-Plath, who opposed the reform.

81 Anthony James Nicholls, *Freedom With Responsibility. The Social Market Economy in Germany, 1918–1963* (Oxford: Clarendon Press, 1994), 305–315.

82 Rutger Claassen and Anna Gerbrandy, "Rethinking European Competition Law – From a Consumer Welfare to a Capability Approach," *Utrecht Law Review* 12, 1 (2016): 1–15.

83 Letter from Joaquín Almunia to Arnaud Montebourg on 19 December 2013, and response on 14 January 2014.

Bibliography

Abdelal, Rawal and Sophie Meunier. "Managed Globalization: Doctrine, Practice and Promise." *Journal of European Public Policy* 17, 3 (2010): 350–367.

Archibugi, Franco, Jacques Delors and Stuart Holland, "Planning for Development." In *Beyond Capitalist Planning* edited by Stuart Holland. Oxford: Basil Blackwell, 1978.

Buch-Hansen, Hubert and Angela Wigger. *The Politics of European Competition Regulation: A Critical Political Economy Perspective*. London: Routledge, 2011.

Bussière, Eric. "Devising a Strategy: The Internal Market and Industrial Policy." *The European Commission, 1973–86: History and Memories of An Institution* edited by Eric Bussière. Brussels: Publications Office of the European Union, 2014.

Büthe, Tim. "The Politics of Competition and Institutional Change in European Union: The First Fifty Years." In *Making History: European Integration and Institutional Change at Fifty* edited by Sophie Meunier and Kathleen R. McNamara. Oxford: Oxford University Press, 2007.

Carree, Martin, Andrea Günster and Maarten Pieter Schinkel. "European Antitrust Policy 1957–2004: An Analysis of Commission Decisions." *Review of Industrial Organization* 36 (2010): 97–131.

Cini, Michelle and Lee McGowan. *Competition Policy in the European Union*. Basingstoke: Palgrave Macmillan, 2008.

Claassen, Rutger and Anna Gerbrandy. "Rethinking European Competition Law – From a Consumer Welfare to a Capability Approach." *Utrecht Law Review* 12, 1 (2016): 1–15.

Ehlermann, Claus-Dieter. "Reflections on a European Cartel Office." *Common Market Law Review* 32 (1995): 471–86.
Gerber, David J. "Two Forms of Modernization in European Competition Law." *Fordham International Law Journal* 31, 5 (2007): 1235–1265.
Goybet, Catherine. "La CEE a-t-elle une politique industrielle?" *Revue du Marché Commun* 352 (1991): 753.
Jenny, Frédéric. "Droit européen de la concurrence et efficience économique." *Revue d'économie industrielle* 63 (1993): 202–3.
Joana, Jean and Andy Smith. *Les commissaires européens. Technocrates, diplomates ou politiques?* Paris: Presses de sciences-po, 2002.
Kassim, Hussein and Handley Stevens. *Air Transport and the European Union: Europeanization and its Limits*. Basingstoke: Palgrave Macmillan, 2010.
Mollet, Guy. "La construction européenne . . . vue par un socialiste français." *Documentation socialiste* 156, April 1965.
Moravcsik, Andrew. *The Choice for Europe: Social Purpose and State Power from Messina to Maastricht*. Ithaca: Cornell University Press, 1998.
Nicholls, Anthony James. *Freedom with Responsibility: The Social Market Economy in Germany, 1918–1963*. Oxford: Clarendon Press, 1994.
Petrini, Francesco. "Demanding Democracy in the Workplace: The European Trade Union Confederation and the Struggle to Regulate Multinationals." In *Societal Actors in European Integration: Polity-Building and Policy-Making, 1958–1992* edited by Wolfram Kaiser and Jan-Henrik Meyer. Basingstoke: Palgrave Macmillan, 2013, 151–172.
Pollack, Mark. *The Engines of European Integration: Delegation, Agency, and Agenda Setting in the European Union*. Oxford: Oxford University Press, 2003.
Ross, George. *Jacques Delors and European Integration*. Cambridge: Polity Press, 1995.
Schot, Johan and Wolfram Kaiser, *Writing the Rules for Europe. Experts, Cartels, and International Organizations*. Basingstoke: Palgrave Macmillan, 2014.
Spector, David. *La gauche, la droite et le marché*. Paris: Odile Jacob, 2017.
Thatcher, Mark. *Internationalisation and Economic Institutions: Comparing the European Experience*. Oxford: Oxford University Press, 2007.
Van Miert, Karel. *Le marché et le pouvoir. Souvenirs d'un commissaire européen*. Brussels: Racine, 2000.
Warlouzet, Laurent. "Towards a Fourth Paradigm in European Competition Policy? A Historical Perspective (1957–2022)." In *The Transformation of EU Competition Law – Next Generation Issues* edited by Adina Claici, Assimakis Komninos and Denis Waelbroeck. Alphen: Kluwer, 2023, 33–52. https://papers.ssrn.com/sol3/papers.cfm?abstract_id=4426768.
Warlouzet, Laurent. "The Centralization of EU Competition Policy: Historical Institutionalist Dynamics from Cartel Monitoring to Merger Control (1956–91)." *Journal of Common Market Studies* 54, 3 (2016): 725–741.
Warlouzet, Laurent. "Competition Policy." In *The European Commission, 1973–86* edited by Eric Bussière et al. Luxembourg: Publications Office of the EU, 2019, 268–280.
Warlouzet, Laurent. "The Difficult Quest to Implement Cartel Control: Grundig-Consten (1966) and Philip Morris (1987)." In *EU Law Stories: Contextual and Critical Histories of European Jurisprudence* edited by Bill Davies and Fernanda Nicola. Cambridge: Cambridge University Press, 2017, 261–277.
Warlouzet, Laurent. *Europe contre Europe: Entre liberté, solidarité et puissance*. Paris: CNRS éditions, 2022.

Warlouzet, Laurent. *Governing Europe in a Globalizing World: Neoliberalism and Its Alternatives Following the 1973 Oil Crisis*. London: Routledge, 2018.

Warlouzet, Laurent. "La contribution européenne aux projets de régulation mondiale de la concurrence (1945–2005)." In *Régionalisme européen et gouvernance mondiale au XXe siècle* edited by Éric Bussière. Paris: Cahiers de l'IRICE, 2012, 105–116.

Warlouzet, Laurent. "When Germany Accepted a European Industrial Policy: Managing the Decline of Steel from 1977 to 1984." *Economic History Yearbook/Jahrubuch für Wirtschafsgeschichte* 58, 1 (2017): 137–162.

11 Rules and exceptions in the recent history of competition law, 2003–2017

Technocracy or scope for a social-democratic perspective?

Wolf Sauter[1]

Introduction

Antitrust, merger control and state aid are the mainstays of EU competition policy that all went through a significant development in the twenty-first century. Each of these components followed a serious reform process which brought EU competition in line with then mainstream assumptions following the so-called more economic approach developed by the law and economics tradition which reached its zenith during the first decade of the twenty-first century. These reforms were carried out to a large extent during the mandate of the Commission presided by the Italian Christian democrat Romano Prodi with the appointment of another Italian professor of economics, the liberal Mario Monti, as commissioner for competition.

The position of director general for competition remained until 2002 into the hands of the German liberal, Alexander Schaub, who had been appointed in 1995 as successor of Claus-Dieter Ehlermann, and therefore, directing the DG for most of the time when the Belgian socialist Karel van Miert was commissioner. He was replaced from that moment by a British competition specialist, Philip Lowe, who had served in various cabinets of Labour Commissioners, including as head of cabinet of the former Labour leader, Neil Kinnock. In nominal terms during this period, the balance between liberals and social democrats in the leadership of competition policy was maintained.

On substance, however, there was an increasing convergence toward a liberal conception of competition policy, which became evident with the appointment by Monti to the new influential position of chief economist, of the German Professor Lars-Hendrik Röller until 2006, replaced by the Belgian Damien Neven until 2011. This coincided with an increasing demand of the ECJ for more evaluation of quantitative analysis.

During this period, after the adoption of Regulation 1/2003, the modernization of antitrust was implemented at the national and central levels, mobilising resources, and arguably augmenting this policy in terms of effectiveness and legitimacy. In the field of merger control, which was introduced as a centralized policy only in 1989, a reform was carried out in 2005 whereby a more effects based approach was adopted with an evaluation in 2009. In the two fields of state aid and services of

DOI: 10.4324/9781351010573-11

general economic interest (SGEI), with the 2003 Altmark ruling of the European Court of Justice on the criterion of advantage, the impact of EU competition policy on the state aid side has likewise increased markedly with legislative packages in 2005 and 2011 which expanded the Altmark logic to introduce distinct state aid regimes for social services and utilities.

This clear trend against state intervention was accentuated by the successor of Monti, the liberal Dutch Commissioner, Neelie Kroes, who was in office during the first Commission led since 2005 by the conservative José Manuel Durao Barroso. It was only during his second Commission term that a social democrat, the Spanish socialist Joaquín Almunia, again obtained the portfolio for competition. He was flanked by the new Dutch director general, Alexander Italianer, an economist who had been deputy head of cabinet of President Barroso. In this context, the possibilities for a substantive social-democratic influence were limited, regardless of the intentions of the Spanish Commissioner, who was an economist and former secretary general of the Spanish Socialists and represented the liberal line closer to New Labour in relationship to the more left-leaning fraction incarnated by Josep Borrell.

Moreover, Almunia had been already Commissioner for Financial and Economic Affairs during the big recession. His role was largely limited to applying the reforms decided before his arrival to this portfolio that he quit after one term, replaced by the Danish liberal Margrethe Vestager in 2015. The position of director general went back to a German conservative, Johannes Laitenberger, former chief of staff of President Barroso.

As dissonant statist backlash on antitrust and state aid policies that occurred during this period were the so-called Sarkozy amendments in the 2007 Lisbon Treaty. These aimed to reduce the purported constitutional significance of these policies and to promote instead the exception for SGEI to obtain a positive approval of the treaty in the French Parliament after the rejection of the Constitutional Treaty in France, as this requested a reinforced majority in both chambers of the French Parliament.

This article attempts to do two things: firstly, to provide an account of the implementation of antitrust modernization as well as merger control and the developments regarding state aid and services of general economic interest in the 2003–2017 period, and second, to combine this with reflections on the role of social democrat politicians and policymakers during the relevant period, notably Commissioner Joaquín Almunia (2009–2014). The main research question is whether the implementation of antitrust modernization, merger review and the development of SGEI were a success on their own terms; in relation to the so-called Sarkozy amendments; and whether a social-democratic element can be perceived that was relevant to this outcome.

Implementation and the outcomes of modernization

The development of EU competition policy shows an expansion of its scope to include new topics and sectors, as well as the more economic approach and themes like market power. Combining several of these features constitutes the so-called modernization of antitrust. Next, as in previous work, my perspective on modernization and its implementation is primarily that of its coherence. This variable is also relevant in relation to the social-democratic context because it co-determines the scope for variation and exceptions to competition law.

A brief outline of modernization

The three main dimensions to modernization are (i) decentralization to national authorities and courts; (ii) a more economic approach based on the effects of the practices concerned; and (iii) the modernization of the instruments, or toolkit, available to competition authorities. However, these three variables are not all pulling in the same direction.

Decentralization may pose a risk to the coherence of EU competition policy, that increases or decreases with the availability of effective overall coordination. It can also improve the effectiveness (scope) and legitimacy (both input and output) of EU competition law. The quality of the European competition network (ECN) of national competition authorities (NCAs), the Commission's success in attracting the key cases, and the success of *amicus curiae* efforts are key compensating variables here. So is effective judicial review at national and EU level. The *more economic approach* on the one hand streamlines the enforcement efforts of the Commission and the NCAs, but on the other hand, it also makes their work more complex. It allows them to focus on hard-core cartels, but considering that an increasing number of cases require complex economic evaluations, it becomes more difficult for all parties involved (including undertakings) to know the law beforehand, and to act accordingly. The work of national courts also becomes more complicated for the same reasons. *Updating the Commission's toolkit* strengthens the power of the Commission by reconstituting it as the linking pin in ECN, providing coherence in terms of effectiveness. It promotes the Commission as the locus of control and its ability to decide hard cases and set the general direction. The extent to which increased investigative powers raise issues of legal protection, and therefore of input legitimacy, remains to be examined. Assessing these three dimensions of modernization jointly, we can say that they literally achieved the modernization of EU competition law. Next, I will look at the way modernization was applied and at its outcomes in more detail.

Implementing modernization: reports from the network participants

Procedurally as well as substantively, modernization of the antitrust rules was framed by implementing Regulation 1/2003.[2] The European Commission's services (DG competition) have reported on the five-year (2009,[3] a report that was required by Article 44 of Regulation 1/2003) and ten-year (2014,[4] at its own initiative) anniversaries of the entry into effect of Regulation 1/2003. The tone of these reports is uniformly upbeat. The five-year report (2009) states three important related claims in this respect.

> The EC competition rules have to a large extent become the '*law of the land*' for the whole of the EU. Cooperation in the ECN has contributed towards

> ensuring their coherent application. The network is an innovative model of governance for the implementation of Community law by the Commission and Member State authorities.

The assertion that EU competition law has become the (i) law of the land is therefore combined with (ii) its coherent application by the ECN and (iii) a new mode of governance for the implementation of Community law.[5] In the Ten-year report (2014) the Commission repeats the aforementioned 'law of the land' claim and advances it further by stating that 'the work carried out by the ECN has become increasingly important to ensure coherent enforcement and to allow stakeholders to benefit from a more level playing field'.[6]

A level playing field is important to the parties that are subject to the relevant rules. The Commission underscores that a dynamic development of close cooperation within the ECN underpins the coherent application of EU competition law throughout the EU.[7] However, evaluating these claims is complicated. Formal hierarchical instruments of control have not been used yet. This regards notably the Commission taking over a case previously handled by an NCA to prevent a decision that it opposes based on Article 11(6) of Regulation 1/2003, or indeed vis-a-vis undertakings a finding of inapplicability based on its Article 10. However, we do not know if their use has been contemplated and discussed or threatened either bilaterally or within the ECN.

The Commission staff working paper that accompanies the 2009 five-year report explicitly details 'the ECN as a forum to promote coherent application',[8] and discusses work on horizontal issues as well as coordination on individual cases and decisions.

> Overall, it clearly results from the feedback received by the Commission . . . that the mechanisms provided by Article 11 of Regulation 1/2003 function very well and have led to the largely coherent and consistent application of the EC [now EU] competition rules in the ECN over the last five years. The concerns related to a major risk of incoherent and inconsistent application of EC competition law in a decentralized system that have been raised at the time of the adoption of the modernization package have certainly not been realized.[9]

Although the Commission also acknowledges that a few cases showed inconsistencies, it does not identify them or the issues concerned.

Types of commission and NCA competition decisions

For the ten-year period 2003–2014 the Commission reports having taken 122 decisions where it applied Articles 101 and/or 102 TFEU, the latter sometimes in conjunction with Article 106 TFEU on legal monopolies and services of general economic interest. Of these decisions 73% involved Article 101 TFEU and 48%, so almost fully half of Commission decisions, involved cartels. (Only 9% of decisions involved vertical restraints.) Three quarters of cartel decisions were based upon leniency applications – the remainder being accounted for by *ex officio* investigations. This is consistent with claims that the Commission has been able to focus more on its priorities, namely the most serious antitrust infringements, mainly cartels.[10] That in turn means that one of the main objectives of EU antitrust modernization appears to have been realized.

During the same period, the NCAs notified 665 envisaged enforcement decisions to the Commission. The joint pattern for the NCAs (which may well obscure significant differences between individual NCAs) is that Article 102 TFEU cases, on dominance, are most numerous at 36%, cartels at 27% measure only half the comparative share reached by the Commission. This is with only 34% of cartels coming in under a leniency program – again about half of that reported by the Commission itself. A relatively large share of 18% of the total number of NCA cases (double that of the Commission) is accounted for by vertical agreements. The dominance cases brought by the NCAs in large part involved the utilities sectors: energy, telecommunications and transport, with for example refusals to deal by vertically integrated monopolists.

These figures suggest that the joint decisional mix of the NCAs is more traditional, and (possibly wholly appropriately) biased towards the utilities, and to some extent verticals, whereas the Commission is ahead of the curve, or at least headed in the direction it had set out as its objective for modernization. This could also be read as a division of labor between the NCAs and the European Commission.

Regarding Article 102 TFEU, the Commission has acted against exclusionary abuses (foreclosure) in 84% of its decisions, and only in 16% (or five actual cases over ten years) against exploitation.[11] This is in line with its general approach to Article 102 TFEU in recent years and the focus on exclusion expressed most explicitly in its 2009 paper on that topic.[12] However, this economics-centred approach was called into question by the General Court in its 2014 *Intel* Case (although largely reversed by the European Court of Justice in 2017).[13] Interviews by the then new Commissioner for competition Margrethe Vestager,[14] and cases opened at the time similarly suggested that exploitation issues would be addressed more frequently.[15] The NCAs appear to have been more evenhanded with regard to exploitation from the outset in part because taken together with cases in which both types of abuses were found, these account for 27% of their Article 102 TFEU decisions. Such cases were found especially in the energy, media and transport (airport services) sectors.

The Commission also reports that industrial products (especially chemicals) no longer form the lion's share of cartel activity; that cartels are more diverse; more sophisticated; and more likely to operate globally. In this context, there is increasing cooperation between the European Commission and the International Competition Network (ICN). In addition, the data collected is increasingly voluminous – reflecting the more general societal trend of having to deal with 'big data' to produce workable conclusions instead of relying on a convenient (but now cartel participants are usually more circumspect generally unavailable) 'smoking gun'.

The net gains for modernization

When compared with pre-modernization data, the above figures show a considerable net gain for antitrust enforcement because of modernization. In a 2013 paper, Wouter Wils found an eightfold increase in the number of substantive decisions based on Articles 101 and 102 TFEU. However, in numerical terms, nearly all the gains are realized by the new cases brought by the NCAs so every NCA decision counts as a gain, and not by additional cases brought by the Commission. Wils has shown that the number of Article 101 and 102 TFEU Decisions taken by the Commission has barely increased since modernization: under Regulation 17/62, the Commission on average adopted 7.5 prohibition decisions and 2 exemptions per year, and under Regulation 1/2003 on average, it adopted seven prohibition decisions and three commitment decisions per year.[16]

An increase might have been expected based on the Commission's claim that modernization was necessary to liberate its services from dealing with low-caloric notifications that kept them away from the red meat of key antitrust infringements. Wils presents explanations, for instance, that the Commission services now must focus more on state aid and merger cases, where they retain an exemption monopoly. Also, the increased stress on economic analysis in competition cases might make case handling more time consuming and managing the ECN is also a time consuming task. Alan Riley has described abolition of the notification procedure as not the radical step that it was presented to be but 'merely the abolition of an already irrelevant procedure with marginal impact on the operation of EC [now EU] competition rules'.[17]

That does not mean there has been no change. The types of cases DG COMP is now handling are more complex and time consuming, its internal quality checks are more rigorous (factors that Wils mentions as well), as are the standards required by the General Court and the Court of Justice of the European Union. Difficult infringement cases are now addressed by teams with economic expertise on board. Because the total number of staff has remained largely constant, this more intense effort is consistent with the number of decisions remaining broadly constant. It also squares with a picture of unchanged quantity but higher quality of Decisions, as well as with the modernization narrative of the Commission taking its responsibility as *primus inter pares*.

It is not clear what the gains from modernization have been in real terms such as annual consumer savings as a percentage of gross domestic product (GDP). Recently, such data are being collected in several jurisdictions (EU, some NCAs and US) for competition policy at large. The available figures for the period 2008–2013 suggest percentages ranging between 0.87 and 0.37 of GDP for the European Commission, which is in line with the findings for the other competition authorities surveyed. However, there are likely to be more significant indirect effects including those based on deterrence, and improved quality.[18]

Coordination instruments

Article 10 of Regulation 1/2003, which enables the Commission to adopt a finding of inapplicability in exceptional cases (without reintroducing the Commission's exemption power under Article 101(3) TFEU that was abolished by modernization), has so far not been applied yet. Article 10 explicitly states that such a Decision must be required by the public interest. An Article 10 Decision is binding on national courts and NCAs and has become the only way for the Commission to positively apply Article 101(3) TFEU.

However, the NCAs have no Article 10 powers themselves. Instead, they are empowered more narrowly by Article 5 of Regulation 1/2003 to decide that there are no grounds for action in cases where the conditions for the application of Article 101 or 102 TFEU are not met. Unlike the Commission's Article 10 Decision, such NCA decisions are not binding on other NCAs, nor on national courts or the Commission. Unlike NCAs, national courts can apply Article 101 TFEU fully, including Article 101(3) TFEU.

The fact that vis-á-vis the NCAs the Commission has a monopoly over findings of inapplicability of EU law under Article 10 (even if national competition law provides otherwise) was settled in the *Tele2 Polska* Case (2011) in relation to Article 102 TFEU.[19] The same outcome was reached concerning Article 101(3) TFEU in *Schenker* (2013).[20]

Meanwhile, there are no known examples of the application of Article 11(6) of Regulation 1/2003 which empowers the Commission to take over a case at any time and is reinforced by its Articles 15 and 16. The latter provides that NCAs and national courts cannot take decisions that contradict Commission decisions. They are even required to consider the possible outcome of pending Commission procedures, which may require them to suspend their own cases. Effectively, this is a codification of the *Masterfood* doctrine,[21] which also includes that the national courts may request a preliminary ruling from the Court of Justice in such cases. There does not appear to be documentation of how this works in practice.

The 2009 Commission services report that forms the basis for its five-year evaluation claims that as an ex-ante measure ensuring consistency Article 10 has been overtaken by events. This is because the ECN has proven to be such an unexpectedly successful forum for discussing issues of competition policy.[22] Hence, soft forms of coordination (albeit in the shadow of binding rules) appear to have obviated the need for the Commission's use of its primacy and preemption tools.

Effects of the ECN on the position of its network members

Effects on the NCAs

Prior to modernization, there had already been widespread spontaneous harmonization of national competition rules to the EU standard. However, the stature of the NCAs has increased both in their domestic setting and within the EU. This growth in stature is to do with the application of norms that are developed at EU level and in the context of the network of peers that is the ECN. It also enables the NCAs to have a direct relationship with the European Commission. This takes the NCAs to some extent outside the national context and protects them from the pressure and influences (political or otherwise) to which they are subject there.

The ECN provides a forum for debate and consensus building where members obtain valuable input, often based on practical experience, that they could not easily obtain within their national legal frameworks. Best practices are developed and shared. This, in turn, helps NCAs to build up a position of enhanced independence vis-á-vis their national governments not only with respect to the application of EU law but also with spill-over to the application of national competition law in cases that lack an EU dimension.

In the ECN, the discussion on the enforcement methods applied relates to the need for effective powers. This led to a lobby for a standardized minimum set of instruments as well as for the allocation of adequate resources.[23] Article 5 of Regulation 1/2003 already provided a minimum set of powers that helps the effectiveness of NCAs. In 2017, a new Directive was proposed to further harmonize enforcement powers (the ECN+ Directive).[24] Hence, it appears that the NCAs can use their participation in ECN to bolster their position, enhancing both their legitimacy and effectiveness.

Effects on the European Commission

The Commission too is an ECN member. As a *primus inter pares*, it disposes of the legal tools to override the other members in the pursuit of actual cases: it can enforce its primacy by preempting conflicting decisions. Also, its decisions are binding on the other members (NCAs), whereas the decisions of the NCAs are valid only within their own Member States and do not have such binding force on the Commission or on each other.[25]

For the Commission, the ECN is not just a network of peers but also a constituency on which it can draw for support in formulating and executing its policies. Moreover, the NCAs form the hands and feet of the Commission in the Member States, making it more effective than if it would have to act as the sole enforcer of EU competition policy. For every Commission antitrust decision, there are between five and six NCA such decisions. The influence of Commission's policy notices is amplified by NCAs following suit and its Decisions can trump national courts. As a result of modernization, the power of the Commission appears to have increased, not decreased.[26]

The increasing clout of DG competition creates some friction with the activities of the college of Commissioners as a whole – for instance, when large multinational corporations are involved with the EU across multiple policy dimensions such as concerning industrial policy. Nevertheless, there is a risk that in the College of Commissioners, the increased competition policy powers enjoyed by the Commission may be influenced by political considerations from other policy aspects. If this risk actually does increase over time this is likely to lead to renewed pleas for DG competition to become an independent authority itself, perhaps structured as part of a European public prosecutor's office.[27] This has not happened yet, although as there is a regular request of the European Parliament for more accountability of Commission's decisions in this field, typically raised at the presentation of the annual report by the commissioner of competition.[28]

What effects on coherence?

The Commission has claimed that modernization has led to the growth of a culture of competition, and that competition law is now 'the law of the land' throughout the EU.[29]

Jointly the aforementioned effects lead to the construction of an EU policy sphere on competition. In the modernization framework as specified in the 2002 joint statement by the Council and the Commission, effectiveness and consistency are the leading objectives of the ECN structure.[30] This is pursued by a mixture of hard (Commission primacy, or preemption) and soft (exchange of information and best practices) instruments.

Nevertheless, it is difficult to estimate to what extent this effort has been successful. Just as increasingly effective competition law enforcement is spreading globally outside the context of the EU so it might have spread and intensified at national level within the EU, even in the absence of modernization. As mentioned, widespread spontaneous harmonization of national competition law already occurred prior to modernization. Some form of coordination might have been construed even in the absence of common enforcement of EU competition rules at national level.

Yet applying the same rules and striving toward doing so consistently and having instruments to enforce that consistency must have enhanced coherence. Also, the common goal has been safeguarding the internal market. The fact that for NCAs, procedures and remedies remain governed by national law is a possible source of divergence. However, there has been a voluntary harmonization effort on leniency, and formal harmonization has been achieved regarding damages, effective from December 2016.[31] Finally as mentioned, proposals were made for a Directive on harmonising the NCAs enforcement powers, including their application of *national* competition rules alongside EU law.[32]

Evaluating the findings so far

So far, at least the picture that emerges from the Commission's own reporting on the functioning of the ECN is positive. The Commission Services in their 2009 report that underpins the five-year evaluation have also stated that 'the Regulation reconciled the requirements of substantive coherence with the existing procedural diversity amongst European Competition Authorities'.[33] Another claim is that a 'common competition culture' has now been founded in Europe.[34] No less importantly the overall productivity regarding the application of Articles 101 and 102 TFEU has increased significantly, primarily due to the new cases brought by the NCAs. The Commission's output in quantity has not increased but it may well have done so on quality.

The ECN has clearly become a policy network with elements of cooperation and hierarchy in place. The latter – the Commission's preemption powers – have so far not been used, at least not explicitly. So far, coordination (perhaps in the shadow of preemption) has sufficed to keep the system on track and moving in a direction consistent with the Commission's aims. This means that the network favoured convergence and coherence – notably its goals of effectiveness and consistency. Taken as a whole, these findings are consistent with EU competition law's dominant objective of protecting the internal market, as it has been since the so-called Sarkozy amendments discussed further in the text.

The Sarkozy amendments: success or failure?

A reader of the aforementioned account of the implementation of modernization might be forgiven for having obtained the impression that there was a consensus underlying the meaning and importance of the competition rules. Although this may be true at the level of the policy community and the ECN network involved that would be a mistaken conclusion regarding politics at large.

The Constitutional Treaty for the EU that was not approved in referenda in the Netherlands and France in 2003–2004 led to the negotiation of the new Lisbon Treaty that was adopted in 2007. On most counts, this did not differ substantively from the failed constitution except from the so-called Sarkozy amendments, named after the French center-right president at the time. He needed a qualified bipartisan majority in the French Parliament to ratify the reformed treaty, which required a modification of the French constitution. Therefore, it was not submitted to a new referendum as the text had been precisely modified in such a way that it could not be seen as the same text rejected in the referendum, and it had been examined in the French Constitutional Court. These amendments formed a Statist backlash that lowered the status of competition from the constitutional plan of making is an objective to merely one of the instruments of the Union. In this context, Protocols 26 on SGEI and 27 on competition and the internal market (nominally with the same binding value as the main text but with less prestige) were added to the Lisbon Treaty. Moreover, Article 36 on access to SGEI in the chapter on solidarity of the Charter of Fundamental Rights of the European Union (adopted in 2000) became binding with equal effect as the Treaties when the Lisbon Treaty came into force in 2009.

Were these Statist amendments a success of a failure? They were certainly successful in terms of allowing the Lisbon Treaty to be passed and innovations to the legal structure to be introduced without engaging in a further potentially painful review of the integration process and its democratic support at the national level. They were less successful in curtailing the scope of EU competition policy, and in this sense a failure as compared to their stated intentions.[35] Arguably, the changes imposed fortified the competition rules by linking them more closely to the sacrosanct internal market objective. Thus, antitrust passed relatively unscathed. The (primarily State aid-oriented) exception for SGEI rebounded following these changes as we shall see further in the text, and this might be regarded as a success. However, this development does not primarily appear to be a consequence of the Sarkozy amendments. Moreover, the very emphasis on SGEI as an exception to the rules on antitrust and State aid suggests that the competition rules that created the friction with national economic policies themselves were accepted or at least not effectively contested.

As an aside, at the same time (albeit not by the hand of Sarkozy) the Lisbon Treaty added achieving a highly competitive social market economy as one of the main objectives of European integration in Article 3(3) of the Treaty on European Union (TEU).[36] The success of the social market economy objective, which evidently extends well beyond the scope of EU competition law, is more difficult to gauge. On the one hand, there is an (ordo)liberal tradition which has charted successive betrayals of (ordo)liberalism since the 1992 Maastricht Treaty.[37] On the other hand, defendants of the welfare state charge the integration process with the erosion of the former.[38] Elsewhere and earlier, I have argued that truth lies in the middle, and we enjoy a mixed economic constitution.[39]

In this chapter, I will limit myself to the dimensions of antitrust and State aid thereof, a combination notably enabled by the existence of an exception for SGEI.

State aid and services of general economic interest

The state aid rules contained in Articles 107 and 108 TFEU aim to ensure that the Member States do not distort competition in the internal market by conferring discriminatory advantages upon undertakings. These rules therefore address Member States although the beneficiaries of the aid are undertakings: in this sense, the state aid rules occupy a middle ground between the competition and the free movement rules. State aid exists if four conditions are met. A measure must: (i) at a cost to the public purse (ii) confer a selective advantage[40] on only some undertakings (iii) that distort competition and (iv) have an effect on trade. Since 2005, the Commission has taken a more refined economic approach to state aid based increasingly on an analysis of market failures, aiming to direct the Member States to awarding less and more targeted state aid.[41] In its state aid action plan, the Commission stated this as follows:

> State aid measures can sometimes be effective tools for achieving objectives of common interest. They can correct market failures, thereby improving the functioning of markets and enhancing European competitiveness. They can also help promote e.g. social and regional cohesion, sustainable development and cultural diversity, irrespective of the correction of market failures.
>
> However, state aid should only be used when it is an appropriate instrument for meeting a well defined objective, when it creates the right incentives, is proportionate and when it distorts competition to the least possible extent. For that reason, appreciating the compatibility of state aid is fundamentally about balancing the negative effects of aid on competition with its positive effects in terms of common interest.[42]

The focus of this change in approach is the so-called balancing test in Article 107(3) TFEU which is used to decide whether state measures are compatible with the internal market. As sketched out in the quotation above this test asks: (i) whether there is a well-defined common interest objective (defined in efficiency or equity terms), such as market failure; (ii) whether the aid effectively addresses this objective, provides the right incentives and is itself both necessary and proportionate); and (iii) whether the resulting restrictions on competition and on trade are limited so on balance the measure has a positive effect.[43]

The state aid regime has come to fruition much later than antitrust, with effective enforcement widespread only since the early 1990s.[44] In contrast to the competition rules that since 2004 have been characterized by decentralized enforcement, the Commission retains the monopoly on declaring aid compatible with the internal market under Article 107(3) TFEU by means of individual decisions. This frustrates the application of the state aid rules by national courts who can declare that state aid exists but cannot exclude that the Commission might exempt the aid by declaring it compatible. To solve this problem, the Commission relies on block exemptions (just as had been the case in antitrust prior to 2004), which the national courts are authorized to declare applicable or not.[45] In recent years, therefore, it appears that state aid is progressing down the same track as antitrust did, starting with a centralized exemption system based on individual decisions and block exemptions for specific favored types of aid.

Like antitrust, state aid aims at promoting undistorted competition, but it is much more intrusive regarding state measures and therefore decision-making and democratic accountability at national (or even regional or local) level. For this reason, the rules on services of general economic interest, or SGEI, are important here. They allow a directly effective exception for state aid provided a legitimate public interest is pursued in a proportionate manner. In the period 2003–2017, the law on SGEI has grown exponentially.

The Altmark case

Coincidentally, this landmark state aid case was handed down in 2003 by the European Court of Justice just as the implementation of antitrust modernization was getting started.[46] In *Altmark*, the court introduced a cumulative four-part test to determine whether financing of a public service amounts to conferring on a public undertaking an advantage, which is a necessary element for a finding of state aid.

1. The recipient undertaking must discharge a clearly defined public service obligation.
2. Objective and transparent parameters for the calculation of the compensation are established before the compensation is granted.
3. The compensation is limited to the costs of providing the public service obligation, considering receipts and a reasonable profit.
4. If the undertaking involved is not chosen by public procurement procedure, the level of compensation needed is determined based on the costs of an efficient undertaking.

Two years later, in 2005, the Commission based its so-called Monti/Kroes Package on the Altmark criteria to establish whether a state aid once granted should benefit from an exemption as an SGEI.[47]

Markets, market failure, and SGEI

Competition Commissioner Almunia promoted and completed the adoption by the Commission of its second package on SGEI.[48] This SGEI initiative was the reverse of the centralization that I just noted regarding state aid and mergers. This is because it allows public authorities at all levels (including local or regional governments) throughout the EU to define their own public service tasks with which they may charge private undertakings under proportional derogations from the competition rules (which often regards State aid regarding funding). Almunia presented this reform as the Commission's contribution to defending Europe's public services and preserving them for the future.[49] Although the second SGEI package was in line with earlier plans and established case law, it was welcome also from a political perspective, given both spreading Euroscepticism and widespread criticism of the financial sector bailouts.

The conditions for deciding whether state aid is involved in public service compensation (the Altmark test under Article 107(1) TFEU) may be contrasted with the question whether, if aid is involved, this may merit an exemption under Article 106(2) TFEU (as aid that is compatible with the internal market). The relationship between the two has been addressed in the 2015 *Viasat* case.[50] Here the General Court pointed out that these two tests are distinct and must be applied sequentially. The first test is whether there is an aid, because there an advantage is conferred; if this is so, the second question is whether it should be exempted. The issue regarding the relationship between the two dimensions arose because the Commission's decisional practice under Article 106(2) TFEU was inspired by the Altmark test. Yet the General Court clarified that the questions concerned remain separate and serve different aims. This means they may eventually diverge.[51]

Balancing markets and public policy

The pivotal role that it assigned to SGEI within the overall scheme of competition policy makes sense also regarding the broader balance between the market and public policy set out by Almunia in his speeches on the topic.[52] Here Almunia has sketched competition policy as bridging generally functioning markets and more occasional market dysfunctions, or market failures, which require correcting by public policy. This view is broadly in line with that on the function of competition policy more generally within DG competition, as well as the European and international antitrust community.[53]

The concept of SGEI however goes one step further to emphasize that markets need correction in more ways than one, because they under supply certain goods (either regarding access or affordability).[54] Moreover deciding which public goods must be supplied requires an adequate democratic justification. This means public justifications and political decision-making are again on the agenda – albeit by way of exception to the general rule that competition law applies unabridged to undertakings, and subject to the general administrative law requirement of proportionality. At the same time, the providers of the public services involved are private undertakings functioning according to market principles to the greatest extent possible while compatible with their public task. Hence, SGEI are a particularly European solution to the problem of supplying public goods by means of private undertakings that is solved in other jurisdictions (such as the United States) by variants on State action doctrines or by more overtly political means.[55]

This raises the question of whether the politics behind this strand of competition policy are identifiable based on ideological preferences.

Reviewing merger control

The context and background to EU merger control

Although today merger control is one of the key pillars of competition law, the EU Treaties themselves did not provide a regime for merger control but were restricted to doing so for antitrust and state aid. Merger control was introduced based on secondary legislation in 1989 (the Merger Control Regulation, or MRC)[56] in the wake of the internal market drive,[57] and the Singe European Act (1987) which streamlined decisions-making procedures. Both sought to reinvigorate European integration based on an administrative push to promote free market principles. This development could be described as driven by the unlikely tandem of the arch liberal British Prime Minister Margaret Thatcher and the statist French socialist, Commission President Jacques Delors.[58] The resulting model based on liberalization-powered growth has served to propel European integration forward until the 2007 banking crisis.

Merger control, originally excluded from the scope of EU competition law for reasons of national industrial policy, played part in this process because it was finally deemed necessary to introduce centralization on this point. European industry favored such a move because national merger control was thought to have stood in the way of EU-wide consolidation which was held necessary to meet industrial challenges from the United States, and increasingly Japan. A one-stop shop was sorely needed instead of time-consuming multiple filings in national jurisdictions with potentially contradictory and time-consuming procedures.[59] In addition, the Court of Justice had found in the 1973 *Continental Can*[60] and especially the 1987 *Philip Morris*[61] cases that Article 102 TFEU (dominance abuse), respectively 101 (the cartel prohibition) could be applied to some mergers. Because antitrust was a very blunt instrument for this purpose and above all featured high risk ex post controls – mergers would already have been consumed before scrutiny was exercized and might have to be unwound at considerable cost – most interested parties came to prefer a bespoke regime that might reduce the risks by having checks done in advance (ex ante).

The first MRC

Such a regime was indeed set out in the original 1989 MCR including a two-phase procedure with short timeframes and fatal deadlines (to the advantage of the companies involved: if the Commission did not decide within these time-limits, the merger was cleared automatically), and a test that was based on preventing the emergence of dominance. With its notification requirement and centralized nature, based on a Commission monopoly on dealing with mergers above a certain turnover threshold, the system of the MCR was (and remains until today) in some important ways like that of pre-modernization antitrust. The difference is that it cannot easily be decentralized – although coordination regarding procedures below the threshold could potentially be improved.

The Commission most clearly signalled that competition would prevail over industrial policy in *Aerospatiale-Alenia/de Havilland*,[62] the first merger blocked in the 1991, the first year of operation of the original MCR.[63] Since then, especially US firms have been critical when their mergers were subject to conditions,[64] or blocked,[65] but no EU industrial policy based on strategic use of its merger control has emerged. Instead, the Commission raised plaudits for executing by means of its Merger Task Force (MTF) a highly efficient policy which processed complex mergers within tight deadlines and based on teamwork and interaction with industry at an intensity that was new to DG competition and came to set standards also for state aid and antitrust.

Legal problems and the 2004 review

However, the MTF ran into problems when its pursuit of an increasingly active merger policy (especially on the contested theory of joint dominance) led to overreach and more generally elicited criticism that the economic effects of mergers were not duly considered. Eventually, the Commission suffered three high profile defeats in merger cases reviewed by the General Court in 2002 (in *Airtours*, *Schneider*, and *Tetra Laval*).[66] This led to the disbanding of the MTF and reorganization of DG competition during the mandate of Commissioner Mario Monti, linking decentralized merger units more closely to antitrust and state aid in the different sectors.

In the context of this reform, Commissioner Monti introduced further changes that involved DG competition as a whole. He created the new position of chief economist staffed by academic economists and introduced an internal review procedure based on the fresh pair of eyes (also called devil's advocate). The role of the nominally independent hearing officer (who remained however an official within DG competition) was reinforced. The 2002 events also lead to a revision of the MCR in 2004, notably a different test that allegedly clarified the role of coordinated versus uncoordinated behavior (previously cover by joint dominance, but not pursued with a notable degree of success before or since).[67] The threshold system was also refined. The overall features of the system, centralized control over exemptions based on a notification requirement and turnover thresholds, remained.

Developments in (the review of) merger control

During the mandate of Joaquín Almunia, the Commission issued in 2014 a White Paper with proposals on merger reform for a third generation of merger powers. It is seeking further review powers, notably with regard to non-controlling (minority) share holdings.[68] The norm proposed in the Commission's 2014 White Paper is that of a 'competitively significant link' based on stakes in a competitor or vertically related undertaking between 5 and 20%. This would trigger a *sui generis* procedure. Apart from this major substantive change, the proposals also sought to streamline (in general) the referrals of merger cases between the NCAs and the Commission. This process is also intended to involve increased information exchange regarding merger cases between NCAs. If this leads to greater coherence of national and EU policies, it would be of great significance to the cohesiveness of competition policy as a whole. It might also lead to a degree of harmonization of national rules and practices.

Other innovations that were the subject of consultation in the context of the White Paper follow-up were alternatives for turnover to determine the notification threshold. This concern was caused by mergers involving pharmaceutical companies, where the value of patents might far exceed turnover of smaller undertakings, and information technology companies, where value of the number of users and the volume of data could equally be understated by turnover. A significant example was the *Facebook/WhatsApp* merger in 2014,[69] which was only handled by the Commission at the request of the notifying parties when it was subject to national controls in at least three Member States, not because it independently met the standard turnover thresholds of the MCR. Coincidentally, this merger has also led to massive fines (over 100 million euros) being imposed on Facebook for supplying false information as part of the merger procedure.[70] More substantively pertinent meanwhile national competition and data protection authorities had rung the alarm over this type of merger.

Possibly, this may lead to the Commission becoming more sensitive to issues such as big data, and online privacy in the context of merger control.

Scope for a social-democratic perspective? The case of Joaquín Almunia

Career and achievements

The main Social Democratic leader with an impact on competition law at the center of EU decision-making during the implementation period of modernization was Joaquín Almunia. An economist and lawyer by training, he started his political career as economic adviser of the Socialist trade union, UGT, before becoming the socialist minister for Labour affairs and social security in the first government of the Spanish Socialist Party directed by Felipe González, carrying out an unpopular pension reform (1982–1986). He shifted to the position of Minister of public administrations in the second González government (1986–1991), before becoming whip of the Socialist group at the Spanish Parliament (1994–1997). Elected secretary general of the Spanish Socialist Party in 1997, he was candidate for Prime Minister representing the social-liberal wing close to the Third Way, after having lost the primaries against Josep Borrell, who represented the neo-Keynesian tradition favorable to state intervention and public enterprise.[71]

He lost the general elections in 2000 before becoming in 2004 Commissioner for economic and monetary affairs during the height of the banking and Euro crisis (when Dutch liberal Neelie Kroes was heading DG competition, notably dealing with state aid to banking). Next Almunia became competition commissioner and vice-president of the European Commission from 2010 till 2014. During his tenure at DG competition, aside from the implementation of antitrust modernization the Commission pursued several high-profile high technology cases: (Microsoft, Intel, Google) and blocked several high-profile mergers (such as that of NYSE Euronext/ Deutsche Börse).

Moreover, Almunia carried forward both (substantive and procedural) state aid modernization and the reform of merger control. In stark contrast to antitrust, even within the context of reform, these two areas remained highly centralized and under Commission control with all the related advantages – such as consistency and relative immunity from (primarily national) political pressure – and disadvantages, such as capacity constraints and the disabling of national procedures. At the same time, both policies were to become more economics oriented and effects based under the influence of the new Chief Economists he appointed, Kai-Uwe Kühn (2011–2013), who had spent most of his academic career at the University of Michigan in the US.

Did his socialism make a difference?

Is it indicative of his social-democratic background that Almunia was the Commissioner to bring these initiatives to fruition while he was presiding over the implementation of modernization? The beneficiaries in all cases are European consumers, and in the SGEI case, in their dual role as citizens. It is true that competition law is a far stretch from the redistribution of wealth as a political and social objective. However, the operationalization of the concept of SGEI notably allows for forms of solidarity (including between generations and social-economic groups) and leaves decisions on that front to the national (or even sub-national) sphere. In that sense, it comes closer to accommodating political decision-making, including from a Social Democratic perspective which may be especially interested in public policy and public goods.

It would be going too far to draw clear inferences here regarding the relevance of the social economic heritage with regard to Almunia's actions as competition commissioner. There is no clear evidence that he created a break from the previous liberal line put forward by his predecessors. Nevertheless, he does appear to represent a new generation of socialist politicians from Southern Member States who have embraced or have become representatives of stringent competition law enforcement by means of or in parallel with EU law.

This is more in line with controlling market forces as market power than with harnessing undertakings for public policy as put forward by another key social-democratic heavyweight, the Italian socialist Giuliano Amato. This former leader of the PSI led by Bettino Craxi, served as secretary of the Cabinet Office (1983–1987) and deputy prime minister (1987–1988) before becoming prime minister of Italy (1992–1993). That year he was appointed as head of the Italian Antitrust Authority (1993–1997) and produced from his experience an intellectual reflection which symbolized the increasing conversion of classical social democrats towards social-liberalism of the Third-Way.[72] This meant that competition policy shifted from being an instrument to serve various purposes to protecting competition and efficiency as such, reducing the original regulatory purpose.[73] This process involved these men becoming conversant with EU competition law concepts and instruments in a manner that may have influenced their politics just as their politics might influence their policies. Given the increasing institutional and economic constraints involved, the former may have occurred even more than the latter.

Conclusion

In the period 2003–2017, the two main developments in competition law have been the implementation of antitrust modernization and the elaboration of the regime of SGEI regarding State aid. I have examined these developments on their own terms as well as in relation to the statist revisions of the Treaties known as the Sarkozy amendments, and the tenure of the Social Democrat Almunia as Commissioner for competition policy.

Modernization

The modernization of EU antitrust and its implementation can broadly be regarded as a success in its own terms. It was truly an upgrade of the Commission's instruments and a successful decentralization combined with new coordinating powers. This meant that ultimately little effective control at the central level was sacrificed but much was gained in terms of impact. This result is politically acceptable also because at its heart is a policy network that ensured it was not necessary to exercise hard power, at least so far. In terms of output, the results indicate that the Member States' authorities are carrying the bulk of the enforcement burden albeit with a more traditional caseload than the Commission, which is focusing on hardcore antitrust and high-profile cases. Although the Commission is not dealing with more cases than before, it is looking at more complex ones.

SGEI

Regarding SGEI, the Altmark package and Almunia package especially really set up two regimes: a mild one for social services (general block exemption type decision) and a strict one for the utilities (the framework) based on arm-twisting and individual decisions. This reflects the Commission's assessment of which areas are too politically sensitive to hazard intrusive intervention (social services), and those where a strict approach may pay off (utilities) in terms of promoting market-based provision of infrastructure and services.

From a systemic perspective, it is worth noting that the Court's Altmark test is a structured rule of reason because it all revolves around the state aid criterion of *advantage* applying or not. By contrast, the Altmark package and Almunia package are a centralized exception applied by the Commission albeit partly in the form of the block exemption. This is to say that the organizational model of pre-modernization antitrust is applied regarding SGEI in the state aid context, after it was abolished as ultimately counterproductive in antitrust.[74] This raises the question whether further developments might at some point also be similar.

Merger control

As we have seen, although it is based on a Regulation (and not the Treaty itself), the system of merger control since the 1990s until today has been remarkably stable regarding its main structure, although there has been constant tinkering at the margins. The principle of centralized control by the Commission based on a notification system (like antitrust before modernization) remains unchallenged. Yet important innovations such as economic effects-based competition analysis have their roots here. More recently, there is a search for more coherent application of powers of national authorities, implying a degree of harmonization of national laws and practices. Finally, as regards the EU level, the question has become whether the MCR is up to the challenges of the on-line world.

The Sarkozy amendments

As we have seen, after the failure of the proposed Constitutional Treaty, the 2007 Lisbon Treaty linked antitrust more closely to the internal market instead of making it a Treaty objective and glorified the scope for state intervention in the market in the form of SGEI at various levels. Notwithstanding Sarkozy's intentions, the result of these amendments appears to be more in conformity with the free market orientation of the Commission than with the state-oriented ambitions of its critics. In fact, the system established for state aid and SGEI closely resembles that of pre-modernization antitrust: a system of stringent rules where exceptions are applied in a centralized manner. A broader integration logic may thus be at play.

Also, the emphasis on SGEI as an exception to the logic of competition law implicitly assumes that the rule itself is established as acceptable. Following the Sarkozy amendments therefore, it may be possible to say that the effectiveness and legitimacy of antitrust increased in line with the enhanced practical application of the State aid rules. However, with the development of SGEI, an important public policy exception to the latter took shape during the same period. This indicated how state aid and public policies might be compatible.

A social-democratic perspective?

It appears that with Karel van Miert and Joaquín Almunia, both being regarded as successful competition commissioners, antitrust has moved into the mainstream as part of the socialist compromise with open markets. In turn, the acceptance of Southern Europeans and socialist politicians (or both) serving as competition commissioners can be seen as reflecting the degree to which they themselves formed part of the market-oriented mainstream typical of the acceptance of general economic principles by the tenants of the Third Way in a European context.

These developments are compatible with a view of competition policy as policing markets to make them efficient and deliver consumer benefits and keeping undertakings honest by controlling market power – the first and dominant strand of competition policy. Yet this does not just mean protecting consumers in free markets instead of distributing wealth. Especially in the context of SGEI, there is scope for pursuing public policies based on solidarity consistent with the competition rules – provided the measures involved are proportionate. This can be seen as a second strand of competition policy that is compatible with social-democratic policies.

In conclusion, there is no evidence of a specific social-democratic perspective or discourse introduced in EU competition policy in relation to either of these trends. Instead, the development of EU competition policy appears to be shaped by economic theory, international peer review (notably within the ECN) and the legal controls exercised by the EU courts. It seems that the policies of liberal and social-democratic commissioners for EU competition law have become largely interchangeable. This is illustrated by the fact that the current director general for competition, the Frenchman Olivier Guersent, has served in the private offices of both van Miert and Neelie Kroes.

Whether SGEI are nevertheless being deployed by social democrats at national, regional or local level to counterbalance market forces and soften the requirements of competition law (albeit within proportionality constraints) would be an interesting problem for further comparative research.

Notes

1 Professor of law, markets and behavior, Vrije Universiteit Amsterdam, and Authority for Consumers and Markets (ACM). ORCID ID: 0000-0001-9989-4419. I am grateful for research assistance by Michelle Rijnen and suggestions by the editors. The opinions expressed here are personal. This chapter largely relies on elements of my books Wolf Sauter, *Coherence in EU Competition Law* (Oxford: Oxford University Press, 2016), notably chapters 2 and 6, and Wolf Sauter, *Public Services in EU Law* (Cambridge: Cambridge University Press, 2015).

2 Council Regulation (EC) No 1/2003 of 16 December 2002 on the implementation of the rules on competition laid down in Articles 81 and 82 of the Treaty, OJ 2003, L1/1.

3 Commission staff working paper SEC(2009) 574, Commission staff working paper accompanying the Communication from the Commission to the European Parliament and Council – Report on the functioning of Regulation 1/2003, paras 264–268. See Communication from the Commission to the European Parliament and the Council, Ten Years of Antitrust Enforcement under Regulation 1/2003: Achievements and Future Perspectives, COM(2014) 453, paras 8 and 23.

4 Commission staff working document, Enhancing competition enforcement by the Member States' competition authorities: institutional and procedural issues, accompanying the Commission Communication Ten Years of Antitrust Enforcement under Regulation 1/2003: achievements and future perspectives, SWD(2014) 231.

5 *Ibid.*, at 9–10.

6 Ten years of antitrust enforcement, above n. 3, at 9.

7 *Ibid.*, at 11.

8 Commission staff working paper SEC(2009) 574, above n. 3, paras 244–268.

9 *Ibid.*, para 260.

10 Ten Years of Antitrust Enforcement, above n. 3, at 4: "The Commission and the NCAs have prioritized the most serious and harmful anticompetitive practices, in particular, cartels."

11 An example is Case T-301/04 *Clearstream Banking AG, Clearstream International SA v Commission* [2009] ECR II-3155.

12 Communication from the Commission: Guidance on its enforcement priorities in applying Article 82 of the EC Treaty to abusive exclusionary conduct by dominant undertakings, OJ 2009, C45/7.

13 Case T-286/09 *Intel Corp v Commission*, Judgment of 12 June 2014 ECLI:EU:T:2014:547. See Paul Nihoul, "The Ruling of the General Court in Intel: Towards the End of an Effects-Based Approach in European Competition Law," *Journal of European Competition Law & Practice* 5 (2014): 521–530; Wouter Wils, "The Judgment of the EU General Court in Intel and the So-Called More Economic Approach to Abuse of Dominance," *World Competition* 37 (2014): 405–434. See Case C-413/14 P Intel Corp v Commission, Judgement of 6 September 2017, ECLI:EU:C:2017:632.

14 Margrethe Vestager, "Speech: Protecting Consumers from Exploitation." Chillin' Competition Conference, Brussels, 21 November 2016.

15 Press Release, Antitrust: Commission Opens Formal Investigation into Aspen Pharma's Pricing Practices for Cancer Medicines, Brussels, 15 May 2017 (IP/17/1323).

16 Wouter Wils, "Ten Years of Regulation 1/2003 – a Retrospective," *Journal of European Competition Law & Practice* 4 (2013): 293–301.

17 Alan Riley, "EC Antitrust Modernization: The Commission Does Very Nicely – Thank You! Part One: Regulation 1 and the Notification Burden," *European Competition Law Review* 24 (2003): 604–615, at 604.

18 Fabienne Ilkovitz and Adriaan Dierx, Ex Post Evaluation of Competition Policy Enforcement: What Can We Learn from the Literature and from the Experience of Competition Authorities? *Competition Policy Brief*, June 2015; and European Commission, Ex-Post Economic Evaluation of Competition Policy Enforcement: A Review of the Literature. Available at: http://ec.europa.eu/competition/publications/reports/expost_evaluation_competition_policy_en.pdf

19 Case C-375/09 *Prezes Urzędu Ochrony Konkurencji i Konsumentów v Tele2 Polska sp. z o.o., devenue Netia SA* [2011] ECR I-3055, para 28.

20 Case C-681/11 *Bundeswettbewerbsbehörde and Bundeskartellanwalt v Schenker & Co. AG and Others*, ECLI:EU:C:2013:404.

21 Case C-344/98 *Masterfoods Ltd v HB Ice Cream Ltd*, ECLI:EU:C:2000:689.

22 Commission staff working paper SEC(2009) 574, above n. 3, at 36.

23 Such as Resolution of the Meeting of Heads of the European Competition Authorities of 16 November 2010, Competition Authorities in the European Union – the Continued Need for Effective Institutions. Available at: http://ec.europa.eu/competition/ecn/ncas.pdf

24 Proposal for a Directive of the European Parliament and of the Council to empower the competition authorities of the Member States to be more effective enforcers and to ensure the proper functioning of the internal market, COM(2017) 142, 22 March 2017.

25 Imelda Maher, "Functional and Normative Delegation to Non-Majoritarian Institutions: the Case of the European Competition Network," *Comparative European Politics* 7 (2009) 414–434, at 428.

26 For fears of a different outcome see Claus-Dieter Ehlermann and Isabella Atanasiu (eds.), *European Competition Law Annual 2002: Constructing the EU Network of Competition Authorities* (Oxford: Hart Publishing, 2005).

27 There is in fact a 2013 proposal to create such an office, albeit so far only with relation to prosecuting fraud against the EU budget. Commission Communication, Proposal for a Council Regulation on the establishment of the European Public Prosecutor's Office, COM(2013) 534. Earlier, Claus-Dieter Ehlermann, "Reflections on a European Cartel Office," *Common Market Law Review* 32 (1995): 471–486; Stephen Wilks and Lee McGowan, "Disarming the Commission: The Debate Over a European cartel office," *Journal of Common Market Studies* 33 (1995): 259–273.
28 European Parliament, Committee for Economic and Monetary Affairs, Report by MEP René Repasi (Germany, SPD) on the Annual Competition Report 2022, 9 May 2023.
29 Ten years of antitrust enforcement under Regulation 1/2003, above n. 3, para 23.
30 Joint statement of the council and the commission on the functioning of the network of competition authorities. Available at: http://ec.europa.eu/competition/ecn/joint_statement_en.pdf.
31 Directive 2014/104/EU of the European Parliament and of the Council of 26 November 2014 on certain rules governing actions for damages under national law for infringements of the competition law provisions of the Member States and of the European Union Text with EEA relevance, OJ 2014, L349/1.
32 Adopted as Directive (EU) 2019/1 of the European Parliament and of the Council of 11 December 2018 to empower the competition authorities of the Member States to be more effective enforcers and to ensure the proper functioning of the internal market, OJ 2019, L11/3.
33 Commission staff working paper SEC(2009) 574, above n. 3, at 61.
34 *Ibid.*, at 74.
35 Wolf Sauter, "Public Services and the Internal Market: Building Blocks or Persistent Irritant?," *European Law Journal* 21 (2015): 738–757.
36 The Union shall establish an internal market. It shall work for the sustainable development of Europe based on balanced economic growth and price stability, a highly competitive social market economy, aiming at full employment and social progress, and a high level of protection and improvement of the quality of the environment. It shall promote scientific and technological advance.
37 Cf. Manfred E. Streit and Werner Mussler, "The Economic Constitution of the European Community: From 'Rome' to 'Maastricht'," *European Law Journal* 1 (1995): 5–30.
38 Cf. Fritz W. Scharpf, *Community and Autonomy: Institutions, Policies and Legitimacy in Multilevel Europe* (Frankfurt am Main: Campus, 2010).
39 Wolf Sauter, "The Economic Constitution of the EU," *Columbia Journal of European* Law 4 (1998): 27–68.
40 This can involve all types of advantages as long as they can be expressed at a monetary value such as interest free loans, loan guarantees, tax deferrals, preferential awards of land as well as more straightforward cash injections and periodic subsidies.
41 Communication from the Commission, State aid action plan: Less and better targeted state aid: a roadmap for state aid reform 2005–2009 (Consultation document) COM(2005) 107, 7 June 2005. Cf. Natalia Fiedziuk, "Towards a More Refined Economic Approach to Services of General Economic Interest," *European Public Law* 16 (2010): 271–88; Damien Neven and Vincent Verouden, "Towards a More Refined Economic Approach in State Aid Control," in Wolfgang Mederer, Nicola Pesaresi and Marc Van Hoof (eds.), *EU Competition Law – Volume IV: State Aid* (Deventer: Claeys and Casteels Publishing, 2008).
42 State aid action plan, above n. 41, paras 10–11.
43 Cf. Common principles for an economic assessment of the compatibility of state aid under article 87.3, Commission non-paper, para 9; Fiedziuk, above n. 41; Neven and Verouden, above n. 41, para 1.3.
44 Herwig C.H. Hoffman and Claire Micheau (eds.), *State Aid Law of the European Union* (Oxford: Oxford University Press, 2016).

45 Commission Regulation (EC) No 800/2008 of 6 August 2008 declaring certain categories of aid compatible with the common market in application of Articles 87 and 88 of the Treaty (General block exemption Regulation), OJ 2008, L214/3.
46 Case C- 280/ 00 *Altmark Trans GmbH en Regierungspräsidium Magdeburg v Nahverkehrsgesellschaft Altmark GmbH* [2003] ECR I- 7747.
47 Commission Decision on the application of Article 86(2) of the EC Treaty to state aid in the form of public service compensation granted to certain undertakings entrusted with the operation of services of general economic interest, OJ 2005, L312/ 67; Community framework for State aid in the form of public service compensation, OJ 2005, C297/4).
48 Communication from the Commission on the application of the European Union State aid rules to compensation granted for the provision of services of general economic interest, OJ 2012, C8/4; Commission Decision of 20 December on the application of Article 106(2) of the Treaty on the Functioning of the European Union to Sstate aid in the form of public service compensation granted to certain undertakings entrusted with the operation of services of general economic interest, OJ 2012, L7/3; Communication from the Commission, European Union framework for state aid in the form of public service compensation, OJ 2012, C8/15; Commission Regulation on the application of Articles 107 and 108 of the Treaty on the Functioning of the European Union to de minimis aid granted to undertakings providing services of general economic interest, OJ 2012, L114/8.
49 SGEI Reform: Presenting the Draft Legislation, *Almunia Speech Bruges*, 30 September 2011 (College of Europe).
50 Case T-125/12 Viasat Broadcasting UK Ltd v Commission, ECLI:EU:T:2015:687.
51 See Leigh Hancher and Wolf Sauter, "Public Services and EU Law," in Catherine Barnard and Steve Peers (eds.), *European Union law*, 2nd ed. (Oxford: Oxford University Press, 2017).
52 The Power of Markets, the Role of Public Policy, *Almunia Speech Bucharest*, 21 October 2011 (Academy of Economic Studies).
53 Trends and Milestones in Competition Policy Since 2010, *Almunia Speech Brussels*, 2014 (Amcham).
54 Wolf Sauter, *Public Services in EU Law* (Cambridge: Cambridge University Press, 2015).
55 Daniel A. Crane, "Hard Look Review of Anticompetitive State Action," in Philip Lowe, Mel Marquis and Giorgio Monti (eds.), *European Competition Law Annual 2013: Effective and Legitimate Enforcement of Competition Law* (London: Hart Publishing, 2016).
56 Council Regulation (EEC) No 4064/89 of 21 December 1989 on the control of concentrations between undertakings, OJ 1989, L395/1.
57 Completing the internal market, White paper from the European Commission to the European Council, COM(85)310, 14 June 1985.
58 Georges Ross, "Inside the Delors cabinet," *Journal of Common Market Studies* 32 (1994): 499–523.
59 Damian Neven, Robin Nuttall and Paul Seabright, *Merger in Daylight: The Economics and Politics of European Merger Control* (London: Center for Economic Policy Research, 1993).
60 Case 6–72 *Europemballage Corporation and Continental Can Company Inc. v Commission* [1973] ECR 215.
61 Joined cases 142 and 156/84 *British-American Tobacco Company Ltd and R. J. Reynolds Industries Inc. v Commission* [1987] ECR 4487. See K. Banks, "Mergers and Partial Mergers Under EEC Law," *Fordham International Law Journal* 11 (1987): 255–309.
62 Case M.23 *Aerospatiale-Alenia/de Havilland* [1991] OJ L334/42. Cf. Giorgio Monti, *EC Competition Law* (Cambridge University Press, 2007) at 6ff.
63 Council Regulation (EEC) No 4064/89 of 21 December 1989 on the control of concentrations between undertakings, OJ 1989, L395/1.
64 Case M.877 Boeing/*McDonnell Douglas* [1997] OJ L336/16.

65 Case M.2220 *General Electric/Honeywell* [2004] OJ L48/1.
66 Case T-342/99 *Airtours plc v Commission* [2002] ECR II-2585; Case T-77/02 *Schneider Electric SA v Commission* [2002] ECR II-4201; Case T-80/02 *Tetra Laval BV v Commission* [2002] ECR II-4519. A negative clearance was overturned by the General Court but upheld by the Court of Justice in Case T-464/04 *Independent Music Publishers and Labels Association (Impala, association internationale) v Commission.* [2006] ECR II-2289; Case C-416/06 P *Bertelsmann AG and Sony Corporation of America v Independent Music Publishers and Labels Association (Impala)* [2008] ECR I-4951.
67 Council Regulation (EC) No 139/2004 of 20 January 2004 on the control of concentrations between undertakings, OJ 2004, L 24/1.
68 White paper, Towards more effective EU merger control, COM(2014)449. Preceded by Commission Report on the functioning of Regulation No 139/2004, COM/2009/281.
69 Case No COMP/M.7217 – FACEBOOK/WHATSAPP, 3 October 2014.
70 Mergers: Commission fines Facebook €110 million for Providing Misleading Information about WhatsApp Takeover, Brussels, 18 May 2017 (IP/17/1369).
71 Joaquín Almunia, *Memorias políticas* (Madrid: Aguilar, 2001); Joaquín Almunia, *Ganar el futuro, Cómo Europa y la socialdemocracia pueden salir juntas de la* crisis (Madrid: Taurus, 2018).
72 Giuliano Amato, *Antitrust and the Bounds of Power: The Dilemma of Liberal Democracy in the History of the Market* (Oxford: Hart Publishing, 1997); Oles Andriychuk (ed.), *Antitrust and the Bounds of Power: 25 Years On* (London: Bloomsbury, 2023).
73 Barry E. Hawk, "Giuliano Amato, Antitrust and the Bounds of Power," *Fordham International Law Journal* 21, 4 (1997): 1670–1675.
74 Case T-674/11 *TV2/Danmark A/S v Commission*, ECLI:EU:T:2015:684; Case T- 125/12 *Viasat Broadcasting UK Ltd v Commission*, ECLI:EU:T:2015:687.

Bibliography

Publications

Almunia, Joaquín. *Ganar el futuro, Cómo Europa y la socialdemocracia pueden salir juntas de la* crisis. Madrid: Taurus, 2018.

Almunia, Joaquín. *Memorias políticas*. Madrid: Aguilar, 2001.

Almunia, Joaquín. The Power of Markets, the Role of Public Policy. *Speech Bucharest* 21 October 2011 (Academy of Economic Studies).

Almunia, Joaquín. SGEI Reform: Presenting the Draft Legislation. *Speech Bruges*, 30 September 2011 (College of Europe).

Almunia, Joaquín. Trends and Milestones in Competition Policy Since 2010. *Speech Brussels* 14 October 2014 (Amcham).

Amato, Giuliano. *Antitrust and the Bounds of Power: The Dilemma of Liberal Democracy in the History of the Market*. Oxford: Hart Publishing, 1997.

Andriychuk, Oles (ed.). *Antitrust and the Bounds of Power: 25 Years On*. London: Bloomsbury, 2023.

Commission Communication, Community Framework for State Aid in the Form of Public Service Compensation, OJ 2005, C297/4.

Commission Communication, Proposal for a Council Regulation on the Establishment of the European Public Prosecutor's Office, COM(2013) 534.

Commission Communication, State aid Action Plan: Less and Better Targeted State Aid: A Roadmap for State Aid Reform 2005–2009 (Consultation Document) COM(2005) 107, 7 June 2005.

Commission Communication, Ten Years of Antitrust Enforcement Under Regulation 1/2003: Achievements and Future Perspectives, para 23.

Commission, Ex-Post Economic Evaluation of Competition Policy Enforcement: A Review of the Literature. Fabienne Ilzkovitz and Adriaan Dierx (DG COMP), June 2015. Available at: http://ec.europa.eu/competition/publications/reports/expost_evaluation_competition_policy_en.pdf

Commission Press Release, Antitrust: Commission Opens Formal Investigation into Aspen Pharma's Pricing Practices for Cancer Medicines, Brussels, 15 May 2017 (IP/17/1323).

Commission Press Release, Mergers: Commission Fines Facebook €110 million for Providing Misleading Information about WhatsApp Takeover, Brussels, 18 May 2017 (IP/17/1369).

Commission Staff Working Document, Enhancing Competition Enforcement by the Member States' Competition Authorities: Institutional and Procedural Issues, Accompanying the Commission Communication Ten Years of Antitrust Enforcement Under Regulation 1/2003: Achievements and Future Perspectives, SWD(2014) 231.

Commission Staff Working Paper SEC(2009) 574, Commission Staff Working Paper Accompanying the Communication from the Commission to the European Parliament and Council – Report on the Functioning of Regulation 1/2003, paras 264–268.

Commission White Paper, Towards more effective EU merger control, COM(2014)449. Preceded by Commission Report on the Functioning of Regulation No 139/2004, COM/2009/281.

Communication from the Commission, European Union Framework for State Aid in the Form of Public Service Compensation, OJ 2012, C8/15.

Communication from the Commission: Guidance on its Enforcement Priorities in Applying Article 82 of the EC Treaty to Abusive Exclusionary Conduct by Dominant Undertakings, OJ 2009, C45/7.

Communication from the Commission on the Application of the European Union State aid Rules to Compensation Granted for the Provision of Services of General Economic Interest, OJ 2012, C8/4.

Communication from the Commission to the European Parliament and the Council, Ten Years of Antitrust Enforcement under Regulation 1/2003: Achievements and Future Perspectives, COM(2014) 453, paras 8 and 23.

Competition Authorities in the EU, Resolution of the Meeting of Heads of the European Competition Authorities of 16 November 2010, Competition Authorities in the European Union – the Continued Need for Effective Institutions. Available at: http://ec.europa.eu/competition/ecn/ncas.pdf

Completing the Internal Market, White Paper from the European Commission to the European Council, COM(85)310, 14 June 1985.

Council and Commission, Joint Statement of the Council and the Commission on the Functioning of the Network of Competition Authorities. Available at: http://ec.europa.eu/competition/ecn/joint_statement_en.pdf.

Crane, Daniel A. 'Hard Look Review of Anticompetitive State Action'. In *European Competition Law Annual 2013: Effective and Legitimate Enforcement of Competition Law* edited by Philip Lowe, Mel Marquis and Giorgio Monti. London: Hart Publishing, 2016.

Ehlermann, Claus-Dieter. "Reflections on a European Cartel Office." *Common Market Law Review* 32 (1995): 471–486.

Ehlermann, Claus-Dieter and Isabella Atanasiu (eds.). *European Competition Law Annual 2002: Constructing the EU Network of Competition Authorities*. Oxford: Hart Publishing, 2005.

European Parliament, Committee for Economic and Monetary Affairs, Report by MEP René Repasi (Germany, SPD) on the Annual Competition Report 2022, 9 May 2023.

Fiedziuk, Cf. Natalia. "Towards a More Refined Economic Approach to Services of General Economic Interest." *European Public Law* 16 (2010): 271–88.

Hancher, Leigh and Wolf Sauter. "Public Services and EU Law." In *European Union Law*, 2nd edn edited by Catherine Barnard and Steve Peers. Oxford: Oxford University Press, 2017.

Hawk, Barry E. "Giuliano Amato, Antitrust and the Bounds of Power." *Fordham International Law Journal* 21, 4 (1997): 1670–1675.

Hoffman, Herwig C.H. and Claire Micheau (eds.). *State Aid Law of the European Union*. Oxford: Oxford University Press, 2016.

Ilkovitz, Fabienne and Adriaan Dierx. Ex post Evaluation of Competition Policy Enforcement: What Can We Learn from the Literature and from the Experience of Competition Authorities? *Competition Policy Brief*, June 2015.

Maher, Imelda. "Functional and Normative Delegation to Non-Majoritarian Institutions: The Case of the European Competition Network." *Comparative European Politics* 7 (2009): 414–434, at 428.

Monti, Giorgio. *EC Competition Law*. Cambridge: Cambridge University Press, 2007.

Neven, Damian, Robin Nuttall and Paul Seabright. *Merger in Daylight: The Economics and Politics of European Merger Control*. London: Center for Economic Policy Research, 1993.

Neven, Damien and Vincent Verouden. "Towards a More Refined Economic Approach in State Aid Control." In *EU Competition Law – Volume IV: State Aid* edited by Wolfgang Mederer, Nicola Pesaresi and Marc Van Hoof. Deventer: Claeys and Casteels Publishing, 2008.

Nihoul, Paul. "The Ruling of the General Court in Intel: Towards the End of an Effects-Based Approach in European Competition Law." *Journal of European Competition Law & Practice* 5 (2014): 521–530.

Riley, Alan. "EC Antitrust Modernization: The Commission Does Very Nicely – Thank You! Part One: Regulation 1 and the Notification Burden." *European Competition Law Review* 24 (2003): 604–615, at 604.

Ross, Georges. "Inside the Delors Cabinet." *Journal of Common Market Studies* 32 (1994): 499–523.

Sauter, Wolf. *Coherence in EU Competition Law*. Oxford: Oxford University Press, 2016.

Sauter, Wolf. "The Economic Constitution of the EU." *Columbia Journal of European* Law 4 (1998): 27–68.

Sauter, Wolf. "Public Services and the Internal Market: Building Blocks or Persistent Irritant?" *European Law Journal* 21 (2015): 738–757.

Sauter, Wolf. *Public Services in EU Law*. Cambridge: Cambridge University Press, 2015.

Scharpf, Fritz W. *Community and Autonomy: Institutions, Policies and Legitimacy in Multilevel Europe*. Frankfurt: Campus aM, 2010.

Streit, Manfred E. and Werner Mussler. "The Economic Constitution of the European Community: From "Rome" to "Maastricht"." *European Law Journal* 1 (1995): 5–30.

Vestager, Margrethe. "Protecting Consumers from Exploitation." Speech Chillin' Competition Conference, Brussels, 21 November 2016.

Wilks, Stephen and Lee McGowan. "Disarming the Commission: The Debate Over a European Cartel Office." *Journal of Common Market Studies* 33 (1995): 259–273.

Wils, Wouter. "The Judgment of the EU General Court in Intel and the So-Called More Economic Approach to Abuse of Dominance." *World Competition* 37 (2014): 405–434.

Wils, Wouter. "Ten Years of Regulation 1/2003 – A Retrospective." *Journal of European Competition Law & Practice* 4 (2013): 293–301.

Legislation

Commission

Regulations

Commission Regulation (EC) No 800/2008 of 6 August 2008 declaring certain categories of aid compatible with the common market in application of Articles 87 and 88 of the Treaty (General block exemption Regulation), OJ 2008, L214/3.

Commission Regulation on the application of Articles 107 and 108 of the Treaty on the Functioning of the European Union to de minimis aid granted to undertakings providing services of general economic interest, OJ 2012, L114/8.

Decisions

Commission Decision of 20 December on the application of Article 106(2) of the Treaty on the Functioning of the European Union to State aid in the form of public service compensation granted to certain undertakings entrusted with the operation of services of general economic interest, OJ 2012, L7/3;

Commission Decision on the application of Article 86(2) of the EC Treaty to State aid in the form of public service compensation granted to certain undertakings entrusted with the operation of services of general economic interest, OJ 2005, L312/67;

European Parliament and Council

Regulations

Council Regulation (EC) No 1/2003 of 16 December 2002 on the implementation of the rules on competition laid down in Articles 81 and 82 of the Treaty, OJ 2003, L1/1.

Council Regulation (EC) No 139/2004 of 20 January 2004 on the control of concentrations between undertakings, OJ 2004, L 24/1.

Council Regulation (EEC) No 4064/89 of 21 December 1989 on the control of concentrations between undertakings, OJ 1989, L395/1.

Directives

Directive 2014/104/EU of the European Parliament and of the Council of 26 November 2014 on certain rules governing actions for damages under national law for infringements of the competition law provisions of the Member States and of the European Union Text with EEA relevance, OJ 2014 L349/1.

Directive (EU) 2019/1 of the European Parliament and of the Council of 11 December 2018 to empower the competition authorities of the Member States to be more effective enforcers and to ensure the proper functioning of the internal market, OJ 2019, L11/3.

Proposal for a Directive of the European Parliament and of the Council to empower the competition authorities of the Member States to be more effective enforcers and to ensure the proper functioning of the internal market, COM(2017) 142, 22 March 2017.

12 A social-democratic dilemma

Swedish competition policy in the 21st century

John Lapidus

Introduction

Competition policy has emerged as one of today's major critical issues for Swedish Social Democracy. From having affirmed competitive measures such as the prohibition of cartels and the public sector's opening-up to competition in the 1990s, the 2000s is rather characterized by a growing distrust of free competition mainly in areas that were previously sheltered from private actors.

Over the last years, the battle of competition policy revolves around the increasing weight of private providers within the Swedish welfare system, especially the providers of welfare services such as health care, education and elderly care. The battle goes under the name of *profits in welfare*.

Profits in welfare is an issue that cuts deep into the social-democratic soul, especially since one of the most distinctive features of the social-democratic welfare model was precisely the public monopolies on delivery and funding of welfare services. Until the early 1980s, Swedish Social Democrats even regarded "public sector expansion as equivalent to democratization."[1]

The rise of private actors in the welfare sector was made possible by new laws and regulations from the 1990s onwards. The competition law from 1993[2] banned all sorts of company cartels as well as many other forms of restricting competition. It is important to note that the concept of *company* was changed in order to include state and local agencies engaged in all sorts of activities, not least the provision of welfare.

Hence, Swedish competition law now includes large parts of the welfare sector. The legislator "consciously wanted to let competition law principles as far as possible also apply to activities in the public sector."[3] The law, inspired by EU competition law, was "a paradigm shift in Swedish competition law with a heightened competition law as a result."[4]

The competition law was implemented by the center-right wing government of 1991–1994, but the law was accepted by the Social Democrats. In the parliamentary debate,[5] the social-democratic MP Axel Andersson said that "a unanimous committee stands behind this report on a proposal for a new competition law."

As a matter of fact, the Social Democrats had done a lot of preparatory work in terms of opening up the public sector for private actors. One of these groundworks

DOI: 10.4324/9781351010573-12

was the social-democratic bill *Economic policy for growth*[6] from 1990, signed by Prime Minister Ingvar Carlsson and Industry Minister Rune Molin. Later on, by the end of the 1990s, the party went even further in opening up the public sector for private actors. The process culminated with a bill entitled *Competition policy for innovation and diversity*[7] in 1999, signed by Third Way–inspired politicians Göran Persson and Mona Sahlin.

The quest for opening up the public sector was never uncontested within the Social Democratic Party. Bearing the party's traditional views on the public sector in mind, it is not surprising that the new competition policy has been more or less contested ever since it was implemented.

On occasion, the internal critique has reached all the way up to the top of the party. For example, the national debate on *profits in welfare* got wind in its sails in 2011–2012 when a number of private sector abuses were highlighted in the media.

In 2014, the new coalitional government (Social Democracy and the Green Party) agreed with the Left Party to appoint a welfare commission, which would review profits in welfare and propose restrictions on them. According to the directives, the welfare commission should come up with proposals on how "profits shall be returned to the operation in which they have occurred."

From the very start, the commission was politically contentious. In 2015, the center-right parties voted for a so-called parliamentary announcement, according to which the welfare commission was urged to focus on factors like quality and follow-up rather than profits in welfare. In 2016, the same parties demanded the welfare commission be shut down altogether.

The welfare commission presented its report on November 8, 2016. It proposed a cap of 7 percent on profits in the welfare sector, which was not exactly in line with the directives according to which "profits shall be returned to the operation in which they have occurred." In other words, the investigation wanted to neither ban nor fully allow for profits in welfare. In 2018, the proposal was made into a bill which was rejected by parliament.

The proposal is a good example of social-democratic indecisiveness on competition policy. This indecisiveness is partly due to constant compromising and balancing between opposing wills and interests of different societal actors. According to the employers' organizations as well as the center-right political parties, the idea to restrict profits in the welfare sector is an unsound political intrusion into private property and business. According to the Left Party and parts of the trade union movement, on the other hand, the social democrats have often been too soft on profits in welfare.

First and foremost, however, the indecisiveness is due to ideological differences within the "broad church"[8] of Swedish Social Democracy. The same goes for the affiliated unions. Over the last decade, competition policy has thus created a number of hot debates at social-democratic and trade union congresses.

Furthermore, there are tactical and strategic aspects of the issue. On the one hand, the issue can be seen as potentially election-winning, where critique against profits in welfare is traditional social-democratic politics which appeals to many voters and creates a clear line of conflict with the opposite political block. On the other hand, it can be seen as a potential election-losing issue where large parts of the middle class have alienated themselves from the traditional welfare model and embraced the possibilities that emerge from a private welfare market.

Background

The Swedish welfare regime is strongly associated with the era of social-democratic governments in the 20th century. In order to distinguish this Scandinavian type of model from *the Liberal welfare regime* and *the Conservative welfare regime*, it is simply termed *the social democratic welfare regime* in the most famous categorization of different types of welfare models.[9] In explaining the rise of the Swedish type of welfare model, those who give the most crucial importance to social democracy are the power resource theorists. They argue that working-class mobilization through active trade unions had its political expression in social-democratic governments, a fundamental power resource that also rested on the ability to create alliances with related organizations.[10]

Although few would dispute that the Swedish welfare model got many of its characteristics from and because of the era of social-democratic governments, their importance has been nuanced by those who indicate that employers were also a driving force in many of the overall compromises that were decisive for its emergence.[11]

Eventually, however, the employers' willingness to compromise came to an end, both in the labor market and in the welfare state arena.[12] Already in the early 1970s, employers began to question Sweden's solidaristic wage policy. In the following decade, they were "able to play different union interests against each other in their efforts to reorganize wage bargaining."[13] Meanwhile, the employers' offensive started to target many other elements of the Swedish welfare model, an offensive that coincided with the international wave of neoliberalism.[14] The Swedish labor movement was surprised by the employers' counterattack and was unable to stand up against it, partly because it was "assumed that the issue could be resolved through the normal tripartite channels of mediation and compromise."[15]

Equally important, there had been a liberal turn among the influential party economists at the Ministry of Finance. In the literature, these social-democratic economists – most notably Kjell-Olof Feldt, Erik Åsbrink and Klas Eklund – are termed *Kanslihushögern* (The Treasury Right). They belonged to a corps that had been given expert status when it came to welfare sector efficiency, and they often defined the public sector as "constituting a problem."[16] For various reasons, they were the ones who made the important decisions and, accordingly, "the shift towards a social democratic compensatory neoliberalism in the mid-1980s, . . . although it had profound effects on Swedish society, was never established as policy through the procedures of mass politics."[17]

The ideological turn within Swedish Social Democracy had a big impact on competition policy. The public monopolies delivering welfare services were the most distinctive[18] and most socialist[19] features of the Swedish welfare model, but, in the 1980s, they started to be exposed to competition from private actors. There was a time when Social Democrats regarded "public sector expansion as equivalent to democratization"[20] but now they gradually affirmed or even took the lead in the trend toward an increased marketization of welfare services.

The affirmation of increased marketization was based on the aforementioned ideological shift, which meant that social democrats embraced a new view of competition policy and a new view of the relationship between equality and efficiency investigated by Birgit Karlsson in this book for an earlier historical period.[21] Furthermore, the social policy ideas from the 1960s and 1970s, including elements such as a "broadening of the social security systems, an expanded responsibility for the state vis-à-vis the individual's welfare and social rights, as well as solidarity with vulnerable people," was now replaced with increased emphasis on the individual's own responsibility and duty vis-à-vis society.[22]

Meanwhile, the ideological turn was part of an international trend. Within European Social Democracy, there was a significant shift in political and economic thinking from the 1980s onwards,[23] often referred to as the Third Way.[24] And even though some attempts were made to chart a different course, especially in the Scandinavian countries and not least in Sweden (e.g. via the so-called wage earner funds which were supported by trade-union economists such as Rudolf Meidner but discouraged by Third-Way social-democratic economists such as Kjell-Olof Feldt), the international trend was quite clear. This was so not least in Britain, where it was "social democrats themselves who were the first to abandon Keynesianism for monetarism, beginning with the Callaghan government."[25]

The discussion within Swedish Social Democracy was often very *Swedish* in its character, but of course, Swedish Social Democracy was influenced by developments in their sister parties all around Europe. Besides, Swedish Social Democracy was influenced by Sweden's gradual approximation to the European Union, which in itself was a threat to traditional values since the social-democratic "compromise and model were national structures and created at that level."[26] The adaptation of a social-democratic model at the European level was difficult since there was a lack of a voluntaristic and political dimension backed by a social movement. The left-wing parties "lost the ability to intervene and provide impetus to social tendencies," which became even more pronounced the more that "legislative and executive powers at national level lost their prerogatives to the European Union and other international bodies."[27]

The 1993 competition law is a good example of this kind of harmonization of Swedish legislation with the competition policy of the European Union (Sweden became a member in 1995). In the center-right government bill[28] preceding the new competition law, it is thus said that it is "the Swedish movement towards the EU," which is the starting point for a new competition policy. It is also said that many countries, such as Belgium, Italy and Ireland, have already adopted national competition laws that constitute a direct harmonization with the EU. Here, leading social democrats agreed with the center-right government. In a parliamentary proposal from 1992,[29] signed by party leader Ingvar Carlsson and many other social democrats, there is thus a certain focus on the need for harmonization with the EU.

On a more direct level, the changing competition policy and especially the changing attitude toward the public sector was made possible by the fact that social democrats, in the early 1980s, began to question the public sector from two different directions. First, there was a critique of bureaucracy and centralization, which had its representatives not least in the Ministry of Public Administration. Second, there was a criticism of inefficiency and unproductiveness, which came first and foremost from the Ministry of Finance.

Initially, the Ministry of Public Administration did not see privatization as the solution to the problem, but instead the public sector would be made more democratic for example by raising the level of service and create more participation via so-called user participation (*brukarmedverkan*). User participation was considered then to be an alternative to privatization.[30] Organizationally, however, the emphasis on decentralization and self-management meant that the public sector was opened up for the Ministry of Finance's demands for marketization.[31] In this context, the aforementioned influential social-democratic economists are often mentioned.

Less noticed is that both types of criticism of the public sector also came from political scientists. An example of this is one of the most well-known interpreters of the Swedish welfare model, Bo Rothstein. In the social-democratic magazine *Tiden*, he attacked the aforementioned public monopolies, which he considered to be "unfair in terms of distribution, politically uncontrollable, inefficient and unjust," and argued that it was best to close down as many of them as possible.[32] Furthermore, he claimed that "because of ideological blindness, Social Democracy has created a privatization ghost [i.e., an unmotivated fear of privatization] and ended up in a sterile discussion of how welfare is to be organized."[33]

Much later, Rothstein changed his opinion on *profits in welfare*. In 2011, he was thus very critical of the effects of privatization in the Swedish welfare sector.[34]

There were other actors, for example, the employers' organizations, who already at an earlier stage advocated a new competition policy in the welfare sector. To them, it was crucial to bring social democracy along because it was seen as the bearer of the traditional Swedish welfare model, and the party had a certain trust capital in this area.

Besides, changes have often occurred with reference to the compatibility with the Swedish model. Here, Cox[35] has introduced the useful concept of *the path-dependency of an idea*, that is, that the Swedish model rests on values (universalism, solidarity and decommodification) so important to so many that "scholars and policy-makers are compelled to justify their observations and proposals for reform by making reference to those values."[36] Hence, the values are allegedly shared even by those who have a completely different agenda. There is thus a political-tactical dimension aiming to change the system not by an open attack but instead by various forms of incremental and "hidden" means, which can be a much more successful way to fundamentally change popular institutions.[37]

The concepts layering, drift and conversion are useful tools to describe this type of incremental and sometimes "hidden" institutional change.[38] Layering takes place when new rules are implemented alongside old rules, conversion takes place when old rules are interpreted in new ways and drift takes place when expenses are not updated in accordance with existing rules. These three concepts can perhaps be also applied to actors and their way of changing over time. When it comes to social democracy, new ideas have been implemented alongside old ones, while old truths have been reinterpreted and/or not updated.

Social democracy agreement on a new competition policy

The 1993 competition law implied both a ban on cartels in private industry and an opening up of the public welfare sector for private actors. The Social Democrats had no problems with the first part of the law, that is, banning company cartels in the private sector. As a matter of fact, the party – cheered by the trade unions and consumer organizations – had been in favor of a restrictive attitude toward monopolistic associations in the private sector ever since the idea of socialization was abandoned in the 1930s.

The Social Democrats remained clear on that point and pushed for a further tightening of the law even after 1993. They referred particularly to consumer interest and emphasized the negative effects of cartels in a more pronounced way than was done for example by the Conservatives. The social-democratic bill entitled *Competition policy for innovation and diversity* in 1999, signed by Prime Minister Göran Persson and Labor Minister Mona Sahlin, stated:[39]

> In view of the serious harm done by cartels, the Government claims that it is not acceptable that cartels causing significant harm to consumer interest whatsoever exist. The bill thus proposes that various measures to streamline tracing and prosecution of cartels be made subject of a special investigation.

From a social-democratic point of view, the sensitive part of the competition law was not the ban of cartels in private industry. A ban on cartels would not create internal tension. But opening up the public sector for private actors, the other part of the competition law, definitely had such a potential.

Including the public sector in the competition law, that is, opening up the public sector for private actors, was an old demand of the Conservatives. Already in 1953, the Conservatives wanted competition law to be directed not only against restrictions on competition in the private sector but also in the public sector. The Conservatives were supported by the Liberals and large parts of private industry in criticizing the state's special status in the 1953 legislation. The Liberals argued that "restrictions of competition related to state regulation should . . . be judged basically on the same grounds as restrictions in other areas?"[40]

The Conservatives continued to raise the issue. The proposed motion, *On economic policy*, from 1975/76 highlighted state involvement in "the business sector," which was said to increase the risk that the state would confuse their "public functions and the private law duties arising from serving as business owner." This was considered to be a problem partly of legal character. The motion also emphasized requirements for "equality in terms of competition between different kinds of companies," an equality threatened by increased state entrepreneurship and the fact that the state was not included in competition law.[41]

The Conservatives finally had their request granted in the 1993 legislation, in which the term *businessman* was replaced with the term *company* to clarify that it comprised all activities of an economic or commercial nature.

The Conservatives thus got what they long wanted. But how did the Social Democrats come to agree on opening up the public sector for private actors?

During the first years of the 1980s, the social democrats were still quite firm on keeping the welfare services publicly delivered. As late as 1985, social-democratic Prime Minister Olof Palme warned about the consequences of private delivery of welfare services.[42] Up to then, gradually, public monopolies had strengthened their position within the Swedish welfare model. One example is healthcare. Due to different reforms in the 1970s and 1980s (e.g. the "seven-crown-reform" and the "dagmar-reform"), the possibilities for doctors to deliver healthcare on a private basis were much restricted. Instead, they were – not without resistance – incorporated into the publicly delivered and publicly funded system.

Palme warned about the consequences of privatization and, exactly in line with traditional social-democratic thinking on the issue, he regarded the public sector as a kind of democratization process. On the other hand, Palme was not very interested in economics and he often let the evermore influential Third-Way politicians and economists such as Kjell-Olof Feldt have the final saying on economic policies, including policies related to the public sector.

The Third-Way party economists, together with the international zeitgeist, influenced the next generation of social-democratic party leaders such as Ingvar Carlsson and, even more so, Göran Persson and, perhaps most of all, Mona Sahlin. In 2011, this series of Third-Way social-democratic politicians was broken by the election of Håkan Juholt. He was more in line with traditional social-democratic views on the public sector, but due to some scandals and also (foremost) internal criticism from the Third-Way-inspired fraction of the party, he was soon replaced by the more pragmatic leader Stefan Löfven.

Hence, by the late 1980s, the Social Democrats had taken a new position on competition policy. And by the late 1990s, that new position was articulated more than ever before or after. The 1999 social-democratic bill *Competition policy for innovation and diversity*, signed by Prime Minister Göran Persson and Labor Minister Mona Sahlin, made it clearer than ever that competition should permeate every aspect of society.

It has been argued that Social Democrats now gave competition policy an even firmer ideological ground than in the 1992 Conservative bill, and that it is "a remarkable difference" compared to the neutral and pragmatic tone of earlier legislative work on competition.[43] Furthermore, the social-democratic bill has been seen as the prime example of a "strong position in favor of an active competition policy and competition as a guiding star."[44] And, finally, economic historian Torbjörn Lundqvist claimed[45] that the Social Democrats delivered a bill with

> more economic liberal features than ever. It was a document of liberal utopian thinking, in my view based on the economic theory of perfect competition,

arguing for the positive effect from competition on the whole society. The vision for the future seemed to be the invisible hand.

It is true that the social-democratic bill contains some utopian features. On no less than six different pages, it gives mention to "the new man" who will arise as a result of free competition. For example, it is said, "Re-regulation and opening up of new markets brings out new ideas, new companies and not least new men." It is also stated that opening up new markets provides an opportunity for "new businesses, new men and new ideas to challenge old and inefficient structures."[46]

The 1999 bill has much to say about the growing need to include even more of the public sector in competition policy. It applies to state monopolies and regulations, but also to local government procurement:

> Now it is urgent to examine the possibility of opening new areas for competition, areas where monopoly currently exists or where the regulatory regime excludes competition between suppliers of different goods. In areas where freedom of establishment of competing companies for various reasons is not possible, models with elements of competitive mechanisms should be tested and developed; models such as the procurement of publicly funded services by independent providers or other operations in alternative forms.

As mentioned earlier, however, even before 1999, the Social Democrats had accepted the claim that the public sector should be included in competition law. One example is the previously mentioned *Competition for more welfare*, published in 1991, which is the public inquiry preceding the 1993 legislation. The person who signed the directive for the investigation was the social-democratic Minister of Public Administration, Bengt K. Å. Johansson. The directive states:[47]

> Specifically, the Committee shall analyze the conditions of competition in regulated sectors and propose measures to increase competition. It shall also examine whether competition law, to a greater extent, can be applied in these sectors.

In an additional directive to the Competition Committee, also signed by Johansson, the Committee is urged to put more focus on enhanced competition for municipal operations, which should be done in close collaboration with representatives of the local government.

The directives mentioned earlier were already deeply rooted in the social-democratic government. Similar thoughts can be found in the 1990 social-democratic bill entitled *Economic policy for growth*, signed by Prime Minister Ingvar Carlsson and Industry Minister Rune Molin. Under the heading "Increased competition and more efficient markets," there is a discussion about the lack of "effective safeguards against cost increases" in the public sector, and it is said:[48]

> The public sector must therefore be exposed to more market-like conditions. This means that producer and client relationships should be developed and

> that contracts and procurement should be systematically considered in the public operations. As part of this effort, the competition committee should – in its continuing efforts to revise state regulations – highlight the idea of alternative activities in the public sector. The increased use of contracts should lead to increased efficiency and the market will be broadened when it is opened up also to individual producers.

According to the bill, social-democratic governments in the 1980s had already done a lot to deregulate the Swedish economy. But much was still to be done:

> In recent years, extensive work has been carried out to deregulate the Swedish economy. The most profound changes have been in the financial markets, agriculture, transportation and the textile and clothing industry. Now the work must go on.

The above has demonstrated that the Social Democrats were highly active in including the public sector in the new competition policy. In the next section, we shall discuss how and why the Social Democrats have started to question the competition law that they once were so keen on implementing.

Social democracy questioning the new competition policy?

It is often said that legislation from the 1990s and onward gradually opened up the public sector to competition from private operators. Another way of expressing it is that new legislation gave private operators the opportunity to use state capital as a source of income and profit for their activities.

The dependence of state capital refers to companies within all three major welfare service sectors (healthcare, education and elderly care), and it involves big companies such as the healthcare company Capio, the education company Academedia and the elderly care company Attendo.

For example, Academedia depends on the *Free school reform* (1992), which stipulates that private education companies can use state capital as a source of income and profit through school vouchers. The reform meant that the Swedish school system was organized according to a voucher system where privately (and publicly) run schools were given a certain amount of money for each student. Similarly, the healthcare company Capio and the elderly care company Attendo depend on state capital either through a voucher system regulated by the *Law on the Freedom of Choice* (LOV) or through municipality and county council procurement of services, regulated by the *Public Procurement Act* (LOU).

The tendency toward increased integration of the public sector in a competitive type of competition policy has continued in the 21st century. This has occurred either through new laws related to the Competition Law, such as the LOU and the Act on System of Choice in the Public Sector, or it has occurred through a direct extension of the 1993 Competition Law. One example is the so-called rule on public sales that restrict competition from 2010. The rule will "create a more level playing field between private and public actors who sell goods or services on the market." The rule means that the competition authority "can go to court with cases where public actors – municipalities, counties or state agencies – conduct operations or act in a way that is judged to distort competition between the public and private sectors."[49]

However, during the same period, the development toward a more competitive competition policy has become increasingly contested. It is primarily the Trade Union Confederation (LO) and political parties to the left of Social Democracy (i.e. the Left Party) that have been critical of the fact that competition policy has been increasingly used against the public sector. But the issue has also been increasingly debated within the Social Democratic Party, for example at the congresses in 2013 and 2017 where more or less vague proclamations were made on the importance to restrict profits for companies engaged in the welfare service sector.

The LO began questioning Swedish competition policy soon after the implementation of the Competition Law in 1993. In its response to the public inquiry,[50] LO spoke of "Competition as a dogma" and attacked the Competition Authority, which it considered to be carrying out the law in a counterproductive and "one-eyed, doctrinaire way, without regard to the negative effects its work to promote competition may have in other regards."[51] According to LO, the Competition Authority had an "evil eye especially towards activities in the public sector." That applies to virtually all public services except the police, customs, military forces and justice systems. The LO regrets that the Competition Authority received support for that "extreme view" in its operations manual. It also criticized that the Competition Authority's goal has been that "everything must necessarily be subject to competition, a goal that is the parent of all other goals of society. Privatization, corporatization and deregulation of public services have therefore become an ideal, an end in itself."

According to LO, it was "more important to maximize welfare than to keep competition perfect." In its response to the public inquiry, the LO raised objections to competition itself. The LO argued that principles of competition often stand in the way of other and far more important principles such as the idea that "public goods should be distributed fairly and be accessible to all citizens; [and] that all citizens, regardless of their place of residence, shall be entitled to the same social services on equal terms."

All in all, the LO has been critical of the development of competition policy and especially of the Competition Authority. It said that the Competition Authority, in its deregulation fervor, cares less about whether deregulation leads to "increased criminality, higher unemployment, poorer working conditions, lower real wages and poorer service for the citizens." Competition comes above everything else. Furthermore, still according to the LO, the Competition Authority has the general idea that "competition is good because competition is good."

Over the past 20 years, the LO has continued to criticize the implementation of competition policy. In 2012, the LO congress decided to push for a ban on profits in health care, education and social services. The congress also wanted to tear up the Act on System of Choice in the Public Sector (LOV).

Within the Social Democratic Party, there has also been increased criticism against the conduct of competition policy. As we have seen, the social-democratic bill in 1999 was very friendly to competition. But ever since the 1993 Competition Law, parts of the party have been highly critical of some aspects of competition policy, especially its focus on deregulation in the public sector.

At the 2013 social-democratic congress, *profits in welfare* was thus a hot topic. In 2015, the decision to start a welfare commission was another step in the new yet old direction. The welfare commission was led by the Social Democrat Ilmar Reepalu, an experienced politician who had long been a leading figure in southern Sweden. His task was to make proposals aimed at "securing that public means are used for the operations that they are intended for and that any surplus, as a main rule, must be reinvested in the operation they originated from."

The welfare commission presented its first report in November 2016. The main suggestion was a 7 per cent cap on profits in the welfare sector. In other words, the investigator wanted to neither ban nor fully allow for profits in welfare.

As mentioned in the introduction, the proposal is a good example of social-democratic indecisiveness on competition policy. To forbid or not to forbid profits in welfare? Or maybe to compromise? The 2017 congress decided to "put an end to the profit hunt in the welfare sector," but as a matter of fact, it is not at all determined or defined how such a stop shall be accomplished.

Along with this indecisiveness comes a striking discrepancy between rhetoric and practical policy. When it comes to profits in welfare, leading social-democratic representatives have talked tough on profits in some places while being much more tolerant in others. For example, when the education company Academedia was about to be introduced on the stock exchange, the then social-democratic Prime Minister Stefan Löfven said it was horrible to sell out 60,000 kids and young persons.[52] In practice, however, he has had a much more tolerant attitude to profits in welfare. Here it is interesting to note that his predecessor leader of the Social Democratic party, Håkan Juholt, had a much more critical stance toward profits in welfare. That was something that contributed to his drastic downfall in 2012, since the welfare industry and the social-democratic Third-Way-politicians turned against him.

Another example is the rapid rise of private health insurance, a phenomenon intimately related to competition policy and the emergence of private delivery in the welfare sector. Here, the Social Democrats have been highly critical in rhetoric while proposing legislation not in line with the same rhetoric. The Stop Law in 2006, for example, was supposed to force private healthcare providers to choose between publicly and privately funded healthcare. According to the then responsible Social Democratic minister, "The government will no longer accept fast-track lanes within the publicly funded healthcare."

In summary, however, the Stop Law was far less draconian than its reputation. The law applied only to hospitals and only to certain hospitals, but it was doubtful whether the law would even apply to these hospitals since there was an opportunity both to redefine them as something else and to separate parts of their activities from the hospital organization. If the county council made decisions contrary to the Stop Law, there were no direct means to override them.[53]

In practice, the Stop Law would not constitute a major threat to the possibilities for purchasing priority for some patients. At the end of the same social-democratic bill, there is actually a reassuring message to all private healthcare providers:

> The Government's assessment is thus that only a small portion of the privately run healthcare funded by county councils will be affected by the government's proposal. . . . As described above, the vast majority of private healthcare providers can thus continue to accept patients whose treatment is funded with private health insurance or own resources.

The above suggests that the Social Democrats, in 2006, criticized fast-track lanes while almost giving them the green light. The same has happened when it comes to profits in welfare, where there have been many proclamations but few bills or other practical policy suggestions.

What are the reasons for the discrepancy between rhetoric and practice? Why do the Social Democrats say they are setting up a law to stop fast-track lanes in health care while creating a law that does not stop the fast-track lanes in health care? Why do they say they want to get rid of profits in welfare, while on other occasions being very tolerant toward them?

When it comes to competition policy and the related issue of profits in welfare there is, first of all, a public opinion that still embraces the idea of the traditional Swedish welfare model. In poll after poll, a majority of the electorate is critical toward profits in welfare. Even within the Social Democratic Party, there has always been an opposition to the Third-Way politicians who have had an almost uninterrupted power position over the last decades.

The radical rhetoric has thus had an important function. The rhetoric of the party leadership has often been directed toward an external opinion and also to an internal opposition, which surprisingly often has accepted words without much substance on these matters. Meanwhile, the party has played a key role in privatizing the welfare sector.

It was the internal opposition and the external opinion that made Prime Minister Stefan Löfven speak out and speak tough about profits in welfare, even though he had no intention of actually doing all what he was saying. In short, it is about a leadership that may preserve a certain measure of radicalism but withholds it in practice for a wide range of reasons: one does not want to bump into middle-class voters who benefit from profits in welfare, one does not want to confront the welfare-industrial complex, which oneself has been involved in building up, one does not want to challenge media which often supports the welfare industry in heated situations, one has developed into an economic elite that has a self-interest in inequality, or one does not want to be too radical during one's term of office, risking losing potentially high-paying jobs awaiting them after they end their political career (in Sweden, there are no quarantine rules for politicians who would like to join private industry after their political careers, and many leading social democrats have done so in the last decade).

Meanwhile, the party is becoming less of a people's movement and more of a voting machine, where it is hard to make a career without falling in line with the party leadership. Signs can be seen at social-democratic congresses. The delegates arrive there with tough motions on – for example – profits in the welfare, but, before the actual debate in the congress hall, the party board gathers the delegates in theme groups where a consensus is molded into phrasings that can be interpreted in any way by the party leadership. Unanimous decisions are taken without debate but all cheer together over words that are so ambiguous that nobody can say what they mean.

The 2017 Congress, for example, decided to put an end to the profit hunt in the welfare sector. How? By what means? Nobody has a clue how it shall be achieved. It is up to the party leadership to pragmatically determine how the will and the decision of the congress shall be interpreted.

One of the explanations mentioned earlier for recent social-democratic policies on competition are strong interest groups and actors that benefit from the new competition policy. Let us discuss some of these actors, for example, the employers' organizations, parts of the trade union movement and parts of the middle class.

The awareness of state capital as a source of income and profits, as well as compact opposition to restrictions in the legislation, is shared by the employers' organizations (for example *the Confederation of Swedish Enterprise*) in which the welfare companies are organized. While the unions' attitude to the rise of a welfare industrial complex has been characterized by a certain ambivalence (see further), the private employers' stance has been clear ever since they seriously began to question the public welfare monopolies at a congress in 1980.

The greater the welfare industrial complex has become, the more employers' organizations have themselves grown in strength. As long as there was no welfare industrial complex, there were also no private employers in these industries. For decades, therefore, the central employers' organization SAF had to rely on related organizations such as the think-tank Timbro, which was founded in 1978 by the right-wing political strategist Sture Eskilsson, and SAF itself.

In recent years, private employers' organizations are themselves much more active in the formation of opinion in the welfare sector. When it comes to healthcare, for example, the company Capio and other private employers in the healthcare sector have organized themselves into a chain with strong links at every level, from the central organization, *the Confederation of Swedish Enterprise*, through the welfare employers' organization *Almega* down to the healthcare employers' organization *Vårdföretagarna* (The Association of Private Care Providers).

But also within the trade union movement, closely related to Social Democracy, there is a certain ambivalence toward restrictions of profits in welfare. One example is the Swedish Municipal Workers' Union (Kommunal), where it has long been an open question how to relate to competition policy and to profits in welfare. Its congress in 2010 ruled that the union must "take up an active struggle against continued competition and for a re-democratization and expansion of the public sector." The congress also decided that the "union board will draw up a plan for the fight," which resulted in a report published two years later.[54]

The congress' decisions were interpreted by many as a no to profits in welfare, but the authors of the report actually took a relatively permissive attitude to them. This attitude was further emphasized by the union's president in a series of interviews on the topic, where she also challenged other unions' stances on the issue.[55] In this regard, the president was questioned by a number of representatives of her own union and also of the Swedish Trade Union Confederation, who argued that she must follow democratic decisions and not promote her own position on profits in welfare.[56] Meanwhile, there was continued criticism of profits in welfare from the majority of union members, with the result that the permissive stance was voted down once again in 2013.[57]

What is the reason for the unions' ambivalence on profits in welfare? In general, just like the Social Democratic Party, the trade-union movement has long had this type of internal antagonism. More specifically, however, there are a number of points of contact between the welfare industrial complex and a union like the Swedish Municipal Workers' Union. The most obvious one is that a growing share of union members are directly employed in the welfare industrial complex. As long as the Swedish welfare model rested on public monopolies with its public delivery of welfare services, welfare workers were almost exclusively publicly employed. This has changed with the emergence of the welfare industrial complex. In the early 1990s, 12 percent of the members of the Swedish Municipal Workers' Union were employed by private sector employees. By 2011, this figure had risen to 23 per cent, that is, 115,000 private sector employees and 355,000 employees in municipalities and county councils.[58] It is likely that the share of private sector employees has increased further in recent years.

The private welfare industry employs an increasing share of the union's members, which means that the two actors must approach each other in new ways. A small but visible example is that the large welfare companies and their employers' organizations are now represented with staff and booths at the union's congresses. Of much greater importance is the fact that the welfare companies are now a bargaining partner. The union's wage negotiations in 2016 included about 50 collective agreements, several of which concern private welfare companies. Under the heading "State of the wage negotiations for your career" are listed six professions of which two are directly related to the private welfare companies, namely "Private schools and private preschools" and "Private healthcare and personal assistance companies."

The fact that the private welfare companies are major employers may be one of the reasons for the union to avoid the friction that a clear no to profits in welfare would entail. It could also be imagined that such a position would be rejected not only by the owners of the welfare companies but also by the members who actually work there. However, this does not seem to be the case. A survey made by the union showed that 84 percent of private sector employees think that profits in tax-funded activities essentially should be reinvested in operation and not distributed to the owners as dividends.[59]

As for the unions, they have different motives for their ambivalent attitude toward state-subsidized topping up possibilities offered under the welfare industrial complex. A union like the Swedish Municipal Workers' Union has mainly focused on the employment aspect, that is, the fact that its own members work in these sectors. The former president of the union, Annelie Nordström, defended the state-subsidized topping up possibilities, arguing that it has a gender dimension where the women-dominated Rut sector (tax-subsidized household services) is always allowed to be questioned, but not the male-dominated Rot sector (tax-subsidized construction services).[60]

For the white-collar unions, it is more that members demand the new topping up possibilities for welfare services provided via the welfare industrial complex, for example, private health insurance. This has made leading representatives vacillate between a defense of the principles of the Swedish welfare model and an embrace of a new model, built on increased private funding of welfare. An example of this is a representative of the Swedish Confederation of Professional Employees (TCO), who contemplated the union's decision to offer private health insurance to their members in these terms: "There is a moral problem when the law states that healthcare shall be provided based on needs, while we in parallel establish a system where you basically buy healthcare."[61] Another example is the TCO-related intermediary Teachers' Insurance, which took the most "controversial but also the most humanitarian and thoughtful decision – to offer you private health insurance as a teacher."[62]

This is the socioeconomic reality in which Social Democracy has to navigate, and it is a reality where it has become more difficult to reach compromises with some other societal sectors. For example, there used to be a social-democratic tradition of cooperation rather than confrontation with private industry. When it comes to profits in welfare, however, private industry has a very firm position, making it difficult to reach any sort of compromise. In some regards, the same goes for parts of the middle class, which is now getting used to a partly privatized welfare sector. And finally, as we noticed, even parts of the trade-union movement have tight links to private actors in the welfare sector.

The above suggests that even though social democrats have started to question the competition policy they agreed to in 1993, there are strong interest groups that will definitely oppose any return to a competition policy where the public sector has a special status.

Conclusion

The new Swedish competition policy, implemented in 1993, consisted of two parts: first, private sector cartels were banned; second, the public sector was opened up to private actors.

Social Democracy had long sought the first. As for the other, on the other hand, it marked a startling break with previous perceptions of the public sector's special position in terms of competition.

For some time, Social Democracy was determined to develop the new competition policy, including opening up the public sector to private actors. As a matter of fact, Social Democracy went beyond center-right wing parties in this regard, and in the late 1990s, social-democratic ministers wrote bills and motions that were almost utopian in their faith in the market economy.

The new view of competition policy was based on the same ideological reversal that characterized Social Democracy in several European countries. During a previous period, Swedish Social Democracy attempted to develop traditional reformist policies, including the so-called wage earner funds in the early 1980s. But in the long run, it was obviously hard to resist the neoliberal offensive. One of the reasons is that during the heydays of the Swedish welfare model, from the 1960s onward, Swedish Social Democracy became accustomed to tripartite compromises with employers' organizations and trade unions. Then, when the employers' organizations suddenly did not want to compromise anymore, Social Democracy was somewhat left without strategy and ideology. They went with the neoliberal flow.

Gradually, however, there was a social-democratic swing back toward a more traditional view of competition policy, with its distinction between the public and the private sectors. Internally, there was always a criticism of the new competition policy and not least a criticism of profits in welfare, which gradually has become a very important issue in Swedish politics. The issue was debated at social-democratic congresses in 2013 and 2017, where more or less vague proclamations were made about the need to restrict profits in the welfare sector.

What are the reasons for the social-democratic vagueness and indecisiveness when it comes to profits in welfare? One answer is that the Third-Way politicians still face a strong position in the party. Another answer is that the criticism of profits in welfare no longer has a parliamentary majority behind it. The majority shifted when the far-right Swedish Democrats changed their view and started to back the center-right wing parties on the issue.

References to the parliamentary situation, however, are not very convincing. With a majority of the electorate supporting a tough stance against profits in welfare, it seems more tactically advantageous to make a sharp left-wing proposal and blame the other parties when the proposal falls in the parliament.

Or is it so tactical? With the emergence of a private welfare industry, there is a new power block with a strong interest in continuing in the current direction. The tone is strident and sometimes anti-intellectual in its character. Furthermore, the private welfare industry is supported by a number of new and old interest groups – a machinery that can turn the public opinion in another direction.

One of several answers is thus that Social Democrats have let the private welfare industry grow so strong that they do not dare to mess with it. Frightened by its power and burned by the debacle of former party leader Håkan Juholt, who fell partly because of the hullabaloo created by his critique of profits in welfare, Social Democrats have refrained from demanding a more traditional competition policy.

In summary, competition policy in the 21st century is a dilemma for Swedish Social Democracy. It is an issue that has inspired a lot of political maneuvering, including a striking discrepancy between rhetoric and practical policy. It is an issue where Social Democracy is in continuous search of which political party it is and wants to be.

Notes

1 Rune Premfors, "The 'Swedish Model' and Public Sector Reform," *West European Politics* 14, 3 (1991): 83–95.
2 Competition law, Konkurrenslagen 1993: 20, 1993.
3 Ulf Bernitz, *Svensk och europeisk marknadsrätt 1* (Stockholm: Norstedts juridik, 2011), 88.
4 Eva Edwardsson, *Konkurrenslagen och konkurrensbegränsande offentliga regleringar* (Uppsala: Uppsala Universitet, 2003), 61.
5 Parliamentary publications, 1992/93:47, 1993.
6 Parliamentary publications, 1990/91:87, 1991.
7 Parliamentary publications, 1999/2000:140, 2000.
8 Lee Miles, "Making Peace with the Union? The Swedish Social Democratic Party and European Integration," in Geyer Robert, Christine Ingebritsen and Jonathon Moses (eds.), *Globalization, Europeanization and the End of Scandinavian Social Democracy?* (London: Palgrave Macmillan, 2000), 218–239.
9 Gøsta Esping-Andersen, *The Three Worlds of Welfare Capitalism* (Cambridge: Polity, 1990).
10 Korpi, Walter, *Den demokratiska klasskampen: Svensk politik i jämförande perspektiv* (Stockholm: Tiden, 1981); Gøsta Esping-Andersen, *Politics Against Markets: The Social Democratic Road to Power* (Princeton: Princeton University Press, 1985).
11 Peter Swenson, "Bringing Capital Back in, or Social Democracy Reconsidered: Employer Power, Cross-Class Alliances, and Centralization of Industrial Relations in Denmark and Sweden," *World Politics* 43, 4 (1991): 513–544.
12 Mark Blyth, *Great Transformations: Economic Ideas and Institutional Change in the Twentieth Century* (New York: Cambridge University Press, 2002).
13 Jonas Pontusson and Peter Swenson, "Labor Markets, Production Strategies, and Wage Bargaining Institutions. The Swedish Employer Offensive in Comparative Perspective," *Comparative Political Studies* 29, 2 (1996): 223–250.
14 David Harvey, *A brief history of neoliberalism* (Oxford: Oxford University Press, 2005).
15 Magnus Ryner, *Capitalist Restructuring, Globalization and the Third Way: Lessons from the Swedish Model* (London: Routledge, 2002), 173.
16 Agneta Hugemark, *Den fängslande marknaden: Ekonomiska experter om välfärdsstaten* (Lund: Arkiv, 1994), 210.
17 Ryner, *Capitalist Restructuring, Globalization and the Third Way*, 174.
18 Rune Premfors, "The 'Swedish Model' and Public Sector Reform."
19 Jonas Pontusson, "Radicalization and Retreat in Swedish Social Democracy," *New Left Review* 165, 1 (1987): 5–33.
20 Rune Premfors, "The 'Swedish Model' and Public Sector Reform."
21 Jenny Andersson, *Mellan tillväxt och trygghet: Idéer om produktiv socialpolitik i socialdemokratisk socialpolitisk ideologi under efterkrigstiden* (Uppsala: Acta Universitatis Upsaliensis, 2003), 11.
22 Malin Junestav, *Socialförsäkringssystemet och arbetsmarknaden: Politiska idéer, sociala normer och institutionell förändring – en historik* (Uppsala: Institutet för arbetsmarknadspolitisk utvärdering, 2007), 41.
23 Herbert Kitschelt, *The Transformation of European Social Democracy* (Cambridge: Cambridge University Press, 1994).
24 Anthony Giddens, *The Third Way: The Renewal of Social Democracy* (Cambridge: Polity Press, 1998).
25 Joe Guinan, "Social Democracy in the Age of Austerity and Resistance: The Radical Potential of Democratising Capital," *Renewal: A Journal of Labour Politics* 20, 4 (2012): 9–19.
26 Pascal Delwit et al., *Social Democracy in Europe* (Brussels: Éditions de l'Université de Bruxelles, 2005).

27 *Ibid.*
28 Parliamentary publications. 1992/93:56, 1993.
29 Parliamentary publications, 1991/92:U504, 1992.
30 Stig Montin, "Privatiseringsprocesser i kommunerna – teoretiska utgångspunkter och empiriska exempel," *Statsvetenskaplig tidskrift* 95, 1 (1992): 31–57.
31 Peter Antman, "Vägen till systemskiftet – den offentliga sektorn i politiken 1970–1992," in Rolf Gustafsson (ed.), *Köp och sälj, var god svälj? Vårdens nya ekonomistyrningssystem i ett arbetsmiljöperspektiv* (Stockholm: Arbetsmiljöfonden, 1994), 37–38.
32 Bo Rothstein, "Socialdemokratin och välfärdens institutioner," *Tiden* 88, 8 (1988): 467–474.
33 *Ibid.*
34 Bo Rothstein, "Forskare har varnat för vinstdriven vård," *Expressen*, 24 November 2011.
35 Robert Cox, "The Path-Dependency of an Idea: Why Scandinavian Welfare States Remain Distinct," *Social Policy & Administration* 38, 2 (2004): 204–219.
36 *Ibid.*
37 Jacob Hacker, "Privatizing Risk without Privatizing the Welfare State: The Hidden Politics of Social Policy Retrenchment in the United States," *American Political Science Review* 98, 2 (2004): 243–260.
38 Wolfgang Streeck and Kathleen Thelen (eds.), *Beyond Continuity: Institutional Change in Advanced Political Economies* (New York: Oxford University Press, 2005).
39 Parliamentary publications, 1999/2000:140, 2000.
40 Parliamentary publications, 1953:21:166, 1953.
41 Parliamentary publications, 1975/76:1979, 1976.
42 Peter Antman, *Olof Palme: Den gränslöse reformisten* (Stockholm: Prisma, 1996).
43 Edwardsson, *Konkurrenslagen och konkurrensbegränsande offentliga regleringar*, 59.
44 Bernitz, *Svensk och europeisk marknadsrätt 1.*
45 Torbjörn Lundqvist, *Competition policy and the Swedish model. Arbetsrapport 2006: 8* (Stockholm: Institutet för Framtidsstudier, 2006).
46 Parliamentary publications, 1999/2000:140, 2000.
47 Parliamentary publications, 1989:1989:12, 1989.
48 Parliamentary publications, 1990/91:184, 1991.
49 Swedish Competition Authority, Addition to competition law KL 2008:579, 2010.
50 Konkurrenslagsutredningen, *Konkurrenslagen 1993–1996: betänkande* (Stockholm: Fritze, 1997).
51 The Swedish Trade Union Confederation, Response to: Konkurrenslagsutredningen, *Konkurrenslagen 1993–1996.*
52 Jonas Löfvenberg, "Hårt tonläge i partiledardebatten," *Aftonbladet*, May 29, 2016.
53 John Lapidus, "Private Health Insurance in Sweden: Fast-Track Lanes and the Alleged Attempts to Stop Them," *Health Policy* 121, 4 (2017): 442–449.
54 The Swedish Municipal Workers' Union, *Vägval välfärd* (Stockholm: Kommunal, 2012).
55 "Kommunal: Varför är LO mot vinster enbart i välfärden?," *Dagens Opinion*, 17 October 2012.
56 Dan Gabrielsson, "Tror Nordström på demokrati?," *Arbetet*, 5 October 2012.
57 Johanna Wreder, "Kommunal ska kämpa mot vinster i välfärden," *Arbetet*, 30 May 2013.
58 The Swedish Municipal Workers' Union, *Vägval välfärd.*
59 The Swedish Municipal Workers' Union, *Privatanställda i välfärden om vinster* (Kommunal: Stockholm, 2015).
60 "Kommunal: Varför är LO mot vinster enbart i välfärden?," *Dagens Opinion.*
61 Tidningen Vision, "Privata försäkringar splittrar TCO-facken," *Tidningen Vision*, 12 October 2011.
62 Lärarförsäkringsbloggen, 28 May 2012.

Bibliography

Andersson, Jenny. *Mellan tillväxt och trygghet: Idéer om produktiv socialpolitik i socialdemokratisk socialpolitisk ideologi under efterkrigstiden.* Uppsala: Acta Universitatis Upsaliensis, 2003.

Antman, Peter. *Olof Palme: Den gränslöse reformisten.* Stockholm: Prisma, 1996.

Antman, Peter. "Vägen till systemskiftet – den offentliga sektorn i politiken 1970–1992." In *Köp och sälj, var god svälj? Vårdens nya ekonomistyrningssystem i ett arbetsmiljöperspektiv* edited by Rolf Gustafsson. Stockholm: Arbetsmiljöfonden, 1994.

Bernitz, Ulf. *Svensk och europeisk marknadsrätt 1.* Stockholm: Norstedts juridik, 2011.

Blyth, Mark. *Great Transformations: Economic Ideas and Institutional Change in the Twentieth Century.* New York: Cambridge University Press, 2002.

Competition law. Konkurrenslagen 1993: 20, 1993.

Cox, Robert. "The Path-Dependency of an Idea: Why Scandinavian Welfare States Remain Distinct." *Social Policy & Administration* 38, 2 (2004): 204–219.

Dagens Opinion. "Kommunal: Varför är LO mot vinster enbart i välfärden?" October 17, 2012.

Delwit, Pascal et al. *Social Democracy in Europe.* Brussels: Éditions de l'Université de Bruxelles, 2005.

Edwardsson, Eva. *Konkurrenslagen och konkurrensbegränsande offentliga regleringar.* Uppsala: Uppsala Universitet, 2003.

Esping-Andersen, Gøsta. *Politics Against Markets: The Social Democratic Road to Power.* Princeton: Princeton University Press, 1985.

Esping-Andersen, Gøsta. *The Three Worlds of Welfare Capitalism.* Cambridge: Polity, 1990.

Gabrielsson, Dan. "Tror Nordström på demokrati?" *Arbetet*, 5 October 2012.

Giddens, Anthony. *The Third Way: The Renewal of Social Democracy.* Cambridge: Polity Press, 1998.

Guinan, Joe. "Social Democracy in the Age of Austerity and Resistance: The Radical Potential of Democratising Capital." *Renewal: A Journal of Labour Politics* 20, 4 (2012): 9–19.

Hacker, Jacob. "Privatizing Risk Without Privatizing the Welfare State: The Hidden Politics of Social Policy Retrenchment in the United States." *American Political Science Review* 98, 2 (2004): 243–260.

Harvey, David. *A Brief History of Neoliberalism.* Oxford: Oxford University Press, 2005.

Hugemark, Agneta. *Den fängslande marknaden: Ekonomiska experter om välfärdsstaten.* Lund: Arkiv, 1994.

Junestav, Malin. *Socialförsäkringssystemet och arbetsmarknaden: Politiska idéer, sociala normer och institutionell förändring – en historik.* Uppsala: Institutet för arbetsmarknadspolitisk utvärdering, 2007.

Kitschelt, Herbert. *The Transformation of European Social Democracy.* Cambridge: Cambridge University Press, 1994.

Konkurrenslagsutredningen. *Konkurrenslagen 1993–1996: betänkande.* Stockholm: Fritze, 1997.

Korpi, Walter. *Den demokratiska klasskampen: Svensk politik i jämförande perspektiv.* Stockholm: Tiden, 1981.

Lapidus, John. "Private Health Insurance in Sweden: Fast-Track Lanes and the Alleged Attempts to Stop Them." *Health Policy* 121, 4 (2017): 442–449.

Lärarförsäkringsbloggen. *Lärarförsäkringsbloggen*, 28 May 2012.

Löfvenberg, Jonas. "Hårt tonläge i partiledardebatten." *Aftonbladet*, 29 May 2016.

Lundqvist, Torbjörn. *Competition Policy and the Swedish Model. Arbetsrapport 2006:8*. Stockholm: Institutet för Framtidsstudier, 2006.
Miles, Lee. "Making Peace with the Union? The Swedish Social Democratic Party and European Integration." In *Globalization, Europeanization and the End of Scandinavian Social Democracy?* edited by Robert Geyer, Christine Ingebritsen and Jonathon Moses. London: Palgrave Macmillan, 2000: 218–239.
Montin, Stig. "Privatiseringsprocesser i kommunerna – teoretiska utgångspunkter och empiriska exempel." *Statsvetenskaplig tidskrift* 95, 1 (1992): 31–57.
Parliamentary publications. 1953:21:166, 1953.
Parliamentary publications. 1975/76:1979, 1976.
Parliamentary publications. 1989:1989:12, 1989.
Parliamentary publications. 1990/91:87, 1991.
Parliamentary publications. 1990/91:184, 1991.
Parliamentary publications. 1991/92:U504, 1992.
Parliamentary publications. 1992/93:47, 1993.
Parliamentary publications. 1992/93:56, 1993.
Parliamentary publications. 1999/2000:140, 2000.
Pontusson, Jonas. "Radicalization and Retreat in Swedish Social Democracy." *New Left Review* 165, 1 (1987): 5–33.
Pontusson, Jonas and Peter Swenson. "Labor Markets, Production Strategies, and Wage Bargaining Institutions. The Swedish Employer Offensive in Comparative Perspective." *Comparative Political Studies* 29, 2 (1996): 223–250.
Premfors, Rune. "The 'Swedish Model' and Public Sector Reform." *West European Politics* 14, 3 (1991): 83–95.
"Privata försäkringar splittrar TCO-facken." *Tidningen Vision*, 12 October 2011.
Rothstein, Bo. "Forskare har varnat för vinstdriven vård." *Expressen*, 24 November 2011.
Rothstein, Bo. "Socialdemokratin och välfärdens institutioner." *Tiden* 88, 8 (1988): 467–474.
Ryner, Magnus. *Capitalist Restructuring, Globalization and the Third Way: Lessons from the Swedish Model*. London: Routledge, 2002.
Streeck, Wolfgang and Kathleen Thelen (eds.). *Beyond Continuity: Institutional Change in Advanced Political Economies*. New York: Oxford University Press, 2005.
Swedish Competition Authority. Addition to competition law KL 2008:579. 2010.
The Swedish Municipal Workers' Union. *Privatanställda i välfärden om vinster*. Stockholm: Kommunal, 2015.
The Swedish Municipal Workers' Union. *Vägval välfärd*. Stockholm: Kommunal, 2012.
The Swedish Trade Union Confederation. *Response to: Konkurrenslagsutredningen. Konkurrenslagen 1993–1996: betänkande*. Stockholm: Fritze, 1997.
Swenson, Peter. "Bringing Capital Back in, or Social Democracy Reconsidered: Employer Power, Cross-Class Alliances, and Centralization of Industrial Relations in Denmark and Sweden." *World Politics* 43, 4 (1991): 513–544.
Wreder, Johanna. "Kommunal ska kämpa mot vinster i välfärden." *Arbetet*, 30 May 2013.

Conclusion

Vera Šćepanović and Brian Shaev

Introduction

Competition policy had already become the most supranational economic policy in Europe by the 1960s, but many scholars have argued that from the 1980s, a strengthened competition policy turned into a weapon to compel member states to move in more neoliberal directions.[1] Yet the relationship between neoliberalism and competition policy is not entirely straightforward. The term *neoliberalism* is sometimes used to capture both the ordoliberal Freiburg school and the neoliberal Chicago school, but these need to be clearly distinguished. Ordoliberals argued for state intervention to protect competition, while neoliberals like Robert Bork and Richard Posner attacked the progressive US antitrust tradition by arguing that monopolies and dominant market positions were justifiable, even beneficial, as long as they kept consumer prices low. Neoliberals advocated therefore a narrower standard of consumer welfare for competition, whereas ordoliberals demanded that competition policy protect competitive markets. There was a series of clashes between neoliberals and ordoliberals over European competition policy in the 1980s, as Chicago school scholars criticized European policies for their formalism and for not keeping up with modern economics.[2] As shown in our chapters, prior to the 1980s, social democrats occupied a distinct position in this debate. They supported consumer interests and efficiency, and often advocated for competitive markets, including through encouragement of "countervailing powers" such as producer or consumer cooperatives. However, they also wanted competition policy to constrain capital through market regulation (like ordoliberals), and supported the use of public power, in the form of direct ownership or control over investment policy (unlike ordoliberals) to achieve public interest goals.

Scholarly literature on the relationship between social democrats and neoliberalism presents a complicated picture ranging from the reinvention of social democracy to its betrayal. Sitting in between is accommodation, whether skillful or not, to the rise of the new right in the 1980s–1990s and a reassertion of forms of market fundamentalism. Gerassimos Moschonas presents the betrayal thesis, arguing that "*social-democratic parties without social democracy* – are in the process of emerging" because "social democracy has made the decisive ideological leap: for the first time so openly and systematically, it has elevated the market and devalued the

DOI: 10.4324/9781351010573-13

utility of the economically active state."[3] By contrast, Jenny Andersson is more in line with the reinvention or accommodation theses in arguing that

> it is clearly not possible, from any reading of social democracy's history, to argue that the Third Way's embracing of the market signifies a decisive break with old social democracy because social democracy has always grappled with questions of markets and capitalist efficiency.[4]

Still though Andersson agrees with Moschonas that the Third Way was "a fundamental ideological change in social democracy's outlook on capitalism" because it "abdicat[ed] central principles of democracy and equality – all in the name of the market."[5] Particularly insightful is Andersson's argument that the Third Way sacrificed an older social-democratic imperative to "discipline capital" and replaced its former "public ethos" with a "market ethos." The concept of competition was core to this as she argues that "the Third Way does draw on important elements of neoliberalism, particularly the idea of competition as driver of social progress."[6] Sociologist Stephanie Mudge helps explain the background for this shift by emphasizing policy experts as "central players" in this evolution of social democracy. We have seen in our book the core role played by economic experts, whether it be the Dutch Pieter VerLoren van Themaat and the German Heinrich Deist in the 1950s–1960s or the Finnish Erkki Liikanen and social democrats in the European Commission in the 1980s–1990s. The first two Mudge considers "economist theoreticians" (she mentions Deist specifically), who became economic experts in a period in which there was a progressive rapprochement between mainstream Keynesian economics and center-left social-democratic and labor parties. In the 1980s–1990s, however, economist theoreticians were replaced by "transnational, finance-oriented economists," who were educated and socialized in milieux linked to international economic institutions like the International Monetary Fund (IMF) and Organisation for Economic Co-operation and Development (OECD). This new generation of party experts reinvented social democracy by bringing neoliberal dogma, language and values into social-democratic parties, according to Mudge. The result of their influence was a "neoliberalization of center-left politics," she argues, even if many of these party experts did not consider themselves to be neoliberal.[7] In our chapters, we also see social democrats in senior leadership positions, many of whom had backgrounds in law or economics, adopting such positions in the 1980s–2000s.

In this conclusion, we analyze changes in the history of social democracy's relationship with competition policy since Regulation 17/62, which established European-level competition policy in 1962. The introduction demonstrated that social democrats had reasons to support bans or restrictions on anticompetitive practices for economic, social, and political reasons. They became increasingly restrictive over time, contributed to the formation of national competition laws, and were the strongest advocates for establishing a supranational competition policy at the European level in the 1950s–early 1960s. The recession of the 1970s often led socialists to relax competition rules to support crisis-stricken industries to preserve employment. This era however also shows growing socialist discomfort with massive levels of state aid and, especially among those working for supranational institutions, a conversion toward a more ordoliberal stance. From the 1980s, European competition policy increasingly drifted away from social-democratic preferences. Following a period of increasing cohesion in which transnational socialists coalesced around antitrust, restraints on multinationals and merger control in the 1950s–early 1970s, as this book shows, by the 2000s–2010s, European socialists parties displayed a wide span of preferences on competition, ranging from the Austrian social democrats' support for "vigorous enforcement by independent institutions" to the Belgian socialists' support for incorporating social policy and political discretion.[8] We trace here how European socialists reacted to the evolution of competition policy in neoliberal directions in the 1980s–2000s, the competition offensive of the European Commission in the 2010s, and the return of industrial policy in the 2020s.

For the sake of clarity, we define a neoliberal competition policy as one that (a) restricts or forbids national state aid, (b) attacks publicly-owned enterprises by seeking to introduce market actors into areas of public monopoly, *and* (c) maintains a narrow consumer interest and economic efficiency concept of competition policy. As we have seen for the 1970s, social democrats could support one or more of these policies without necessarily being neoliberal. Given the uneven development of European economic integration, with minimal capacity to pursue industrial policies, raise taxes and engage in redistribution, and build community welfare at the European level, competition policy was the strongest economic tool available to the European Commission. Following the accommodation or reinvention thesis, socialists working there would be tempted to strengthen competition policy further as a means of pursuing specific goals like lower prices or to prevent wasteful spending on industries that were not going to survive anyway. When all three elements are combined (an attack on state aid and public monopolies and a narrow consumer welfare and efficiency standard), though, we argue that the policy is neoliberal even when those who practiced the policy contest this characterization. We argue this because older social-democratic competition preferences like political discretion in service of public policy goals and instrumentalizing competition policy in pursuit of a holistic socioeconomic policy that combines price policy, industrial policy, and welfare become impossible under such restrictive conditions.

The uneasy relationship between competition and industrial policies in Europe, 1960s–1980s

Regulation 17/62, which established European-level competition policy, is generally considered to have a German ordoliberal origin, but this picture is incomplete to the point of distortion. First, the French government was able to insert some of its preferences into the regulation against German wishes, specifically a ban on exclusive dealing and a focus on vertical integration.[9] The Commission's first cartel ban in 1964 focused on exclusive dealing, as did the first major European Court of Justice (ECJ) ruling on competition in the 1966 Grundig-Costen case, which largely confirmed the Commission's ban. Second, Shaev shows that social democrats (and not Christian democrats or liberals) were the major backers of a strong supranational competition law in the early European Parliament (EP).

Ernst-Joachim Mestmäcker, an ordoliberal working in Hans von der Groeben's DG for Competition in the European Commission in the 1960s, later wrote that there was 'bipartisan support for competition policy in Germany.'[10] This is true but misleading, as Schröter's chapter shows that social democrats emerged as stronger supporters of competition policy in the 1950s than Christian democrats, who were split between a pro-cartel business wing and anti-cartel ordoliberal wing. Social-democratic competition policy, in any case, differed from ordoliberal visions. This difference can be seen in the contrasting reaction of social democrats and ordoliberals to French Commissioner Robert Majorlin's effort to launch a European-level macroeconomic planning initiative in 1962, the same year that Regulation 17/62 was published. Social democrats saw Marjolin's planning proposal as compatible with and complementary to competition policy whereas ordoliberals saw it as mutually contradictory. Social democrats hence supported a strong European competition *and* planning policy in the 1960s.

Sigfrido M. Ramírez Pérez argues in our book that Keynesianism was the dominant influence for the form and practice of competition policy in the 1960s–mid-1970s. Keynesian competition policy differs from ordoliberal policy, he argues, by its subordination to social and industrial goals, its toleration of state aids and cartels if they enhance efficiency, and by its emphasis on the need for merger control. While Anselm Küsters shows an 'ordoliberalization' of Commission and ECJ language over the 1960s, there was less in practice. Small and medium businesses were largely allowed to cooperate with each other by the Commission and ECJ,[11] in line with ordoliberal *and* social-democratic preferences. Von der Groeben was replaced as commissioner for competition in 1967 by Emmanuel Sassen, who Ramírez Pérez argues had a more Keynesian and instrumentalist idea of competition policy than von der Groeben. This view accords with Thomas Freyer's argument that the European Commission primarily used competition policy as a tool to pursue "social welfare capitalism" until the Single European Act of 1986.[12]

The Commission opened an obligatory cartel register on the basis of Regulation 17/62, which social democrats supported (see Shaev's chapter), but Laurent Warlouzet has shown how it was quickly overwhelmed by the huge number of notifications, which encumbered its work.[13] To relieve its load, the Commission soon gained the right to issue block exemptions. The cartel ban channeled concentration efforts into a wave of mergers, which rose rapidly over the next decade. This merger wave did not escape social democrats' notice. Intra-EEC mergers had deep support among policymakers following the success of Jean-Jacque Servan-Scheiber's *The American Challenge* in 1967, the same year that a new DG was set up for Industrial Affairs. Euromercantilism became dominant in European economic policy as a means of building technological economies of scale to compete with US airplane manufacturers and computer companies.[14] Social democrats in principle supported the idea of mergers to create scaled-up "European" companies but wanted them to be subject to supranational prior approval and supervision against abuses of dominant market positions.

Historians Anselm Doering-Manteuffel and Lutz Raphael write of a "symbiotic bond" between social democracy and Keynesianism that peaked from 1966 to 1971/72 as Europe launched into a "social-democratic decade,"[15] with the elections of social-democratic-led governments in Austria, Belgium (for a short while), Denmark, Germany, the Netherlands, Sweden, and later Portugal, Spain, and the UK. This was the political context for an ambitious "industrial policy." Literature has long highlighted the "tension"[16] between competition and industrial policy, but the 1973 proposal for a wide-ranging community industrial policy by Altiero Spinelli, then Commissioner for Industrial, Technological and Scientific Affairs, presented them as complementary. At the same time, though, the term *multinationals* increasingly replaced "cartels" as a pejorative in social-democratic parlance as an internationalization of the economy accelerated at the turn of the 1970s, marked especially by the implantation of overseas subsidiaries of large US corporations.[17] Spinelli's industrial policy proposal was accompanied by a plan to study and control multinationals at the European level, a view that was strongly supported by socialists in the EP and in international congresses.[18]

This merging of competition and industrial policies was social-democratic in the context of the early 1970s. Social democrats not only supported Spinelli but were also the firmest backers of a European merger control regulation in the EP. This regulation was proposed under the influence of Keynesian and social-democratic commission officials in 1973. It coincided with initiatives to create a European company statute to facilitate cross-border intra-EEC mergers, which social democrats in principle approved but wanted to be subjected to supranational authorization and supervision. The European merger regulation failed in the Council of Ministers, however, while the SPD-led German government succeeded in passing a national law in 1973.[19] This first merger control law in continental Europe was part of a widespread legislative offensive in which competition laws were strengthened in many European countries during the 1970s. This coincided with a growing prominence of employing state aid as a means of managing crises in the coal, light manufacturing, steel, and textile sectors.

The first major case against abuse of dominant position (EEC Article 86), also bears marks of combining antitrust with broader socio-economic considerations. Spinelli successfully pressured his fellow commissioners to launch an abuse of dominant position case against IBM, the US information technology firm that captured 90% of the European computer market in the early 1970s. The case was finally settled in 1984 after IBM made concessions. Arthe Van Laer argues that the IBM case, by far the Commission's largest antitrust case in the 1970s–1980s, should be seen as part of EEC industrial policy because it was meant to foster a home-grown competitive computer industry. He writes that Spinelli launched the IBM investigation to "complement other common actions [designed] to render the EEC computer industry competitive."[20] This supports Dimitri Zurstrassen's portrayal in our book of Spinelli's concept of competition policy as a means not merely to pursue lower prices, but also balanced growth, as well as environmental and regional structural policies. In this social-democratic period in the early 1970s, competition and industrial policies were considered to be complementary and both

DG III (industry, technology, and research) and DG IV (competition) supported the IBM case and the goal of building a European computers industry.

For the same reasons, Spinelli supported the use of subsidies, but he wanted the Commission to gain greater approval and supervision powers in order to pursue a common EC-level industrial policy. By the mid-1970s, economic recession had deepened. The Commission accepted national state aid programs at the height of the crisis, but also worried that fragmented national support would delay the necessary restructuring and result in weaker European firms overall. As Warlouzet argues, having no basis in the EEC Treaty to actually pursue a Community industrial policy, the Commission tried at first to nudge governments into aligning with common EC goals through consultations and threats rather than launching state aid cases. As a matter of fact, under the UK Labour Commissioner George Thompson, it even succeeded in establishing a Community-level fund to aid regions especially hard hit by industrial crisis. State aid maintained jobs in high-employment sectors at a time when double-digit unemployment, largely unknown in Western Europe in the 1950s–1960s, reemerged in dramatic fashion. However, it also came at enormous expense and was largely focused on declining industries (shipbuilding, steel, and textiles) rather than new technology areas that might enhance European competitiveness over the long term in the context of rising competition from developing countries (textiles) and industrialized countries like Japan and South Korea (manufacturing, shipbuilding, and steel).

In January 1977, Spinelli was replaced as Commissioner for Industrial Affairs, Internal Market and Customs by the Belgian Christian Democrat Etienne Davignon. Shortly before that, Luxembourg Socialist Raymond Vouel became commissioner for competition, with German Social Democrat and trade unionist Willy Schlieder as director general for competition. Zurstrassen describes how the two took an ambiguous stance on crisis supports, expressing concerns about the social costs and "decadence" of restricting competition, but acknowledged the need to apply competition rules flexibly in times of economic crises. State aid was thus largely tolerated, even if accompanied by attempts to bind governments to agreements that would make such aid strictly temporary and linked to restructuring commitments. In an article on crisis in the Dunkirk shipyards, Warlouzet notes that under Vouel, the Commission only prohibited six cases of state aid out of 487 investigated, and frequently accepted fairly loose promises from governments.[21]

Crisis cartels were a thornier matter. Davignon pushed for a plan that would allow for sectors in structural crisis – textiles, shipbuilding, and steel – to coordinate prices and market shares. The first proposal for a textile cartel tabled by DG industry was blocked, however, by DG competition. The sector was already benefiting from other forms of support, including state and regional aid, and protection from foreign competition orchestrated through the 1973 Multi-Fibre Agreement at the GATT.[22] However, socialist commissioners lacked the influence to defend their approach amid the rising crisis or the tools to directly intervene in industry. Vouel vacillated between opposing the cartel plans and working with Davignon to prepare the regulation that would make them possible. In 1978, all socialist members of the College of Commissioners – Vouel, Commissioner for Economy, Finance and Budgets Wilhelm Haferkamp, and Commissioner for Employment and Social Affairs Henk Vredeling – voted against the proposal, but the president of the Commission Roy Jenkins came out on the side of Davignon, who won the vote in the College of Commissioners. A crisis cartel for steel was also formed in 1977, based on import restrictions, voluntary production quotas and binding minimum prices until a "manifest crisis" was declared by the Community in 1980, evoking a European Coal and Steel Community (ECSC) Treaty article that allowed for greater state intervention in the sector.[23]

The late 1970s thus show the social democrats in the European Commission torn between the still prevalent vision of competition policy as a tool to be used instrumentally in the pursuit of broader socioeconomic goals, a gradual turn toward a neomercantilist vision of industrial policy, and a more liberal view that such goals might best be served by a stricter application of competition law. There are multiple explanations for this shift, some more individual and some more structural.

On an individual level, it probably mattered that both Haferkamp and Schlieder had occupied various positions within the Commission since respectively 1963 and 1958, and were likely socialized into the "ordoliberalizing" economic language of the Commission that Küsters identifies in the 1960s and 1970s.[24] Unlike Spinelli, who as Zurstrassen discusses was well embedded in the structures of transnational socialism – both in the EP Socialist Group and in international congresses – and who had the political authority to promote an essentially social-democratic vision for industrial policy at the EU level, their efforts remained largely defensive, geared toward protecting the wallets of European consumers and taxpayers against what they saw as an aggressively pro-business stance of Davignon. For Vouel, it probably also mattered that he came from the smallest EC member state, Luxembourg. Industrial policy has long been seen as giving economic advantage to larger member states like France, Germany and Italy that could afford to finance large economic projects that smaller member states could not.

On a more structural level, this shift among European-level social democrats is also linked to the tension between national and supranational objectives of competition-as-industrial policy. It is clear that all three figures were deeply dedicated to advancing European integration through the deepening of the internal market. This pro-polity stance during a period marked by rhetoric about "Eurosclerosis" seems to have taken precedence over the advance of socialist-inspired economic policies. It also mattered that many of the traditional tools that social democrats used to balance support for industry with broader social goals, in particular various forms of public control of supported companies, were not available at the Community level. After all, Spinelli's proposal to give the Commission the ability to guide and oversee mergers was defeated in the Council, and there was no option to finance restructuring from a common budget. Another proposal to check private power at the EU level by allowing worker participation in multinational companies based in the EEC (the "Vredeling directive") met with the same fate. Strict application of competition policy where the Commission allowed member states to support industry but set conditions under which they could do so thus began to look like an appealing second-best option.

The restrictive stance toward national industrial policy instruments began to sharpen in the 1980s, when Dutch Christian Democrat Frans Andriessen replaced Vouel as Commissioner for Competition. Andriessen was in many ways a transitional figure on state aid because, though he was mostly lenient, he massively increased the Commission's information-gathering and inquiry competence, which gave his successor Peter Sutherland the tools with which to launch a community-wide attack on state aid from 1985. In 1981, the EC approved an updated regulation on state aid that expanded the Commission's scope for intervention.[25] The rules on state aid now included strong preference for so-called horizontal measures (e.g. regional policy and research and development policy) over vertical ones designed to protect specific company sectors, which had been widespread since the start of the recession. Approval of state aid was increasingly made conditional on restructuring plans, overseen by the Commission and often requiring divestment and reduction of output and employment.

The divergence of views between the "national" and "European" politicians, even those in the social-democratic family, should not, however, be exaggerated. The critique of "picking winners" and wasteful "money pits" into which governments threw money to finance "dinosaur" industries that would never be profitable again also began to spread within social-democratic parties from the beginning of the 1980s. As Zurstrassen shows in his chapter, European capitals accepted the impositions from Brussels surprisingly meekly. François Mitterrand's government, elected in 1981, attempted to swim against the tide but its "turn to rigor" in 1983 led it to acquiesce to Commission's demands. This meant a break with the French Communist Party and Jean-Pierre Chevènement, a forceful advocate for a socialist industrial policy since the 1960s.[26] Mathieu Fulla argues that this rebalancing was in large part caused by "a growing transnationalization of networks of 'policy experts' and 'experts'," who progressively displaced the generation of socialist economics who entered the party with the re-founding of the French Socialist Party in 1971, though he emphasizes that this did not amount yet to a turn to neoliberalism.[27] Warlouzet's research on the restructuring of the shipyards in Dunkirk has also shown how socialists in government became split between maintaining employment and concerns about its spiraling expense.[28] The incentive was all the greater for socialists in the South European accession countries. Spanish socialists largely followed the Commission's demands to wind up state aid in the steel sector, Zurstrassen shows, and led the way in the restructuring and privatization of manufacturing.[29]

The chapter by Susanna Fellman shows how a similar evolution within social-democratic ranks took place even in Finland, where the pressures of restructuring and Europeanization were milder. The position of the Finnish Social Democratic Party long embodied the usual ambivalence between a more radical pro-competitive stance favored by consumer interest groups and smaller cooperatives and a more lenient industrial policy position advocated by worker organizations in big export industries. In the early postwar decades, the party concentrated less on competition policy proper, in the sense of managing business concentration and policing dominance, and more on managing the consequences of market dominance, such as abuse of power and the impact on consumer prices. This resulted in domestic legislation evolving along the lines of prevention of abuse, with registers and supervision bodies put in place to monitor price developments and collusive agreements. Third Way ideas, which came to fruition in the European center-left in the 1990s but which were in many ways pioneered in Nordic countries in the 1980s amidst the challenge of deindustrialization, led social-democratic parties to accept privatization and the withdrawal of the state as an active participant in the economy in many sectors. Price monitoring and regulation were abolished in favor of market forces, and special laws that governed sectors such as banking and insurance were abandoned in favor of a more liberal approach. A stricter competition policy therefore came to be favored as a replacement for the former tools of market regulation.

"Modernization," consumer welfare and the triumph of neoliberalism, 1980s–2010s

The Finnish experience shows that social-democratic competition policy was already changing in national spheres but the largest sea change in the 1980s–2000s took place at the European level. It was in these years that European competition policy reached its zenith but was also transformed into a neoliberal form that differed from both ordoliberal and social-democratic visions. The main developments in this period include the passing of a new merger regulation in 1989, very different from the one proposed by social democrats in the early 1970s; attacks on publicly owned enterprises like national airlines and postal systems and a narrowing of the scope for public involvement in the "services of general economic interest"; the "modernization" of competition policy in the early 2000s; and, finally, the broadening international influence of European competition policy, especially in the context of the EU enlargement toward Nordic and Central and Eastern European states. This section explores the evolution of competition policy in neoliberal directions and argues that social democrats responded to it in a disjointed manner, with some participating in the neoliberal turn and others resisting it.

By the end of the 1970s, social-democratic views on competition aligned with important tenets of the ordoliberal approach to competition policy. This involved the need for state intervention to restore balance among market actors and prevent dominance by individual firms. Though social democrats shared this wariness of market dominance, particularly when it translated into political dominance, they had a more flexible view of the instruments needed to control it. Market dominance could be opposed not only through competition but also through the use of public power, if necessary through nationalization, and by internal democratization of the companies to give more power to workers. For this reason, competition policy could also be subordinated to political discretion in service of political goals and a holistic socioeconomic policy that combines price policy, industrial policy and welfare. As other tools of democratic control of companies such as organized labor and public ownership eroded in the wake of the 1970s crises, social-democratic views came ever closer to those of the ordoliberals, reifying market competition as the main way to keep the power of capital in check and protect consumer interests.

Neoliberals took this a step further, positing a narrow definition of consumer welfare as the sole objective of competition policy, which ordoliberals opposed, and attacking public enterprises as an obstacle to the market's objective to deliver value to consumers rather than as a way to counteract the power of private capital – which ordoliberals supported. We argue that the reason some social democrats fell into step with this new trend can be found in the structural obstacles to the deployment of older social-democratic tools in a multilevel supranational polity and, following Mudge, in the emergence of transnational expert communities that saw technocratic solutions as a suitable and even superior alternative to democratic accountability.

That said, the conversion of social democrats to the notion of competition as the engine of capitalism in its own right came gradually and largely in reaction to developments set in motion by their liberal counterparts. The real revolution in European competition policy in the 1980s–early 1990s occurred under the leadership of Peter Sutherland and Leon Brittan, who opposed social and neomercantilist ideas of competition[30] despite the Commission being led by President Jacques Delors, a French Socialist who was the first major social-democratic heavyweight in the Commission since Jenkins and Spinelli. Delors served as a bridge between two eras. He considered an active industrial policy and, famously, "Social Europe" to be essential ingredients of European integration, opposed fiscal rules for the Euro, and also wanted more political discretion over monetary policy.[31] On competition policy too, he presented an alternative social-democratic vision to "synthesize market-oriented, socially-oriented and neomercantilist features," Warlouzet writes in our book. Though Delors brought postwar social-democratic competition goals into the Commission, much like Spinelli before him he lacked the political backing to turn them into policies. It was under his leadership that Sutherland and Brittan turned DG competition into the fierce department it is today. Delors had made the creation of the single market the paramount aim of his presidency, but, as observed by Warlouzet, the proposal barely mentioned competition policy. Nevertheless, the overriding objective of creating the single market gave competition commissioners the opportunity to go after, with new vigor, anything that was perceived as working against it.

Investigations into state aid grew ever more rigorous. Sutherland began his mandate in 1985 by creating a task force on state aids. The aim was not merely to improve the scrutiny of ongoing cases, but also to review all aid granted to Community firms in the preceding crisis years. The resulting *First Survey of State Aids in the European Community*[32] compiled meticulous data on aid, which allowed easy comparison across cases and countries. This served not only to call out states that were seen to be overly generous[33] but also to introduce the notion that a more standardized approach to aid was needed. Armed with statistics, the Commission could point to "excess aid" and even demand that it be repaid, as Brittan famously did in 1991 in the case of the French government's aid to Renault.[34] As reported by Warlouzet, socialist commissioners, including Delors, occasionally tried to oppose this hardening stance, but were regularly outvoted. As in industrial, monetary, and social policy, Delors' social-democratic vision for the Single European Market gradually lost vigor in the early 1990s.

DG competition under Sutherland and Brittan also stepped up the supervision of cartels and other restrictive practices, raising fines to record levels and developing more proactive investigations.[35] It also made another attempt, this time successful, to take control of Community-level mergers. The Commission received help in this direction from the ECJ, which ruled, in the Philipp Morris/Rothman case, that in some cases Article 82 of the EEC governing cartels can be extended to mergers. The ensuing legal uncertainty rendered the business community more receptive to the Commission's idea of centralizing merger control, eventually swaying even the Council.[36] The contrast to the proposal tabled under Spinelli is instructive: whereas the previous Commission wished to use merger supervision to orchestrate the development of internationally competitive European companies and ensure balanced regional and social development, the 1989 Merger Regulation is entirely focused on securing "effective competition."[37] As noted by Hubert Buch-Hansen and Angela Wigger, this makes the merger regulation quite distinct from other competition articles in the treaties, which all tend to make exceptions for other objectives of "community interest."[38] Still, the French Socialist government supported it, Warlouzet shows, despite misgivings. Brittan, who famously declared that "companies can be competitive abroad only if they are used to competing at home,"[39] immediately demonstrated what he thought of using mergers for industrial policy by blocking the proposed takeover by an Italian-French aviation industry consortium of the Canadian firm De Haviland, a move which would have placed European industry in a dominant position in the global market for commercial aircraft. Despite protests from Delors, who supported the merger, and very public opposition by French and German politicians, the College of Commissioners upheld Brittan's ban.

In fact, while Brittan's approach to enforcement may have been deliberately abrasive, his beliefs had come to be widely shared within DG IV. From 1990, the director general for competition under Brittan was a German social democrat Carl Dieter Ehlermann, and in 1993 Brittan was replaced as Commissioner by Karel van Miert, a Dutch Labor politician. At the time, this was seen as heralding a possible change of direction: as Warlouzet describes in his chapter, in his previous position as Commissioner for Transport, van Miert had locked horns with Brittan on several occasions, and many feared that he was willing to take a more "political" approach, that is, give space to non-competition objectives in his decisions.[40] These warnings proved to be unwarranted: van Miert and Ehlermann continued the strict line taken by their predecessors, and, in Ehlermann's own words, even took pride in not allowing their political preferences to influence their work.

In fact, it was under van Miert that the Commission opened up a new front in European competition policy, one that cut at the core of the former social-democratic vision of the economy. Public enterprises and especially utility services had remained until then outside the jurisdiction of DG competition. One rather tentative exception was a 1980 directive binding member states to greater transparency in their relationship with publicly owned enterprises, but this was understood to mainly target large manufacturing firms.[41] From 1991 onward, however, DG competition applied the competition rules ever more aggressively to the publicly owned sectors of telecommunications, energy, transport and postal services, as part of a broader effort to bring these under the rules of the Single Market.[42] A series of directives adopted throughout the 1990s introduced the principles of separation of ownership, operational independence, strict limits on budgetary support and third-party access which prepared these sectors for eventual privatization. As noted by Warlouzet, van Miert did not consider this campaign to be contrary to the aims of social democracy, as he argued that the ultimate goal was to benefit consumers and fight vested interests in these highly protected industries. It is notable, however, that the emphasis on consumer interest in his speeches was couched in a strongly ordoliberal discourse, emphasizing the importance of the European economy becoming more "competitive," and consumers having the freedom to choose their supplier as the ultimate form of exercising accountability. He even won the Ludwig Erhard Prize as a reward for his efforts.[43]

This was not out of character for many European social democrats at the time. In his chapter on Sweden, John Lapidus examines how Swedish social democrats came around to support the 1993 Swedish competition law passed by a center-right government that opened up not only general economic services but also welfare services such as healthcare and education to private competition. He argues that the social-democratic argument often drew not only on efficiency as a source of consumer welfare but also on ideas of accountability and participation, that is, political control of the service provision, even though this was to be exercised mainly by consumers voting with their feet. He also credits the transformation, in line with Mudge's argument, to "Third Way economists" in the Social Democratic Party that acquired disproportionate influence under the leadership of Olof Palme and especially later under Göran Persson and Mona Sahlin. According to Lapidus, these leaders viewed competition through a utopian lens and supported introducing it in different dimensions of the public sector. Giuliano Amato, writing from his position as the head of Italy's antitrust office in 1997, just before joining the left-wing government of Massimo D'Allema as Minister for Institutional Reform, also cited approvingly the European Commission's tendency to take a stricter stance against public monopolies than against private ones. From the position of a country embroiled in corruption scandals, which saw public power subverted for private aims, using supranational tools to create competition in public services must have appeared to be in the general public interest, and Amato's book makes a powerful case for the use of antitrust to check against abuses of both private and public power.[44]

The emergence of effective competition as the ultimate guarantor of consumer welfare and the main objective of European competition policy was also helpful to another cause the Commission began to champion in this period: the "modernization," or professionalization, and concomitant depoliticization of competition enforcement. Van Miert's director general, Ehlermann, was the driving force behind this campaign. A social democrat with a tenure in the Commission services dating back to 1961, he proposed a way to rationalize the enforcement system to allow DG competition to effectively cover its ever-expanding portfolio. This involved delegating responsibility to national competition authorities to process notifications of agreements between companies in order to concentrate the Commission's resources on more proactive cartel investigations and the ever-growing numbers of cross-border mergers, as Wolf Sauter discusses. The Commission also mobilized private actors: the 1996 Leniency Notice granted immunity to companies that acted as "whistleblowers," and the involvement of national courts also incentivized market actors to seek legal redress against companies suspected of collusion.[45]

One major concern such a decentralization posed was potential inconsistency in the application of competition law. This was resolved by establishing a network of independent national competition authorities (NCAs) that often received direct training from DG competition. The Commission was to regularly exchange information with the NCAs, act as an advisor, and be allowed to act as amicus curiae before national courts.[46] Standardizing the objectives of competition policy into a single yardstick of effective competition and promoting uniform methods of assessment through institutional exchange and case law ensured consistent application, but it also led to the emergence of a broad epistemic community consisting of Commission officials and state bureaucracies as well as private lawyers socialized into the same narrow and seemingly "apolitical" understanding of competition policy. Though acknowledging the origins of antitrust in the need to check the political dominance of private capital, Giuliano Amato welcomed the "liberation of the antitrust law from other purposes it has served in the past" that emerged out of the consolidation of the EU competition policy.[47] As Sauter writes in our book, this "meant that competition policy shifted from being an instrument to serve various purposes to protect competition and efficiency as such, reducing the original regulatory purpose." Amato even championed taking responsibilities for competition entirely from the hands of Commission and investing it in an independent authority in order to further insulate it from political discretion – a position also supported by Ehlermann. Whatever role for social objectives may still have existed in the single market, it was going to have to be pursued by other DGs. A rather lukewarm attempt was made in this period to revive Vredeling's idea to have organized labor act as a countervailing power to the rapidly consolidating European multinationals. The resulting 1994 Directive on European Works Councils did succeed in establishing transnational workers' organizations in all large companies operating in multiple EU countries, but confined their role to information and consultation rights, depriving them of the possibility of collective bargaining.[48]

The narrowing and professionalization of competition enforcement also proved useful for another purpose: the export of competition policy principles for which European industry clamored. The 1994 agreement establishing the European Economic Area largely took over the EU's competition regime, and established an institutional framework mirroring the one inside the EU, including a separate Surveillance Authority within the European Free Trade Association. As noted in Fellman's chapter, even in the absence of direct intervention from the Commission, these transformations in the transnational regulatory sphere influenced domestic debates and gave additional weight to the pro-competition fraction within the Finnish SDP in its push for stricter policies. A much more hands-on transformation took place in Central and East European countries, where alignment with the EU's competition rules, especially in the domain of state aid, was a pre-condition for accession. This significantly affected the direction of the post-socialist transition, with many governments accelerating the privatization and sale of former industrial champions under the threat of delayed membership.[49] DG competition was involved in the accession negotiations from the start to ensure that competition authorities in the new states were properly trained and fully independent – a remarkable success of externalized institution-building if one is to judge by the record low levels of infringement procedures and reclaimed aid, as well as the marked absence of anything resembling "national champions" in these countries after the accession.[50]

Van Miert and Ehlermann also attempted to influence the development of competition policy globally, though this initiative was far less successful.[51] In 1995, the Commission published a report setting out its vision for the global coordination of competition policies, dubbed the "Van Miert Report."[52] With the former Commissioner Sutherland as director general of the WTO and Brittan as the EU Commissioner in charge of trade, European officials managed to lay the seeds of the WTO's incipient policy on subsidies (Ehlermann himself would go on to serve on the WTO Appellate Body from 1995 until 2001).[53] This was more difficult terrain, however, partly because of the growing divergence in the competition principles espoused by the EU and the United States. The relationship soured especially after Van Miert's decision to block the merger between Boeing and McDonnell Douglass in 1997, though the case did lead to a renewed bilateral agreement on competition matters between the European Union and the United States. The merger had been cleared by US authorities, and the fact that the European Commission intervened in a merger between two American companies was viewed as overstepping the boundaries at best, and at worst as an outright protectionist intervention in the interests of Airbus. Once more, however, comparison to the Intel case of the early 1970s is instructive. While at the time industrial policy objectives were openly discussed in connection to the decision to force Intel to reduce its dominance of the European market, this time, the Commission defended itself scrupulously in the language of effective competition, though plenty of accusations of protectionism were hurled Van Miert's way.[54]

The drive toward the depoliticization of competition policy reached its peak with the appointment of the non-partisan technocratic figure, Mario Monti, to the post of the competition commissioner in 1999. An economist, Monti went ahead to implement Ehlermann's vision of modernization and invested further in the professionalization of procedures used to identify violations of effective competition. During this period, DG competition, traditionally staffed by lawyers, radically increased the number of economists in its ranks and its assessments started to rely on ever more sophisticated econometric simulations, as neoliberals had long demanded.[55] Küsters argues that this represented a neoliberal displacement of ordoliberalism in EU competition policy in the early 2000s.[56] This was in line with Van Miert's ambition of establishing a "more economic approach," one that presumably replaced formalistic preoccupation with dominance with a more pragmatic inquiry into its effects on consumers. The question is not, however, merely one of measurement sophistication. The previous concern with dominance, which the modernization policy displaced, has roots in both the legalistic ordoliberal approach and social-democratic concerns over the links between market dominance and political dominance, and the intuition that elevated levels of market dominance must therefore be counterbalanced by public power and scrutiny.

Reducing the yardstick to consumer welfare and economic efficiency alone implies thus in practice a narrow focus on price in accordance with neoliberal views. Though consumer welfare is not formally defined in EU competition law (the 2004 Merger Regulation refers instead to a "significant impediment to effective competition"),[57] such considerations have been incorporated into subsequent Commission strategies. From 2005, for example, DG competition under Commissioner Neelie Kroes from the Dutch Liberal Party initiated a public consultation that resulted in the "Priorities Paper" of 2009, which highlighted the Commission's intention to prioritize consumer welfare in its enforcement of Article 85 EC (Article 102 TFEU – abuse of dominant position).[58] In other words, whereas all forms of abuse of dominant position remained in principle *illegal*, the Commission would only actively prosecute conduct leading to demonstrable harm to consumers, which represented a de facto adoption of neoliberal views of competition.

Revealingly, the one area in which the Commission has chosen to maintain a more formalistic focus on dominance concerns so-called services of general economic interests (SGEI). There is no general definition of SGEI in the Community law – the Treaty of Rome refers loosely to "undertakings entrusted with the operation of services of general economic interest or having a character of revenue-producing monopoly."[59] Traditionally, they are understood as referring to public services where concerns over quality, access, and affordability have long limited the scope for market operations. The treaty excluded them from the scope of community law in so far as the application of competition rules would "obstruct the performance of the particular tasks assigned to them," and to the extent that such exemption would not affect the development of cross-border trade "to such an extent as would be contrary to the interests of the Union."[60] This double qualification became the lever by which the Commission attempted, from the 1980s on, to introduce competition into the domain of public services in contrast to postwar social-democratic ideas that sought to shield them.

The Commission's tools for doing so proved to be even more controversial than its objective. Article 90, which allows the Commission to issue authoritative interpretations of how to apply the law to utilities and other public undertakings, was used in the 1980 Directive on transparency and in the set of directives adopted between 1988 and 1990 that introduced competition requirements into the telecommunications sector. Both the Council and the Parliament objected to the use of Commission directives, arguing that they effectively amounted to legislation by the Commission, an overreach by the EU executive.[61] Though the ECJ upheld the Commission's right to issue directives under Article 90, their further use was found to be too risky. Instead, competition principles were subsequently introduced through Council directives in the energy, transport and postal services sectors, albeit under the shadow of the Commission's threat to use its unilateral powers if the member states failed to agree.[62] In domains where no agreement seemed possible due to widely differing national traditions of service provision, the Commission continued to probe the limits of the application of competition principles by going after cases even in sectors such as healthcare, education, welfare, and social housing. The case law has produced a fairly broad definition of principles such as the "economic nature" of an activity, which now covers not only activities that are provided on the market but also those that could in principle be provided on the market, even if no market presently exists in that member state.[63] It also introduced very narrow criteria under which the financing of public enterprises could be exempted from state-aid rules, putting them de facto on par with the rules governing private companies.

The European Parliament, and especially the Socialist Group, has been especially concerned about this state of affairs. The use of Commission directives and Council directives to regulate competition rules in public services sidelines the EP, which has surprisingly few competences in competition policy. Socialists have also frequently complained that the reliance on case law creates legal uncertainty over which public sector practices may be declared illegal, and that this has led to a more conservative application of competition law in social services than would be necessary, as well as to a preoccupation with proportionality and cost-effectiveness of services over quality and reliability.[64] The Rapkay Report, prepared for the Parliament by German social-democratic rapporteur Bernhard Rapkay, therefore called for a framework directive to properly delineate "economic" from "services of general interest" that would be exempt from liberalization through the application of competition law. These calls came in response to the Commission's sweeping proposal of a 2004 "Bolkestein Directive" on services, which went into effect in revised form in 2006. It extended the application of community rules on competition and freedom of movement to practically all services, including SGEI. Amid the uproar that followed, the Commission was forced to withdraw and substantially revise its proposal.

By implying that a strengthened European Union would undertake a radical liberalization of public services, the public controversy contributed to the rejection of the European Constitutional Treaty in Dutch and French referenda in 2004. Jean-Luc Mélenchon, then still a member of the French Socialist Party, emphasized the Bolkestein directive, especially in his campaign against the Constitution, which was supported by moderate French socialists. He criticized that "the first principle that [the Constitution] lays down is 'free and undistorted' competition in all fields," which would prevent social harmonization between countries. Furthermore, evoking "services of general commercial interest," he argued that "in every field, neoliberalism tries to transform what was, until yesterday, considered free: postal services, education and health," and condemned the Constitution for "prohibit[ing] subsidies for any kind of product or service."[65] Largely due to this political pressure after the constitution was voted down, the center-right French President Nicolas Sarkozy demanded that the revised Lisbon Treaty include two protocols that defined more precisely how SGEI and SGI (services of general interest) could be exempted from competition law. The right to public services was even put in the Charter of Fundamental Rights and Freedoms, though Sauter discusses in his chapter how these changes had little direct effect on the implementation of competition policy in the 2010s.[66]

Between the 1980s and the end of the 2000s, European competition policy developed into a powerful domestic and international force. Internally, it crystallized around a narrow set of principles focused on the protection of competition and consumer welfare, and imposed those on an ever broader range of subjects and sectors. Externally, the EU attempted to export its vision of competition through international and bilateral agreements, although with varying degrees of success. In the process, although socialist and social-democratic politicians participated actively in shaping the policy at both national and European levels, competition policy in Europe lost any distinctively social-democratic character. At the EU level, this was partly driven by an institutional logic that prioritized supranational market integration and sought to harmonize the application of the law across the Community. But, like at national levels, it was also a result of the spread of neoliberal and "Third Way" ideas that considered traditional social-democratic ideals of balanced growth, employment, social welfare, and control of political power as possible to deliver through the mechanisms of market competition.

A social-democratic competition policy for the 21st century?

The first decade of the new millennium marked the peak of neoliberal economic doctrine and, with it, neoliberal competition policy. The global financial crisis of 2008/2009 did not immediately bring that edifice down, but it signaled the beginning of a long process that has increasingly placed European competition policy under strain. These challenges came in different flavors, reflecting both social and neomercantilist concerns. In both camps, some maintain that competition policy has gone too far, while others worry that it has not done enough. The reopening of discussions at the EU level is an opportunity for social-democratic forces to reclaim European competition policy away from its narrow neoliberal focus and toward support for a broader range of socioeconomic goals. At the same time, this book stands as a reminder that building a competition policy in service of broader public interest is fraught with difficulties in a supranational setting where the "public" is not so easily defined and where there is a lack of alternative tools to pursue the objectives of social welfare and economic and political equality.

Social welfare and equality are indeed at the core of the first set of arguments that challenge the neoliberal competition consensus. If earlier years saw competition policy reaching far into the realm of public services, the global financial crisis and the austerity policies that followed it – and especially the COVID-19 pandemic that revealed the extent of underinvestment in healthcare across the EU members – saw mounting demand for public intervention to ensure accessibility of basic services. As discussed in John Lapidus' chapter on Sweden, social democrats abandoned their trust in the market to criticize the effects of privatization, which was now seen to be generating excessive profits in social services and creating inequality in treatment as wealthier citizens benefit from greater choice while poorer ones are confined to the increasingly overburdened public option. Similar arguments were behind the renationalization of private pension funds in East Central Europe[67] and post-pandemic calls to renationalize healthcare providers across the EU. As Sauter argues regarding the 2012 regulations published under Spanish Socialist Competition Commissioner Joaquín Almunia, the European Commission took a more permissive stance toward SGEI in social services while maintaining a tougher one toward public utilities. The Almunia reforms allowed public authorities at both national and local levels to define for themselves the public services under which they may derogate from some competition provisions when it is necessary to ensure the affordability and accessibility of services.[68] On balance, though, Sauter argues that socialist commissioners in the 2000s–2010s pursued mainstream competition policies that reflect the market-oriented tenants of the Third Way.

Lapidus' chapter also shows how difficult it has been for Swedish social democrats to translate broad agreement on the importance of public services and condemnation of "profits in welfare" into a coherent policy response. An attempt by the newly elected leader of the SAP Håkan Juholt in 2011 to impose old-fashioned forms of intervention such as banning profits in public services and regulating access resulted in him being ousted from leadership only a year later. A broad middle-class base in the SAP constituency appreciated the advantages of the differentiated system and even some trade unions opposed an outright restriction on the operations of private businesses – a combination that resulted in policy stalemate on the issue. Across Europe, renationalizations and a strengthening of public control remain minority responses. Instead, the return of public intervention to safeguard public services and employment in the face of crises largely took the form of massive injections of state aid into private enterprises – from banks to airlines and from the pharmaceutical to the automotive industry. These interventions have been accommodated by the European Commission through a series of temporary frameworks that allowed member states to authorize state aid in case of "serious disturbances" in their economies.[69] Further allowances for public spending for industry were created under the horizontal exceptions for state aid for the purposes of technological investment and environmental protection in order to encourage the "greening" of European industry.

The use of national state aid to support economies in crisis also led to a series of conflicts between the Commission and member-state governments that point to the difficulty of defining public interest in a transnational polity with tightly integrated markets but without the capacity to conduct supranational industrial policy. In 2009, declarations by the French government that the EUR 7.3 billion aid to carmakers will be used to repatriate jobs to France were met with fury in the Commission and in East European states that saw it as an attack on French subsidiaries there, even if those calls seem to have been little more than posturing necessary to "sell" the bailouts at home.[70] Under "asymmetric" European integration, individual states are prevented from using state aid to pursue national social objectives such as employment. Without such control, however, many of the support schemes have amounted to little more than corporate welfare.[71] Meanwhile, the persistent disparity in the ability of some states to spend generously while others cannot afford to do so, often due to the constraints of European fiscal governance, is generating serious discrepancies in the development of industrial capacities of different member states, which has increasingly worried the Commission.[72]

This situation in which the withdrawal of state-aid rules is not matched by the ability or willingness of member states to impose conditions and control over the private recipients of this largesse chimes well with the second strand of the leftist critique of competition policy: that in fact it has done too little. Since the 1970s, despite the strengthening of competition policy in Europe, corporate concentration has proceeded vertiginously, accompanied by increases in corporate profit margins and a declining labor share of GDP.[73] While the neoliberal competition doctrine tolerated such concentration as long as it did not lead to increased prices for consumers, more recent discussions echo older ordoliberal and social-democratic concerns with market dominance and its political consequences. In the United States, the concern with political power of large corporations became the touchstone of a renewed antitrust policy championed by the head of the Federal Trade Commission Lina Khan. In the EU, however, this discussion has been more subdued and focused predominantly on digital services. The principle of consumer welfare, understood mainly as the price of services, has been of little use in a sector where most companies offer end-users their products for free. Echoing ordoliberal principles, the focus of the newly adopted Digital Markets Act (DMA) is therefore on protecting *competition* and consumer *choice*, as well as many non-competition objectives such as privacy and right to information.[74] Even more remarkably, the DMA aims to achieve this by imposing different standards and obligations on very large firms than on smaller digital businesses, a position that accords with ordoliberal and social-democratic competition policies before the 1980s.[75]

The fact that regulatory efforts have been focused on the digital "giants" – almost all of them US companies – has also meant that the discussion in Europe of market dominance very easily becomes merged, and even subsumed into the neomercantilist worry about fading competitiveness of European industries. This is reflected in the now widespread discourse of "digital sovereignty"[76] and calls to unleash a new industrial policy in Europe. This concern spreads well beyond the digital industry and has resulted in yet another set of challenges to existing competition policy. The most paradigmatic case was the proposed merger of two European railway giants, the French Alstom and German Siemens, which the Commission blocked in 2019 over concerns that it would create an excessive dominance in several European regional markets.[77] The result was a political outcry, with French and German ministers for industry proposing to weaken the Commission's monopoly on competition policy and create more space for political discretion.[78] This proposal was soon shelved, but a different piece of legislation did allow member states a degree of political discretion in balancing economic with security concerns in cases of foreign takeovers. Research shows that the Commission has recently become more willing to expand its definition of relevant markets to "global" rather than just European markets when assessing the competition implications of mergers.[79] The COVID-19 crisis, concerns with the instability of global value chains, and mounting pressure to respond to the climate crisis have also multiplied demands to adapt competition policy to serve broader social aims. Examples include exempting vertical agreements to allow for "reshoring" of production in crucial industrial sectors and loosening anti-cartel policies to allow for more inter-company cooperation on sustainability goals, even when these may lead to higher consumer prices.

On the face of it, these multiple challenges dovetail with the traditional social-democratic view that competition policy ought to be subordinated to broader societal goals. As argued by Matthew Guidi and Yannis Karagiannis, this is a position that many social-democratic parties in Europe continued to champion even as they conformed with evolutions in the neoliberal supranational policy.[80] This book argues, however, that equating such objectives with social-democratic competition policy is a historically incomplete view, and one that may easily end up being counter-productive. Equally important is that the pursuit of public interest must be accompanied by a public control of capital to ensure that these interests are met. The research presented in this book shows that the concern with counter-balancing market power was not hoisted upon social democrats by ordoliberals, but was a position that emerged organically from social democrats' own concerns with the dominance of private capital. Historically, this concern has been addressed in different ways: by imposing public control directly through nationalization in the postwar period; by encouraging countervailing forces such as strong worker organizations, small and medium enterprises, and cooperatives in some countries in the 1950s–1960s; or by supporting supranational competition policy to check the runaway power of multinationals from the 1970s. However, the book shows that the erosion of alternative tools of public control, especially at the supranational level, is partly responsible for the social democrats' convergence toward a more liberal view of competition policy. These constraints should not be forgotten as social democrats consider a reorientation of competition policy for the 21st century. Declaring public interest objectives without creating effective oversight mechanisms that impose democratic control and accountability on the actors presumed to be pursuing those objectives will only result in yet more corporate welfare and inequality.

Notes

1 Lee McGowan and Stephen Wilks, "The First Supranational Policy in the European Union: Competition Policy," *European Journal of Political Research* 28 (1995): 141–169; Hubert Buch-Hansen and Angela Wigger, *The Politics of European Competition Regulation: A Critical Political Economy Perspective* (London: Routledge, 2011); Laurent Warlouzet, *Governing Europe in a Globalizing World: Neoliberalism and Its Alternatives Following the 1973 Oil Crisis* (London: Routledge, 2018); Matthieu Montalban, Sigfrido N. Ramírez Pérez and Andy Smith, "EU Competition Policy Revisited: Economic Doctrines within European Political Work," in Bernard Jullien and Andy Smith (eds.), *The EU's Government of Industries: Markets, Institutions and Politics* (London: Routledge, 2015), 141–164.

2 Laurent Warlouzet, "Towards a Fourth Paradigm in European Competition Policy? A Historical Perspective," in Adina Claici et al. (eds.), *The Transformations of EU Competition Law – Next Generation Issues* (Alphen: Kluwer, 2023), 33–52.

3 Gerassimos Moschonas, *In the Name of Social Democracy: The Great Transformation: 1945 to the Present* (London; New York: Verso, 2002), 293, 301.
4 Jenny Andersson, *The Library and the Workshop: Social Democracy and Capitalism in the Knowledge Age* (Stanford: Standford University Press, 2009), 9.
5 *Ibid.*, 12.
6 *Ibid.*, 36–42.
7 Stephanie Mudge, *Leftism Reinvented: Western Parties from Socialism to Neoliberalism* (Cambridge, MA: Harvard University Press, 2018), 1–42.
8 Mattia Guidi and Yannis Karagiannis, "Social Democratic Parties and Antitrust Policy: Evidence from Western Europe (2002–13)," *European Political Science Review* 8, 4 (2016): 495–515.
9 Neil Rollings and Laurent Warlouzet, "Business History and European Integration: How EEC Competition Policy Affected Companies' Strategies," *Business History* 62, 5 (2020): 717–742, 721.
10 Ernst-Joachim Mestmäcker, "Towards a Concept of Workable European Competition Law: Revisiting the Formative Period," in Kiran Klaus Patel and Heike Schweitzer (eds.), *The Historical Foundations of EU Competition Law* (Oxford: Oxford University Press, 2014), 191–206, 198.
11 Tony A. Freyer, *Antitrust and Global Capitalism, 1930–2004* (Cambridge: Cambridge University Press, 2009), 286–287.
12 Freyer's fifth chapter is titled "Antitrust in Postwar European Social Welfare Capitalism," in Freyer, *Antitrust and Global Capitalism*, 245–314, 245.
13 Laurent Warlouzet, "Competition Policy in the European Economic Community, 1957–1992," in Susanna Fellman and Martin Shanahan (eds.), *Regulating Competition: Cartel Registers in the Twentieth-Century World* (London: Routledge, 2015), 48–65.
14 Warlouzet, *Governing Europe*, 121–135.
15 Anselm Doering-Manteuffel and Lutz Raphael, "Der Epochenbruch in den 1970er-Jahren: Thesen zur Phänomenologie und den Wirkungen des Structurwandels 'nach dem Boom'," in Knud Andresen et al. (eds.), *"Nach dem Strukturbruch"? Kontinuität und Wandel von Arbeitsbeziehungen und Arbeitswelt(en) seit den 1970er-Jahren* (Bonn: Dietz, 2011), 25–40, 25, 37.
16 Thorsten Käseberg and Arthe Van Laer, "Competition Law and Industrial Policy: Conflict, Adaptation, and Complementarity," in Kiran Klaus Patel and Heike Schweitzer (eds.), *The Historical Foundations of EU Competition Law* (Oxford: Oxford University Press, 2013), 162–190, 162.
17 See Aurélie D. Andry, *Social Europe, the Road not Taken: The Left and European Integration in the Long 1970s* (Oxford: Oxford University Press, 2022).
18 Warlouzet, *Governing Europe*, 68; Andry, *Social Europe*.
19 Brian Shaev, "International Cartels in the Political Origins of German Competition Policy, 1949–1953," in Susanna Fellman and Martin Shanahan (eds.), *A History of Business Cartels: International Politics, National Policies, and Anti-Competitive Behaviour* (New York: Routledge, 2022), 83–102.
20 Arthe Van Laer, "The European Lilliputians Attacking IBM: Balancing Innovation and Competition in the European Commission's First Big Antitrust Case (1973–1984)," *Business History* 62, 5 (2020): 837–857, 839.
21 Laurent Warlouzet, "The Collapse of the French Shipyard of Dunkirk and EEC State-Aid Control (1977–86)," *Business History* 62, 5 (2020): 858–878.
22 Freyer, *Antitrust and Global Capitalism*, 282–283.
23 Käseberg and Van Laer, "Competition Law and Industrial Policy," 177.
24 Anselm Küsters, "The Making and Unmaking of Ordoliberal Language: A Digital Conceptual History of European Competition Law," PhD dissertation, Goethe University Frankfurt am Main, 2022, 261.
25 Warlouzet, *Governing Europe*, 111.

26 Mathieu Fulla, *Les Socialistes français et l'économie (1944–1981): Une Histoire économique du politique* (Paris: Presses de Sciences Po, 2016), 213.
27 *Ibid*., 413; Mathieu Fulla, "The Neoliberal Turn that Never Was: Breaking with the Standard Narrative of Mitterrand's *tournant de la rigueur*," *Contemporary European History* (FirstView 2023): 1–22.
28 Warlouzet, "The Collapse of the French Shipyard of Dunkirk," 869, 873.
29 Otto Holman, *Integrating Southern Europe* (London: Routledge, 1995), 182–221.
30 Montalban, Ramírez Pérez and Smith, "EU competition Policy Revisited."
31 Dermot Hodson, "Jacques Delors: Vision, Revisionism, and the Design of EMU," in Kenneth Dyson et al. (eds.), *Architects of the Euro: Intellectuals in the Making of European Monetary Union* (Oxford: Oxford University Press, 2016), 212–232.
32 Commission of the European Communities, Directorate-General for Competition. First survey on state aids in the European Community. SEC(88) 1981 final, 13 December 1988.
33 Buch-Hansen and Wigger, *The Politics of European Competition Regulation*, 80.
34 Michelle Cini and Lee McGowan, *Competition Policy in the European Union* (Basingstoke: Macmillan, 1998), 157; Official Journal 91/C 11/03 State aids case no. 38/87 France.
35 Lee McGowan, *The Antitrust Revolution in Europe: Exploring the European Commission's Cartel Policy* (Cheltenham, UK: Edward Elgar Publishing, 2010).
36 Simon Bulmer, "Institutions and Policy Change in the European Union: The Case of Merger Control," *Public Administration*, 72 (1994): 423–444.
37 Council Regulation 4064/89/EEC of 21 December 1989 on the control of concentrations between undertakings.
38 Buch-Hansen and Wigger, *The Politics of European Competition Regulation*, 85.
39 Leon Brittan, *Address to the Bar European Group – London: The Law and Policy of Merger Control in the ECC* (London, 3 May 1990). https://ec.europa.eu/commission/presscorner/detail/en/SPEECH_90_36.
40 Cini and McGowan, *Competition Policy*, 45.
41 Commission Directive 80/723/EEC of 25 June 1980 on the transparency of financial relations between Member States and public undertakings.
42 Cini and McGowan, *Competition Policy*, 145.
43 Angela Wigger, "Competition for Competitiveness: The Politics of Transformation of the EU Competition Regime," Dissertation, Department of Political Science, Faculty of Social Sciences, Vrije Universiteit Amsterdam, 73.
44 Giuliano Amato, *Antitrust and the Bounds of Power: The Dilemma of Liberal Democracy in the History of the Market* (Oxford: Hart Publishing, 1997), 109–129.
45 Angela Wigger and Andreas Nölke, "Enhanced Roles of Private Actors in EU Business Regulation and the Erosion of Rhenish Capitalism: The Case of Antitrust Enforcement," *Journal of Common Market Studies* 45, 2 (2007): 487–513; Simon Brenner, "An Empirical Study of the European Corporate Leniency Program," *International Journal of Industrial Organization* 27, 6 (2009): 639–645.
46 Wolf Sauter, *Coherence in EU Competition Law* (Oxford: Oxford University Press, 2016), 143–170.
47 Amato, *Antitrust and the Bounds of Power*, 116–117.
48 Jeremy Waddington, "What do Representatives Think of the Practices of European Works Councils? Views from Six Countries," *European Journal of Industrial Relations* 9, 3 (2016): 303–325.
49 Dorothee Bohle and Dóra Husz, "Whose Europe is It? Interest Group Action in Accession Negotiations: The Cases of Competition Policy and Labor Migration," *Politique Européenne* 15, 1 (2005): 85–112.
50 Laszlo Bruszt and Visnja Vukov, "Making States for the Single Market: European Integration and the Reshaping of Economic States in the Southern and Eastern Peripheries of Europe," *West European Politics* 40, 4 (2017): 663–687.

51 See David J. Gerber, *Global Competition: Law, Markets, and Globalization* (Oxford: Oxford University Press, 2010).
52 Officially European Commission, "Competition Policy in the New Trade Order: Strengthening International Cooperation and Rules," Report of the Group of Experts, Brussels, July 1995.
53 Buch-Hansen and Wigger, *The Politics of European Competition Regulation*, 128.
54 Lee McGowan and Michelle Cini, "Discretion and Politicization in EU Competition Policy: The Case of Merger Control," *Governance* 12 (1999): 175–200.
55 Buch-Hansen and Wigger, *The Politics of European Competition Regulation*, 108.
56 Küsters, "The Making and Unmaking of Ordoliberal Language," 456.
57 Council Regulation (EC) No 139/2004 of 20 January 2004 on the control of concentrations between undertakings.
58 Neelie Kroes, "Preliminary Thoughts on Policy Review of Article 82," Speech at the Fordham Corporate Law Institute, New York, 23 September 2005 (SPEECH/05/537); Communication from the Commission – Guidance on the Commission's enforcement priorities in applying Article 82 of the EC Treaty to abusive exclusionary conduct by dominant undertakings, [2009] OJ C45/7.
59 Article 86(2) EC.
60 *Ibid.*
61 Cini and McGowan, *Competition Policy*, 162.
62 *Ibid.*
63 Communication from the Commission on the application of the European Union State aid rules to compensation granted for the provision of services of general economic interest OJ C 8, 11 January 2012. For an example, see also Vincent Gruis and Hugo Priemus, "European Competition Policy and National Housing Policies: International Implications of the Dutch Case," *Housing Studies* 23, 3 (2008): 485–505.
64 See especially European Parliament – Report on the Commission White Paper on Services of General Interest ('Rapkay Report'), 2005/2101(INI), 14 September 2006.
65 "A Tale of Two Treaties," debate between Alain Lipietz and Jean-Luc Mélenchon, Red Pepper, 1 March 2005. www.redpepper.org.uk/A-tale-of-two-treaties/ (accessed 30 July 2023).
66 Wolf Sauter, *Public Services in EU Law* (Cambridge: Cambridge University Press, 2015).
67 Marek Naczyk and Stefan Domonkos, "The Financial Crisis and Varieties of Pension Privatization Reversals in Eastern Europe," *Governance* 29 (2016): 167–184.
68 Communication from the Commission on the application of the EU state aid rules to compensation granted for the provision of services of general economic interest, OJ 2012, C8/4
69 Based on Article 107 (3b) TFEU. See Philip Lowe, "State Aid Policy in the Context of the Financial Crisis," *Competition Policy Newsletter* 2 (2009): 3–8.
70 The Financial Times, 21 March 2009. https://www.ft.com/content/83fc9542-1599-11de-b9a9-0000779fd2ac.
71 Fabio Bulfone, Timur Ergen and Manolis Kalaitzake, "No Strings Attached: Corporate Welfare, State Intervention, and the Issue of Conditionality," *Competition & Change* 27, 2 (2023): 253–276.
72 See open letter by Commissioners Thierry Bretton (Internal Market) and Paolo Gentiloni (Economy) published in newspapers across the EU in October 2022. https://www.irishtimes.com/opinion/2022/10/03/germanys-latest-response-to-energy-crisis-raises-questions/.
73 Jan De Loecker, Jan Eeckhout and Gabriel Unger, "The Rise of Market Power and the Macroeconomic Implications," *The Quarterly Journal of Economics* 135, 2 (2020): 561–644.
74 Warlouzet, "Towards a Fourth Paradigm."
75 Michelle Cini and Patryk Czulno, "Digital Single Market and the EU Competition Regime: An Explanation of Policy Change," *Journal of European Integration* 44, 1 (2022): 41–57.

76 State of the Union 2020 Address by President Ursula von der Leyen, European Commission. https://ec.europa.eu/info/strategy/strategic-planning/state-union-addresses/state-union-2020_en.
77 Commission decision of 6 February 2019 declaring a concentration to be incompatible with the internal market and the functioning of the EEA Agreement, Case M.8677 Siemens/Alstom.
78 See Bundesministerium für Wirtschaft und Energie, "A Franco-German Manifesto for a European industrial policy fit for the 21st Century," available at https://www.bmwi.de/Redaktion/DE/Downloads/F/francogerman-manifesto-for-a-europeanindustrial-policy.pdf.
79 Sophie Meunier and Justinas Mickus, "Sizing Up the Competition: Explaining Reform of European Union Competition Policy in the Covid-19 Era," *Journal of European Integration* 42, 8 (2022): 1077–1094.
80 Guidi and Karagiannis, "Social Democratic Parties and Antitrust Policy."

Bibliography

Amato, Giuliano. *Antitrust and the Bounds of Power: The Dilemma of Liberal Democracy in the History of the Market*. Oxford: Hart Publishing: 1997.

Andersson, Jenny. *The Library and the Workshop: Social Democracy and Capitalism in the Knowledge Age*. Stanford: Stanford University Press, 2009.

Andry, Aurélie D. *Social Europe, the Road Not Taken: The Left and European Integration in the Long 1970s*. Oxford: Oxford University Press, 2022.

Ben Clift. "Le Changement? French Socialism, the 2012 Presidential Election and the Politics of Economic Credibility amidst the Eurozone Crisis." *Parliamentary Affairs* 66, 1 (2013): 106–123.

Bohle, Dorothee Bohle and Dóra Husz. "Whose Europe is It? Interest Group Action in Accession Negotiations: The Cases of Competition Policy and Labor Migration." *Politique Européenne* 15, 1 (2005): 85–112.

Brenner, Simon. "An Empirical Study of the European Corporate Leniency Program." *International Journal of Industrial Organization* 27, 6 (2009): 639–45.

Buch-Hansen, Hubert and Angela Wigger. *The Politics of European Competition Regulation: A Critical Political Economy Perspective*. London: Routledge, 2011.

Bulfone, Fabio, Timur Ergen and Manolis Kalaitzake. "No Strings Attached: Corporate Welfare, State Intervention, and the Issue of Conditionality." *Competition & Change* 27, 2 (2023): 253–276.

Bulmer, Simon. "Institutions and Policy Change in the European Union: The Case of Merger Control." *Public Administration* 72 (1994): 423–444.

Cini, Michelle and Patryk Czulno. "Digital Single Market and the EU Competition Regime: An Explanation of Policy Change." *Journal of European Integration* 44, 1 (2022): 41–57.

Cini, Michelle and Lee McGowan. *Competition Policy in the European Union*. Basingstoke: Macmillan, 1998.

De Loecker, Jan, Jan Eeckhout and Gabriel Unger. "The Rise of Market Power and the Macroeconomic Implications." *The Quarterly Journal of Economics* 135, 2 (2020): 561–644.

Doering-Manteuffel, Anselm and Lutz Raphael. "Der Epochenbruch in den 1970er-Jahren: Thesen zur Phänomenologie und den Wirkungen des Structurwandels 'nach dem Boom.'" In *"Nach dem Strukturbruch"? Kontinuität und Wandel von Arbeitsbeziehungen und Arbeitswelt(en) seit den 1970er-Jahren* edited by Knud Andresen et al. Bonn: Dietz, 2011, 25–40.

Freyer, Tony A. *Antitrust and Global Capitalism, 1930–2004*. Cambridge: Cambridge University Press, 2009.

Fulla, Mathieu. *Les Socialistes français et l'économie (1944–1981): Une Histoire économique du politique*. Paris: Presses de Sciences Po, 2016.

Fulla, Mathieu. "The Neoliberal Turn that Never Was: Breaking with the Standard Narrative of Mitterrand's *tournant de la rigueur*." *Contemporary European History* (First View 2023): 1–22.

Gerber, David J. *Global Competition: Law, Markets, and Globalization*. Oxford: Oxford University Press, 2010.

Gruis, Vincent and Hugo Priemus. "European Competition Policy and National Housing Policies: International Implications of the Dutch Case." *Housing Studies* 23, 3 (2008): 485–505.

Guidi, Matthew and Yannis Karagiannis. "Social Democratic Parties and Antitrust Policy: Evidence from Western Europe (2002–13)." *European Political Science Review* 8, 4 (2016): 495–515.

Hodson, Dermot. "Jacques Delors: Vision, Revisionism, and the Design of EMU." In *Architects of the Euro: Intellectuals in the Making of European Monetary Union* edited by Kenneth Dyson et al. Oxford: Oxford University Press, 2016, 212–232.

Holman, Otto. *Integrating Southern Europe*. London: Routledge, 1995.

Käseberg, Thorsten and Arthe Van Laer. "Competition Law and Industrial Policy: Conflict, Adaptation, and Complementarity." *The Historical Foundations of EU Competition Law* edited by Kiran Klaus Patel and Heike Schweitzer. Oxford: Oxford University Press, 2014, 162–190.

Küsters, Anselm. "The Making and Unmaking of Ordoliberal Language: A Digital Conceptual History of European Competition Law." PhD dissertation, Johann Wolfgang Goethe University, 2022.

Laszlo Bruszt and Visnja Vukov. "Making States for the Single Market: European Integration and the Reshaping of Economic States in the Southern and Eastern Peripheries of Europe." *West European Politics* 40, 4 (2017): 663–687.

Lowe, Philip. "State Aid Policy in the Context of the Financial Crisis." *Competition Policy Newsletter* 2 (2009): 3–8.

McGowan, Lee. *The Antitrust Revolution in Europe: Exploring the European Commission's Cartel Policy*. Cheltenham, UK: Edward Elgar Publishing, 2010.

McGowan, Lee and Michelle Cini, "Discretion and Politicization in EU Competition Policy: The Case of Merger Control." *Governance* 12 (1999): 175–200.

McGowan, Lee and Stephen Wilks. "The First Supranational Policy in the European Union: Competition Policy." *European Journal of Political Research* 28 (1995): 141–169.

Mestmäcker, Ernst-Joachim. "Towards a Concept of Workable European Competition Law: Revisiting the Formative Period." In *The Historical Foundations of EU Competition Law* edited by Kiran Klaus Patel and Heike Schweitzer, Oxford: Oxford University Press: 2014 191–206.

Meunier, Sophie and Justinas Mickus. "Sizing up the Competition: Explaining Reform of European Union Competition Policy in the Covid-19 Era." *Journal of European Integration* 42, 8 (2022): 1077–1094.

Montalban, Matthieu, Sigfrido Ramírez Pérez and Andy Smith. "EU Competition Policy Revisited: Economic Doctrines within European Political Work." In *The EU's Government of Industries: Markets, Institutions and Politics* edited by Bernard Jullien and Andy Smith. Oxon: Routledge, 2015, 141–164.

Moschonas, Gerassimos. *In the Name of Social Democracy: The Great Transformation: 1945 to the Present*. London; New York: Verso, 2002.

Mudge, Stephanie. *Leftism Reinvented: Western Parties from Socialism to Neoliberalism*. Cambridge, MA: Harvard University Press, 2018.
Naczyk, Marek and Stefan Domonkos. "The Financial Crisis and Varieties of Pension Privatization Reversals in Eastern Europe." *Governance* 29 (2016): 167–184.
Rollings, Neil and Laurent Warlouzet. "Business History and European Integration: How EEC Competition Policy affected Companies' Strategies." *Business History* 62, 5 (2020): 717–742.
Sauter, Wolf. *Coherence in EU Competition Law*. Oxford: Oxford University Press, 2016.
Sauter, Wolf. *Public Services in EU Law*. Cambridge: Cambridge University Press, 2015.
Shaev, Brian. International Cartels in the Political Origins of German Competition Policy, 1949–1953. In *A History of Business Cartels: International Politics, National Policies, and Anti-Competitive Behaviour* edited by Susanna Fellman and Marti Shanahan. New York: Routledge, 2022, 83–102.
Van Laer, Arthe. "The European Lilliputians Attacking IBM: Balancing Innovation and Competition in the European Commission's First Big Antitrust Case (1973–1984)." *Business History* 62, 5 (2020): 837–857.
Waddington, Jeremy. "What Do Representatives Think of the Practices of European Works Councils? Views from Six Countries". *European Journal of Industrial Relations* 9, 3 (2016): 303–325.
Warlouzet, Laurent. "The Collapse of the French Shipyard of Dunkirk and EEC State-Aid Control (1977–86)." *Business History* 62, 5 (2020): 858–878.
Warlouzet, Laurent. "Competition Policy in the European Economic Community, 1957–1992." In *Regulating Competition: Cartel Registers in the Twentieth-Century World* edited by Susanna Fellman and Martin Shanahan. London: Routledge, 2015, 48–65.
Warlouzet, Laurent. *Governing Europe in a Globalizing World: Neoliberalism and Its Alternatives following the 1973 Oil Crisis*. London: Routledge, 2018.
Warlouzet, Laurent. "Towards a Fourth Paradigm in European Competition Policy? A Historical Perspective." In *The Transformations of EU Competition Law – Next Generation Issues* edited by Adina Claici et al. Alphen: Kluwer, 2023, 33–52.
Wigger, Angela. "Competition for Competitiveness: The Politics of Transformation of the EU Competition Regime." Dissertation, Department of Political Science, Faculty of Social Sciences, Vrije Universiteit Amsterdam.
Wigger, Angela and Andreas Nölke. "Enhanced Roles of Private Actors in EU Business Regulation and the Erosion of Rhenish Capitalism: The Case of Antitrust Enforcement." *Journal of Common Market Studies* 45, 2 (2007): 487–513.

Index

abuse: doctrine 12, 14, 53–54, 74, 79, 81, 84; of dominant position 147–148, 156, 158–159, 166–167, 190, 208, 303 monitoring 7, 9, 20, 43, 52, 133, 135–136; of power 60, 65, 108, 307; *see also* IBM
Adenauer, Konrad 73, 75–77, 81, 98, 109
ADGB *see* German Trade Union Confederation
Adroher, Enric 161; *see also* Gironella, Henri
Agartz, Viktor 43, 82–83
Agrarian party (Center Party) 178, 195
air transport 238, 242
Airbus 243, 312
Albrecht, Ernst 166, 209
Allgemeiner freier Angestelltenbund (AfA) 10
Allied: decartelization 80, 84, 108; powers 72, 78
allocation of resources 37, 190, 204, 206, 259
Almunia, Joaquín 244, 253, 264, 267–270, 316
Altmark ruling 253, 263–264, 269–270
Amato, Giuliano 268, 310–311
Americanization 3, 29
Andriessen, Frans 213, 233–234, 236, 306
anticompetitive practices 15, 17, 20–21, 131, 134, 179, 216, 300
antitrust: laws/provisions 70, 77, 80, 82–85, 100, 116, 149, 151, 208, 311; modernization 253, 256, 263, 268–269; policy 70–71, 80, 85, 87, 115, 234, 317
Archibugi, Franco 233
Armengaud, André 151, 153
Association technique d'importation charbonnière (ATIC) 106–107
ATR (aircraft company) 237, 244
Auriol, Vincent 12, 151
auto industry 3, 115, 149–150
Baade, Fritz 8, 10, 101
Bangemann, Martin 240
bankruptcy 55, 194, 236
Barre, Raymond 215
Barroso, José Manuel Durao 253
BDI *see* Federation of German Industries
Bebel, August 36
Belgium 97, 128, 148, 153, 156, 159–160, 163–164, 213, 282, 303
Bérégovoy, Pierre 234
Berenguer Fuster, Luis 243
Bernstein, Eduard 17, 34, 36, 40–41, 45
Birkelbach, Willi 106, 114, 117
Blankenhorn, Herbert 75
Blum, Léon 12, 234
Böckler, Hans 72–73
Boeing 242, 312
Bork, Robert 299
Borrell, Josep 253, 267
Borschette, Albert 166–167, 170, 207–208
Boussac (textile firm) 236
Brandt, Willy 1, 166–167, 238
Briand, Aristide 5
British Labour Party 2, 13, 30, 209
Brittan, Leon 233, 236–237, 240–242, 244, 308–309, 312
Bundeskartellamt (independent competition authority) 85, 239
Bureau for Freedom of Commerce 188
Bureau of Monopoly *(Monopolutredningsbyrån)* 65

Calvo-Sotelo, Leopoldo 219
capitalism 7–8, 10, 12, 17, 29, 31; development 31, 33, 37; regulation 130, 154, 180; socialism and 42–43; view of 53, 55
capitalistic mode of production 31, 34
cartel: abuse 7, 54; agreements 9, 53, 100, 132, 134, 151, 154, 157, 178, 187;

anti-cartel law 2, 15, 44–45, 72, 84, 98, 100, 106; anti-cartel policy 34, 45, 87, 99, 108, 115; authority 79–80, 83, 239; control 10, 186; crisis cartel 210–212, 221, 305; definition of 31; international 6, 8–9, 132; interwar 5; law 40, 43, 77–78, 80, 83–85, 88, 100, 178–179, 184; policy 4, 15, 70, 101–102, 104–105, 114, 127–128, 130, 132, 136; practices 112, 127, 133–134; private 6–7, 107; register 3, 6, 9, 14, 20, 40, 65, 100, 115, 127–128, 302; regulations 6, 18–19, 53, 105, 181, 234; secretive nature 6, 18; state interventions 64, 233; theory of abuse 53
Cartel Bureau 182, 185–186; *see also* Bureau for Freedom of Commerce
cartelization: anti-cartel positions 6, 70; evolution/support 29, 36–38, 42, 45; international 3, 5–8, 13, 32; merits of 7, 33; *see also* decartelization
CDU *see* Christian Democratic Union
CEEP *see* European Centre for Public Enterprises
Central Union of Consumer Co-operatives (KK) 179, 181–182, 185, 187, 198
CFTC *see* French Catholic trade union
Charter of Fundamental Rights and Freedoms 261, 314
Cheysson, Claude 206
chief executive officers (CEOs) 148–149, 158, 160, 164
Christian Democratic Union (CDU) 20, 43–44, 73, 84
Christian Democrats 1, 20, 73, 81, 110, 147, 151–152, 233, 304, 306
Clement, Bernard 164, 171
Clinton-Davies, Stanley 237
coal industry: cartelization 13; double-pricing practice 98–99; imports 106–107; Ruhr coal sales 78, 98, 105–106, 126
Coal Sales Syndicate (DKV) 76, 78, 102, 105
Cockfield, Arthur 235
Collard, Leo 164
College of Commissioners 205, 210, 213, 259, 304–305, 309
collusion 3, 29, 170, 181, 311
Colonna memorandum 206
commodities 56, 58, 62, 64, 127
commodity board 12, 18
Communist Party 10, 20, 31, 38, 54, 213, 215, 306
Communist Party of Germany (KPD) 38–39, 45
Community: application of 103, 106, 108, 204–205, 225, 314; institutions 214; policy 108–109, 221
company cooperation 59, 63, 318
competition: history 3, 21; Keynesian concept 124, 146–147, 161, 166, 172; lack of 182, 188, 196; legislation 18, 20, 66, 125, 130, 151, 179–183, 187, 190–193, 196–199; long-term perspective 17, 29, 42, 74, 172, 194, 218, 238; portfolio 165, 237; regulation of 4, 53–54, 100–101, 151, 197
Competition Authority (Finnish/Swedish) 193–194, 299
competition law: enforcement 170, 243, 305, 311, 314; history of 252; as law of the land 254–255, 260; opposition 20
Competition Ombudsman 189–190
competition policy: history 2–4, 21, 124, 137, 161; implementation 193, 288, 302, 315; modernization 237–238; national/supranational 4, 21, 111, 113, 124, 136, 300, 318; market-oriented 232, 240, 243–244; profits in welfare 279–280, 283, 289–294, 316; strengthening of 97, 207–209, 221–222, 231, 317
competitiveness 57, 74, 80, 85, 107, 149, 166, 210, 215–216, 218, 262, 304, 317
Confédération générale du travail (CGT) 11, 164
Constitutional Treaty 253, 261, 270, 314
consumer: cooperative 62, 108, 115, 170, 179, 181, 183, 299; interests 18, 63, 65, 115, 188–189, 299, 307; prices 32, 125, 137, 186, 196, 299, 307, 318; welfare 190, 242, 299, 301, 307–308, 310, 313, 315, 317
consumption 37, 56, 62, 64–65, 130, 181
Control of Practices Restricting Economic Competition 185
Council for Freedom of Commerce 188, 190
Council of Europe 80, 129, 154
Council of States of the American Occupation Zone 73
covenants 180, 182, 184–187
Craxi, Bettino 268
Cresson, Edith 236

Dalton, Hugh 14
Davignon Plan 214

Davignon, Etienne 210–212, 214, 220–221, 232, 304–305
De Havilland (aircraft company) 237, 244
De Man, Henri 11–12
de Vries, Frans 131–132
decartelization 29, 72, 76; *see also* Allied
decentralization 72, 254, 269, 283, 311
Deist, Heinrich 104, 106–110, 300
Delors, Jacques: Delors Commission 240; European Commissioner 231; French socialist 236; Maldague report 233; policy promotion 232, 234
Denmark 61, 207, 213, 303
deregulation 213, 288–289
Deringer, Alfred 116
Deutscher Gewerkschaftsbund see German Trade Union Confederation
DG *see* director general
DGB *see* German Trade Union Confederation
director general (DG): appointment/ position of 165–166, 208, 232, 235, 237; of competition 21, 112, 124, 160, 238, 252, 271, 304; Statistical 74k
dominance 256, 265–266, 306–307, 311–313, 317–318
dominant positions *see* abuse
Dreyfus, Pierre 159–160
Dubois, Jean 241
Dutch: competition policy 124, 126, 130, 134, 137; government 126, 134–135, 137–138
Dutch Economic Competition Act 100, 125, 128
Dutch Labor Party (PvdA): competition policy 133–134, 137; foreign policy 98; leadership 100, 102–103, 106, 112, 116, 128, 131–132; postwar 19, 21, 128
Dutch social democrats 128, 134, 138

Ebert, Friedrich 38
ECJ *see* European Court of Justice
ECN *see* European Competition Network
economic: coordination 72, 161, 204; crisis 31, 34, 56–57, 128, 170, 172, 205, 209, 221; democracy 8, 19, 42–43; downturn 194–195; efficiency 13–14, 166, 301, 313; experts 7, 11–12, 14, 83, 87, 96, 233, 242, 257, 300; interdependence 204; liberalism 126; management 18–19; modernization 214, 222; oligarchy 11–12; planning 5, 13, 75, 86, 88, 113, 129, 302; policies 4–5, 14, 125, 146, 165–166, 172, 231, 242, 261, 285, 305; policymaking 10, 125, 128, 130; system 9, 19, 78, 82, 85, 89, 212
Economic Competition Act 1956 100, 125, 130
ECSC *see* European Coal and Steel Community
EEA *see* European Economic Area
EEC/EU *see* European Economic Community/European Union
Ehlermann, Claus-Dieter 232, 237–240, 242–244, 252, 309–312
Engels, Friedrich 36
ER *see* European Parliament
Erhard, Ludwig 20, 43–44, 74, 82, 84, 101, 106, 114, 133, 149, 156, 165, 310
ETUC *see* European Trade Union Confederation
Etzel, Franz 103
European Bureau of Consumers Unions (BEUC) 170
European Centre for Public Enterprises (CEEP) 164–165, 168–169
European Coal and Steel Community (ECSC): competition policy 20, 80, 107, 218; Treaty 70, 77, 99, 111, 135, 155, 158, 160, 168, 210, 214, 304
European Commission: competition policy 3, 5–6, 21, 124, 147–148, 205, 232–233, 235–236, 238, 244; economic policies 164–167; regulatory powers 97, 112, 157–159, 170–171, 207; restructuring policy 214, 216, 220; structural crisis 209, 211–212
European Competition Network (ECN) 241, 254–255, 257–261, 271
European Confederation of Free Trade Union (ECFTU) 169
European Court of Justice (ECJ) 86, 134, 157, 167, 170, 239, 253, 263, 301
European Defense Community (EDC) 80, 156
European Economic and Social Committee 83–84
European Economic Area (EEA) 179, 194–195, 197–198
European Economic Community (EEC): competition policy 3, 111, 117, 124, 163, 234–237; merger control 235, 302–303; Treaty 80–81, 110–111, 126, 135, 210–212, 216, 304
European Economic Community/ European Union (EEC/EU): Block

Exemption Regulation 242; college of commissioners 236&237; competition policy reform 231–232
European Free Trade Agreement (EFTA) 185, 197
European integration: cartel law 179; competition policy 2, 17, 70–71, 80–81, 96, 113, 236, 305; legal history 146–147; merger control 265; opposition 114, 117; private monopolies 155, 162; prohibition principle 193–194
European Labor Movement 161
European Parliament (EP) 232–233, 243, 302–303, 305, 314
European Planning Commissariat 162–163
European Political Community (EPC) 80
European Regional Development Fund 207
European Trade Union Confederation (ETUC) 168–172, 234–235
Evalenko, René 106, 116
experts: cartel research 38; economic 11–12, 14, 87, 233, 300; legal 162–164, 182; new establishment 65; technical 157, 160

fascism 11, 128
Faure, Edgard 155
Faure, Maurice 158
Fayat, Henri 105, 108–109, 115–116
Federal Ministry of Economics and Technology 75
Federation of German Industries (BDI) 74, 78–79, 82
Fette, Christian 77
financial crisis 194, 315
financial markets 190, 204, 287
Finland 2, 20, 178, 183–185, 190, 192–195, 197, 232, 306
Finnish: consumer cooperative 179, 181, 183; economy 181, 190, 192, 197; government/parliament 189, 191, 193–195; legislative initiatives 180–182, 185, 191, 193; workforce competition 180
Finnish Trade Unions (SAK): legislation 1964 185–186, 188–190, 193, 196–197; policy reform 199; price regulations/inflation 183–184, 186, 193
Flemish Socialist Party (SP) 240
food industry 15, 18, 37, 62, 183, 196
foreign direct investment (FDI) 159
France: coal monopoly 103, 109–110, 112; competition policy 20, 96, 99, 148–150, 152–155; Schuman plan 75, 77
free market competition: concepts 2, 64, 66, 73, 97, 99, 106, 133; economic doctrine 53, 84, 103, 136, 155, 185, 235; elimination 9, 17, 154; rationale 43, 74, 79, 124, 131
Free Trade Zone 113, 162
Freitag, Walter 77–78, 164
French Catholic trade union (CFTC) 158, 233
French Communist Party 213, 215, 306
French Socialist Party (PS/SFIO) 98–99, 213, 233

Gaitskell, Hugh 14
Galbraith, John Kenneth 162
GATT *see* General Agreement on Tariffs and Trade
Gazier, Albert 99, 104, 151, 153
General Agreement on Tariffs and Trade (GATT) 80, 197, 243, 304
General Union of Workers (UGT) 218, 267
GEORG *see* Ruhr sales syndicate
German: cartels 134, 138; economy 39, 42, 72, 87, 98, 101, 108
German Cartel Office 1, 160
German Competition Act (GWB) 82–85, 87
German Social Democratic Party (SPD): discourse on cartelization 34, 36, 40; historical materialism (Histomat) 32–33; pro-competition 20; reputation 30; supported cartels 29, 45
German Trade Union Confederation (DGB): ADGB 8, 10–11, 41–42; cartel/antitrust law 79–83; trade unions 85–89
Gironella, Henri 161, 164, 168–169, 171
Giscard d'Estaing, Valéry 215
González, Felipe 217, 219, 267
Gozard, Gilles 109
Great Depression 9, 11, 13–14, 18
gross price system 65
Grosse, Franz 75–76, 80
growth: capitalist 204; economic 57, 157, 161, 192, 206; harmonious 162
Gundelach, Finn Olav 207
GWB *see* German Competition Act

Haferkamp, Wilhelm 166, 207, 209, 212, 305
Hallstein, Walter 153, 164–165
Havana Charter 16, 80–81, 131, 137
Heimann, Eduard 42
Helle, Ceikko 183, 185, 187, 192
Herle, Jakob 32
High Authority (HA): competition policy 3; independent 77; proposals 102–105

Hilferding, Rudolf 8, 10, 36–37, 40–41, 45
Hillery, Patrick 207
Holkeri, Harry 191
Holland, Stuart 233
Hoover, Herbert 32
horizontal agreements 191, 194, 239
Houssiaux, Jacques 162–163
Houtman, Anne 241
Huunonen, Emil 184

IBM (US information technology firm) 208, 303–304
ICC *see* International Chamber of Commerce
ICFTU *see* International Confederation of Free Trade Unions
IFTU *see* International Federation of Trade Unions
IG Bergbau 76, 78, 104
IG Metall 76–78, 164
IMF *see* International Monetary Fund
Immenga, Ulrich 243
industrial policy: Community 205–206, 221–222, 303–304; EEC 237, 244, 303
industrial restructuring 172, 204–205, 210, 214, 221
industry: computer/technology 75, 237, 267–268, 303–304; private owners/ownership 66, 284, 290, 293; *see also* steel industry
inflation 39–40, 155, 183, 188, 207, 209, 213–215, 218, 231, 233–234
international: business activity 3, 194; trade 70, 126, 194
International Chamber of Commerce (ICC) 3, 6, 32, 160, 167–168, 170
International Confederation of Free Trade Unions (ICFTU) 70–71, 75–76, 81–82, 85, 89, 164
International Federation of Trade Unions (IFTU) 9–10, 18–19
International Labour Organization (ILO) 5, 234
International Monetary Fund (IMF) 197, 300
International Ruhr Authority (IAR) 73
International Trade Organization: 16, 131, 243
Interparliamentary Union (IPU) 9
Ireland 207, 282
Italian Socialist Party (PSI) 164, 213, 268
Italianer, Alexander 253

Jenkins Commission 209
Jenkins, Roy 208, 212, 305, 308
Josten, Paul 73–74, 78
Jouhaux, Léon 234
Juholt, Håkan 285, 289, 294, 316

Kapteyn, Paul 103, 105–106, 109, 111–112, 134, 164
Karleby, Nils 56
Karliski, Julius 37
Kautsky, Karl 34, 36–37, 39–41
Kawasaki Steel Corporation 219
Keynesian policy 21, 57, 124, 133–134, 146–148, 161–162, 165, 172, 222, 302
KK *see* Central Union of Consumer Co-operatives
Kleinwächter, Friedrich 31
Koivisto, Mauno 190
Korthals, Henk 100
KPD *see* Communist Party of Germany
Kreyssig, Gerhard 104–105, 107–110, 112–113, 116–117
Kroebel, Gerhard 83
Kroes, Neelie 253, 271, 313
Kühn, Kai-Uwe 268
Kuhne, Karl 164
Kurlbaum, Georg 44
Kutscher, Hans 238

Laakso, Jalmari 181–182
Labour and Socialist International (LSI) 2, 5–11, 19
Labour Party 6–8, 13–16, 19–20, 30, 38, 114, 148, 155, 164, 207, 209
Lacoste, Robert 12
Laitenberger, Johannes 253
Lamoureux, François 236, 243
League of Nations 5–7, 9–10, 19, 32, 150, 180
Lefaucheux, Pierre 149
legal: history 2–4, 54, 146; objectives 166; power 98, 102, 104; security 131–132, 135–136; service 162, 212, 236, 238; solutions 221; structure 158, 261
Legien, Carl 18, 37–38
legislation: competition regulations 3, 65, 70, 88, 136, 159; Law on Restrictive Trade Practices *(Konkurrensbegränsningslagen)* 54, 65; zero-tolerance 179, 183, 193, 195, 198
leniency 103, 241, 256, 260
Lenin, Vladimir 37, 41
Lewin, Leif 55
Liikanen, Erkki 192–193, 196, 300

Lindroos, Reijo 193
Lipponen, Paavo 192–193, 195–197
Lisbon Treaty 253, 261–262, 270, 314
lobby groups 29, 43–44, 86, 114, 184, 187, 193, 259
Löfven, Stefan 285, 289–290
Loucheur, Louis 5–8, 19
Louekoski, Matti 195
Löwe, Adolf 42
Lowe, Philip 239, 252
LSI *see* Labour and Socialist International
Luxembourg: Prime Minister 213; Socialist Workers Party 208
Luxemburg, Rosa 34, 36

Maastricht Treaty 262
MacDonald, Ramsey 13
Mansholt, Sicco 165, 170
Marchal, André 115, 162, 172
Marin, Manuel 237
Marjolin, Robert 12, 115, 158–160, 165, 302
market-domination 1, 79, 116
Marshall Plan Administration 152
Marx, Karl 17, 31, 34, 38, 41, 44
Marxism 30, 32, 36, 43, 45, 213–214
mass production 58, 66, 79, 82
Mauroy, Pierre 216, 222, 233
McDonnell Douglas 242, 312
merger: ATR/De Havilland 237, 244; blocked 167, 172, 266, 268; Bochumer Verein 109; Boeing/McDonnell Douglas 242, 312; conditions of 110; Facebook/ WhatsApp 267; Krupp 109–110; legal issues 266; regulations 232; Thyssen-Rheinrohr 110
merger control: cartel 77, 161; developments 266, 268; leveraging 235; reform 252–253; regulations 118, 157–158, 166–168, 171–172, 196, 270
Merger Control Law 1
Merger Control Regulation (MRC) 265
Merger Task Force (MTF) 266
Merl, Wilhelm 85–86
Mestmäcker, Ernst-Joachim 302
middle-class 11, 37, 281, 290–291, 293, 316
Mitterrand, François 215, 222, 233, 306
Moch, Jules 12
mode of production 31, 33–34, 52
modernization: antitrust 253, 256, 263, 268–269; dimensions of 254, 259, 268; economic 192, 214, 222; implementation and outcomes 253–254
Möller, Gustav 55
Mollet, Guy 98–99, 104, 156–159, 234
Monnet, Jean 20, 76, 78, 98, 102, 115, 149–153, 156, 158, 171
monopolies: cartels and 8, 17–18, 52, 74, 78–79, 159, 161, 181–182; partial 9; private 14, 38, 72, 147, 155, 161, 187; public 111, 158, 279, 281, 283, 285, 292, 301, 310; socialization of 57
Monopolies and Mergers Act 15–16
Montan Co-determination Act 1951 77
Montebourg, Arnaud 244
Monti, Mario 241, 252–253, 263, 266, 312
Moutet, Marius 9, 12
Müller-Armack, Alfred 80
Müller, Hermann 40
Myrdal, Gunnar 56–57, 65

Napthali, Fritz 7–8, 10, 41
Narjes, Karl-Heinz 213
National Board of Trade and Consumer Interests 188–189
national competition authorities (NCAs) 254, 256–260, 267, 311
nationalization 11–15, 19–21, 70–71, 107, 184, 215, 222, 307, 318
Nazi (National Socialism) 11, 14, 30, 42, 71–72
Nederhorst, Gerard 19, 100, 102, 104–107, 109–111, 114, 117, 128–130, 132–135, 164
neoliberal: concepts 3, 146; directions 299, 301, 307; drift 231–233, 244
neoliberalism 133, 193, 240, 281, 299–300, 306–307, 314
Netherlands 2, 20–21, 97, 100, 124–126, 134, 153, 164, 166, 261, 303
New Deal 153, 156
Nölting, Erik 101
Norway 194

OEEC *see* Organization for European Economic Cooperation
Ohlin, Bertil 54, 56, 63
oligopoly 2, 86, 108, 113, 150, 166, 169, 172, 233
ordoliberal: competition 2–3, 21; policy 303; thinking 73, 97, 112, 124, 133, 138, 146, 166
Organisation for Economic Co-operation and Development (OECD) 190, 197, 243, 300

Organization for European Economic Cooperation (OEEC) 148, 158, 162
Organization of the Petroleum Exporting Countries (OPEC) 204
Ortoli Commission 168, 205–206, 208, 221
Ortoli, François-Xavier 168–169, 209

Palmstierna, Erik 58–59
Panhellenic Socialist Movement (PASOK) 213
patents 8, 62, 182, 267
PBO *see* Publiekrechtelijke Bedrijfsorganisatie
People's Democratic League of Finland (SKDL) 178–179, 184, 187
Petersberg Declaration 73
Petersmann, Ernst-Ulrich 243
Petsche, Maurice 152
Philip, André 12, 99, 149, 151, 153–156, 159, 161, 164, 171–172
Piette, Jacques 116, 164
Pineau, Christian 12
planned economy 43, 55, 57, 79, 85, 128, 150
Poisson, Ernest 6
Poos, Jacques 243–244
Posner, Richard 299
postal service 238, 240, 242, 310, 313–314
Posthumus, Siep 116
price: maintenance 15–16, 20, 54, 65, 78, 84–86, 182–189; regulation 179, 184, 186, 188–189, 191–193, 196–199
Price Monitoring Act 188–189
private: enterprise 11, 13, 316; ownership 11, 53–54, 56; property 33, 38, 40, 280
privatization 190, 192–193, 197, 204, 213, 215, 283, 288, 306, 310, 312, 315
Prodi, Romano 252
prohibition principle 14, 78, 80–83, 88, 191, 193–196
Promotion of Competition Act 186–187
PSI *see* Italian Socialist Party
PSOE *see* Spanish Socialist Workers' Party
public: investigations 52–54, 56, 62–64, 66; monopolies 111, 158, 210, 279, 281, 283, 285, 292, 301; policy 4, 71, 231, 264, 268, 270, 301; powers 111; spending 213, 316; works 11, 56, 128
public policy 4, 71, 231, 264, 268, 270, 301
Public Procurement Act (LOU) 287
Publiekrechtelijke Bedrijfsorganisatie (PBO) 19, 127–128, 130–133, 137
PvdA *see* Dutch Labor Party

quotas, suppression of 76, 112, 211, 214, 305

Ramadier, Paul 150
Rapkay, Bernhard 243, 314
Rathenau, Walter 18, 37
Reagan, Ronald 193
regulatory powers 1, 6, 12, 96–97
Renault 149, 159–160, 164, 308
resale price maintenance (RPM) 15–16, 20, 54, 65, 85, 182, 184–189
restrictive practices 7, 14, 16, 178, 186, 191, 194–195, 234, 309
Restrictive Trade Practices Act 14, 16, 65
restructuring process 172, 204–205, 210, 214–216, 218–222, 304–306
retail: price maintenance/monitoring (*see* resale price maintenance); shops/stores 15, 78
Ripa di Meana, Carlo 236–237
Rocard, Michel 234
Röller, Lars-Hendrik 252
Rosenburg, Ludwig 82–83
Rosenstock-Frank, Louis 156
RPM *see* resale price maintenance
Ruhr sales syndicate (GEORG) 102–107
Russia 37, 54, 56; *see also* Soviet Union

SAK *see* Finnish Trade Unions
Salolainen, Pertti 192–193, 195
sanctions 16, 111, 188, 194–195, 241
SAP *see* Swedish, Social Democratic Party
Schaub, Alexander 240, 252
Schippel, Max 36
Schlieder, Willy 166–168, 170, 172, 208–209, 211, 232, 304–305
Schmidt, Robert 40
Schöne, Joachim 44, 101–108, 111, 115
Schönlank, Bruno 36
Schröder, Wilhelm 36
Schumacher, Kurt 43, 98–99
Schuman Plan 72, 75, 81, 96, 98
Schuman, Robert 75–76
SER *see* Social Economic Council
services of general economic interest (SGEI) 110, 253, 255, 261–265, 268–271, 278, 307, 313–314, 316
SFIO *see* French Socialist Party
SGEI *see* services of general economic interest
Sherman and Clayton Acts 53
Sieber, Günther 110, 115
Simonet, Henri 208, 214

SKDL *see* People's Democratic League of Finland
Smith, Adam 31
Sociaaldemocratische Arbeiders Partij (SDAP) 128
social democratic: competition 7, 17, 242, 244, 301, 307–308, 315, 317–318; government 55–56, 63, 222, 281, 286–287; identity 197; ideology/thinking 53, 55, 124, 128–130, 133, 137–138, 285; leaders 54, 231–232, 243, 244; parties 4, 6, 17, 19–22, 39, 125, 285, 299–300, 306–307, 318; perspectives 171, 252, 267, 270–271; policy/policymakers 4, 56, 204, 253, 271, 291
Social Democratic Party (SDP): Finnish 178, 181, 306; German 1, 6, 20, 29, 34, 161; Swedish 53, 57, 60, 280, 288, 290, 292, 310
Social Economic Council (SER) 130, 132, 135
social-democracy: background 4, 11–12, 17, 52; dilemma 57; ideological development 55–56; Marxist 17, 30, 32–34, 36, 38–41, 43–45, 52, 55, 213; policy 64, 66, 284; postwar planning 57, 96; thought/thinking 3–4, 281; vision 179; *see also* Third Way
social-democratic: commissioners 221, 236–237, 271, 303; concept 21, 97, 148, 170; governments 55–56, 63, 222, 281, 286–287; ideology 53, 55; interventions 137; leaders 54, 231–232, 243–244; members 210; supporters 172
Socialist Movement for a United States of Europe (MSEUE) 115, 151
Socialist Party of Belgium (PSB) 163, 240
socialization: alternative 64–66; committee 42; ideology 53–56, 129, 137, 284; international 110; private property 33, 38–39; proposals 12, 17, 19, 89
Solchaga, Carlos 218–220
Sorsa, Kalevi 189, 191
Soviet Union 16, 182, 194
Spaak, Paul-Henri 80–81, 135, 156–157, 160, 164
Spain 2, 214, 217–220, 303
Spanish Communist Party (PCE) 213
Spanish Ministry of Industry and Energy 218
Spanish Socialist Workers' Party (PSOE) 213–214, 217–220, 222
SPD *see* German Social Democratic Party
Spinelli, Altiero 205–207, 214, 221, 303–305, 308–309
stagflation 204, 209
state aid: market failures 262, 264; rules 262; rulings 253, 263, 269
Steel Aid Code 215–216, 220
steel industry: hot-rolled products 217, 219–220; Spanish 218
Stresemann, Gustav 39
structural crisis 209, 211, 304
Sutherland, Peter 233, 236–237, 306, 308–309, 312
Suurhoff, Ko 100
Sweden: elder care 279, 287; healthcare 279, 288–291; legislation 54; welfare system 2, 279
Swedish: economy 287; Municipal Workers' Union 291–292; Parliament *(Riksdag)* 53, 58; Social Democracy 18, 279–282, 294; Social Democratic Party (SAP) 4, 52–53, 57, 285, 288–290, 292; Trade Union Confederation 292
synthetic fibers crisis 210–212, 221

Tanner, Väinö 182–183, 185
technology 216, 237, 267–268, 303–304
telecommunications 232, 238–239, 256, 310, 313
Temple-Lang, John 238–239
Tervo, Penna 184–185
TFEU *see* Treaty on the Functioning of the European Union
Thatcher, Margaret 193, 265
Third Way: capitalism/socialism 42–43; politicians 280, 282, 285, 289–290, 294; social democracy 179–180, 192, 196, 198, 300, 307, 310, 315–316; social-liberalism 267, 269, 271
Thomson, George 206–208
Thorn, Gaston 213
trade union: non-profit 75; Socialist 163, 267; steelworker 73; WTB-Plan 10–11
Trade Union Confederation (LO) 288
Trade Union Congress (TUC) 15, 167; *see also* European Trade Union Confederation (ETUC)
Treaty of Amsterdam 239, 242
Treaty of Paris 3, 77, 147, 149, 154–155

Treaty of Rome 84, 147–148, 150, 156, 160–162, 165–166, 239, 313
Treaty on European Union (TEU) 262
Treaty on the Functioning of the European Union (TFEU) 255–258, 260, 262–265, 313
trusts: cartels and 36–37, 52–53, 58–60, 64–65, 112, 115, 127, 183; milk and sugar 59; national/international 6, 9–10; regulations 13, 58–59
Tschierschky, Siegfried 32

UGT *see* General Union of Workers
Uyl, Joop den 106, 129–130
UNICE *see* Union of Industrial and Employers' Confederations of Europe
union: coal miners' 76, 88, 104; white-collar 10, 34, 184, 196; *see also* trade union
Union of Democratic Centre (UCD) 218–219
Union of Industrial and Employers' Confederations of Europe (UNICE) 3, 167–168, 170
United States: bilateral agreement with EU (Competition Cooperation Agreement) 243; Department of Justice Antitrust Division 183; US Federal Trade Commission 160; US multinationals 170, 245
Uri, Pierre 149, 152, 156–157, 171
USSR (Union of Soviet Socialist Republics) *see* Soviet Union

van Ameringen, A.A. 115, 131
van den Brink, Jan 100
van Miert, Karel 232, 237, 240–244, 252, 270–271, 309–310
Van Schendel, Robert 164
Varfis, Grigori 237
Varga, Eugen 37
VerLoren van Themaat, Pieter 21, 112, 114, 124–127, 129–131, 133, 135–136, 138, 160–161, 300
Verret, Alexandre 158
Vestager, Margrethe 245, 253, 256
Virtanen, Viljo 184
vom Hoff, Hans 75–76
von der Groeben, Hans 81, 111–112, 116, 124, 156, 160, 165–166, 302
von Moellendorff, Wichart 39
von Schmoller, Gustav 32
Vos, Hein 111, 129
Vouel, Raymond 205, 208–212, 221, 232–233, 244, 304–306
Vredeling directive 235, 305

Wagenführ, Rolf 43, 74, 76, 113
Webb, Sidney 13
Wehner, Herbert 103
Weill-Raynal, Étienne 105
Westman, Karl Gustaf 54
whistleblower 241
White Paper (publication) 21, 218, 235–236, 241, 266–267
Wigforss, Ernst 56, 64
Wilson, Harold 13, 15–16
Wirtschaftswissenschaftliches Institut (WWI) 74, 82
Wissell, Rudolf 39
Work Council Constitution Act 88
Works Constitution Act 77, 89
World Economic Conference 1927 5–7
World Federation of Trade Unions (WFTU) 70
World Trade Organization (WTO) 238, 243, 312
Woytinsky, Wladimir 10–11
WTO *see* World Trade Organization

Zijlstra, Jelle 130, 132–135, 137

For Product Safety Concerns and Information please contact our EU representative GPSR@taylorandfrancis.com
Taylor & Francis Verlag GmbH, Kaufingerstraße 24, 80331 München, Germany

www.ingramcontent.com/pod-product-compliance
Ingram Content Group UK Ltd.
Pitfield, Milton Keynes, MK11 3LW, UK
UKHW020154200926
475702UK00016B/2700

* 9 7 8 1 0 3 2 7 6 9 9 8 1 *